S0-BOG-136

WITHDRAWN
L. R. COLLEGE LIBRARY

975.01
D29i

110652

DATE DUE			

WITHDRAWN

Intellectual Life

in the Colonial South

1585–1763

.

RICHARD BEALE DAVIS

Intellectual Life
in the
Colonial South
1585-1763

Volume Two

THE UNIVERSITY
OF TENNESSEE PRESS
Knoxville

CARL A. RUDISILL LIBRARY
LENOIR RHYNE COLLEGE

975.01
D29₂
110652
July 1979

Intellectual Life in the Colonial South
is published as a set of three volumes.

·

Subventions from the National Endowment for
the Humanities, Washington, D.C., and the John C.
Hodges Fund of the English Department of the University of Tennessee, Knoxville, toward publication
of these volumes are gratefully acknowledged.

·

Copyright © 1978 by The University of Tennessee Press.
All rights reserved.
Manufactured in the United of America.

·

Library of Congress Cataloging in Publication Data

Davis, Richard Beale.
    Intellectual life in the Colonial South, 1585–1763.

    Bibliography: p.
    1. Southern States—Intellectual life—Colonial
period, ca. 1600–1775. I. Title.
F212.D28   975'.01   77–1370
ISBN 0–87049–210–1

CHAPTER FOUR

Books, Libraries, Reading, and Printing

CONTENTS

———◄◆►———

Introduction	491
Books and Libraries in the Seventeenth Century	500
The Chesapeake Colonies	501
The Carolinas	514
Books and Libraries in the Eighteenth Century	517
The Collections: Public or Club	520
The Collections: Private	526
Reading Tastes: The Books and the Uses Made of Them,	
Especially in the Eighteenth Century	579
Religious Reading	580
Educational Reading	584
Occupational Reading	586
Recreational Reading	589
Reading on the Functional Artistic	590
Historical, Political, and Philosophical	591
Printing	595
Establishment of the Presses: Maryland to Georgia	596
The Provincial Gazettes: Function, Form, and Policy	609
Conclusions	622
Bibliography	991
Notes	1001

~~~ The Author has made a general Observation among all Natives in America; they are in general of very elevated Spirits, and most of them with very little Education; yea some by reading good Authors only, acquire real knowledge and great Wisdom. . . . He was often surprised at the good Judgments and Argumentations of Men whom he knew had been brought intirely to Mechanism without any more Education, than reading and writing, they, after acquiring Estates, being in easy Circumstances of Life, and in a Country not as yet debauched by European Luxuries such as Balls, Masquerades, Operas, Plays, etc., they applied themselves to reading good Authors, of which (yea the best) America has no reason to complain of a Want. There is scarcely a House in the Cities, Towns, or Plantations, but what have some Choice Authors, if not Libraries of Religious, Phylosophical, and Political Writers. Booksellers endeavour to import the newest Editions, and take Care to commission the best, well knowing they will not incumber their shops long, but soon find Admirers and Purchasers; besides that, many of their Books they write for are commissioned by the Inhabitants. This Province was scarce thirty years settled, before it had three fine libraries in the City of Savannah; the fourth at Ebenezer, and a fifth 96¾ miles from the Sea upon the Stream of Savannah. In these Libraries could be had books wrote in the Caldaic, Hebrew, Arabic, Siriac, Coptic, Malabar, Greek, Latin, French, German, Dutch, Spanish, besides the English, vide, in thirteen languages.

—*De Brahm's Report of the General Survey in the Southern Department of North America*, ed. Louis DeVorsey, Jr. (Columbia, 1971), pp. 143–144.

~ ~ ~ The best way that I know of to avoid those fatal
consequences which you suppose may Result from Errors in
Opinion on yᵉ Subject of Government, is first to gett well
grounded in yᵉ Original End & design of Government in General, by reading the best Historians and other books which
treat on the Constitution of our mother Country on which we
so much depend, and next to Consider what Arts or Steps
have been regularly taken among ourselves toward making
a difference between the English Constitution & our own here,
& what not; & when all this is done, a man ought to be well
aware of Byasses from Interest Passion friendship Authority
or any other motive but yᵉ pur dictates of Right Reason.

—Stephen Bordley to Matthias Harris, February 22, 1739 [quoted in
Joseph T. Wheeler, "Reading Interests of the Professional Classes
in Colonial Maryland, 1700–1776: Lawyers," *Maryland Historical
Magazine*, XXXVI (1941), 281–286].

Books, libraries, and printing were as significant as formal education
in the transmission of Old World culture to the southern colonies. Printing
came relatively late, and even when it was firmly established in the one or
two generations before 1764 it was used primarily for purposes other than
book production. Therefore what the South Atlantic settler read, except
for provincial gazettes and volumes of local laws, was usually printed in
Great Britain or on the European continent. At least until the 1850s,
as far as books are concerned, his mind was shaped and directed by the
world from which he or a recent ancestor had come.

That many white colonials of every class read is obvious to anyone who
has taken a glance at book inventories, diaries, letters, and local communications to eighteenth-century newspapers. Perhaps even more than
in most other aspects of their development in America, their reading habits
were affected by their agrarian existence, their living in isolation from
others who might share their interests. That they were usually planters did
not necessarily cause them to devour books on husbandry or farming, on
fertilization of the soil or on the cultivation of indigo or tobacco. They
gathered some books on these subjects, but on the whole such works form
a relatively insignificant proportion of the volumes they owned or showed
in other ways they knew.

One investigator of southern colonial libraries goes so far as to say that
in one colony the collectors of books seemed utterly indifferent to guides
or manuals which might help them in farming, and that in inventory lists
he examined he found only one or two instances of practical studies which

assist the cultivator of the soil. This is an exaggeration, for an examination of book lists for the same colony indicates that almost every good-sized library of a hundred or more titles, or even volumes, did contain books on the problems of husbandry. The fact is that in this and other southern colonies book collections moderate or large, with the exception of those of professional men such as clergymen, lawyers, and physicians, and even many of theirs, were what might be called general collections.

From the beginning to the end of the colonial period books and reading in the South were strongly purposeful, even though in the two generations just before the Revolution the recreational—especially verse, drama, and fiction—had become an appreciable part of many libraries. One must agree with Louis B. Wright that for the whole colonial period, with not more than half a dozen possible exceptions, the planter or professional man or government official or merchant brought and bought books to be used. He was not a collector in any nineteenth- or twentieth-century sense.

Even from the beginning a surprisingly large number of people owned a moderate number of usable titles. Bruce estimates that in Virginia alone, in the last quarter of the seventeenth century, there were about one thousand book collections and at least twenty thousand volumes.[1] Most frequent were pious or religious or theological titles, for the greatest use the colonist made of books was to prepare himself for the future world.[2] Next in order of importance to him were the matters of establishing a civilization or a nation in the New World and in making a career and if possible a fortune in this strange environment. A remarkable variety of books he found useful in furthering both these aims. Then if he had derivations from or aspirations to the upper class, he was likely to heed the admonitions in certain other kinds of books frequent especially in the early colony—Henry Peacham's *The Compleat Gentleman* (1622) or Henry Scudder's *The Christians Daily Walke in Security and Peace* (1628) among them—as to what he brought or bought and how it or they should be read.[3] Along with or ahead of all these subjects save religion was history, for the present and the future must learn from the past about everything from personal ambition to civic or political organization and the concomitant bases for a philosophy of living.

Then there was more obviously utilitarian reading, much of it, though it often touched only obliquely on the book owner's principal occupation. For every man—planter, lawyer, merchant, craftsman, or official—had to care for a household and his own property in matters today looked after by outside specialists. Thus from the beginning there were a few essential manuals or handbooks for home treatment of sickness and disease, and sometimes even technically detailed medical books appeared in lay libraries. With these aids laymen attempted to treat their spouses or children or servants in a region where professional physicians were very scarce indeed. After medicine usually came law, compilations of acts and statutes, and handbooks for simpler cases. In hundreds of libraries were one or more of these manuals for the country or county justice of the peace. Every man of any substance had to be able to pass judgment in elementary legal matters, for he was almost sure to be called to service at one time or another as a justice on a county commission of the peace, a much more prestigious and responsible position than it is today. Also, in a highly litigious age every man wanted to know how he could retain his own property and acquire title to more. It is not strange, therefore, that books with such titles as *Every Man His Own Lawyer* were to be found in many households.

The southern colonial, for practical reasons and out of sheer Renaissance or Enlightenment curiosity, also wanted to learn as much as possible about this strange western world to which he had come to stay. Accounts of travel or voyages of discovery even from somewhat earlier times were often still the only extant printed materials on things he wanted to investigate. Books translated from the Latin or Spanish which were concerned with Central or South America, dictionaries or encyclopedias or other works dealing with natural history in all its forms, and the historians of English North America or of parts of it, from Hakluyt and Purchas to the late colonial observers, were frequent in southerners' collections. Books on ideal commonwealths (experiments attempted even in southern Indian country), already indicated such as More's *Utopia* or Bacon's *New Atlantis* are among the earliest of Renaissance and later utopian writings to be found.

Since they rightly considered themselves as heirs to a part of the Renaissance European heritage, these colonists were much interested in the various works of Erasmus and Grotius, in English or in Latin, and of other contemporaries or near-contemporaries, as well as of medieval schoolman St. Thomas Aquinas. Classical writers on rhetoric—Aristotle, Cicero, Quintilian—stood alongside more recent critics of eloquence or written style such as Peter Ramus. Other classics, including historians such as Herodotus and Sallust—and Ovid, Horace, Tacitus, and all the rest, especially Cicero—were to be found in scores of libraries from Maryland to Georgia.

History was closely connected with politics. Once their provincial governments were established, the colonials found themselves involved in one way or another with party government. As a late seventeenth-century observer put it, they had at that time no parties in name, and yet the settlers were dividing or forming their allegiances to one group or another partially as a result of events in the mother country, such as the Bloodless Revolution, and partly from local conditions. The shelves of the medium-sized and larger libraries held many books which in one sense or another may be called political, from some of the contemporary editions of the classics and Hooker's *Ecclesiastical Polity* (1594–1597) through Rapin de Thoyras' multivolumned Whiggish history of England to Bolingbroke's discussions of parties and patriot-kings on to the Whig-vs.-Tory writers just before the American Revolution. Hobbes, Filmer, and Hume appear, but far more frequent are Locke and what Caroline Robbins calls the eighteenth-century "Commonwealthmen,"[4] the "Real Whigs," some of them avowed republicans.

There were almost surely, from the beginning of these southern libraries, a few belletristic works, and as time went on titles in this area increased even proportionately a great deal, though the extent to which they were taken as utilitarian, or to which many were taken as didactic, is a moot question, which will be considered in somewhat more detail below. That many surely were read merely for delight or for ornament seems fairly obvious.

But so far the collections broadly characterized have been private, and one must remember that from Jamestown on there were, sporadically at first and later more or less continuously, public or semi-public libraries—parochial, provincial, lending-social, and college. The contents were much the same as those of private gatherings, though frequently with natural or curious differences in emphasis. Inevitably all these libraries, private and communal or institutional, must be compared with those of the New England and Middle colonies. As yet no comparison of any real validity can be made. First to be prepared are scores of basic studies and analyses of libraries north and south. This can be done properly only after detailed inventories yet remaining in manuscript have been published. A recent interesting analysis of South Carolina colonial collections fails to present any complete inventories and announces several book figures or statistics which the present writer's generous sampling of dozens of inventories, many not even mentioned in the study, leads him to view with uneasiness. Worst of all, the reader of the same study gets very few interesting or direct examples or proofs of what books really contained or how they were used, though the author declares his intention of showing both.[5]

By the end of the eighteenth century, and probably at the beginning, the Harvard library was superior to all other institutional collections in numbers and quality. Dartmouth, Brown, Yale, and Columbia had approximately three thousand volumes, and William and Mary about the same number, the last despite destruction by fire or pillage of several previous collections. The Virginia college had far more books then than either the University of Pennsylvania or Princeton.[6] One brief and quite superficial attempt has been made to compare in quality and quantity New England, middle Atlantic, and southern libraries. The author did not take South

Carolina or Georgia into account at all, though the former is especially significant. Using a few fairly large libraries of certain colonies as a basis for his tables and conclusions, his subject-matter figures for southern colonial libraries show applied science as 24 percent, literature as 22 percent, theology as 19 percent, history as 18 percent, and six other categories ranging from 1 to 5 percent each. For the middle colonies his order of content is history, theology, literature, and applied science; for New England, theology, history, applied science, and literature. It is not clear what he considers applied science and literature, but under any conceivable definition he is wrong about the southern colonial libraries in placing applied science foremost. He acknowledges that he had far more southern libraries (including ten large Virginia collections) available than for the other areas. Having examined all the Virginia inventories he lists, the present writer is at a loss to understand either implied defintions of subject matter or the percentages. His conclusion that "private libraries were more common in colonial Virginia [he might have said the whole South] than in the North" is probably correct, but proof is simply not presented.[7]

But local printing as well as book collections became an important reading source in the eighteenth century. All the major printers of the South Atlantic region through 1763 were legally or implicitly agents of provincial government. Even the first of them, William Nuthead, who set up a press in 1682 in Virginia, probably came to the colony with the encouragement of the House of Burgesses. For some reason, while he was printing legislative acts and journals, the governor and council became alarmed and forbade his publishing or printing anything, an edict made formal and final when Governor Lord Effingham arrived in 1684 with a specific order forbidding any printing in his government. Nuthead removed to Maryland and by 1685 had his press set up at St. Mary's as an authorized agent of government. Though there are gaps of a few years, Maryland was to have successful and even distinguished printing from such men and women as Dinah Nuthead, widow of William, William Parks, and various members of the Jonas Green family well into the nineteenth century. Parks, who probably began his American career at Annapolis, had by 1730 opened a second establishment at Williamsburg in Virginia. In South Carolina three printers set up presses in 1731, but within eighteen months two were dead and the third had disappeared from view. One of them was succeeded by Benjamin Franklin's protégé Louis Timothée (Lewis Timothy), the story of whose press is outlined below. At New Bern, North Carolina, James Davis was printing for the provincial government in 1749, and at Savannah, Georgia, James Johnston was turning out copies of laws and a gazette by 1762/1763.

Most or all of these printers had contracts with legislative assemblies and other agencies of provincial government to print everything from laws to legal blank forms. These contracts usually assured the printer of an adequate and even comfortable income, but they also tacitly or specifically imposed a sort of censorship. The otherwise quite successful (from our point of view) gazettes, especially of Maryland, Virginia, and South Carolina, the newspaper-journals issued for personal profit by these official printers, seem to have been produced on the assumption that they could not contain anything that might be taken as criticism of the conduct of either branch of the general assemblies or of the governors, though they might publish quite harsh attacks on representatives of religion or ecclesiastical bodies or economic matters outside legislative concern, especially on which provincial opinion was divided. Thus the Reverend John Camm had to get his reply to the political attacks of two prominent Virginia leaders printed in Maryland, and during the French and Indian War devastating personal indictments (in literary form) of Governor Dinwiddie of Virginia could be circulated only in manuscript. This was late in the game, and certain Whiggish Virginia legislators (for reasons hardly connected with Dinwiddie or Camm) saw to it that a rival printer was invited to Williamsburg to set up a "free" newspaper. In Maryland much of the controversy between a Dulany and the Bishop of London's Commissary was published in Philadelphia newspapers and pamphlets. Hermon Husband of North Carolina had at least two of his three major political tracts printed outside his province, in Philadelphia and in Boston.

Yet all three of the southern gazettes just mentioned published much on both sides of the Whitefield-vs.-Established Church controversy. Whatever political implications the controversy had were either not visible to "authority" or to the printer, or were not considered derogatory to Crown or Proprietary government. In Virginia and Maryland especially, a number of essays arguing the tobacco-tax question were published, probably either because legislators were divided and governors wanted to see how the wind blew or the latter may have been actually in sympathy with the attitudes of a majority of the colonists, as Sharpe of Maryland, Glen of South Carolina, and Fauquier and Botetourt of Virginia seem to have been.

The newspaper-chronicles are among the most fascinating and significant emanations of the southern colonial mind. For, despite their being politically inhibited, they represented and presented most of the interests and tastes and abilities of the thousands who subscribed to them over the years. Advertisements reveal much about books, theaters, servants, and slaves. A remarkable coverage of foreign news indicates that the readers were not parochially or provincially minded. Belletristic materials, from poems to bawdy or moral essays, might be reprinted from British newspapers and magazines or composed locally. The serious utilitarian essays on indigo or cotton or tobacco or rice growing, on Indian policy, on social conditions, were usually of American and local origin, and frequently were written by men and women who had a sense of style as well as a point to make.

The printer's other two major functions, private publishing of books or tracts and operating a bookstore, will be enlarged upon later, as will the character of the gazettes. Typographically the presses of the three colonies each produced some distinguished books, of which also more below.

One must remember that individual tastes changed with European civilization and with the steady development of the southern colonies during the almost two centuries of their history. In books and printing there was really no cultural lag, for the colonial received the latest volumes only a few months after his relatives back home did. As noted elsewhere, in several instances he knew of forthcoming books and ordered them before they appeared. Though the southern library often contained volumes with seventeenth- and even sixteenth-century imprints, so did similar collections in Great Britain. Standard authors all the way back to Herodotus or Homer might have been present in Renaissance editions, but in most instances when dates and places of publication are given in southern inventories, they indicate that these classics and most medieval and Renaissance authors normally appeared in recent contemporary editions with quite up-to-date annotation. Both the southern colonial and his British contemporary ordinarily preferred the freshest printing. The colonial's letters to his friends in London or his relatives in other parts of Britain usually request the "latest edition" of a desired book, sometimes by name of editor or publisher.

Inventories of books for many counties of these seaboard colonies simply do not exist, for the ravages of British troops in the Revolution and the War of 1812 and, far more often, the accidental fires which consumed so many colonial buildings, destroyed book lists along with the other records. This is true for counties such as Gloucester in Virginia, where for a variety of reasons we believe fairly large book collections existed. Another fact that will forever prevent anyone from seeing the whole picture is the too-frequent method of representing libraries in inventories with such terse and tantalizing phrases as "a parcel of books," "a parcel of old books," and "some old books," for the fairly obviously smaller collections to "a study full of books" or "a study of books" representing the library of an educated lawyer-planter such as William Fitzhugh. Even in several inventories which list some titles there will appear such a phrase as "and 42 books in French" or "and his law books" or "his books on medicine and surgery" or "forty theological works" or "twenty books of sermons." Well into the eighteenth century such abbreviated listings are the rule rather than the exception, though in the generation before the Revolution some colonies, such as South Carolina, passed laws requiring the listing of books in any collection above a certain value. Whether from legal compulsion or something else, the records in most colonies from the 1740s and 1750s on are much more complete and detailed.

The inventories which give titles vary greatly in accuracy of title, length, matters of publication, and number of volumes per title. The bibliographical description depends on the degree of education of the person or persons making the inventory, and unquestionably often on the purpose for which the listing was made. Rarely does one find place and date of publication given except in such printed catalogs as those of 1770–1772 for the Charleston Library Society of South Carolina,[8] and even more rarely any direct mention of the publisher. The largest and perhaps most significant of southern colonial libraries, that of the three William Byrds (primarily of the second of the name) is listed only by abbreviated titles, size of the volumes, and bookshelves and bookcases in which located. This was a very late list, made primarily for sales purposes, and one may be fairly sure that William Byrd II's librarian Proctor made in the years around 1740 a somewhat different list of the books at Westover. There is plenty of evidence that sales catalogs were printed for or of southern libraries from the 1740s well into the nineteenth century, but so far no one of them is known to be in existence. The William Byrd list appears to have been printed, as was the Ralph Wormeley list in the early nineteenth century, but all copies have disappeared. The gazettes contain notices that catalogs will be or have been printed and may be obtained by calling or writing for them, but all that remains of printed evidence is in abbreviated lists appearing in advertisements in the newspapers themselves.

The inventories that do exist, from one line to dozens of pages, indicate a great deal. The "parcel of books" or "one Bible, one Common Prayer, one Whole Duty of Man, one odd volume of sermons" from the very fact that they appear so often, suggest or prove that a great many families, in these cases usually but by no means always humbler folk, owned books, and that they could read. These phrasal lists are recorded almost from the beginning of the Virginia colony (complete records do exist for a few Tidewater counties) to the very end of the period, in every province from Maryland through Georgia. The more detailed lists reveal much more, and suggest much more still. It is obviously easy from only an abbreviated title to pinpoint a sixteenth-century book printed in only one known edition as to place and date of publication, and there are a number of traces of such volumes which would form a most valuable collector's library were they still extant. But naturally most books owned by southern colonists appeared in more than one edition before the date of the inventory, and suggesting particular editions is usually only guesswork. Almost surely many early as well as later relatively affluent colonists, or even poorer men and women who knew they were making a permanent move to the New World, brought old and treasured family books with them. These are occasionally suggested by titles in inventories, which include early sixteenth-century imprints or such rarities as the quarto edition of *Macbeth* of 1673 (perhaps the earliest recorded copy of Shakespeare in America) in a Virginia list. But fire, dampness, carelessness or indifference, and loss through lending have caused these potential bibliographical treasures to disappear.

The present study is based first of all on a generous personal sampling of manuscript library inventories in the archives of every one of the southern colonies, in the Public Records Offices of London and Belfast and Dublin, in the British Museum, the university collections in this country and England and Scotland, the Lambeth Palace and S.P.G. collections in London, and others which will be noted. Printed sources in all the state historical journals and the published archives, including letters and diaries as well as inventories, have been useful, as have pioneer studies, some still unpublished, such as those mentioned in the bibliography for this chapter. The history of southern printing has been fairly well covered by a number of distinguished investigators, but since they published their findings a few additional imprints of books and issues of colonial newspapers have appeared.

Some of the books mentioned in the extant inventories are school texts and thus in a sense or to a certain degree connect this chapter with the preceding one on formal education. But the vast majority of the titles mentioned represent the reading choices, or tastes, of adults and in so doing suggest the informal education which extends through life. It has often been said that Thomas Jefferson's education in the main came not from Maury's school or the College of William and Mary but through what he read. The same may be said for most other colonial thinkers and writers, political or belletristic. Commissary Bray of Maryland was recognizing the potentialities, especially for religious education, when he founded the parochial and provincial libraries. The promulgators of the Charleston Library Society and of other private or commercial lending libraries throughout the southeast were aware of the educative value of books, as were the colonial printers.

BOOKS AND LIBRARIES IN THE SEVENTEENTH CENTURY

Englishmen had libraries in America before the seventeenth century, but one may be sure that not a single volume brought in the sixteenth century has survived. John White, the Roanoke Island artist of the 1580s, returned in 1590 to the coast of North Carolina in search of the colony which for various reasons had been abandoned for several years. The story of what he and his companions found is famous—the word CROATAN cut into the bark of a tree—and what they did not find, the people of the colony. Few historians note that among the remains of the lost Englishmen were five despoiled chests, three of them White's own. Rusted armor and ruined household furniture interest us less than the frames of pictures, maps rotten and spoiled by rain, and above all, in White's words, "my bookes torne from the covers."[9] One can be fairly sure from Thomas Hariot's writings that he too had a number of learned tomes with him, especially scientific ones, and other literate colonists certainly must have had a number of religious works. At least one can know that the first British settlement in North America had books and that there were literate and even some learned men to use them.

Thus in books as well as other matters this was in some sense an abortive beginning, for there is no further record of printed matter in what is now North Carolina for more than a century. Again as in other matters, it is at the Jamestown settlement of the Virginia Company of London, 1607–1624, that the American and southern story of books and reading must begin.

THE CHESAPEAKE COLONIES

There is considerable evidence of books in the Virginia colony throughout the years when it was controlled by the joint-stock company. Undoubtedly that first expedition reaching the site of their settlement in the spring of 1607 had books with them, for John Smith's 1612 *A Map of Virginia* tells of the carelessness of the first additional supply, who set the town on fire, and of what was apparently the greatest casualty, the loss of the library of "our preacher" Master Robert Hunt, "yet none ever see him repine of his losse."[10] Then there is the 1608 testimony for and against the tragicomical Councilor and whilom President of the little group of settlers, Edward Maria Wingfield, who was accused of being an atheist because he had no Bible with him. Wingfield searched frantically among the books he had brought in a trunk but found that it had been broken open and rifled before it even left London.[11] At least two deductions are obvious from this little episode: Wingfield was not a daily reader of the Bible, and most or all the settlers possessed at least this book.

In another decade, when both King and Company were planning the college at Henrico, as related in the preceding chapter, a great deal of evidence of books and a number of specific titles survive.[12] In 1619, for example, when George Thorpe was preparing to come to America to take charge of the college lands and the building of the institution, his "supplies" included two church Bibles, two copies of the Book of Common

Prayer, three copies of Lewis Bayley's *The Practise of Pietie* (by then in its third edition),[13] and three of *The Plain Man's Pathway* (probably originally printed in the late sixteenth century). One recalls that the first purpose of the college was to convert the red men through education. In 1620–1621 an English agent listed books sent to Virginia as "Babington's works . . . french surgeon . . . Enchiridion medicn . . . [and] Smith of doctrines," an interesting combination of directions for the healing of soul and body. About the same time the ship *Supply*, sailing in 1620, carried the utilitarian works of Gervase Markham on husbandry and housewifery (two separate titles) and Barnaby Googe's equally popular late sixteenth-century book on husbandry. A volume on silkworm culture, a topic which would absorb the attention of southern settlers through the rest of the colonial period, was also sent in the *Supply* in 1620.[14]

At a quarter court of the Virginia Company meeting in London January 30, 1621, an announcement was made that among other gifts for the East India School were a small Bible, a large Church Bible, and the Book of Common Prayer, by the same person who had the year before sent for the use of the college "S. Augustine De Civitate Dei, Master *Perkins* his workes, and an exact Map of America." St. Augustine's and Puritan William Perkins' works were to remain popular in the southern as well as the northern colonies well into the eighteenth century.[15] At the same time the Company announced the first bequest or gift of a library or gift of books to a public institution in English America, that of the Reverend Thomas Bargrave, deceased, whose library was valued at one hundred marks and was to go to the new college.

Individuals who probably had some books wrote to various persons or agencies in England pleading for more. John Pory, translator, and speaker of the 1619 Assembly of Burgesses, asked for some pamphlets to keep himself informed of events at home. George Thorpe made an earnest plea for legal books, for the resident Council was often perplexed for lack of reports or precedents.[16] Thorpe's request perhaps marks the beginning of the ubiquitous and astonishingly large legal libraries of the southern colonists. He wanted Stanford's *Pleas del Coron divisees in plusieurs titles* (1557 and later editions), a new abridgment of English statutes, and William West's "presidents" [precedents], of which there had been ten editions beginning in 1590. He also wanted a book already famous in Europe and destined to become one of the most popular botanical items in southern colonial libraries, John Gerard's *The Herball, or Generall Historie of Plants*, used by generations of colonials in identifying or attempting to identify the flora of the South Atlantic region.

Just a year before the Company was dissolved, in 1623, it sent "three great Bibles, Two Common prayer bookes and Vrsinaes Cathechisme, being the guift of an unknowne person for the use of those Churches that most need them."[17] That even by 1621 there was a considerable number of theological works in Virginia is suggested by the London officials' letter to the Council in Virginia of September 11 of that year, which recommends highly the new clergyman Thomas White, who comes, they warn, with a very small allowance. They add, "as for bookes we doubt not but you wilbe able to supplie him out of the lybraries of so many [clergy] that have died."[18]

There can be no doubt that Treasurer George Sandys, completing his translation of Ovid's *Metamorphoses* on the banks of the James, was surrounded by a number of Renaissance editions of the classics and commentaries upon them, and probably by a moderately large number of other books of several kinds. Sandys' display of learning in his earlier 1615 *A Relation of a Journey* and in the commentaries of the second folio edition of the Ovid, not to mention his other works, indicates that he was the sort of man who would always be surrounded by books.[19] The same thing may be said, perhaps less emphatically, of many of the other university men in the early colony, including Secretary Christopher Davison the poet, or the philosophical Governor Sir Thomas Wyatt. Perhaps the best known and certainly most eloquent reference to reading in this first period of southern settlement is that of John Pory, writing to an unidentified nobleman in England on September 30, 1619. Near the end he remarks, "I am resolved wholly to minde my business here, and nexte after my penne, to have some good book alwayes in store, being in solitude the best and choicest company. Besides among these Christall rivers, & odoriferous woods I doe escape much expense, envye, contempte, vanity, and vexation of minde." Yet it is almost in the next breath that he requests "pampletts and relations" which will keep him abreast of European news.[20] For the next century and a half books served for diversion, acquaintance with the classical authors, knowledge of contemporary Europe, religious devotion, and the American world and everyday occupations. Not all but most varieties for most purposes were present before the Crown assumed control in Virginia.

After the death of Davison and the departure of Wyatt and Sandys in 1625 and 1626 there is still evidence of books already present or just arriving. The early clergyman Richard Bucke left "a library of books" in 1626, and in 1627 Lady Temperance Yeardley presented "ffower divinity books wth brasse bosses" among other gifts to the college, one of the proofs that in some sense that institution was still alive.[21] In 1635 the first detailed surviving inventory was made as a result of a lawsuit by the father of a young clergyman, John Goodbourne, who had died on the way to Virginia. The schedule of Goodbourne's wearing apparel and books appears to be in his own hand, and was probably drawn up just before the son left

England. At the time of the suit the books were in storage in Virginia, where they were probably disposed of. An early twentieth-century editor has expanded and identified the titles. As many tables later do, the table gives the cash value of the books, sums almost impossible to transfer into modern currency values.[22] Naturally the great majority are theological, quite interesting in themselves for a number of reasons, though some of the nontheological titles may be of even more concern.

Libraries of well over one hundred titles will usually in this chapter be designated as "major," and the Goodbourne collection of about two hundred titles and five hundred volumes qualifies for the category. Most of the titles were to be repeated scores of times in later listings of theological writings, though some are fairly unusual. At least two works of St. Augustine, one each by Aquinas, Hooker (*Ecclesiastical Polity*), Erasmus, the Puritan William Ames, William Fulke, Nicholas Byfield, the comments of Vives, and the sermons and tracts of various Anglicans, were among the dozens of biblical or doctrinal exegeses. Among the ancients Plutarch, Seneca, Caesar, and other Greeks or Romans were present. Brinsley's "Grammar Schoole," noted in the preceding chapter, is alongside Ascham's *The Schole-master*, Greek and Latin grammars, dictionaries, and additional books which might be used in teaching or by the teacher personally. Among the names to appear many times later, besides most of those just mentioned, are Aelianus, Justinian, Quintilian, Bellarmine, Camden, Ursinus, Calvin, and John Prideaux. "A marriage prayer" and a few medical books complete a list obviously intended for teaching and preaching and for preserving life. The volumes on eloquence, however pagan in origin, were edited by Renaissance scholars in forms designed for use in homiletics. As one might expect, the theology leans toward puritanism or Low-Church Anglicanism, representing the thought and form which has remained dominant in the Episcopal church in Virginia.

No inventory comparable in size for Virginia books remains for the next generation, though there are indications that men such as Richard Watson of York County in 1643 owned probably two hundred volumes, including thirty folio titles and fifty quartos. In 1643 Dr. John Holloway of Northampton County bequeathed a sizable collection of physic and surgery books, Latin and Greek volumes, and a Greek testament in folio.[23] Scattered or casual mentions are made of parcels or chests of books, of four hundred copies of a volume on silkworms sent in October 1652 to teach Virginians how to grow these useful little creatures, and of one hundred copies of "the Second part of Crums of Comfort with groanes of the Spirite and Handkerchiefs of wet eies, ready bound to be distributed among poor children that can read" sent over in a bequest from Michael Sparke, London stationer.[24]

Bruce and Mrs. Stanard, the former at least working from actual inventories, have found several other lists of titles during the next two decades as well as some tantalizing brief descriptions, such as William Brocas' (Lancaster County) description of a parcel of old Spanish, Italian, and Latin books. In 1669 the first of the later opulent and distinguished Carter clan, Colonel John, left a large library which went in large part to his eldest son, John, with a few books to his last wife, "David's Tears and Byfield's *Treatise* and the *Whole Duty of Man* and her own books." [25] Puritan Nicholas Byfield's various theological writings, including *A Learned Treatise on the Sabaoth* (1630, etc.), appeared in several Virginia libraries into the eighteenth century; and [Richard Allestree's] devotional volume *The Whole Duty of Man* (1660 and later editions) appeared in every southern colony and almost every moderately large library (and *many* smaller) up to the time of the Revolution. The latter is an Anglican work which rivals even the Bible and the Book of Common Prayer in popularity.

Meanwhile Argall [sometimes Argoll] Yeardley, son of Sir George and brother of Francis, had died in 1655 in moderately affluent circumstances, yet leaving little evidence of any reading interests. Bibles, the works of Perkins, and a copy of Lucan's *Pharsalia* are the only books listed. He had been reared in England by an uncle after his parents died in 1627 and 1628 and probably obtained at least a grammar school education there. He may have given his five children other books before his death. The Lucan is a little strange in association with the religious works and it probably is no real indication of any interest in learning.[26] Then Bruce lists scores of other libraries before 1670, some of which appear in the inventories without titles. But worth noticing are the books in the 1667 estate of Matthew Hubbard of York County, which contained such items as Ben Jonson's *Remains* in folio; *Astrea, A French Romance*; Donne's *Poems*; and Aesop's *Fables*. Of these Aesop appears most frequently later, but also Jonson and Donne were in several collections. This library also included under "Travel" the works of John Smith and Purchas' *Pilgrimage*; under "Religion and Morals" a dozen titles including a Latin Bible; five books of "Physick"; and a number of miscellaneous works.[27] In 1667 too Richard Russell, a Quaker of Lower Norfolk County, ordered his twenty-five titles (of about sixty volumes) to be divided among seven friends of his own sect.

Two collections owned by persons named Willoughby, in different counties, are perhaps large enough to be counted among major libraries, especially for the seventeenth century. Of these the earlier is that of Mrs. Sarah Willoughby of Lower Norfolk County, who died about 1673. She possessed fifty-five titles in about 110 volumes. Included are folio and quarto Bibles, Eusebius' *Ecclesiastical History*, and seven more religious titles, including sermons. She had history and biography, Sandys' *A Relation of a Journey* (travels in the Middle East), a volume on midwifery, a grammar, dictionaries, books of navigation and geography, a book on mulberry-tree planting (perhaps Hartlib's), Aesop, and Latin authors including Ovid, Virgil, and Cicero. Dr. Henry Willoughby of Rappahannock County, who died about 1677, had forty-four medical titles, seventy-four books of divinity, thirty-eight law titles, and a fair representation of history and classics. This is an early indication of the broad interests suggested by the contents of physicians' libraries in the southern colonies.[28]

For the last quarter of the seventeenth century in Virginia, Bruce's estimate of the number of inventories, titles, and volumes has already been noted. Many on the Eastern Shore had libraries. Colonel Southey Littleton's for example, contained Aesop, sermons, histories, laws of Virginia (printed in England), and other legal and medical volumes. On the western shore James Porter of York County, who may have tried his hand at writing, left in 1675 forty-two books and twelve manuscripts.[29] During this period Governor Effingham imported special Bibles and Prayer Books for his chapel. The foundations of such later great libraries as those of the Byrds, Carters, and Wormeleys were laid in this last quarter of the century. William Byrd I was ordering regularly from England and also acquired the fine library of the scientist John Banister, who had been killed in a hunting accident. In 1690 John Carter II left sixty-two titles in six languages, of which twenty-one titles were religious, nineteen medical-scientific-utilitarian, five history, ten reference, and seven belletristic or classical. Of these all in Latin or relating to law went to Robert Carter, who was to augment the collection considerably.[30] Among the religious works were the familiar Byfield, six of Puritan Richard Baxter, Bayley's *The Practise of Pietie*, and Quaker William Penn's *No Cross, No Crown*, the last appearing in a number of southern libraries into the eighteenth century. A treatise by Aelianus was military in subject matter; the scientific and agricultural included three works by Gervase Markham on husbandry or farriery, Bacon's *Sylva Sylvarum*, and *A Way to Get Wealth* (agricultural); books on medicine and surgery had among them two of the popular *Dispensatories*, those by Culpepper and Salmon, both appearing in scores of libraries. In the categories of history and biography were standard works such as Josephus' *History of the Jews* in seven volumes, North's translation of Plutarch (1579 and later), and the familiar *Collections* of proceedings in Parliament by Rushworth, which in several volumes covered the century from 1618 on. Among the standard dictionaries and books of instructions was Thomas Spencer's *The Art of Logic Delivered in the Precepts of Aristotle and Ramus* (1628), a volume of rhetorical criticism combining the classic with the more recent Ramean precepts. Ovid, Virgil, and Homer were represented in famous English translations, and there were several early novels, some French.

The prominent clergyman Thomas Teackle of Accomack County had certainly one of the larger libraries of the seventeenth century. By the time of his death in 1696 he had acquired some three hundred titles in about five hundred volumes.[31] More than one hundred volumes are primarily religious, ninety-odd Latin but not always classics, fifty medical (some in Latin), and about eighty-five nonscientific miscellaneous English. The list deserves a thorough study and analysis, but here there is space for only a few comments on titles and contents. Worthy of note is the evidence of Puritanism, for there is a great deal of John Calvin besides two works of John Cotton, something of Richard Baxter, William Prynne's *Anti-Arminianisme* (1629 and later editions), and two books by Dr. Sib(b)s which may also be considered Puritan. As will be noted in this volume several times, the Eastern Shore of Virginia was to a considerable extent settled by Englishmen who came directly from the Netherlands and the Separatist or Puritan groups there, and for several generations a constant communication and shift of settlement went on between persons of the Eastern Shore and New England. The presence of these and other books which might be labeled Puritan or puritan (see the distinction made in the next chapter) is also entirely in keeping with the Low-Church Anglicanism of Alexander Whitaker and his colleagues and successors in the James River area of Virginia. Alongside those puritan volumes in Teackle's collection are dozens of orthodox Anglican sermons and doctrinal tracts by English clergy such as Jeremy Taylor, Jewel, and Ussher.

Mixed among other works are classics such as Juvenal, Ovid, Lucan, Suetonius, Cicero, Sallust, Martial, and Lucian. Two editions of Salmon's *Dispensatory* are perhaps the most obvious of the medical books; but works by William Harvey, one of them on the circulation of the blood, and other Latin medical tomes may interest the historian more. On Teackle's shelves was Burton's *Anatomy of Melancholy*, read by millions from its first publication in the earlier seventeenth century on through Herman Melville and Paul Hamilton Hayne (to name but two American authors who used it in the mid-nineteenth century). Hugo Grotius' *De jure belli* ("The Law of War"), Dr. John Heydon's *The Rosie Crutian*, the 1641 edition of English *Statutes* printed by Beale and Hearn; a history of New World discovery printed by John Norton also in 1641, and a small "Herball" are among his lay books. By no stretch of the imagination may one call Teackle's a recreational library.

The third major known collection of the last decade of the seventeenth century is that willed by Governor Francis Nicholson to the newly established College of William and Mary.[32] The governor began by turning over seven items to the college, including books by Sherlock, Burnet, Sir Thomas More (an English translation of the *Utopia*), and John Locke's *Some Thoughts Concerning Education*. When Nicholson returned to Virginia in 1698 to resume the government, he apparently donated the remainder of the library. About 158 volumes are mentioned by title, classified as folios, quartos, octavos, and duodecimos. A large proportion were printed after 1690, as Jennings' analysis shows, a fact which suggests that Nicholson formed the collection between 1692 and 1694 which he was in England. It is a strongly theological library of Protestant caste such as could be found in other public and private collections: for example, Hooker's *Ecclesiastical Polity*, the sermons of Edward Stillingfleet, William Cave's *Antiquitates Apostolicae* and his *Primitive Christianity*, Allestree's *Works of . . . the . . . Author of the Whole Duty of Man*, Matthew Hale's *Contemplations Moral and Divine*, and Tillotson's *Rule of Faith*. Sherlock, Wilkins, Jewel, Samuel Clarke, and more Tillotson were also there. Books quite rare in other southern libraries were Strype's *Memorials of . . . Thomas Cranmer* and Towerson's *Explication of the Decalogue*. There were several books against the Quakers, perhaps the largest assemblage in the colonial South on this subject. Raleigh's *History of the World*, Camden's and Bohun's studies of Queen Elizabeth or her age, histories of war in the Netherlands or in Ireland and the "memorable actions" of William III show the wide geographical and perhaps military interests of the donor. Histories or travel books on Germany, Ceylon, China, and the Levant, several accounts of America (including Increase Mather's *Brief History of the Warr with the Indians* and de Acosta's *Natural and Moral History of the East and West Indies*) further reflect Nicholson's interests and what he thought young colonials should know about their world.

Weak in the classics, the collection was strong in trade and commerce. Gardening and husbandry books included two by Evelyn, Meager's *English Gardener* and de la Quintinie's *Compleat Gard'ner*, Blount's *Natural History*, and Peachey's *Compleat Herbal*. Grotius' *Law of Peace and War* in English, the *Works* of Sir William Temple, the *Essays* of Montaigne, a *Catalogue* of the nobility of England, Milton's *Letters of State*, and courtesy books round out other facets of human interest. As Jennings observes, this was a good nucleus for a library, not a well-rounded collection in itself.

Among other late seventeenth-century Virginia collections Dr. Thomas Cocke's thirty-odd titles seem rather well balanced.[33] But the last large library of the century for which there is any detailed inventory—as well balanced as Cocke's and larger—is that of lawyer-planter Arthur Spicer, who died in 1699[34] in Sittenbourne Parish, Richmond County.

He owned about fifty-three legal titles, twenty-nine religious, eight historical, three medical, and some miscellaneous individual items worth
commenting upon. His legal volumes were usual—Coke, Dalton, laws of
Virginia, manuals, reports. In religion he had Perkins, Ussher, Prynne, and
Bayley's *The Practise of Pietie,* Peter Heylyn's *History of the Sabaoth*
(1636), Thomas Fuller, Samuel Clarke, and a number of middle-of-the-
road Anglicans. More interesting were several books on war, Browne's
Religio Medici, and the one known item of Shakespeare in the seventeenth-century colonies, the first quarto of *Macbeth* of 1673, as mentioned
above. Shakespeare was probably read and owned earlier, but not by the
record. Then there were Cicero's and Socrates' *Orations,* Lady Mary
Wroth's *The Countess of Montgomery's Urania* (a popular romance),
a few more pieces of fiction, and Bacon's *Advancement of Learning.* The
scattered outside records of Spicer's life and this inventory suggest that he
was a man of considerable intellectual curiosity. Along with the inventories mentioned above and others which suggest if they do not specify,
Spicer's list offers evidence that there were more books read in Virginia
than Parson John Clayton thought.[35] And there is good evidence in early
Virginia correspondence and commercial records of an insatiable thirst
for more. Even a schemer and sinner like William Sherwood had so many
divinity books that he directed his wife to share them with Joseph Pottit,
and he distributed his history and legal works among various friends, including Dionysius Wright.[36]

The adjoining Chesapeake colony of Maryland, founded in 1634, has
records of brief inventories at least as early as 1637. Though titles are
frequently given, they indicate for the first two decades only small collections, though it is quite possible that there were other sizable libraries
before 1657. As it is, the story of books in early Maryland is inextricably
bound up with the friction between Protestants and Catholics. In 1638 a
Catholic planter's overseer named William Lewis of St. Mary's was haled
into court for forbidding the indentured servants to read Protestant books,
and in 1641 prominent Dr. Thomas Ger(r)ard was convicted and fined
for locking a Protestant chapel against would-be worshippers and for
removing the religious works therein.[37] The Lewis servants appear to
have been reading the sermons of the famous puritan cleric, "Silver-
Tongued" Smith.

As for the legal records, as in other colonies they usually lump together
without further identification "a parcel of books," "a parcel of English
books," or in a few instances "small books in French."[38] These often belonged to substantial planters such as Richard Lee, Gentleman; Justinian
Snow; Captain Robert Wintour; and John Cockshutt. In 1638, on Kent

Island, held and garrisoned by Virginians under doughty William Claiborne, Church of England services were held, and there were a number of legal volumes and "1 great booke of Mr Perkins," the perennial favorite of the Low-Church Anglicans as well as of the Puritans. When Governor Leonard Calvert died in 1647, the list of his worldly possessions included only thirteen books. In 1656 the estate of Thomas Hawkins showed "2 Bibles, 1 Practis of Pietie I Sermon Book: & A Concordance."[39] In 1657, however, Thomas Hill, who owned two plantations and an astrolabe, old desk, and inkhorn, had chests apparently containing some three hundred books, referred to as "His Library."[40]

In the 1660s inventories continued to mention old books or parcels of books, and in 1669 Presbyterian clergyman Matthew Hill wrote to Richard Baxter in England begging for some theological works which might assist him in his ministry.[41] By far the most interesting of the early Maryland inventories is that of the Presbyterian Reverend Nathaniell Taylor of Upper Marlborough, including more than five hundred volumes. Principally religious, they are notable for the mixture of puritan and conservative Anglican divines represented (from Baxter to Tillotson and including John Prideaux, Stillingfleet, and Chillingworth and Cudworth as well as Barrow) and for the number of anti-Quaker pieces. Among other books were John Guillim's *Display of Heraldry* (best edition the London folio of 1724 but first about 1660), two works of Sir Thomas Browne, many by Robert Boyle (both religious and scientific), many scientific and philosophical works including Boethius; various rhetoricians such as Quintilian and Ramus; and Steele and Hobbes and Grotius and Barclay, along with some of Milton's prose. Also included were globes and atlases and mathematical works. The list compares most favorably with the Anglican Reverend Thomas Teackle's of Virginia. Taylor, whose origins are somewhat obscure, came to Maryland with his congregation about 1703 and with other ministers formed the Philadelphia Presbytery about 1706. He may have been Scottish or the son of a famous English nonconformist clergyman of the same name in London. He has been discussed here with the group primarily of the seventeenth century because his books so obviously represent the end of that century. Probably such able and learned nonconformists as Taylor gave some impetus to Dr. Bray's determination to attempt to strengthen Anglicanism in that colony, principally, or at least appreciably, through reading matter.

In the spring of 1695 the Proceedings of the Council contain an account of six sets of books sent over by the Bishop of London and indicate to whom and where they were delivered.[42] Something of Bray's work in organizing the Anglican church in Maryland is told below, in the next two chapters. But his establishment of parochial libraries and a provincial library to aid clergy and laymen is perhaps the most significant part of it. Realizing that he could induce able clergymen to undertake the arduous and lonely tasks of missionary priests only if they had encouragement for intellectual development, he conceived the idea of parochial libraries, an idea which proved to be so good it was expanded to include all the English-speaking plantations and even lending libraries for English towns, especially seaports. By 1695 he had printed a prospectus in five thousand copies for establishing the parochial collections.[43] The first proposal is that the Bishop of London be pleased to prepare a catalog (Bray himself took over the job) of particular books which might be needed by a parish clergyman. The first edition of the *Bibliotheca Parochialis* (spring of 1697) was given to potential donors. Shortly afterward Bray published an essay suggesting lending libraries in England, to begin with sixty-three titles, more than half theological works.

Although the catalogs of parochial libraries and of the provincial library sent by Commissary Bray to Maryland before 1700 are now lost, there is a 1702 (?) table of the number (1095) and value of books for the provincial library at Annapolis and from 10 to 314 in the parish libraries, a total of 2,566 books valued at £808.7.6, as opposed to a total of 1,504 books for all other colonies combined with a value of £964.6.0. Joseph T. Wheeler, who has made an analytical study of eighteenth-century Maryland books and reading, in "Thomas Bray and His Maryland Parochial Libraries,"[44] prints the list for the parish library of St. James in Anne Arundel County for May 1698 as representative. It is naturally overwhelmingly theological, with Hooker, Taylor, Tillotson, Burnet, Allestree, Hale's *Contemplations Morall and Divine*, and polemics against Quakers and Papists and atheists. Bray's own *Catechical Lectures* (1697) and his *Bibliotheca Parochialis* are here, and Thomas Aquinas, Du Pin's *Ecclesiastical History* (1696), the popular scientific-religious Ray's *Wisdom of God in the Works of Creation* (1692). Histories were Blome's *Geography and Cosmography* translated from Varenius (1693), an abridgment of Raleigh's *History of the World*, Sir Richard Baker's ubiquitous *Chronicles of the Kings of England*, Xenephon, Hennepin on America (1698), Grotius' *De Jure Belli et Pacis* (1651) and his *De Veritate Religionis Christians* (1675). There were eighty-seven titles in all, 90 percent of them printed (usually reprinted) in England in the 1690s. This may or may not be exactly Bray's proposed list of 1695 which the Bishop of London did not like and had modified.[45] When compared with private clerical and other religious collections, it proves to be comprehensive and useful—from an Anglican point of view.

The laymen's libraries for Maryland, like those for England, both Dr. Bray's ideas, were designed for inhabitants of isolated districts seldom visited by clergyman. They were also intended as antidotes for the rampant Quaker doctrines in late seventeenth- and early eighteenth-century Maryland. Thus they too were essentially religious or theological collections, though designed less learned than the parochial libraries. Bibles, pastoral letters, catechetical lectures such as Bray's own, Allestree, Sherlock *On Death*, sermons covering many centuries, Leslie's anti-Quaker *The Snake in the Grass* (1697), were usually in multiple copies. A few asterisked items of more complexity of argument appear in one copy only, designed for "persons of better condition."[46] The cost of the collection was designed to be less than £10. Bray planned for various Maryland clergymen to write books for these libraries and even gives the initials of his prospective authors, who were to be Hugh Jones, Henry Hall, Joseph Colebatch, Thomas Cockshutt, Stephen Bordley, and perhaps a dozen others, most of whose names appear in other connections in the following chapters. In a revised plan of 1701 the titles to be written by local parsons were omitted. In 1701 eleven of these laymen's libraries were sent to parishes. The inventories differ somewhat from the proposed list, and three of the libraries (St. Mary's, St. Michael's, and St. George's) received about twice as many titles as the other eight.[47]

Much more significant to the intellectual historian or bibliophile than the smaller parochial and laymen's libraries is the Bibliotheca Provinciales, or Annapolitan Library, begun about 1696 and largely financed by a grant of one hundred guineas from Princess Anne. It contained 1,095 books (probably titles) and cost £350, serving as a model for smaller libraries sent to Boston, New York, Philadelphia, and Charleston. Though its catalog has not been preserved, a manuscript volume forming a register of the other libraries set up in imitation of it does give a good idea of its contents. And fortunately St. John's College at Annapolis, successor to King William's School, which became custodian of the collection, still possesses more than four hundred volumes from this library.[48] The first part of the Annapolitan Library arrived in 1697, three years before Bray himself set foot in Maryland. It is an orthodox Anglican theological collection. Unlike many of the private libraries of staunch Church of England men in this and other southern colonies, it seems not to have contained books which might be labeled outright Puritan. There is no Bunyan's *Pilgrim's Progress*, nor *The Theatre of God's Judgments* (by Cromwell's tutor), nor Reynolds' *The Triumph of God's Revenge on the Crying and Execrable Sin of Murther*, pious nonconformist works in favor in Puritan and certain Low-Church Anglican families.[49] *The Whole Duty of Man*, orthodox Anglican guide to religion reprinted for a hundred years, was here as it was in Bray's smaller libraries. The collection was designed primarily for the use of clergymen, but Bray's idea of what a parson should know was fairly broad and comprehensive, including "all parts of Useful Knowledge, both Divine and Human." Though "Theology, Metaphysicks, and Pneumatology" is the largest division, there are works on "Ethicks, Moral Philosophy, and Oeconomicks,' '"Politic and Law," "Voyages and Travails," "Physiology," "Chemistry," "Pharmacopy," "Anatomy and Chirurgery," and 'Mathematicks, Trade and Comerce," as well as a division on "Words" (including Grammar or Rhetoric, Poetry, and Logic). The Church Fathers, including Ambrosius, Athanasius, Augustine, the *Corpus Juris Canonici*, Pearson on the Creed, Burnet on the Thirty-Nine Articles, and Sherlock *On Death*, appear alongside the works of the chemist Robert Boyle (including something on theology) and the Platonist Henry More, Bishop Gilbert Burnet's *History of His Own Time*, and Grotius and Pufendorf on war, peace, and the law of nature and nations.

Going through the card catalogue of the surviving volumes will impress one with the variety and number of sixteenth- as well as seventeenth-century theological works. Church Fathers, medieval English churchmen such as Matthew Paris and Robert Grosseteste, stand beside later pulpit orators or tractarians already mentioned in other libraries. Three authors with a Puritan tinge were William Ames, Richard Baxter, and William Perkins.

The nontheological titles, probably borrowed more frequently in the two and a half centuries between Bray's time and ours by college students and laymen, were likely once present in greater proportion. But surviving are Aristophanes and Euripides, Dante and Descartes, Aristotle and Quintilian, Ovid and Plutarch, the already-mentioned More, and Bayle and Pufendorf, Robert Horne's *A Brief Description of Carolina on the Coasts of Florida* (1666), and one novel in Latin, Barclay's *Argenis* (1634). Many of these volumes still show stamped on one cover of the original binding DE BIBLIOTHECA ANNOPOLITANA.

It is more than probable that up to the time of his death in 1730 Dr. Bray added to the original Annapolitan Library as he did to the smaller laymen's and parochial collections. At any rate, books which he may have sent, now housed with the presumably pre-1697 gatherings, are works by Sir Robert Cotton, Rushworth, Thomas Rymer, John Selden, Sir Henry Spelman, Cicero, Thomas Burnet, and Pierre Bayle's *Dictionnaire*, some of which are in eighteenth-century editions. James Hanway's *An Historical Account of Trade over the Caspian Sea*, published in 1754, was too late to have been a Bray donation, but it was a book found in the colonial period in both Virginia and South Carolina as well as Maryland.[50] It was probably a donation to King William's School, which after the Revolution became St. John's College.

The original Annapolitan Library was clearly intended for public use and as a research library for Maryland clergy who might need for some of their sermons or tracts many of the great theological materials it contained. Apparently it was moved many times, and it is amazing that almost half of it should have survive fire, weather, and war. One wonders how much the galaxy of able Maryland clergy, who have left us sermons and other writings that contain varying degrees of reference to authorities, may have used it—a point to be brought up a bit later when homiletic appeal to authority is considered. One may say, however, if this remainder of a great collection be the criterion and test of use when compared with extant sermons or tracts, that Dr. Bray came much closer to meeting American clerical needs and laymen's religious needs in his smaller libraries. But there must be much further investigation before one can be sure.

THE CAROLINAS

Though books are mentioned in inventories in both Carolinas from the 1670s or the 1680s, they were generally until the 1690s few in number and insignificant save that they showed colonists had books and were enough interested in them to consider them as valuable property. Weeks notes North Carolina inventories in the 1676–1680 period, apparently all of the "parcel of books" or "Bible, Common Prayer, and *Whole Duty of Man*" variety.[51] The first library of any moment in the upper Carolina was the parochial-provincial library sent to the town of Bath by Commissary Bray, most of it arriving after 1700, though part of it by 1699.[52] In size it was more nearly like the parochial or laymen's collections in Maryland than like the Annapolitan provincial collection. Why Bath, which was not the provincial capital, was chosen to be the recipient of this first donation is not entirely clear, but actually, as one reads between the lines and learns of the Reverend Daniel Brett's bequest, it looks as though the intention was in 1699/1700 to found a public parochial library. In 1703 Governor Walker called it a public library, the personal gift of Dr. Bray and the bequest of Brett, "a minister appointed to this place." Both Bray's and Brett's collections were naturally predominantly theological. The inventory of Brett's books is extant and at least suggests the kind of subjects the whole library contained. Classified by size, the *Works of the Author of the Whole Duty of Man* and the *Cambridge Concordance* were among the folios, and the usual divines in the smaller volumes, along with tracts against Quakers and other nonconformists.

But Brett's library also contained useful nonreligious works such as Guillim's *Display of Heraldry*, dictionaries, books on weights and measures, Whiston's *New Theory of the Earth*, classical authors, Wingate's

Arithmetick, works on history including Baker's *Chronicles,* Fuller's *Worthies,* a handbook for carpenters, a manual of hunting and hawking and fishing, and *The Merchant's Map of Commerce.* If Bray added to it the usual laymen's and parochial library's titles, this was a respectable library. Brett's part alone came to about 163 volumes.[53] This library had a chequered and ultimately disastrous history. Legislative efforts for its maintenance were made, especially in 1715, though earlier two S.P.G. missionaries had declared it in ruinous condition. The suggestion has been made, though not very convincingly, that this was the collection which Edward Moseley, a trustee of the Bath library, tried in 1723 to present to the town of Edenton. As it is, the legislation introduced by its existence was certainly among the earliest legal enactments (but see South Carolina below) for libraries in the southern colonies, and its known titles indicate or suggest that there were literate and even well-educated men capable of using them.

South Carolina, much more thickly populated than North Carolina from the beginning, and with plans for a real city, trade, and large-scale plantation agriculture, has for the seventeenth century much more evidence of interest in books and reading, especially for practical purposes. Chronologically the first significant record of a desire for useful books, in this instance for a kind which would be in demand throughout the South for the rest of the colonial period, is to be found in a letter of May 29, 1682. Young Thomas Newe, formerly of Exeter College, Oxford, and son of the Butler of the College, wrote to his father a series of letters describing South Carolina and Charleston. In this one he asked that "you would be pleased by the next opportunity to send me over the best herbalist for Physical Plants in as small a volume as you can get. There was a new one just come out as I left England, and I mistake not in 8.vo that was much commended, the author I have forgot, but there are severall in the Colledge that can direct you to the best."[54] Though the young man was dead within six months, one may be fairly sure the book reached the American shore and was put to good use in a colony later noted for its botanists.

In 1685 Landgrave Morton, one of the leading early settlers and governor from 1682, left to his son and daughter fifteen books by title, and in a later provision "the rest of my books" to his son Joseph. All those specifically named are religious, and the books as well as other details denote that the owner was a dissenter. Stern Calvinist determinism is evident in Puritan William Twisse's huge folio *The Riches of God's Love* (1653), evidently a reply to Anglican Samuel Hoard's book arguing for God's mercy.[55] Other seventeenth-century inventories are not as specific as this one. John Godfrey in 1689/90, for example, simply left all his law books to his son Captain John. In 1693 Thomas Smith, Sr., left his instruments of chirurgery and half his books on medicine to his son George. Merchants, locksmiths, and others rarely specified titles but did bequeath books. Intriguing is the 1697 inventory of Robert Adams, a practitioner of medicine, which lists two works called *London Dispensatory*, a *Practice of Physick*, and several other books with registered but now indecipherable titles.[56]

The other recorded library of seventeenth-century South Carolina, usually referred to as "The Provincial Library" in Charleston, probably deserves to be classified among major colonial collections. Again this was in part the direct result of Dr. Bray's efforts in 1696. There are at least 233 titles in Bray's slightly later "A Register of the Library of Charles Town Carolina, / A Register of the Books Sent tow^ds Laying the Foundaçon of a Provincial Library at Charles Town in Carolina."[57] The books began to arrive in 1698, and Bray estimated their value at £300. The South Carolina Assembly in the same year, in gratitude for Bray's work, itself voted £53 toward payment for certain of the books, an amount owed Robert Clavell, London bookseller, probably part payment of a pledge made by the province toward the library benefaction. Bray's accounts show further shipments in 1699 and 1701, and in 1700 the provincial Assembly passed a law regarding the care and place of deposit for the books. They were to be under the charge of a churchwarden and clergyman of the Anglican communion in Charleston. The Assembly also laid down rules for borrowing and returning. Commissioners were to visit and examine the books each year.

As might be expected, the list very much resembles in basic materials those Bray prepared for other provinces and his parish libraries. Theological titles are in the overwhelming majority. This time the "Register" or Catalogue is not by size but by subject, beginning with Scripture and commentaries, Church Fathers and ancient writers, and many other religious themes on to the Doctrine of the Covenant of Grace and the Creed. There were nonreligious groupings such as humanity, polity and law, history and its appendages, voyages and travels, physiology and medicine, mathematics and trade, grammars and lexicons, logic, poetry, and two other headings without books. The usual Aquinas, *Cambridge Concordance*, St. Augustine and St. Jerome, Grotius, Hale, Bray himself, Puritans Baxter and Perkins, Calamy, Heylyn, Barrow, Henry More, Sherlock (at least six titles), Taylor, Sanderson, Tillotson, and Leslie, are a few of the items.

Under humanities the titles are all classical. The histories and travels include Raleigh, Lawrence Echard's *Roman History*, Esquemeling on the buccaneers, Dampier's *Voyage Around the World*, Henepin's *A New Discovery of the Vast Country in America*, Camden's *Britannia*, Baker's *Chron-*

icles, Fuller's *Holy Warre,* Guicciardini's *History of Italy,* Cave's *Lives of the Fathers of the Church,* Burnet's *History of the Reformation,* and Bellarmine's *De Scriptoribus Ecclesiasticus.* Under medicine and kindred subjects were books by Salmon and Read. Hans Sloane's *Catalogus Plantarum quae in Insula Jamaica . . .* (1696) and Ray's *Historie Plantarum Universalis* (3 vols., 1684–1701) were among the famous botanical works. Dictionaries, lexicons, and only two volumes of verse, made up the rest, though the subject headings for rhetoric and logic indicate the intention of supplying books in those areas.

This collection increased steadily for a time. In 1705 Governor Nicholson of Virginia sent money for South Carolina parish libraries which was perhaps expended on this provincial library, and Nicholas Trott in 1703 stated that Dr. Bray had sent more volumes, together with some books for a layman's library. More restrictive rules about borrowing, as already noted, had to be passed in 1712. John Urmstone wrote to Nicholson in 1714 that the "Famous Library sent by Dr. Bray's direction" was largely destroyed, a statement which was almost surely an exaggeration. But the books did gradually disappear, and when in 1724 Schoolmaster Morritt searched for them they were not to be found. From 1698/1699 to at least 1712, however, this library was a major resource for religious and secular intellectualism in South Carolina.[58] Placed at the heart of the colony's life, the capital city of Charleston, it was used by anyone who felt the urge or need to read. Among the southern colonies only Maryland equalled or surpassed it in having a general public provincial library, and even then such a collection did not come anywhere nearly so early in the colony's history as it did in South Carolina's. Books and reading had at least a good start in South Carolina. And the S.P.G. never forgot the colony but continued to send books and pamphlets to individual clergy or parochial libraries for at least the next half century.

BOOKS AND LIBRARIES IN THE EIGHTEENTH CENTURY

As population and territory expanded in the southern colonies between 1700 and the Revolution, so did books and reading. At the very end of the period, in 1763, when frontiers had been pushed so far west that intellectual communications had been stretched thin, books as well as schools were scarce west of the Blue Ridge. But there were books in the Great Valley of Virginia and with the Carolina-Georgia traders among the mountain Cherokees, as James Adair's writing gives evidence, for there were educated men in the west who wanted to read. In the Tidewater and Piedmont older settlements literacy remained apparently at a rather high ratio, and thousands of inventories great and small, with institutional and society libraries, newspapers, and provincial writing and publication prove that there were books. Especially in families grown prosperous or even relatively opulent by the end of the seventeenth century the foundations for quite remarkable collections had been made.

The usefulness mentioned earlier as a principal criterion in book collection is as evident in the large extant inventories as in the more modest ones. In the ongoing *Papers of Thomas Jefferson* the editors remark in Volume One that they have been constantly impressed by the third President's evaluation of everything by its degree of usefulness, and they hasten to add that the word or the idea behind it, *usefulness*, was much more comprehensive in its meaning in the eighteenth century than it is today. Everything that brought men virtue and happiness was useful. And Jefferson's great collection, the nucleus of our national library, was built not only on his lifelong purchases through booksellers but on what he could pick up from the old Virginia libraries of John Banister, the three William Byrds, Richard Bland, George Wythe, John Wayles, and his own Randolph relatives, among others, as will be discussed. But everything he selected from these older colonial libraries was chosen for its usefulness in one way or another, as his biographers have shown. Even the library of William Byrd II, sometimes characterized as the first southern bibliophilic library, gathered primarily for the love of books for themselves, is basically also a utilitarian collection. Byrd may not have read and used all of it, but in his seventy years he made a mighty effort to do both, as his diaries attest.

A short time ago Edwin Wolf, 2nd, a distinguished librarian and bibliophile who has spent a lifetime studying and analyzing older major American libraries, published a most interesting and provocative monograph on "Great American Book Collectors to 1800."[59] Of a dozen great collections from those of the New England Mathers and Winthrops through middle-colony James Logan and Benjamin Franklin, he found only two in the South, those of Byrd and Jefferson. Some of his northern representatives, such as John Adams and Thomas Wallcut and William Bentley, were contemporaries of Jefferson or younger. But if southern records were intact or the actual contents survived, perhaps a dozen great libraries from below the Susquehannah might stand beside these northern ones, and every one of them was collected before the Revolution. As it is, the fragments of inventories and purchase and sales lists of the library of John Mercer of Marlborough in Virginia would indicate in themselves that this collection must stand among the great ones. The no-longer-extant sales catalogues of Peter Manigault and Nicholas Trott of South Carolina, of Ralph Wormeley of Virginia, and many others including those of Randolphs and Carters, might also indicate that their books should be listed among the once-great colonial collections. Wolf is writing mainly about books or libraries which have survived, at least in part, into the present time. The Manigault and Mackenzie and Charleston Library Society original collections have disappeared except for a few isolated volumes, though a catalogue exists for the latter two. Maryland clergy such as Samuel Skippon and Thomas Bacon and Jonathan Boucher had more than respectable collections which survive for the first two only in inventory lists, and the Tory Boucher lost his valuable library (only generally described) when he had to flee the country in 1777. In the same province there were several other gatherings worth well over £100. Of all the Marylanders, the younger Daniel Dulany may have owned the most extensive and expensive and useful library, though only a portion of it has been recorded; but as far as extant lists are concerned the private library of Robert Morris may have exceeded it in variety and value.[60] In North Carolina there were a dozen libraries which might be called major, from Edward Moseley's in 1723 to that left by James Hasell in 1786 (primarily a pre-1764 collection), but even Governor William Tryon's hardly seems to have approached the Byrd-Jefferson class. There were more than a score of large South Carolina libraries besides those of Manigault (d. 1773) and Trott (d. 1739), though no evidence that they were in the group of great collections. Some of these notable lists are considered below. The great Georgia libraries seems to have been public or institutional, though two or three private ones deserve notice.

W.B. Edgar has found 154 presumably private libraries in South Carolina (all in the eighteenth century before the Revolution) valued at £50 or more,[61] but he is not counting certain large societal collections and apparently has not included some other potentially large collections for which he could find no attached valuation or appraisal. These last may be a serious omission from his study, as certainly his failure to include a single inventory of one of his 154 libraries is. One may guess from extant evidence, printings and samplings of manuscript records, that Maryland and Virginia each contained at least as many libraries of this minimum value, and the latter probably more. The kind of analysis Edgar has done is useful up to a certain point and is referred to below. Similar studies should be done for each colony, as suggested at the beginning of this chapter, but only after the publication and/or examination of *every* known book inventory and after the weighing of certain other factors not considered in the study mentioned. What Wheeler for Maryland, Edgar for South Carolina, to a lesser extent Weeks for North Carolina, and various persons for Virginia do show is that people of many occupations and conditions read and owned books and what sort of books they had. A brief survey of these libraries should be made before one turns to the matter of reading tastes and the uses made of the books available.

THE COLLECTIONS: PUBLIC OR CLUB

As already indicated, many or most of the libraries which were more or less open to the colonial general public were founded before or by 1700. The collegiate institutional collections of Henrico in 1619–1624 and William and Mary in the 1690s, and the provincial and parochial and laymen's libraries primarily of Maryland but also of the Carolinas late in the 1690s, were in operation as the new century began, of course with the exception of Henrico. The original library of the college at Williamsburg survives in only one or two books, though later donations kept the library open to students and to permanent or temporary residents of the town most of the time up to the Revolution, and the library improved after the signing of peace. The Charleston provincial collection survives only as a list, but the Annapolitan collection, thanks to King William's School and St. John's College, is more than 40 percent extant. It seems to have been in continuous use at least into the middle of the nineteenth century. Bray's parochial and laymen's collections today survive if at all only in fragments, and the Bath-Brett library of North Carolina primarily through Brett's list of books. Though some of the smaller group collections probably continued to be used by some individuals throughout the eighteenth century, parish clergymen's reports to the Bishop of London two decades and later after 1700 often indicate that the volumes have disappeared. Whatever safeguards had been made for their preservation were not enough.

Though undoubtedly the loss of books and collections was to a considerable extent the result of neglect, both in physically preserving and in mode of lending them, these first public libraries served communities which to some extent appreciated the opportunities the libraries afforded them. Letters to ecclesiastical authorities in England from colonial clergy frequently complain that borrowers have failed to return books, not an entirely bad thing in itself. One learns from other letters, as those of William Fitzhugh, that borrowed books might be passed on without the permission of the owner and consequently lost. This instance relates to private ownership; books known to be public or church property were probably handled even more carelessly. In a country of relatively few books, this situation was natural. In other words, usable tomes on husbandry or surveying as well as the more abundant and at least equally popular religious works such as sermons were in constant circulation. The borrowers were first probably clergymen, and second avid or curious or pious lay readers not prosperous enough to buy everything they wanted to peruse. It is perhaps significant that the surviving remnants of the great private collections seldom if ever contain a volume stamped with the name of a public institution or club or having such denotation of ownership within its covers, though Jefferson and Byrd and Landon Carter and other major collectors had books bearing the autographs of various persons. Certainly most of these last had been bought at inventory sales but just as certainly some had been borrowed from individuals and never returned.

The history of the Annapolitan Library is indicated by the card catalogue of the original volumes surviving and the books that were added to them at least up to 1847, and the story of the vicissitudes of the William and Mary collection has recently been well told by John M. Jennings.[62] As far as "public" libraries founded in the eighteenth century are concerned, the story is almost entirely of social-club lending collections or commercial ventures in circulating books. The story may well begin in Maryland, which has the oldest and longest continuous printing history, for both private-club and commercial lending are in one way or another connected frequently with printing establishments.

Maryland printers from Evan Jones in 1700 had been booksellers, offering for sale books and pamphlets printed by themselves as well as imported volumes. But it was not until 1762 that William Rind advertised his proposed lending library, a year before New York's first and three years before Boston's first, for the "great Utility of diffusing a Spirit of Science thro' the Country." His initial list was of 150 titles, of which half were on English literature or the classics or language. Thomson, Swift, Shakespeare, Fénelon, Voltaire, Defoe, Fielding, and Richardson were among his belletristic authors.[63] Terms were that each subscriber should pay twenty-seven shillings in Maryland currency annually in order to borrow two books at a time. Time limitations were imposed according to size, the borrower of a folio naturally being allowed four times as long to read it as the person who took an octavo. Anyone passing a book on to others would have to forfeit the full cost of the volume, another evidence of the loose lending-borrowing habits of the period and region. Rind got too few subscribers to warrant establishing his circulating library on the scale originally proposed, and on January 13, 1763, he announced a modified plan which included the stipulation that he would lend only to persons who lived within a thirty-mile radius of Annapolis and that only one book at a time might go to a subscriber. This plan worked for the moment and he issued a catalogue, though at the end of the year subscription renewals were insufficient. First he decided to auction off the entire library; finally he had to resort to selling the books by lottery.

In 1773 William Aikman in Annapolis and Joseph Rathell in Baltimore each attempted a circulating commercial library. Loyalist Aikman moved to Jamaica in 1775, and Rathell never got enough subscribers. It was not until the Revolution that a successful lending library was operated in Baltimore. That the idea of the circulating library had taken firm hold in America—and in at least some of the southern colonies—is evident from a 1787 Baltimore newspaper poem written by a local citizen on "The Circulating Library; or, Advantages of Reading."

In South Carolina, there seems to be no record of a public lending library until George Wood opened one in connection with his new bookshop, at the end of the period, in 1763–1767;[64] he first advertised his venture in April 1763. In 1772 Samuel Gifford opened a circulating library, and there is some evidence that Samuel Carne, a physician, operated some sort of lending library from the 1740s. Carne's books appear to have been almost entirely medical.[65]

A public library of limited circulation was that established about 1756 for the Council and Commons House of Assembly. It was located in the new state house and was primarily if not entirely juridical, including statutes and legislative journals, parliamentary history and debate, and other works which could have been extremely useful to working legislators especially if they were not professional lawyers.[66] Edgar suggests that the noted Redwood Athenaeum of Newport, Rhode Island, may have supplied summer residents from South Carolina, of whom there were many into the nineteenth century, with reading matter. Even if this is true, the Redwood had only a relatively minute part in the reading of Carolinians.

Perhaps the greatest of southern colonial public-club libraries was that established in 1748 in Charleston by a group of young would-be intellectuals from every element of the city's literate classes. Among the seventeen promoters were several Scots, some French Huguenots, and several Englishmen. There were nine merchants, two planters, a schoolmaster, a printer, a doctor, a peruke maker, and two lawyers.[67] Among them were at least three (James Grindlay and Joseph Wragg, Jr., and Samuel Wragg) who themselves possessed excellent private or personal libraries, of which more later. More than any other collection of the South, this Charleston library was a product of an urban environment, and perhaps for this reason has flourished, allowing for periods of pillage and neglect, to the present day. It is said that the seventeen young men banded together so that they could purchase all the recent magazine and pamphlets. And though there were other obvious reasons, Dr. George Milligen-Johnston was surely right in observing (in 1770) that through the Society's means "many useful and valuable Books have been already introduced into the Province, which probably would not otherwise have soon found their Way here, private Fortune not being equal to the Expence."[68] Though couched in rather pompous or at least grandiloquent language, the preamble to its rules is a manifesto of intellectualism, declaring that the Society was created to prevent future generations from sinking into the savagery of the red men and to preserve the European heritage of knowledge in this New World. They invited any and all who agreed with them to join. It was then ostensibly a democratic organization, aiming to emulate the mother country's "Humanity, as well as her Industry."

In other words, here was to be a circulating library neither theological nor commercial. Its first president, John Cooper, was a distiller and a Quaker, and John Sinclair, the first librarian, a merchant and a Quaker. The first published notice of a meeting appeared in the *South Carolina Gazette* of July 24–31, 1749. By 1750 the rules were published with a list of 129 members. By 1754 the Society was incorporated and its first £1,600 laid out in books. As in the case of the Annapolitan Library, covers were stamped in gold with the name of the owner, here the CHARLES-TOWN LIBRARY SOCIETY. Edgar declares the library more balanced than any owned by individuals,[69] and if one follows simply the 1770–1772 catalogue perhaps this may be true. This invaluable list is really in three parts, the 1770 catalogue, a 1772 appendix, and a 1772 addition-on-deposit of the fine collection of John Mackenzie. The grouping is once again by size, with some 172 folio titles (the original numbering is often inaccurate) in 311 volumes; 107 quartos in 196 volumes; "octavo et infra" 506 titles in 1161 volumes. The appendix lists about 70 more titles in 129 volumes. One thus counts almost 1,000 titles in nearly 1,800 volumes by 1772, not including the excellent Mackenzie collection of about 318 titles in 655 volumes.[70] History is the category best represented in the library, with perhaps religion or the classics next. There are indeed some fifteen or more periodicals. Verse and belles lettres generally are represented in English plays (Congreve, Cibber, Gay, Farquhar, and Johnson's Shakespeare, *inter alia*), in Montaigne and Corneille, Aristotle's *Poetics* and other works on rhetoric and aesthetics, and Butler's *Hudibras*, with fiction English and French. Trott's *Laws* may have been the only book printed in South Carolina in the library, but there were dozens of other books concerned with America, including Milligen-Johnston's and Cove's descriptions of Carolina, a history of Louisiana (partially about South Carolina), Lahontan, Douglas, Raleigh, and Ulloa; Hutchinson's *History of Massachuesetts Bay* and Colden's *History of the Five Nations* (of the Iroquois) and even a *Natural and Civil History of California* in two volumes; Eliot's *Indian Bible*, and Samuel Quincy's *Twenty Sermons* (preached in South Carolina but printed in New England). Some conservative and a considerable amount of liberal or Whiggish political philosophy is here, including *Cato's Letters*, *The Independent Whig*, Gordon's edition of Tacitus, Molesworth's *An*

Account of Denmark, Algernon Sidney's *Discourses on Government,* Shaftesbury's *Characteristicks,* Locke's *Two Treatises on Government,* Montesquieu, Rapin, and many others who could be used in Whiggish argument. Hume and Bolingbroke may or may not have represented the other side. Certainly both sides used Bolingbroke. But of this more in a later chapter.

The titles lost and the titles listed belie certain alleged observations (somewhat twisted in the retelling out of context) that Josiah Quincy on a trip to Charleston in 1770 is quoted as having made concerning "the mental abilities" and anti-intellectualism of these Charlestonians,[71] and a Charlestonian is quoted out of context to support him. The Charlestonian knew better, and if the vain and self-righteous Quincy had probed a little deeper, he might have altered his statements, which even as they stand are almost all weak when read in context. The Charleston Library Society, along with other book collections, newspapers and other writings, and encouragement of the fine arts, showed the city to be much more than an acquisitive urban center for trade and exports, though it was certainly that.

There is one instance in North Carolina of what might be called an abortive attempt to found a public library, referred to specifically at the time as a provincial library. It is a curious and somewhat puzzling story. In 1723 Edward Moseley, one of the North Carolina commissioners for surveying the boundary described in William Byrd's classic *History of the Dividing Line,* offered to present a collection of books to the S.P.G. as the nucleus or foundation for a "Provincial Library to be kept at Edenton, the Metropolis of North Carolina." There were seventy-six volumes of folios, quartos, and octavos entirely theological and naturally suited to a clergyman's research collection.[72] The offer was apparently never accepted. At least no record survives of its existence or use at Edenton. As for booksellers' lending libraries before 1763, there seem not to have been any. Presumably the population was too scattered to make it practicable to operate a commercial lending library such as was tried in the village-city metropolises of Annapolis, Baltimore, and Charleston.

Georgia's late start makes the story of its books and reading almost outside the picture given in this study, but not quite. The German Salzburgers seem to have organized their religious library at Ebenezer by 1738 and continued to add to it, with titles in Latin, German, and English, at least until the American Revolution. There survives in Germany a list of 104 titles sent to this community, the books bearing imprints from the seventeenth century to 1776, though only two have dates before 1763.[73] It must have been useful to Lutheran clergy but not at all attractive to most laymen. Before this Ebenezer library was in operation there seems to have been between 1736 and 1757 a "Parson's Library" at Savannah. During the era of the Trustees, or Proprietary ownership, it grew by leaps and bounds as boxes full of books poured in (nine cases, for example, in 1749) and by 1757 the "parson's books" took fifty-six folio pages to catalogue. If one estimates this by the twenty-three pages and 1,200 books of Whitefield's Bethesda Orphanage Library (1771), the Savannah collection may have numbered above four thousand volumes.[74] Frederica also had a German theological collection, and at Augusta by 1751 a library for public use had been organized. The engineer William G. De Brahm, in his great *Report of the General Survey of the Southern District of North America*, included a delightful "history" of Georgia which mentions five fine libraries (see the epigraph at the beginning of this chapter), three in Savannah, this one at Augusta, and the collection at Ebenezer mentioned earlier.[75] The highly educated and intelligent De Brahm was presumably praising without prejudice, and at least three of the five were public or semi-public collections. Probably only the Ebenezer Library was at the beginning purely theological, and it may not have remained so. The "Parson's Library" almost surely was as general as the Annapolitan's if not the Charleston Library Society's; and the Augusta collection, the history of which is little known except that it still continues (with book replacements), almost surely was a balanced representation of various areas of knowledge.

The beginning of the Augusta library appears to have been in 166 volumes sent by the Trustees aboard the *Charming Nancy*, religious and educational and philosophical works (e.g., Plato),[76] and was intended primarily for educational purposes, for it contained from six to fifty of each of the titles named. There can be no doubt, as Fleming suggests, that all these libraries gradually became more and more secular. As for rules for borrowing or lending and who was eligible to use the books, one can only guess. De Brahm may be understood as implying that anyone who wished might use them, though perhaps under restrictions.

The Bethesda Orphanage Library just mentioned, with its twelve hundred volumes burned with the buildings soon after Whitefield's death, does survive as a list or in categories.[77] One recalls that Whitefield planned to make Bethesda into a college, and the volumes there in 1773 seem to indicate that such was his aim. It was before Whitefield's death an academy, and most probably many of the library books were donated by admirers of the great evangelist and his institution. Of the 45 or more works he had earlier placed on a sort of proscribed list not one appears in the Bethesda collection.[78] Three-fourths of the 1,200 are religious—including dictionaries, lexicons, encyclopedias, commentaries, concordances, Biblical translations, sermons, and theological and philosophical writings. Some church history, 25 volumes by the Wesleys and 26 by Whitefield, are among this same group. The remainder have been analyzed as 45 reference works, 108 history and biography (including 8 in natural history and 10 in American), 10 geography and travel, 75 belles lettres ("literature," poetry, and mythology), 23 music (principally hymns), 3 theoretical and practical education, 19 science, 7 medicine, 13 law and government, a dozen "secular" philosophy, and some young people's books and periodicals.[79] As the analyst of this library points out, from the point of view of collegiate education the collection compares quite favorably with those of Harvard (5,000 in 1764), William and Mary (3,000 in 1776), Yale (4,000 in 1766), Princeton (1,281 in 1760), King's (Columbia, 2,000 about 1760), Pennsylvania (1,670 in 1832), Brown (250 in 1772), and Dartmouth (355 in 1775). Bethesda was not open to everyone, but a great many "liberal" or nonconformist laymen and clergy in Georgia must have used it.

Virginia, the oldest of the colonies, seems to have left no trace of commercial or public lending libraries before the Revolution, and actually only slight hints that they may have existed before the end of the century. The scores if not hundreds of modest private collections and the large number of varied personal libraries, combined with the habit of lending to neighbors, may have been major reasons why they seem not to have existed. But as already noted, permanent or transitory inhabitants of Williamsburg might have used the college's books. And it is quite evident that most of the literate persons, from great planters to Presbyterian preachers to craftsmen, felt that they could purchase what they needed straight from England or through the bookstore connected with the *Virginia Gazette* office. That is, at mid-eighteenth century it was in general a society which had felt for several generations that it could afford to buy its own books. And though there is little way of comparing even fairly precisely the William and Mary library of 1750 with that of the Charleston Library Society or the Annapolitan of the same year, William Byrd II's books alone surpassed any of these public collections. At mid-century there were probably a dozen private libraries in Virginia which equalled in size and variety the public and society collections of any of the other southern colonies.

THE COLLECTIONS: PRIVATE

Several suggestions have been made at the beginning of this chapter, perhaps most of them indirectly, as to why anything like the complete story of colonial southern private libraries has not yet been told, and also as to why the full story can never be told because of total destruction of many records and most of the books themselves. But for all the colonies there is at least some detailed information, including the invaluable inventories already available in print. And for three colonies at least a great quantity of information regarding titles, size of collections, and number of volumes appears in periodicals and book-length studies. In other instances photographic reproductions are available, though prohibitive costs have prevented their extensive use. But already for the southern colonies perhaps more than for the northern, private libraries have been listed and analyzed in such books as Wright's *First Gentlemen of Virginia* or for a later period Sowerby's great five-volume *Catalogue of the Library of Thomas Jefferson.* From these, further analytical studies have grown.[80]

What is now available on private libraries shows several things. For some there are fairly exact lists of what they contained, often with information as to size and number of volumes per title and occasionally with prices of purchase and place and date of publication. For each colony there is enough detailed listing to prove that there were, as noted at the end of the previous section of this study, several fine collections. Other libraries probably as large and varied and useful are represented by only a few tantalizing details, such as the amount at which they were appraised, enumeration of the number of folios, quartos, octavos, and duodecimos, more rarely a numerical analysis according to subjects or areas represented, and here and there partial lists of what were clearly collections many times as large as the lists enumerate by title.

For Maryland Joseph T. Wheeler has given enormous amounts of information about libraries and reading habits from 1700 to 1776. Wheeler points out that in this province inventories before 1715 are scarce and fragmentary, for it was not until that year that executors and administrators were *required* to make inventories in the presence of creditors and relatives of the deceased as witnesses.[81] The estimates given are naturally conservative, for books might be overlooked but none would be invented to be placed in lists in the presence of such witnesses. For the period 1720–1770 more than 60 percent of the inventories examined included books. Usually an inventory listed only a Bible or a parcel, or less than ten titles, with some groups of twenty or so. Wheeler finds, and anyone who has worked in such materials must agree with him, that the proportionate or actual monetary value of the books is difficult or impossible to estimate in modern terms. As will be shown below, perhaps only in South Carolina, and then only relatively and quite inclusively, do appraisal values indicate much about libraries. For the purposes of this study, what the southern colonial owned and thus could read or lend to others to read is the more important thing.

But it is worth noting that the value of books varies greatly in proportion to total assets. A poor man might die possessed of a good library. It might be professional, but more often than not it contained general religious, belletristic, and professional works. Using George K. Smart's classifications according to subject matter,[82] in twenty-five *larger* (here nineteen or twenty to several hundred titles representing many more volumes) private libraries the largest category proves to be religion; next, history-travel and law; then literature, classics, medicine, science-arts, "doubtful," and philosophy in descending order. In many instances titles may be placed under more than one category, as John Ray's books on science and religion, and the designation has to be somewhat arbitrary. The Bible, the Book of Common Prayer, and *The Whole Duty of Man* were the almost omnipresent religious books in these libraries. The Bishop of London and the Society for the Propagation of the Gospel poured copies of *The Whole Duty* into the Atlantic colonies for general distribution, though moderately prosperous individuals ordered their own from London or (by 1746) were buying the reprint by William Parks of Williamsburg in Virginia. Lewis Bayley's *The Practise of Pietie*, so popular earlier in the Chesapeake colonies, had by 1700 lost favor, perhaps because it was considered too Puritanical in its depiction of God's wrath.

The Quakers, who were still strong in some parts of the Chesapeake and Carolina colonies in the eighteenth century, owned and read devotional books published by their own sect. But judging by the extant listings, far more popular in the southern colonies generally, including Maryland, was Charles Leslie's anti-Quaker tract *The Snake in the Grass* (1696).[83] Perhaps a typical religious library is represented in the 1734 inventory of Arthur Miller of Kent County, Maryland, who had among his books William Penn's *No Cross, No Crown* (first edition, 1669), as did other good Anglicans, *A Treatise on the Sacrament and Divine Art of Prayer*, *The Whole Duty of Man*, and a Bible.[84] The same man had both Michael Dalton's and William Nelson's standard *Justice of the Peace*, and *The Independent Whig*, all popular legal and political works. Appearing in Maryland and other southern libraries was a third manual for the country squire, Richard Burn's *The Justice of the Peace and Parish Officer*, which did not appear until 1755 but then went through twenty-nine editions in ninety years. Other legal aids were *The Young Secretary's Guide*, *The Compleat Clerk*, Godolphin's *Orphan's Lawyer* and other books for executors, evidently all found useful in Maryland and the colonies to the south. Many more titles will be noted below.

History was throughout the eighteenth century an absorbing topic to the Marylander and other southern colonists, perhaps even more than it had been in the preceding century. Raleigh, Burnet, and Rushworth continued to be popular. But read increasingly were books written or translated more recently, as Voltaire's three major histories (in English or French); Josephus' *Works* on the Jews; Lawrence Echard's *Ecclesiastical History*; Charles Rollin's, Lediard's, and Humphrey Prideaux' histories; and many voyages, especially Anson's and Cook's.

The *Spectator*, the *Tatler*, the *Guardian*, and the *Rambler* were in most larger libraries of Maryland as well as Virginia and the deeper South. Pope, James Thomson, Swift, even Stephen Duck; the playwrights Beaumont and Fletcher, Ben Jonson, Dryden, Farquhar, Otway, Congreve, Cibber; Rabelais, Le Sage, Fielding, and Smollett were all in one moderate-sized Maryland library of 1757.[85] Shakespeare, Bacon, Quarles (*Emblems*), But-ler's *Hudibras*, and Milton increased in popularity as the years passed, and new editions continued to appear. Political writings, all to be considered in some detail below, were in eighteenth-century Maryland collections, even in some of the groups of twenty titles or fewer. In later years Bolingbroke and Hume appeared beside the more liberal writers.

Mathematics practical and theoretical was in many libraries. Books on navigation and bookkeeping were vital for practical purposes. Perhaps less obviously utilitarian were the editions of Euclid, trigonometry, or general mathematical principles. Only a few American imprints of any sort appeared in Maryland collections, most of them legislative acts and laws, but a few belles lettres were included.

Naturally the clergy owned at least fair-sized collections and were perhaps at the same time the least prosperous generally of the bookholders among professional groups. Their inventories vary from parcels containing a few specifically titled religious works to a hundred and even many more volumes on varied subjects, some showing titles and some not. When the Reverend Stephen Bordley died in Kent County in 1709, he left some 150 volumes, most of them untitled but including Grotius' *Works* in four volumes, and sermons. The Reverend Edward Topp had at least as many, including Tillotson, Grotius, and "Old [church?] Musick books," besides ten untitled folios, of which two were in Latin. Welsh Evan Evans of St. George's, Harford County (d. 1721) had fewer books but more variety, for besides forty "Sermon books," a biblical concordance, and ninety-two sermons in one folio, he had a volume of the laws of Maryland, *The Life of the Duke of Marlborough*, and a history of Charles I and II and James II. Samuel Skippon, dying in 1724, left about 150 volumes, again including music and sermons and history, Pliny's *Natural History*, a number of books in Latin, Maryland Acts of Assembly for 1717 (probably the Jones-

Bradford collection of Laws of 1718), and "Chaucer's Poetry in English folio." The owner had been described by his Commissary as "A Whig, & an excellent scholar and good liver."[86]

Perhaps the most valuable and diverse clerical library of the mid-eighteenth century belonged to the Reverend Thomas Bacon, certainly one of the major Maryland figures of his age, compiler of the *Laws of Maryland*, to be noted elsewhere, as well as poet, pulpit orator, educator, and musician. His private library, as might be expected, was unusually large and varied.[87] It included lexicons and dictionaries, an assorted collection of medical books, religious or theological commentaries (including Chillingworth, Stillingfleet, Stackhouse, James Blair of Virginia, Hooker, and Sherlock), history (Raleigh, Pufendorf, Rapin, and William Stith of Virginia), science (Newton, geographies, etc.), mathematics, classics, law (as John Mercer's *Abridgement* of the Laws of Virginia), Whig political works (Shaftesbury's *Characteristicks*, Rapin, Stith), some philosophy, some books on gardening, and a few novels. Thirty percent were medical, one of the evidences of the fact that early clergy and other educated men perforce practiced the healing art within limits. Untitled parcels of Greek, Latin, Italian, French, and Dutch books and manuscripts are listed. What must have been a considerable musical library is unlisted except for "Medleys," perhaps because his widow had bestowed most of it on one or more friends. Virginia items already listed and a "History of Pennsylvania," along with his own *Laws of Maryland*, are the principal representatives of American materials and are, in the instances of his own *Laws* and the Stith and Mercer, American imprints.[88]

The Reverend James Sterling, Irish playwright and poet, Maryland customs official as well as Anglican priest, must have had a large library. Even if one judges only by the allusions in his American writings including his verse, he must have had on the Eastern Shore a considerable collection, though the inventory of his £1,500 estate contains only an unlisted group of books valued at a mere seven pounds. The last of the major colonial Maryland clerical libraries, that of the Reverend Jonathan Boucher, already mentioned in Chapter III above, was a valuable one, as shown by the advertisement in the *Maryland Gazette* of June 5, 1777, after he had had to flee because of his Loyalist sympathies and activities. It is said to have contained

> a complete set of the Greek and Latin Classics, Dictionaries, Lexicons, and a Variety of other school-books, entertaining Miscellanies and Novels, a choice collection of English and French poets, the most approved writers on Agriculture, Biography, Chronology, History, Geography, Mathematics, Philosophy natural and moral, Law, Physic, and Divinity.[89]

Whatever dissenting clerical libraries of value or variety there were, except for some more connected with Virginia than with Maryland, usually came in the inventories so long after the colonial period that they almost surely were not brought together before 1763. Presbyterian Nathaniell Taylor mentioned above is a notable exception. Other Presbyterians and Quakers, however, certainly had libraries at least in part theological, and there may have been reasons for not recording them in legal inventories.

Alan F. Day of the University of Edinburgh, while completing his doctoral dissertation on "A Social Study of Lawyers in Maryland, 1660–1775," found that before 1690 there were hardly any law libraries in Maryland. Of ninety-eight lawyers who listed their books in the colonial period, only nineteen (19.5 percent) were before 1690. But after the Revolution of 1688/1689 the legal volumes began to multiply. Day finds the most popular law books to have been Coke's *Institutes* (first and third parts), Godolphin's *Orphan's Legacy*, Bridgeman's *Conveyances*, Wentworth's *Office and Duty of Executors*, William West's *Symbolaeography*, and frequently for maritime-law practitioners Molloy's *De Jure Maritimo et Navali*. Compilations of cases in King's Bench, Common Pleas, and Chancery, and handbooks of procedure and dictionaries, were also present. Day has found that Maryland lawyers' libraries were overwhelmingly professional. Stephen Bordley, for example, had non-law titles but they were not estimated at more than one-fifth the value of his total library. William Bladen's were nearly completely legal. Maryland barristers, earnestly desiring to improve their profession in the colony, attempted from 1678 to procure standard manuals or sources such as Keble's *Statutes* and Dalton's *Country Justice* for all the commissions of the peace, and were later in the eighteenth century a major force in getting provincial law and procedure into print.[90]

Among these Maryland practitioners were several dozen able and learned men. The education of dozens of them at one or another of the Inns of Court has been mentioned in the preceding chapter. One of the earliest of the period to have left a catalogue of his books is William Bladen, trained at the Inner Temple, secretary and attorney-general of Maryland, who arrived in the colony in 1692 and died in 1718. He had a considerable part in bringing the printer Thomas Reading to Annapolis in 1700 and getting the first collection of provincial laws published. His was one of the major law libraries of the colony in the century. Nine-tenths of the collection is made up of *Reports*, including Coke's, Bulestrode's, and Keble's; commentaries and statutes; histories and dictionaries. He had in all forty-eight of these titles in many more volumes. He had also Beaumont and Fletcher (six volumes), Bacon's *Atlantis* (two volumes), the *Spectator* (three), Shakespeare (six), and a "Compleat Gardiner." His professional titles suggest what all other American legal libraries do, the close affiliation of the American juridical system with the British. George Garnett of Kent County had books worth £190 out of a total estate value of £300. Again it was predominantly a collection of legal reports, commentaries, and statutes. But Butler's *Hudibras*, a book against deistical writers (Leslie's?), some natural history, Johnson's *Dictionary*, Montesquieu's "Reflections on the Roman Empire," John Harris' *Lexicon technicum* (1704, here called "Lexicon of the Arts & Sciences"), and Watts' *Logick* (1725) are also here. Richard Chase of Baltimore (died 1757), though his titles differ somewhat from Garnett's, had a parallel collection of reports and statutes.

The aforementioned Stephen Bordley (1709–1764), educated in Great Britain and making frequent short trips back there, tells in his letter-books much about what was perhaps a major library of 184 legal titles besides other sorts of volumes. He was nephew of the Reverend Stephen Bordley and son of the lawyer Thomas Bordley. The surviving correspondence shows him sending plays, classical authors, the *Gentleman's Magazine*, and other journals from England. When he was back in Maryland he wrote for the works of Machiavelli, Gordon's *Tacitus*, Salkeld's *Reports*, Quintilian's *Oratory*, Polybius, Herodotus, La Bruyère's *Characters*, various reports, Pufendorf, Tillotson, the *Craftsman*, Rapin, Bayle's *Dictionary*, and much other history. Some few he secured from a friend in Kent County, the prominent planter Matthias Harris. One of the many primary evidences of political reading—content, cause, and effect —is included in a letter of February 22, 1739, from Bordley to Harris quoted as one of the epigraphs for the present chapter.[91] There will be more on reading as background for politics, but one should note that Bordley also read Sale's translation of the Koran, specifically mentioning the "Preliminary Discourse" which was to be of use to a later Baltimorean, Edgar Allan Poe, in composing some of his major poems and tales.

Less is known generally of the medical profession in early Maryland than, for example, in Virginia and South Carolina. In the colonial period almost all known Maryland physicians had been educated by proceeding through apprenticeships to independent practices. Just a little later they were to go to organized medical schools in Philadelphia or Edinburgh. There were a few "professional" writers among them who contributed to British journals observations on fauna and flora and meteorology. Dr. Richard Brooke, for example, who published in the *Philosophical Transactions* of the Royal Society and in the *Gentleman's Magazine* in the 1750s and the *Maryland Gazette* in the 1760s, must have had a good library, judging from his allusions. Dr. Alexander Hamilton, frequently mentioned elsewhere, in his *Intinerarium* and his *Defence of Doctor Thomson's Discourse on the preparation of the body for the small pox* (1750) shows a wide knowledge of medical and scientific books and theories. His letters, his unpublished minutes and mock history of the Tuesday Club, and his *Maryland Gazette* essay on Maryland authors, all reveal a varied and recent reading—that is, reading continued in the colonies after his rearing and education in Edinburgh.[92]

Dr. Robert Holliday of Baltimore County left few titled medical books in his library; probably most of them had been disposed of by previous arrangement, though there is a "parcell of Physic Books." But he did list or had listed histories by Rapin, Lediard, Josephus, and Voltaire; a volume of plays; voyages, dictionaries, Bibles, *The Whole Duty of Man*, Locke on the *Human Understanding* and *On Government; Pamela*, the *Spectator* and *Tatler* (twelve volumes), and the usual miscellaneous "parcell of old Books."[93] More interesting, perhaps because more titles are listed, is the collection of Dr. John Jackson of Queen Anne's County, who died in 1768. The medical books, unnamed, were valued at more than £10, but the remainder show by their titles some variety: Shakespeare, Thomson's *Seasons*, "Arabian Tales," Swift's *Tale of a Tub* and a biography of Swift, Le Sage's *Gil Blas*, one volume of Pope's *Works* and a biography of him, Cervantes' *Don Quixote*, and collections of plays. History was represented by ancient and Roman accounts, and by books on China, the Netherlands, Guernsey, and the New World (Raleigh), and biographies and memoirs of Charles XII, and others, and Anson's, Harris', and Roberts' voyages. Along with some religious and legal works were political titles, Marana's *The Turkish Spy*, Shaftesbury's popular *Characteristicks*, Trenchard and Gordon's *The Independent Whig*, and other works perhaps denoting Whiggish inclinations. Among other items are Boccalini's *Advices from Parnassus*, fellow Marylander the Reverend Thomas Cradock's *New Version of the Psalms of David* (1756), Sherlock *On Death*, and the frequently mentioned John Campbell's *Life of the Duke of Marlborough*. There are other physicians' libraries, at least one a notable collection, to be considered with planters', for several prominent physicians in this province and elsewhere were first of all farmers.

In the Chesapeake colonies those who were planters were in general the most prosperous people, with perhaps merchants next. But certainly the most interesting intellectual-cultural story from these two groups in Maryland is that of tobacco factor and small planter Henry Callister, who was hardly what might be called prosperous. Much of his correspondence has been preserved by the Maryland Diocesan Library and the Maryland Historical Society. He was the provincial representative, under chief factor Robert Morris, of the Liverpool firm of Foster Cunliffe and Sons.[94] Callister was perhaps more interested in books and music, in playing in ensembles with the Reverend Thomas Bacon and even the governor, than he was in his occupations or livelihood. A number of documents show what books Callister ordered from London, and a curious advertisement in the *Maryland Gazette* requests the return of dozens of volumes he had lent to friends. In February 1744, for example, he ordered from Parson Bacon's merchant brother in England four histories of various parts of America from Greenland to the Spanish colonies, Newton on Daniel and Revelation, Defoe's *True-Born Englishman*, the *Gentleman's Magazine*, some French works, and naturally some music. He continued to ask for periodicals, voyages, dictionaries, maps, and prints, and for an engraved heraldic bookplate. His missing-books list shows that he owned Swift, Bolingbroke, Richardson's *Clarissa*, *The Independent Whig*, and Colden's *History of the Five Nations*, among other works.[95]

Living not far from Callister on the Eastern Shore was William Carmichael, whose principal estate was near Chestertown. The two were great friends. Carmichael's correspondence with Callister refers to books, as one on Bolingbroke, periodicals, Antonio de Ulloa's *Voyage to South America* (trans. London, 1758, later a favorite of Madison and Jefferson), several on California, the popular Burn's *Justice of the Peace and Parish Officer*, Smollett's *History of England*, the *North Briton* of John Wilkes, and Jethro Tull's *Horse-Hoeing Husbandry; or, an Essay on the Principles of Tillage and Vegetation* (1733–1744), a *must* for every agriculturist including Washington and Jefferson throughout the rest of the century. Callister himself gathered books on gardening, as Miller's *Gardener's Dictionary* with the additional illustrations, the pictorial part of which he appears to have sold to Governor Sharpe. Callister died a bankrupt, though enough of his books remained in 1785 for his daughters to advertise an imposing list. Included are twenty volumes of the *Universal Magazine*, three of Fielding's *Works;* the multivolume *Nature Delineated*, Molière's *Comedies*, *The Independent Whig*, *Deism Revealed*, Swift's *Works*, *Hudibras*, a Latin-English Ovid's *Metamorphoses*, British statutes, and a number of novels and periodicals. He had Bisset's *Laws of Maryland*, Cradock's version of the Psalms noted above, and, most intriguing, "Version of Psalms by Mather and Wells N. England 1640." In other words, he had a copy of the great American rarity, *The Bay Psalm Book*, the earliest surviving printed book of English America.[96] As every student of Maryland local general or intellectual history has agreed, Henry Callister was a remarkable man. Since he was not only merchant but small planter, his papers show how wide and deep the interests of a middle-class colonial might be and how intimate he could become with the governing class of the colony.

The letterbooks and other materials regarding the Carroll family afford evidence of the reading interests of definitely upper-class Marylanders. In this instance most of the booklovers and bookowners were Roman Catholics, educated at home and in France in Catholic schools and colleges, and occasionally showing the influence of their religion on their book collecting and reading. The first member of the family to be considered, however, was Protestant Dr. Charles Carroll (1691?–1755), who came to the Chesapeake region in 1715 to practice medicine. Like many others, he soon became as much interested in agriculture, shipbuilding, and land speculation as in his profession. His 1723–1755 letterbooks show many things about early Maryland, including reading interests. Like others, he ordered his books directly from England. They included a considerable number of legal items which might have been useful in his business affairs. He also wanted maps of Europe, Asia, and Africa as well as America, perhaps partly out of curiosity and perhaps partly to plan voyages. He had a terrestrial globe; North Carolinian Edward Moseley's "A Mapp of North Carrolina made in 1743 dedicated to Gabriel Johnson [*sic*] Govr sold at the 3 Crowns over against Minceing lane in Fan Church street"; various histories; the latest book on the peerage of England, Scotland, and Ireland (at least he ordered this); and Plutarch, Pope, and Dryden.

Dr. Carroll's letters to his son at Cambridge and then at the Inner Temple give more about his book interests. He wanted the young man to get for him Bacon's abridgment (of laws), laws and statutes against Papists, "The Wigg Spectacles," Bolingbroke, Charles Boyle the Earl of Orrery's remarks on Swift, and a new planisphere. The son in turn wanted in 1752 a good edition of Maryland laws, though there was not really a good one until Parson Bacon's some years later. Curiously the physician requested no medical books. For his second son, educated in the colonies, he ordered a good collection of the classics, even though the boy was destined to be a merchant.[97]

Charles Carroll, barrister (1723–1783), who returned to Maryland only a few months before his father died, continued the family habit of interest in books. His letterbooks 1755–1769 show him writing for a complete set of the *Gentleman's Magazine*; a book on taxes; Philip Miller's *Gardening* [*sic*] *Dictionary* and Thomas Hale's *Complete Body of Husbandry*, both used frequently by his wife and himself, and three or four other books on husbandry. In 1760 he asked his agents to pick up the monthly reviews and any good pamphlets on current affairs for him, and he continued collecting at least until the Revolution. In 1760–1764 he asked for Tindall's continuation of Rapin's Whiggish *History of England*; the four-volume edition of Sir William Temple; the same number of volumes of Lord Shaftesbury; Lord Molesworth's *Account of Denmark* (1692), and histories of Sweden, Ireland, and France; Tacitus, Voltaire as historian, Montesquieu's *Spirit of the Laws* and D'Alembert's *Analysis* of the law, Smollett's continuation of his history, and apparently Oldmixon's *British Empire in America* (2nd edition, 1741). He bought a few religious titles but was more interested in periodicals, the classics, Machiavelli, even medicine. And he purchased Matthew Prior's *Dialogues of the Dead* and Johnson's *Dictionary*.[98]

Charles Carroll of Carrollton (1737–1832), signer of the Declaration of Independence and heir of the Catholic branch of the family, used books all his long life. The first record is of 1750, when he was a thirteen-year-old student at St. Omer's. He had already begun to read law and was struggling with Justinian's *Institutes* and enjoying Horace, Virgil, Racine, and history. He began to make what he hoped would be a complete collection of all the Latin authors. He wrote his father for a list of the French literature they already had. He did not wish to duplicate any of it. He intended to have Boileau, Rousseau, and Voltaire, and the best dramatic poets. Though as a Catholic he could not formally be admitted, he read law at the Middle Temple, with the aid of family legal works his father sent him from his grandfather's library. In England before he returned to Maryland in 1765 he bought Hume's *History*, a natural history of Kamchatka, Orme on Hindustan, the second volume of Warner's Irish history, and a number of pamphlets and almanacs. Later correspondence between father and son in America concerns volumes of Vitruvius Britannicus, the architectural author whose manual and drawings were used by many planters, and Arthur Young's *Tour* of Wales and south England. He continued to secure whatever interested him from England and France, including Pope, Milton and Farnsworth's translation of Machiavelli. Voyages always fascinated him, as they did most British and Americans of the eighteenth century.[99]

An examination of wills and inventories of the members of the famous Tuesday Club of Annapolis reveals that these professional and business men were in every known case lovers of books. A few have already been noted. But among the others wealthy Daniel Dulany the elder, pamphleteer and lawyer, left books at each of several of his plantations when he died. At one stood "the new London Dispensary" (medical) beside volumes on bookkeeping, a Hebrew lexicon, a treatise on architecture, and Annapolitan Richard Lewis' translation from the Latin of Holdsworth's Welsh satire *Muscipula*. At another place he had Raleigh's *History of the World* in folio, Dryden's Virgil, the usual Bible, Book of Common Prayer, and *The Whole Duty of Man*, Blackmore *On the Creation*, Burnet and Sherlock (half a dozen by the latter), Bates in religious tracts or sermons, and the "History of Tom Jones in His Married State." In his study were biographies and histories ancient and modern (including Rapin), Pope's *Iliad* and *Odyssey*, [Tull's?] *Horse Husbandry*, Plutarch's *Lives*, the abridged *Philosophical Transactions* of the Royal Society, some dictionaries, many legal works, Butler's *Hudibras*, Milton's *Paradise Lost* and *Paradise Regained*, Humphrey Prideaux's *Old and New Testament connected in the History of the Jews and Neighboring Nations* . . . , Montaigne, another Raleigh's *History*, Grotius, Molesworth's *Account of Denmark*, Orrery on Swift, Waller's poems, and about two hundred books in parcels, ninety-five of them in French. Here and elsewhere were volumes on architecture and husbandry, mariners' guides, and schoolchildren's elementary textbooks. Though the total collections may not be said to be distinctly Whiggish, the titles lean in that direction, as is suggested by Dulany's one major essay.[100]

Another of the more interesting collections is that of the Callister's friend and benefactor Robert Morris, founder of the great financial family. It contained more belletristic titles than any other located by the man who has investigated Maryland libraries most fully, though the Lloyd family collection may have contained almost as many.[101] Planter-merchant Morris was evidently a man of as varied tastes as his whilom assistant Callister. Religious and medical books include the usual Sherlock, dispensatories, a life of King David, Brady's *Psalms*, sermons, and Bibles. Histories appear frequently, as Rapin's of England, Oldmixon's *The British Empire in America*, accounts of Germany, the Reformation, Europe, the Rebellion, Rome, and others. Besides Oldmixon, other accounts of the New World are a history of Virginia, Esquemeling (on buccaneers), Lediard, Pufendorf, and Vertot. There are lives of Czar Peter, [Campbell's] the Duke of Marlborough and Prince Eugene, Suetonius, and half a dozen more besides some memoir biographies. Hill's *Natural History*, Harris' voyages, travels in Egypt and Africa, Ramsay's *The Travels of Cyrus*, and Anson's voyages, are not unusual in other larger southern libraries. Political disquisitions are prominent, among them Shaftesbury's *Characteristicks*, Bacon *On Government*, *The Independent Whig*, *Cato's Letters*, [Bolingbroke's?] "Dissertations on Partys," and Locke's *Two Treatises on Government*, all more or less Whiggish on the British Constitution. There were books on agriculture, anatomy, chronology, poetry and painting, midwifery; on moral philosophy; and on methods of studying history. Belles lettres include Montaigne, Rollin, Molière, and Cervantes, among continental authors; Addison's periodicals, Thomson's *Poems* and his *Seasons*, Swift's *Works*, Temple's *Works*, Milton's major poems, Gay's *Fables* and *Poems*, Glover's *Leonidas*, Prior's *Poems*, Congreve's *Works*, and dozens of plays including the *Beggar's Opera* in a separate edition. Perhaps significant are the volumes of literary criticism, such as Bysshe's *Art of Poetry, Reflections on Poetry*, and Addison's Notes on *Paradise Lost*. Among the novels are *Clarissa, Tom Jones, Pamela, Joseph Andrews*, and a few lesser known. *Hoyle's Games* reflects recreational interests more than anything else save the belles lettres.

Later Maryland clubs, such as the Forensic (founded 1759) and the Homony (c. 1770), had perhaps as many intellectual men as did the Tuesday Club and men even more prominent in provincial and national history, but the story of their activities belongs generally to a later period, and most of their records seem to have disappeared, anyway. Two Homony Clubbers, George Chalmers and Jonathan Boucher, are known to have had large book collections, but only a few hints as to what they contained survive,[102] for as Loyalists they fled at the beginning of the Revolution.

From these samplings it is obvious that the sorts of books mentioned as popular in other colonies and indeed in Great Britain were popular in Maryland. Professional libraries, especially the clerical and legal, were often quite good. History, biography, and travel were both recreational and useful in occupations and in politics. The great English figures of literature, from Chaucer through Congreve, Pope, and Fielding, were on their shelves. Their owners had the facts as well as the formal education from which to speak and write effectively, and in the eighteenth century a number of them did become most articulate. Maryland's individually significant early resident authors naturally reveal much of their reading in their writings, but so far no inventory of the library holdings of these writers has been discovered.

For several fairly obvious reasons more has been written about private book collections in colonial Virginia than about those of all the other southern colonies combined. First, there is a longer history and record of libraries in county archives than for any other colony, despite the destruction of all early papers for whole counties such as Gloucester and the partial destruction of others such as King William. Those for York and Northampton are virtually if not entirely complete, and there are some inventories for almost all other colonial counties. Second, the existence for a century and more of various local, regional, and state historical journals in Virginia has afforded opportunity for the publication of book lists long and short from hundreds of estates. Besides these journalistic documents, others have been printed as appendices to books, as the libraries of William Byrd II and Robert Carter of Nomini Hall. Third, as a result of the preceding two factors, several useful and stimulating studies of reading interests and books have been made, such as Wright's *First Gentlemen of*

Virginia, George K. Smart's "Private Libraries in Colonial Virginia," John M. Patterson's "Private Libraries in Virginia in the Eighteenth Century," E. Millicent Sowerby's *Catalogue of the Library of Thomas Jefferson*, and others mentioned in the bibliography for this chapter. Then there is such material as the "*Virginia Gazette* Daybook 1750–1752, 1764–1766" (Univ. of Va. Lib. Microfilm Publications, no. 5, 1967), Lester J. Cappon and Stella Duff's *Virginia Gazette Index* (2 vols., Williamsburg, 1950) to the files of that newspaper on microfilm, Swem's *Virginia Historical Index*, and the microfilm copy of the Landon Carter title pages from Sabine Hall. Despite these riches (perhaps the largest group of available book titles among all the American colonies), the readily available printed materials are by no means comprehensive. Many manuscript lists are still to be published and analyzed.

But obviously much can be said now about Virginia colonial libraries, far more than there is space for in the present study. Perhaps one should begin by noting a few facts about the small libraries, of which Bruce found a great many from the seventeenth century. In the eighteenth century the library inventories or references continue to multiply in the records and continue to tantalize the interested searcher in frequent terse phrases such as "all his books" or "a parcell of books." A few of them which include titles are of great interest because of what is already known about their owners, such as Charles Stagg (d. 1736), the veteran theatrical producer and actor of a Williamsburg troupe, a man who left seven volumes of Bolingbroke's *The Craftsman*, a Bible, prints and maps, and two books on the art of dancing, one by John Weaver and the other by James Essex.[103]

Those libraries which may be designated as of medium size (usually below a hundred volumes) may in some instances actually have been larger, or may represent the remnant of a once major library reduced appreciably in size by widespread gifts to others before the owner's death or by deliberate or careless dispersal in the months or years between the death of the original collector and the filing of the inventory. This diminution may be expected or was probable in lists filed by widows some years after the deaths of their husbands. Proportionate to total number of recorded collections, as many of these medium-sized libraries existed in the seventeenth as in the eighteenth century.

What was at least a moderate-sized collection was William Fitzhugh's "a study of books," mentioned in the 1701 inventory of Fitzhugh's estate. It may actually have been as large as or larger than that of his friend Arthur Spicer, who died just two years earlier. It was of course a seventeenth-century collection, and the few titles known are to be found in Fitzhugh's correspondence with the London agents or friends who procured books for him, or in his citations of various authors in his letters. In giving legal advice in his role as a lawyer he often mentions the usual Bracton, Keilway, Fleta, and Britton, most of which he could have taken secondhand from complete editions of Coke's *Reports, Institutes,* and *Commentaries on Magna Carta.* But there were other authorities he could hardly have repeated from memory or from Coke. From England he ordered Thomas Burnet's *Theory of the Earth* (1684), Robert Boyle's *The Sceptical Chemist* (1661), Joseph de Acosta's *Natural and Moral History of the East and West Indies* (transl. 1604), Cornelius Agrippa's *Occult Philosophy,* Tacitus, Polybius, Virgil, Horace, Juvenal, and Persius (in Latin and/or English). Though he preferred English translations, he clearly had no trouble with Latin or French. He wanted Francis Bacon's *Remains* (1648), Cotton's *An Abstract Out of the Records of the Tower Touching the King's Revenue* (1642); a large quarto Bible, a folio Prayer Book, and all the works of the author of *The Whole Duty of Man.* In one letter he abjectly apologizes for having lost a book he has borrowed from a neighboring planter. In another he orders a work from England which had not yet appeared, though he knew it was scheduled to do so. Fitzhugh's known books are not at all unusual, but his dated references are one of the proofs that there was no cultural lag in reading among southern colonists.[104]

In this first decade of the eighteenth century several other medium-sized libraries are of some interest. In 1706 Fitzhugh's lifelong enemy the Reverend John Waugh left a library appraised at £75 sterling, quite a considerable sum. In 1701/2 Edmund Custis on the Eastern Shore left forty-one rather usual titles and one quite intriguing "Scarum muche" (Scaramouch, the buffoon character opposite Harlequin from Italian, in English drama by 1673); in 1709 John Hay of Middlesex had seventy-seven books in Latin and English; and in 1710 Hancock Lee of Northumberland had over fifty volumes, religious, medicinal, and legal, including the first three parts of *Pilgrim's Progress.* In the second decade of the century the Reverend Josias Mackie, a Presbyterian minister, in 1716 left books in Latin, Greek, and Hebrew to be divided among three nonconforming ministers of "Poatomoake or thereabouts." In 1713 Vincent Cox of Westmoreland left "a walnut table and form and 54 books." In 1716 in the same county Thomas Thompson, a surveyor among other things, left six books on his profession, seven law books, three on navigation, five theological or religious, Sir Richard Baker's *Chronicles of the Kings of England* (1643), "Glanceck of Witches Observances," and three singing books. In 1718 St. John Shropshire also of this county left a large library, unidentified, valued at £60.[105]

In the 1720s men like Charles Colston (d. 1724) and John Dunlop

(d. 1728) left modest libraries with the usual variety, except that Dunlop had a few religious books and a number of romances and plays suggestive of items to be found in later libraries. In 1728 the rather elusive figure Dr. Mark Bannerman, versifier and friend of the Scottish poet Allan Ramsay, bequeathed fifty-three English and Latin books. Listings for scores of medium collections exist, but very few give the titles or even number of volumes. Many of the testators' names are of interest, for they have connections with other matters of intellectual and historical concern. Among them by mid-century were Nathaniel Harrison and John Cargill of Surry, Mathew Hubard of York, Sterling Clack of Brunswick, Richard Chichester of Lancaster (who had two hundred varied works), and Charles Pasture of Henrico, whose fairly large library is listed by titles, covering the usual religion-to-dictionary range, with Leslie against deism, Erasmus, and the plays of Aphra Behn. Then there was John Buckner of Stafford, probably related to Fitzhugh's friend of that name, who in 1747 had eighty-seven volumes.[106]

Later in the century in 1760 one woman, Mailana Drayton of Middlesex, owned a number of volumes of French and Latin books, probably for her children or for use in teaching. In the same year and county Alexander Reade left two hundred titles and a parcel of pamphlets and magazines, all valued at £61. Many of these libraries belonged to the clergy. The Reverend Bartholomew Yates of Middlesex, mentioned in Chapter III as a cultured and able cleric, had a library valued at only £7. Schoolmaster Donald Robertson's collection of books, acquired 1758–1775, is difficult to assess, for it contained multiple copies of classical and mathematical school texts. A partial list of single-copy titles survives, however, showing varied Latin classics, Pope, Fontenelle, Burnet's *Theory of the Earth*, Montaigne, Fénelon's *Telemachus,* Aesop, Montesquieu, Dodsley, Thomas à Kempis, Boerhaave, Locke *On the Human Understanding*, Smollett's *History*, and other works which might attract the curious mature mind and excite the youthful. These were all popular books, but Robertson's possession of them probably assured his pupils of the opportunity to become acquainted at an earlier age than they might otherwise have done with the thinking of the world in which they lived.[107] Goronwy Owen, Welsh clergyman and poet, sometime Oxonian and member of the faculty of the College of William and Mary from about 1757, is among the most distinguished owners of private libraries. What his appraisers in Brunswick County listed was twenty-six actual titles and "A parcel of Old Authors . . . in Number 150." Of the twenty-six exactly half are religious, including several volumes of sermons. There are also dictionaries (English and Welsh), a book on medicine, Milton's *Poems*, Terence's *Comedies* in English (edited by Echard), a few magazines, and a book of travels in Asia. His theological authors included Jeremy Taylor, Humphrey Prideaux, John Leland, William Sherlock, and Thomas à Kempis. A knowledge of the 150 old authors might shed light on the intellectual habits and diet of one of the more romantic figures among southern colonials, a man of gifts and weaknesses reminding us of Edgar Allan Poe and Owen's twentieth-century countryman Dylan Thomas.[108]

Only rough patterns of interest, popular authors, and some book values can be determined from these piecemeal, fragmented, or lumped inventories of modest but usable libraries. The titles already mentioned all reappear in most of the larger libraries, only slightly changing their complexion as the decades passed. That is, these Virginia colonials held onto or even bought from England seventeenth-century authors up until the Revolution, as already suggested. Often they bought them in new editions at the same time they acquired the latest or recently composed works. Perhaps patterns of taste at least are more discernible in the larger collections. Certainly George K. Smart, John M. Patterson, and W.D. Houlette seem to think so.[109] Patterson's examination of selected eighteenth-century libraries results in a five-group classification: law, medicine, religion, science and mathematics, and dictionaries-lexicons-grammars. This division given in an appendix does not include the many philosophical and political, literary and historical, agricultural and gardening, classical, and periodical items which he discusses in his study. Houlette separates William Byrd II's books into history, law and medicine, entertainment-poetry-translations, classics, and religion, suggestive but not all-inclusive for Byrd or other southern colonials. Smart's classifications—philosophy and law, science-medicine-practical arts, classics and languages, history-biography-travel, religion and divinity, English literature, and "unclassifiable" is perhaps the most useful of these three, though Walter B. Edgar's divisions in his study of South Carolina libraries, admittedly suggested by Smart's for Virginia, is much more indicative than any of the three above for all southern collections. Edgar's thirteen include religious and philosophical, literature, legal and political, practical, classics, medicine and science, history, magazines, geography and travels, memoirs and biography, music and art, general information, and "unknown."[110] The "practical" division is an umbrella which may cover secretary's manuals, gardener's dictionaries, books on farriery or planting or particular trades, and a multitude of other works. Again many books may fall into two or even more categories. These analyses are useful because they are suggestive of the breadth or comprehensiveness of most of the larger libraries of Virginia and the rest of the South Atlantic provinces.

Of major or large Virginia libraries begun or completed from 1700 to 1764 but perhaps not inventoried until a decade or two later, publications in print and microfilm and examinations of original records reveal a great deal, but it is by no means comprehensive. One hopes it is at least representative. About forty-four libraries, from Ralph Wormeley's and William Colston's recorded in 1701 to George Washington's inventoried in 1799, not including Thomas Jefferson's conglomerate libraries (also to be noticed briefly), have been examined or counted in one way or another. Perhaps the library of Signer George Wythe, who bequeathed books to Jefferson when he died in the early nineteenth century, should be included, for certainly his collection was large even during the colonial period.[111]

Of the forty-four libraries which almost surely included from one hundred to a possible several thousand volumes, one-fourth, or about eleven, have been determined only by contemporary reputation and clues such as advertisements of sale, the known and recorded learning and reading of their owners, and other miscellaneous information. In most instances these collections were probably quite large indeed, several of them probably rivaling if not equaling in number and variety of titles the libraries of the very largest of recorded-title inventories. There can be little doubt, for example, that the books of Sir John Randolph, distinguished scholar and King's Attorney, ran into the hundreds and perhaps thousands. He himself brought together a great historical and legal collection for use in his projected political history of the colony. His nephew William Stith used them when preparing his own *History of the First Discovery and Settlement of Virginia.* Though Sir John's library was probably divided between his two sons Peyton and John (the latter the Loyalist King's Attorney and writer on gardening who may have carried his books to England), when Peyton (first president of the Continental Congress) died in 1776, he left a library valued at the unusually large sum of £250.[112] Undoubtedly the younger John Randolph had added to whatever his father had left him. Their relative Thomas Jefferson was to buy a large number of legal books from the Sir John-Peyton Randolph library, some fifty titles in all.[113]

Of even greater monetary value than Peyton Randolph's, and probably larger, was that of Henry Fitzhugh of Stafford (c. 1706–1742), the son of the second William.[114] Henry's books were appraised in 1743 at £258 sterling, a quite considerable sum before mid-eighteenth century.[115] Governor Alexander Spotswood in 1740 left "all [his] books, maps, and mathematical instruments" to the College of William and Mary. This surely large collection was one of the several of that college burned or pillaged with little or no trace.[116] A single volume has survived. One of the most tantalizing clues to what was probably a great library is the notice in the *Virginia Gazette* of April 17, 1746, of the sale of Dr. John Mitchell's (1690?–1768) collection, as he was about to "return" to England (where he was educated, though he was born in Virginia). Physician, zoologist, botanist, cartographer extraordinary, writer on political as well as scientific subjects, he lived at Urbanna on the Rappahannock. He became increasingly dissatisfied with the lack of the kind of intellectual companionship he craved. But the fact that he was in very bad health probably caused the removal to England. This many-sided man, who published voluminously on many subjects even before he left America, probably had a large library. It might be traced through the allusions in his writings better than through the general "notice" in the *Gazette*.[117] Though there were two William Dunlops among the eighteenth-century Virginia bookholders, it was the later one, who died in 1769 in King and Queen County, who was possessed of the larger library, if the description "several thousand volumes in most arts and sciences" be accurate.[118]

The man known as "The Virginia Antiquary," usually considered one of the most learned of American colonials as well as a trenchant writer on political subjects, the close kinsman of Jefferson and the Randolphs, was Colonel Richard Bland, who had the reputation of owning a varied and extensive collection of books. After this cousin's death in 1776 Jefferson purchased a number of volumes from the library, among them Filmer, Hakluyt, and Woolaston, and secured some of the old Virginia documents Bland had preserved.[119]

Professor Clyde S. Henson of Michigan State University, in making a general study of Bland, gathered all he could about the books in the Colonel's library. Naturally most of these he has found are through the Jefferson catalogue, but there are others, some eighty-odd titles in all. As might be expected, even in this fragmentary list, the politico-philosophical is most prominent. About one-fourth of Henson's list belong in this group, including the allegedly or genuinely "liberal" Burlamaqui, Shaftesbury, Grotius, Harrington, Mandeville, Oldmixon, Rapin, Sir Thomas More, Sidney, and Pufendorf, and among others of different complexion Filmer, Fortescue, Machiavelli, William Petyt, Thomas Pownal, Speed, and Squire. Early Virginiana, including manuscript laws and journals preserved eventually through Jefferson, the 1589 Purchas, Hakluyt (already mentioned), Beverley, and George Sandys (through his *Travels*, not at all a product of the New World), were among his collections. And there are other Americana. The surviving belletristic list is astonishing. Besides the classics, there are Chaucer, Langland's *Piers Plowman*, Spenser, Pope, Temple, and others. This fragmentary surviving representation suggests what Bland must have had.[120]

William Stith, cousin of both Bland and Jefferson, Oxford educated, president of William and Mary, and historian, apparently had a good library which he used in his writing, though he also browsed in the collections of Byrd and Sir John Randolph, as he acknowledges. His predecessor as president of the College and his brother-in-law, William Dawson, also Oxford educated and a poet, probably had several hundred books. And it was during the colonial period that George Washington began the collection which was not concluded even with his death. Though not any great number of the more than nine hundred volumes surviving and shown in his inventory date before 1764, he had a few books from the earlier John Custis and Daniel Parke Custis libraries. Perhaps the most interesting items now among the 354 of his volumes in the Boston Athenaeum are the items of Virginiana, including Beverley's *History* (1722), Bland's *A Letter to the Clergy of Virginia* (1760), John Camm's *A Review of the Rector Detected* (1764), James Horrocks' sermon *Upon the Peace* (1763), Landon Carter's *A Letter from a Gentleman in Virginia* (1754), his *Letter to the Right Reverend Father in God, the B——p of L——n* (1760), and his *Letter to a Gentleman in London from Virginia* (1759), and William Dawson's *Poems on Several Occasions. By a Gentleman of Virginia* (1736). Judging by these volumes alone one would characterize the Mount Vernon collection as that of a military and agricultural gentleman who wished occasional printed amusement.[121] The last of these large but inexactly recorded colonial Virginia libraries is that of Jefferson. Though his libraries numbered two and three (if one includes the University of Virginia collection) belong in large measure to the period after 1763 and indeed after 1800, one does know that the gentleman of Monticello had an unrecorded first library burned at his birthplace, Shadwell, and that the sort of books represented in the great collection turned over to the nation in 1814 was already being gathered while Jefferson was a student in Williamsburg. As noted, it contained works from older Virginia private collections, from Randolph, Bland, Wythe, John Banister, Byrd, Reuben Skelton and John Wayles, and several now-famous manuscripts basic for any study of colonial Virginia history. There are probably more pre-1764 imprints, English and continental, than in any earlier southern library, with the possible exception of William Byrd II's or John Mercer's.[122]

These do not quite exhaust the possibilities of large libraries on which there is little information. Almost surely the great Tidewater planter John Page, heir of several generations of wealthy and educated men who lived in spacious and gracious mansions not too far from Williamsburg, had at least a thousand and possibly several thousand volumes on his shelves. Page himself was a scientist, poet, and essayist of ability. Benjamin Waller (1716–1786) of Williamsburg, legal mentor of George Wythe, patron of the poet James Hansford and himself a poet, burgess and judge, was a sprightly, intellectually curious man who according to his grandson Littleton Waller Tazewell "was an excellent scholar and kept alive his scholarship, learning until his death."[123] He seems to have possessed a collection used by his law students and himself for recreation as well as legal research.

Robert Bolling "of Chellowe, Buckingham county" (to distinguish him from his cousin Robert Bolling of Blandford, Petersburg), who had attended Yorkshire grammar schools and the Middle Temple before returning in 1755/1756 to Williamsburg to study law near home, was probably by 1765 Virginia's most prolific poet.[124] He was also learned in languages and in law, and an effective essayist. Though there remains what is probably only partial evidence in the records, he also must have had a good library. At least a part of Bolling's library of the mid-1760s is listed in an extant manuscript in the Huntington Library, along with two pages of books he was ordering. Of the forty-odd books he sent for, thirty-three were in Latin, Italian, and French and were principally histories. He had already fifty poetry titles in three or four languages; thirty-two in astronomy, physic, natural philosophy, geography, and geometry; seventy-one on morality, politics, rhetoric, entertainment, and commentaries; and thirteen on logic, grammar, and reference. The titles of this collection are not so unusual as the fact that most of it is in French, Latin, and Italian.[125]

The learned Presbyterian preacher Samuel Davies of Hanover County shows in his poems and sermons that he had a number of books, and the *Virginia Gazette* daybook or ledger of 1750–1752 shows that he was a frequent purchaser. When he became president of Princeton, one of his first tasks was to prepare for the printer a catalogue of the college library, which he prefaced with a classic statement as to what he considered the functions or purposes of academic book collections, the "literary wealth" of the institutions.[126]

Of the remaining thirty-odd major libraries of which there is some specific record almost half contained between one hundred and five hundred titles, though a few instances (to be noted) may have had more than this maximum. What is chronologically the first of them may have been large, for Mungo Ingles, Master of the Grammar School of William and Mary, wrote in 1707 of the loss by fire of his study full of books, "which has cost me many a deep sigh. . . . I cannot enough lament the loss. . . . 18 boxes or shelves crammed as full as could hold."[127] More specific, for the book inventory with titles survives, is the 287-title and at least 300–400-volume collection of Richard Lee II, friend of William Fitzhugh (their children married) and opulent planter of the Northern Neck. Since exact number of volumes per title apparently is indicated only occasionally, it is possible that this library runs into the 500–1000-volume group. The editor of the *William and Mary Quarterly* in 1910 (XIX, 48) puts it in the group of great libraries with the Byrd and Dunlop collections mentioned above. The inventory shows some seventy-three schoolbooks or learned scientific titles, fifty-seven religious, thirty-five classical, twenty medical, twenty belletristic, five on ethics and philosophy, ten on government and politics, five on conduct and heraldry, a few legal works, and some miscellaneous. The taste of the owner was conservative, but his interests were diverse. Louis B. Wright has called him a "belated Elizabethan," partly on the basis of the library and its early editions.[128] Bacon and Erasmus, Aristotle and Lyly, are listed among his older authors, some in sixteenth-century editions. His classical authors were of many varieties, with of course Cicero and Caesar in greatest number, with Horace, Ovid, Tacitus, and Xenephon. The law books included Coke's *Reports*, maritime laws, Keble's *An Assistance to the Justices of the Peace*, and a 1662 edition of the *Laws of Virginia Now in Force*. His histories included Bacon on the reign of Henry VII, Boyer on Queen Anne, Raleigh's *History of the World*, Rushworth's *Collections*, and Ussher's *Annals of the World*. The medical books were such as might be used by the educated planter in attempting to cure or care for members of his household. Many of his belletristic volumes represented continental authors such as Ariosto, Boccalini, Guarini, and de Voiture; but there were also Butler's *Hudibras*, poems of Cleveland and Cowley, even the Massachusetts 1668 *Daily Meditations* (verse) of Philip Pain. Montaigne's *Essays* are listed, and in politics volumes of Thomas Hobbes, Richard Hooker, and others. Utilitarian volumes considered everything from cooking to surveying. The library indicates that Lee read Greek and Latin and was probably a devout Anglican in religion and a Tory in politics, a man who did not seem to have owned Chaucer, Spenser, Shakespeare, or Milton. He was one of those from whom his neighbors borrowed, for Fitzhugh's apology for losing a book was directed to Lee in 1679.

In 1716 the library of another Virginian who possessed more than one hundred volumes was inventoried. Godfrey Pole had served five years as a clerk to an attorney at one of the London Inns of Court and was clerk of the Virginia House of Burgesses from 1718 to 1727 and of Northampton County from 1722 to 1729/30. For some reason his books were listed by title and format in 1716, some thirteen years before his death. In the nineteenth century, when his papers were presented to the Virginia Historical Society, it was discovered that he had been a belletristic writer, or litterateur, as well as a legal expert.[129] Pole probably enlarged his library during his remaining thirteen years, but as it is his 115 titles include the first recorded Virginia copies of Chaucer and Milton's *Paradise Lost* (almost surely at least the latter was in the colony earlier), *Hudibras*, Erasmus, Waller's, Cowley's and Drayton's poems, a scattering of classics and orthodox religious works (including *The Whole Duty of Man*), and many on law and history. Written after at least sixteen titles are the names of the persons to whom he had lent them, including the attorney general, Dr. Cocke, Mann Page, and other prominent Virginians. Dalton, Crook's *Reports*, Coke's *Institutes*, Swinburne, and Godolphin are among the legal books. He had a history of Virginia and of "York Heraldry." Pole is a figure who merits further investigation, but his library here noted is remarkable principally for the two first-in-Virginia English poets or poetry it contained.

In 1718 died Edmund Berkeley of Barn Elms, Middlesex County, member of the Council, whose inventory of June 1719 shows a hundred titles in considerably more volumes. In many respects it is a normal educated gentleman's library—practical legal and medical manuals, orthodox Anglican religious works and sermons, several histories, Aesop, Locke's *On the Human Understanding*, and a few classics. More intriguing titles are Shakespeare's *Works* and "Mr. John Banister's Works," the latter quite possibly a transcription of the Virginia scientist's unpublished natural history catalog which the author himself may have made.[130] In 1724 the books of Colonel Daniel McCarty of Westmoreland and Captain Charles Colston of Richmond County were listed. These were relatively small libraries, McCarty's running to 110 titles, of which exactly half were law, and Colston's consisting of even fewer titles but including a parcel of old books, perhaps many of the more than one hundred left by his father, William, in 1701.[131] Colston's had the usual legal-historical-religious character, including Beverley's *Abridgement* of the Virginia laws, one volume of William Perkins' works, and *The History of America* (and one of several books). McCarty, a member of the House of Burgesses and a wealthy planter, had more variety, at least as indicated in titles, though modern histories and scientific and political tracts are missing. He had the usual classical authors, something of Erasmus, Addison's later popular tragedy *Cato* (1713), the popular Francis Quarles' *Emblems* (1635), a few medical books such as Sydenham's *Physician* and the London *Dispensatory*, both frequent in southern households. He had also an *English Gardener*.

Robert "King" Carter, whose books were inventoried in 1732, was for at least a third of the century the wealthiest man in Virginia and one of the most influential. In 1690 he had inherited the Corotoman estate and library of his brother John II, who had in turn inherited a sizable collection from their father, the first John. Robert Carter, burgess, councilor, agent for the Fairfax family for the Northern Neck Proprietary, militia colonel and commander-in-chief for two counties, naval officer (customs collector) for the Rappahannock River district, was to be with the Lees and Randolphs the founder of one of the great Virginia dynasties. His library of 269 titles reveals something of the owner's intellectual interests, though one should always bear in mind that some of it was inherited. Carter's letters show his personal eagerness to procure from England a variety of books. His collection was proper for the intellectual interests and recreations of a gentleman and was also a good working collection for the plantation household. Over one-third of it was law books, for like other planters he felt he must know how to defend his own land and obtain more, and in addition protect the rights of his employer, Lord Fairfax. Many of his legal volumes were first in print before 1650, about 50 percent were of the 1650–1700 period, and twenty were first published in his own century. He had all the standard works present in smaller libraries and a great many more, including William Sheppard's *Whole Office of the Country Justice of the Peace* (1652) to supplement Dalton's earlier work. Swinburne, Godolphin, Coke, Dyer, Bohun, maritime law, colonial laws including those of Massachusetts were there. Though a Royalist, like other conservatives and liberals he owned volumes with which he almost surely did not agree—William Prynne, Algernon Sidney, and Nathaniel Bacon (strongly against royal prerogative). But he also had the antidotes for these, such as Sir Robert Filmer.

The classics and history are strong in the Carter collection and as in other instances are quite overlapping, as Laurence Echard's *Roman History* (1698–1699), and he had the Whiggish interpretation of Tacitus in the Thomas Gordon edition (1728–1731), then quite new. English historians were present, including Camden, Bishop Gilbert Burnet, John Rushworth, the Earl of Clarendon, and others giving Whiggish interpretations of national history, such as Tindall's translation of Rapin's *History of England* (1725–1731). Carter's seventy-two theological works were unexceptionable, including both sides of recent deistical disputes along with the older books and several on the problems of nonconformity (he had the antagonists Calamy and Hoadly, as many southerners did). Sermons, such as Tillotson's, abounded. Scattered among the various categories were Americana, such as Esquemeling on buccaneers, statutes of various colonies, Commissary Blair's sermons (5 vols., 1722), and Sandys' translation of Ovid's *Metamorphoses* (1626 or 1632, probably). This is not a great library; it is short on science and medicine, fair on philosophy (six works), strong on nondoctrinal theology and history-biography, and best on government and law. Carter's son Landon, of greater imagination and intellectual curiosity than his father, was to surpass the parent also in the variety of his learning and interests. But then the son was also a major pamphleteer of the decades before the Revolution.

Richard Hickman died in the same year as Robert Carter;[132] he was clerk of the Council in Williamsburg, a lawyer by profession, who left what may have been up to that time the largest legal collection in Virginia. Of his approximately 250 volumes, about two hundred were concerned with the law, including the laws of Maryland. But he also had Brooks' *Heraldry*, [Gordon's?] Tacitus, Bibles and Prayer Books, "Purchas' Pilgrimages," a somewhat puzzling "History of Virginia, 2 books," the *Works* of William Perkins, and Fénelon's *Telemachus* in French. Though this was essentially a professional library, one must remember that Hickman had access to other reading at the college.

In February 1733/4 in Spotsylvania County was recorded the inventory and appraisal of the books and other property of Robert Beverley of Newland in that county. Son of Captain Harry Beverley, third son of the immigrant Robert I, this Robert has been called "an exceptional instance of a Virginian of large estate who never held public office"; he did, however, accumulate great landed property.[133] He left about 250 volumes, a collection about the size of Hickman's but differing greatly in that it is hardly a legal library at all. History, natural science (accompanied by globes and planispheres), religion, government, classics, gardening, and philosophy are well represented. But he was perhaps strongest in belles lettres, from "Harnaby's Rhetorick" through Fénelon and Erasmus and Aesop to the *Tatler* and *Spectator*, Milton's *Paradise Lost*, Pope's *Homer*, Butler's *Hudibras*, Manly's novels, and Pomfret's *Poems*. "A Flute Book," two sets of Virginia laws, Keil's "Astronomy," and various volumes on logic and other branches of philosophy are perhaps the most interesting. This Beverley, like his namesake and cousin the historian, was apparently a man of at least moderately broad interests who could read Latin and French with ease.

The Reverend Lewis Latané, who died in 1734, member of a prominent French Huguenot family, left a collection of more than 130 titles. Included was a good deal of Calvin as well as many French works on divinity, ninety-five religious works in all. Medical, mathematical, legal, and scientific made up most of the rest, though his collection included an occasional French play, Swift's *Tale of a Tub*,[134] "Playford's Music," Marana's *The Turkish Spy*, Locke and Erasmus, a volume of the *Spectator*, Governor Sir William Gooch's *A Dialogue between Tom Sweetscented and Will Oronoco* (1732, an interesting discourse on the Virginia Tobacco Law of 1730), and an *Abridgement* of Virginia laws. In 1739/40 in Prince William County a William Dunlop, perhaps related to the later King and Queen County book owner noted above, left some 106 titles in about two hundred volumes, almost half of them in French. Shaftesbury's *Characteristicks*,[135] Fénelon's *Télémaque*, Rapin's *History*, Gordon's Tacitus, the *Whig Examiner*, were all liberal political works.

But there were sermons, classics, contemporary English poets and play-wrights, periodicals, science from botany to astronomy, Mandeville's *Fable of the Bees* (also political), Le Sage, Molière, and Racine, indicative of the interests of this son of the professor of Greek at Glasgow. Dunlop had in his home pictures or portraits of Sir William Temple, Lord Shaftes-bury, the Duke of Buckingham, Lord Godolphin, Lord Oxford, Lord King, Milton, Gay, and Rowe.[136]

Captain Samuel Peachy in 1750 had about seventy titles in about one hundred volumes, fifteen titles in law, thirteen in religion, and smaller numbers in other areas, including history (such as Rapin, Rollin, Stith).[137] Inventoried in 1755 were at least two interesting libraries. Of these per-haps the smallest but most significant is that of musician and teacher and friend of organist Peter Pelham of Williamsburg, Cuthbert Ogle. About sixty-two of his titles have been quite well identified (though the somewhat garbled list is difficult), but there were more, including several manuscripts. Ogle's music was probably bought by Pelham, Councilor Carter, John Randolph the Loyalist, and other interested amateur mu-sicians and musicologists in Williamsburg.[138] This Ogle inventory is of vital importance in determining the musical taste of eighteenth-century colonial Americans, for rarely in any colony are as many actual composers or titles named. In this year John Waller of Spotsylvania, father of the more noted Benjamin of Williamsburg mentioned above, owned at least 134 books, thirty-six history, thirty-two belles lettres, twenty-five religion, and the remainder scattered through five other areas of interest. Two items of Virginiana and "Ab^t Witchcraft," Shakespeare, Milton, Suckling, Congreve, Quarles, Butler, are included.[139]

Daniel Parke Custis of New Kent County and Williamsburg, first hus-band of Martha Washington and father of Jacky (John Parke) Custis, whose education gave the stepfather some concern, left in 1757 a large library. A few items, as noted above, survive in the Washington collec-tions in the Boston Athenaeum, but the greater number afforded a foun-dation on which John Parke Custis was to build a distinguished library. As it is, the elder Custis owned some 460 volumes, including thirty-three on medicine, and a great deal of history, belles lettres, and classics. Among his politico-philosophical tomes were three volumes of the *Free-Thinker*, and Trenchard and Gordon's *Cato's Letters* and *The Independent Whig*. One is not surprised that the library of the son of the great amateur horticulturist contains a number of volumes on gardening beginning with Mark Catesby's *Natural History*.[140] Another library of some 160 books including at least eleven on gardening, and generally a varied and po-tentially useful collection in many areas, especially law, was that of John Herbert of Chesterfield (appraised 1761).[141] In 1765 the Reverend John

Moncure of Stafford, some of whose able sermons are extant, left 137 titles. In 1770 Jefferson's old teacher, the educator and essayist the Reverend James Maury, left some 400 titles and forty-four pamphlets, a number which probably places him in the class of those who owned more than five hundred volumes.[142]

Several libraries gathered in the main before 1763 were not inventoried until their owners' deaths after the Revolution. About 310 titles and five hundred volumes comprised the library of John Parke Custis just mentioned, a collection based in part on his father's and grandfather's collections.[143] Many of the garden books seem to have disappeared, but the medical group is enlarged, and there is an increase in the number of plays and histories. Southern Americana include Commissary Blair's *Sermons* and a *Natural History of Florida* in folio. Though Voltaire and Hume are here, one suspects that Jacky bought few books because he was interested in their contents or in reading per se. According to Parson Boucher, this Custis was the sort of Virginian Henry Adams described Rooney Lee as being. But the fact remains that when at Mount Vernon he had a quite respectable if somewhat outdated library.

Dozens of collections in the 100–500 group were gathered before 1763. Among them are those of Dabney Carr the elder, Jefferson's brother-in-law, who had some 135 titles in 1773, and in the same year Dr. David Black of Blandford in Dinwiddie near Petersburg left almost an equal number. [144] Easily the most interesting and significant of these libraries is that of the diarist and pamphleteer Landon Carter of Sabine Hall, who departed this life reluctantly and almost surely truculently. No complete inventory of the library as it was at the time of his death exists, but what probably made up about one-third of his collection still remains at Sabine Hall, one of the few libraries in all America to survive from this period. Since the extant title pages of the library largely collected by him (a few volumes were added apparently by his son) have been microfilmed along with his signatures and marginal comments from other pages, one can see for himself how and why Carter used his books. Another strong evidence of his intellectual interests lies in the considerable number of titles and quotations throughout the 1752–1778 diary, now available in printed form.[145] On the film one finds approximately 175 titles in three hundred volumes.[146] The references in the diary supply scores of other titles. It is still a balanced library, with at least twelve fairly distinct categories. Of these the largest number, thirty-one, represent the classics; then there are thirty in verse and belles lettres generally; about twenty-seven on politics, perhaps the most significant as representative of Carter the writer and intellectual; about ten in philosophy and aesthetics; fifteen in theology, nine of miscellaneous reference; fifteen in history and voyages, many involving politics and philosophy; at least seven to nine in law, gardening, husbandry, and natural history; six in mathematics, surveying, physics, and astronomy; files of five or six periodicals; and three titles of heraldry and genealogy. Of these books referred to, quoted, or ordered from England in the diary, the vast majority, about seventy-five, are no longer in the Sabine Hall library, another indication of the collection's probable much greater original size. Most of the medical works, many classics, a number of volumes on husbandry and most of the newspapers Carter mentions in direct references, items he must have had in hand, are no longer in the collection. Among the last, for example, are five different Philadelphia newspapers he seems to have received. The agricultural volumes referred to would increase his list in this area into one of the larger gatherings on the subject. One recalls that he wrote and published several essays on the farmers' problems. Addison's *Cato* and two essays of Pope are mentioned or quoted in the diary, but the texts are no longer at Sabine Hall. One would give much for the political essays mentioned in his journal but not to be found, especially because they include several of his own, on which he probably made the kind of marginal commentaries he did on everything else.

Carter's extant theological volumes are orthodox Anglican, as indeed his diary shows he was—Tillotson, Sherlock, Allestree, and the rest. A first edition of Johnson's *Dictionary* is among his reference works. History and voyages include much Rollin, and Smollett, Herodotus, Robertson, and Ramsey's *The Travels of Cyrus*. Even this fragment of the library is rich in the classics, with a great deal of Cicero and at least a dozen other authors. The political works, most of them published during his lifetime and several after 1763, include many on English liberties and the right to tax the colonies. Among them are Volumes I and II (1763) of John Wilkes' *North Briton*, with some interesting marginalia which certainly reflect arguments Carter used in his own essays on liberty and taxation. Henry Care's *English Liberties* (1719 edition) bears marginal notations, as does Edmund Burke's *Thoughts on the Cause of the Present Discontents* (n.d. shown). In law Carter had some of the usual Acts and Reports and Richard Starke's *The Office and Authority of a Justice of the Peace* in a Williamsburg edition of 1774. The books extant and mentioned in the diary show that Carter was first of all a hard-working farmer, anxious about crops, planting, weather, diseases of tobacco and wheat and of sheep and cattle. The volumes on natural history, mathematics, astronomy, and surveying indicate the mixture of innate intellectual curiosity and utilitarianism which most of these books catered to. In belles lettres this moody, introspective man read and quoted Milton and his own contemporaries Aaron Hill, Pope, Parnell, Thomson, Young, even Rousseau, among others, and also Erasmus and Molière. His books on philosophy and aesthetics are often tinged with the political—reflecting Locke, Sir Thomas More, and Bolingbroke—but in Edward Bysshe's *The Art of English Poetry* (1725) and R.P. le Bossu's *Traité du Poeme Epique* (Hague, 1714) he had volumes on literary form and theory. Also Thomas Stanley's *History of Philosophy* (4th ed., 1743), was probably perused with profit and pleasure. The newspapers and periodicals, six or seven British ones including the *Guardian*, the *Adventurer*, the *London Magazine*, and the *London Mercury*, with his American newspapers, probably kept him abreast of thinking and events on both sides of the Atlantic and must certainly have suggested or afforded points of departure and models of style for his own essays. Finally, his volumes on heraldry, peerages, and titles indicate that like most other southern gentlemen he was interested in social hierarchy and probably family ties between colonial Americans and British gentry and nobility. Carter's writing will be referred to later. But it should always be considered with the known and probable titles of his library in mind.

Though when Landon Carter used his library it may have included a thousand or more volumes, there is no final proof that his collection was one of the truly "great" ones reaching at least millenary numbers. Before turning to the few that one can be sure did belong to that group, some notice should be taken of the almost-great in size, first of the Reverend Francis Makemie, the father of Presbyterianism in America, who spent most of his mature life on the Eastern Shore of Virginia and Maryland. He wrote and preached with eloquence. The inventory of his estate taken on August 4, 1708, shows that he owned "896 books VIZt: Latin Greek English & hebrew & c" valued at £20, and a parcel of old books and some paperbound books, about ninety-six in all.[147] Makemie, who is believed to have studied at one of the Scottish universities and was born in Ireland, was apparently like most clergy of his church a quite learned man. One would give much for a list of titles in this library. In fact, that he bequeathed his law books separately to the barrister Andrew Hamilton (who later defended Peter Zenger) may mean that his library actually did run well over a thousand.[148]

Though the libraries of several physicians have been noted, what was apparently the largest and most varied was that of Dr. Charles Brown of Williamsburg, who in 1738 left all his estate, including books, to his friend William Stith, then rector of Henrico Parish. Though only a few books are given titles, it was in number an impressive list: 82 folios, 128 quartos, 407 octavos, and 3 or 4 medical books found later (and listed by title), a total of some 620 volumes.[149] The list would help to support the surmise made above that Stith apparently had a good library. And at least one other major collection must be noticed, that of William Fitzhugh's friend Ralph Wormeley II in 1701. Later generations of Wormeleys added to this collection for more than another century, though the printed early nineteenth-century sales catalog of the final accumulation seems no longer extant.[150] This Ralph Wormeley II of Rosegill in Middlesex County has been called by Louis B. Wright an ideal colonial cultivated gentleman,[151] and his library inventory of between five and seven hundred volumes would tend to support this characterization.[152] The largest subject-matter group is religion and morals, some 123; then history and biography, sixty titles in eighty-five volumes; many on statecraft and law; twenty-two on medicine; many classics, travels, grammars, English plays and poetry; eighteen works in French, and general acts. Of Americana there are Ogilby's *America* (1671) in folio, three or four collections of Virginia laws, Morgan Godwyn's *The Negro's & Indians Advocate*, and John Smith's *Generall Historie of Virginia, New England, and the Summer Isles*. The later letters of the Wormeleys, ordering and discussing books, show us that the cultivation of the mind through reading was for this family during at least a century and a half both a recreation and an employment. Even this early library indicates their variety of interest, and in its concentrations in several areas the possibility of in-depth study.

Three indisputably great Virginia eighteenth-century libraries remain to be considered, those of William Byrd II of Westover, John Mercer of Marlborough, and Councilor Robert Carter of Nomini Hall. Byrd's is the earliest and largest of these collections, as it is one of the greatest of all American colonial libraries. It has been written about many times, but so far there has been no surviving accurate and complete printing of the manuscript catalogue which survives, though this list was once printed in the eighteenth century and distributed for sales purposes.[153] This manuscript catalog was written by John Stretch, then in Williamsburg, and presumably bound by him, between 1751 and 1757, the latter year the date of William Byrd III's bankruptcy.[154] In it are listed at least 2,345 short and at times tantalizing titles in some 3,513 volumes, all roughly classified by subject (and size) in keeping with their order on the shelves. Since the titles seem to have been taken from the binders' titles on the spines, they naturally fail to include individual pamphlets and even all but one of several small books bound together. Thus the actual count of titles of separately printed works is probably a great deal more than the number just given. Twenty or more years after the catalog was made, on December 19, 1777, the unfortunate widow, Mary Willing Byrd, advertised in the *Virginia Gazette* that "This Day is published a Catalogue" of almost four thousand volumes of the library at Westover. Edwin Wolf, 2nd, has told well the story of the collection's purchase as a whole by Isaac Zane, Jr., its removal to Philadelphia, and its piecemeal sale and disappearance. Mr. Wolf's efforts to locate individual titles had by 1958 resulted in his bibliographical catalog of 402 volumes (more than 10 percent of the original) and since then he has located many more. Jefferson, Madison, and Edmund Randolph are known to have been purchasers of certain volumes, though only Jefferson's are now identified. To sum up briefly, most of the known copies of Byrd's library are now in Philadelphia repositories, especially the Pennsylvania Hospital and the Library Company of Philadelphia. Through Jefferson, priceless early Virginia official manuscript records came directly and indirectly from Byrd to enrich the Library of Congress.

As already mentioned, Byrd's has been called the first great collector's library in English America, and he has been described as the first man to gather books because he loved them principally as books, as a pure bibliophile would (if there ever were such a person). This is not even a half-truth, for like the other collections sketched or noted in the preceding pages, this one was chosen largely to be *useful*, in the larger sense of the term. In one sense it is simply the largest southern collection of the sort of books to be found in other libraries of the period in Great Britain and America. That is, Byrd managed to gather in one group books which otherwise might be assembled if a score of moderate or even large libraries were brought together. They were on the whole, from religion to science to history to belles lettres, what most people read. But there were esoterica, there were great gatherings of Americana and Virginiana of many kinds, there were surprising concentrations in areas which show what were Byrd's interests and uses for these books. So far there has been no real analysis of the contents of his library, a research project requiring and deserving a scholar who has breadth and depth in his knowledge of seventeenth- and eighteenth-century writings or publications in at least half a dozen languages.

Byrd's letters and diaries show his ordering (purchasing) and reading of his books, and even his arranging them in his library. He was a bibliophile. He did love books per se. He did have his plain vellum-bound volumes richly gilded. But one may be sure that almost every book he secured helped him to safeguard the health of his kin and household, to protect legally his property, to design his house and gardens and plant his crops, to entertain himself and his neighbors, or to stimulate his mind in other ways. Like Jefferson later, William Byrd II and his father before him obtained books whenever and wherever they could. Clearly the son bought a great many personally on his several trips to Great Britain or during his long stay there, and several while he was learning business methods in Holland. The first William Byrd probably had secured the library of the aforementioned scientist John Banister, and volumes from that seventeenth-century collection survive in several instances today.[155] On the Westover shelves were the precious manuscript copies of the records of the Virginia Company of London (c. 1619–1624), acquired by William Byrd I from the estate of the Earl of Southampton, already quoted many times in this study. Near them were manuscript Virginia laws and statutes, such as the Virginia Company papers acquired eventually by Jefferson (some through Bland) and preserved for posterity in the Library of Congress. Yet from the surviving printed volumes, which have since Byrd's time often passed through several hands, it is evident that the Westover collection is based less on older Virginia libraries than was Jefferson's. Inheriting the Banister and Virginia manuscript items and a small general and useful library from his father, William II built or expanded his holdings into the most impressive cultural assemblage in rural surroundings in British America.

This library like others could be classified and divided into many different areas, each at least a little overlapping one or more other areas. But until a careful and perceptive analysis is made any one of several arbitrary divisions will aid in showing what the library contained. One commentator assigns 700 titles to history, 350 to law, 300 to divinity, 225 to science, and 200 to physic or medicine. One weakness in this kind of division is that it does not indicate the subject matter or genres within the area of "classics" or "French" or "science." But a glance at individual titles is revealing in several ways, the first of which is that in each area a wide variety of interests and subjects are represented.

Though some of Byrd's own writings place him squarely in contemporary English literary traditions, others show an absorbing interest in the reflection of the New World in forms and ideas somewhat different from the British. The hundreds of histories cover Europe and even parts of Asia from antiquity to his own time. But Byrd also owned Smith's *Generall Historie of Virginia* and Beverley's *History*, Purchas' *Pilgrimage*, Hennepin's *Travels*, Lahontan's *Voyages*, and both Mathews' and Neal's *History of New England*. He had several editions of Virginia laws, Beverley's *Abridgement* and Mercer's, Dr. Tennent's *Epistle* to Dr. Mead, Sandys' Ovid, Esquemeling's *Buccaneers*, [Jones' *Present?*] *State of Virginia*, John Fox's *Mottos of the Wanderers*, and Catesby's *Natural History*, all these to some extent or in some way Virginiana. There were other accounts of New England, New York, and Pennsylvania, Ogilby's *America*, many early European voyages to America, and descriptions of Peru and the Caribbean.

Byrd, who had been admitted barrister in London while attending the Middle Temple, had a formidable and rich legal library. More nearly political than legal, however, were the works of Locke, Sidney, Hobbes, Harrington, and Shaftesbury. His wide assortment of medical volumes undoubtedly were frequently referred to when there was illness or disease on his home plantation. His classical works were perhaps even more varied, certainly more imposing in format, than those of the later John Randolph of Roanoke, and that is saying a great deal. Byrd's diary tells us he read in them regularly. Of poetry, drama, and translations, Chaucer, Spenser, Shakespeare, Jonson, Dryden, Defoe, Swift, Milton, Pope, Ovid, Fontaine, Rabelais, and Corneille are a few authors among many. In religion were Tillotson, Taylor, Prideaux, Baxter, and the rest of the divines, and a number of anti-Quaker writings.

Byrd had several books on painting, on gardening (Catesby helped him lay out the Westover gardens), and on architecture (Palladio, Vitruvius, Alberti). Scattered about were dozens of periodicals and dictionaries and lexicons. Mathematics, physics, surveying, geography, natural history, astronomy, music, and heraldry were all here, as was geological theory. All these were contained in twenty-three walnut bookcases. If he did not read all his books, he certainly read something on every subject represented, in Greek, Latin, French, Spanish, Dutch, and Hebrew. "As a carefully balanced collection of the best literature and learning of the day it had no equal in America," says Louis B. Wright,[156] and one is inclined to agree, though Mather and Logan had probably an equal or almost equal number of volumes. If one wishes evidence that Byrd used his library for practical, everyday purposes and in the form and subject of what he wrote, he should examine the histories of the Dividing Line, the three portions of the diary, the miscellaneous essays and poems, the graceful and sardonic letters, and his legal arguments.[157]

The collection of John Mercer (1704–1768), Irish-born and -educated, legal scholar, eminent practicing attorney, poet, land speculator, and builder of one of the most original and elaborate houses of colonial America,[158] is scarcely known at all. There is no even roughly complete catalog, as there is for William Byrd. The number and nature of his titles is to be pieced together from his manuscript lists and daybooks and writings, the last to be discussed in a later chapter. An advertisement in the *Virginia Gazette* of December 1768 soon after his death claims that there were sixteen hundred volumes in the collection.[159] Though not all of them can be counted or identified in the several inventories, sales lists, and other source manuscripts, no two of which are identical but all of which are somewhat overlapping, this figure seems fairly accurate, and may even be an underestimate.

Law was naturally the area best represented in the collections of *the* legal scholar in Virginia in his generation; in fact Mercer's *Abridgement of Virginia Laws* has been said to stand next to the Bible in popularity among his fellow colonists after its publication in 1737–1739. In one list alone are about 278 titles (four to five hundred volumes). The 1771 list of "remainders" after sales shows 341 legal volumes together with 213 sets of the *Abridgement*. The belles lettres group, including poetry and plays and some classics, is especially strong. The novels, among others, are *Rasselas, Tristram Shandy*, and *Tom Jones*. Here was one of the rare American colonial copies of George Sandys' *Paraphrase upon the Divine Poems* (first edition, 1638). Scores of reference works, periodicals, sermons, religious tracts, philosophical-political treatises, medicinal works, and agricultural manuals (especially on brewing) indicate another owner who held diverse interests. Every one of the authors referred to in the "Dinwiddianae" poems (to be discussed later) is represented in the title lists of inventories or of his purchases from the *Virginia Gazette* bookstore. There is a good deal of Anglo-Irish history and literature. Mercer had Cadwallader Colden's "History of the Indian Nations" (*History of the Five Nations*), many editions of Virginia laws and perhaps some manuscripts, Stith's *History* and *Sermons* (probably the three latter bound as one), and the poems of Samuel Davies. Many more of his purchases in Williamsburg were of general works, especially classics and history, than of legal volumes, and the bookstore entries show that he paid for the binding of many others besides those he purchased. He owned many of the Whig histories, as Molesworth's *Account of Denmark*, which must have been quite useful as he wrote his essays and political verse. On its somewhat smaller scale, even allowing for the preponderance of legal works, Mercer's library like Byrd's was varied, useful, and entertaining. As his volumes were scattered after his death, his armorial bookplate became familiar in many households from Pennsylvania to Virginia and even beyond. His library as well as Byrd's should be cataloged as accurately as possible and analyzed as to content, always with his intellectual interests as shown in his writing in mind.

The third and last great library is known not from a complete inventory made after the death of the owner, but from a list drawn up when that owner was in the prime of life, a list which undoubtedly continued to be enlarged up to the time of his death. This was the library of Robert Carter (1728–1804) of Nomini Hall in Westmoreland, councilor and grandson of "King" Carter and nephew of Landon Carter. In 1774 the tutor for his children, Philip Vickers Fithian, today well known for the diary he kept during his stay with the Carters, made a catalog of the books at Nomini Hall, approximately 1,066 volumes, and comments that Carter had left behind at his Williamsburg house 458 additional volumes besides music and pamphlets.[160] This Robert Carter is more appealing in character than his aggressive grandfather, for the reader of Fithian's diary sees him as a gentle, generous, thoughtful, musically gifted man who preferred his harpsichord and violin and musical composition to the management of his estate, which incidentally he seems to have handled capably. Fithian found him widely read in many fields and fully conscious of the educational and other social and intellectual limitations of the colony.

As was customary, Fithian catalogued the books at Nomini Hall by size—folios, quartos, octavos, and duodecimos. Patterson feels that the subjects were too diverse to represent the genuine interests of one man, a judgment the person who knows of the Byrd, Mercer, and Jefferson collections can hardly agree with. Fithian, just out of Princeton, calls the councilor a good scholar "even in classical learning, and a remarkable one in english grammar." He continues, "Mr Carter has an overgrown library of Books of which he allows me free use. It consists of a general collection of law, all the Latin and Greek Classicks, a vast number of Books on Divinity chiefly by writers of the established Religion; he has the works of almost all the late famous writers, as Locke, Addison, Young, Pope, Swift, Dryden, & c." [161] Later Fithian frequently mentions the great number of volumes of musical compositions and of pieces of sheet music as well as books of musical theory. Handel's "Operas for Flute" in two volumes and a "Book of Italian Music," and Dryden's "Alexander's Feast" set to music by Handel, are among them. Carter probably should have been a good student of grammar, for he had fifty-eight dictionaries, grammars, and lexicons. Besides the authors Fithian mentions in the quotation above, the inventory shows dozens of others, as Chaucer, Gay, Donne, Montaigne, Molière, Shakespeare, Waller, Congreve, Milton, Wycherley, and Vanbrugh, and novels by Sterne, Smollett, and others. Here are the liberal political writers, Sidney, Shaftesbury, Montesquieu, Molesworth, Gordon, and Locke, with the more conservative Hobbes and Hume. American and Virginia colonial interests are suggested by Webb's *Virginia Justice*, Virginia laws, and Thomas Cradock's (Maryland) *Version of the Psalms*, though he does not have among the Nomini books the proportion on America exhibited in the Byrd or Jefferson collections. Along with texts of the belletristic writers are other volumes of criticism of them, including a study of Shakespeare and Lord Kames' *Elements of Criticism*. The histories vary from ancient to contemporary. Books on science, mathematics, and mechanics are few indeed, though there are some works on natural history. There are more on husbandry, gardening, and agriculture, but not so many Byrd and Mercer possessed, even proportionately. On painting and the other fine arts Carter had more than his peers, with the possible exception of Byrd. This inventory of a library approximately the size of Mercer's and almost as varied, shows with the latter's that two colonial planters of means not only had intellectual interests but individual and distinct ones. Mercer's titles reflect and are reflected by his writing, usually on legal or philosophically liberal political points of view. Carter's list indicates a leaning toward aesthetics and the fine arts, especially music, which was a lifelong source of pleasure for the squire of Nomini Hall. But any of these three greatest of Virginia colonial libraries presented potential constant and varied stimulation to the "curious" mind of its owner, offered sources or background for the education of children in the home, and was eminently useful in the performance of daily plantation duties, from planting to purging. The dozens of large libraries of their contemporaries and neighbors clearly, though perhaps to a slightly lesser extent, were employed in the same way.

The story of colonial private libraries in North Carolina is quite different from that of its neighbors to both the north and the south. It was in part a matter of population. Perhaps not more than ten thousand people were in the province at the end of the Proprietary period in 1728, and no town west of what became the Wilmington and Weldon Railroad was settled before 1750.[162] Between 1749 and 1786, quite late in the colonial period, there were inventoried at least ten private libraries which exceeded one hundred volumes and indicate something of their owners' interests, and from the first decade of the eighteenth century to 1790 some eighteen smaller collections of some significance are recorded.

Many of these latter smaller libraries belonged to the clergy, especially those of the earlier decades. The S.P.G. missionaries John Urmstone in 1708, James Adams in 1710, and Giles Rainsford in 1712 had collections which went with them when they moved to other colonies or, as in the Adams case, which they left in the hands of a planter who refused to deliver them to the new parish clergyman.[163] These and other S.P.G. missionaries brought books with them or managed to obtain them from Great Britain, not locally.

Frederick Jones of Chowan in 1722 left "all [his] Library of Books" to be divided among his three sons except those his wife used.[164] Probably John Hodgson (fl. 1739–1741 but died much later) gathered most of his books before 1763. A lawyer, he had such volumes of general literature as Young, Congreve, Sterne, Le Sage, Cervantes, Addison and Steele's periodicals, Pope, Swift, and Molière, all still in existence at the end of the nineteenth century.[165] Daniel Blinn in 1753 left the frequently listed "1 Box & Parcel of old Books," but Henry Snoad, who had come from Boston, left a modest list of about fifty diverse volumes, from sermons to verse to gardener's manuals, marine calendars, military works, and periodicals.[166] In 1759 prominent and prosperous Colonel James Innes of Point Pleasant, near Wilmington, left his property, including a good library, for the use of a free school for the youth of the colony.[167] In 1762 the Reverend John Macdowell sent the secretary of the S.P.G. in London a comprehensive list of the books of which he was in dire need. Most were the usual theological works, such as Sherlock *On Death* and Allestree's *The Whole Duty of Man*, but he also included an abridged Johnson's *Dictionary*.[168] More interesting to the layman is perhaps the inventory in 1769 of Richard Eagles, which included Raleigh's *History*, Ulloa's *Voyages*, various sermons, a life of Mahomet, Rapin's *History of England*, one volume each of *Pamela* and the *Gentleman's Magazine*, two copies of the *Annual Register* and one *Compleat House Wife*, among others. The libraries inventoried between 1777 and 1790, such as those of Tory Governor Josiah Martin (sold in 1777), John Penn and William Hooper, the signers of the Declaration of Independence (1777 and 1790), and James Iredell, were probably collected for the most part after 1763; Hooper at least had a varied and strong library probably running into the hundreds.[169] The largest of the moderate libraries for which there is a good list of titles is that of Governor Thomas Burke (c. 1747–1783), physician, poet, and political liberal, most of whose books were legal. Of approximately sixty-eight known titles, forty-eight were in law, nine in classics, and a scattering in history, philosophy, mechanics, and miscellaneous.[170] The books in these smaller collections are much the same as would be found in libraries of the same size in the Chesapeake colonies. There are simply not as many of the North Carolina inventories, though suggestions in local and county histories indicate that perhaps proportionately even more of them have been lost for this colony than for Virginia and Maryland, for a variety of reasons.

The ten larger private libraries inventoried or described in wills or elsewhere in North Carolina are worth some attention, especially in certain instances because of the known character of their owners. First in time was that of Edward Moseley, a gentleman already there in 1705, in which year he was a member of St. Paul's Parish vestry and became a member of the governor's Council. Recent investigations by George Stevenson of the North Carolina Department of Archives and History confirm William Byrd's characterization of Moseley as "bred in Christ's Hospital," for the records of the famous blue coat school show him as a student there from 1687 to 1697. Though he may have been related in blood to the Virginia Moseleys of the southeastern corner of the province (they had come directly from the Netherlands half a century earlier), the North Carolinian probably reached the colony by way of Barbadoes and South Carolina.[171] His attempted gift of a public or parochial library for the North Carolina colony has been described above.

Even the somewhat cynical William Byrd II recognized Moseley as a well-educated man of intelligence. Like Byrd, the North Carolinian was variously gifted. In 1744 Dr. Charles Carroll ordered from London Moseley's map of North Carolina dedicated to Governor Gabriel Johnston.[172] Whatever may have happened to the early library offered by Moseley to the public, at the time of his death in 1749 he owned over four hundred volumes, probably the largest library of the time in the province.[173] Perhaps, as some historians believe, the books offered earlier to the province were included in it. In the will he gives by title only a few volumes. His two hundred law books were to go to the son who would study that subject, for he averred that every family must have at least one member who was legally trained. To his wife he left eight volumes of religious works and "all the books of physick"; to a daughter, Ann Humfries, three folios of the Old and New Testament and the *Works* of the author of *The Whole Duty of Man*, which last should be bought for her. To the eldest son who did not study law he left Chambers' and Miller's dictionaries, Locke's works, and a book on gardening. The rest, some 150, were to be divided among the other three sons. One may be sure that works in Latin, including various classics, a number of historical and geographical volumes, and other works on gardening and agriculture besides the one named were in this library.

A year later, in 1750, an inventory of the estate of Eleazar Allen was recorded.[174] Born in Massachusetts in 1692 of English parentage, he moved to South Carolina and was married there in 1722 to Sarah Rhett. By 1725 Allen had a grant of land on Cape Fear, where he made his residence, calling his plantation Lilliput. In 1726 he returned to Massachusetts and finished work for a degree he had begun years before, and then went to South Carolina for a time before he made his permanent home in North Carolina in 1734, in which year he was sworn a member of the Council of Governor Burrington. Like Moseley, Allen was a dividing line commissioner, though in the latter case between North and South Carolina.

Allen's library contained at least three hundred volumes in English and Latin and fifty in French. It was the collection of a man of taste and diverse interests. Relatively, it was low in law and even in the ordinary belles lettres, including fiction, high in volumes supposedly indicating liberal political sentiments, unusually large in philosophical and political studies generally. Accompanying the books were pictures and maps. The books as usual were classified by size—folios, quartos, small quartos, octavos, etc. There were volumes on shipbuilding, architecture, and printing, on gardening and mathematics. The travels included Dampier, Lawson's *Carolina*, and one of the several works titled *Description of Carolina*. He had six periodicals in varying numbers of volumes, thirty-four classics, thirty-three collections of plays, twenty books of poetry, twenty in the political-philosophical area mentioned, and forty in religion. The Whiggish writings included Rapin's *History*, Trenchard and Gordon's *Independent Whig*, and *Cato's Letters*.

One collection which grew through the century is usually known as the

Governor Gabriel Johnston library. It had its foundation in the library of Governor Eden (d. 1722), though of this only a single book, Montaigne's *Essays*, survives. Governor Johnston (d. 1752) married Penelope, the daughter of Eden, and presumably inherited the collection and built upon it. His nephew, Governor Samuel Johnston (d. 1816), seems to have inherited and augmented the library. Later it was inherited by James Cathcart Johnston (1782–1865), who continued to add to it. A partial catalog made before the Civil War shows 1,527 volumes, but Weeks declares that by 1860 the collection contained 4,500 books.[175] One may surmise that before 1764 it contained at least between five hundred and one thousand volumes. In 1896 Weeks names many titles then extant from Governor Gabriel Johnston's library, including much travel-voyage and historical writing, Plutarch's *Lives*, *The Turkish Spy*, Cicero, Prior—in all, sixty-three volumes sure to have been his. The library also contained books from the collections of other men well known in North Carolina history. Weeks divided what he saw into eleven groups totaling more than five hundred volumes. Since he gives the dates of publication of most of them, it is evident that the majority were published before 1764 and were probably in the Johnston library before that date. Law is represented by only 34 titles, agriculture and household affairs 7, general literature 129, fiction 27, theology and sermons only 6, reference works 30, biography and travel 37, history and politics 153, classics 36, and poetry and drama 56. As it survives, then, it is predominately a belletristic and historical collection and quite rich in works published before 1764. Thus the Johnstons and their wide kin had access to the standard literature in print in the eighteenth century.

Somewhat smaller, but presumably gathered by one man, is the library of Jeremiah Vail of New Bern, the inventory of whose estate was taken in 1760.[176] Judging by the proportion of law books, the owner was probably a barrister by profession. The inventory shows some 178 titles (in about 225 volumes), 73 of them concerning the law. But there are as many histories as legal works, and 20-odd titles in theology. There is little out of the ordinary in the collection, but it does contain "N England Psalms 2 Books," a "History of Georgia," and *Cato's Letters*.

Perhaps the largest and most remarkable library of eighteenth-century North Carolina is that of Governor Arthur Dobbs, who died in 1765 three years after his first paralytic stroke and perhaps as he was preparing to return to the British Isles. Dobbs (1689–1765), sometime surveyor general of Ireland and a proprietor of thousands of acres in and governor of North Carolina, promoter of expeditions searching for a northwest passage, advisor to the Crown on matters of national finance, was an imperialist, a robust

Protestant, and a thoughtful writer in several areas.[177] It is difficult to count his books, for the listings were prepared for different purposes and to some degree overlap. Some lists number each item, some are written without any count. Some few indicate cost or value. At first glance it seemed questionable whether the lists included both books Dobbs had in North Carolina and those he had left in Ireland. Experts at the Public Record Office in Belfast and the Southern Historical Collections felt they could not tell. A fairly close study of the lists, however, by the present writer, seems to indicate that these books were all in North Carolina at the time of Dobbs' death. That there was an intention of shipping them back to his children by his first wife may be implied in the letters between the second wife and his children in Great Britain, but neither his biographer nor the present writer has ascertained what happened to them, though Captain Richard Dobbs of Castle Dobbs has stated that many were shipped back to Dobbs' son or sons. Certainly there was available in this colony, over the extensive period of Dobbs' governorship (1754–1765) a large and varied collection. At least he personally used it in writing verse, scientific treatises, theology and philosophy, histories of exploration, promotion literature, and business surveys, most of them of significance.

In the eighteen or nineteen sheets of listings, several are double pages, and all contain from two to four columns of titles. In addition, there are two brief purchase records of a single column each. The count of actual titles goes over 2,100, but there are so many repetitions that the lists reduce to a library of about 1,200. All Dobbs' interests seem to be represented. The voyage literature alone runs into hundreds, from Purchas and Hakluyt through Dampier and Cook to most of his contemporaries. Of course others as well as these reflect his interest in finding a northwest passage. There were scores each on history, gardening, and mathematics, and dozens on metals, telescopes, meteors, optics. On America, especially Carolina and Virginia and other southern colonies, there were again dozens, including Ogilby's *America*, Catesby's *Natural History of Carolina*, and the *Laws* of North Carolina. Dictionaries, periodicals, *Philosophical Transactions* of the Royal Society (to which he contributed essays on bees and other subjects), medicine, politics, religion, belles lettres, the classics, and architecture are well represented. Evidently he planned to build public and private edifices in North Carolina, for here are Gibbs, Palladio, Vitruvius, Evelyn, Le Clerk, a "Builder's Dictionary," Bellidore, and other architects. Music was not neglected (one recalls that he wrote a hymn of thanksgiving to be sung in the churches throughout his province). Among his manuscript remains is an "Essay upon the Grand Plan of Providence and Dissertations Annexed Thereto," a 250 page effort, probably written in Carolina with constant reference to the theological volumes in his library.[178] Dobbs' book titles are suggestive of one of the most active and curious minds of the colonial South.

The library which Governor Tryon, Dobbs' successor, had in his New Bern Palace survives in at least one insurance list. In recent years the Tryon Palace Commission and its staff have obtained 84 percent of the titles Tryon held, in nineteen different categories. The insurance claim lists only 259 titles in perhaps 294 volumes.[179] Since Tryon was a soldier, he had more books on military science than his predecessor, but his largest group was history, next literature or belles lettres, then law, novels, politics, sermons, dictionaries, novels and fables, geography, architecture, and agriculture. The books ranged in size from folios to duodecimos, from thick tomes to pamphlets. Like Dobbs, Tryon had a number of books of American interest or association, such as George Sandys' *A Relation of a Journey* (1637/8 edition), Virginia and New York laws, Francis Bacon's *True Interest of Great Britain with Respect to the North American Colonies* (1766 edition), John Brickell's *The Natural History of North Carolina* (1737), Edmund Burke's *An Account of the European Settlements in America* (1765), and several others. Like Dobbs and the Chesapeake colonists, Tryon showed an interest in heraldry, the peerage and baronetage, and genealogy. Though these books were in North Carolina during 1764–1771, immediately after the period under study, they so nearly parallel the titles in the libraries of slightly earlier residents that they seem worth noting here.

One of the significant libraries largely collected in the colonial period and indicative of the calibre of the intellectual circle of Wilmington at the middle of the eighteenth century, is that of Dr. John Eustace, who died in 1769. The Wilmington talkers, says Malcolm Ross, "were of the same breed as the disputants of the Raleigh Tavern and Faneuil Hall." Dr. Eustace had the contemporary reputation of uniting wit and genius with real learning.[180] The inventory is divided between general and professional, with about 135 books on various subjects and 130 on medicine. Dictionaries and encyclopedias are prominent, as are histories and voyages, belles lettres, classics, and periodicals. Contemporary or near-contemporary poetry and fiction are prominent, and it is not surprising that this colonial who corresponded with Sterne had a complete set of *Tristram Shandy* and works of Fielding and Smollett. He had nine volumes of Voltaire "in blue paper." His Swift's *Gulliver*, Descartes, Pope, Hume, and Montesquieu are among other favorites of his time.

A larger and even more interesting library is that of John Milner (d. 1772), though until quite recently far less was known about the owner than about Dr. Eustace.[181] Milner, who had come to Virginia at least as early as 1760 and had been a friend of Robert Bolling of Chellowe, in October 1766 had contributed to the *Virginia Gazette* under the pseudonym of "Dikephilos" on the famous Colonel Chiswell case. In the year of his death he had been elected a representative of North Carolina in its legislature, as the *Virginia Gazette* bears witness. He left a collection of almost 650 titles in perhaps a thousand volumes, and several containing his armorial bookplate are extant. His inventory also includes maps, musical instruments, globes and astronomical instruments, walnut bookcases, and desks, concomitants of a good library. That Milner was a lawyer is borne out by some 182 legal titles, including the usual Hale, Godolphin, Swinburne, and Grotius as well as five volumes of Virginia laws, George Webb's *The Office and Authority of a Justice of the Peace . . . adapted to the Constitution of Virginia* (1738), two volumes of Carolina laws, and more than a hundred volumes of reports and legal dictionaries and manuals. He also had a lawyer's wig. Travels, classics, medicine, religion, and mathematics and physics ran from nine to thirty-three volumes each. Six books on gardening, two on building or architecture, and one on surveying were surely useful. Novels, verse, and other forms of belles lettres numbered more than sixty. Perhaps most unusual were his thirty-nine volumes of periodicals and his more than thirty music books (used in connection with his flutes, violins, and other instruments). In philosophy he had Voltaire, Hutcheson, Watts, Shaftesbury, Locke, Gerard (*On Taste*), Haller, Aristotle's *Ethics*, and the political Machiavelli, Mandeville, and Pufendorf, inter alios. This was a sophisticated library of a sophisticated gentleman.

In 1777 died the Reverend James Reed (Reid?), who became the first regular rector of Christ Church Parish in New Bern in 1753.[182] He was an active S.P.G. missionary and advocate of free schools, as his tombstone inscription indicates, and as chaplain of the General Assembly for some years was known as an eloquent preacher. He left behind him a library of about 456 books and pamphlets, including an unusually large collection of sermons and theological works (about 389). He also possessed fifteen volumes of classics, several grammars, histories, periodicals, works on natural philosophy and medicine, and dictionaries and grammars. The collection was hardly varied save within the area of theology. He had the working materials for learned preaching.

Last of the larger North Carolina libraries to be noticed is that of James Hasell of Wilmington, member of Governor Josiah Martin's Council just prior to the Revolution. Hasell died in 1786, but most of his surviving books show the probability of having been secured before 1764. This library was built in part, like several in the Chesapeake region, from older libraries. Many of the volumes carry the bookplates or inscriptions of four members of the Lillington family and of Sampson and Edward Moseley.

Like Landon Carter's in Virginia, Hasell's is the only known library of any size in this colony to survive into our time, even though here only in a fragment. One may actually see and examine ninety volumes now in the North Carolina Collection of the University at Chapel Hill.[183] These are relics of the several families whose names occur inside their covers. They are quite diverse in subject, thirteen representing belles lettres, ten each religion and periodicals, eight the classics and oratory, five geography, four each criticism and gardening, three each political philosophy and voyages, and history, drama, dictionaries and encyclopedias, natural history, and general philosophy. Bolingbroke's *A Dissertation upon Parties* (1743) bears the Hasell bookplate, as do Shaftesbury's *Characteristicks* (1744–1745), *A Collection of Political Tracts* (the real title, 1748), Marana's *Letters Writ by a Turkish Spy* (1741), and Molesworth's *An Account of Denmark* (1745), all political. Most of the others also bear the Hasell bookplate (a few only his name or inscription), some with the inscribed name of a Lillington or a Moseley. Though the works are not unusual in themselves, their diversity indicates that their owners had been as representative sons of the Enlightenment as were Governor Dobbs or James Milner.

Not to be ignored, as an appendix to these major libraries, is the list of 324 volumes Scottish North Carolinian Alexander McLeod submitted to the Loyalist Claims Commission after the Revolution. It probably goes back at least in part to the colonial period. In the list of 129 titles were history, philosophy, poetry, drama, religion, a biographical dictionary, *Tom Jones, Joseph Andrews, Robinson Crusoe*, books on husbandry, *The Scots Peerage*, and bound volumes of the *Scots Magazine*.[184] This library is especially significant as representative of the Highland Scots Piedmont culture as opposed to or compared with the Anglican Tidewater civilization. The books of both groups were, allowing for Scottish national pride, much the same.

Considering North Carolina's small population and relatively small agricultural or industrial production before 1764, the books and libraries in private hands in the first century of the province's history are really quite impressive. Especially in the New Bern and Cape Fear regions an inquisitive mind in search of historical information, theological doctrine, voyages and travels, and many other subjects might find answers on his own shelves or those of his neighbors, who seem to have been only too willing to lend.

More opulent and populous South Carolina, centered culturally as well as economically, socially, and politically in the seaport city of Charles-Town, or Charleston, apparently contained scores of private libraries between 1700 and 1764. These fall into the categories of small, moderate, and large, as did those of the Chesapeake colonies. As noticed somewhat indirectly above, many of the inventories of these collections still remain in manuscript, though Walter B. Edgar in his "Libraries of Colonial South Carolina" has analyzed the contents of 154 pre-Revolutionary libraries valued at £50 or more (54 of these were registered after 1763).[185] He finds that in the 1736–1776 period some 2,051 inventories out of a total of 4,700 in the provincial secretary's office mention books or libraries and an additional 263 seventeenth- and eighteenth-century inventories list books in the miscellaneous records of this secretary of the province. His inclusive dates in neither instance coincide with those used in this study, and the criterion for analysis, the £50 value in local currency, seems a most doubtful or unreliable yardstick for measuring larger libraries. His failure to present sample inventories of major libraries is his study's major weakness, however, for the reader needs to visualize at least representative lists. In some instances the present writer has found inventories or lists of books in the period, potentially quite significant ones, which Edgar appears for some reason not to have used. Though his classifications are neither entirely clear nor convenient, they are of use occasionally, as will be evident in this discussion. The author spent many days in South Carolina repositories gathering materials long before Edgar's work appeared, and again since, and generally this study has had to rely on his own finds in Columbia and Charleston repositories.

Except perhaps for their indication of greater interest in shipping and navigation, and in indigo and rice as opposed to tobacco cultivation, the South Carolina books are much the same as those in Virginia and Maryland in the same period. Between 1700 and 1764 there are the same scores of small inventories (less than fifty-volume here) by title, besides those which mention "a parcel of books" or "a library of books." In the correspondence of the S.P.G., missionary Dr. Francis LeJau[186] names books he has or needs, usually theological. There is also in the S.P.G. correspondence in its London library frequent mention by title of books sent to South Carolina in this period, to individuals, presumably not to be included in the public parochial libraries. In 1722 the library of the Reverend Francis Merry[187] was left with a Colonel Moore of St. James, Goose Creek, a collection of some thirty works, all theological and orthodox Anglican, including a few Church Fathers. On October 16, 1723, Ebenezer Taylor left about fifty theological works, including Baxter and Foxe's *Martyrology* and a biblical concordance.[188] In 1727/29 Major William Blakeway left a seven-page inventory of about fifty books, the majority in law, but also including *A Short Account of Carolina*, Bacon's *Henry VII*, Ovid's *Metamorphoses*, something of Erasmus, Milton's historical-political works, and a *Historical Account of Pensilvania*.[189] In 1734 Dr. Thomas Cooper of

Charleston left to his friend Dr. Kilpatrick [or Kirkpatrick], and to Dr. John Lining and others, various volumes of Greek, Latin, and English, including Greek lexicons, dictionaries, a "Lexicon Technicon," and mathematical works.[190] In the fourth decade of the century the manuscript inventories and will books show many "parcels" and "old books" legacies[191] as well as detailed title lists. Though as in other colonies the theological books are frequent even among laymen, here there are many more French religious books in mixed English-French gatherings and in Huguenot libraries than are to be found in the other southern provinces. James le Chantre (d. August 1732), for example, had two large French Bibles and twenty or so French sermon volumes. René Ravenel, Madame D'Hariette and Madame Jean du Pre seem to have had *The Whole Duty of Man* and other English religious works along with French psalm books.[192] Philip Combe in 1737 had a large French Bible and twenty-one other French titles in his library.[193]

In the next two and a half decades the inventoried small libraries continued to be primarily religious, though such political items as *The Independent Whig* began to appear in them.[194] Some persons had Rapin's *History of England,* the usual books on gardening, voyages, *Tatler*s and *Spectator*s, Hervey's *Meditations,* Young's *Night Thoughts,* Shakespeare, Rollin's *Roman History,* Swift, Fénelon, and various classics. Two libraries which listed few books are placed at a relatively high value and may have been much larger than the given titles indicate. In 1746 in Georgetown County Noah Serré left a fine library with nineteen titles, a parcel, and twelve old books. He had Clarendon on the Rebellion, Rapin, Trott's South Carolina laws, Molière's plays, Butler's *Hudibras,* Dryden's Juvenal, at least two periodicals, a French Bible, and one of Thomas Burnet's Latin works, with a dictionary. The library, valued at £91.5, probably contained other fine books.[195] The Reverend James Tessot's 1763 collection was valued at £200, though his books were in a "parcel."[196]

The moderate-sized libraries follow a similar pattern of some variety, though until the end of the period the largest segment of most was theological or religious. Among them were probably the majority of clergymen's libraries, but many Anglicans and some nonconformists held such a large number of titles they may be placed in the "major" category. Of collections of about fifty to one hundred volumes or slightly less or greater, some two dozen have been considered. Several are represented by "lots" or "parcels" valued high enough to place them tentatively in this category. Besides the clergy, the list of owners of these "moderates" here includes merchants, planters, silversmiths, woodcarvers, carpenters, and architects. Among them was probably the collection of James Child, the benefactor of education, who bequeathed his books to his grandson and as a nucleus for a library at the school he endowed. Perhaps larger was the collection of nonconformist clergyman James Parker, who died in 1742 possessed of 126 titles, 104 of them being theological. The remainder were primarily historical and classical.[197] Thomas Hepworth, like Blakeway perhaps a lawyer, possessed in 1728 about one hundred printed volumes and four manuscripts. He probably indicates his personal origins by showing among his legal volumes Thornton's *Antiquities of Nottingham*.[198] Thomas Gadsden, father of Christopher, left behind him in 1741 some 135 volumes,[199] at least one-third religious. Apparently a good Whig, he had among his books *Cato's Letters*, *The Independent Whig*, the *Freethinker*, Rapin's *History*, and Shaftesbury's *Characteristicks*.[200] Law is conspicuously absent, though he may have disposed of legal works before he died. John Rich and Leonard Urquhart were carpenters who had books on architecture, as did woodcarver-architect Ezra Waite, who may have worked on the Miles Brewton House.[201] There is no sure evidence that Eliza Lucas Pinckney ever owned a great library, but the small collection she mentions in her earlier letters undoubtedly was enlarged after her marriage to Pinckney. As it is, her letters reveal the considerable variety of her reading and seem to indicate that she had constantly before her during her married life most of the books mentioned. She is also at the same time good evidence of how the planters' habit of borrowing books existed in South Carolina.[202] John Laurens' 1747 inventory is hardly that of a private library, for it shows principally sets or duplicates of from two to twenty-five, though there are a few scattered periodicals and histories.[203] It is simply a merchant's inventory. More typical were the hundred-odd books of John Ouldfield, Jr., inventoried in 1751 and left in his Craven County house. They included Tull on husbandry, Congreve's plays, Locke *On Education*, Butler's *Hudibras*, Milton, Dryden, Prior, Tillotson, the *London Magazine* (four volumes), and four musical miscellanies.[204] Even more secular, and musical, was the library of Paul Jenys (a planter along the Ashley) numbering about 133 volumes (seventy-five titles) valued at £185.5.[205]

Interesting for various reasons was the library of Charles Purry, son of the founder of Purrysburgh. His estate was settled in 1755 and shows twenty-four titles in 109 volumes. A Swiss converted to Anglicanism, he was, judging by his library, a staunch churchman. Thomas Bray, Benjamin Hoadly, Charles Leslie, and other militant Anglican theologians were represented among his books, 63 percent of which were on divinity.[206] Planter Edward Croft of Christ Church Parish had fifty-six titles (106 volumes), a mixture of religion, law, history, politics, natural history, periodicals, classics, and a few volumes of verse.[207] Slightly smaller but similar in variety is David Hext's 1759 list of forty-seven titles (ninety volumes and a parcel).[208] These and other modest collections suggest how typically British Whig-oriented the South Carolinians were, whether Anglicans or nonconformists.

Several of the major libraries of South Carolina have already been considered, for they were in one sense or another public collections, missionary-parochial provincial, or organized society. The major private libraries naturally included all the books found in the smaller libraries, but there were some more or less significant additions. Perhaps the earliest of these private large eighteenth-century collections is that of the Reverend Richard Ludlam, rector of St. James, Goose Creek, mentioned in the preceding chapter for his contributions to education.[209] His inventory of 1728 shows 226 titles in 248 volumes.[210] Of these, about one-half (114 titles) are in theology, including the sermons of the great Anglican divines past and contemporary, Hooker's *Ecclesiastical Polity*, Cave's *Primitive Christianity*, Calvin's *Institutes*, Allestree's *The Whole Duty of Man*, Jeremy Taylor, Thomas à Kempis, Donne's *Letters*, Burnet, Ray, Wilkins, Grotius, St. Augustine, and others to be expected in a clergyman's collection. Belles lettres include Burton's *Anatomy of Melancholy*, Mandeville's *Fable of the Bees*, Peter Ramus (religious rhetorician), Erasmus, Quarles, Bacon's *New Atlantis*, Fénelon's *Telemachus*, and Butler's *Hudibras*, among others, most of them representing morals and religion as well as "pure" literature. Ludlam had four sets of histories and voyages, more than a dozen classical authors, dictionaries and almanacs, and some mathematics and science, the latter including John Ray's semireligious *The Wisdom of God in the Works of Creation*.

James St. John, appointed surveyor-general for the Crown in 1731, in 1743 left an inventory of some 215 volumes worth £237.7.6.[211] He had thirteen folios, seven quartos, 125 octavos, sixty-four duodecimos, and six pamphlets. The 1747 inventory of the Reverend Robert Betham, assistant rector of St. Philip's in Charleston, lists seventy-four titles in 135 volumes and some smaller Latin tracts.[212] It is essentially a professional theological collection. Much larger is the library of the nonconformist clergyman and theological writer the Reverend Isaac Chanler. This Baptist preacher owned thirty-two titles in thirty-seven volumes, a parcel of pamphlets, and 445 "sundry books." An ardent supporter of Whitefield, Chanler had six of the twenty books especially recommended by that evangelist, and a five-volume set of Whitefield's works. The books *named* are with a single exception religious. When he died in 1749, Chanler left to his children *Emblems for Youth* and *Pilgrim's Progress*. He had a few books on medicine and several of general reference. The books he wrote show how he used his library.[213]

The collection of physician and litterateur Dr. Thomas Dale is designated simply as a "library of books" and 915 pamphlets, all together worth £880. The *South-Carolina Gazette* of January 7, 1751, offered a printed catalog to prospective purchasers. Dr. Waring says that there were 2,273 books, divided into 325 on medicine and botany, 101 on natural philosophy and gardening, 308 on the classics and grammar, 177 on poetry-wit-humor, 150 on divinity, 83 on law-ethics-commerce, 74 on history-geography-voyages, 42 on mathematics, 98 "Epistles of Learned Men," and the 915 pamphlets.[214]

Dying about the same time was Joseph Wragg, merchant, who left in 1751 over two hundred volumes appraised at more than £300. Wragg had about thirty law books. Next in number were the histories and literature, including Raleigh's *History*, Pufendorf's *Introduction to the History of Europe* (frequent in southern libraries), Rapin's *History*, Shakespeare, Dryden, Pope, Waller, Addison, Fielding, and some others. The voyages of Anson, Bayle, Frazier, and Northleigh, and atlases, would have interested a seaport merchant. But he also had Locke's writings and eight volumes of the *Philosophical Transactions* of the Royal Society, at least eight books on gardening and five on architecture. It was a practical library, but it also showed its owner's varied cultural interests.[215] It is perhaps worth noting that like some others it seems to have been heavily weighted toward political liberalism, as Sidney, Trenchard and Gordon, Marana, Pufendorf, Bolingbroke (the *Craftsman*), Rapin, and many more therein contained were at least used by the eighteenth-century Whigs in arguing for their cause.

In 1753 Peter Porcher had some 150 titles including several of those recommended by Whitefield, and others showing his Huguenot background.[216] This wealthy rice planter seems to have been primarily concerned—if one judges by his books—with his spiritual welfare. More varied, at least in surviving titles, was the 1757 library of Colonel Edward Flower, merchant.[217] Besides the sixty-nine old French books there are listed by title a number of significant works. Here are the Whiggishly interpreted Shaftesbury's *Characteristicks*, Trenchard and Gordon (*Cato's Letters* and *The Independent Whig*), Fénelon's *Telemachus*, Pufendorf, the *Craftsman*, and the *Freeholder*. Besides a number of other periodicals, Swift, Pope, Dryden, Thomson, Addison, Butler, Rochester, Milton, Voltaire, and Smollett, biographies, and histories are also listed.

Another merchant, Daniel Crawford of Charleston, in 1760 left some 215 titles in 349 volumes and a large parcel of Latin, Greek, French, and Hebrew books.[218] From Hooker's *Ecclesiastical Polity* on through Steele's *The Christian Hero* and Doddridge's and Watts' nonconformist works, along with Whitefield's, the religious titles are here in quantity. But also present are secular titles such as Playford's *Introduction to the Skill of Music*, Evelyn's *Sylva, or a Discourse on Forest Trees*, Locke *On Education*, Montaigne's *Essays*, several books on liberty, Montesquieu, Vertot, Fénelon, Scarron, Cervantes, and the usual poems, plays, and novels. Listed are at least five books on gardening, a history of Virginia, Mrs. Lennox's *The Female Quixote*, Fontenelle's *Plurality of Worlds*, and a treatise on dreams and visions, among many worth noticing. Crawford reached out intellectually in several directions.

In 1765 two library collections made in the previous generation were probated. One is that of Dr. James Crokatt, who appears to have owned 145 titles in 203 volumes.[219] He lived in Prince Frederick Parish and was a country member of the Charleston Library Society. His books were about one-third professional (medicine). But along with the classics, histories, dictionaries, periodicals, and theological works including sermons, were Mandeville, Swift's *Gulliver*, Marana, Dryden's plays, and a few volumes of verse. In the same year James Grindlay, a Charleston lawyer of Scottish ancestry and a Presbyterian, left in his house on Tradd Street 312 titles in 518 volumes besides a parcel of books and magazines. This library was given the presumably high valuation of £810.4.6. Edgar calls it the second largest he located possessed of a complete inventory.[220] Of the total, about 187 titles in 288 volumes seem to be legal. They include the usual treatises, Trott's *The Laws of South Carolina*, and editions of the laws of Virginia, Jamaica, Scotland, and England. The Indian Bible here is perhaps John Eliot's. The histories are concerned as much with the ancients and continental Europe as with England. Grindlay had a book on "The Art of Painting in Oil," Colden's *History of the Five Nations*, and [Wilson's?] "Instruction for Indians," and complete sets of the *Critical Review*, *Tatler*, *Rambler*, and *Spectator*, and partial sets of the *Guardian* and *Negotiator* were on his shelves. Addison's *Cato*, Molière, Sydney "On Poesy," Congreve, Butler, Shakespeare, Fielding, Pope, Fénelon, and Montaigne represented various belletristic and perhaps other interests. Grindlay is reputed to have been far from wealthy, but his library shows a man of considerable intellectual curiosity who found somehow the means to satisfy it.

Francis Stuart (d. 1765), leading merchant of the Beaufort-Port Royal region, was a Scot of Jacobite leanings and brother of the famous John Stuart of the colonial frontier. His library was the largest known from his region, containing 122 titles in 233 volumes and valued at £306.7.6. He had the *Laws of Scotland* and a *History of Scotland*, the usual inexact titles of works both of which were by Sir George Mackenzie, and David Hume's *History of England*. Somewhat surprisingly he had the *Sermons* of Isaac Chanler and the *Sermons* of George Whitefield, as well as various belles lettres, periodicals, and Anson's *Voyages*.[221] The Reverend John Green (d. 1767), rector of St. Helena's and an M.A. of St. Peter's College, Cambridge, possessed 369 titles and almost five hundred volumes, 60 percent of the whole being religious. History was also strong, as were the classics. There were only twenty-nine titles other than these, including Montesquieu, Cervantes, Shakespeare, Buchanan, and Nelson's *Justice of the Peace*.[222] Physician William Pillans, who died in 1769, had 119 titles in 278 volumes and detached music. The latter is described as "one of the most complete collections of chamber music in colonial South Carolina," including Archangelo Corelli's concertos and other works, Carlo Marino's sonatas for violin, sonatas for German flute and violin by William McGibbon, and John Lates' sonatas for pianoforte. Almost 64 percent of all titles were medical or scientific.[223] But there were periodicals, classics, Pope, Swift, Addison, Smollett, and Molière. In the same year George Seaman, Charleston merchant-planter, left some 156 books and pamphlets, 50 percent theological. Stith's *History of the First Discovery and Settlement of Virginia* was the only really unusual volume. The library leaned more toward seventeenth- than eighteenth-century books, a fact which may indicate it was primarily an inherited collection.[224] And in 1772 Dr. William Fyffe of Georgetown left an inventory showing sixty-six titles in ninety-eight volumes, with eighty-one old books. Though medical titles are the major segment, here are also the Scottish poets Blacklock and Ramsay, and Shakespeare, Congreve, Molière, Swift, Pope, and Plutarch; and a few books on religion and travel, four sets of histories, and Boyer's *French Dictionary* are among the lot.[225]

At least five other large libraries existed in colonial South Carolina, most if perhaps not all of them gathered but not necessarily appraised before 1764. The earliest is that of Chief Justice Nicholas Trott (1662/63–1739/40), one of the remarkably learned men of his age and a legal scholar of the first order. His volumes of laws of the American plantations and of South Carolina earned for him honorary doctorates from Oxford and Aberdeen. Other writings of his are well known, and his manuscript remains in Charleston have been edited for publication. The latter will be discussed below. Though he died in 1739/40, the bulk or remainder of his library, one is not sure which, was not put up for sale until the death of his wife, Sarah, in 1745. Though no itemized inventory exists in the South Carolina Archives, it is one of the six Edgar has listed as valued at £1,000 or more. It was surely worth a great deal more than £1,000. As Trott's most recent editor has shown, the jurist quotes a huge number of learned and esoteric tomes in many languages. His Hebrew,

Greek, Latin, French, and other languages, his enormous range of reference and quotation, are an indication that his was the greatest library in the province in the first half of the eighteenth century.[226]

Charleston lawyer James Michie (d. 1761) left a library valued at £1,750, of which law books were appraised at £1,120 and miscellaneous at £630. His collection was advertised in the *South Carolina Gazette* of October 17, 1761, as "a very complete collection of law, civil, statute, and common, most of the Classicks, *notis variorum*, and others of the best editions. And a very large collection of the best *English* Poets, Historians, &c. &c.—The Books are in very good condition, many of them in elegant bindings."[227] Another lawyer, James Rattray of Charleston, had a library valued in 1761 at £1,200.[228]

Peter Manigault, who was collecting books for his father and himself while he was in Great Britain in 1752, was still building his library when he died in 1773. Its appraisal value, £3,000, was the highest of all South Carolina colonial collections. Manigault's early letters tell us something of his books, but the "parcel" inventory leaves us without any sure knowledge of the great library. How much was collected through 1763 one can only guess.

The John Mackenzie library of 1772, left in care of the Charleston Library Society for the future use of the projected college in the city, is the largest of the inventories of books collected principally in the colonial period, and the inventory, noted above, was printed probably along with the 1772 appendix of the Society's collection, though the catalogue title pages are distinct. There are some 418 titles in from 600 to 800 volumes in the printed catalogue. Edgar, giving the appraisal value at £2,350 (with £250 in Charleston and £2,100 at the Goose Creek plantation) may be referring to a larger collection.

As it is, in the printed list one finds seventy law titles, sixty-four classics, forty-five belles lettres, forty history, thirty politics and economics, twenty-six theological, and fifteen reference. The number of Whiggish writings, or books that both Caroline Robbins and H. Trevor Colbourn have shown could be considered liberal, is the largest recorded in this or perhaps any other southern colony. Trenchard and Gordon, Fénelon, Molesworth, Shaftesbury, Montesquieu, Sidney, volumes of "American Tracts containing letters against taxing the colonies," are only some of them. Mackenzie had Bolingbroke on political parties, Pufendorf, and Mandeville. Other sorts of books concerned gardening and husbandry, the art of painting, architecture, and Hogarth's *Analysis of Beauty* (London, 1753).[229] How Mackenzie as an ardent Whig used his library in the pamphlet warfare of the times is noted elsewhere in this chapter.

Walter B. Edgar has been able to find and analyze a number of middle-

or artisan-class libraries, some of which have been touched upon above along with other moderate or small collections. The reader is referred to his fairly extensive listing and discussion of these libraries as indicative of the quality of mind and of interest of these skilled workmen.[230]

Taken all together, for the generation just before the Revolution South Carolina books indicate that a significant segment or proportion of the population was literate, sophisticated, and probably predominantly Whiggish. They parallel to some extent the greatly accelerated search for formal education in Europe which came in this period. It is evident that any citizen of Charleston or its environs might buy or borrow almost any book he wanted. The bookseller lists in the *Gazette* indicate that all the books mentioned save a few older volumes were for sale throughout the century, and that most of the old authors might be found in new editions alongside the contemporary writers.[231]

As indicated in the discussion of public libraries, almost all the largest early Georgia collections were probably parochial, community, or institutional.[232] There were, however, several private libraries worth noting. In an inventory of May 6, 1756, the booklist of Nicholas Rigby of Savannah shows about ninety titles in more than 120 volumes.[233] Rigby, categorized as "Gentleman," left his personal estate to his wife and two daughters. Items under religion, belles lettres, political-legal, medical, reference, history, periodicals, classics, navigation, business, philosophy, travel, and music are varied but the titles are not unusual. He had *Pilgrim's Progress* and *Robinson Crusoe, Paradise Lost, Arabian Nights*, Dryden, Congreve, Ramsay, Pomfret, Fénelon, Bacon's *Atlantis*, and Joe Miller's *Jests*. He had Bishop Thomas Wilson's *Essay towards an Instruction for the Indians* (1740), which was in libraries in Maryland, Virginia, and South Carolina; and as a Georgian not surprisingly he had Whitefield's collected *Sermons*. His other religious books indicate Anglican background.

Thomas Burrington, clerk and sporadical member of the Common House of Assembly of the province, died in 1767. His collection of about 425 volumes in four languages may have been one of the three large Savannah collections De Brahm saw and used in the early 1760s.[234] About two hundred were legal works, the rest the normal variety from classics to reference, with a considerable proportion by ancient and modern belletrists. Trenchard and Gordon, Lennox's *The Female Quixote*, Voltaire, Shaftesbury, Rollin, suggest some of his interests. It was indeed the sort of library the enquiring mind of De Brahm would have found useful.

Other collections largely gathered before 1764 included Chief Justice William Simpson's library (d. 1768/9), consisting of about 220 books, more than half in law.[235] The library of the Reverend John J. Zubly (1724–

1781), who had come to South Carolina in 1736 and removed to Savannah in 1760, was certainly gathered largely in America, or from America.[236] A Presbyterian, Zubly was awarded the D.D. by the College of New Jersey (Princeton). His library is described in the journals of Lutheran Henry M. Muhlenberg (1711–1787), who was most enthusiastic, declaring that the books and manuscripts were not inferior to those of the most famous collections in Europe.[237] There were of course many more small libraries in private hands, principally of clergy, but also of lawyers, merchants, physicians, public officials, and others.[238] Harold E. Davis has found 188 inventories from the royal period alone which indicate ownership of reading materials.[239] For example, in 1758 John Robinson's inventory showed five books, one legal, the others Dryden's *Poems*, a volume of voyages, Rowe's *Letters*, and the *Memoirs of Fanny Hill*.[240] Robert Hamilton, with no date shown, had fifty-four volumes including history, politics, and belles lettres. He also left ninety-four gallons of rum.[241]

Perhaps more comprehensive and indicative of popular or general reading in Georgia is the advertisement of James Johnston, bookseller and printer, in the *Georgia Gazette* of November 10, 1763 (no. 32). The two-column list of titles includes from two to eight volumes each of the *Spectator, Adventurer, Guardian, Tatler, Rambler, World, Idler,* and *Female Spectator,* among other periodicals. Books on trade and husbandry, manuals of guidance for young men, and dictionaries were utilitarian. There were Joe Miller's, Falstaff's, and Tom Brown's *Jests* for sale. Swift, Pope, Defoe, Addison, Milton, Young, Ramsay, Blacklock, Dodsley, Sterne, Lennox, Richardson, Congreve, Bacon, Shakespeare, Smollett, Gay, and Fielding were among the English playwrights, poets, and novelists offered. Boileau, Molière, Voltaire, and Vertot, often in more than one title, could be bought. There were the usual religious works, though not in large proportion, including seven by Isaac Watts alone, and Tillotson, Sherlock, and the rest, including many collections of sermons. The classics are present but not in great abundance. Americana is represented by an account of the Spanish settlements (illustrated and including a map) and sea charts for the coasts of South Carolina, Georgia, and Florida. Since the *Georgia Gazette* was begun only in that year and Johnston was Georgia's first printer[242] and probably bookseller on an extensive scale, this seems a good list. There is hardly the abundant variety offered in the advertisements in the provincial *Gazettes* of the other southern colonies of this date, but it is a varied offering. It indicates the needs and interests of literate men who already had begun libraries of their own or wanted to acquire them. Many of the interests Georgians showed in private and public libraries already mentioned are barely if at all represented here, but if the titles of the general religious German library at Ebenezer and of the general and private libraries of Augusta and Savannah and Ebenezer are added to this, it becomes obvious that by 1763 Georgians were reading.

READING TASTES: THE BOOKS AND THE USES MADE OF THEM, ESPECIALLY IN THE EIGHTEENTH CENTURY

Though scholars such as Perry Miller have shown us a great deal about the uses of books in New England libraries, especially of theological works, very little indeed has been done to show how the southern colonists employed their libraries. Louis B. Wright in several books, notably his *First Gentlemen of Virginia*, has considered individuals in relation to some of the specific titles in their personal collections, with strong implied or explicit suggestions as to how they may have used them, though there is very little on their attitudes toward the body of theological writings they possessed and read. In "The Libraries of Colonial South Carolina," unpublished (except on microfilm), and the briefer, published "Some Popular Books in Colonial South Carolina," Walter B. Edgar has listed by subject-matter categories hundreds of books read in South Carolina, and in the former work has, like Wright, suggested some probable uses made of certain subject groups if not of individual items.[243]

The suggestions, indirect or direct, in Wright's *First Gentlemen of Virginia*, Robbins' *Eighteenth-Century Commonwealthman*, and Colbourn's *The Lamp of Experience* are to sources of ideas and make some specific references to particular works which went into pre-Revolutionary pamphleteering. Colbourn's, the most recent and in content most specifically directed study as far as America is concerned, notices titles of books and gives library lists (public and private collections) in an appendix. Colbourn includes a little on South Carolina books in this appendix but in his text fails to analyze books, speeches, and writing south of Virginia. Thus in this most obvious area of southern active intellectuality only a trifle has been done to connect books and ideas.

Richard Gummere in two books has shown something of the widespread southern attention to the classics, and in the preceding chapter something of southern colonial educational theory and its origins has been pointed out. A dozen books on individual colonials of the South Atlantic region, such as John Smith, William Byrd, and the Dulanys of Maryland, give some indication of how reading influenced their reading and writing. But no comprehensive study of the impact of books on the southern colonial mind has been done. Perhaps there can be no such study. It may be too large a subject. But once all the inventories are printed and the owners of libraries are as clearly identified as is possible at this distance in time, there must be at least a series of studies, of printed page to mind back to printed page or to oral declaration, before the southern intellect can be understood reasonably well. In the following pages only a few suggestions can be made, based on the inventories already discussed and certain other knowledge of the reading of individuals or groups below the Susquehannah and certain of their publications.

RELIGIOUS READING

For most of the nearly two centuries of the colonial period in the South religion was the one subject on and in which every literate man and woman, white or black or red, was sure to read. For much of the period it was for most colonials the invitation to, explanation of, and pathway toward eternal salvation. The next two chapters are concerned with the nature and history of religion in the southern mind and society and its manifestations in sermons and tracts. Though here the relationship between the theological printed page and southern colonial belief and expression can only be touched upon, it must be noticed, if only as a suggestion for needed future studies.

Already has been emphasized the most obvious of facts about colonial books of the South Atlantic region—that the largest single area represented among them was religion or theology. The small libraries of the humbler or poorer literate colonists were likely, as already suggested, to contain, first of all, one or more editions of the Bible, next, the Book of Common Prayer and Anglican catechisms, and, third, the pious book of Anglican devotionals called *The Whole Duty of Man*. The same volumes form the nuclei of larger libraries, of the person with a grammar school education who knew Latin, as well as of the individual of university or professional training who had learned even more. The Presbyterians, the Huguenots, and the Lutherans, even the Quakers, ignored all these titles except the Bible, but their catechisms and manuals of moral instruction were not greatly different from those of members of the established church. All these Christians read and reread the Bible and the concomitant works to the point where, much more even than in the nineteenth century, these books were consciously memorized and come down to us as they were employed in official records of courts and legislatures, newspaper essays and verses, and private correspondence.

When the educated and more prosperous added to their book collections, in almost every instance they added religio-moral treatises, from the complexities of Calvin's *Institutes* and Richard Hooker's *Ecclesiastical Polity*

NULLA PALLESCERE CULPA

William Byrd of Westover
in Virginia Esqr.

Virginia State Library

Bookplate of William Byrd II

JAMES HASELL

DE ME · OLIM
PRÆSAGIA

North Carolina Collection, University of North Carolina, Chapel Hill

Bookplate of James Hasell of North Carolina

through such popular tracts as Sherlock *On Death*, Grotius' *The Truth of the Christian Religion*, the ecclesiastical histories of Bishop Burnet, and rational explanations such as Humphrey Prideaux's *Connections*,[244] most of them first published in the seventeenth century and often purchased in the Latin versions. Puritan William Perkins' *Works*, presented to the college at Henrico in the first years of the Jamestown colony, continued to be found at least occasionally in southern libraries up to the Revolution. Perkins and Calvin and other Calvinist-puritan writers were read in the earlier southern generations probably with at least one of two attitudes, either without paying much attention to the doctrine but paying a great deal to ethical ideas, or with great enjoyment because of agreement with the Calvinist doctrines thus expressed. In southern libraries early and late, next to the Bible and Book of Common Prayer on their shelves, were volumes of tracts and sermons by the great preachers, from Perkins and Andrewes through Jeremy Taylor and Stillingfleet, Ussher and Tillotson, of the seventeenth century to the later Jonathan Edwards and James Blair and Samuel Davies and George Whitefield.[245] The Cambridge Platonists, moderate Arminians, later English Calvinists, and anti-Calvinists might be found in the same library.

In the laymen's libraries, in a country where there were never regular weekly sermons save in the capital towns, these books were read to comfort or strengthen faith or to regenerate. On bad-weather Sundays, or when his parson was conducting services in other parts of the parish, William Byrd II was wont to read a sermon or two from Tillotson, who was far and away the most popular preacher among Anglican readers of the century before the Revolution. As late as 1802 a wealthy Anglican plantation matron thanked her son for sending her a new edition of sermons by Hervey, which she read with professed edification. Those less inclined to read for themselves were likely to hear at service on an *average* Sunday (for then the clergyman was likely to be at another place) some one of the sermons of a great English preacher read by a layman (lay reader) in charge of the service—a poet blacksmith such as Thomas Hansford or a wealthy planter-pamphleteer such as Landon Carter.[246] Even when in the mid-eighteenth century many men such as Sir John and Peyton Randolph and Thomas Jefferson had the reputation of being deistically inclined, their theological titles were more often than not orthodox, though frequently with a sprinkling of deistical writers among them. Perhaps Jefferson is the exception among the readers and book collectors here noticed. He bothered little about printed commentaries on Christian doctrine; he had several, but there is little evidence that he read them more than once, and then with impatience at their expressed doctrines.

The anti-deistical books which were present even in the Randolph libraries and in many of the clergymen's collections were not designed merely to furnish argument for locally composed sermons. There are as many of these in surviving laymen's libraries as in the clergy's—the books were meant to be and were read. Anti-Quaker tracts were read and used in much the same way by clergymen, governors, legislative debaters, and letter-writers secular or ecclesiastical.

The hundreds of theological titles, from St. Augustine through Thomas Aquinas and Thomas à Kempis to a seventeenth-century French archbishop or an English divine, have already been noted. They are remarkably varied in subject, shades of doctrine, theme, and form, from hymns to Jesuitical casuistry, to reconciliations of science-revelation, to expositions of witchcraft, from Indian Bibles to Mohammedan Korans. The great proportion of such books in clerical libraries warrants a direct if brief look at a few surviving southern colonial sermons to show certain uses that were made of the theological works—uses perhaps implied but not emphasized elsewhere in this book.

From the beginning in the seventeenth century the Anglo-American southern colonial preacher employed his religious library as did his brethren in Great Britain. Alexander Whitaker's 1612/1613 sermon from Virginia is studded with marginal references to specific passages of the Bible, almost every argument in this strong missionary sermon being buttressed by Scripture.[247] The text of the sermon indicates extensive knowledge of contemporary books on witchcraft, though none is named. The other extant sermon of the seventeenth-century South, Deuel Pead's "A Sermon Preached at James City in Virginia . . . 1686,"[248] written at the other end of the century for a quite different purpose, suggests that homiletic scholarship and practice had changed very little in three-quarters of a century. Pead uses scriptural allusions much as did Whitaker, but he adds in his text Hebrew quotations and references to theological works, as of the Jewish grammarian David Kimhi, and to the more secular and non-Christian Stoics and Empedocles, the first Earl of Shaftesbury, and recent European historians.

In the eighteenth century an effective and learned Maryland Anglican preacher such as the Reverend Thomas Bacon continued this page-by-page reference to the Bible, as in his *Four Sermons . . . [on] Negro Slaves . . . ,*[249] discourses in which he was concerned with the recurrent southern problem of the African slaves' relation to Christianity and Christian doctrine. The manuscript sermon book of the Reverend Robert Paxton[250] of Virginia in 1710 likewise shows continuous marginal scriptural reference, some of it from the biblical concordances noticed in the inventories. Presbyterian Samuel Davies had his collected as well as individually printed sermons appear with copious biblical reference, usually printed as footnotes. In other instances, as that of South Carolina Anglican Samuel Quincy's *Twenty Sermons* (1750), the marginal annotations (if there ever were any) have disappeared in the transposition to type. In several other instances the scholarly notes have disappeared, but the texts themselves of Baptist or Anglican or Presbyterian homilies contain reference after reference indicating direct use of the Bible and concordance or biblical dictionary or encyclopedia as the sermon was composed.

One of the most heavily annotated sermons is *Popish Zeal inconvenient to Mankind, and unsuitable to the Law of Christ,* preached by Anglican William Brogden in 1754 and printed at Annapolis by Jonas Green in 1755.[251] Brogden in the preface or dedication addressed to his parishioners refers to "this plain Discourse" which they have desired that he have published. Plain style it is in the body of his discourse, but he buttresses his reasoned arguments with annotations or references to authority. He quotes Cardinal Bellarmine (for various reasons popular among Protestants), he refers to Spanish history and the lives of the popes, Louis E. DuPin's ecclesiastical history, Pufendorf, the Church Fathers, Burnet's *History of the Reformation,* Foxe's *Book of Martyrs,* various Roman Catholic theologians of his own or recent times, sermons by White Kennet, W. Lloyd, Tillotson, and Stillingfleet, and numerous anti-Papist tracts of the times, together with the usual scriptural citations. His numerous notes are far more than citations, however, for he explicates or attacks other persons' interpretations at some length in most of them. The author, rector of Queen Anne Parish in Prince Georges County, evidently had available an excellent personal and perhaps parochial library. Of these authorities cited (and they are not all) DuPin, Burnet, Pufendorf, Stillingfleet, and Tillotson are among the writers Commissary Bray had listed in his proposed catalogue of lending libraries for market towns for "The Use of the Clergy . . ." and others.[252] They were also, of course, in many clergymen's private collections, as were the Church Fathers. This sermon is one of a number Brogden preached against the Roman church, as did other of his Maryland Anglican brethren, partly because of the French threat and the still considerable Catholic element in that province.[253]

In their tracts the southern colonial clergy vary in the amount of reference to authority just about as they do in their printed sermons. Baptist South Carolinian Isaac Chanler's long and somewhat curious *Doctrines of Glorious Grace . . . defended* (Charleston, 1744) relies primarily on scriptural citation as basis for argument throughout its 445 pages, and there are almost no footnote or marginal annotations. But in the text, along with the biblical citations, are references to the works of contemporaries who support or oppose Chanler's Whitefieldian position, most of them pamphleteers whose works seldom if ever appear by title in book inventories. Quite different is one of Samuel Davies' tracts, an answer to a sermon by William Stith, and a work which for various reasons remained in manuscript until it was published in 1941.[254] *Charity and Truth United: Or, The Way of the Multitude Exposed: in Six Letters to the Rev. Mr. William Stith* . . . is a dignified, scholarly, reasoned essay. The catalogue of names Davies marshals in support of his argument is most impressive: Plato, Socrates, Hesiod, Aristotle, Cebes, Cleanthes, Epictetus, Porphyry, Virgil, Horace, Seneca, Juvenal, Cicero, Eusebius, Athanasius, Lactantius, St. Augustine, Hilarius, Theophylact, Guyse, Wolfius, Maloratus, Poole, Grotius, Locke, Sir George Littleton, Doddridge, Atterbury, Jenkins, Clarke, Cave, Watts, Brennius, Jacob Böhme, Sir Thomas More, Swift, Young, and Pope, with dozens of others. They appear in both text and notes, with specific citations by volume and chapter or other division. Interlarded with the learned theological and philosophical authorities are biblical citations. Some of the notes are entirely in the Greek or Latin of Davies' source. In text or notes Davies gives rather lengthy quotations from the verse of Pope, Edward Young, and English versions of Juvenal and Horace. He shows himself familiar with various contemporary theories of the earth's origin, a plurality of inhabited worlds, millenarianism, and the Great Chain of Being. Yet with all this heavy annotation and impressive learning, there is no complex, involved doctrine, but the clear and carefully reasoned discourse of the pulpit orator. This single essay proves several points—Davies' own considerable learning, the effective education given by the log colleges to the Presbyterian New Lights, and Davies' access to and probable ownership of an impressive library.

Finally, as far as religious works are concerned, the scores of letters from Anglican missionaries back to the S.P.G. headquarters in London begging for libraries for themselves and their parishioners—and naming the necessary books—are strong proof of what the clergy had read and of their attempt to get their laity to study books specifically designed for the layman. Francis Makemie and Davies and Josiah Smith were learned Presbyterians who also wanted their flocks to have available catechisms, Bibles, Calvin, and other, simpler doctrinal writings.

EDUCATIONAL READING

Since this subject has been discussed at some length in the preceding chapter, it will be given only brief attention here. From the beginning schoolmasters were reading Brinsley on the grammar school and with their students Lily's and others' grammars, usually in Latin. In the eighteenth century Lily was still used, though there were additional new grammars. Several of the private inventories list multiple copies of textbooks—

grammars, editions of the classics, mathematical works from arithmetic through algebra and geometry and astronomy and navigation, and manuals for composition or writing, for learning trades, for morals and manners. For teachers, there were pedagogical works, such as Clarke "on Learning" and "upon Study" and Turnbull "on Education" and *Reflections on Learning*;[255] and there were various and varied books on rhetoric, some fairly elementary texts and some as complex or sophisticated as Aristotle and Peter Ramus and certain later writers. In geography and science there were numerous books, often in Latin or translated from that language. Edgar found in the larger South Carolina libraries that next to the *Spectator* in actual number of volumes to be counted were the English dictionaries (there were three variant titles) of Nathan Bailey.[256] Certainly every plantation tutor or parochial schoolmaster needed one or more of these English dictionaries, as he probably did Abel Boyer's French-English *Royal Dictionary*, also frequent in colonial libraries public or private. Besides the Latin classics, the Latin colloquies of Erasmus and Corderius and the elementary Latin books of Corderius were used as textbooks.[257] The account books of the Scot Donald Robertson's school, mentioned in the preceding chapter, show something of what eighteenth-century schoolboys had to purchase as textbooks.[258] Those named are principally on Latin and Greek and "Mathematicks," but there were surveying and some "business" texts or manuals, as well as geographies. The school itself may have supplied histories and dictionaries as reference works. "Lilly's gr." is a frequent item. Quintilian, Cicero, and Aristotle were used in secondary schools and at William and Mary in teaching oratory and forensics. Rapin, Raleigh, and Bacon were required historical reading in some southern schools, apparently, though only in the College of William and Mary does one know of actual curricula, and then for a late period. All these books had the effect one might expect: of giving some knowledge of the classics (including ancient history), of learning English grammar via Latin grammar, of mastering basic arithmetic and frequently algebra, and of acquiring perhaps somewhat obliquely a knowledge of modern history and geography, and of going on from grammar to rhetoric, again English via Latin.

Besides these orthodox teaching and text materials were the practical guides and manuals. The courtesy books from the Renaissance and their later seventeenth- and eighteenth-century descendants were present in most gentlemen's libraries, as were clerk's guides, the latter of which might be used by indentured accountants or apprentice lawyers, or simply by literate persons wishing to learn how to write business or professional letters and keep records or tally. There were dozens of these, and it is clear that they were effective as models for various kinds of epistles.[259] The dictionaries in English were supplemented by encyclopedias in several languages and by biographical dictionaries in the same languages. These were reference tools for schoolboy and adult alike, but scarcely textbooks. The effectiveness of various grammars, including Lily's, is sometimes commented upon adversely by schoolmasters, but the fact is they gave appropriate examples and drills which helped to make effective writers of many men. Despite Maury's opposition in principle to classical learning for the average Virginia boy, he and his textbooks made of Jefferson an excellent Latin scholar who read the ancients for relaxation as well as philosophical and political theory. Donald Robertson and his schoolbooks did much the same thing for James Madison. Landon Carter imported orthodox textbooks for the school he held for his grandchildren at Sabine Hall, and, as noted in the previous chapter, "King" Carter's ideas of what constituted an effective grammar text were most positive. The elder Carter considered the textbook as important as the teacher.

Naturally books on many other subjects might under peculiar circumstances or from peculiar needs be employed in the same manner as textbooks. Probably many of the occupational, recreational, and politico-philosophical works were used in educating youth, and the poetic and prose belletristic miscellanies almost surely were. Perhaps equal to Lily's grammar as a teaching text was the Book of Common Prayer, from which the illiterate white or the black slave or red Indian might learn both English and Anglican Christian doctrine and thus learn to read English and sometimes to write it.

OCCUPATIONAL READING

From the survey of book inventories above it is evident that the average or moderate-sized library was usually a professional or occupational collection. The clergyman's use of books in his sermons and tracts has been noted. The lawyer was the same—his case must be based on cited authority. Thus the great legal collections. They might be considered occupational even by the planter, who knew he must have legal knowledge to protect his personal interests. The legal works were of particular use to the justices of the peace, most of whom did not have formal juridical training. Their many manuals have been noted. These were an absolute necessity to provincial general courts or supreme courts, which usually established their separate libraries. To the compilers of the laws, men like Mercer in Virginia, Bacon in Maryland, and Trott in South Carolina, the legal library was indispensable. To a governor such as Sir William Gooch or a chief justice such as Nicholas Trott, both of whom charged grand juries, legal knowledge was the source of ideas. Relying largely on his own library, Trott in his

"Charges" to the South Carolina Grand Jury in the first decade of the eighteenth century produced one of the most beautifully composed and profound legal treatises or commentaries of the colonial period.

Law libraries in all the southern colonies were used in the years immediately preceding the Revolution as sources for arguments for and against the right of taxation without representation, and earlier still as the bases for tobacco tax or vestry-vs.-governor debates, among others. Knowledge of the law and quotations from statutes, reports, or institutes are to be found in newspaper essays, separate pamphlets, and recorded legislative proceedings. There can be no doubt that legal libraries were used for more than trial argument.

Medical libraries were owned principally by practicing physicians, but also by affluent planters who had the health of large households to protect. Some of these titles and libraries have already been examined. There is certainly need for a more extensive analysis by a qualified medical historian. As it is, Joseph I. Waring's *History of Medicine in South Carolina, 1670–1825*, in mentioning the medical books advertised for sale by Charleston dealers,[260] gives the usual list, including Boerhaave, Sydenham, various dispensatories, botanical dictionaries, Smellie's *Midwifery*, Keil's *Anatomy*, and Huxham *On Fevers*, and suggests some but not all the works available to Dr. Thomas Dale, practitioner and medical author, who in 1750, among 2,273 titles, shows 325 "Medical Anatomical & Botanical Books," or later to the remarkable Dr. Lewis Mottet, who in 1762 offered his considerable medical library for sale.[261] These and other South Carolinians wrote or spoke trenchantly and voluminously on medical subjects, including inoculation, and in doing so combined personal experience with reading. Virginia physicians from 1621 or earlier brought with them medical books. In the seventeenth and eighteenth centuries these volumes were, in this colony as in all the others, a means of consultation where no colleagues were easily available. For the first century no strictly medical writing came from Virginia, though physicians and other educated men sent to the Royal Society essays which were related to medicine. Published in the *Philosophical Transactions* was William Byrd's report on the Negro with dappled spots. Banister's "Catalogue" of Virginia plants appeared in John Ray's *Historia Plantarum* (1686). Then there was the Reverend John Clayton's essay on medicinal plants.[262] In the eighteenth century, however, while the learned and curious still gathered and labeled and shipped plants, several actually did a good deal of writing, even before 1764. The most prolific author was Dr. John Tennent, who wrote on such topics as epidemical diseases in Virginia and the efficacies of the rattlesnake root (it could cure pleurisy, among other ills), and produced such books as *Every*

Man His Own Doctor; or the Poor Planter's Physician (second edition, Williamsburg, 1734), a household manual. Again Tennent's is an instance of combining American experience with his reading.

Blanton's comment that Virginia medical libraries were "surprisingly large and well chosen" is documented by his printing of several inventories and the summarizing of others.[263] Dr. John Mitchell, the younger John Clayton, and Mark Catesby, though the latter two were not physicians, are among those whose works on natural history, including its medical aspects, were published in Great Britain. Of their work more in a later chapter. These men and others, some physicians and some not, used their volumes on materia medica and general botanical works as a basis for major contributions to British or continental scientific knowledge. The same is true for other colonies, especially South Carolina, where Dr. John Lining and Dr. Thomas Dale and others wrote copiously, frequently directly on such medical subjects as inoculation, basing their arguments on recorded precedent and personal experience. But again, more of this in Chapter VII.

At this distance, and with few records of individual farming or provincial crop totals and with the total absence of southern books on agriculture in the colonial period, the effect of Gervase Markham's *Way To Get Wealth* (fourteenth edition, 1683), Jethro Tull's *Horse-Hoeing Husbandry* (1731), and Thomas Hale's *A Complete Body of Husbandry* with a score of similar works is impossible to measure. There are indications that some planters did try to follow British-recommended procedures in plowing and fertilizing. But in a country of newly cleared fields, crops strange to Europeans such as tobacco and maize, and special or peculiar problems of limitation of market imposed by the home government, far less heed could be paid to Tull or Hale or the rest than the literate farmer in Great Britain probably paid. A number of essays in the southern newspapers on tobacco, indigo, rice, cotton, mulberry silkworms, and other American agricultural items show a knowledge of general agricultural principles perhaps derived from books on farming, but of the details certainly from personal experience. It is true that many books on husbandry were in evidence in colonial libraries, and a thorough study through farm accounts and correspondence could and should be made.

There were as many or more books on gardening as on farming on a larger scale. Kitchen gardens of herbs and simples are among the subjects with which they were concerned. But more frequently than not Gerard's *Herball*, Evelyn's *Sylva* or his books on domestic gardens, Miller's ubiquitous *Gardener's Dictionary*, Vanosteen's *The Dutch Gardener* and half a dozen other such books concerned with useful and ornamental gardens were put to real use, for both kitchen and ornamental gardens might be modeled entirely, except for a few native plants included, on the British varieties. The ornamental garden, romantically "wild" or geometrically patterned, such as Byrd's or Carter's or Custis' or the governor's in Virginia, the Dulanys' and Lloyds' in Maryland, the Middletons' and others' in the Carolinas, was laid out and cultivated with care. Byrd undoubtedly studied his books on the subject, though it was Mark Catesby who gave him the technical advice he needed. Again, from a combination of environmental experience and Old World books southern colonials produced something of their own, the garden both useful and ornamental, as attractive to the palate as to the eye and ear. Thyme and marjoram stood a little aside from blossoming tulips or roses and the hummingbirds flitting about them, but books imported from Europe helped to develop both in the southern botanical paradise.

The average South Atlantic colonist lived, as did his British ancestor, on the banks of salt rivers or bays or ocean or within a few miles of at least some sort of body of water. Any member of any family from the upper through the middle to the indentured classes might become a sailor. Many planters were former sea captains. Therefore there were books on navigation. From them Captain Isham Randolph, son of William of Turkey Island and a friend of William Byrd II, probably got his first training. Even if a boy might not become a professional seaman, he was likely to need some knowledge of navigation as he sailed about in the sylvan Venice of the Chesapeake area, the coasts and sounds and inlets of North Carolina, or the rivers and coasts of South Carolina and Georgia. It is not out of character that a descendant of seagoing Huguenot Fontaines and Maurys should within a century after the end of the colonial period become the great Pathfinder of the Seas, the man who charted the ocean currents, the man to whom air as well as sea pilot will always be obligated.

Other full-time or part-time occupations were represented in the volumes of colonial libraries, occupations such as cartography. But more can and will be said about them later. In the most modern practical sense, many colonial libraries were useful, even utilitarian.

RECREATIONAL READING

The Britisher or German or Frenchman trying to establish himself in a primitive world did not have much time for recreation. But he took some time from the beginning, and as the first century passed into the second was as hedonistic—perhaps not quite the word—as he is today, and more given to fine arts than he was again until the present century. His games he usually brought with him in his mind or adapted from those of his red neighbors. But he liked to browse in books of heraldry, genealogy, and peerage, and for this pastime or hobby he imported dozens of distinct titles. He had books on music and dancing, to be noticed again in a moment. Above all he enjoyed reading British poetry from Chaucer to Pope, drama from Shakespeare to Cibber, novels from Scudéry and La Calprenède to Fielding and Smollett and Henry Brooke, history and biography and memoirs from Raleigh's *History of the World* to Baker's *Chronicle of the Kings of England* to Voltaire, including scores of works concerned with the western hemisphere from Spanish America to Canada, but especially with the provinces in which he lived or with the Indians around him. In the larger South Carolina libraries Edgar found that Shakespeare was the most popular belletristic author, but Pope and Swift there and elsewhere were at least close rivals. Into the colonial's writing early or late some of these men's verses creep, or emerge, sometimes for serious or didactic purposes, on other occasions purely as entertainment, to enliven.

People who flocked to capital towns during the professional theatrical season and performed plays at home in the country were likely to own volumes of the dramatic poets, and they did. In the Chesapeake colonies playwrights Congreve and Gay stood among the most popular authors, often equalling or surpassing Shakespeare. Steele, Rowe, Cibber, Jonson, Steele, Molière, Corneille, Aphra Behn, Vanbrugh, Farquhar, and Wycherley were frequent. Addison's *Cato*, for several reasons, was popular reading, viewing on the stage, or quoting in support of human rights. There were also fables and allegories which might amuse as they served other purposes.

READING ON THE FUNCTIONAL ARTISTIC

Close to the genuinely and usually fully recreational were the functional arts, which often though not always combined the aesthetic and the practical. Architecture, gardening, painting, music, rhetoric appeared as the subjects of scores or hundreds of volumes. In a land of beautiful if modest edifices—governors' palaces, churches, country and town mansions, and court houses (especially in the eighteenth century) one might expect books on architecture. In public and private libraries of any size they were present, from the so-called *Builder's Companion* and *Builder's Dictionary* to the design or pattern books of James Gibbs, William Salmon (his *Palladio Londoniensis*), Evelyn's *Architecture*, Vitruvius (including *Vitruvius Britannicus*), Andrea Palladio's *First Book of Architecture*, and Le Clerc's *Principles L'Architecture*. They were to be found in Virginia and Maryland and both Carolinas and probably existed in Georgia libraries as yet untallied. With their aid John Mercer might plan his mansion at Marlborough, the Pages and Wormeleys their houses at

Rosewell and Rosegill, William Byrd II his at Westover, the Lloyds and Dulanys theirs in Maryland. These books were used in planning the beautiful adapted-to-the-terrain dwellings of old Charleston in South Carolina; the governors' palaces of Maryland and Virginia and South Carolina; the main building of the College of William and Mary; the courthouses of Hanover and King William counties in Virginia; the grandly simple churches of rural South Carolina, Maryland, and Virginia, and the more stately temples of Charleston and Williamsburg and Annapolis; the small but graceful houses of modest men of moderate means. Without these books these surviving or vanished buildings would never have existed in the forms they assumed. But more of them in another chapter.

Gardening has already been discussed and certain books on and of music mentioned. From music teachers and wealthy amateurs such as Councilor Robert Carter of Nomini to humbler farmers, physicians, or clergy, men and women owned musical instruments, sheet music, musical grammars, miscellanies and hymnals, and books of theory. In fact, music was an almost always audible presence in colonial life. Governors composed hymns, dignified provincial administrators or prominent clergy played on fiddles and hautboys, tobacco factors might join the others in string quartets or in singing on the steps of town houses.

Rhetoric, oratory, and aesthetic theory overlap into other areas. There were books on all of them in the South. Rhetoric, with texts in Latin and English, remained a part of required secondary as well as university education throughout the colonial era. It influenced the adult writer in newspaper or magazine as much as it did the schoolboy learning to express himself orally or in written discourse. Lawyer and clergyman in particular attempted to master the rules and practice of rhetorical expression, which went along with oratorical expression. Latin and English editions of Demosthenes, Quintilian, and Cicero have been noted in many libraries. Along with them were a few books on aesthetics, as Webb, de Piles, and Algerotti on painting, and perhaps a dozen others. There were only a few itinerant painters and a miniaturist or two in the colonial South, but everybody owned pictures, and most owned at least a few portraits and landscapes. The books were aids to both comprehending and imitating the latter.

HISTORICAL, POLITICAL, AND PHILOSOPHICAL

From the point of view of intellectual history most significant were perhaps the uses made of volumes of political history and political philosophy. Even in the seventeenth century, when little or nothing was actually printed in the South and not too much in England, considerable evidence exists in legislative and judicial records unpublished until this century, in letters, and in pamphlets that the rights of individual Englishmen, especially those removed to foreign parts, were a matter of continuous concern. The problem crops up first in the records of the Virginia Company of London, when Treasurer Sir Edwin Sandys is quoted as declaring that he considered the republican government of the city of Geneva in Switzerland the best on earth, and when an intransigent James I dissolves the Company and declares its charter void. Questions were raised on both sides for a full generation, and then again by William Stith in his *History*, as to whether King or Company more nearly represented the individual rights of freeborn Englishmen. In southern libraries a little later were More's *Utopia*, Bacon's *Atlantis*, and Raleigh's *History of the World*, books which with their authors may have been taken as symbols of rights or the abnegation of them. Accounts of the insurrections in Maryland in the 1650s and at the time of the Bloodless Revolution, and of Virginia in 1676, produced a flutter of pamphlets of many complexions, some expressing alarm at the challenges to constituted authority and others defiantly declaring (and reasoning) that entrenched arbitrary authority was not constitutional. Whatever may have been the more basic causes of these conflicts, the ideological literature which sprang from them brought up again a subject never to be forgotten in colonial assemblies, the rights of transplanted Englishmen.

In 1682 William Fitzhugh, employing his legal knowledge and library to support his argument, made a complaint on the floor of the Virginia House of Burgesses concerning the manner in which provincially enacted laws were treated in London. It was merely one query of hundreds. Though personally Fitzhugh was a Tory inclined to the Stuarts, here he was in the main Whiggish tradition, which was to dominate southern colonial thinking in the Revolution. Southern colonials got their ideas of government at least in great part from what they read, and they read and possessed books presenting varying interpretations. In the late seventeenth and very early eighteenth centuries Sir Robert Filmer, John Locke, Harrington, and Algernon Sidney might stand side by side. And slightly later Bolingbroke's *Patriarcha*, Henry Care's *English Liberties*, Pufendorf's *Law of Nature and Nations*, Montesquieu's *Persian Letters* and *Spirit of the Laws*, Mandeville's *Fable of the Bees*, and Bishop Hoadly were to be found together on the shelves of libraries. Though most of these authors were Whiggishly inclined or so interpreted, believing in constitutional monarchy or a semi-republic, few of them were genuine Whig radicals, those whom Caroline Robbins calls the "Real Whigs," who were outspoken in their desire for a republican form of government. These "Real Whigs," too, stood on southern shelves, and in great numbers—Trenchard and

Gordon's *Cato's Letters* and *The Independent Whig*, Gordon's editions of Tacitus and Sallust, Milton's political writings, Shaftesbury's *Characteristicks*, Lord Molesworth's *An Account of Denmark*, Sidney's *Discourses*, even at the end John Wilkes' *North Briton*. Along with them were the Whig historians Oldmixon, Rapin, and Stith, together with Clarendon, Rushworth, Rollin, and Catherine Macaulay, who might be and were interpreted as genuine if not "Real" Whigs. Even Sir Henry Spelman's earlier research work in Anglo-Saxon history, suggesting that Norman tyranny had overcome Saxon freedom, was present in southern libraries. H. Trevor Colbourn, borrowing his title from Patrick Henry and William Wirt, has in *The Lamp of Experience* attempted to show that the colonials' study of English history and institutions through the books mentioned above was a vital force impelling Americans to revolt. His quite convincing proof comes from no farther south than Virginia, as already noted, but from the samples of libraries given above this writer would suggest that there were more of these books and authors in the South from Maryland through Georgia than in the northern and middle colonies. The most effective political pre-Revolutionary polemical writing came from the South, in this writer's opinion, and it was, as Colbourn argues for other regions, in considerable part impelled by what Whiggish or liberal political history and philosophy on library shelves suggested.[264] Colbourn does indicate how much the printed expression of the Dulanys, the Carrolls, Richard Bland, Patrick Henry, George Mason, and Thomas Jefferson reflects the ideas of the liberal historians. He should have added, in Virginia alone, Edmund Pendleton, Landon Carter, and Peyton Randolph, and in South Carolina Mackenzie, Laurens, and half a dozen others. It is probable indeed that the southern colonial's careful perusal of the "historical" volumes on his shelves—most of which he had chosen for himself—was in the long view the most significant part of his reading. Home government mismanagement of colonial affairs moved him to secure certain political and historical works, and these in turn confirmed him in pursuing his path toward liberty, all within English terms.

Perhaps a word should be said of the European writers, especially the politico-historical named above, who have been declared to have had a special vogue and often tremendous influence in America at some time during the eighteenth century. Those who have been singled out for attention in essays or whole volumes are Marmontel and Voltaire, John Locke and John Milton, Joseph Addison and Samuel Butler, and Montesquieu and Rousseau.[265] The works on Marmontel, Rousseau, and Voltaire give us nothing pertinent to the colonial period and subject. They present later instances. The study of Butler's *Hudibras* offers only the obvious suggestion that Cook's *The Sot-Weed Factor* was modeled on it. The commentator on Montesquieu's potential influence in the colonies has a good deal to say about his subject's "presence" in the South, but almost all of it is concerned with the post-1763 eighteenth century. Leon Howard and George Sensabaugh point out that some of Milton's prose work reached America before *Paradise Lost* was printed, and that outside New England the earliest recorded American copy of any of Milton is Godfrey Pole's recorded in Virginia in 1716. They suggest the probable influence of Milton's verse on Samuel Davies' lines and perhaps on William Dawson's, though the evidence is not usually conclusive.

More impressive is the proof that Addison's *Cato* was performed by professionals and collegians in the South in the earlier half of the eighteenth century, that it was in most larger Virginia libraries, and that the southern colonial, from Charleston in South Carolina to Upper Marlborough in Maryland, saw it on the stage and quoted from it when he spoke or wrote on liberty or tyranny. Furthermore, a great deal of scattered material exists arguing for or against the presence of Locke in the colonies. Some of it consists of vague or negative assertions as to American or southern possible familiarity with the *Two Treatises on Government* before the mid-eighteenth century. One historian in effect declares that a cultural lag prevented the colonists' knowing and using Locke on government before about 1750, and actually doing so to any extent even after that.[266] Ralph Wormeley had Locke's *Two Treatises*,[267] and dozens of southern libraries during the next half century had the *Works of Locke*, which from 1714 always contained the governmental essays. Marylander John Webb(e) of Kent County was ridiculed repeatedly in the *Pennsylvania Gazette* of the 1740s for his dependence on Locke's ideas of government. Daniel Dulany, Sr., used the *Treatises* along with Coke and Rushworth and others to make his points in his 1728 *The Right of the Inhabitants of Maryland to the Benefit of the English Laws*, citing specifically the "Learned Mr. Locke."[268] Commissary Blair developed a personal friendship with Locke and corresponded with him. All this leads to the strong likelihood that the Williamsburg circle knew Locke's ideas on government from the 1690s and that Blair's affiliation or alliance with local interests may be partially responsible for their joint essay on the Virginia situation, recently published. This piece indicates how familiar Blair had to have been with Lockean political philosophy. Blair was a power in the colony, one recalls, up to the time of his death in 1743.

William Byrd II and other colonists in Maryland and the two Carolinas had the *Treatises*. Bland refers to them, or it, in his 1766 *An Inquiry into the Rights of the British Colonies* (Williamsburg) as do dozens of other southern pre-Revolutionary political essayists. Some of Locke's theories undoubtedly filtered in through the Trenchard and Gordon and other Whig discourses and histories. Most of these provincial writers, who were using British liberal arguments extensively by the 1750s and 1760s, almost surely read them before 1750, and probably much earlier.[269] Thus there was no cultural lag in the South in the matter of reading current political philosophy and employing it in argument, as there was no cultural lag in other artistic and intellectual areas.

PRINTING

Printing in the southern colonies is a complex story of men and presses, of paper mills, of publishing local materials from manuscript, of reprinting and editing foreign or British books, of newspapers, and of many other matters. On a sound and continuous basis it began relatively late when compared with the Massachusetts press, for its first newspaper production came in the 1720s. But a press was operating, albeit without license, in one colony as early as 1682, and in another neighboring province by 1685. In chronological sequence one may place the Virginia-Maryland first attempts second only to the Stephen Daye press of 1639 at Cambridge, Massachusetts.[270] But in actual extant publication it drops below Bradford's Philadelphia and New York presses. In the last year of the colonial period, 1762/1763, the last of the southern colonial presses was set up in Savannah, Georgia. Almost every year new and earlier products of southern presses are being discovered or identified, and it is possible that eventually something may turn up from the 1682 Virginia press and something more than blank forms from the early years of the same printer and his press when they transferred to Maryland before 1685. Perhaps not even the Massachusetts presses or the Philadelphia presses of Bradford and Franklin have a more interesting history than the various southern printing establishments and the remarkable men who operated them. Certainly in the generation and a half before the Revolution the gazettes produced in the South equalled at least in literary quality and quantity and in polemical writing any of the northern newspapers. Perhaps no finer body of political essays on current topics of vital interest appeared than those in the Chesapeake newspapers of the period. They influenced thought in Virginia and Maryland and, in reprinted form, in the northeastern and middle colonies. Yet except in one instance all southern newspapers were official or semiofficial voices of government— fortunately for the liberal-minded, more often of the House of Burgesses or Commons House of Assembly than of the governor and Council, though through the colonial period they showed due respect for the latter.

Individuals made presses and newspapers as well as books. The southern roll of printers is a list, almost without exception, of able and versatile men and women, from William and Dinah Nuthead through Parks and Green, Purdie and Dixon, Rind, James Davis, and Lewis Timothy to James Johnston of Georgia. They were usually efficient as business managers and executives, tactful in their dealings with provincial authority and independent individuals, shrewd in their insights into what their readers wanted, and, in a few notable instances, themselves writers of ability. Through their presses they both reflected and molded taste and public opinion in their respective provinces.

ESTABLISHMENT OF THE PRESSES: MARYLAND TO GEORGIA

The chronological beginning of printing in the South Atlantic region was in 1680 or 1682, when John Buckner of Virginia, merchant and planter, attempted to establish a press, probably at Jamestown, to be operated by William Nuthead. Early accounts assume that Buckner set up the printing equipment on his own plantation in nearby Gloucester County, but recent scholars argue rather convincingly that the Buckner-Nuthead operation was set up openly in the capital town, for everyone seems to have known that it began printing at once the acts of the recently adjourned Assembly and "several other papers." No license had been applied for or issued, probably because the promoter knew of no need for official sanction. Buckner was himself a burgess in 1680–1682 and later. For reasons now obscure, the Virginia governor and Council in 1682 ordered Buckner to give bond to print nothing further until the royal wishes were known.[271] Two years later Lord Effingham arrived, bearing the order that "no person be permitted to use any press for printing upon any occasion whatsoever." As far as Virginia was concerned, the mandate remained in effect until 1730.

The reasons, though obscure, may be guessed at. Not many years had passed since Bacon's Rebellion, when the House of Burgesses had passed a number of acts somewhat erroneously known as "Bacon's Laws." There were still prominent in the colony men of doubtful loyalty as far as the governor was concerned. Laws were not in full effect, or were not permanent, until they were approved by the Crown. The home government, and perhaps the local Council, may not have wanted Virginians to see or to have their own legislative acts in cold print and then to have them nullified or vetoed (though in view of later printings immediately after adjournment and before subsequent veto, this seems dubious as a possible reason). And there is the simple fact that at the time no other colony except Massachusetts had a press, it being the result of early and special circumstances.[272] So far, nothing has been identified as a product of this first southern press.

That by 1685 Nuthead was comfortably established in Maryland and was official printer for that colony, receiving payment for services to the Assembly, makes the Virginia action all the more perplexing. Probably Nuthead forestalled local objections by offering his services before he began printing. He was settled by November, 1685, at any rate, in St. Mary's, and was the first of a long line of southern printers to survive by becoming official agents of government.

Isaiah Thomas' pioneer *History of Printing in America* (original edition 1810)[273] states that William Parks' 1726 press was the first in Maryland, but Lawrence Wroth has proved quite conclusively that the Nuthead press was in the colony forty-odd years earlier. The latter scholar has traced Nuthead's activities in the colony, including the payments made to him by the Maryland Assembly. Nuthead's earliest known surviving product is a 1685 blank form for St. Mary's County business use, dated August 31.[274] Surviving also is a 1689 broadside printed by order of the Assembly to be sent to the King, the only known copy being in the Public Record Office in London. In the same year, during the Protestant revolution in the colony, Nuthead printed *The Declaration . . . for . . . Appearing in Arms* of the Protestant Association, in this instance surviving only in a London reprint which states as a colophon that it was originally printed by William Nuthead of St. Mary's in Maryland. Sermons on public occasions by the Reverend Peregrine Coney in 1694 and 1696 are known to have been printed by the Nuthead press, though no copy is extant. Following Nuthead's death in 1694, his widow, Dinah, carried on for a few years, moving the press when the government moved to Annapolis, but publishing nothing that is known save for a few official forms. By 1700 a new publisher and new printers were in the new capital. Such is the story of the southern colonies' only printer in the seventeenth century.

Dinah Nuthead's successor as printer was Thomas Reading, who was sponsored by William Bladen, clerk of the Lower House, who was to be publisher and financier of the enterprise. Bladen was given permission or encouraged to reestablish the press at the end of 1696, but it was not until May 1700 that he was able to announce to the Assembly that the printer was ready for business. Within the seven months remaining of 1700, Reading produced three known works of some importance—Commissary Bray's sermon to the Assembly on *The Necessity of an Early Religion*, a provincial *Act for the . . . Establishment of Religion in this Province according to the Church of England*, and *A Complete Body of the Laws of Maryland*. In 1702 he printed several sorts of forms for the use of provincial officers, in 1703 George Keith's sermon *The Power of the*

Gospel, in 1704 *An Abridgement of the Laws in Force and Use in Her Majesty's Plantations* (printed in Latin) and sermons by Thomas Cockshutt and James Wooton, and from 1705 through 1709 more laws and some official speeches.[275]

For two years, 1718–1719, Andrew Bradford of Philadelphia printed Maryland's laws, and in 1720 the later famous John Peter Zenger became the resident printer in Annapolis, about seven years after Reading's death. His extant product consists of editions of laws and acts in 1720 and 1721. Again there was no resident printer for several years, and then in 1726 William Parks arrived to inaugurate a distinguished program of printing and publishing in this and the other southern colonies.

Parks is probably the best-known printer of the colonial South, though his Annapolis successor Jonas Green may have been intellectually more gifted.[276] Born in Shropshire and in 1719 the first printer in the town of Ludlow in that county, between 1719 and 1723 Parks published in Ludlow, Hereford, and Reading several extant titles, including sermons, theological tracts, and a newspaper. At least it is presumed by this American printer's biographer that the English Parks whose imprint appears in these three places is the same man.[277] In 1725 Thomas Bordley, who had struggled with the editing of Assembly debates printed by Bradford in Philadelphia, sent for a printer. Whether Parks came directly from England or was working in Bradford's establishment or in some other American office is not known, though the last situation seems likely. As Wroth insists, Parks' arrival in Maryland produced for the office of public printer a dignity it had not before possessed. It was marked, for one thing, with the enactment of a law fixing the duties and salary of the printer and thus giving him legal status and position. He was to remain in Maryland public service for eleven years, though during that period he had set up the office in Williamsburg to which he was eventually to devote all his time. But in the smaller Chesapeake colony he did quite remarkable work.

Though there was some haggling between the two branches of the Maryland provincial Assembly as to the terms to be made with Parks, the debate did not prevent his printing the Acts of Assembly (which the governor had wished deferred) and the laws enacted, as well as *Proposals for a Tobacco Law . . . In a Letter from a Gentleman,* all in 1726. In 1727 he continued with *A Compleat Collection of the Laws of Maryland;* the laws enacted at a legislative session; the proceedings of the Assembly; a broadside, *A Letter from a Freeholder, to a Member of the Lower House of Assembly in the Province of Maryland;* and the first southern newspaper, the *Maryland Gazette.* He continued to print annually official provincial publications through 1737, but beginning in 1728 he began to expand and vary his production. The *Maryland Gazette* marked Parks' initial plunge into "literary" publishing, and he continued it at least until 1734. But in 1728 he printed one of the first great political pamphlets of the American colonies, Daniel Dulany, Sr.'s, aforementioned *Right*; Richard Lewis' remarkable translation of Edward Holdsworth's satiric *Muscipula . . . the Mouse-Trap*; John Warner's *Almanack* for 1729, and a two-page address of the Upper House and the governor's reply. The next year he brought out an English primer-catechism, a new almanack, three religious devotional tracts bound together, more addresses, Henry Darnall's *A Just and Impartial Account of the Transactions of the Merchants in London, for the Advancement of the Price of Tobacco*, and two sermons in separate pamphlets.

In 1730 Parks printed one of the significant works of a major Maryland author, Ebenezer Cook's *Sotweed Redivivus*, a sort of sequel to the poet's *Sot-Weed Factor* of 1708. Also appeared pamphlets concerning politics and economics such as the Tobacco Law, and one item in the Henderson-Dulany exchange, Henderson's *The Case of the Clergy of Maryland*. In 1731 Ebenezer Cook reappeared in *The Maryland Muse* (containing two distinct poems); in 1732 Richard Lewis' poem *Carmen Seculare. . . . To . . . Lord . . . Baltimore*, the same author's *A Rhapsody*, and a speech of Governor Ogle; in 1733 a reprint of the British Charles Leslie's popular *A Short and Easy Method with the Deists* (called the fifth edition), already noted as present in scores of colonial libraries; and in the remaining years through 1737 the laws and proceedings of the Assembly and the almanacs.

In personal activities Parks' successor in Maryland was a much more versatile man than the founder of the first *Maryland Gazette*. Jonas Green, who was in business in Annapolis by 1737 and was to remain there until his death in 1767, was the great-grandson of the Samuel Green who in 1649 succeeded the Dayes as the first printers of English America. The family had continued in printing, and Jonas served his apprenticeship under his father, Timothy, in New London and later worked with his brother, partner in the printing firm of Kneeland and Green in Boston. In 1735 Jonas Green's name appeared alone on the imprint of a Cambridge *Grammar of the Hebrew Tongue*, by Judah Monis, the first Hebrew grammar brought out in America. In 1736 "Mr. Jonas Green of Philadelphia" was a subscriber to Thomas Prince's *Chronological History of New England*. He married his Dutch-born wife, Anne Catherine Hoof, in Christ Church in Philadelphia. The three of his sons who reached manhood carried on with their descendants the family business in Maryland into the nineteenth century.[278]

Wroth feels that Green's work as a printer shows a tendency toward studied simplicity, even austerity. After he obtained the handsome font of Caslon type in 1764 for setting the edition of Bacon's *Laws of Maryland*, Green produced some beautiful examples of his art. Even before this his work was always neat. Curiously for the versatile son of the Enlightenment that he was, Green as a publisher was less versatile than Parks had been. But he was postmaster, auctioneer, clerk of the races, Mason, vestryman, alderman, and moving spirit in the Tuesday Club both socially and literarily. He wrote well for his own newspaper, for he revived the *Maryland Gazette* in 1745 and carried it on until his death. He made his *Gazette* into one of the sparkling periodicals of America, rich in literary prose and verse and in its discussion of political and economic and social problems local and imperial.

As a printer, Green's greatest achievement was *The Laws of Maryland at Large,* compiled by the Reverend Thomas Bacon and appearing in 1765/66. Bacon as clergyman and musician is discussed elsewhere, and this work is dated after the period covered by this study had passed. But the *Laws* were gathered and arranged before 1764 and in press from at least 1764.[279] This most handsome of colonial printed books, done with new fonts of type, though now outdated by the series of *Archives of Maryland,* remained until the closing years of the nineteenth century the single most important source of information on the colony's past. If Green the printer had done nothing else, he would deserve remembrance for having produced it.

But Green did do other printing. He continued acts and journals of the Assembly, addresses to and by governors, and official recruiting notices, among other official documents. In 1742 he printed the Georgia Trustees' *Account* of the progress made in that colony. In 1743 for his good friend Dr. Alexander Hamilton he printed an advertisement requesting the physician's debtors to pay up, as Hamilton planned to go to England. In 1745 the press brought out the Reverend Hugh Jones' sermon *A Protest against Popery,* in 1746 a thanksgiving sermon by the Reverend John Gordon, in 1747 Thomas Cradock's *Two Sermons,* in 1748 *Extracts from the Essays of the Dublin Society* and *The Situation of Frederick Town* and *Prince George's County is so very large . . .* (both the latter broadsides), in 1750 Masonic sermons by William Brogden and John Gordon. So goes Green's printing record—acts, journals, official addresses, sermons, almanacs—to the end of the colonial period. Among the more unusual items are James Sterling's sermon of 1755 and the Tuesday Club notice of the same year, with a broadside invitation to its meeting, Thomas Cradock's *A New Version of the Psalms of David* in 1756, Abraham Milton's *The Farmer's Companion, directing how To Survey Land . . .* in 1761, and the Reverend John Camm's *A Single and Distinct View of the Act, Vulgarly entitled, the Two-Penny Act* in 1763 (a major item in the Virginia Camm-Bland-Carter controversy). Later, after the colonial period, he printed a Daniel Dulany, Junior, pamphlet in 1765, another by him in 1766, and in the latter year Samuel Chase's broadside about local Annapolis affairs. As the Revolution approached, there were more and more petitions and polemics in broadside or letter form by or to the clergy of the established church.

The story of Maryland pre-1764 printing must include William Rind, who for almost eight years (1758–1766) appeared on the *Maryland Gazette* imprint as the partner of Jonas Green. He also conducted a large bookstore on West Street in Annapolis and was one of those already mentioned who attempted a circulating library. At the solicitation of Jefferson and others in Virginia who wanted a free newspaper outside official control, Rind moved to Williamsburg and set up a second Virginia newspaper with the same title as the one already there, the *Virginia Gazette*.[280] Then there was Thomas Sparrow, the first Maryland engraver, who did not get into his craft until 1764/1765, producing most of his wood and copper engravings between 1765 and 1780, including a number of bookplates. His work is crude, but he is to be remembered as the designer of the armorial seal of the province on the titlepage of Bacon's *Laws*.

Virginia printing, except for Nuthead's abortive project, came after that of Maryland was well established and was derived from her sister colony. William Parks, who rightly saw in Virginia's larger population and greater wealth more abundant opportunities for the exercise of his craft, was negotiating with the Williamsburg legislature as early as 1727/28 for an edition of the collected laws of the colony (it did not appear until 1733). He actually began printing operations in Virginia in the early fall of 1730. Apparently he had gone to England earlier in that year to secure the printing equipment he needed, for at least at first he seems to have planned to operate permanently in both colonies. By 1731, in the *American Weekly Mercury* of Philadelphia, Parks noted that he was living "at his House, near the Capitol, in Williamsburg," probably indication that he had changed his place of permanent residence. As far as is known, the earliest issue of the Williamsburg press in 1730 was the first book or paper to be printed and published in Virginia.

Parks advertised in the *Maryland Gazette* of October 20, 1730, that he had for sale three books printed in Williamsburg: the laws of the May session of the General Assembly, a separate issue of the Tobacco Law of the session, and a book of rates and tables under the title *The Dealer's Pocket Companion*, no copy of any one of which has been discovered. Probably none of the three was as interesting as two other 1730 imprints which do survive, J. Markland's *Typographia, an Ode to Printing* and Governor Sir William Gooch's *A Charge to the Grand Jury*.[281] In 1731

A Virginia Miscellany was advertised to be published by subscription, but it probably never materialized. In 1732 Sir William Gooch's tract, *A Dialogue between Thomas Sweet-Scented, William Oronoco and Justice Love-Country*, two copies of which have turned up within the last half-century, was printed. It is a discussion of the Virginia Tobacco Law of 1730, in which arguments for and against the law are put in the mouths of these typical figures, the author clearly being in favor of the act. Probably the most ambitious printing project Parks ever undertook was the 1733 *A Collection of All the Acts of Assembly, now in Force, in the Colony of Virginia*. In 1734 the aforementioned Dr. John Tennent had printed in Williamsburg the second edition of *Every Man His Own Doctor*. In 1736 the college's William Dawson had Parks print his *Poems on Several Occasions . . . by a Gentleman of Virginia*.[282] George Webb's *Office and Authority of a Justice of the Peace*, printed in the same year, was in most legal libraries in the province for the next generation. The most educationally valuable work of 1736 was *The Charter and Statutes of the College of William and Mary, in Virginia*. Parks reprinted many English works, theological, moral, agricultural, and military, for which he saw a need and a sale. Individual sermons by Whitefield were among the separate reprints, as were American-composed utilitarian works such as (Robert Biscoe's) *The Merchant's Magazine: or Factor's Guide, The Compleat Housewife*, and *An Address to the Inhabitants of North Carolina*. Two or three of Stith's sermons, several legal compilations of John Mercer, Samuel Davies' *The Impartial Trial* (1748), and John Thomson's *Explication of the Shorter Catechism* (1749), the last two representing New Light and Old Light Presbyterianism, were among the publications written in Virginia. By far the most significant book Parks printed, from a historiographical and literary point of view, is William Stith's *The History of the First Discovery and Settlement of Virginia*, discussed in Chapter I above. The printer died in 1750 on a voyage to England. His successor, William Hunter, his journeyman in former days, completed the printing of *The Acts of Assembly* in 1752. In a sense this was Parks' last book. His *Virginia Gazette* founded in 1736 a few years after he settled in Williamsburg will be noticed in this chapter a little later.

Hunter was public printer from 1750 to 1761. He was deputy postmaster-general for the colonies, and he published or continued to publish the *Virginia Gazette* during his tenure as government printer.[283] He and his successor, Joseph Royle, continued Parks' policy—or necessity—of not criticizing the local government, a policy which eventually led to some trouble. Hunter was the first native southerner to hold such a public position. He was born in Virginia, probably at Yorktown, and was perhaps in his twenties when Parks died. He was trained under Parks or his own brother-in-law John Holt, who had printing establishments in Connecticut and New York before he was connected with Virginia. Though for some reason the *Virginia Gazette* was suspended for a few months after Parks' death, Hunter soon resumed publication with a new series of numbers and some minor changes in format.

Hunter included almanacs as well as laws and legislative journals among his official or semi-official publications from 1750, even though he was not legally appointed as provincial printer until 1752. He also operated the old Parks bookstore, and his daybook or ledger of purchases by Virginians great and near-great, including Samuel Davies, George Wythe, and John Mercer, is an invaluable indication of reading tastes in the period.[284] When his official appointment was made in 1752, he asked for and received an increase in salary over what Parks had had, and was raised in pay again a little later. He was especially distinguished as deputy postmaster-general for the colonies and then in his joint postmaster-generalship with Benjamin Franklin. Poor Richard and the Williamsburg printer became warm personal friends, and Hunter was instrumental in obtaining for Franklin an honorary degree from William and Mary.

Hunter issued at least seventy-five imprints besides his newspaper. Sermons and other religious works, cookbooks, the beautiful charter of the college, letters, pamphlets, a collection of poems, and the journal of youthful Colonel George Washington were among them.[285] Some of the more significant pamphlets of the Pistole Fee and Two-Penny Act controversies were his work, including Landon Carter's *A Letter to a Gentleman in London, From Virginia* (1759) and *A Letter to the Right Reverend Father in God, the Lord B——p of L——n* (1759) and Richard Bland's *A Letter to the Clergy of Virginia* (1760). He also printed two of the three sermons by William Stith ever published (1752 and 1753), which with the polemical essays are the best-known issues from his press.[286] Apparently Hunter was financially more successful than Parks, though his individual imprints are hardly more distinguished.

In his will of 1761 Hunter requested that his foreman, Joseph Royle, carry on the business for the benefit of Hunter's natural son, another William Hunter, and Royle himself. Royle was born and trained in England and may have been brought to Virginia by Parks. He married one of Hunter's half-sisters and had two sons, both named after his friend Hunter. He operated the press, including the *Gazette*, for only five years, and left only twenty-six known imprints besides the newspaper. As in Hunter's case, a portion of his booksale ledger is extant, 1764–1766, and it shows that he sold a variety of works, including many which were belletristic.

Of his imprints, perhaps those which will be remembered longest are the polemical pamphlets, actually a continuation of the series begun by

Hunter. He issued Bland's classic *The Colonel Dismounted: Or the Rector Vindicated* (1764), Tory John Camm's *Critical Remarks On a Letter ascribed to Common Sense* (1765) and *A Review of the Rector Detected: Or the Colonel Reconnoitred* (1764), and Landon Carter's *The Rector Detected: Being a Just Defense of the Twopenny Act . . .* (1764).[287] Royle marked the end of an era in Virginia colonial newspaper publishing, for the year in which he ceased operation and was succeeded by another official printer of the official *Gazette*, Williamsburg obtained a "free" or independent rival, the William Rind of Maryland mentioned above.[288] Under other printers, Alexander Purdie and Clementina Rind, were to appear such pamphlets as Bland's *Inquiry into the Rights of the British Colonies* (1766) and Jefferson's *A Summary View of the Rights of British America* (1774). But they more than the essays just mentioned emphasized a new era, albeit a legitimate descendant of the Parks-Hunter-Royle period.[289]

North Carolina publishing history before 1764 is much briefer than that of the Chesapeake colonies, for its first printer, James Davis, set up shop in New Bern as late as 1749. Davis was public printer from then until 1777.[290] The colony had considered establishing an official printer as early as 1745, but only after four years more of argument and agitation was a bill passed and approved by the governor, April 14, 1749. The terms of contract were the usual ones: Davis was to print the speeches and addresses, journals and proceedings, and laws enacted by each Assembly with copies for all concerned parties. An early writer on the subject claimed 139 imprints in North Carolina before 1800. McMurtrie was able to locate only 39, though he records some 290 titles.[291] Of the latter number a clear majority, 172 of 288, were official documents, a not-at-all unusual proportion. There were also almanacs, some funeral orations, military manuals, Revolutionary polemical pamphlets, sermons and religious tracts, and a scattering of titles of other sorts. The 1749–1752 items are all official, but in 1753 the Reverend Clement Hall had Davis print what may be called the first North Carolina book, *A Collection of many Christian Experiences . . .* , a little volume of rather simple devotions by an S.P.G. missionary.[292] Among other items of the press in the colonial period are the Reverend Michael Smith's *Sermon, Preached in Christ-Church, in Newbern, in North-Carolina . . . Before The Ancient and Honourable Society of Free and Accepted Masons* (1756), Governor Arthur Dobbs' 1757 and 1758 *Proclamations*, the Reverend Alexander Stewart's *The Validity of Infant Baptism* (1758), and Quaker Thomas Nicholson's *An Epistle to Friends in Great Britain* (1762).

There are other records before 1764 of sermons, and in 1765 began the political polemical tracts, such as Maurice Moore's.[293]

Chronologically, printing in South Carolina came almost immediately after Parks set up his Virginia press in 1730. For by 1731, after years of sporadic effort, Charleston suddenly had three printers—George Webb, Thomas Whitmarsh, and Eleazar Phillips, Jr.[294] They all came as the result of a subsidy of £1,000 offered by the provincial Assembly in 1731 to induce a printer to settle in Charleston. Phillips came directly from Boston and Whitmarsh (a former employee of Franklin) from Philadelphia, and George Webb may have been from Philadelphia, Virginia, or Maryland.[295] Webb's name appears on one public document of 1731 with a "Charles-Town" imprint and then disappears from view. Phillips and Whitmarsh were more tenacious, and each started a newspaper in the city. The first issue of Whitmarsh's *South-Carolina Gazette* appeared on January 8, 1732, the Phillips *South-Carolina Weekly Journal* probably about the same time, though there is no known copy of the latter. Both Phillips and Whitmarsh petitioned the Assembly for remuneration. Phillips was awarded £500 of the premium, and the Lower House requested he be allowed to begin public printing. But Whitmarsh, who had Franklin's backing and even a partnership agreement, secured the favor of the Council, which made the proposal that both men print copies of the Quit-Rent Roll Law. Though all copies have disappeared, there is good evidence that Phillips did print this second South Carolina publication. At the same time he was authorized to print this law, Phillips was also asked to print the votes of the Commons House of Assembly. Except for these two items and his *Weekly Journal*, nothing more is known of his work, and not a scrap seems to have survived. He died July 10, 1732.

Whitmarsh's recorded activities have to do almost entirely with his attempts to secure the Assembly's premium, which went to Phillips and to his heirs. Whitmarsh did finally obtain £200. From January 8, 1732, until his sickness and death in the summer of 1733 he published his *Gazette*, operated an office-supply and book store, and printed legal forms, pamphlets, and broadsides. McMurtrie lists two broadsides not included in Ray O. Hummel's recent *Southeastern Broadsides before 1877*, and though he found no copies of several other Whitmarsh items he lists, there is plenty of contemporary evidence, as in the *South-Carolina Gazette*, that they were printed.[296] Among them are *A Dialogue between a Subscriber and a Non-Subscriber* (second edition), presumably religious or sectarian; *Proposals for the Opening of an Insurance Office Against Fire*; an almanac for 1733; *A Full and Impartial View of Mr. Bow-*

man's Visitation Sermon. In a Conference between a Church of England Man and a Dissenter in South-Carolina; and *A More Impartial View, or the Annotations on the Vicar of Tewsbury's [sic] Sermon Paraphrased in a Letter to Mother Bavius,* the last surely satiric.[297]

On Whitmarsh's death Franklin sent another printer from Philadelphia to carry on the business. This was Louis Timothée, a French refugee who had learned his printing in Holland and married there. He has been called America's first professional librarian because he was for a time in 1732 in charge of the Philadelphia Library Society's collections.[298] Charleston and vicinity, with its numerous French Huguenots, must have been a most congenial region for this man who nevertheless soon anglicized his name to Lewis Timothy. Franklin in his *Autobiography* describes this new business partner as a man strong in learning but weak in accounting, and adds that he never got a satisfactory financial statement from Timothy during the South Carolina printer's life.

But Timothy set to work in Charleston with vigor. He resumed weekly publication of the *South-Carolina Gazette* in February 1734, and in the same month he was acting as public or official printer. The first nonperiodical publication of his press was *An Essay of Currency, Written in August 1732,* a pamphlet which until McMurtrie's discoveries was long accepted as the earliest extant South Carolina imprint. By April 1734 he was advertising the proposal to publish Nicholas Trott's monumental *The Laws of South Carolina, of Force and Use . . .* , the handsome book with the rubricated title page. In this last he was strongly supported by legislative grants, for it was to be a costly undertaking. The first volume was announced as complete in 1736, and both volumes bear this date, though it seems clear that the second came in January 1737. Meanwhile Timothy was printing the separate Acts of the Assembly, a reprint of the London *The Gentleman's Pocket Farrier* (subsequently to be found in many South Carolina libraries); a pamphlet on the treatment of slaves; a Josiah Smith sermon; and a work on South Carolina-Georgia relations, all before the end of 1736.

The year 1737 is marked by Timothy's publication of one of the American and world firsts, a volume edited by John Wesley under the title *A Collection of Psalms and Hymns,* the first hymnal by the great founder of Methodism.[299] This most remarkable book, composed of original, adapted, and translated hymns, is one of the highlights of southern colonial publishing. In subsequent years Timothy continued to print almanacs, medical polemical or explanatory tracts, broadsides on many subjects, trenchant sectarian or religious letters by George Whitefield and Commissary Alexander Garden, and more sermons by Garden and nonconformist Josiah Smith. The medical pamphlets by eminent practitioners of the city such as

Dr. Thomas Dale and Dr. James Kilpatrick (or Kirkpatrick) are historically professionally significant; but Timothy's most important publications, in the long view of intellectual history, were Wesley's *Hymns* and
Trott's *Laws*, the latter like Bacon's for Maryland one of the more handsome books from colonial presses. By December 1738 Timothy was dead,
and his Dutch-born wife for a time took over his business.

Elizabeth proved to be better at business than her husband, much to
partner Benjamin Franklin's relief. The length of tenure is a little uncertain but apparently lasted from her husband's death until 1746, when her
son, Peter Timothy, reached his majority. She was the first woman in the
colonies to publish a newspaper, but by no means the last even in the
South. After her retirement as publisher she conducted a small book and
stationery shop, but left Charleston in 1748, to return again by 1756. She
died in 1757. During her time as province printer she continued the usual
laws and proclamations, and unofficially the medical controversial pamphlets by some of the same authors her husband had printed, letters and
sermons in the Whitefieldian controversy—from both sides—burlesque
verse, broadsides, a pamphlet on the cultivation of indigo, and other matters of local concern. Of greatest literary interest is the attack by Patrick
Tailfer et al. on General Oglethorpe and the Trustees of Georgia, one of
the more significant literary evidences of colonial disenchantment with the
New World, prefaced by one of the ablest and most biting satires of colonial America, the scathing tongue-in-cheek "Dedication" to the founder
of Georgia.[300]

Peter Timothy, born in the Netherlands in 1725, became editor of the
Gazette and manager of the printing house, living a relatively uneventful
existence for many years well past the end of the colonial period. He was
a pillar of Charleston church and society, official printer, postmaster, a
founder of the Library Society, member of the South Carolina Society, a
Mason, and a pew holder in St. Philip's Church. He was in subsequent years
to become an ardent supporter of the Revolutionary cause, placing his
newspaper at the disposal of the Whig faction, but that is a later story. He
died in 1783, his widow and son carrying on his book and (when they were
able) his newspaper business until 1807.

Over Peter Timothy's long tenure naturally much was printed, but only
that appearing before 1764 will receive any degree of attention here.
Almanacs, laws, the Whitefield controversy, catechisms, Indian-white af-
fairs,[301] a collection of psalm and hymn tunes, Garden's farewell sermon,
Zubly's *The Real Christian's Hope in Death* (see Chapter VI below), ex-
tracts from a poem on Indigo, Richard Clarke's *The Prophetic Numbers of
Daniel and John Calculated* (again see Chapter VI), many more Josiah
Smith sermons, Gadsden's *Some Observations on the Two Campaigns*

against the Cherokee Indians, in 1760 & 1761 [signed Philopatrios]. A few interesting "proposals" to publish never materialized, as De Brahm's "A Map of South-Carolina and Georgia" (advertised January 29, 1753), and "A Collection of Poems" (August 25, 1757, with a specimen of a poem entitled "Indico"; see also December 1, 1758).[302] Thus South Carolina printers rivaled those of the Chesapeake area and perhaps showed even greater variety. Judging by what they printed separately, Carolinians seem to have shown much more interest in the Great Awakening–Whitefieldian controversy than did Virginians or Marylanders. For Presbyterian Samuel Davies' sermons and tracts never received the attention in the Chesapeake Bay region (at least during his lifetime) that nonconformist Josiah Smith's did in South Carolina. Perhaps because Charleston was less dominated by the established church than were Annapolis and Williamsburg, a great many more nonconformist sermons appeared in South Carolina than in Virginia or Maryland, both in separate pamphlets and in some sort of newspaper form.

Richard P. Morgan, who has composed a checklist of South Carolina imprints to 1800,[303] has analyzed them by subject. The large majority appeared before 1764. He tabulates five or six satires before the terminal date for this study, three or four views or maps, four or five strictly belletristic works, scores of official and legal pieces, between twenty and thirty religious books, a French edition of Catesby (see Sabin, nos. 11508 or 11514), eight or more medical pamphlets, letters, and some pamphlet essays on trade and politics.

There were other booksellers than the printers mentioned above, men like Richard Wells, who also started his own newspaper in 1758[304] and printed other things as well. And from the wording of certain imprints there are indications that other printers may have set up shop for brief periods in South Carolina. Books and pamphlets published in Charleston seem to have sold in the colony rather well, though few of them are extant in other American provinces.

The story of printing in Georgia before 1764 is brief, for there was less than one year of it.[305] Georgia was the last of the thirteen colonies to set up its own press, just as it was the youngest of those colonies. As in other colonies, there had been efforts for a year or more before printing was established to see that an official publisher was obtained, with financial inducements eventually determined upon. Scot James Johnston, who was to take the position, had arrived by way of the West Indies late in 1761. In 1762 he was offered £100 annually for four years after establishing his press to do the official printing. It took over a year to set up the equipment, if one agrees, as Johnston's biographer does, that the first issue of the *Geor-*

gia Gazette in April 1763 probably came very soon after the press was put into operation.[306]

Johnston, though only twenty-four when he went into printing on his own, soon showed himself a sound, careful, though not brilliant, craftsman. He also conducted a bookstore and advertised his wares in his newspaper. One of the earliest products of his press was *An Act to prevent stealing of Horse and Neat Cattle.* . . . Extra-official extant pamphlets begin in 1764 with an almanac by John Tobler and in 1766 continued with the Reverend J.J. Zubly's *The Stamp-Act Revealed; A Sermon.* . . . McMurtrie states flatly that the first issue or imprint of the press was the first number of the *Georgia Gazette.*[307] Thus the printer and his press belong primarily in the history of the Revolutionary era proper.

THE PROVINCIAL GAZETTES: FUNCTION, FORM, AND POLICY

Even more significant for general or intellectual history than the official governmental and individual titles of the southern colonial presses were the newspapers they issued before 1764. Since the subject matter (especially specific literary, social, and political qualities) will be considered in their appropriate places in other chapters of this work, here the primary consideration will be of their function, form, and editorial and sometimes business policy.

William Parks began his *Maryland Gazette* probably in 1727, though the earliest extent issue is number 65 of December 10, 1728.[308] Almost surely he began his first issue with the statement, or the kind of statement, with which he opened the first issue of the *Virginia Gazette:*

> The Design of these Papers, is to inform the Reader of the most material Occurrences, as well of Europe, and other Foreign Parts of the World, as of these American Plantations, which relate to Peace and War, Trade and Navigation, Changes of Government; Parliamentary Affairs, Births, Marriages, Promotions and Deaths of Persons of Distinction, with many other Transactions of Consequence; by which the Readers may be improv'd, amus'd or diverted: which I shall faithfully collect, as well from the Public Prints, which I have ordered to be transmitted to me, from several Parts of England and the American Plantations, by all Opportunities, as from the private Accounts I may receive from my Correspondents. . . . And if any Ingenious Public-spirited Gentlemen, who have time to spare, will employ their leisure Hours in the Service of the Public, by Writing any Speculative Letters, Poems, Essays, Translations, &c. which may tend to the Improvement of Mankind in general or, the innocent Diversion or Entertainment of either Sex, without Offence to any in particular, they may depend on a Place in this Paper; and their names concealed if desired.[309]

This is an accurate statement of what he and his successors among southern colonial newspaper editors attempted to do. These periodicals included a remarkably large amount of foreign news from all over the world, some of it several months old, but most of it fairly fresh, for Parks and his contemporaries exchanged, as did their successors, both provincial and European or other world news which came to them. Like other southern and American editors, he reprinted speeches by governors and significant actions and addresses by legislatures and legislators all along the Atlantic coast, though when he began he had only a few northern newspapers to rely on. All the subjects of peace and war, personal data on eminent persons, significant local or world business transactions, received some notice in his papers. He and others did reprint, with and without acknowledgment, anything they found in the public print of the rest of English America and of England, Scotland, Ireland, and sometimes the Continent, the curious or significant event but more often the amusing or contemporarily pertinent "literary" work, from essays on every subject to verses and whole plays and an occasional tale. To this day it is impossible to separate all the originally American, especially that native to the colony in which the newspaper was located, from borrowings from all the well-known writers mentioned in the library inventories above or pieces from newspapers anywhere and in the *Gentleman's Magazine* and *Scot's Magazine* and a dozen other periodicals. Yet a great many native American essays and verses have already been identified, and certainly many more will be attributed to their actual authors as more and more is known about the extant papers of these writers.[310]

One thing difficult to determine from this 1727/1728 *Maryland Gazette*, as well as from all other southern colonial newspapers, is the extent to which they were considered by their editor-publishers as mouthpieces of government. Since official publications were their greatest single source of revenue and since at least one classic instance—that of a John Camm pamphlet—was refused publication by a printer presumably for fear of official repercussions, and since Jefferson and others just after the colonial period engaged Rind to come to Williamsburg and publish "a free paper," one judges that some sort of censorship existed, though it was most probably designated and determined by the printer-editor himself. But a concomitant question remains—to what branch or branches of government did the publisher feel he was most indebted? One is tempted to say first of all to the House of Burgesses (or Commons House of Assembly), which voted funds for official publication. But there are numerous evidences that certain politico-literary pieces were never printed for fear of offending the governor (or lieutenant-governor)[311] and members of the Council, at least until late in the period when, for instance, in the *Virginia*

Gazette of the 1760s Robert Bolling, Jr., felt he could attack Colonel Chiswell, though it may be that Bolling represented another faction as powerful as Chiswell's.[312]

As already suggested, controversial questions of religion and economics (as tobacco or indigo laws) or even of government which presumably might not or would not tread on local toes were published everywhere at any time, but especially in Maryland, Virginia, and South Carolina. Individuals were often insulted with impunity, provided the insult was expressed in humorous tones and had no political suggestiveness.

One other matter Parks does not mention in his statement of policy— what he does or will do about advertising. In practice he and his successors did just what the newspaper still does—advertise anything not related to immorality or outrage. Ships advertising imported cargo or desiring outgoing cargo, notices of runaway indentured servants or slaves, lost or stolen horses and cattle, books and music, playbills including actors and titles, medicines, crafts, and scores of other things appeared uually on the latter two pages of a four-page newspaper.

Parks' earliest extant *Maryland Gazette* is a single sheet printed on both sides. But in January 1728/1729 it had grown to four printed pages, perhaps one folded folio sheet, the size at least in pages of most newspapers before 1764. Some grew, however, to six or eight pages, often with supplements considering specific and large subjects and carrying further advertising. The sheet varied somewhat in size and ranged from two to four columns of printed matter on each page.

Though the subject matter of newspaper essays will be considered with that of other prose pieces in later chapters, one series in the earliest extant issues of the *Maryland Gazette* illustrates Parks' editorial and authorial habits, habits characteristic of other editors. This is his "Plain-Dealer" essays occurring in extant nos. 65, 66, 67, 69, 70, 71, and 74 and three others recovered from Franklin's *Pennsylvania Gazette* (incidentally showing that they were well written or timely enough to be copied). Aldridge has seen them as strongly deistic, reflecting the views of Parks and Franklin. Joost points out that deism in 1728 was barely if at all discernible in America, and in examining the numbers of the "Plain-Dealer" decides that they are more nearly assertions of free thinking on social and political matters than on religion. Lemay sees the series as rationalistic, perhaps deistic, and points to other printed expressions of deistic attitudes in America just before and after these essays.[313]

But there are other qualities of the "Plain-Dealer," the fourth periodical series in America, says Lemay. Most of the essays are simply reprintings of papers from Ambrose Philips' *Free-Thinker* (1718–1721), which has been shown to have been in several southern libraries, though perhaps not in a great many in Maryland at this early date. One essay Parks used was written by Bishop Burnet, and one must agree with Joost that it is hardly deistic.[314] It and others are certainly rationalistic. Two or three seem to have been written by Parks (at least they do not appear in the *Free-Thinker*), but an English source, or one translated from the French, may yet be discovered for them, as has been the case for other essays. There are new and individual touches by Parks, such as new introductory quotations or epigraphs from classical authors. One of the more interesting, original or not, defends the role, or the product, of the literary author, who is too often ridiculed for anything and everything he has printed. Subjects of the series include "Philosophical Doubting" (*Maryland Gazette* nos. 65 and 66), "Poetry and Painting" (no. 67), "Religion" (no. 69), on the "Efficacy of Dreams" (no. 70), and on political liberty (no. 74). Such series were to continue to appear in southern newspapers, some wholly derived from British periodicals (occasionally acknowledged to be so), some by individuals as groups who worked together, as the Meddlers Club of the *South-Carolina Gazette*, and the "Monitor" and the "Virginia Centinel" of the *Virginia Gazette*, though "the Centinel" may all have been by one man. This last series was reprinted in almost every American colony.

Thus Parks in these first essays was setting a southern precedent or following one already set in the northern colony of Massachusetts. But in poems such as "Elegy on the Death of the Honourable Nicholas Lowe," by Ebenezer Cook, which appeared in the December 24, 1728, issue, Parks was perhaps initiating in print though continuing in actual practice the southern colonial tradition of the secular elegy, a form of verse quite different from the lugubrious gnarled Calvinist lines of New England versified mourning for the departed. Other locally authored material included a Tobacco Law "letter" by Henry Darnall, a declaration against the London merchants for the avaricious and grasping modes of buying and selling tobacco by Nicholas Ridgely, amid others on the same subject (including one from "Oppressed Planter" and another from "Oroonoko"), an avowedly "original" poem on "Cupid Wounded," an essay on determining longitude at sea, the George Seagood-Arthur Blackamore poem on Governor Spotswood's transmontane expedition, and a Pennsylvania-authored piece on the necessity for a paper currency. "Somerset English" wrote almost a full-page poem, "Verses on St. Patrick's Day, Sacred to Mirth and Good-Nature." Subsequent issues contained more elegies and a governor's speech from Massachusetts. After a brief suspension from about March of 1731, the *Gazette* was revived for 1732–1734. In these few years some of colonial Maryland's best verse and some able essays appeared in Parks' *Gazette*. Though in its later years perhaps handicapped by its owner's growing interest in his Virginia enterprise, this first *Mary-*

Courtesy of the Carolina Art Association

Plan of one of the finest gardens of Colonial North America

Courtesy of The College of William and M

James Blair, First Commissary for Virginia and Founder and
President of The College of William and Mary

land Gazette is a distinguished milestone in the development of southern publishing, a model for the *Virginia* and later South Atlantic *Gazette*s.

There was no newspaper in Maryland from 1734 until January 17, 1745, when Jonas Green refounded, or founded, a periodical with the same name.[315] Green had been printer for the colony since 1737. With the inaugural issue of his *Maryland Gazette* that province's literary golden age had begun. The first four-page issue included advertisements and an editorial on the advantages of a newspaper, which makes public "whatsoever is useful and entertaining, at home or abroad." Green stressed his intention of publishing as much American material as possible, especially that concerning his own colony. At the same time he began the *Gazette*, he stepped up his publication of local literary materials in separate form, many of which he advertised for sale in his new medium. Like his predecessor and now neighborly contemporary William Parks, he devoted much of each issue, especially early, to foreign news. The second number, one of April 26, for example, fills three of its four pages with non-American news. A few weeks later Green has excerpts from the *Gentleman's Magazine* and news from Virginia, along with some Maryland General Assembly data. This *Gazette* evidently reached a great many Virginia planters along the southern shore of the Potomac, and indeed through the whole of the Northern Neck. The Virginia news, of course, would interest many Marylanders, but the number of literary and other contributions, including advertisements, from northern Virginia indicates that Green's paper had a number of subscribers in that region.

In no. 7 of June 7, 1745, appeared in the form of a letter to the editor the first belletristic work, an essay by "Phil-Eleutherus" on the uses of history, one of the many positive proofs, besides those already noted above, of the almost universal interest in the South in that subject. The author points out history's double purpose of instruction and entertainment, and suggests that the degree of a man's interest in history may correspond with "the Degrees of Virtue and Vice he possesses." A week later Green printed a poem now included in anthologies of colonial writing, "Juba's" "To the Ladies of Maryland," a fairly witty piece which warns the fair sex of affectation in manner or dress. Then there were reports of a naval engagement against the French in which an old Marylander played a heroic part and an epitaph for him, notes on runaways (some amusing), and recipes for Indian salve and sassafras water. Before the year was out, what was to become a major colonial literary group was represented by verse of "Philo-Musus," Dr. Adam Thomson, and the first volley of the playful literary skirmish between the "Baltimore Bards" and the "Annapolis Wits" was fired in the issue of December 17. In the latter some member of Dr. Alexander Hamilton's Annapolis circle satirized the poetry of the Reverend Thomas

Cradock. And the year ended literarily with "Emolpus's" mediocre poem "To the Ladies."

From the beginning of 1746 the Annapolis Wits were in full swing (as was the Tuesday Club to which most or all of them belonged), and sprightly satire by Dr. Hamilton and other writings by Dr. Thomson, former schoolfellows in Edinburgh, enlivened its pages, as did a continuation of the mock warfare between the Baltimore and Annapolis literati. Scientific essays or notices, Tobacco Law essays, several Franklin prose pieces (the two printers had continued to correspond), and a long discourse in several installments by Daniel Dulany, who said it was written before the Tobacco Law was passed, were among the miscellaneous offerings in prose. Green reprinted Virginia-South Carolina writer Joseph Dumbleton's "A Rhapsody on Rum" in the issue of November 1, 1749.

From 1749 scores of essays anticipating later arguments and the principles behind them leading to the Revolution began to appear.[316] By 1748 Green was doing bookbinding and advertising the fact in the *Gazette*. A few of the joint efforts of the Tuesday Club appeared as well as a number of poems, serious and satiric essays, and miscellaneous pieces by individuals who were members of the group. Verse fair and mediocre was in abundance, much by Adam Thomson as "Philo-Musaeus" (he varied the spelling), by James Sterling (usually identified by his dateline address, Kent County), and by Green himself (much more of it was left unpublished in the manuscripts of the Club); a poem possibly by Green (though there seems evidence in the Club records that another wrote it) published on August 22, 1754, "Memorandum for a Seine-Hauling in Severn River";[317] a recruiting song probably by John, son of the Reverend Thomas Bacon, "The Stage-Coach from *Bourn*, Imitated" by a Virginia bard; and dozens of other elegies and mock-epic verses.

But Green's *Gazette* is a mine of information on other phases of Maryland life and taste. By his time the traveling professional troupes of actors were performing at Annapolis and Upper Marlborough and their advertisements tell of plays and playwrights, actors and actresses. In March 1760, a news notice describes the opening of the theatrical season and quotes the prologue and epilogue for the play, both apparently local in origin. Frequent accounts of the success of collecting for Bacon's charity school (discussed in Chapter III above) and advertisements of or for teachers reveal something of the state of education. There are also a good Indian captivity narrative in the issue of April 1, 1756 (no. 569), a poem from the "Virginia Centinel" noted above in the August 12, 1756 issue, lists of books to be sold or which have been lost, essays on agriculture including remedies for various ravages of grain by insects, and Landon Carter's essays on lucerne.[318]

Hamilton died in 1756 and Sterling in 1763; they were Green's two most frequent and perhaps ablest belletristic contributors. Poems and essays continued to appear, but the remarkable outpouring of art and ideas in several literary forms was diminishing rapidly after 1760. Green patriotically wrote against the Stamp Act and published essays on the subject. He died in 1767. Though his *Gazette* continued under his family, its literary content and literary renown were never again the same. One curiosity about Green's literary materials is, as Lemay points out, that in many instances instead of being imitations of current styles at home they were mockeries of, or satires on, those English forms. The principal serious verse he did include, namely the elegy, is so entirely different in form from New England graveyard verse that it marks a separate genre in America, the beginning of what would become a peculiarly secular form of the elegy, pastoral in form and imagery, very often then and later with mocking or ironic overtones.[319] At a glance there seems to have been fewer political pressures on Green than on his contemporary printers in Williamsburg, for he printed in his *Gazette* what appear to be both sides of certain very sensitive political questions, and in at least one instance printed separately a pamphlet the Virginia printer was afraid to touch because he thought it reflected on his House of Burgesses and other officials. Green, thoroughly identified personally with the life of a colony perhaps more evenly balanced politically and officially than Virginia, *seems* to have printed in his newspaper and elsewhere about what he pleased, though one states this with reservations and a few questions unanswered. This is another subject deserving further investigation.

The officially declared purpose of William Parks' *Virginia Gazette*, begun in 1736, has already been quoted at length above as indicative of the purpose also of his earlier *Maryland Gazette*. "The Design of these Papers" was indeed to present foreign and domestic news and to print local belletristic writings as well as reprint occasionally British essays or poems. Much of the provincial news, and some of the foreign, was certainly political, drawn in the former instance from the documents Parks printed for the local government under contract.

Parks had been printing in Virginia for six years before he issued the first *Virginia Gazette*, his most significant contribution to American literature, journalism, and printing. Its avowed function of amusing as well as informing was usual for most British and American newspapers of the period, as already indicated. He planned perhaps even more than he had done in Maryland to give offense to no one and thus to attract many readers.[320] The journal he printed up to the time of his death in 1750 bears witness that he lived up to his intention, as has also already been shown in contrasting and comparing his journal and policies with Green's. The *Virginia Gazette* contents were chiefly literary pieces, news accounts, and concise advertisements in the *Maryland Gazette* pattern, a pattern which continued under his successors, William Hunter (1750–1761) and Joseph Royle (1761–1766).

Again as in Maryland but now with more American newspapers to draw from, his accounts were often taken verbatim from other American journals but more frequently from British and continental media. Sometimes readers, especially ship captains or regular provincial subscribers to European periodicals, furnished items. The greatest fund or body of news apparently came from the first source mentioned, journals he received, probably on an exchange basis, from their publishers.[321] Ship arrivals and departures, speeches of governors and Indian chiefs and European or British monarchs, occasionally legislative enactments, wars and battles, strange occurrences from St. Petersburg in Russia or the coast of Africa were among the news items.

Some of the reprinted materials were literary pieces, especially essays on happenings in Great Britain, which were usually anonymous. But even in the first year Parks ran a series of moral and instructive essays by "The Monitor," which appeared twenty-two times from the first issue of the *Gazette* on August 6, 1736.[322] These essays, though they are obviously modeled on *Tatler-Spectator* pieces, are probably all original products of the colony, unlike the "Plain-Dealer" series of the *Maryland Gazette* somewhat earlier. Though the essays will be discussed with others in a later chapter, it should be pointed out here that the author or editor used the old device of a group of tag-name people, in this case principally six "ladies" such as Miss Leer, Miss Sly, Miss Fidget, and Amoret, who contribute letters, poems, billets-doux, or "remarks" for each issue. Each of the six (daughters of an oddly dressed dame who introduces them) specializes in a particular genre such as manners, morals, theaters, literary criticism, and character sketches. Parks probably used various persons to contribute particular numbers, though there is a certain unity of tone.

Political essays on the Tobacco Law are fairly numerous. Perhaps the ablest political discussions came after Parks' time, the "Virginia Centinel" series. Only number X (September 3, 1756) survives in extant copies of the *Gazette*, but several others remain in various other provincial newspapers.[323] One historian believes that number X is an attack on George Washington and his Virginia regiment,[324] but there seem other underlying theses or aims. "The Centinel" is better writing than "The Monitor." Incidentally by no means all the Centinel's discourses are on military or political subjects, for religion is prominent. The religious or theological or moral essays appear over many pseudonyms in Parks' newspaper.[325] One of the most famous literary exchanges is that between the learned Samuel Davies and his friends, who defend the Presbyterian's recently (1751) published volume of verse against the vitriolic attacks of "Dymocke," since identified as an Anglican clergyman. This was during Hunter's editorship. There is much of real literary criticism here, as well as of religious jealousies and rivalries and some social class animosities.[326] If the Parks-Hunter-Royle *Virginia Gazette* had printed only the Monitor, Centinel, and Dymocke-Davies essays, its literary respectability would have been established.

As it is, from long before 1750 to 1766 there were, as in Maryland, a number of modestly gifted poets who presented elegies, mock-heroic verse, acrostics, love lyrics, ballads, translations, and "odes." Few of these poetasters have been identified, but certainly among them were William Byrd, William Dawson, and Samuel Davies, all of whom also published elsewhere. There were also letters, most merely formally so and designed for other purposes than simple friendly or business communication. They discussed the same subjects as did the essays (most were really essays), though the epistolary authors were often conscious of their obligation to observe certain rhetorical rules for the form as presented to them by the *Clerk's Guides* and *Secretary's Guides* in their libraries. They are speculative, satiric, playful, religious, moral, scientific—just as are the more strictly formal essays.

One should not forget that the *Virginia Gazette*, like other colonial papers, carried a considerable amount of material on science, a subject in which planters, physicians, clergymen-botanists, and others of the "curious" were much interested. Most of the essays or notices were concerned with medicine, remedies and cures, new developments in treatment, or epidemics in Europe and America. Dr. John Tennent was a principal contributor of both essays and advertising of his books and remedies, but there are many other writers, especially on fevers and smallpox. Natural history, particularly botany, in its relation to materia medica or ornamental gardens of exotic plants in the Old World or the New, was another popular subject. Astronomy received much attention after 1768, but something on the fascinating comet or meteor appeared somewhat earlier. In the sparse extant issues of the late 1740s and 1750s relatively little is concerned with the new interest in electricity, though after 1768 there is a great deal on the subject.[327]

There were also the theater advertisements, dramatic criticism, and notices and news of actors and actresses. The first theater preceded the first newspaper by twenty years, and it lasted under Stagg just long enough in 1736 to have notices of its performances in the *Gazette*. After Stagg's death there were notices of performances of Addison's *Cato* by college amateurs and other plays by "the gentlemen and ladies of the country." In 1751 the second theater opened. Its history is recorded at least in part in the continuing *Gazette*. Concerts, balls, and other social gatherings are advertised along with the dramatic performances.[328]

Though the Williamsburg coterie of amateur writers between 1735 and 1765 rivaled that of Annapolis, much more of the literary material in Parks-Hunter-Royle's *Virginia Gazette* is appropriated from British sources than the parallel material in Parks' or Green's *Maryland Gazette*, especially as far as verse is concerned. After 1750, when the Pistole Fee and Two-Penny Acts had stirred Virginians deeply, there were indeed more and more political essays, and from 1751 to 1766 and beyond some of the ablest written in America appeared first in the pages of the *Virginia Gazette*, presumably because authors and publishers knew that they had the sympathy of the majority of the House of Burgesses and even of several governors. The *Virginia Gazette* has continued to the present day, and the Rind version of the later 1760s, independent entirely (at least theoretically) of Crown government influence, printed more or less what it pleased. But the great body of Virginia writing which appeared in newspapers at all, including much of the political, is contained in the thirty years of this newspaper founded and formulated in policy by William Parks. It was the voice, by no means a full and complete one, of the intellectual golden age of colonial Virginia.[329]

James Davis' first North Carolina press, in operation from 1749, in August 1751 brought out the first issue of *The North Carolina Gazette* and continued it for about eight years. Today only six known issues of this journal are available to indicate its contents.[330] They are dated in 1751, 1752, 1753, 1757, and 1759. These isolated issues show that the editor was producing what was in general the same sort of newspaper the surrounding colonies did. There is in the November 15, 1751, issue, for example, a prose allegory on page one, "The Temple of Hymen. A Vision," selections from the *Westminster Journal* and the *Old Woman's Magazine* on page two, foreign news on page three, and more foreign news, shipping dates, and advertisements of books and other merchandise on page four. The 1752 issue of March 6 begins with an essay, "Reflections on Unhappy Marriages," and continues with foreign and domestic news and advertising. A fragmentary 1753 issue has on page three a poem, "Hymn to the Supreme," which may or may not be an original American composition. The 1757 and 1759 issues consist of reprinting from English papers such as the *Bristol-Journal*, in one a proclamation of a fast by Governor Dobbs, and news from all over the world. Any real evidence of the intellectual groups existing in New Bern and Wilmington is missing, though this proves little. Not until 1764 did Davis make another journalistic effort, *The North Carolina Magazine*, which in 1768 changed its name to the *North Carolina Gazette*, though in this period Davis had a rival newspaper and printer in Wilmington (in the person of Andrew Steuart, who arrived in 1764 and died in 1769).[331]

Of South Carolina newspapers much more is known because many more issues are extant and because there has been a book-length study of the longest-lived of them. Though Phillips' few issues of the *South-Carolina Weekly Journal* have been lost, a number of issues of Thomas Whitmarsh's *Gazette* are extant.[332] The earliest is dated January 8, 1731/1732. It includes on page one a statement of purpose and policy, inviting contributions, quoting Horace, and urging promotion of commerce and manufacturing. Whitmarsh's prose statement is similar to those in the Chesapeake gazettes, but his rhymed statement of policy is more specific:

> I'm not High-Church, nor Low Church, nor Tory, nor Whig,
> No flatt'ring young Coxcomb, nor formal old Prig.
> Not eternally talking, nor silently queint
> No profligate Sinner, nor pragmatical Saint,
> I'm not vain of my Judgment, nor pinn'd on a Sleeve,
> Nor implicitly any Thing can I believe.
> To sift Truth from all Rubbish, I do what I can,
> And, God knows, if I err—I'm a fallible Man.
> I can laugh at a Jest, if not cracked out of Time,
> And excuse a Mistake, tho not flatter a Crime.
>
> . . . .
>
> Cool Reason I bow to, wheresoever 'tis found,
> And rejoice when found Learning with Favour is crown'd,
> To no Party a Slave, in no Squabbles I join
> Nor damn the Opinion, that differs from mine.
> Evil Tongues I contemn, no mob Treasons I sing;
> I dote on my Country, and am Liege to my King.
> Tho' length of Days I desire, yet with my last Breath,
> I'm in hope to betray no mere Dreadings of Death,
> And as to the Path, after Death to be trod,
> I rely on the Will of a MERCIFUL GOD.

Though Whitmarsh printed his paper for only a little more than a year and a half before he died, his successor, Lewis Timothy, beginning with a new serial number in February 1734, resumed publication in the same spirit. Whitmarsh's invitation brought immediate response, for his second issue of January 15, 1732, carries an essay on the usefulness of hemp and the proper planting time for it, and a letter on gay young blades, both of pseudonymous authorship. Under Whitmarsh and his successor, Timothy, essays lean toward the utilitarian, though there are some notable exceptions. Verse appears often. Controversial essays on smallpox inoculation are more frequent in the *South-Carolina Gazette* than in the newspaper to the north, perhaps because there was more of the disease in this colony and certainly because two opposing methods were advocated by eminent Carolina physicians. One of the literarily graceful and cogent essays is on the uses of satire, written by "Publicola," who used the dateline address of Goose Creek.

Then there were essays on silkworms, poems on the ladies, a facetious piece from "Mary Meanwell" of Port Royal. Much of the verse is doggerel or heroic couplet or Hudibrastic in form, and in subject matter appropriate to these measures. There is a relatively large proportion by female contributors, or males using female pseudonyms. In Whitmarsh's *Gazette* in April 1732 was an essay on the virtues of a good education, with a follow-up a few weeks later in a deliberately dialectal and pretendedly illiterate letter prefacing couplets beginning "LEARNING that Cobweb of the Brain, / Profane, erroneous, and vain. . . ." The next issue returns seriously again to literature and learning in an essay signed "F.S." of Crowfield. All together, Whitmarsh's *Gazette* is a lively affair, full of locally authored essays and verses and a scattering of reprinted foreign and some local news. It has pieces celebrating the settlement of Georgia and a welcome to the inhabitants of the new province. There are discussions of printing in prose and in verse, announcements of vocal and instrumental concerts, offers to teach foreign languages and to decorate fans, something on paper currency and on religion and liberty. Then there are the official legislative records, the speech of the chief justice, another speech by General Oglethorpe, and a speech by the South Carolina governor.

In his issue no. 1 of February 2, 1734, Lewis Timothy began with a long inaugural essay. Like his predecessor Whitmarsh, he maintained close ties with his Philadelphia partner, Franklin, exchanging and printing news from the northern province. Hennig Cohen has analyzed the contents of the *South-Carolina Gazette* as it was published successively under Lewis, Elizabeth, and Peter Timothy, the last of whom carried the newspaper far beyond the colonial period. They remained official printers and became strong patriots and quite substantial citizens. The *Gazette* reflects their developing personal distinction in the growing city and province. Humor, theatrical notices, religion, oratory, miscellaneous essays, dignified occasional poems (and sprightly prologues for plays), and book advertisements are prominent on their pages. During the Indian wars and the Stamp Act and other pre-Revolutionary disturbances the

Gazette published essays on two sides of many questions, such as the Grant-Middleton policies about Indian fighting, the James Adair-Governor Glen divergences in Indian policy, and other polemics—all of which seem to indicate at least that these South Carolina editors were less fearful of official disapprobation than were the publishers in Virginia and even in Maryland, perhaps reflecting the balance of power and influence existing in South Carolina.[333]

There is much in this *Gazette*, as noticed elsewhere, on the Whitefield-Anglican controversy, in this case surely because of the immense interest created by the evangelist's frequent appearances in the colony. The Anglican Commissary Alexander Garden's attitude is represented because he was after all the head of the established church which had a number of strong supporters in Charleston and the colony generally. On the other hand, Whitefield had the powerful support of Josiah Smith, son of a former Proprietor, and other nonconforming ministers, who when banded together must have been at least equal in influence to the Anglicans. Timothy's newspaper was indeed neither Tory nor Whig in any theological applications of the terms.

Verse as well as prose was provincially strongly patriotic. On October 19, 1738, for example, appeared a long poem signed James Reid beginning "HAIL, *Carolina*, hail! Fill up the Bowl," which is not only chauvinistic but an advertising of the author's recently arrived cargo of wares which ladies and gentlemen may enjoy. "Sweet William" praises the Duke of Cumberland, who defeated the Scottish rebels. Other poetasters are elegiac, satiric, pious, facetious (as in Dumbleton's praise of rum), philosophical, even scientific.

Advertisements are much as in the Chesapeake papers, except that there are more on portrait painters and miniaturists; music, dancing, and language instruction; concerts and plays; and social clubs of various origins and affiliations. As befitted a seaport serving a great hinterland of Indian fur traders, cotton and rice and indigo planters, importers of useful and luxury items, the business advertising is considerable. As Hennig Cohen has shown, the Timothys' *South-Carolina Gazette* is a faithful reflection of the microcosm which was early Charleston and South Carolina.

But during the period there was one other interesting newspaper, founded and conducted by Robert Wells, who has been called the greatest bookseller (in volume and variety) of Charleston's eighteenth century.[334] Wells, a Scot, began operation of the *South-Carolina Weekly Gazette* in 1758, changing its title to the *South Carolina & American General Gazette* in 1764. Wells was a Loyalist in later years and suffered accordingly. Though his newspaper came earlier than Rind's did in Virginia as rival to the "establishment" newspaper, like Rind's it resembled in general content the politically opposing journal. Sometimes in the later years the Royalist had access to political news materials the Timothys did not. But typical of the growing sense of American identity in all the colonies, whether Loyalist or separatist Whig, are lines in Wells' journal in 1766:

> When poets shall adorn these new-born climes;
> When Popes and Miltons shall successive rise,
> And charm the savage as they civilize[.][335]

There is very little more to be said concerning the *Georgia Gazette* of the colonial period, founded by James Johnston in April 1763, beyond the brief notice of it given above in discussion of the establishment of the southern colonial presses. Johnston's was a more or less typical colonial newspaper, with news items, announcements, and statements which were circumspectly within political bounds. In size it was in the beginning quite small, being printed on a 7¼ by 11¼ inch page with the type matter in two columns. The page and type columns were not enlarged until 1766. There were the usual four pages and the customary occasional six- or eight-page issue. In 1763 Johnston advertised regularly for an apprentice and then for a journeyman, one or the other of which he must have obtained.[336] In the pre-Revolutionary decade he had his personal and publishing troubles, but he managed to print a number of books and pamphlets and his *Gazette* until after the war was in progress.

CONCLUSIONS

In the running commentary on printers and their careers a great deal has already been said about their publishing ventures. Each official printer produced a newspaper, and each brought out the laws and other papers his provincial government wished to have printed. There exist an excellent calendar of Maryland imprints by Wroth in his history of printing in that colony and calendars of varying quality and quantity for each of the other colonies. These are mentioned in this chapter's bibliography. Torrence's *Trial Bibliography of Colonial Virginia* is being revised or redone, a most important project, and the revised edition of *American Bibliography* by Evans et al. now under way should show a number of hitherto unknown imprints. But a separate "complete" calendar of imprints for each colony, from the inauguration of printing in that region to a natural terminal date such as 1763 or 1776 or 1781 would reveal a great deal about the intellectual and general interests of the separate provinces. At it is, what present calendars reveal is that there was a great variety of printing outside the official and the journalistic. Prose pamphlets and volumes of verse, sermons, almanacs, Indian treaty ceremonies, speeches, at least three great legal works (by Bacon, Mercer, and Trott), broadsides on many subjects, at least one major history, college charters, and medical and agricultural manuals are among the materials originating in the colonies in which they were printed or written directly for them. Then there were a number of reprints of British and even Continental works which printers or a segment of their public thought might appeal to many people. In the long view, perhaps the most distinguished of southern imprints are the pamphlets on liberty and taxation which began as early as elsewhere in the colonies, if not earlier.

The printer in the southern colonies was only a little later than his brother in New England in getting started, and in the Maryland instance ahead of any other but the Massachusetts men. With the possible exception of Franklin's *Pennsylvania Gazette*, the newspapers of the two Chesapeake Bay colonies and of South Carolina seem as generally informative, with as high a quality and variety of literary materials, as the newspapers in the north. The southern printer did not often have the type fonts his brethren in Boston, Philadelphia, and New York may have possessed. But when occasion demanded, especially when the occasion of a remarkable book demanded, he secured new fonts from which to print it. One result is the handsome volume of Thomas Bacon's *Laws of Maryland at Large* (1765/6).

The southern printer, from William Parks in Maryland and Virginia to Robert Wells and the Timothys in South Carolina and James Johnston in Georgia, proved to be a remarkably perceptive and adaptable man. Almost without exception he held local office, most often as postmaster but sometimes as alderman and vestryman. He was often moderately convivial and gregarious and made himself a distinguished member of local society. Parks, Green, Hunter, and Lewis Timothy were among the moving spirits in clubs, library societies, Masonic lodges, and patriotic associations. Printing-publishing began on a highly respectable scale in the colonial South and remained there.

Although some European visitors felt, as has already been noted, that southern colonists for want of books read men the more (and they said something of the same thing about other colonials), by the end of the eighteenth century a traveller such as the Duc de La Rochefoucauld-Liancourt observed that "the taste for reading is commoner [in Virginia] among men of the first class than in any other part of America."[337] His observation would have held for most of the southern colonies if one may judge by late-century inventories for literate men of all classes. There was nothing new or really developing or evolving about this fact save that all western society had become gradually more prone to reading, as this chapter has shown. From their first settlement in the seventeenth century the Chesapeake colonists owned and read books, in considerable number and some variety, as the inventories indicate. By the last decade of the century the newly organized Carolinas had a large segment of citizens who had more than decent private libraries and whose clergymen were receiving a steady flow of religious works from the Bishop of London and from the Society for the Propagation of the Gospel in Foreign Parts. Quite soon, in towns and parishes, they were organizing public libraries and library societies. The observation already made holds true, that the planter living in relative isolation was more likely to employ his spare time, from deliberate choice or by force of bad weather, in reading than was the more northern colonist who usually lived even as a farmer in a close-knit community, where social intercourse was possible in any weather. The southern towns and parochial libraries, even commercial lending libraries, were designed to appeal to this isolated planter as well as to the relatively small urban populations—witness the time allowed for possession of an individual book.

Then there was the constant borrowing and willing lending from the larger collections of the opulent or the omniverous collectors (Henry Callister among the latter). From William Fitzhugh's apology for having lost one of Richard Lee's books through the advertisements of owners in the Maryland or Virginia or South Carolina *Gazette* for the return of certain books there is widespread evidence that private libraries were used profitably or for recreation by literally scores of others not fortunate enough to own the volumes these collections contained. The scholar especially profited from the generosity of men like William Byrd, who lent books to Richard Bland which apparently were never returned (though Jefferson gathered them in) and allowed William Stith to use both manuscript and printed materials for the scholar-clergyman's *History of the First Discovery and Settlement of Virginia.* One may guess that a John Lawson, a John W. Gerard De Brahm, or a later David Ramsay used libraries other than their own in composing their studies of the country.

The omnipresence of the basic religious works among most literate southern colonials—the Bible, the Book of Common Prayer, *The Whole Duty of Man* among Anglicans and the sectarian equivalents of the latter two among others—need not be reemphasized. But the reader should be reminded that clerical and parochial libraries, almost every large private library, library societies, and the College of William and Mary possessed large numbers of theological works of a sophisticated and often controversial quality (in the sense of presenting contrasting theory or doctrine). A learned clergyman such as Cradock or Sterling or Bacon in Maryland, Blair or Maury or Davies in Virginia, Garden or Smith or Quincy in South Carolina, and Zubly in Georgia had access to hundreds of religious tomes. The natural philosopher—botanist, zoologist, geologist, ethnologist, meteorologist—might find in southern libraries the European-British imprints he needed and used in his field work. John Banister even in the seventeenth century owned many of the scientific books he needed, and the two John Claytons and Dr. Alexander Garden were among those who owned or easily borrowed them. William Byrd II and his brother-in-law John Custis inherited or bought the books they needed in botanical collecting or horticultural planning.

Some future full study of southern architecture before 1763 must depend to a considerable extent on a careful reading of the builders' and architects' manuals and pattern books in libraries. And the story of music in the colonial South admittedly so far must rely largely on book and sheet-music inventories printed or still in manuscript. The story of dramatic composition and performance public and private is again related to certain volumes in these libraries and to the newspaper advertisements and notices and critiques.

The relation between libraries and political ideas, the presence of histories, especially Whig and libertarian, has been commented upon, and at least one mention has been made of an excerpt from *Cato's Letters* taking up several columns of a newspaper. There are scores of such excerpts, though many come at the end of the period or just after it. They represent in several ways both a summing up and a look into the American future. The reading and use of the classics for themselves and as lessons in liberty, tyranny, rhetoric, style, and a dozen other matters has been at least touched upon. Classical influences were pervasive, including architecture through the Renaissance Italians and their British imitators.

Through almost two centuries the southern library in some respects remained constant or static, in others changing or dynamic. To the end of this colonial period, and from the beginning, Richard Hooker's *Ecclesiastical Polity* was present, quoted, and clearly read, as were Ovid (often in Sandys' translation after 1626), Purchas and Hakluyt, Cicero and Horace. After 1680, sometimes or in some instances, Newton and Locke, Algernon Sidney, Filmer, Hobbes, Harrington, Milton in his prose, Molesworth, and other conservative and liberal politico-social writers appeared on the same shelves. Later Trenchard and Gordon, Addison (especially in his *Cato*), Oldmixon, Bolingbroke, Hume, and other politico-philosophical "historians" joined them, though after 1720 the "liberals" predominated on the shelves and in the newspaper excerpts.[338]

Much of this is mere recapitulation to lead to some sort of suggestive conclusions. The chapter has really been little concerned with the frontier and its reading problems, for before 1764 the border settlers as a whole were not far enough removed from towns or great plantation libraries to make distance the separate problem it later became. The small extent of frontier in the Turner sense one does see here. The Carolina-Cherokee land to which white traders journeyed was to a considerable extent, as the cases of James Adair and Edmund Atkin mentioned in Chapter II indicate, a land where sufficient learned volumes were available as reference to produce a few remarkable books.

What remains now should be obvious: that from the seventeenth century a great number of southern colonists owned and read books; that by 1700 there were a few impressive libraries and that in the next half-century these increased or came into being in every southern province; that the S.P.G. was instrumental in making religious and some practical secular reading matter available through all these colonies except Virginia; that small libraries multiplied at least as rapidly as large ones, thanks to the proliferation of reading-writing instruction and many types of schools in each province; that the titles of books in dated inventories and in letters ordering them prove once and for all that there was no cultural lag; that from Spicer and Wormeley in 1700 to Jefferson (the beginnings of his great collections) there were in some eighteenth-century libraries sixteenth- and earlier seventeenth-century imprints, books treasured and read as they have been in all countries; and that in such men as William Byrd II and Thomas Jefferson and John Mercer and Peter Manigault and John Mackenzie there were in the colonial South book collectors in the best sense, men who bought first for use and then for entertainment and then for ornament. Each colony had its binder (usually the printer) who did elaborate gilding, conflated or otherwise rearranged, and hand-tooled his leather and vellum covers. Out-of-doors men these southern colonials were indeed, but they also spent many hours in the chimney corner of paneled Georgian library or of rough log-walled greatroom taking delight in their books.

CHAPTER FIVE

———◆———

Religion: Established, Evangelical, and Individual

CONTENTS

———————◆———————

Introduction   629

The Seventeenth Century   632
   Witchcraft: The Devil in the Southern Colonies   653
   Bishops and Commissaries   662

The Eighteenth Century through 1763   669
   The Anglicans   670
   Anglican and Other Attitudes toward Christianizing
     the Negro   679
   The Presbyterians and the Great Awakening   684
   The Baptists   694
   German and Swiss Sects   694
   The Quakers   696
   The Huguenots   696
   Deism and Rationalism   697

Bibliography   1028

Notes   1033

~ ~ ~ You shall have made this Iland, which is but as the
Suburbs of the Old World, a Bridge, a Gallery to the new; to
joyne all to that world that shall never grow old, the
Kingdome of heaven. You shall add persons to this Kingdom,
and to the Kingdome of heaven, and adde names to the
Books of our Chronicles, and to the Booke of Life.

—JOHN DONNE, *A Sermon Upon the VIII. Verse of The I. Chapter
Of The Acts of the Apostles* 1622, preached to the Virginia
Company of London, November 13, 1622.

AS THE PROMOTION and exploration literature examined in Chapter I so
strongly indicates, from 1584 to 1733, from Roanoke Island to Savannah,
the southern colonist established himself with religion strong in his conscience and consciousness. From Maryland to Georgia, one of the repeatedly
avowed purposes in colonization was the spread of Christianity. Each individual knew that he was expected to increase and multiply, and thus
people the wilderness with white civilized Christians. He also knew that
it was his moral duty to convert the red man. And after a time he had to
consider the possible salvation of his black pagan slaves as well.

But concerning even the latter two purposes he sometimes had reservations, and beyond them any common acknowledged aim in religion ceased.
The Church of England was from the beginning the established church in
Virginia, and long before 1763 it had become the official church of the
other four provinces. Yet much that was happening in Great Britain and on
the European continent had effects on the southern seacoast settlements
which prevented the kind of unified, albeit changing, religious and theological unity New England possessed, at least relatively, during the same
period. And the very social and economic nature of the five colonies was
to develop within and without the Church of England qualities in religious
organization and relationship to government which left them in 1763 well

along the road to the sort of denominationalism, evangelicalism, and independence which has marked American as well as southern religion down to the present time. In most colonies there was from the beginning a kind of religious tolerance, but by the mid-eighteenth century the Europeans who had become Americans had given a new meaning to the term.

Maryland, planted a generation after Jamestown, with a Roman Catholic Proprietor under a Protestant King, for obvious reasons declared tolerance on first planting. Gradually its ruling group became predominantly Anglican, and within two generations the whole colony officially so. But strong Roman Catholic elements, considerable Presbyterian and especially Quaker groups, and even for a time an influential Puritan community, together with the Puritan and Bloodless Revolutions in England, prevented the northernmost southern colony from ever being dominated by Anglicanism. The Carolinas, with eight Proprietors, were tacitly and unofficially Anglican from the beginning, and well before the end of the period officially so, but steady streams of Scots, Scotch-Irish, Germans, French, and smaller national groups gave the opportunity for Presbyterians, Lutherans, Huguenots, and Puritans to develop and establish ways of thinking which differed widely from those of the establishment. In North Carolina especially, the Quakers had a golden age as the dominant religious sect, and there were Quaker and other "tolerant" governors in both Carolinas. Georgia, settled by a philanthropic group, was also tacitly Anglican in its genesis, but German and Swiss forms of Lutheranism and a tiny outpost of New England Congregationalists were soon very significant indeed in the development of religious thinking. And almost simultaneously with the founding of Georgia came the Great Awakening with an effect in that colony immediately, for through it George Whitefield entered the American evangelical pulpit. Though in the colonial period the Baptists were never felt in proportion to their numbers, they were present from the seventeenth century, and by the year of the Stamp Act had prominent members in all classes of society.

To trace even in the seventeenth century the theological and religious cerebrations of the southern colonist, from governor to indentured servant, is a much more complex and confusing matter than it is of the New Englander, and much more spadework must be done before there can be first ventures at a firm interpretation. The sermons and tracts to be discussed in the next chapter afford certain evidences of the southern religious mentality and activity. What can be done in the present chapter is to trace in somewhat broad outlines the religion of these seaboard colonials as it manifests itself in charters from Great Britain, in local legislation, in the activities of bodies of men and of individuals; and along with this to note, usually by implication, the effect of way of life, of scattered farms and isolated frontiers, of national and sectarian European origins, on their degree or kind of piety or the absence of it.

That the white European who settled south of the Susquehannah was less interested in his personal relation to his God than was his Pennsylvania or New England contemporary is naturally not easy to determine. If a theocratic state and iron covenant (even a halfway one) or the Inner Light as guide are hallmarks of real Christian faith, the average southern settler was not the Christian most of his northern neighbors were, though one recalls that Puritans existed in the Anglican provinces and that Quakers were enormously active in several of them. Though Quakers labeled both New England and Virginia Anglican clergy "hireling priests," the latter never governed as a theocracy. Men were persecuted, whipped, and imprisoned from Maryland to Georgia for religious observances or the lack of them, but the church did not control the state, and even under the most zealous High-Church governors in provinces of the Anglican establishment there never was the interference of God's representatives (self-appointed) in daily life such as existed in New England. As will be shown, an element one may call puritan, within the Anglican church, was from Jamestown's first years always strong, with a strength perhaps later accentuated by the puritanism of Presbyterian or Huguenot or Lutheran neighbors. But its manifestations, strong as they are in individuals and certain societies to the present time, never assumed doctrinal forms which were imposed on every individual. This puritanism has had its effect on the liturgical observances and certain beliefs of the Episcopal Church in the South to this day, but at the same time that church has been by and large latitudinarian, a quality derived from its ancestry and its environment. Presbyterian (or Baptist or Methodist or radical evangelical) puritanism, as William Faulkner so frequently demonstrates in his novels, is still a pervasive social and moral and even political force in the region. But this lowercase-*p* puritanism is not and has never attempted to be organizational or formally political in such a way as to control men's personal religious lives.

There was no all-absorbing form of religion or religious way of thinking because the southern colonial had this world as well as the next on his mind. Neither the illustrious Elizabethan and Jacobean commentators on exploration, from Hakluyt to Purchas, nor the series of eminent divines exhorting Londoners to work for God and themselves beyond the sea, nor the balladeers who made the best of the worst as they sang the news of the New World, ever dreamed—much less said—that the individual motivated to worship as he pleased emigrated for this reason alone. He might avow that this adventure, as all man's actions, was indeed ultimately for God's glory. But he included in the same breath at least one other good reason for his errand into the wilderness or the terrestrial paradise.

THE SEVENTEENTH CENTURY

The religious history of the colonial South falls rather naturally into two periods, the years before and after 1701, when the Society for the Propagation of the Gospel in Foreign Parts was founded in the mother country. During the seventeenth century all the five colonies except Georgia were settled and organized, the Anglican church had assumed or was assuming official status, and Roman Catholics and several forms of dissenters had begun to appear. Even Puritans* had for several reasons a share in the South's religious development: the dominance of their coreligionists in England under the Commonwealth, their small though active bodies in the region, and the predilections of many of the early Anglicans.

A few sixteenth-century Englishmen, as we have seen, lived for a time on the sandbanks of what is today North Carolina. That they were orthodox Anglicans is evident from the pious comments of their eyewitness chroniclers and from the fact that first Manteo the Indian and then the infant Virginia Dare were christened. Since there is no record of a resident clergyman in the colony, a chaplain from the ship anchored nearby must have performed the sacrament.[1] Manteo is thus the first North American Indian known to have been admitted to the Church of England, and Virginia Dare the first British child baptized in the New World. Manteo was baptized, says the chronicler, at the insistence of Sir Walter Raleigh. Thus a pattern was set which, if it had been pursued more vigorously during the whole of the succeeding century, might have altered the story of Indian-white relations a great deal. The comment that the christening had to be insisted upon appears to suggest some opposition from other English leaders or from the Indian himself. Parallels may be found later.

Then there was the Chesapeake Bay colony of Virginia. It was founded, as noted in an earlier chapter, by a joint-stock company of pious and patriotic men, leaders among the nobility, gentry, and merchants, and moti-

---

* The words *Puritan* and *Puritanism* throughout this chapter refer to the extreme Calvinist groups such as the Massachusetts Bay Colony which in effect were separated from the Anglican church. The words *puritan* and *puritanism* refer to the extremely Low-Church movement within Anglicism and kindred communions which believed in cleansing or purifying the Church of Roman rituals and doctrines and its members of immoral practice. Both Puritans and puritans in the beginning were Calvinists, strict moralists, and not by nature (though sometimes by force) tolerant. In the South puritanism has remained not always Calvinist but zealous for what it considers morality and for minimizing or abolishing formalistic manners of worship. Outside the Episcopal church in the South puritanism as a moral and antiritualistic force was and is a dominant quality of the Presbyterian, Methodist, and Baptist groups, among others.

vated, as their records[2] and printed proclamations prove, much as their Elizabethan predecessors had been. If their earlier executive officer, Sir Thomas Smith, was more profit-seeking than pious, his successor, Sir Edwin Sandys, was probably the opposite. Certainly Sir Edwin—son of an archbishop, himself once in holy orders, author of a widely read survey of religion in Europe, genuinely anxious for the spiritual welfare of this first permanent colony of Englishmen—was the leader who saw to it that the people in the first little fleet landed well equipped with authority to propagate their religion and with a clergyman. The authority came from a charter issued in 1606 and in the sealed instructions to the first governor. The phrases of King James' first Virginia Company charter set the tone and intent followed in most later papers from Company or from Crown:

> We, greatly commending, and graciously accepting of, their Desires for the Furtherance of so noble a Work, which may, by the Providence of Almighty God, hereafter tend to the Glory of his Divine Majesty, in propagating of *Christian* Religion to such People, as yet live in Darkness and miserable Ignorance of the true Knowledge and Worship of God, and may in time bring the Infidels and Savages, living in those Parts, to human Civility, and to a settled and quiet Government; DO . . .[3]

The second charter, that of 1609, reiterates the "principall Effect" as conversion of the heathen and the true worship of God in the Christian religion and adds that for this reason no one suspected of adherence to the Church of Rome may "pass in any Voyage."[4] Therefore any would-be emigrant had to take the Oath of Supremacy[5] before he was allowed to embark. In the "Instructions Orders and Constitutions . . . to Sir Thomas Gates knight Governor of Virginia" of May 1609 appears a statement which is at the same time firm in establishing the Church of England but somewhat elastic on points other than "fundamentall." In other words, it frequently allows the clergy their own choice in form of service or dress. It also exhorts specific attempts to convert the red men through their children and expresses fear of pagan priestcraft (of which more later):

> You shall take principall order and Care for the true and reverent worship of god that his worde be duely preached and his holy sacraments administred accordinge to the constitutions of the Church of England in all fundamentall pointes, and his ministers had in due observance and respect agreeable to the dignity of their callinge. And that all Atheisme Prophanes Popery or Schisme be exemplarily punished to the honor of God and to the peace and safety of his Church, over which, in this tenderness and infancy, you must be especially solicitous & watchefull.

> You shall, with all prepensenes and diligence, endeavour the conversion of the natives to the knowledge and worship of the true § god § and

their redeemer Christ Jesus, as the most pious and noble end of this plantation, which the better to effect you must procure from them some convenient nomber of their Children to be brought up in your language, and manners, and if you finde it convenient, we thinke it reasonable you first remove from them their Iniocasockes or Priestes by a surprise of them all and detaynge them prisoners, for they are so wrapped up in the fogge and miserie of their iniquity, and so tirrified with their continuall tirrany chayned under the bonde of Deathe unto the Divell that while they live amounge them to poyson and infecte them their mindes, you shall never make any greate progres into this glorious worke, nor have any Civill peace or concurre with them.[6]

So they were to begin education and instruction in Christianity. For the devilish qualities of the priests, more below. But Charter and Instructions then and later expressed or implied that, whatever might be missionary or nationalistic aims, the colonists were themselves to live the religious lives of normal Englishmen. To this end their titular but nonresident parish rector, Richard Hakluyt, chose to send the Reverend Robert Hunt to be his vicar in Virginia.[7] Master of Arts of Oxford, devout and gentle, Hunt served the group of adventurers, from Earl's son and brother to humblest laborer, as he would have served his village flock in England. In the accounts of the hard first year in Jamestown, Captain Smith, Wingfield, and others comment, always favorably, on this true shepherd. One sees him ministering to the sick and perplexed on shipboard, losing his whole library without complaint in the great fire of the bitterly cold first winter, or preaching his usual sermon at the end of a day made arduous by Indian alarums. Smith vividly describes his first church services:

> When I went first to Virginia, I well remember wee did hang an awning (which is an old saile) to three or four trees to shadow us from the Sunne, our walles were rales of wood, our seats unhewed trees till we cut planks, our Pulpit a bar of wood nailed to two neighbouring trees. . . .
> Yet wee had daily Common prayer morning and evening, every Sunday two Sermons, and every three moneths the holy Communion, till our Minister died: but our Prayers daily, with an Homily on Sundaies, we continued two or three yeares after, till more Preachers came: and surely God did most mercifully heare us.

And Smith summarizes: "Master *Robert Hunt*, an honest, religious and courageous Divine; during whose life our factions were oft qualified, our wants and greatest extremities so comforted, that they seemed easie in comparison of what we endured after his memorable death."[8]

To this picture others may be added: the serio-comic spectacle of Edmund Maria Wingfield's search in his trunkful of books for his (stolen) Bible, the lack of which had allowed his enemies to whisper "atheist"; the same gentleman's more dignified account of the saving of the colonists' last two gallons of sack for the communion table;[9] the touching and eloquent though long and tedious prayer, morning and evening, prepared probably by Crashaw or Whitaker,[10] in accordance with but not from the Book of Common Prayer.[11] The tone of the prayer may suggest the puritanism of the Anglicans who composed it. A brief excerpt will indicate its tenor:

> Merciful Father, and Lord of heaven and earth, we come before thy presence to worship thee in calling upon thy name, and giving thanks unto thee....
> And now O Lord of mercie, O Father of spirits of all flesh, looke in mercie upon the Gentiles, who yet know thee not, ... And seeing thou hast honoured us to choose us out to beare thy name unto the Gentiles: we therefore beseech thee to bless us, and this our plantation, which we and our nation have begun in thy feare, & for thy glory.... And whereas we have, by undertaking this plantation undergone the reproofs of the base world, insomuch as many of our owne brethren laugh us to scorn, O Lord, we pray thee fortify us against this temptation. ... Lord, bless England, our sweet native countrey, save it from Popery, this land from heathenisme, & both from Atheism. And Lord heare their praiers for us, and us for them, and Christ Jesus, our glorious Mediator for us all. Amen.[12]

But one more description from the colonists themselves. This time, after the terrible period of starvation had been ended by the timely arrival of Lord de la Warr and Hunt's replacement, one sees a church and service in more style, but hardly more dignity, than Hunt's. This account appears in William Strachey's "A True Reportory," the same famous letter in which the author described the wreck in the Bermudas, a vivid portrayal employed by Shakespeare in *The Tempest*. The year is 1610.

> In the midst [of Jamestown] is a market place, a store-house, and a *corps de garde*, as likewise a pretty chapel, though (at this time when we came in) as ruined and unfrequented. But the lord governor and captain general hath given order for the repairing of it, and at this instant many hands are about it. It is in length three-score foot, in breadth twenty-four, and shall have a chancel in it of cedar and a communion table of the black walnut, and all the pews of cedar, with fair broad windows to shut and open, as the weather shall occasion, of the same wood, a pulpit of the same, with a font hewn hollow, like a canoe, with two bells at the west end. It is so cast as it be very light within, and the lord governor and captain general doth cause it to be kept passing sweet and trimmed up with divers flowers, with a sexton belonging to it. And in it every Sunday we have sermons twice a day, and every Thursday a sermon, having true preachers,[13] which take their weekly turns; and every morning,

at the ringing of a bell about ten of the clock, each man addresseth himself to prayers, and so at four of the clock before supper.

Every Sunday, when the lord governor and captain general goeth to church, he is accompanied with all the councilors, captains, other officers, and all the gentlemen, and with a guard of halberdiers in His Lordship's livery, fair red cloaks, to the number of fifty, both on each side and behind him; and, being in the church, His Lordship hath his seat in the choir, in a green velvet chair, with a cloth, with a velvet cushion spread on a table before him on which he kneeleth; and on each side sit the council, captains, and officers in their place; and when he returneth home again he is waited on to his house in the same manner.[14]

Quite an advance in color and fanfare in a short three or four years! But there was not to be another nobleman as resident governor for two generations or more, and one may doubt that so elaborate a spectacle occurred on Sundays after de la Warr's short stay. One notes that this account tells nothing of the clerical garb or manner of service conducted, though from other inferences one may surmise that it was Low-Church or puritan, and the clergy may or may not have worn the surplice. Nor does it tell much about individuals and their devoutness and attendance at church services.

Dale's *Laws*, from which the prayer for and by the guard quoted above is taken, included explicit provisions for Sunday morning prayer and sermon, Sunday afternoon catechizing, two briefer services every weekday, and a sermon again on Wednesdays, not quite as Strachey in his letter records them. It was the minister's duty to keep records of all christenings, marriages, and deaths. It was the duty of the laity to repair to the church upon the tolling of the bell, twice every weekday as well as Sunday. The punishment for absences was harsh, as was that for profaning the Sabbath by gaming and other such pastimes. For the third offense in not attending the two Sunday services the punishment was death. Sacrilege, such as stealing from the church, false witness, and certain other offenses, were likewise punishable by death. Even the minister, upon pain of losing his week's supply of provisions, had to read these laws every Sunday before catechizing.

Dale's *Laws* seemed infamous to nineteenth-century historians, but today even the theological commentators tend to defend these laws as merely typical of an age and a situation which required an iron hand from both man and God. They reveal much of the detail of daily life, with religion at its center. And they brought order out of chaos. Neither Roman Catholic nor Separatist could have objected on religious grounds to any of them save that making the minister of the parish the judge over the sufficiency of the layman's faith.

But more than Jamestown had to be provided for, and the tolling of the bell for daily worship could not be heard by all settlers. Up the river was laid out in 1611 "The City of Henricus," later Henrico. Helping with the plans for streets, houses, and fortifications was a remarkable clergyman, Alexander Whitaker, who remained a rural parish minister-missionary until his death by drowning six years later.[15] This most able and energetic of the early Anglicans was the son of a Regius Professor and Master of St. John's College, Cambridge. He attended Trinity, his father's old college, where the great puritan William Perkins died soon after Whitaker's arrival in 1602. Puritanism and puritanism were everywhere around him at the university. The Emmanuel College people at this time did not, for example, use the Book of Common Prayer or wear the surplice. Whitaker received the M.A. in 1608 and the next year, at the age of twenty-four, was ordained. Soon he felt the missionary call to Virginia. A friend asserted that he was learned enough to write with elegance in Greek or Latin as well as English, and there is evidence that he was in easy material circumstances.

Whitaker left in writing a record of himself and his work. From it one learns something of the man and definite things about the puritan leanings of the clergy and perhaps the laity of the time. Zeal to spread and to live Christianity, disregard for liturgical forms, regard for providences, and belief in witchcraft are among the qualities Whitaker shows were as characteristic of the early Virginia Church of England as they were of the religion of the later settlers to the northeast. Though some of these qualities were common to all Christianity, others are distinct enough to suggest that the Low-Church pattern which has marked the Episcopal Church in Virginia to the present day was already being set. Three personal letters and a letter-sermon by Whitaker, the last printed in London in 1613, are all that have survived from his pen.[16] His notable sermon will be discussed at length in the next chapter. Like the letters, it reveals him as a moderate puritan and an acute observer of Indian life and character who was sure that for the moment the red aborigines were outside the covenant of grace.

In his letter to William Gouge in 1614 he tells of his daily "preaching ministry" at Henrico: "Every Sabbath day wee preach in the forenoone, and Chatechize in the afternoon. Every Saturday at night I exercise in Sir Thomas Dale's house. Our Church affaires bee consulted on by the Minister, and foure of the more religious men. Once every month wee have a *Communion*, and once a yeer a solemn *Fast*." In another version of the letter, in place of the above lines, Whitaker comments pointedly: "But I much more muse, that so few of our English Ministers that were so hot against the Surplis and subscription: come hither where neither is spoken of. Doe they then not wilfully hide their Tallents, or keepe themselves at

637

home for feare of loosing a few pleasures. . . . and I though my promise of 3 years service to my country to be expired, will abide in my vocation here untill I be lawfully called from hence." [17]

Both passages seem to indicate Whitaker's puritanism, though in the first only the rudimentary congregational organization (which also may be a small vestry) is probably pertinent, for the fasts and catechisms were normal for the Church of England. The Saturday night "exercise" may suggest some puritan preparation for the Sabbath. The second passage (from the first issue of the printed letter), much better known to historians, is more explicit in its moderate puritanism and indeed proves that Whitaker tolerated if he did not follow the nonsubscribers to the Thirty-Nine Articles and Book of Common Prayer.

Brydon states positively that Richard Bucke of Jamestown was also puritan,[18] but mainly on the grounds that he endowed his children born in Virginia with names "worthy of bluest New England": Mara, "bitterness"; Gershom, "a stranger here"; Benoni, "the son of sorrow" (apparently mentally defective); and Peleg, "divisions . . . for in his days the earth was divided." The 1623 report that in 1619 there were five ministers "in orders and two without" [19] probably indicates that the "two without" were of Genevan or Presbyterian ordination. If so, here is further evidence of probable puritan leanings.

Actually there is too little surviving evidence of the character of the clergy before 1624, when the Virginia Company of London was dissolved by the King, to prove much about their doctrinal attitudes. Except from Whitaker, there appear to be no surviving religious writings from them. A few times their names do appear in court records of civil or social matters. Of nineteen ministers whose Christian names as well as surnames have come down to us, there is good evidence that six attended Cambridge, five Oxford, and one either university (his name appears in both). Of the others one may be sure that most if not all attended one of the universities. Those whose backgrounds are known were from families of prominence, often of distinction. Thomas Bargrave of Henrico was nephew of the Dean of Canterbury; David Sandys of Hog Island in Surry County was closely related to Sir Edwin and George the poet (also Treasurer in Virginia); Hawte Wyatt of Jamestown was brother of Governor Sir Francis and descendant of the poet Thomas.

A hundred years later the Reverend Hugh Jones observed that surplices, for a long time in disuse, were returning to fashion in Virginia, though not without difficulty. The same was true of kneeling to receive the sacrament.[20] Most parishioners had become accustomed to the Presbyterian form of receiving it sitting. It seems likely that these and other unorthodoxies in liturgical practice go back in part to the puritan habits or inclinations of the first generation of clergy and their communicants.

Missionary endeavor, as already noted, was encouraged in the beginning by all kinds of Anglicans. It loomed large in the minds of the Virginia Company Council in London and of the earliest settlers at Jamestown. Some of the explicit instructions concerning it have already been noted. Its core was education, and the founding of the College of Henrico in 1619, of the East India school, and of the Indian segment of the College of William and Mary have been noted in other chapters. Some few red men or red children were sent to England to be educated. The baptism and marriage of Pocahontas brought a period of good will during which some Christianizing may have been done. It ended for a time with the great massacre of 1622. It is worth recalling that a converted Indian, Chanco, saved the colony from total destruction in this year. Persistent and what was considered necessary destruction of Indian crops and villages during the next two years naturally made the heathen reluctant to send their children to the English for Christian instruction.[21] Thus things stood when the King dissolved the Company in 1624 and Virginia became a royal province. The tempered idealism of the Virginia Company had come to an end.

The first General Assembly of 1619 had enacted only a few ecclesiastical laws[22] growing out of customs by then fairly well established. They concerned the reading of divine service and the exercise of other ministerial functions according to the Church of England, such functions as the keeping of the records of baptisms. Churchwardens were given fairly specific instructions as to their duties to the poor, the impious, and the lawbreaking. Thus there are indications that churchwardens were already functioning in accordance with English usage. All ministers were required to meet with the governor four times a year as a sort of ecclesiastical court to try certain offenders. Some legislative steps were taken toward converting the Indian.[23] In the next two years under the Company further laws about church attendance and the duties of the clergy were passed, with fines for nonadherence. After the massacre, March 22 was proclaimed a holiday for worship and thanksgiving.[24]

The first decade under the Crown saw transition and change. The cities-shires[25] became counties, evidence of a realization that at least for some time the colony would not have even a reasonably concentrated or urban population. New parishes had to be created and others had to be extended. By law each had to have its own minister. King, Privy Council, and General Assembly recognized the weaknesses of a strung-out series of farms without urban centers, and again and again acts were passed creating

towns. Most never existed except on paper, and the few in which buildings were erected carried on a struggling existence through the first century. Parishes, beginning as the villages of the first decades, were gradually
stretched to include long strips of sparsely settled wilderness, and then as
new counties were created so were new parishes. By 1629/30 stricter laws
requiring specifically that the clergy should conform to the canons of
the Church of England were passed, but nothing prevented dissenters
from living unmolested by civil authority provided they obeyed the original
laws governing religious behavior.[26]

In 1632 the laws were assembled in a code and definite advances were
made in church organization, particularly in regard to ministerial conduct
and duty. Between 1633 and 1636 vestries appear to have been set up,
though the records for the period are missing. The first vestry act in Hening's *Statutes* is that passed at the session of March 1642/43. Minister
and churchwardens were to choose the vestry, and henceforward the
"Vestrie of evrie parish [were to] ... have power to elect and make choyce
of their ministers," the latter clause the basis for civil-ecclesiastical contention for the remainder of the colonial period. There is plenty of evidence
in county records[27] that a vestry act had been passed some time before
1636. Apparently vestries were chosen originally by justices of the peace
sitting as county courts, though in 1644/45 an act empowered each parish
to elect its own vestry directly. In a relatively short time most of these
vestries, whatever their origin, had become self-perpetuating. They func-
tioned whether or not there was a minister; they had control over the
poor and certain other secular as well as ecclesiastical affairs. The surviving vestry books, of which there are many now in print, reveal the varied
duties and governing functions of these bodies. They also show how strong
as civil powers these technically ecclesiastical organizations were, exercis-
ing their rights in defiance of governor, commissary, or king. Their contentions with their own clergy, the later commissaries, and governors to
preserve their independence in local affairs religious or civil never ended.

The chief function of the vestries as they understood it was ecclesiastical and social—to preserve their parishes from unworthy ministers. For
this reason they fought what came to be the governor's right by law to
"induct" a clergyman,[28] which gave that clergyman tenure and power to
go his own way. This right many vestries simply refused to acknowledge.
The records for 150 years show that usually the vestry won—despite
even some adverse attorney-general's opinion from England—and elected
their ministers from year to year. When the first commissary, James Blair,
was appointed in Virginia in the late seventeenth century, he more often
than not sided with the vestry instead of his clergy on the matter of induction. Obviously this was partly because his own powers were so vague

and yet limited that he felt clergymen with tenure might defy him at will. Even when the governor commanded a particular induction, Blair supported the vestry. So acrimonious did this dispute become, and such was Blair's ability to maneuver politically back home in England, that he caused directly or indirectly the ousting of three strong governors—Andros, Nicholson, and Spotswood.[29] On the other hand, Spotswood refused to induct Blair at Williamsburg when the vestry presented him. With strong British legal opinion to support both sides, the case was never settled.

Though the clergy justly claimed that this failure to induct hampered candid preaching of the gospel and morality and resulted in financial insecurity, in the whole colonial period in Virginia very few incumbents were ever dismissed. A survey questionnaire of 1724 shows that, though only a few were inducted, the twenty-nine clergy reporting had on the average held their parishes for twenty-one years and had served in the colonies for twenty-five years.[30] Undoubtedly there were injustices, especially in matters of salary, but this system based on self-government worked. Well might Bishop Meade make the comment that the battles of the American Revolution had already been fought by the Virginia vestries for 150 years: "*Taxation and representation* were only other words for *support and election of ministers*. The principle was the same."[31]

There were clergy intimidated by wealthy and powerful parishioners who lived dissolute lives. There was a great inequality in salaries, which theoretically were almost all the same. They were originally fixed by law at £200 sterling but later at 13,333 pounds of tobacco and about 1700 at 16,000 to 20,000 pounds.[32] Crops varied greatly from year to year in quality and quantity, and the parishes in which the more desirable Sweet-scented was raised were considered vastly preferable to those in which Orinoco was the staple. But the records of the Executive Council and the General Assembly as well as of local vestries indicate that the continuous probational status as a whole tended to make the clergymen more energetic and faithful to duties and more circumspect in behavior.[33] The timid clergymen were well balanced by the fearless ones, such as the Reverend Anthony Panton, minister of York and Chiskiack parishes about 1639–1640. Panton expressed a highly derogatory opinion of unpopular Governor Harvey's secretary of state, Richard Kemp. He was tried and convicted of mutiny, fined, condemned to banishment from Virginia, and given other severe penalties. Panton appealed to the Privy Council in England, however, and a new trial was granted, resulting in his triumphant vindication.[34] The interesting point is that the governor might deprive him of income but could not deprive him of his parish, or depose him.

But here one should turn to the neighboring province of Maryland, founded in 1634. Some of the territory granted Lord Baltimore had been within Virginia's patent, and naturally the older colony resented the intrusion. Even before the first fleet of the Catholic Calverts arrived, stout old William Claiborne had set up a community on and claimed Kent Island in Chesapeake Bay for Virginia. Here, two years before mass was celebrated at St. Clement's, Church of England services were held. Claiborne's account books show charges for Bibles, Prayer Books, a pewter communion service, and the salaries of two ministers, Richard James and William Cotton (the latter only an occasional visitor from the puritan Eastern Shore of Virginia).[35] Since Claiborne was within a few years to have a part in Cromwellian government in Virginia, it seems evident that Anglicanism more than tinged with moderate nonconformity preceded the planting of the Calverts' flag in what is Maryland.

The charter granted by Charles I to these Calverts included *ordinary* powers, that is, the powers a bishop has in his jurisdiction over such matters as patronages and licensing for erecting places of worship, "and of causing the same to be dedicated according to the ecclesiastical laws of our kingdom of England."[36] Many Protestants in England looked with misgivings and suspicion upon the powers and opportunities offered Roman Catholicism in this new colony. Whatever the original motives of Lord Baltimore and the Jesuits who landed and said mass on Lady Day 1634, the Protestants need not have worried. Recent historians find that the great majority of even this first group of Calvert settlers were strongly Protestant, and that the Protestants continued to come in greater numbers, for a variety of reasons, than did Romans. The charter not only implied that if any church were established it must be the Church of England; it also provided that any Christian might worship without molestation from civil or church authority.

In practice it did not always work out this way at first. Much was made in the colonial courts and by earlier historians of the 1638 case of Catholic Captain Cornwallis' overseer's forbidding indentured servants' reading aloud to each other certain Protestant books and his calling Protestant ministers servants of the Devil.[37] The overseer, Lewis, defended himself by stating (correctly) that the books read called the Pope anti-Christ. The case, tried before the governor, was decided in favor of the Protestants. In another instance prominent Catholic Thomas Ger(r)ard took the key and the books away from a Protestant chapel (presumably on or adjacent to his land) and was tried before the General Assembly. These and other cases indicate, among other things, that the first upper-class landowners may have been predominantly Roman Catholic.[38]

The Calverts trod softly until the deposing and in 1649 the beheading of their friend Charles I. Now opposed directly by an overwhelmingly Protestant nation and as far as power was concerned a non-Anglican people, they approved a proposal of the Maryland Assembly for "An Act Concerning Religion." It resembled Virginia basic enactments in its penalties for blasphemy and Sabbath-breaking but differed a little in that it included punishment for speaking reproachful words of the Blessed Virgin or for the use of epithets such as *Roundhead, Jesuit, Antinomian,* and *Separatist.* Finally it provided for the exercise of any Trinitarian Christian religion. Apparently Lord Baltimore, since he had to make a choice, was supporting the Independents (believers in nonestablishment for all) rather than supporters of a strict presbytery.[39] Thus only could the Proprietary survive. Five years later, when Puritans attained control of the Assembly, both Romanism and Anglicanism were proscribed, but in another three years the colony was restored to the Proprietor and the Act of 1649 reenacted.

Such was the state of religious affairs in the two Chesapeake colonies when Charles II was restored in 1660. Besides a puritan element within Anglicanism, both had felt a Puritan element. The latter, difficult to extricate from the lower-case puritanism, left no enduring organization but did leave a strong spiritual influence on social and political forms and on individual southern thinking such as moral taboos. Its close relative, Presbyterianism, carried many of its ideas into future generations. Therefore a little should be said of the Puritans present in the earlier years of the two colonies. The story is a joint one, for the histories of these people in the sister provinces overlap and converge.[40]

In both colonies there were actually some Puritans of the radical Pilgrim of Plymouth type, as opposed to the conservative Massachusetts Bay type. In Virginia most of them were gathered in communities on the south side of the James River. They went back to a London and Amsterdam group which resembled the Pilgrims of 1620 in almost every way. One hundred and eighty of them sailed for Virginia on August 24, 1618, but only thirty survived a painful six months' voyage. All except seven of the remainder were killed in the massacre or died from illness before 1623. In the same year Christopher Lawne and associates were more successful in an Isle of Wight settlement, soon after Nathaniel Basse established a third group near Lacone's. Both men represented their plantations in the House of Burgesses.

Another Puritan settlement was founded by opulent Edward Bennett, who had been an elder in the Ancient Church at Amsterdam. His 1621 patent lay between Lawne's and Basse's and was almost wiped out in the 1622 massacre, though thirty-three people were living there in 1623.[41] A few years later Bennett himself came to Virginia and in 1628 was a member of the House of Burgesses. The elder Daniel Gookin established a plantation above Newport News, and in 1635 the second Daniel Gookin, later to be famous in New England, settled fifty people on a 2,500-acre tract in Nansemond. Their first clergy all seem to have been of Puritan tendencies or were outright Puritans. The Reverend Thomas Bennett was the only Nansemond minister for some years until their settlement called upon New England for clergy. William Thompson, Thomas James, and John Knowles were sent to assist.[42] All three were English university men. Though they were heartily welcomed, they did not tarry long in Virginia, for Berkeley was now in power and a new, stricter law regarding conformity was passed.[43] Another strongly though not entirely Puritan community existed in Lower Norfolk County, the second minister of which was the Reverend Thomas Harrison, a Cambridge man who had first gone to New England and arrived in Virginia in 1640. The parish churchwardens brought charges in 1645 that he was not using the Book of Common Prayer or following the liturgical practices of the Church of England. Thereupon Harrison shifted his ministrations to Nansemond, where he was welcomed. By this time Pilgrim and Puritan, Plymouth and Boston types, are impossible to distinguish in Virginia. Berkeley apparently attempted to bring the eloquent preacher to conform and allowed him three years before forcing his departure, though there is no evidence for the oft-repeated statement that he was at one time Berkeley's chaplain and then turned nonconformist. Harrison married Governor Winthrop's niece on a trip to Boston and then returned briefly to Virginia in 1649. Soon he was in Ireland as Henry Cromwell's chaplain.[44]

Though Virginia was more intolerant of Puritan elements in the 1640s than it had been before, the opposite was happening in Maryland, perhaps because Lord Baltimore would have had much more to lose than Governor Berkeley if he strenuously opposed the rising Puritan power in England. The Proprietor appointed a Puritan or puritan from the Eastern Shore of Virginia, William Stone, as governor of Maryland, one of the conditions being that Stone bring in five hundred more settlers. The Nansemond group later claimed that they were "invited and encouraged by Captain Stone to remove to Maryland and that they were promised liberty of conscience."[45] During 1648 some three hundred nonconformists journeyed from Virginia to the Severn River in Maryland.[46] Evidence indicates that this was less than half the Puritans in Virginia and that the rest remained. Richard Bennett held property in both colonies and in a few years returned to Virginia. The two speakers of Virginia general assemblies under the Commonwealth were both Nansemond men. Meager existing evidence suggests that the Nansemond-Isle of Wight region continued to be Calvinist, though royalist refugees moved into these counties in the 1650s. In the 1680s Francis Makemie, the Presbyterian, wrote that he found a "[Scotch-]Irish minister" and flock in Lower Norfolk. The Eastern Shore of Virginia has a parallel history, with Puritan clergy like William Cotton, Nathaniel Eaton, John Rosier, and Francis Doughty (Doughtie), the last of whom has his place also in New England history for his arguments which anticipated the Half-Way Covenant.[47]

Apparently there were always nonconformists in Maryland, even clear-cut Puritans, though how many or what percentage of the population they represented it is impossible to say. As early as 1643 the Proprietor had invited settlers from Massachusetts Bay, with inducements of special privileges and the allurement of a warmer climate. Both the first major groups probably came from Virginia, however, and settled on the Severn at Providence (later Annapolis) and on the north side of the Patuxent River. The latter group had Puritan neighbors from other sources. Also English Puritans, Scots, and Welsh Puritans were settled among continental European peoples of Calvinist or Lutheran persuasions. The 1649 act forbidding such epithets as *Anabaptist, Independent, Roundhead,* and *Jesuit* show how heterogenous the Maryland nonconformists were, that they were by no means all Puritans or Congregationalists.

Not until the 1650s did the Cromwellian government in England take over Virginia and Maryland. Virginia and Berkeley had capitulated under extraordinary terms which in effect gave the government greater independence than it had before enjoyed. Berkeley retired as governor, and the House of Burgesses *elected* a governor, the Council, and the county commissioners. The colony was careful never to identify itself with the Commonwealth, though from time to time it had to acknowledge its supremacy. With the Restoration Governor Berkeley was back in office.

In Maryland the situation was somewhat different and evoked a polemical pamphlet warfare still worth perusing. Leonard Strong, in *Babylon's Fall in Maryland: a Fair Warning to Lord Baltamore* (1655), speaking for former Virginia Puritans settled at Providence, tells the story of Stone's invitation and promises and of Lord Baltimore's retraction or rejection of them. Stone led the Proprietor's forces in the battle of Severn against the Providence forces. A conflicting report and reply, John Langford's *A Just and Cleere Refutation of . . . Babylons Fall in Maryland . . .* (1655), with additional information from other sources, indicates that both sides exaggerated numbers participating and casualties in their actual resort to arms. There are several other contributions in prose to this struggle, each blaming the other for inciting it. The belligerent obstinacy, even bigotry, of the Providence group in their unwillingness to tolerate Roman Catholics and even certain other Protestants in a land to which the two latter had welcomed them shows them true blood-brothers of their New England coreligionists.[48] But, as in Virginia during the Commonwealth, nonconformists never ruled long in Maryland, probably because they were divided in their loyalties. A few years later, in the 1660s, George Alsop observed that Marylanders were carried in many directions by religious fads, including Quakerism.

It is perhaps significant to note in passing that in the later seventeenth century Virginia Anglicans were much more tolerant of Roman Catholics than were their Maryland neighbors, certainly partly because there were too few in the province to present any threat to the establishment political or religious. The most interesting case is that of the Brent family, some of whom moved across the Potomac from Maryland in 1651. Acquiring vast acreage and other property, they were apparently never bothered by the anti-recusant laws, partly because they were as fervent royalists as Sir William Berkeley himself. In 1686–1687 one of them, Captain George Brent, served as the King's attorney-general in Virginia. In 1688, upon his election to the House of Burgesses and refusal to take the oaths then tendered on a voluntary basis, his colleagues, instead of recoiling in horror, at once elected him to several committees. Amid the Maryland uprisings of 1688/89 Brent had some trouble, but the Virginia authorities supported him completely. He lived on ten years, most of them spent as an agent for Lord Fairfax's Northern Neck Proprietary. This "practical toleration" by the Anglicans was to continue for the Brents in Stafford County up to the American Revolution.[49]

Despite the political upheavals and temporary triumph of Puritanism in England in the mid-seventeenth century, outright Puritanism never had the popularity in Virginia and Maryland that Quakerism did. Babette Levy classifies Quakers as merely variant Puritans (she uses the capital *P* form to include almost any kind of nonconformist), and though in New England Puritans and Quakers clashed throughout the century, in Virginia's old Puritan settlements the Quakers had their first great successes in the province.[50]

The members of the Society of Friends, "the people called Quakers," believed intensely that they had rediscovered a spiritual principle which they thought would revolutionize society, government, and religion. They exalted personal experience, and they insisted on certain outward forms, as sitting indoors in meetings with their hats on, and in certain principles of conduct and morality, as refusal to swear a civil or legal oath or bear arms for their country or attend any other church's services. All these qualities sooner or later got them into some degree of trouble with civil and ecclesiastical authorities.

It has been frequently said that in New England Quakerism won its first converts from among those revolting against establishment, and in the South from among the unchurched. This is only partially true, especially for Virginia and Maryland. The first Quaker missionaries appeared in New

England and in Virginia at about the same time, 1656–1657. They were so successful in winning converts in Virginia within a year or two that in 1660 "An Act for Suppressing Quakers" was passed and the two men were ordered out of the colony.[51] Before this the master of a ship bringing outside Quakers was fined and ordered to carry them back whence they had come. Some Virginia Quakers were allowed to go to Maryland, and one woman with child was pardoned; but frequently they were whipped and imprisoned. One man died in the Williamsburg prison because of its unsanitary conditions and inhumane treatment in other ways. New laws attempting to compel conformity were passed in 1662, but they proved as ineffectual in the next decades as the previous punishments had been. Quaker ministers came and went as they pleased, and people continued to be "convinced." These preachers kept up a continuous shuttle from Virginia to Maryland or North Carolina and back.

Three great internationally known Friends were the real founders of the Meetings in the South. John Burnyeat in 1665, George Fox in 1672, and William Edmundson slightly before Fox, were great proselytizers in Virginia, Maryland, and North Carolina. Their greatest success in Virginia, as noted above, was from the southeastern side of the James River to the North Carolina boundary, the old Puritan stronghold.

By 1672 the first Maryland Yearly Meeting was held in Baltimore, apparently organized by Burnyeat and attended by Fox, just after the latter's arrival in America. This appears to have been the turning point toward a status of respectability in the Maryland colony. During the next few years these preachers moved among the northernmost southern provinces, organizing and "convincing." Then there was another period of Quaker suffering in Virginia between 1675 and 1680, terminated by the arrival of a sympathetic governor, Lord Culpeper. One Anglican minister noted that they had most converts in Virginia and Maryland in counties where the established church had no ministers. In North Carolina theirs were the first ministers of any kind to visit large unchurched areas of population, and there they were even more successful than in the Chesapeake provinces.

Finally in the Quaker connection should be mentioned here Thomas Story, educated intellectual and officeholder under William Penn in Philadelphia. His journal will be discussed later. But his account of his travels, discourses, and debates, and his courteous reception by Virginia and Maryland governors in 1698–1699 and 1705, point to an intrenched Quakerism in the Chesapeake colonies by the latter date. It also indicates considerable tolerance and even sympathy from Anglican laity, including some prominent persons, and the fact that this Quaker could hold his own in debate or discourse with the educated clergy of other groups. Evident here are the qualities which would insure Quaker survival into the national period and an apparent promise of broader expansion in the Chesapeake area than ever came. His observations at least bear out those of others who testify to the strength of the Friends in the Tidewater region at the beginning of the eighteenth century.[52]

Before a return to the Anglican church in Virginia and Maryland at the end of the century it should be noted that other religious groups had before 1700 made some progress in these colonies. The Presbyterians were of course the strongest. It is extremely difficult, especially for the early decades of both colonies, to draw a distinction between them and the Puritans, from whom they differed primarily in matters of organization, not doctrine. Though the Reverend Matthew Hill in Maryland has been called a Presbyterian-Puritan, the first Presbyterian pastor to devote his life to his co-religionists in the Chesapeake Bay area and in America was Francis Makemie (1658–1708).[53] He was in Maryland in 1683, and before 1698 there are traces of him in North Carolina, Virginia, Pennsylvania, and the Barbadoes. His missionary activities on the Eastern Shore led to the formation of four or five churches, including Rehobeth and Snow Hill in Maryland. Some time before 1698 he married the daughter of a wealthy Accomac, Virginia, landowner and permanently settled on the Maryland-Virginia boundary of the peninsula. He continued his work to the northward, however, until his death. His great achievement was the organization in 1706 of the Presbytery of Philadelphia, which brought together scattered Presbyterian ministers in Maryland, Delaware, and eastern Pennsylvania. His principal literary work, to be considered in the next chapter, was his sermon-form apologia or defense of freedom of worship directed at Lord Cornbury, governor of New York, who had flagrantly violated all acts of toleration by imprisoning Mekemie.

The colonial Baptists of the upper South belong primarily to the eighteenth century, though they too were in Maryland at least fairly early in the seventeenth. Huguenots had reached Virginia as early as 1688 and many came between 1700 and 1701, but theirs too is an eighteenth-century story. The Lutherans and other German groups likewise belong in the second century. Jews seem to have arrived in Virginia is early as 1621, and here and there is evidence of their presence in the Chesapeake Bay area throughout the century,[54] but they apparently were absorbed into the Christian population, died out, or migrated. The Labadists of Bohemia Manor in Maryland, who procured a large tract from Augustine Herrman in 1684 and lasted until well into the third decade of the eighteenth century, are remembered as experimenters in an early American utopia. Though of French origin, the communal organization was made up principally of Scandinavians, Germans, and Dutch.[55]

Another incident of the politico-religious history of the seventeenth century primarily concerns Maryland, though it had at least repercussions in Virginia. It occurred in 1689 along with and as a concomitant of the struggle for the Protestant succession in Great Britain. It is frequently called "the Maryland Revolution," for it represents a rebellion of a Protestant "Party of Resistance" ("Protestant Association") against the intrenched "Proprietary Party." It was primarily political and economic in origin, but its effect on religion was impressive.[56] A generation of conflict lay behind it. Maladministration of justice, flagrant discrimination of patronage including offices, and the economic distress of certain groups were sparked into fire by the unwise insistence of Governor William Joseph that the Assembly swear allegiance a second time to Catholic James II. Involved too was a fear, repeated in countless letters, of a Papist-French-Indian uprising on the western frontier.

Leaders of the rebellion were themselves men of substance, the three principal ones, John Coode, Kenelm Cheseldine (Chiseldine, or Chyseldyne), and Nehemiah Blakiston (Blackiston), all sons-in-law of Catholic Thomas Gerard (Gerrard), had held various offices in the colony and all had been members of the Assembly. Coode, the nominal leader, has been as much written about pro and con as any colonial political figure.[57] Hot-tempered, avaricious, blasphemous Coode certainly was. But he was popular, intelligent, educated, a natural leader who could stand firm. Cheseldine and Blackiston, even more than Coode, were men of substance and education, the former attorney-general before this uprising and the latter governor several years after the revolution. Henry Jowles and Ninian Beale, the latter a Presbyterian, were also prominent in the affair.

Coode, finding that the Maryland government had delayed recognition of the new Protestant monarchs in England (a messenger with the news of the accession had died en route) and yet in the preceding year had joyfully proclaimed a Catholic heir to the throne, led the militia company of the "Protestant Association," of which he was captain, to Annapolis and seized the government. He and his colleagues represented to the King that the Proprietor had forfeited his rights and that the Association had acted only in the Crown's behalf. He called an election of an assembly and to this body he and his associates surrendered the power they had seized. With Cheseldine he sailed for England in 1690 to prove the charges against the Proprietor. Coode was later on in much personal trouble again and was refused a seat in the Council because he was said to be an Anglican priest (it has now been proved that he was ordained by the Bishop of Exeter). He died in 1709, leaving six children and four plantations.

But the colony was placed under royal government, Lord Baltimore being allowed only his income from it. The majority of the new governor's Council in 1692 were anti-Proprietary. Cheseldine was speaker of the house. One of the Assembly's first acts was for "the Church of England as by law established" in the mother country, with descriptions of the powers of the vestry, the setting up of thirty parishes in the ten counties, with other forms quite similar to those in Virginia's establishment. An additional act in 1695 provided for churchwardens, organizing of vestry, and appointment of clerks, all of whom were to take oaths appointed by Parliament instead of the old "Oaths of Allegiance and Supremacy" and to submit to the test. The last qualifications were difficult for Jacobite clergymen, and some of the clauses of the bill were passed over to the next session. A new act in 1696 with further details for an establishment was, like that of 1695, disallowed in Great Britain. In fact, no church act had been approved in England. In 1701, after Dr. Thomas Bray appeared as Commissary, an act similar to those preceding was sent off to England and, after Dr. Bray's tactful intercession and some amendments, was approved in both Great Britain and Maryland by March 16, 1701/2. It applied only to Anglican churches and specifically provided freedom of worship for all Protestant dissenters (Roman Catholics remaining under disabilities in all British territory until 1829). News of final approval of the establishment reached Maryland in June 1702, ten years after the Assembly had first passed an act for it.

A few words should be said about the Carolinas in the seventeenth century. The two were originally one colony under eight proprietors, and their "Constitutions" were drawn up by John Locke and Lord Ashley. Tacitly assumed (and later so expressed) was the Church of England as an establishment. So it remained, by tradition and later by official acts. But in practice the Anglicans were never the dominant religious group in numbers in North Carolina, and probably never a full majority in South Carolina. The Charter of 1663[58] to the Lords Proprietors permitted real religious tolerance and freedom of worship outside the Church of England, and not until the revision of the Fundamental Constitutions in 1682 was it explicitly stated that the Church of England be publicly supported by the building of churches and the paying of the salaries of clergy.[59] Though northeastern North Carolina was settled even before the charters by colonists from Virginia, their religious affiliations appear not to have been strong, for no record is known of practicing clergy among them or of appeals for clergy.[60] The terms a little later offered Sir John Yeamans and his Cape Fear settlers seem liberal, in that no person was to be molested for his practice in matters of religion. The first settlers were pretty clearly not Puritans or other dissenters seeking a religious haven, but migrating for economic reasons (good land). The Yeamans terms and subsequent events do demonstrate that dissenters and the unchurched were both present.

The first Christian minister known to have preached in North Carolina was William Edmundson, the Quaker referred to above for his work in Virginia and Maryland. As also noted, in North Carolina he was almost immediately followed or joined by George Fox. This was in 1672, and the area was the northeastern part of the colony adjacent to the strong Quaker and nonconformist region of Virginia. As their journals indicate, these pious men found a Quaker or two but preached largely to people long without any religious instruction, who heard them gladly. If these people had been Presbyterians or other organized nonconformists, as Weeks points out,[61] the Quakers would not have found conversions or "convictions" quite so easy.

The last quarter of the seventeenth century in North Carolina registered the high-water mark of Quakerism in the province and indeed in the southern colonies. The Anglicans did little or nothing in the colony; other dissenting ministers did not appear. In other words, the Quakers had the field to themselves. In 1694 John Archdale, a convert of Fox who had lived in North Carolina since 1683 representing his father, a Proprietor, was appointed governor. When the Anglican church was legally established in 1701 and the S.P.G. missionaries began to arrive, the Quakers became less powerful and perhaps less numerous, but they continued as a strong sect up to the Revolution.

In South Carolina the history of the Church of England is much like that in North Carolina, though the nature of those outside the church differed. Implicitly the colony was Anglican from the beginning, but an act for establishment failed more than once before it became firm in 1706. The first shipload of settlers reaching the site of Charleston was almost entirely English.[62]

Of religion in the very first years little is known. The Reverend Atkinson Williamson, an Anglican, was in Charleston in 1680, and the Reverend Thomas Barret, a dissenter, probably Presbyterian, in 1685. The city was laid out and operating by 1680, and the Church of England had built the first St. Philip's, on the spot where the present St. Michael's stands, by 1681–1682.[63] At the time the S.P.G. appointed its first missionary to the province, in 1702, there was only one Anglican clergyman outside the city, the Reverend William Corbin at Goose Creek.

But in 1680 forty-five French Protestants also arrived, probably among them in the first ship a number of dissenting English Protestants. In 1683 Lord Cardross founded a Scottish colony of ten families (10,000 people had been expected), presumably Presbyterian, near the site of Port Royal. Other French Huguenots drifted in, among them Isaac Mazyck in 1686 and the Reverend Elias Prioleau (naturalized in 1698). French settlements were all along the Cooper and Santee and at Goose Creek, but they rarely formed congregations separate from the Anglicans. From Dorchester, Massachusetts, came in 1695 a Puritan missionary group who settled at a place they named Dorchester. And in Charleston a Congregational-Presbyterian enclave organized and built the "Circular Church." They had a Harvard graduate, Benjamin Pierpont, as their first minister. His immediate successors were a Mr. Adams and John Cotton (1640–1699?), son of the celebrated John Cotton of Boston and also a Harvard graduate. There was also "the White Meeting," almost as old as St. Philip's, and a Calvinist French Protestant church built before 1693. A Quaker meeting house promoted by Governor Archdale was built about 1696. And the Baptist church was probably organized about 1685.[64]

By 1686 a Baptist minister had arrived from Maine, perhaps attracted by the known tolerance of dissenting or otherwise liberal governors. Anabaptists had congregated in Charleston by 1693, and in 1702 an S.P.G. missionary found many along the eastern branch of the Cooper. German and Swiss Lutherans may have filtered in gradually during the period, but their group migrations were to come later. Before 1700 a total of some 438 French Protestants had reached the colony,[65] a relatively small group who with their descendants were to make themselves individually distinguished reputations in the long stretches of South Carolina history.

By 1700 there were in the province two Anglican churches, four Presbyterian-Huguenot, one Presbyterian-Independent-Puritan, one Congregational, and one Quaker.[66] Up to that time these groups and the Baptists had worshipped side by side without known friction. Though it is not easy to judge the numbers in each group, certainly at this time there were more dissenters, taken together, than Anglicans. Though the Anglicans were never to have a clear majority in numbers (40 or 45 percent of total population seems to be as high as they ever reached), with the advent of the S.P.G. in 1702, the Establishment in 1706, and more pro-Anglican governors they grew steadily stronger politically as well as religiously. But the fact that the first generation was almost overwhelmingly dissenting in character was to affect the province's social, political, and spiritual history for the remainder of the colonial period and after.

With the advent of the new century and the foundation of the Society for the Propagation of the Gospel in Foreign Parts, the four existing southern colonies were by no means uniform in their spiritual or religious aspects. Virginia was overwhelmingly Low-Church Anglican, permanently altered away from English orthodoxy by puritan and dissenting elements in its early history. It was beginning to feel the pressures of strong new dissenting elements as Scots, Scotch-Irish, Huguenots, and German Lutherans began to people its frontier. The Anglicans were themselves somewhat divided politically into Jacobites and anti-Jacobites. Maryland, officially Anglican but with firm establishment a few years away, was estimated to have in 1700 about 25,000 people (exclusive of slaves), of whom 15,000 were nonconformist of little positive belief, about 5,070 Anglicans, and the remaining 4,751 Quakers (2,083), Roman Catholics (2,083), and Presbyterians (585).[67] From the reports of the early Quakers in North Carolina and of the first S.P.G. missionaries of 1702–1720 in that province it is probable that the majority of the people in 1700 were still unchurched. The probable South Carolina figures for the date are noted above. One may guess, if he includes the many unstaffed parishes in Virginia and Maryland, that the unchurched percentage for all four colonies was large, perhaps in aggregate one-third of their population. Probably more than another third were active nonconformists of firm convictions. That seventeenth-century Englishmen or Europeans were utterly indifferent to religion is most unlikely. The fault lay first with the Church of England, which never provided adequately for the souls of those they sent to inhabit the New World. Though by 1700 the Anglicans had seen and repented of their remissness, they could never recover certain qualities of their church for these Americans, who indeed by then did not wish them to. The stronghold of Anglicanism, such a recent historian as Carl Bridenbaugh calls the southern colonies in 1700; but if true, it was a vulnerable and poorly manned fortification. Its Anglicanism was adulterated wherever it existed; its people were coerced, lulled, or led into tolerance. The colonial southerner had much yet to undergo in the forms, ideas, and stresses of religion before the Revolution. Presbyterian zeal, Great Awakening enthusiasm, quarrels within the Establishment, deism and rationalism, were to be further factors in altering his spiritual perspective. But the great unchurched one-third were in large part to come back to religion, and with fervor, before these southern people became citizens of the United States.

Conversion of the Indian is touched on in other chapters. Conversion of the Negro will be considered in the present chapter's section on the eighteenth century and in the subsequent chapter. There are two vital religious matters, however, which span both the seventeenth and eighteenth centuries, one dealing with church organization and control and the other with religious superstition and its legal consequences, which should be considered before the story of the various denominations and movements peculiar to the 1700–1763 period are traced. Each tells something of the southern colonial and his religion.

WITCHCRAFT: THE DEVIL IN THE SOUTHERN COLONIES

A very good way of measuring certain features of the southern colonial mind is to examine its attitude toward witchcraft, or the practice of the black arts. That this practice was one of the most damnable of sins was a conviction shared by Roman Catholic and Anglican, Presbyterian and Puritan, by unlettered indentured servant and learned chief justice. The conviction had its roots in the Bible, in folk superstition reaching back into pagan times, and in the writings of contemporary theologians, including King James I.

In his *Daemonologie* in 1597 the future ruler of Great Britain had noted that the Devil was present "where [he] finds greatest ignorance and barbaritie" and that the abuses of witchcraft, derived directly from Satan, were "most common in . . . [the] wild partes of the world" such as Lapland and America.[68] Through the settlement at Jamestown, the sovereign-author became ruler over the barbaric as well as the civilized. He and his subjects became much interested in the form and results of the black arts among both the red and white Virginians. The literature of exploration and settlement is full of allusions to the Indians as followers of Satan in a quite literal sense. Court records give interesting indications of the colonists' attitudes toward instances of the crime among themselves. As the seventeenth century went on, there were fewer references to the Indians as the chief servants of Satan and more to the evil practices of transplanted Englishmen. Though a belief in black magic persisted even among some of the educated well into the eighteenth century, there never was in the southern colonies a "darkest page" of history such as the witch persecution hysteria left in New England's story. There was one (fairly certain) execution for alleged witchcraft in the South; one or two other death sentences were apparently never carried out; three poor old women were hanged at sea on the way to America in at least two instances by the passengers and crew allegedly against the captain's wishes; and some interesting trials took place. The dates of these trials and the execution tell us something, and the charges, jury statements, and jury charges much more.

But to begin with, the colonists took little time looking for the Black Man among their white neighbors. They found him too easily among their fearful and fascinating red neighbors. Even on the voyage of 1606–1607 to Virginia, Master George Percy noted the "Canibals . . . [who] worship the Devill for their God, and have no other belief." [69] That the Indians were devils is stated again and again. Captain John Smith describes their fiendish appearance and manner. Their chief idol, Okee, is usually designated, from Smith to Robert Beverley in 1705, as the inanimate representation of the Devil. Writing in 1612 William Strachey states flatly that the Indians worship only the Devil in this "Idoll which they entitle Okeus." In 1670 the Reverend Samuel Clarke gives a quite similar description, probably drawn in part from Smith, and in 1672 John Lederer, the explorer, notes their god Okee. Some narrators describe child sacrifice to the Evil One, the children, according to the Reverend Patrick Copland, being consecrated to Satan. The good puritan clergyman Alexander Whitaker pictures the natives along the Nansemond River in the very act of witchcraft, persuading the Devil, by their "anticks" and dancing, to bring rain. He thought "their priests . . . no other but such as our English witches are." [70]

For the New Englanders, Kittredge tells us, their Devil-worshipping red neighbors were "a constant reminder of danger from witchcraft." [71] Yet in southern colonies one who follows the record must believe that trials for witchcraft or for dealing in black magic had little connection with any white man's consciousness that the red man was practicing devilish arts. Witchcraft is a subject for discussion in courts from 1626 through at least 1706–07, but in no instances is it related to the demonism of the aborigines.

But for the southern colonists such evil in neighbors of their own race was another matter. Deeply imbedded folk superstitions could be and were buttressed by learned scholars. Even in the latter half of the seventeenth century Joseph Glanvill's *Saducismus Triumphatus; or, a Full and Plain Evidence concerning Witches and Apparitions* (1681) [72] and puritan preacher William Perkins' earlier "A Discourse on the damned Art of Witchcraft" (1603, etc.) were much more in evidence in southern libraries than antiwitchcraft rationalists such as Reginald Scot (1584), John Cotta (1616), and John Webster (1677), though at least Scot appeared in several libraries. William Byrd II owned copies of Glanvill and Perkins, books he may have inherited from his father.

In Virginia, as the colony increased steadily after the 1622 massacre, there were enough people to represent all kinds of sin, as the surviving court books show. Witchcraft was never the most prevalent, but from 1626 it appears sporadically in the General Court record of Jamestown. It and all other cases which reached this superior or supreme court originated before county courts or grand juries. In some instances they were actual trials of accused persons; in some, of persons who allowed executions, such as sea captains; in many others, civil suits brought by individuals defamed as witches against those who spread or made the accusations.

The Virginia case (or hearing) of September 1626 concerns Goodwife Joan Wright. The evidence, perhaps now incomplete, consists of a series of depositions attempting to prove her guilty of practicing witchcraft. [73] Trivial and absurd as these evidences appear today—of spells put on women in childbed, of mysteriously dying flocks of hens, of threats against impudent or lazy servant girls, of the use of red-hot horseshoes in urine to relieve illness—they seem to have been believed by the testators. Poor Goodman Robert Wright, in real perplexity, was only able to swear that in his sixteen years of marriage he had never seen such "evidences." The case was apparently not considered a strong one, for there is no evidence that Mrs.

Wright was ever brought to trial. The most one can gather is that, whenever she lost her temper, she pretended she possessed occult powers.

The next case, and indeed most of those of which record exists in Virginia and Maryland, came during the period of the Puritan Commonwealth in England. Possibly these cases were as much the result of increase in population as of Puritan influence. The first certainly bears no marks of Puritan attitudes or influences. In 1641 in Virginia Jane Rookens accused the wife of George Barker of being a witch. The depositions before the General Court, however, were directed against Jane Rookens as a scandalmonger. "The said Rookens" claimed she did not remember what she had said but was sorry anyway.[74]

That three executions for witchcraft occurred at sea on the way to America during this period has some significance. On June 23, 1654, depositions before the Council of Maryland, acting in its capacity as General Court, concerned a Mary Lee, who the seamen were convinced was a witch. The ship's captain, John Bosworth, claimed that he was holding a conference as to what should be done with her when the crew seized and examined her and found the privy marks of a witch upon her body. She was alleged to have confessed under considerable pressure. Even then the captain refused to order an execution, going into his cabin with orders that nothing should be done without his command. The crew (and probably passengers) went ahead with the execution, however. The hearing concerned the captain's guilt. He was exonerated. It should be noted that in this and the other voyage cases the incident seems to have occurred during a time of danger when a storm threatened to sink the ship.[75]

In the same year in Virginia, in notes taken from documents now lost, is the laconic entry, "Captn Bennett had to appear at the admiralty court to answer the putting to death of *Kath Grady* as a witch at sea." [76] In 1659 in another Virginia case John Washington complained against Edward Prescott for hanging a witch on the latter's ship outward bound from England. Submitting himself to trial, Prescott denied that one Elizabeth Richardson was hanged on his ship, but the record goes on to say that Prescott was not responsible for the action of Master (Captain?) John Greene and the crew and was therefore discharged.[77]

Meanwhile, on October 16, 1654, what was to become a familiar action —suit for slander—was brought to the Maryland Provincial Court. Richard Manship claimed that Peter Godson and his wife had declared Manship's wife to be a witch. After hearing the evidence, Justice Richard Preston ordered that the Godsons should pay all costs and acknowledge themselves sorry for the slander.

Across the Potomac in Northumberland County, Virginia, the Reverend David Lindsay in November 1656 brought accusations against William

Harding for "witchcraft, sorcery, etc." The twenty-four-man jury ordered ten lashes and banishment from the county for Harding, the only instance of actual punishment (except ducking) by a Virginia court. Lindsay, an Anglican Scot of excellent family and the voice of ecclesiastical authority in the parish, was militant puritan enough to have been the personal reason for the conviction.

In Virginia in 1657 Barbara Winborough was tried before the General Court as a witch and acquitted.[78] But by this time in other counties jurors were becoming incensed at the increase in gossip and accusation of witch-craft. On May 23, 1655, a "private court" held in Lower Norfolk ordered that henceforth persons making unproved charges of such a nature were to be fined one thousand pounds of tobacco and censured by the court. Four and a half years later the same court showed that it meant business when it ordered the husband of one Ann Godby, who had accused various women of being witches, to pay a fine of three hundred pounds of tobacco "& Caske" and defray all costs because of her contempt of the 1655 order. Perhaps Thomas Godby and other husbands like him, touched in that tender part the purse, complained to their legislative representatives. Whether moved to action by the Burgesses from Lower Norfolk or not, the General Assembly in 1662 passed "An Act for Punishment of Scandalous Persons" which gave the innocent husbands of such persons some protection:

> Whereas many babling women slander and scandalize theire neighbours for which their poore husbands are often involved in chargeable and vexatious suits, and cast in great damages. Be it therefore enacted by the authorities aforesaid that in actions of slander occasioned by the wife after judgment passed for the damnages, the woman shall be punished by ducking and if the slander be so enormous as to be adjudged at greater damages then five hundred pounds of tobacco then the woman to suffer a ducking for each five hundred pounds of tobacco adjudged against the husband if he refuse to pay the tobacco[79]

Thus at a period when the greatest English witch hunter, Matthew Hopkins, was at work in Great Britain,[80] Virginia colonists were becoming more and more skeptical regarding allegations of witchcraft, if we are to believe their treatment of such matters. And after the Restoration the skeptical treatment continued, as the 1662 enactment indicated it might. Lindsay, the only successful prosecutor in a witchcraft case, surely belonged at least to the puritan-Presbyterian wing of the Church of England, and may have been close to Puritanism. The Puritans, like their contemporaries, believed witches existed. The principal difference between Puritan and non-Puritan was that, though the former found evidences everywhere, the latter was extremely skeptical of alleged manifestations.

Between 1658 and 1662 the Reverend Francis Doughty, erstwhile New England Puritan, New York Dutch Reformed, and Eastern Shore of Virginia Anglican, was noted in his Charles County, Maryland, parish for his witch-hunting proclivities, as he was a little later in Rappahannock Parish in Virginia across the Potomac. He was a troublemaker, but apparently not a very successful one, for in 1661 the records show Joan Mitchell as suing him for accusing her of witchcraft.[81] In 1665 Maryland's General Court returned a bill that Elizabeth Bennett, suspected of practicing the black arts, was "not presentable." She was cleared by proclamation.[82]

In 1668, 1675, 1678/9, 1694, 1695, and 1698 Northumberland, Westmoreland, King and Queen, and Lower Norfolk County grand juries were still trying witchcraft cases or suits for slander, in every case the verdict being in favor of the person originally accused of practicing the Devil's arts.[83] The most famous of Lower Norfolk (Princess Anne after 1691) County cases was that of Grace Sherwood in 1705/6. This woman had as early as 1697/8 sued various persons for slander when she had been accused of witchcraft of various kinds. In her cases the accusers as defendants had the verdicts rendered in their favor. By 1705/6 the county obviously was tired of Mrs. Sherwood as a general nuisance. Two panels of women jurors were ordered to search her house for suspicious images, but both groups refused to serve. On July 5, 1706, a county jury of justices of the peace, wishing to settle this long-drawn-out affair, ordered Grace Sherwood "by her own Consent to be tried in the water by Ducking." On July 10 the order was put into effect and the poor woman floated though bound, a positive sign of guilt. Moreover, she had on her body the incriminating marks of a witch. She was committed to the "Common Gaol" and secured in irons. Here the records end, except for her will dated in 1733 and probated in 1740, which indicates the testatrix and the ducked woman were one and the same. That the name Witchduck, given a site on an inlet of Lynnhaven Bay, still exists is itself good evidence that such methods of trial were extremely rare in Virginia.[84]

The witchcraft story for Virginia ends with the Sherwood episode, and with much the same qualities it showed at the beginning of the Restoration. The Virginian, learned or unlearned, was likely to believe in witchcraft, as did the able lawyer William Fitzhugh,[85] but one may be sure that hundreds were highly skeptical, keeping quiet because they would be needlessly and uselessly opposing canon and biblical law. Believers or unbelievers, the colonial Virginians were rationalists enough, perhaps legalists enough, to demand strong evidence and not to be carried away by an hysteria such as developed among their pious neighbors of New England.

Maryland's record, though much like Virginia's on the side of common sense and rationalism, is not quite so good. In 1674 John Cowman, who was convicted in the General Court for witchcraft on the body of Elizabeth Goodale, was by the petition of the lower house of Assembly reprieved by Governor Calvert.[86] In 1686 Hannah Edwards was tried before the court after being indicted by a panel of justices including the prominent William Digges. The jury, most of whose names are well known in Maryland history, declared her not guilty.[87] In 1712 the Grand Jury considered the case of Virtue Violl, who allegedly caused the body of Elleanor Moore to pine away, and again not guilty was the verdict. But before either of these women had been brought to trial, in 1685 Rebecca Fowler was arraigned before the Provincial Court, which included several of the justices who heard the evidence about Hannah Edwards a year later. A jury found her guilty of practicing the black arts and causing the laming and wasting away of divers persons, including Francis Sandsbury, laborer, all of Calvert County. She was hanged on October 9.[88] One of her jurymen was also to serve on the panel which exonerated Hannah Edwards the next year. Actually the jury hedged on Rebecca Fowler, finding her guilty only of actual "facts" charged. They further stated that, *if* these facts constituted practice of witchcraft, then she was guilty; if the court found that the things charged in the indictment did not make her guilty of sorcery, etc., she was not guilty. The court had a respite until the next day, when the accused was brought in and condemned, presumably by the justices. Thus the one really certain "blot" on the southern colonists' record was decided not by the real jury of ordinary folk, but by a Calvert governor, his attorney-general, and his Council of gentlemen judges. How the evidence in the 1685 case differs from that in the 1686—the charges are quite similar—we do not know.

North Carolina's scattered and largely unlettered folk of the later seventeenth century seem to have retained their witch lore from old England,[89] but the first trials recorded, or preserved, of the crime are of the earlier eighteenth century. Three trials for defamation or for practice of witchcraft, all in the first dozen years, are almost all the evidence that remains. In one, undated but clearly 1702–1712, the plaintiff Ann _____ sues Sarah _____ for £200 sterling for accusing her of witchcraft in "false scandalous words." The verdict is not given. More definitely dated in 1703, Susannah, wife of John Evans of Coratuck Precinct of Albemarle County, was accused of specific arts of witchcraft on the bodies of a servant and the wife of John Bouchier. Apparently she was convicted in some court or at least indicted and had to appeal to a higher one. A few days earlier in the same precinct William Parker charged Martha Richardson with bewitching him and several others.

The general court for the county convened and fifteen men were impaneled to hear the charges against the two women. It is perhaps significant that the panel included Captain Cornelius Jones, a member of the Provincial Assembly, and Robert Wallis, a former member of the Council of State, both presumably educated and intelligent men. The jury deliberated and in both instances the verdict read "Wee of ye Jury find no Bill." [90]

Such is the tally for North Carolina, except for John Lawson's passing reference in *A New Voyage to Carolina* (London, 1709) that only two persons have "ever suffer'd as Criminals," one for murder, the other an old woman for witchcraft. The context mentions both execution and other punishment, though the implication here, in the coupling of witchcraft with murder, is of actual execution.[91]

South Carolina's known recorded history in relation to witchcraft is brief, and all in the eighteenth century. In a province inhabited by so many dissenters, including Puritans, Huguenots, and Presbyterians, one might expect earlier trials; if there were, they have disappeared with the many lost records.

In South Carolina, country folk as late as 1792 thought witches abounded in Fairfield, and in 1813 or 1814 a South Carolina judge silenced a girl for declaring, in an assault and battery case, that an old woman came through a keyhole. Curious evidences of belief in witchcraft also survive in a manuscript from York County in 1790.[92] All this superstition after the colonial period certainly indicates that it lay deep in the folk mind and that its bases were in English law and lore. But the surviving examples of colonial belief in the black arts are from educated Anglicans.

These examples occurred in 1706–1707. Those convinced that the black arts were being practiced were an S.P.G. missionary who was a doctor of divinity, and the chief justice of the province, who was one of the ablest jurists of colonial America. The clergyman, Dr. Francis LeJau, originally a Huguenot but then a firm Anglican, had arrived in the province just the year before. He believed strongly that he should Christianize the Indians and Negroes and convert the whites, and that witchcraft was openly practiced in South Carolina. The last belief came from his literal acceptance of ecclesiastical and biblical law, and it was bolstered by his wide reading in the Church Fathers and in contemporary theology.[93]

As far as we know, LeJau was not active in prosecution or persecution, but in a letter of April 15, 1707, to a friend in London he noted that his parish included "a notorious Malefactor evidently guilty of Witchcraft, & who has killed several Persons by the Devils help [and] was lately return'd Ignoramus by the Grand Jury; this makes me stand amazed that the Spirit of the Devil shou'd be so much respected, as to make men call open Witchcraft Immagination and no more." On July 3, 1707, to the same correspondent, LeJau mentions that "the Judge" was examining evidences relating to the accused witch "that is still in our Prisons, it don't belong to me to judge, but she said she will come off and that she has many friends here. It is a dismal Sight to perceive how powerfully the Spirit of the Devil contrary to that of Christ is here." [94]

In nearby Charleston the chief justice of the province who charged the grand jury probably agreed with him. This was Nicholas Trott (1662/3–1739/40).[95] The malefactor referred to by LeJau was probably a woman who had been confined in the Charleston jail from early 1706. The uncovering of LeJau's letter in this century seems to explain a hitherto puzzling and elaborate "charge" by Trott surviving in a manuscript volume in the Charleston Library Society. It was puzzling because, as Wallace says, "Judges are not accustomed to charge juries on matters not likely to demand their attention." [96]

Nicholas Trott, able but controversial figure in his own time and in ours, was a learned and genuinely devout man who wrote, compiled, and published a great deal which will be considered elsewhere. His charges to juries display his unusual learning in several languages, including Hebrew, and his cast of mind. The manuscript volume includes these words:

> But this I think I may very well assert, that they that have given us good proof of *Apparitions* & *Witches*, have done Service to the common cause of Religion: for if there be such Creatures as Witches, then there is certainly Spirits by whose aid and Assistance they Act, and by consequence then there is an other invisible world of Spirits.
>
> Now though I am not at all inclined to believe every common and [idle?] story of Apparitions and Witches neither would I have you be credulous on things of that Nature, especially when they come before you in a judicial manner; Yet there is such Creatures as Witches I make no doubt, and neither do I think that they can be denied, without denying the truth of the holy Scriptures, and most grossly perverting the sense of them.
>
> Now that the Scriptures do affirm that there are Witches and Magicians, is evident, from so many Places that might be produced out of them, that time will not permit me to recite them to you.
>
> I shall therefore . . . .

Trott continues with innumerable references, and quotes Latin, Hebrew, and Scripture. He endeavors to explain the meaning of the original Hebrew text of the Old Testament upon the subject. He warns not to punish without fully reliable witnesses, and more than one, pointing out Exod. 22:12 and Deut. 17:6 as bases for judgment. In the margin he notes significantly "Perkins of Witchcraft c. 7 & 2, p. 644" and "Mather's Cases of Conscience & concerning Witchcraft." [97]

Trott, a High-Church Anglican, is showing that the skeptical rationalism perhaps present earlier in the Chesapeake colonies and prevalent later
in this century among some of the educated men in South Carolina is not
his way of thinking. Though only these two references from learned men
have survived from early South Carolina, they show among other things
the lingering of belief in literal interpretation of the Scriptures, often called
a puritan trait, among the leading people. The witch accused appears to
have escaped the death sentence or at any rate execution, perhaps because
of or despite the instructions Trott gave the jury. Of course the conviction
that the black arts were practiced in their world was one the two learned
gentlemen shared with thousands of Englishmen of the preceding century,
who had executed many more witches than did the Puritans of New England.[98] The conviction was the common heritage of humanity. Despite
what is apparently LeJau's positive assurance of guilt, the impressive thing
about Trott's charge is his calm, reasonable, and legal way of handling the
question, well worth comparing with our records of procedure in the New
England trials fifteen years earlier.

BISHOPS AND COMMISSARIES

Another great religious problem began in the seventeenth century as
a peculiarly Anglican one, but it was to continue throughout the colonial
period and become of vital concern to dissenters as well as members of the
Church of England. It was the matter of a colonial bishopric, for individual
colonies or for all British America. Two books and scores of essays have
commented upon this problem in its intercolonial and intracolonial aspects,
and almost all histories of the Episcopal Church in early America have perforce discussed it.[99] Involved in it is the commissarial system, which came
into being a decade or so before 1700. Its secular political implications are
also significant.

Some of the backgrounds of the problem lie in elements of the American Anglican system already discussed. What prelate or prelates in England
had jurisdiction over the first scattered Anglican churches in Virginia and
Maryland was not clearly settled by any law. Though the Archbishop of
Canterbury was always interested and often corresponded directly with
American clergy and laymen, as far as existing records indicate the Bishop
of London was the first of the episcopacy to be principally concerned with
the colonies. A tradition of the Restoration period was that the latter's
authority rested on an Order in Council issued in the Laudian era. A more
likely origin for this authority is that it gradually evolved from the Bishop
of London's personal and business interest in the Virginia colony when he
was a member of the old Virginia Company.[100]

In the first years there was little need for episcopal supervision, but, as time went on, the Council for Virginia applied to the Bishop of London for aid in securing more ministers. He responded quickly. Though he was able to do nothing during the Commonwealth, with the Restoration he became very active in colonial affairs. That he was actually in charge of the Anglican church in America is evident in a letter of July 18, 1666, from Thomas Ludwell, secretary of Virginia, to Secretary Lord Arlington, in which Ludwell observes that the clergy "are subject to the see of London and have no superior clergyman among them,"[101] certainly more than a hint that some sort of prelate be appointed to have direct supervision in the colony. A letter from Maryland of May 25, 1676, from the Reverend John Yeo, to the Archbishop of Canterbury, complains more directly of lack of Anglican clergy and need for supervision of those actually in the field.[102] Thus by the last quarter of the century the Bishop of London was at least by precedent the diocesan for America, but the relationship would seem to have been neither ideal nor even mildly satisfactory.

Certain ecclesiastical functions did belong to the bishop in England. He, or one of his peers among the bishops, had to ordain the clergy going out to the colonies. This gave a certain control, but for colonial natives who wished to be ordained, or others such as colonial schoolmasters who decided to enter Holy Orders (and there were many of them), this was a great hardship. Ecclesiastical functions such as consecration of churches, holding visitations or conventions, and superintending the conduct of the clergy were delegated before the end of the century to the bishop's commissaries, of whom more later. Appeals, however, went to the archbishop or some great officer of state, not to the bishop. The civil part of an English bishop's jurisdiction, such as probate of wills, marriage licenses, and collations or inductions to benefices, was vested, as already noted, in the colonial governors, who were within their bounds the "ordinaries" of the Bishop of London or were in limited areas lay bishops.[103] In the royal colonies, it has been observed, the candidates for clerical appointments were presented by vestries and inducted into their cures by governors, or even presented and inducted by governors, at least by law. In practice, the governor sometimes appointed directly and the vestry refused to allow induction (whether the man was presented by some of them or by the governor), for reasons already noted, the principal one being that this power of refusal and of removal was their only safeguard against unworthy clergy. Maryland's proprietary government made for a slightly different system. The Proprietor had the sole right of presentation and induction (the latter through his own appointed governor). Though the bishop might have moral weight, he had no legal or coercive force.

The appointment of Henry Compton as Bishop of London in 1675, a post he held until 1714, resulted in new and direct interest in the colonial Anglican church. Alarmed and amazed when he discovered in 1679 that there were only four Church of England clergymen in North America outside Virginia and Maryland, he found money for a church building in New England and bounties for clergy and schoolmaster going to the colonies. He had a patent issued to him which gave him ecclesiastical authority over the clergy and over matters concerning houses of worship and divine service. Beyond that he had no authority, no right to send a suffragan bishop, no power as regards the conduct of the laity of the church. Even his patent expired at his death. But Compton was a most competent ecclesiastical administrator and a genuinely intelligent man. Despite lack of tangible authority, he did a great deal to strengthen the church in all the colonies, and especially did he strengthen it in Virginia and Maryland and in the last years before his death in the Carolinas.

Searching for some means of supervision, he found that all he could do was to appoint commissaries, or bishop's representatives, to perform such duties as the bishop should assign them. No set of instructions from the Bishop of London to his commissary in Virginia survives, nor does any file of regular reports. The commissaries in Virginia and Maryland were confined to overseeing the lives and character of the clergy and holding clerical conventions or visitations when matters of importance demanded. Issues between minister and vestry or congregation went to the governor and Council of the colony.

The Reverend James Blair, minister of Henrico Parish, was appointed first commissary for the colony of Virginia on December 15, 1689. He is usually considered the first and sometimes the ablest[104] of all the commissaries of colonial America. He served fifty-four years. For Maryland that remarkable missionary spirit, Dr. Thomas Bray, was appointed commissary in 1696, several years before the Anglican church was fully established and three or more years before his own short visit to the colony.[105] Bray did much for his church in America, but less as resident commissary than at home in England. Before he arrived, the Maryland Lower House noted that "when Doct: Bray Arrives in Quality of a Suffragan Bishop the right of Marriage License will properly belong to him."[106] As for the matter of bishopric, which neither Bray nor any other Anglican ever received for America during the colonial period, Bridenbaugh, in *Mitre and Sceptre*,[107] makes the Anglicans who wanted a bishop in America villains, plotting conservatives, and enemies to freedom although he is concerned principally with the colonies in which the church was never established. Actually, established or not, a church which wished for the authority inherent in its laws was hardly insidious, treacherous, or even anti-libertarian in so wishing. The average Englishman at home or abroad was still at least nominally an Anglican, and it was his co-religionists in the colonies who saw the necessity for proper authority if their kind of Christianity was to survive or take the place commensurate with that which it enjoyed in England. From a very early period, earlier and more frequently than Arthur L. Cross discovered in his useful and balanced *The Anglican Episcopate and the American Colonies*, some Virginians saw the only solution for their church problems in a resident bishop. When such a solution was proposed time and again, it met with accident or with opposition, much of the latter outside Virginia and Maryland, in the middle and northern colonies, which feared "infiltration" and Anglican "tyranny," and among the Whig-Dissenter politicians in Great Britain. If even one bishop had been secured, the whole history of the Episcopal church in America might have been different, and of course political history also would have been altered.

The question of an American bishop had been thought of before Ludwell's letter of 1666. Laud's plan to send a bishop to New England, for quite different reasons from those later argued for sending one to the Chesapeake colonies, has been noted. In 1662 Roger Green published *Virginia's Cure; Or, An Advisive Narrative Concerning Virginia*,[108] devoted to the unhappy state of the church and a remedy therefor, which would include a "Bishop . . . so soon as there shall be a City for his See."[109] Though the pamphlet is valuable chiefly for its detailed description of population dispersion, occupied land, rivers, and the present clergy and their problems, it does suggest a township system such as New England's, which would have allowed for the Bishop's See but would hardly have accommodated tobacco planters. Ludwell gave a hint; Green, a suggestion.

In another decade, however, Charles II had gone so far as to have a charter prepared for the establishment of a diocese in Virginia, and an already resident clergyman[110] had been nominated by him to be the first bishop. This was the Reverend Alexander Moray (or Murray), a Scot who had been with the King in 1652 at the battle of Worcester and was in 1672 minister of Ware Parish, Gloucester County. Moray's letters[111] to his relative Sir Robert Moray, one of the founders of the Royal Society, reveal the Virginia clergyman to have been a learned, imaginative man who found exquisite pleasure in the sights and sounds of the Virginia woods, looked for rarities in stones and metals for his friends, and professed his love of country as "nixt the Gospel." In 1672/3, a public intimation was given in London that a meeting on February 6 was to be held at which objections might be raised. This announcement was signed by the Archbishop of Canterbury and the Bishops of London and Worcester. At the same time the prelates wrote to a Colonel Smith of Rappahannock and to others concerning Moray's doctrine. The last document in the case, filed with the others, is a petition from Moray to the archbishop asking that Colonel Smith and the others named be summoned to appear and state their objections to the petitioner.[112]

Brydon and other ecclesiastical historians apparently did not know of requests for information and of the petition. Brydon conjectures that Moray's death the next year put an end to the scheme. Another historian says the plan failed with the fall of Clarendon, another that it excited opposition because the "endowment was payable out of the customs." Any of these would have been reason enough, but it seems far more likely that Moray was accused of Presbyterian or other nonconformist doctrines and that the charges were at least partly substantiated. Apparently the King and Bishops had no other candidate at the time.

After this no formal steps were taken for a southern bishopric for some time. The Reverend Nicholas Moreau in a discontented letter to the Bishop of Lichfield in 1697 stated that if his "Lordship would send here a good Bishop, with a severe observation of the Canons of the Church, and eager for the Salvation of Souls," the Church would flourish.[113] In 1712 in a "Report of the Committee for Bishops and Bishopricks in America," the S.P.G. agreed that there should be two bishops, one seated at Burlington in New Jersey, and the other at Williamsburg in Virginia.[114] Meanwhile Dean Jonathan Swift had been corresponding in 1708/9 with Colonel Hunter, later to be governor of New York, concerning "my Virginia bishoprick," which Swift seems to have taken more than half seriously.[115] In 1724 the Reverend Hugh Jones in his *Present State of Virginia* entered a prolonged plea for the establishment of episcopacy in Virginia, though he admits that "the people's fear" of the abuses of English "spiritual courts" might cause them to oppose it at first.[116] As late as 1756 a layman, Graham Frank, a prominent merchant of the colony, gave the Bishop of London a candid appraisal of the state of the church in Virginia, including the vestry's power, the clergymen's inability to comply with the rubric, the Scottish Presbyterian schoolmasters turned Anglican clergy for the handsome livings, and above all the absolute necessity for a suffragan bishop or someone with more power than the commissary had.[117]

Meanwhile recently appointed Commissary Bray of Maryland between 1698 and 1702 presented "A Memorial Representing the Necessity of Constituting a Suffragan Bishop in Maryland."[118] He gave good reasons: several are the fairly obvious ones used by various people before him; others point out that the Roman Catholic success in other parts of the New World came from sending out bishops, and that in general the people of the colony really wanted a bishop. Apparently the S.P.G. supported Bray in this proposal, though nothing came of it.[119]

After Bray's time, in 1716, two commissaries were appointed for Maryland, the Reverend Jacob Henderson for the Western Shore and the Reverend Christopher Wilkinson for the Eastern Shore. In 1724 one or both the commissaries asked Bishop Gibson, then of the See of London, to appoint a suffragan bishop to administer discipline in America or in Maryland.[120] A number of ways of supporting the prelate were suggested, one being Henderson's offer to sell for £4,000 a 2,000-acre tract with a good house and building, the price a mere fraction of its value. Henderson certainly wanted the position himself, but he had enemies such as Thomas Bordley, the attorney-general, and his brother, the Reverend Stephen Bordley, who were determined he should not obtain the post. Governor Calvert supported Henderson, a Tory, but Bordley and the Whig group won.[121]

Henderson's suggestions were not forgotten, however, and in 1727 the Bishop of London sought to appoint as suffragan for or from Maryland the Reverend Joseph Colebatch (or Colbatch), rector of All Hallows Parish, Anne Arundel County. He was never consecrated. On December 10, 1728, Wilkinson wrote the Bishop of London that Colebatch had been prevented from leaving the country for the consecration by a writ of *ne exeat* issued by the court. The writ has never been found; it is not in the Provincial Court judgments for 1727–1731, and the Anne Arundel court (within whose local jurisdiction Colebatch lived) records are missing for 1724–1733.[122] Colebatch was a Whig and may have been the nominee of Bordley and his fellow Whig clergy. The writ of *ne exeat*, to prevent for various reasons a subject's leaving the realm, was perfectly legal and may have been an act of the governor or State, in Rightmyer's words, "to avert danger to the provincial polity from the admission of a bishop."[123] But it may also have been forced by the pressure of eminent laymen who in turn felt the pressure of lesser laity (nonconformist?) who did not want a bishop under any circumstances. More documentation might certainly determine whether this was a people's, a political party's, or a Proprietary governor's move (the Proprietary having been restored before this).

Though in the eighteenth century both North and South Carolina established the Anglican church, neither said much on the question of the episcopacy in the colonial period, and most of what historians have quoted from their citizens between 1763 and 1775 is anti-Anglican hearsay. That the Church of England did not forget or ignore the absolute necessity of bishoprics if the church was to succeed or prosper in America is borne out in one exchange of letters of 1751 between the then Bishop of London and the great English dissenter and hymn writer, Dr. Philip Doddridge. They were corresponding primarily concerning Samuel Davies and the Presbyterians in Virginia, and on a cordial and candid basis. The bishop took up one of the points Davies had made concerning the bad character of Anglican clergy and laity, suggesting that it was considerably exaggerated but that even if true, the remedy lay in one thing—bishops for America. The prelate pointed out how *intolerant* were the New Englanders when he had proposed two or three bishops for America. One of his telling points lies in the question, "Would they [New England dissenters] think themselves tolerated if they were debarred the right of appointing Ministers among themselves, and were obliged to send all their candidates to Geneva or Scotland for orders? At the same time they give this opposition, they set up a Mission of their own for Virginia, a Country entirely Episcopal . . . ?" Doddridge's reply[124] is a defense of Davies and of toleration as practiced by Presbyterian-Nonconformists, "But I freely acknowledge, my Lord, that I think it is a considerable hardship on those in the Communion of the Church of England there to be obliged to send hither for ordination." He goes on to say he finds among dissenters in the colonies tremendous opposition to Anglican bishops, but admits it originates in their notions of the terrible persecutions their forefathers suffered. And he concludes, "I could by no means satisfy myself in opposing what appears to me so highly reasonable, as that the Church established here at home, in the principle part of the British Dominions should have a full capacity of doing all which they think expedient in religion, with respect to themselves at least, as freely as any other Society or denomination of Christians in those parts." Thus spoke reasonable men in an age of reason.

The American episcopate, or the unsuccessful struggle for it, was not a matter of black and white, of Whig and Tory, of liberal and conservative. It was one thing in one colony and another in another; it was several things in a single colony. Certainly in the South in this period it occasioned no great alarms or antagonisms. And one might pause and say here that *in general* other southern Anglican parishes and vestries were modeled on the Virginia system and would have reacted much as the Virginians did. Most of the clergy were for it (with the probable exception at times of Commissary Blair) *if* they were themselves of good character and ability. Quite clearly most, but not all, the laity were opposed to it, because they rightly felt that it would raise taxes for ministerial support, might bring the dreaded ecclesiastical courts, and would end vestry-congregational control of parish and ministers, and thus their local ecclesiastical, moral, and petty-civil independence. But vestries fought governors' powers of induction more than they did an American episcopate. And some governors opposed the episcopate because it would take from them all the lay powers and perquisites they enjoyed as the Bishop of London's civil "ordinaries." We know that southern dissenters cannily joined with neighboring Anglican vestries in opposing bishoprics. We do not know whether the same governors who fairly consistently championed their constituents against Crown preroga- tive were also opposed to the episcopacy. It seems doubtful that, if estab- lished, a bishop in the southern colonies would have been able, had he so wished, to disturb dissenters in any significant way, and it is certainly true that a stronger clergy, in greater numbers, might have caused the church to prosper as it never did in this country until the twentieth century. What emerges from this confused and confusing issue is the fact of southern con- gregationalism within the Anglican church, a civil-ecclesiastical local gov- ernment of great independence which intended to keep that independence. In other words, what emerges is the same thing that comes out of the three- cornered vestry-governor-commissary matter of induction—the sturdy in- dependence of the people particularly as represented in their vestries, partly for moral but primarily for economic motives.[125] Many of the vestry lead- ers before the Revolution were themselves sons, grandsons, or other rela- tives of the clergy who had wanted an episcopate. Among them was Patrick Henry of Virginia.

THE EIGHTEENTH CENTURY THROUGH 1763

The year 1701 has already been noted as the watershed in the history of the colonial churches, Anglican and dissenter, for the incorporation by royal charter in that year of the Society for the Propagation of the Gospel in Foreign Parts affected all forms of Christianity along the southern sea- board. Increasingly disturbed by the fact that the Anglican church was virtually unrepresented by clergy in the middle colonies and in New Eng- land, and aware of the strength of the Quakers and other nonconformists in the South, Archbishop Tennison and Bishop Compton decided to form a missionary society. All English bishops were to recruit clergymen willing to go to America; those secured were to report to the Archbishop of Canter- bury and the Bishop of London for their blessing (and probably inspec- tion); and each missionary was to submit a report every six months to the secretary of the society on the state of his parish and on the actions and meetings of the clergy.[126] Commissary Thomas Bray of Maryland had a great deal to do with the founding of the society and its sister organiza- tion, the Society for Promoting Christian Knowledge (1699), known usually as the S.P.C.K. The two were joined in 1729 by a third group, "Dr. Bray's Associates."[127]

The missionary function of staffing and conversion in colonies already in existence belonged to the S.P.G. The S.P.C.K. sprang from Bray's desire to educate laymen and supply clergy with needed books, both in the United

Kingdom and in America. It would provide parish and circulating and provincial libraries and do necessary publishing on its own, as it has continued to do to this day. The third organization was designed to arouse interest in the moral and spiritual welfare of the Negro slaves. Though technically Maryland and Virginia were not fields of endeavor for the S.P.G., since the Anglican church was established in them, both they and their three sister colonies to the south were to be affected by these three organizations, in varying degree, throughout the remainder of the colonial period.

The eighteenth century was to be marked by the preaching and other work of able commissaries like Blair and Garden, great dissenters like Samuel Davies and Josiah Smith, and persuasive and eloquent parish and itinerant clergy, and by the well-known though brief labors of Charles and John Wesley, and above all, of George Whitefield. By 1763, through the Parson's Cause and other such incidents, the Anglican church was well on the road to disestablishment. The first Great Awakening affected, at least for the time, no part of the continent more than it did the southern seaboard provinces. And when these colonies had printing presses, clergy and laymen began to write on religion and publish sermons, tracts, catechisms, theological books, and countless newspaper essays. The southerner has never been inarticulate, and from early in this eighteenth century he was as prone to put on paper as he was to orate upon what he believed.

THE ANGLICANS

Before the end of the first decade of the eighteenth century the Church of England was formally established, as we have seen, in the four existing southern colonies. In certain respects it grew and prospered for a time; in others its story is that of lost or wasted opportunities. Though it might have embraced the frontier and the Great Awakening, it almost completely ignored the one and remained hostile to the other, thereby losing a great deal of its strength among all sorts of people. It did something for the Indian and a little for the Negro, though not enough in either case. When its Methodist communicants formed their own church in 1784, it lost for a number of generations its contact with the common people who had, during the colonial era, been its army if not its generals.

Much more information exists about the eighteenth-century Anglican churches than about the seventeenth. The commissarial system had become well established, and records of visitations or conventions and clerical responses to the Bishop of London's questionnaires reveal a great deal. Even more comes from the semiannual required letters, and voluntary letters, from the S.P.G. missionaries. Originally almost all these epistles were

from the Carolinas, to which the missionaries had gone before final establishment,[128] but within a few years men who had gone out to the colonies
as missionaries found established parishes in Virginia and Maryland much
more attractive than labors among a barely settled and often poorer people.
Though they gave up formal affiliation with the S.P.G., they continued to
write to its secretary about church conditions in their new parishes, about
the state of the clergy, and about conversion of Indians and Negroes, and
above all to ask for books for themselves, their parishes, and their provinces.[129] Other clergy, in support of or against their commissaries, or on
the church matters mentioned above, wrote frequently to Fulham Palace
(residence of the Bishop of London), Lambeth Palace (residence of the
Archbishop of Canterbury), or the S.P.G. headquarters in London.

At the visitations or conventions,[130] sometimes held annually but more
often sporadically according to the needs of the province, the clergy and
their commissary *and* governor discussed church business of varying kinds.
In Virginia, in Governors Nicholson's and Spotswood's time in the first
quarter of the century, the conventions were marked by acrimonious debate
between most of the clergy and the governor on one side, and Commissary
Blair and a few faithful to him on the other. In Maryland and the Carolinas
these gatherings were less tumultuous and marked with almost a unanimity
regarding local ecclesiastical problems.[131] In Virginia the clerical convention in 1719 had produced a bitter attack on Commissary Blair, led by the
governor and the Reverend Hugh Jones, and ostensibly concerned with
the question whether Blair had ever received Anglican ordination, though
the clergy really seem to have been attacking Blair for siding with vestries
against official induction as well as showing their general lack of confidence
in him. As already noted, the governor, who had had the power of induction at least since Nicholson's time, was on the side of the clergy. Blair,
who did not want his clergy too individually independent, supported the
vestries.[132]

But the minutes of these meetings do not tell as much about the religious
situation as do the questionnaires returned to the Bishop of London. Probably typical and certainly interesting ones survive for Maryland in 1714
and for Virginia, Maryland, and South Carolina in 1724.[133] That of 1714
for Maryland was composed of seven questions, perhaps drawn up by the
governor (since the general reply was in this instance directed to him).[134]
The combined answers indicate that, in contrast with Virginia custom, all
twenty-one parish ministers replying were inducted; services were held regularly on Sundays and holidays, but salaries were at the bare subsistence
level.[135] Each minister was principal vestryman in his parish (though in
some provinces there was a dispute as to whether he stood within or without
the vestry); all known clergy who administered sacraments were in orders;

the Bishop of London's jurisdiction was acknowledged here; schools were bad and schoolmasters insufficient; there were strict laws regulating marriages (especially incestuous ones); and assistance was begged against blasphemy, polygamy, and the growth of Popery. Other replies tell of the condition of church buildings, frequency of administration of sacraments, and condition of glebes.

Virginia replies are equally interesting. In 1704 forty-seven vestries' reports to Governor Nicholson concerning whether or not they had inducted their minister, and if not what they would do hereafter, were received.[136] This followed British Attorney-General Northey's opinion that the Acts of Assembly and other orders and laws gave the governor the right to induct. Only two had been inducted; a few parishes would consent to induct if absolutely necessary; the rest were strongly against it, some claiming that their clergy were satisfied as they were, others that from time immemorial choice of clergy in Virginia had been the vestries' right.

More generally revealing are the frequently lengthy and sometimes humorously pithy answers in 1724 from South Carolina, Maryland, and Virginia.[137] And it is worthwhile to compare these with the Reverend Hugh Jones' comments on the condition of the church in the same year, in his *The Present State of Virginia.*

South Carolina clergy said a great deal about schools and libraries. From another source (a letter of Commissary Johnston to the secretary of the S.P.G., June 12, 1712), we learn that South Carolina parish or vestry meetings voted on the selection of a minister. Johnston concludes that the church will never succeed in the colony until "Popular Elections are quite taken away." Yet in 1724, of the nine South Carolina clergymen reporting, though two had only recently arrived and had not yet been inducted and one missionary (for four years) had also not been, six had been inducted. These inductions may all have been by the consent of the people. It is perhaps ironic that to this day the "People" (vestry) continue to select and elect their clergy in the American Episcopal Church, while their Methodist descendants, usually considered more democratic at least as individuals, have their bishops select the clergy for particular parishes.

In Maryland the clergy of twenty-two parishes replied, all inducted under the patronage law of the Proprietor. In another generation Maryland laymen were to assume control as they had in Virginia, but the time was not yet. Questions of glebe and salary in tobacco, of sacraments, of size of parishes, of schools and libraries, and other matters are much the same as in the Virginia answers. Probably because they did not possess a college, there do seem to be more "free" and private schools in existence or being built in Maryland than in Virginia.[138]

Curiously, by what Brydon calls a strange perversity of fortune, and a most unusual one, in this particular year Virginia's fifty-odd parishes included fifteen without ministers.[139] From the resident clergy, only twenty-eight reports have been preserved, with three ministers stating that they held two parishes each. Despite the fact that only five were inducted,[140] the average length of service in one place was twenty-one years.[141] Parishes, though now frequently being divided, were still entirely too large for adequate pastoral care. Church buildings built of wood or brick ranged from one to four per parish. The ornaments of the church, lectern Bibles, large Prayer Books, vessels for celebration of the Holy Communion, various cloths, the surplice, and the font appear to have been supplied in most churches, though one lacked both font and surplice. The glebes, supposed to be land of two hundred acres or more provided by the vestry, and with proper buildings, seem to have varied from parish to parish. Too often the clergy report them as worthless, and in general they seem to have been unsatisfactory. Schools are discussed elsewhere.

Though some men reporting in 1724 supplemented their reports with letters going into further detail, and some of the reports spend pages on particular inquiries, the most comprehensive survey of the Anglican situation in Virginia—and in many respects it holds for all the other southern colonies, especially Maryland—is Hugh Jones' *The Present State of Virginia* (London, 1724),[142] in Part III and in Appendix II. Naturally Jones has the clergyman's point of view, and one recalls that earlier in his life he had been a bitter opponent of Commissary Blair.[143] But here his disinterested zeal seems the distinguishing trait of his comment.

Jones had come to Virginia in 1716 as master of the grammar school of William and Mary and the next year was appointed professor of natural history. In 1721 he was back in England for a three-year stay, during which he published his history and *An Accidence to the English Tongue*.[144] Soon after his return to Virginia, probably because of Blair's continued enmity, Jones removed to a parish in Charles County, Maryland, and later to Cecil County in that province. Before his death in 1760 he was well known as official mathematician for the survey of the Maryland-Pennsylvania boundary, for his published sermon against Popery and other writings in magazine and pamphlet form in Maryland and in Great Britain, and as a devout and able pastor. His parishioners clearly loved him, and he was a personal friend of certain of the Calverts.

But in 1724 he was thousands of miles from Virginia, which he could view with a certain detachment combined with zeal. He corroborates in general the individual reports of the clergy made in the same year, pointing out weaknesses in salaries and inadequacies in glebes. He wisely advises clergymen coming to the colonies to expect to adjust in many minor matters, including use of the rubric. He commends the fine brick churches now replacing timber edifices. He feels that the clerk of the vestry too frequently assumes too much power; he suggests that unconfirmed persons admitted to the Lord's Supper should undergo a brief examination before admittance. The baptism of Negroes and Indians, he observes, is still a highly debatable question with many colonials, but he believes that by education the red and the black may be prepared for baptism to everybody's satisfaction. For absolutely wild Indians and newly imported Negroes, he thinks baptism would be prostitution of that sacrament. The children of these people, as other Indians and Negroes, should undoubtedly be baptized after due preparation.

In an appendix Jones offers a solution for the church's governmental problem in Virginia and in North Carolina. He prefers a bishop, but until such time as a prelate can be obtained he suggests a dean, who would have greater powers and duties than a commissary. The same man might have jurisdiction over North Carolina as well as Virginia and improve the church's deplorable condition in the former colony. And he warns that though Virginia might support its own episcopacy, caution should be taken "not to transplant with it the corrupt abuses of spiritual courts," [145] the old fear of most colonials. Above all, he proposes new ways of equalizing clerical salaries.

Such an analysis would without great variation serve for the other southern colonies, though matters of salary, induction, and ecclesiastical courts did differ. Besides the Anglican relation to the Great Awakening, to be discussed along with that of the Presbyterians, two further features of southern Anglicanism should be noted—the character of clergy and people, and the church's attitude toward the Negro.

In the nineteenth century historians general and religious were inclined to charge that the corrupt character and evil living of the clergy sent by the Bishop of London was the greatest cause for the church's loss of membership before and disestablishment after the Revolution began. Even Bishop Meade tended to agree about the truth of the charge. Actually it came almost surely from dissenting elements within the South and from the descendants of New England Puritans who wrote most American history before World War I.[146] There is no doubt about the fact that alcoholics and a few sexual deviates found their way to the southern (and other) colonies in Holy Orders. From the London Company period to the Stamp Act, the church assumed that a troublemaker at home (and he might have been merely a puritan) might employ his energy to better purpose in a foreign field. A fair number of cases against clergy appear in county court records and general court minutes of all the southern colonies, the great majority concerning chronic alcoholism. There were inveterate gamblers, seducers of women, and embezzlers among them, but considering the hardships and relative unattractiveness of the situation to well-established holders of cures in Great Britain, it is remarkable that there were so few.

Another charge made as early as 1697[147] against Commissary Blair, a Scot, was that he gave preference to his countrymen, including several who had no Anglican ordination, and that the Scots were the leading offenders among Virginia clergy. Blair showed clearly that his blackest shepherds were almost all Englishmen, though he did not refute so distinctly the other charges. In fact, after the first generation or two of English clergymen in Virginia, there were always a large number of Scots, including the prominent Alexander Moray and David Lindsay already mentioned. In Maryland and the Carolinas Scottish names are frequent, including that of Commissary Garden of South Carolina. Scotch-Irish and Irish also were represented in considerable numbers. Occasionally a parish complained about the French accent of its formerly Huguenot minister. The S.P.G. missionaries were in general less satisfactory than the men who came under other auspices. And Bishop Meade says flatly that the best of the colonial clergy, with whom there was never any trouble, were the native-born and those who had been educated at William and Mary.[148]

The letters to the Secretary of the S.P.G. often show the natures of unpleasant clerics. John Urmston(e), from 1709 until his death in a drunken fit in 1732, served first as missionary in North Carolina and then in parishes in Pennsylvania and Maryland. His communications are querulous, truculent, demanding. One historian says he did more to retard the spread of Christianity through the Church of England, while he was in North Carolina, than all other causes combined.[149] Bitter Giles Rainsford, beginning in North Carolina as an S.P.G. missionary, never got along with fellow clergy or people there or in Virginia or Maryland. But as the period came to its close, one who examines the records can see that the vast majority had shown themselves throughout the century preceding as earnest, hardworking, devout men who literally gave their lives to the church.

Space allows only a brief discussion of the careers of the most able of the southern commissaries, James Blair, Alexander Garden, and Gideon Johnston. Blair of Virginia has already been noticed several times and will be considered again in his connection with the Great Awakening and in the next chapter in the form and content of his sermons. Much has been written about him, though no study can be called definitive since no really comprehensive assessment of his religio-political role during his fifty-four years as commissary has yet been made.[150] Founder and president of the South's only colonial college, minister of Bruton Parish, active member of the governor's Council, as well as commissary, he and his career have been called by Brydon "a tragic failure." [151] Brydon bases his conclusion on what he considers Blair's inability or refusal to recognize "wherein lay the true strength and power of his position as commissary" and declares that this more than any other one factor was the direct cause of the Church of England's loss of the people of his own and other colonies.[152] Blair's weaknesses as educator and commissary, even of character, have been pointed out in this and in Chapter III. Apparently devout, he undermined governors who supported his clergy and secured their dismissal. By maneuvers in the Council and letters to ecclesiastical and other authorities in England, he blasted the reputations and the work of clergy and laymen who did not see church government as he did. His seriocomic encounters with the fiery but able Governor Nicholson are the raw materials of an entertaining dramatic farce. His inability to keep good men, such as Hugh Jones, in Virginia parishes and his equal inability to secure other good men to fill vacancies was in part his own fault. Yet he was able to found and endow a college and secure some very able professors, though again he was not always able to keep them. And under his ecclesiastical leadership parishes multiplied. He spoke and wrote well. His sermons on *Our Saviour's Divine Sermon on the Mount* are practical as well as apparently sincere. He had some friends and many enemies, among the latter scores of able clergy and the urbane layman William Byrd II.

Irish-born Gideon Johnston (c. 1671–1716),[153] who came to South Carolina as commissary in 1707 and was drowned nine years later, did all he could to get his newly (1706) established church organized and to promote schools which would give Christian education to whites, Indians, and Negroes. His letters to the S.P.G. and to the Bishop of London and his instructions to the clergy afford vital evidence of his exertions. Klingberg believes that it was he who built the church in South Carolina so firmly that it was able to survive the visits of George Whitefield and the Great Awakening, even though what Johnston left was a thoroughly Americanized version of Anglicanism.[154]

Alexander Garden (c. 1686–1756) succeeded Johnston, after two years, as rector of St. Philip's in Charleston. He was appointed commissary in 1726 for both the Carolinas and the Bahama Islands.[155] Pious, devoted, and austere, he controlled with a strong hand until his retirement twenty-three years after appointment. His greatest difficulties were the usual ones, in securing clergy, schoolmasters, and buildings; and an unusual one, his fight with George Whitefield and the nonconformists, of which more later. He did much for the education of the Negro and would have liked to do more; his school for the slaves operated for more than twenty years. He was of assistance to John Wesley when that young man arrived in Charleston on the way to Georgia. He is remembered for his sermons and his tracts, the latter primarily against Whitefield and his followers.

Courtesy of the University of Georgia Libraries

George Whitefield preaching. Engraving by R. Roffe from a painting by N. Hone

Courtesy of Charleston *Evening Post, The News and Courier*

St. Michael's, Charleston, completed about 1760

There were other able commissaries and clergy. Maryland was the working area for men like Thomas Bacon, Peregrine Coney, Thomas Cradock, John Gordon, James Sterling, and (for the latter part of his career) Hugh Jones. Virginia parishes were held by scores of able men, from Alexander Whitaker through Bartholomew Yates and William Stith to James Maury and John Camm. In North Carolina Clement Hall and Michael Smith were men of some distinction. In South Carolina Dr. Francis LeJau, Samuel Quincy, and Richard Clarke were among the parish clergy who showed character and ability. Though many letters to the Bishop of London or to the Secretary of the S.P.G. complain of unlearned clergy, one has only to examine the lists from each province in E. L. Goodwin, Nelson Rightmyer, Frederick Dalcho, W. S. Perry, and other sources to see that the overwhelming majority were English-university educated, with some from the Scottish universities and Trinity College, Dublin, a few from Harvard, and later a few from the College of William and Mary. Some of the first-generation Huguenots were of course graduates of continental universities. One clergyman was a Spaniard. The learned references and general style of Anglican tracts and sermons examined in the next chapter bears out the assumption from biographical data that there was nothing wrong with the education of parish clergy before the American Revolution. The very letters expressing parishioners' complaints of unlearned priests would themselves bear this out: these occasional complaints came from people accustomed to erudite clergy.

Their constituents or communicants as such have left less record, but there is enough in vestry books, county court files, and scattered papers to show a great deal about them in relation to their religion. Since from the revival of the Episcopal Church in the earlier nineteenth century it has usually been considered the church of the socially elite, at least until quite recently, some historians have taken for granted that this was true for the colonial period. But one should recall that it was the only church in Virginia for most of the people for well-nigh a century, and that in the other colonies it attempted to appeal to persons of all ranks and conditions of men, including Negroes and Indians.[156]

In a time when freeholders elected to their Houses of Burgesses the leading gentlemen of their county, parishioners great and humble elected to the vestries the leading laymen—*leading* in the sense of most prominent for political, economic, and social reasons. As already noted, vestries became largely self-perpetuating. In the Chesapeake Bay and Low-Country South Carolina parishes they continued to consist, throughout the period, *in general* of these leading citizens, who performed their duties with the same sense of *noblesse oblige* (together with presumed piety) they showed from that time to the Civil War in their political duties. In North Carolina, so strongly dissenting in proportion to population, when the S.P.G. and the church were established a clergyman complained that his vestry included two professed Anabaptists, three vehement Scotch Presbyterians, one descended from Quakers and never baptized, and no one of them a genuine friend to the Church of England.[157] Everywhere the records show a noticeable difference between backwoods and more settled parishes in the social and educational background of the vestry, though even in the more remote areas there were usually men of culture and refinement to serve as churchwardens and clerks.

The laws regarding church attendance were enforced in the Chesapeake Bay colonies and in the sections of South Carolina most strongly Anglican. The vestry and county court records of fines and other punishment for non-attendance offer excellent examples of the occupations of parishioners. Besides those who pleaded dissent, there were Anglican laborers, small farmers, mechanics, millers, and saddlers. As the nonconformist groups successfully fought for their right to attend only their own church services, parish records continue to reveal that in large part Anglican congregations were composed of the middle and lower classes.

One significant evidence of the composition and occupation of parish laity lies in a petition prepared to be presented by "the poor" of St. Thomas' Parish, Orange County, Virginia, to Governor Gooch asking that their former minister be reinstated.[158] Granted that the parish was not an old settlement, it did present a cross section of colonial society. Allegedly "found" by the priest who himself wished for reinstatement, the document is in crude, somewhat ungrammatical language such as one might expect from a literate but unlearned parishioner. Incidentally, it also pictures graphically the hardships of clergy and laity in holding church services in a widely scattered frontier community. But it is the concluding pages which especially interest us. For here, laid off in columns or spaces for signing according to occupation but not by social rank, it includes persons by professions, many of them not at all usually to be included among "the poor." The alphabetical column-space order with occupational designations which do not begin with the same letter may mean that the author had in mind definite surnames which fitted these alphabetical divisions and the occupations he gives with them. For example, A–B is a column-space for "housekeepers" to sign; C–D for "Freeholder & Hotelkeeper"; E–F for "Planter"; G–H for "Com : of ye peace"; J–K for "Carpenter"; L–M for "Capt. & Vest: man"; N–M–O for "Servant-Mark"; P–Q for "Colo: & Com : of peace"; R–S for "sch : Maj : & ho : kepr"; [G?–U] for "Blacksmith : & ho : kpr"; V–[N?] for "Tailor"; X–Y for "Weaver"; Z–A for "Cooper"; and B–C for "Sh[?]er."

A more amusing example of the unlearned within the fold appears in a letter to Commissary Gideon Johnston of South Carolina dated April 3, 1716.

> Mr. Jonson
>
> I have Received Youre leater and in case I cannot have Mr White-head to Creason my Children at my hows I can have them Cresend by a desenter Minister which I dont Dout but they will git as sone to Heaven that way as the other which is all from him that is a lover of all Christians whilst I am
>
> Cha Burnham[159]

Occasioned by the commissary's refusal to baptize or have baptized except in the church, this is one more key to an understanding of the Anglican's disadvantage in competing with dissent.

Even lay readers and churchwardens were not necessarily men of high social rank. Or rather one might say that parish offices afford another indication that southern colonial society was still, at mid-eighteenth century, quite fluid. An example is Charles Hansford, blacksmith by trade and self-educated, who was lay reader and vestryman in old Tidewater Virginia. That he was kinsman of the rebel leader Hansford of Bacon's Rebellion and close personal friend of prominent lawyer Benjamin Waller of Williamsburg may indicate that blacksmithing was socially acceptable, that Hansford was but another member of "a nice" family (in old Virginia parlance) which had suffered economic reverses but had not lost caste. That he was a fair poet of some erudition may or may not have been known to his fellow parishioners. But the fact remains that here was a rural blacksmith in the golden age of Virginia plantation aristocracy who belonged to the vestry and read the Anglican service or at least lessons Sunday after Sunday.[160]

ANGLICAN AND OTHER ATTITUDES TOWARD CHRISTIANIZING THE NEGRO

Though the white man's, including the Anglican's, attitude toward the Indian has been considered in Chapter II, it is perhaps well to note here the southern colonial attitude toward Christianizing the Negro, for that was largely though not wholly an Anglican enterprise during the colonial period. It was much more than an enterprise: it represented a religious attitude, or attitude toward religion, based on a mixture of economic and social and moral factors.

For the first decades after 1619, usually accepted as the date of the first cargo of black human beings from Africa, the question of Christianizing was not a real one. As countless clergy and laity were to observe during the whole period of the African slave trade, newly arrived Negroes simply could not be communicated with because of language. But the Virginia law of 1632 requiring all masters to send "children, servants, and apprentices" to be catechized by the parish priest soon posed the problem.[161] The Negroes were usually termed "servants" and actually for a time were not under life servitude. Their children clearly fell under the edict anyway. Many masters were aware, however, of an English law which forbade the enslavement of Christians. As the African servant became slave, many planters absolutely refused to allow them to be instructed, catechized, or baptized. For a time it was not a pressing problem because of the language obstacle for newly imported slaves, but by 1667 the Virginia General Assembly found it necessary to pass a law declaring that baptism did not alter the condition of bondage or freedom for the individual.[162] In the revisions of the Fundamental Constitutions of Carolina, the statement added in 1669 that "Every Freeman of Carolina shall have absolute power and Authority over his Negro Slaves, of what opinion or Religion soever" was clear enough, though it was more euphemistically phrased in 1682:

> Since Charity obliges us to wish well to the Souls of men, and Religion ought to alter nothing in any man's civil estate or right, it shall be Lawful for Slaves, as well as others, to enter themselves and be of what Church and profession any of them think best, and thereof be as full members as any freeman; but yet no slave shall thereby be exempted from that Civil dominion his master has over him, but be in all other things in the Same state and condition as he was before.[163]

In the later seventeenth century many Negroes were baptized and some became communicants. Usually but not always these Christians were second or third generation Americans. Then as later their Christianization was largely a matter of what the master desired, despite laws like those of Virginia and the Carolinas. In many instances the master was simply indifferent or seemingly unaware that his Negroes had souls to be saved. In the 1680s and 1690s devout lawyer-planter William Fitzhugh was regularly buying African slaves and mentioning them in his letters, but his long-surviving correspondence of almost a quarter-century shows no concern for their spiritual welfare.[164]

The clergy were another matter. Though in the seventeenth century they recognized the problems attending conversion of the Negro, they showed genuine missionary zeal for bringing all men to Christ. The Reverend Morgan Godwyn, for example, who had served parishes in York and Stafford counties in Virginia for a few years before he returned to England, published in 1680 *The Negro's and Indians Advocate, Suing for their Admission into the Church: or a Persuasive to the Instructing and Baptizing* of *the Negro's and Indians in Our Plantations*, and in 1681 and 1708 published more on the subject. He was probably the first to raise the question in book or pamphlet form.[165] Included in the book's appendix is a heated letter written to Governor Berkeley in 1667, either just before or just after Godwyn returned to England.[166] Among other things, Godwyn blasts at "their *Plebeian Junto's, and Vestries*," which hire and admit ministers. He professes that all this criticism is out of love of the colony, which in many ways he prefers to England. In his view, the underprivileged red and black men had to be Christianized if religion was to survive at all. The young man overstates his case, but he initiates a procedure and attitude the S.P.G. and other clergy were to persist in for a century to come.

In the eighteenth century the S.P.G. and Dr. Bray's Associates, not to mention missionary-minded Bishops of London, spurred on the clergy in conversion and instruction. The periodical reports to headquarters usually commented on this matter. The answers to the Bishop of London's queries of 1724 vary a great deal. In Virginia almost all clergymen replying mention catechizing and baptizing the Negro. Occasionally masters are reluctant, but usually they consent and sometimes encourage. William Black on the Eastern Shore baptized two hundred Negroes and regularly catechized them at their masters' houses. Bartholomew Yates noted that masters allowed time for catechizing and baptizing.[167] In Maryland in 1731, after the Bishop of London had come out strongly about 1727 for conversion of slaves and the commissaries had stated bluntly that the clergy were most blameworthy on this score, the resulting replies of the clergy seem little different except for some evidences of greater activity among the slaves.[168] Among those reporting was Hugh Jones, who baptized both adults and infants at his church. The Reverend Mr. Cox noted that his parishioners allowed Christianization "to be a good thing" but generally excused themselves from promoting it among their own slaves because it was "impracticable."

Yet as the century progressed there was an increasing sense of responsibility for the welfare of the slaves' souls; and more and more Negroes were instructed in the Creed, the Lord's Prayer, and the Catechism, and sometimes in more detailed matters. Under the S.P.G. and Dr. Bray's Associates schools were established for them in the middle and southern colonies, in Virginia at Williamsburg[169] and Fredericksburg. With the S.P.G.'s help Commissary Garden set up in South Carolina a school that endured, as already noted, for more than twenty years, educating numbers of Negroes who were reported as late as 1822 to be sober, industrious folk who had never given "trouble."[170] In Georgia, where slavery was not permitted until 1749, the Trustees were most concerned for the Negroes' religious instruction and baptism. The conscientious minister Zouberbuhler in Savannah urged a school for them. Joseph Ottolenghe, a former Jew, was chosen in 1751 to direct the institution, which operated (with the help of Dr. Bray's Associates[171]) for ten years.

Commissaries such as Henderson and Wilkinson in Maryland, Blair and the Dawsons in Virginia, and Johnston and Garden in South Carolina cooperated with the missionary societies at home and their own clergy in this program of conversion. All of them used Bishop Fleetwood's strong 1711 sermon on the subject as propaganda in every political, social, and ecclesiastical quarter into which they could introduce it. From its founding in 1701 to the British Emancipation Act of 1833, however, the S.P.G. took the stand that a Negro could remain a slave and be a Christian.[172]

Though Commissary Johnston did all he could, he carried with him to London in 1713 a statement from his clergy of the obstacles in the way of conversion. The five points made are (1) that slaves have only Sunday for instruction, a time when it is impossible for a minister to give them time from his other duties; (2) plantations are so scattered it is impossible to get together enough for group instruction; (3) masters are generally of the opinion that a slave grows worse by being a Christian; (4) the legislature does not support the clergy properly in this matter; and (5) many planters allow the seventh day to the slaves only so that they can plant and sow for their own subsistence.[173] It is not strange that a physically ill Johnston was also mentally and spiritually depressed when he laid this statement before the S.P.G.

The surviving documents therefore indicate that the problems of conversion were in all five southern colonies much the same. Small insurrections such as those of 1730 and 1739 did not greatly disturb the onward progress in that colony, but fear of slaves and slave gatherings in the 1760s caused Georgia to prohibit teaching slaves to write and later even to read, laws sometimes imitated in other colonies. But the documents, especially those from Virginia and Maryland, indicate that the picture Commissary Johnston presented to the S.P.G. was exaggerated on the dark side, certainly for the Chesapeake provinces and perhaps even for the Carolinas.

The Anglican planters built their still lovely churches with slave galleries; and sermons for masters and slaves, as the four of Thomas Bacon in Maryland in 1750, were addressed to a black and white congregation, however it may have been segregated.[174] Some letters mention fear of slave insurrections, but almost all the correspondence of the colonial period regarding slaves, except that of the clergy, is not concerned with religion. William Byrd II in his *Diaries* has a great deal to say about his Negroes, and at one time he decided not to invite guests to Sunday dinner because by doing so he would prevent his Negro house servants from attending church.[175] A little later the Carters with whom Philip Fithian lived took their slaves to church with them, and not simply to be of service: "all the Parish seem'd to meet together, High, Low, black, white";[176] and another tutor noted the baptism of newly born Negro infants and his own teaching of the catechism to Negro children at Colonel William Daingerfield's.[177] Another Carter, Colonel Landon, left in his diary of the mid-eighteenth century a number of comments on his slaves and their religion. This complex man, deeply religious, rigidly moral, honestly tried to be fair to all human creatures. Though he had no faith in Negro character—"Indeed, Slaves are Devils"—he treated them as he did his own children, with discipline. The most constant churchman among his slaves was, he felt, a thief, rogue, and drunkard; the most religious displayed the most ingratitude; "some inculcated doctrine of those rascals" the New Lights (of the Great Awakening) he believed was responsible for the fact that throughout the colony the slaves were getting "worse." Yet he remained constantly aware of the Negro's humanity. When one slave had flagrantly abused his trust, he noted, albeit somewhat sanctimoniously, "After all I forgave this creature out of humanity, religion, and every virtuous duty with hopes though I hardly dare mention it that I shall by it save one soul more Alive."[178]

Though the Presbyterians were conscious of the souls of the slaves and felt a responsibility for them, the first considerable activity in conversion seems to have begun during the Great Awakening. The Reverend Samuel Davies of Hanover, Virginia, records in his letters and diary his own interest in the blacks. By 1749 Jonathan Edwards in New England had heard of Davies' "remarkable work of conviction and conversion, among whites and negroes." In 1755 Davies wrote to the London Society for Promoting Christian Knowledge about the poor of the "unhappy Africans" whom their masters were neglecting and whom he was instructing, catechizing, and baptizing in great numbers; he found them overjoyed to receive books of psalms and hymns, "which enable them to gratify their peculiar taste for psalmody."[179] They often spent the night in his kitchen, and he mentions being awakened at two or three in the morning by "a torrent of sacred harmony." Davies admits, with some surprise, that even Anglican masters offered no objections to their slaves' flocking to hear him.

The success of Davies and his immediate colleagues and followers was marked indeed, not only in Hanover but in the Northern Neck of Virginia.[180] John Todd, John Wright, John Caldwell, and other Presbyterian preachers attracted in their mixed congregations a large proportion of Negroes. Since Davies and the others visited North Carolina for long periods, they must certainly have carried on similar work in that province.[181] In South Carolina wealthy planter Hugh Bryan led in founding schools for and having Christian assemblies of Negroes. Perhaps because of the hardships of his early life, the pious Bryan was somewhat unbalanced mentally. He seems to have prophesied the destruction of Charleston and the immediate freeing of slaves, and he was charged with inciting slaves to insurrection under cover of religious meetings. But because of the respect of his neighbors, he was never brought to trial.[182] A young converted stage player, William Hutson, was the teacher in Bryan's school. Hutson was later ordained as a Presbyterian or Independent minister and served for many years.[183] In South Carolina as elsewhere George Whitefield attracted, converted, and baptized many Negroes, most of whom had become Presbyterians. But Presbyterianism in the Carolinas and Georgia slowly lost out to Anglicanism in the Low Country, or Tidewater, and gained in the backwoods and frontier, where there were few if any Negroes.[184] The great period for the evangelical sects in Christianizing or converting the slaves was to come after the Revolution.

Of course the Quakers, ardently for emancipation and proselytizing, also believed in instructing the Negroes in Christianity. Again and again in Yearly Meetings the matter was brought up along with the question of abolition.[185] But few Negroes ever became Quakers, and there is very little information as to what steps the Friends took to instruct them during the colonial period. John Woolman just before the Revolution knew only of a little religious instruction given slaves by New Lights and Quakers.[186] Henry J. Cadbury, the Quaker historian, speculates that the quietism, or quiet manner, of the Friends may have been one cause why few Negroes joined their ranks, but he also finds little evidence of attempts by Quakers at instruction or conversion of slaves before 1763.[187]

Full communion or full Christianization of Negroes in the southern colonies technically and to some extent morally lay with the Anglicans. As an established church, like the Roman and Puritan in other colonies, where there was more nearly complete Christianization, they might have enforced their beliefs and their legal right to bring the Negro into the church. But, as has been stressed here so many times, they were never in the position of absolute authority, or anything approaching it, that the Puritans or Catholics were. Their constituency, the planters and merchants, were too frequently hostile or at least uninterested or indifferent. The evidence would suggest that the clergy did all they could, as they did on the induction question, but that this was not enough.

THE PRESBYTERIANS AND THE GREAT AWAKENING

Though Presbyterianism and the Great Awakening in the South were no more synonymous than they were in the middle colonies, through a series of men and circumstances they were to have a close relationship. Therefore a survey of Presbyterians in the southern colonies from the beginning of the eighteenth century to 1763 must include as a large measure of their story their relationship to the great revivalist movement.

In the first thirty-odd years of the century the presbytery formed by Makemie and his followers continued to develop and branch out in Virginia and Maryland.[188] Groups developed in Stafford and other Northern Neck Virginia counties before 1725, though none seems to have survived for many years. From the Puritan-Presbyterian strength of the Maryland Eastern Shore came one of the four entities which in 1717 organized the Synod of Philadelphia. There were at that time no presbyteries or ministers south of Maryland and the Eastern Shore of Virginia except in South Carolina, too far away to be included in the synod.

The amalgamation, never really fusion, of Huguenot-Independent-Presbyterian elements in newly settled South Carolina has been mentioned. In 1710 a letter from Charleston reports Anglicans as about 42.5 percent, combined Huguenot-Presbyterian-Independents 45 percent, with Baptists 10 percent and Quakers 2.5 percent,[189] and these percentages hold roughly for the number of congregations and ministers. The Presbyterian early history survives chiefly in the form of debates in the 1720s and 1730s over whether or not the Westminster Confession of Faith had to be subscribed to. The Charleston presbytery was, like the Philadelphia synod, greatly divided on this issue, and there are sermons and letters of Josiah Smith[190] against subscription, and of others for. By 1732 the Scotch-Irish were pouring in, settling along the rivers and eventually in many instances making their way to the hill country frontiers. These were not Josiah Smith's group. Apparently the Cainhoy and Charleston Presbyterians were largely of English origin.

Also in 1732 a group of Scottish Highlanders settled along the Cape Fear River in North Carolina, though their greater influx came in the years just before the Revolution. Lowland Scots and Scotch-Irish were also strengthening the Presbyterians in North Carolina. All sorts of Scots and Scotch-Irish joined other Calvinists (Swiss and French and German) in the newly formed Georgia between 1735 and 1755.

Despite this steady flow, the Presbyterian church, as already observed, flourished primarily in the back country of the South. Some of the people came from New England, others through the port of Charleston, and others through Philadelphia. They turned south and southwest from the northern cities and seaports, following along the Appalachian mountain range, sometimes crossing it to the west, sometimes turning east. Land policies attracted them in these hinterlands, and of course freedom from interference by the established church. Militarily for at least two generations they formed the first line of defense against the French and Indians.

Without missionaries to minister to them they would have been lost to the Presbyterian church. The Synod of Philadelphia, especially the New Castle presbytery, recognized this fact. The records of churches like Tinkling Spring (in Augusta County, Virginia) or county histories, which employ minutes often still in manuscript, tell us what happened. In the lower Virginia Piedmont county of Prince Edward, for example, the first group of Presbyterians were Scotch-Irish who were well settled before John Thomson in 1739 and William Robinson in 1743 preached to them. Thomson was an "Old Side" (or "Old Light") Presbyterian as were most of the Scotch-Irish, who did not believe in the new evangelism but did believe strongly that the ministry should be university educated. Robinson, a "New Side" man, held forth in evangelistic terms and manner and was convinced, as were his brethren, that a university degree was not an absolute prerequisite for the ministry, though he and others of the "New Side" did believe strongly in an educated ministry. The latter were practical men who saw that, if Presbyterianism was to flourish or even survive among the people who had grown up in its tenets, there must be missionary clergy at once. Thus the "New Side" people trained their clergy in the later famous schools, the "Log Colleges," largely in Pennsylvania, and sent them forth through the colonies.[191]

These questions of evangelism, education, and subscription to the Westminster Confession, all arising more or less simultaneously, were to be factors in producing in 1741 the first real division in the Presbyterian church. Other beliefs and actions helped to cause the rupture. "Old Side" parsons accused the "New Side" men of invading the parishes of their fellow ministers without permission, of rashly condemning others who did not agree with them, of using terror and other emotional pressures in ways unsanctioned by Scripture, and above all in teaching that all true converts are as certain of their state of grace as a person can be from his outward senses, and that they can judge of others' states of grace. For seventeen years Presbyterians in the South were about evenly divided between the Synod of Philadelphia, which remained "Old Side," opposed the methods of the revivalists, and finally expelled them; and the Synod of New York, which included the principal "New Side" men from the middle colonies, who with Whitefield brought revivalism to the South. Bitter accusations came on both sides, with the "New Side" clergy frequently associating their "Old Side" brethren with most Anglicans as "an unconverted ministry."

The "New Side," as the divisions appear now in perspective, was the more aggressive and on the whole included the abler men. With such leaders as the Tennents and Blairs, Samuel Finley and Samuel Davies, the first of whom founded the most famous of the Log Colleges and trained the others for their great work, the "New Side" was in the end to win. Along with, really in large part directly involved in, the Great Awakening, Presbyterianism in the South was to intrench itself as a major Christian group, though in the later awakenings it was not always as strongly evangelical as were its Methodist and Baptist brethren.

Contrary to many statements by New England scholars that the Great Awakening began with Jonathan Edwards in Massachusetts and had its roots in American Puritanism, the revivalist movement in this country actually began in the middle colonies, "where German pietism had prepared the way by its emphasis upon inner, personal religion." The first great revivalist was Theodore J. Frelinghuysen of the Dutch Reformed churches in New Jersey, whose work reached its height about 1726.[192] Its next phase was the work of the graduates of William Tennent's Log College at Neshaminy in Pennsylvania, the principal names being those mentioned just above. In twenty years (1726–1746) some sixteen to eighteen young men were trained, most of them entering the Presbyterian ministry. Their scholarship was clearly equal to that acquired at the New England colleges or William and Mary, as Davies and Blair alone would attest. The revival grew stronger and stronger in the thirties. Edwards began his work eight years after Frelinghuysen, and near the end of the decade George Whitefield appeared on the American scene, coming ostensibly to be an Anglican missionary in the new southern colony of Georgia. Thus the Great Awakening in America is no more the child of Jonathan Edwards and New England than of any other single man or one region of the colonies.

It clearly was a reaction from the rationalism, sometimes extreme, which had dominated the Anglican and indeed conservative Presbyterian churches for some decades, and it was a natural answer to the clearly seen need by pious Christians of reaching the masses. It had origins in German pietism, in the ancient church, in an Oxford student club, in a dozen socioreligious situations. In America (one must recall that it was also strong in England and had manifestations on the European continent) it was in the first phase strongly Calvinist, at least by lip allegiance of its propagators, but by no means entirely so. And the southern and general American revivalism and revivals, recurring and persisting for two hundred years, have in the end become anything but Calvinist.

The southern mind, so often reexamined and reassessed in this twentieth century when southern literature had become the most distinguished in the nation, is by general critical agreement a religious mind. As the earliest colonial writings attest, in one sense it always has been. But what the theological or literary critic-historian means by "religious" today seems pretty close to what the people of the first Great Awakening thought it was, and made it. This set or frame of mind, most obvious in the ordinary people of the South but clearly part of all manner of southerners, has probably remained firmer in this region than in any other part of America. That it originated as a general American reaction or response and that it had particular and immediate origins in the southern colonies are equally true. For Josiah Smith, Hermon Husband, Alexander Garden, and Samuel Davies are at least as significant as Jonathan Edwards, Charles Chauncey, Samuel Blair, and others of the northern and middle colonies for an understanding of this great wave of religious fervor and reaction or opposition in the generation preceding our war for independence. And one should not forget that it was through the South as gateway that John Wesley left his first slight but unmistakable mark on eighteenth-century America before 1763, that George Whitefield came to be here at all, and that as representative of southern evangelical Presbyterianism Samuel Davies gave his great sermons (published in more than nineteen editions by 1864) and hymns to the dissenters of both England and America.

But all this takes us back to Whitefield in Georgia, where he arrived on May 7, 1738.[193] Most of his first visit was spent, as Anglican minister in charge, in settling the new schoolmaster and preparing for the orphan house he intended to build. On the way back to England he stopped in Charleston and was received cordially by Commissary Garden, who invited him to preach at St. Philip's the next Sunday morning and evening.[194] So far, all was well within the Anglican fold. Whitefield pointed out then and later that he was a Calvinist and quite truthfully that the Thirty-Nine Articles of the Church of England were pretty thoroughly Calvinist too—or could be so interpreted. Then he returned to England to be ordained (he was at that time a deacon) in priest's orders. But he left printed copies and memories of his powerful sermons among the Georgians. In August 1739 Whitefield returned to America, landing at Lewes, Delaware, and beginning his first evangelistic tour in the middle states, where the way had been prepared for him by Frelinghuysen and the Log College preachers. He found his friends and allies among the Presbyterians, partly through congeniality in doctrine and partly through his ignorance of the American ecclesiastical situation.

Why the best-known Anglican clergyman of the eighteenth century, his friends the Wesleys possibly excepted, should have apparently deliberately incited or provoked the hostility of fellow churchmen has no simple or single answer. Certainly, as historians of the Episcopal Church in America admit, failure to participate in the movement, in at least some forms and to some extent, was a mistake from which their church has not yet recovered. One recent scholar analyzes the personalities involved and the situation itself quite well.[195] Social status, he proves, was not a major factor: the average Anglican congregation was as poor as the Presbyterian. The decisive element may have been the clergy. For the most part the Anglican ministers of this time were Arminians, as were their colleagues back in England, and they also had a strong clerical concern for church order and social order. They formed, *as* the revival developed, a pretty solid phalanx against it until the time of Devereux Jarratt, when favorable attitudes within the church gradually went into Methodist Arminianism. But there were two other major factors less often considered. First, the Awakening quite by chance interrupted the "long, sputtering argument" between Anglicans and dissenters, already noted, in such a way as to cause Anglicans to see revivals through the "prism of this controversy," as an attempt by nonconformity to destroy the Church of England. Whitefield, ignorant of these colonial realities, unintentionally presented himself as a turncoat churchman allied with the enemy. And by his doctrine and conduct he sometimes wittingly and sometimes unwittingly supported the nonconformist against every item in the Anglican critique of dissent. He made the experience of the New Birth paramount, he seemed to ignore the Book of Common Prayer, he attacked those basic Anglican books *Tillotson's Sermons* and the *Whole Duty of Man* as unchristian. To begin with, Anglican commissaries from New York and Pennsylvania to South Carolina welcomed him to their pulpits, Cummings and Vesey in the north, Blair and Garden in the South. These men and their clergy were aware that Whitefield might be a great force for Christian good. But through ignorance and arrogance, misunderstanding and untactful sincerity, Whitefield alienated them all. Certainly the burden of alienation is heavily on his side. It is interesting to conjecture what might have been the effect on the conformation of the southern religious mind—for there Anglicanism was strongest—had the Church of England and her great son been able to work hand in hand.

In New England, welcomed by Edwards, the Puritan conservatives, and the Presbyterians, Whitefield was again enormously successful. In the middle colonies, working with the Log College men, things went equally well. From Maryland to Georgia men flocked to hear him and his message, not all of it doctrine. He wrote home of one prominent Maryland Anglican clergyman who was "under conviction" though not temperamentally suited to evangelism,[196] and he was pleased with the results in the Chesapeake colonies. Two of his Oxford college contemporaries were faculty members at William and Mary, and he thoroughly enjoyed his visit in Williamsburg. Old and ailing Commissary Blair welcomed him. Yet in the end he seems to have preached in Virginia during only three of his nine visits to America.[197] North Carolina he seems to have found the "greatest waste" spiritually and temporally. The South Carolinians, he felt, responded much more.[198] In Charleston Presbyterian-Independent Josiah Smith was Whitefield's friend and champion in life and in death. The Georgians, Anglicans though they were, admired him and prided themselves in his accomplishments among them and elsewhere.

Whitefield's preaching style will be commented upon at greater length in the next chapter. Though titles such as "The Eternity of Hell Torments" among these sermons are most frequently remembered, it is equally in "The Almost Christian," "Of Justification by Christ," or "The Benefits of an Early Piety," delivered with tenderness and persuasiveness, that his pulpit oratory deserves remembrance. Like other pre-Romantic thinkers in a variety of areas, he so touched his horror- and awe-inspiring images with grandeur that at his best he comes close to the sublime. The earliest Log College men were more terrifying, raging, and ranting, and were properly the objects of criticism for their forensic style. It is only in the later or younger "New Side" or "New Lights," especially in the Virginian Davies, that the Awakening saw, and heard, its greatest pulpit oratory. It seems safe to say that Whitefield was much more of a model for Davies in delivery and style than were the latter's fellow Presbyterians of the middle colonies.

Whitefield's most direct confrontation with the representatives of his own church came in South Carolina when he and Commissary Garden met head on. The story has been told from several points of view. The dispassionate examiner of the evidence will conclude that Whitefield's fusion of sincerity and arrogance in his denunciation of an "unconverted" Anglican ministry and the cherished Anglican books mentioned above was as unfair as it was impertinent. On the other hand, Garden, who had been gradually aroused against the minister he once welcomed, replied to Whitefield's allegation in a series of sneering, supercilious letters which lack effective dignity. Incidentally, Garden made the mistake of seeing Puritan Calvinists in all Methodists, especially the Wesleys, and saw no difference between their doctrines and Whitefield's.[199] But best remembered is Garden's denying Whitefield the Holy Communion and "trying him" before an ecclesiastical court, an action from which the evangelist appealed successfully on technical grounds, though its verdict was that he be suspended from his priestly functions.[200] A series of sermons by Garden and Whitefield and Josiah Smith, Garden's letters, and a prolonged newspaper controversy remain to aid us in considering or judging the situation.[201] As already noted, Josiah Smith not only invited Whitefield to preach in his church, but for years afterward preached and wrote in defense of the evangelist and his views. Other South Carolina Presbyterians and Independents who supported Whitefield included Baptist Isaac Chanler, who in the cause wrote his province's first theological treatise, *The Doctrines of Glorious Grace . . . Defended.*[202]

And this brings us to the glory of the Great Awakening and of the Presbyterian church in the southern colonies, the work of Samuel Davies and his immediate predecessors. For Davies became a major international figure as preacher, hymn writer, and champion of religious toleration. Though friend and disciple of Whitefield, Davies was possessed of much more tact and warm gentleness than was the great Englishman.

The Hanover County area of Virginia from which Davies' name and fame were to spread was in Piedmont, and the Reverend Patrick Henry, uncle of the patriot, was the Anglican rector of the parish in which the seed of Presbyterianism and the revival flourished. It was a fairly old settled region, not especially noted for the number of aristocratic Anglican planters, perhaps because its soil was not rich. But concatenations of circumstances turned for a time a generally normal rural population of English descent and Anglican church affiliations into one of the great centers of revivalism and Presbyterianism.

In one way it is the old story of the unchurched or the pietistic finding no spiritual satisfaction in their environment. Samuel Morris, a planter probably without religious affiliation, became interested in certain books by Bunyan, Luther, and Whitefield. He and his neighbors began to hold meetings in their homes to discuss their reading; soon they found that they had to build "reading houses" to accommodate the throngs. The dissenters they knew were Quakers. Therefore they were calling themselves Lutherans when William Robinson, "New Side" missionary sent out by the New Brunswick Presbytery, appeared among them. Robinson's substance and style and his revivalistic preaching, convinced these people that his was the religion they wanted. Thus began seriously—though Robinson had earlier unsuccessfully tried to enter the western Scotch-Irish "Old Side" communities—the Presbyterian Awakening in the South. Other Log College itinerants followed—John Blair, John Roan, Samuel Finley, Gilbert Tennent, and finally the young man Samuel Davies.[203]

There were already the Presbyterians in the Valley of Virginia whom Robinson had tried to reach, "Old Siders" who had no opportunity or wish to proselytize Anglicans and began to send their own anti-revivalist missionaries east to counteract the "New Side" people. Despite the efforts of these conservatives, the revival continued to spread, particularly after the arrival of Davies in 1747. For the next eleven or twelve years the story of the Great Awakening in Virginia and North Carolina centered in Samuel Davies and his Presbyterian stronghold in Hanover.

Davies came into a stimulating but by no means entirely favorable situation. His predecessors among "New Side" itinerants had frequently abused the established church and had not bothered to ask for licenses to preach, both matters of behavior contrary to the laws of Virginia. Davies, born in Delaware in 1723 and ordained by the Presbytery of New Castle in 1746, was a Log College graduate (later he was to defend his thesis for the M.A. from Princeton) who always revered his former teachers and classmates and received some of his ardor from their fiery inspiration. When he arrived in Virginia, he and others thought he was in the early stages of tuberculosis (and perhaps he was), but he was determined to do all he could in what he thought would be the three or four years left to him.[204]

At first he did not plan to do that all in Virginia. On this "visit" he remained only about six weeks, during which his first wife died. But he began in the right way, for his first act in 1747 was to secure a license from Governor Gooch to preach at four meeting houses. In 1748 he remarried, this time to a Virginia woman who was related to the publisher of the *Virginia Gazette*, and settled permanently in Hanover. In the latter year Davies had brought back with him an old schoolmate, Rodgers, as fellow-evangelist, and went to Williamsburg to get his friend licensed. Though the governor was favorable, the Council, alarmed at Presbyterian inroads in Anglican parishes, flatly declined. Davies had to work without Rodgers, but from this time until he left Virginia in 1759, he fought for religious toleration. Of course he was acting in great measure from denominational interest, but some of the bases and principles he laid down were to pave the way for later and more successful champions of religious liberty. On the technical side, to oversimplify, one can say he pleaded that the British Act of Toleration did apply in the colonies and that he and his colleagues and followers had the right to worship as they pleased. In addition, he had to prove that "New Side" or "New Light" Presbyterians were a legitimate religious body, not too easy a matter, for their "Old Side" brethren for a long time disclaimed them. And finally, they had to show that itinerating preachers such as they qualified for licenses under the Act of Toleration.

Davies had powerful friends and enemies at home and abroad. The young Peyton Randolph, attorney-general of the colony and later president of the Continental Congress, argued that the act did not apply in Virginia. Davies, acting as his own attorney before the General Court, made his point that if it did not apply the Act of Uniformity also did not. But since dissenters had by enacted laws been allowed to hold meetings in Virginia, both did apply. Commissary Thomas Dawson and Governors Gooch and Dinwiddie were not unfriendly, but the cause was not fully won when Davies went to England in 1753. Both then and later he bombarded governors, Bishops of London, dissenting British leader Philip Doddridge, and others who might have influence, with letters and arguments for his cause.[205] Though Davis and the Presbyterians of Virginia never won a clearcut decision, in December 1755 they did go on to organize the Hanover Presbytery, called by Foote and others "the mother of Presbyteries in the South." Davies was its first moderator.

So this young man's work continued. As a minister, he insisted on conversion of the Negroes, pastoral visitation, and prepared sermons. The greatest pulpit orator of his generation in America he has been called, and he was all of that. When after his return from England in 1755 the French and Indian War touched Virginia in every corner, he began preaching a series of patriotic sermons with an eloquence unequaled in other known literature of the type.[206] Through them he became Virginia's best recruiting officer. These sermons did as much to establish him and his church as all his vigorous epistles and legal arguments had done. They proved once and for all to an Anglican South that dissent could be intensely patriotic.

By 1759, when Davies succeeded his friend Jonathan Edwards as president of Princeton, he had already contributed immensely to that institution by his unprecedented success in Great Britain in raising funds for its endowment and buildings. Undoubtedly he shortened his life by the strenuous efforts in preaching and promoting he did in 1753–1755. But during the eighteen months he held Princeton's presidency he also did much to organize that institution on a sound scholastic basis.

To read Davies' evangelical sermons is still a delight to a lover of cadenced, imaginative, and energetic prose. Orthodox Calvinism Davies preached to his dying day, though his *Diary* indicates that he sometimes had doubts as to some of its doctrines, especially when he found "good" Presbyterians in Great Britain no longer adhering to them.[207] Along with his reminders of the dire punishment of sinners, Davies always emphasized the positive side of his religion, the justification through faith alone, the most sublime of religious tenets.[208] Less austere than Edwards, and usually in his sermons (though not in his tracts) less inexorably logical, Davies represents better than any other minister of the Awakening the attraction that Calvinist sublimity had for the religious mind of his time. When a generation or two after he was gone (he died at thirty-seven) the Wesleyan-English-Arminian brand of revivalism nominally superseded the Calvinist, there remained in all evangelism, and in all evangelical churches including the American Methodist, something of the particular Calvinist sublimity which is a hallmark of American Protestantism. Especially in the southern mind have terror and awe and ineffable grace remained in fusion. The southern mind, if it has remained religious, has done so largely in the tradition of Samuel Davies.

Yet southern Presbyterianism's later history is a study in relative failure, that is, failure as a denomination to grasp the religious imagination of the common folk so as to become the representative and largest American doctrinal body. After Davies' departure, Presbyterianism ceased to be the force in the middle counties of Virginia it had been with him, though the (now divided) Hanover Presbytery exists to this day. The best-organized religious body in the South well into the nineteenth century, the church gradually lost its revivalistic vision. On the frontiers of Kentucky and Mississippi, as its Scotch-Irish peoples moved west, it continued for a time as the leading denomination. But lack of missionaries (partly because of its insistence on a trained ministry) and the relative complexity of its doctrine, not to mention its sternness and rigidity, gave the Methodists and the Baptists the chance to become *the* churches of the American and southern people. Davies' evangelical spirit and the *spirit* of his doctrine, if not the doctrine itself, appear to live on more in them than in his own denomination.[209]

THE BAPTISTS

The Baptists, when Davies died, were still weak in influence if not in members. In Virginia it was not until Elder John Leland and his brethren began work in the 1770s and 1780s that they became a major factor in the revival movement, and that is after the colonial period.[210] In the Carolinas they were largely scattered, though in Charleston and vicinity men like Isaac Chanler had firmly organized congregations and did have a definite part in the Great Awakening. The Baptists had in the colonial period, and apparently still retain, their Arminian and Calvinist branches.

The General Baptists, originally Arminian, were in the 1750s in North Carolina absorbed into the strongly Calvinist Particular (or Regular) Baptists. But when the Reverend Shubal Stearns arrived from Virginia in North Carolina in 1755 he brought the more evangelical, less Calvinist doctrines of the Separate Baptists and carried through the Carolinas in the 1760s and later a Baptist form of the Great Awakening.[211] It was not until 1788 that the major branches of the church were united, and then not necessarily in doctrine.

GERMAN AND SWISS SECTS

A word more should be said about the German groups in the South before 1764, including the German Swiss. However tenuous their connection with the Great Awakening, they were present by the mid-eighteenth century in considerable numbers in Maryland and Georgia, and in a variety of sects.

Pennsylvania was the center from which most of them spread, especially into the South—Moravians, Mennonites, and Dunkers, as well as the more orthodox Lutherans.[212] These four came into western Maryland from western Pennsylvania, and in Maryland many of them stayed. Others followed the Scotch-Irish along the Appalachian mountain chain into east Tennessee and Kentucky, southwest Virginia, and western North Carolina. In the Valley of Virginia many of the Mennonites and Dunkers settled.

The first German Reformed colony in Virginia was established by Governor Spotswood at Germanna in 1714. With them came the Reverend John Henry Haeger. In a few years (1718–1724) they moved to a new site eight miles south of Warrenton in Fauquier County, where they were visited by Moravian missionaries in 1743. They were followed at Germanna by two successive orthodox Lutheran groups in 1711 and 1719–1720. Probably a fairly typical Lutheran of the Dutch church was John Casper Stover, who settled in Orange County in 1739 and left in his will an interesting account of his journey from Danzig to Philadelphia to Virginia.[213]

The Moravians instead of turning southwest pushed directly south from the lower end of the Shenandoah Valley and found a region to their liking in what is today Winston-Salem, then best known as Wachovia.[214] They have remained a small but definite influence in this region in education and music as well as religion. Moravian hymnology has had a great effect on all evangelical church music. Perhaps their strongest influence on the South was indirect, for John Wesley and others of the Great Awakening on both sides of the Atlantic found their form of pietism most congenial.

But there were also German Lutherans in North Carolina from 1745. They settled principally in Catawba County to begin with, and by the 1770s there were almost three thousand German Protestant families in Rowan, Orange, Mecklenberg, and Tryon counties.[215] Both Reformed and Lutheran groups came without pastors, and though they had visiting clergy from South Carolina, it was not until 1768 and 1773 that they obtained resident ministers.

In South Carolina, as already observed, German and Swiss sects were present by 1685. The Swiss were first at Purrysburgh. In 1735 a shipload of German Swiss arrived from Rotterdam and settled principally in Orangeburg. More and more emigrants from various parts of the old German states flowed in as the century progressed. They were in the main humble folk. No distinguished clergy appeared among them in the colonial period.

Georgia, founded for persecuted continental Europeans as well as for the English poor and unemployed, had German settlers soon after Oglethorpe and his vanguard arrived. These were the Salzburgers, led by John Martin Bolzius, who had been fiercely persecuted at home. They settled at

Ebenezer and continued to come to Georgia in small parties until in 1741 there were some twelve hundred. Industrious and frugal Lutherans, they were for a time the largest national-religious element in the colony.

The Salzburgers were followed by a small group of Moravians, who soon removed to Pennsylvania. Other smaller bodies drifted in, but it is the Salzburgers who have left significant records of their settlement and their religious tribulations on the way to America and even after arrival.[216]

THE QUAKERS

The Quakers of the eighteenth-century South have left voluminous records of their Monthly and Yearly Meetings and of their antagonism to slavery, and sad evidence of their lack of dynamic leadership. Men like John Woolman visited and encouraged Friends in the South as well as the middle colonies, but they themselves produced no able leaders nor did great leaders settle among them. With the firm establishment of the Church of England in the Carolinas they finally went entirely out of public life. In this latter part of the colonial period, especially in Virginia and the Carolinas, they continued to live quiet, spiritual lives. How much later Abolitionism owed to them may be an open question, but the strong anti-slavery feeling of many of the southern Revolutionary patriots, notably Jefferson and his friends, almost surely came in part from their Quaker neighbors and kinsmen. Vestiges of early Quakerism include a college in North Carolina and a few schools and scattered communities. They are all that remain in the South of a people who continued to be numerically fairly strong throughout the colonial period, but whose moral conscience and consciousness, if it had any effect on the southern mind, is an effect too subtle and tenuous to trace today.

THE HUGUENOTS

The French Protestants continued to pour into the South in the eighteenth century. From Maryland to Georgia but most strongly in Virginia and South Carolina they settled sometimes in little communities of their own, sometimes on farms, and sometimes beside English or German-speaking neighbors in village or town. Their Calvinist faith endured while they lived together and when, as many did, they joined the Presbyterians. But in Virginia and South Carolina many of their clergy even in the first genera-tion became priests of the Anglican church, clergy whose names echo in southern history to this day, Maury and Fontaine and Marye and Latané and a dozen others. Certainly they brought their Calvinism with them into the Church of England, where it often accentuated the Calvinism of the church's own Thirty-Nine Articles. But if one looks at the sermons of Peter Fontaine and James Maury[217] he sees few of its doctrinal vestiges remaining.

DEISM AND RATIONALISM

About one half of the colonial period in the South, if one begins that half with John Locke, was an age of rationalism and Newtonian science in all the English-speaking world. For England or America as well as for France and Europe it was the Age of Reason. Appeals to the reasonable side of man's nature, application of Lockean principles of rational psychology and philosophy and of Newtonian science permeated the arts, religion, and the beginnings of technology. It was an age of inquiry, of ranging freedom of thought, as the books and science read and taught at Harvard and Yale and William and Mary indicate. Rational principles were applied in sermons and theological tracts, more or less within an orthodox Christian frame of reference, by every sort of Protestant. It was of course what they considered the extremely "cold reason" side of Anglicanism which the Wesleys and Whitefield were reacting from. But one does not have to read Anglican Commissaries Blair and Garden or Parson Maury to find rational terminology and appeals to reason to bring religious conviction. Josiah Smith and Samuel Davies, like their New England friend Edwards, employed it and Locke's psychology for their own "Calvinist" purposes.

There were, however, educated men and women in all Protestant bodies who felt that reason carried them beyond Christianity to what we call deism. Deists accepted the authority of human reason, rejected the miraculous, and denied the Trinity and the authority of the Bible. They further denied the divinity of Christ, though at the same time they revered his teachings. Lord Herbert of Cherbury (1583–1648) had long before Locke enunciated the five points of deistic rationalism: belief (1) that there is a Supreme Power or Benevolent God, (2) that this Power is to be worshipped, (3) that the good ordering or disposition of the faculties of men constitutes the best part of divine worship, (4) that all vices and crimes should be expiated by repentance, and (5) that there are rewards and punishments after this life.[218] To anyone familiar with the writings of Benjamin Franklin or Thomas Jefferson or most other founding fathers of the Republic, these will appear to be the moral or spiritual principles they lived by. Franklin[219] and Jefferson actually enumerated them more than once, despite the latter's frequent protest that a man's religion was nobody's business but his. The question here is, however, how much and in what ways deism was a religion, or a philosophy, in the colonial South during the generations before the Revolution.

Undoubtedly many of those called atheists by their enemies in the court records of the southern colonies were accused out of spite or fear; but in other instances they were probably persons who had in private or in public voiced one or more deistical beliefs or convictions. Probably few pure deists existed in the South or in the rest of America before the 1760s. But there were New England as well as Virginia clergy who argued that Christianity was a rational religion.[220]

Most historians observe that the deistical movement was less conspicuous in the southern than in the northern provinces. Perhaps the word *conspicuous* is the key. There was in the South no vigorous attack on the clergy as such, except the Parson's Cause case of the 1760s, and that was primarily a political-economic matter. But by 1733 there is evidence that Virginia at least was concerned about the spread of something it called deism. Before and after that date, southern clergy writing to the S.P.G. requesting books for parochial libraries frequently asked for tracts which would aid in combatting deism. In a letter of July 21, 1724, for example, the Reverend Mr. Forbes of Isle of Wight County, Virginia, asked the Bishop of London for books which might stop the mouths of "the Quakers and even Deists."[221]

William Parks, the Williamsburg printer, reprinted in 1733 for colonial consumption a book published in England a decade before, Charles Leslie's *A Short and Easy Method with the Deists. Wherein the Certainty of the Christian Religion is Demonstrated by Infallible Proof from Four Rules*, evidence in itself that someone, probably Commissary Blair and the clergy, feared the spread of deistical thinking among the Anglicans. On July 8, 1735, Governor Gooch reported to the bishop that "free thinkers multiply very fast having an eminent Layman for their Leader, and the Current runs in some places without opposition."[222]

The eminent layman may have been Sir John Randolph, the only native Virginian knighted during the colonial period, who had a colony-wide reputation for speaking freely on religious doctrine. In his will of 1737/8 this great lawyer took cognizance of his reputation by giving at length a profession of his own faith. It is an eloquent document, only a small fraction of which may be quoted here:

> Whereas I have been reproached by many people, especially the clergy, in the article of religion, and have . . . drawn upon me names very familiar to blind zealots, such as deist, heretic, and schismatic, . . . I think it necessary in the first place to vindicate my memory from all harsh and unbrotherly censure of this kind and to give this last testimony of my faith.
>
> I contemplate and adore the Supreme Being, the first cause of all things, whose infinite power and wisdom is manifested throughout the world, of which none can entertain the least doubt but fools or madmen.

Sir John goes on to state his belief in Jesus Christ as the Messiah, in the resurrection, and in punishment and reward. The last he thinks will not come because of speculative thinking but "according to the degree of virtue we have practiced in this life." He believes in free will or "perfect liberty . . . exempted from fate and necessity." Simple faith he sees in the gospel, not in the hair-splitting of learned theologians, which does not tend to cause men to amend their lives. If he is wrong, he yearns to be enlightened hereafter, hoping, he says, "that I shalt not be dealt with according to the errors and frailties of my life, but may be admitted to some degree of that everlasting peace which he has promised to those that believe in him." [223]

Such was Virginia deism in its first phase, before it had parted definitely with Christianity. There were undoubtedly many others among the learned and the speculative who had gone as far as this "halfway house," how many one cannot even guess. [224] That it was a matter taken seriously by Randolph's own generation is evident when, less than a year after his death, the House of Burgesses voted to have printed the Reverend Mr. Chichley Thacher's sermon "against the groundless Objections to the Divinity and Dignity of the Blessed Jesus." [225] One thousand copies were ordered to be distributed among the counties of the colony.

Half a generation later, President William Stith of the College of William and Mary, in a sermon discussed in the next chapter, and Colonel Richard Bland, in his pamphlet against the clergy in the Parson's Cause, seem close to deism, though they never declared themselves so openly as did Thomas Jefferson. All three of these men were nephews of Sir John Randolph.

Such beliefs as Sir John's had in their background, or in their foundation, the latitudinarianism of the Anglican church and the temper of the learned in those times. The pattern probably held also for university-educated and well-read men of speculative mind in Maryland, Carolina, and Georgia, though even in the Revolutionary generation it is not so obvious among them as among the gentlemen of Virginia. That there were deists among the half-educated was also doubtless true. But the evangelical Protestantism of the Great Awakening and the moderate Christian rationalism of many southern Anglicans never disintegrated on the scale on which Calvinism in New England crumbled into Unitarianism.

The rational religion of southern leaders of the mid-eighteenth century was inextricably interwoven with their political and social beliefs. It was one of those nephews of Sir John Randolph who was to compose the Virginia Statute of Religious Freedom, disestablish the church in which he was a lifelong vestryman, and make up his own Bible by clipping Jesus' personal words from the rest of the New Testament. Yet when he wished to place a distinguished alleged atheist on the faculty of his infant university, an evangelical Christian denomination, the Presbyterians, were able to prevent his doing so.

Of such mingled yarn the southern religious mind was knit. From the beginning the southern colonist was conscious of religion. In 1763 he still yearned for a Christian heaven, but it was a different heaven for every sect and every individual, and it was earned or arrived at differently. Calvinism often gripped the southern colonial, and it has left its indelible mark. The southerner was a moralist by instinct and by conviction. But he was also a hedonist. For him as for others this life was a path to the hereafter; yet he could and did stop to look at and do a number of other things along the way. For he loved life itself.

CHAPTER SIX

The Sermon and the Religious Tract

CONTENTS

————◆————

Introduction	703
The Seventeenth-Century Sermon	705
The Eighteenth-Century Sermon	721
The Early Preachers	722
The Later Colonial Anglicans	730
Dissenters and the Great Awakening	758
The Religious Tract	775
The Seventeenth Century	777
The Eighteenth Century	783
Bibliography	1052
Notes	1055

~ ~ ~ As for Sermons, tho' they were never so nicely Calculated and adapted to these purposes, yet it is not in the Power of the most Skilfull Preacher to come up to the Case of every Single Person; because for want of time as I have just now observed, he must be too great a Stranger to many of his hearers, so as to be able to speak home to their particular Circumstances: And tho' the minister cou'd do this, yet in many Cases it may be neither safe nor prudent so to do; because it wou'd look too much like pointing, and wou'd disoblige and disgust rather than anything else. I have ever carefully avoided the splitting on this Rock, tho' at the same time my Conscience also bears me witness, that I have according to the best of my Skill and power, rightly diveded the Word of Truth, neither concealing nor prevaricating in, any part of it, for any Worldly Consideration whatsoever. . . . my discourses, according to the necessity of the times, and as my knowledge of the People increases are now more plain and vehement.

—Commissary GIDEON JOHNSTON to the Secretary of the S.P.G., Charles-Town, South Carolina, July 5, 1710.

If New England be called a receptacle of dissenters, and an Amsterdam of religion, Pensylvania the nursery of Quakers, Maryland the retirement of Roman Catholicks, North Carolina the refuge of run-aways, and South Carolina the delight of buccaneers and pyrates, Virginia may be justly esteemed the happy retreat of true Britons and true churchmen for the most part; neither soaring too high nor dropping too low, consequently should merit the greater esteem and encouragement.

—The Reverend HUGH JONES, *The Present State of Virginia* [1724], ed. R. L. Morton (Chapel Hill, 1956), p. 83.

PERHAPS OF ALL THE emanations of the southern colonial mind that which has received least attention is the sermon, and next to it the religious tract. Few general, intellectual, or religious historians seem aware that such works exist, except that occasionally in some context they recall the writings of Samuel Davies. That sermons and religious or theological essays by scores of clergymen, totalling several hundred individual titles, were printed and widely circulated in their time is unknown to most and considered of little or no significance by the few who are dimly aware of their existence. And that several scores of interesting Sabbath homilies still lie in manuscript has apparently been undreamed of.

In this generation of critical re-evaluation of the mind of our past the New and old England Puritan sermon has more than come into its own, for it is seen as *a* key, if not *the* key, to the understanding of the mind and action of a particular people at a particular time. And it is recognized, at least for New England, as the foremost literary genre in artistic form and intellectual impression from the 1620s to the threshold of the Revolution. Alongside it ranks the polemical theological tract, from Cotton and Williams to Bellamy and Darling.

For the South, however, there survives no body of trenchant and eloquent seventeenth-century sermons such as Thomas Shepard, John Cotton, and Increase Mather left to their posterity. The two-or-three-sermons-a-week custom initiated at Jamestown continued in many parishes (usually urban) of the southern colonies through the entire century, and the men who preached were in most cases, as the preceding chapter indicates, as learned as their brethren to the north. In some instances, such as Alexander Whitaker, Thomas Harrison, and Morgan Godwyn, who have left writings or reputation to judge by, they clearly compared favorably in intellect. Of most—either men or their theological thinking—there is little way of knowing. In this seventeenth century in the South there were no burning intra-ecclesiastical issues such as seethed in New England, and there were, perhaps with one questionable exception, no presses which might print powerful or pleasing essays or sermons. Those which were published had to be brought out in London.

But from this first century a few sermons and essays do survive. And along with them should be considered the homilies read at church or on the plantation when there was no minister, and the doctrine and form of the theology in the volumes which composed the largest individual segment of every southern library. For these last are as revealing of the southern religious mind as are the native-bred treatises or sermons.

The eighteenth century in the Southeast is another story, or certainly a larger and longer one. Though most of the colonies did not get printing presses until the century was a third or half over, there survive in both print and manuscript many scores of sermons from the first quarter of the century. And after the presses at Annapolis, Williamsburg, and Charleston got well under way the number multiplied. In the eighteenth century there were burning religious questions which the southern preacher and now and then his congregation took up and wrote upon with vigor, sometimes indignation, sometimes bitterness, sometimes real persuasiveness, and occasionally with beauty and eloquence.

The religious writing of the first century is naturally almost all Anglican, with a little Roman Catholic and Quaker and Presbyterian controversy thrown in. Even after 1707 most of the surviving printed and unprinted material is Anglican, but much Presbyterian and some Baptist expression was beginning to appear in print.

Several significant and perhaps surprising inferences and conclusions arise from this survey. First, the Anglican sermon was *not* the opposite in form of the Puritan, but very much like it. Second, the early Anglican southern sermon was in content usually as Calvinist as any early Puritan sermon. Third, the early Anglican southern colonist, if he was literate (and except for the Negro he usually was), was an avid reader and collector of religious books, especially of certain favorite sermons. Fourth, the characteristic American forms of enthusiasm and the concept of the sublime in religion had their inception and first development most largely in the southern leaders of the Great Awakening. Fifth, the southern religious essay—pulpit oration or polemic tract—indicates a good deal of the temper of the southern mind, how like and unlike that of New England it was, how American it had become by 1763.

THE SEVENTEENTH-CENTURY SERMON

The first and second of the southern seaboard colonies, Virginia and Maryland, came into existence in a generation when puritanism[1] was a dominant, if not the dominant, religious attitude of Englishmen. These establishments followed the age of exploration, which produced much of the literature considered in the first chapter of this book. This literature, assembled, edited, commented upon, and even paraphrased by clergymen, had a religious and forensic and missionary cast. Richard Hakluyt's *Principall Navigations* of 1589 and the enlarged edition of 1598 and Purchas' later continuations, were written avowedly with the hope that thus Christianity —Protestant Christianity—might be spread throughout the world. Their work excited the religious as well as the secular imagination and their volumes were read and placed beside the King James Bible and Foxe's

Book of Martyrs on the most accessible shelf in the Jacobean library.[2]

When the Virginia Company of London received its charters in 1606 and 1609, the clergy—Anglican and Puritan—were already supporting the idea of colonization and trade in their sermons in behalf of the East India Company. Their incentives were several and somewhat mixed, but chief among them was saving the souls of the heathen and checking Spain's conversion of infidels into Roman Catholics. Though ballads, books, and pamphlets supporting the Virginia enterprise have long been noted, the sermons of powerful English preachers have too often been overlooked.

In the crucial year 1609, when the expeditions of Sir Thomas Gates and Lord de la Warr excited great interest in Virginia, there was a burst of pulpit oratory. Some if not most of it was inspired by the Virginia Company, which desperately needed popular support. A series of distinguished sermons or essays in sermon form were printed, and in most instances previously preached, by English clergy, several of whom were puritans or Puritans.

On April 25, 1609, the Reverend William Symonds gave orally the first of these: *Virginia. A Sermon Preached at White-Chappel, in the presence of many, Honourable and Worshipfull the Adventurers and Planters for Virginia* . . . (London, 1609), with a dedication to the "Adventurers" of the Company and a text from Genesis 12:1, 2, 3 :"For the Lord said unto Abram, get thee out of thy country, and from thy kindred, and from thy father's house, unto a land that I will shew thee. And I will make thee a great nation, and will bless thee . . . ."[3] Three days later Robert Gray dedicated an essay-sermon, *A Good Speed to Virginia* (London, 1609), also to the members of the Virginia Company, using as his text Joshua 17:14, a message of promise and of exhortation[4] to the enterprise. On May 28, Rogation Sunday, Daniel Price spoke at Paul's Cross on *Saules Prohibition Staide. . . . And to the Inditement of all that persecute Christ with a reproof of those that traduce the Honourable Plantation of Virginia* (London, 1609), another of the command sermons. Price was a fashionable London preacher and chaplain in ordinary to the Prince; he might teach some people his predecessors had not. His text, Acts 9:4, "Saul, Saul, why persecutest thou me?" was denunciatory of those who had traduced the plantation. Earlier, on March 24, Richard Crakenthorpe, chaplain to the Bishop of London, Fellow of Queen's College, Oxford, and a man of strong puritan leanings, had alluded to Virginia and given encouragement in a sermon ostensibly celebrating the anniversary of the accession of King James.[5] On May 7 George Benson, also sometime fellow of Queen's, in *A Sermon Preached at Paules Cross* . . . (London, 1609), foresaw the spread of the gospel westward by way of Virginia. On April 17 Robert Tynley, like Symonds a Fellow of Magdalen College, Oxford, preached in praise of Virginia and against Rome in what was published as *Two Learned Sermons* (London, 1609). And finally, as a sort of climax for the year, Alexander Whitaker's friend William Crashaw (Crashawe), preacher at the Inner Temple, gave to the departing great fleet a fitting peroration, *A Sermon Preached in London before the right honorable the Lord La Warre ... and the Rest of the Adventurers .... Wherein both the lawfulnesse of that Action is maintained, and the necessity thereof is demonstrated. ... Taken from his mouth, and published by direction* (London, 1610). His text was Luke 22:32. He gives a major defense of the plantation, its legality and its necessity, its aims and its promise. His organization is in terms of "discouragements" and "encouragements." Puritan though Crashaw was, his style in places is more strongly suggestive of that of his younger contemporary John Donne than of William Perkins:

> Thus shall heaven and earth blesse you [Lord de la Warr and Company], and for this heroicall adventure of thy person and state in such a godly cause, the God of heaven will make thy name to bee remembred thorowout all generations: and thousands of people shall honour thy memorie, and give thanks to God for thee while the world endureth.
>
> And thou Virginea, whom mine eies see not, my heart shall love; how hath God honoured thee! Thou hast thy name from the worthiest Queene that ever the world had: thou hast thy matter from the greatest King on earth: and thou shall now have thy forme from one of the most glorious Nations under the Sunne, and under the conduct of a Generall of as great and ancient Nobility as ever was ingaged in action of this nature. But this is but a little portion of thy honour: for thy God is coming towards thee.[6]

This noble sermon is the first to indicate that the frontier will be strong factor in the life of the new "nation," a theme to be developed later in sermons preached in America.

There were during the next ten years religious pamphlets and sermons on the Virginia venture. But in 1622, a crucial year in which catastrophe piled on catastrophe was to lead eventually to the dissolution of the Virginia Company, two of the greatest of Jacobean sermons were delivered on behalf of the colony. The Reverend Patrick Copland, who had raised money for an East India Company free school in Virginia and was at one time scheduled to go there as rector of the college at Henrico, was invited to give at Bow Church what proved to be one of the most effective and quotable propaganda sermons of the whole period of English colonization. *Virginia's God be Thanked, Or A Sermon of Thanksgiving For the Happie successe of the affayres in Virginia this last yeare* (London, 1622) was optimistic with hyperbole, and rich with description (based on letters from thence) of the new Garden of Eden. Ironically, news of the great massacre of 1622 was on its way to England as he spoke.

To counteract the news of the catastrophe, Sir Edwin Sandys and the Company persuaded an eminent member to preach a sermon which might reencourage prospective settlers and investors. Thus Dr. John Donne, Dean of St. Paul's, poet and famed preacher, delivered *A Sermon Upon The VIII. Verse of The I. Chapter Of The Acts of the Apostles* (London, 1622). Donne was rightly proud of the sermon and felt its importance. One of his biographers has called this the first missionary sermon preached in England since Britain became a Christian land. It is indeed an eloquent plea for conversion of the Indians, an encouragement of the Company, and a fair example of Donne's sermon rhetoric. Its magnificent climax, the conclusion of which is printed at the beginning of Chapter V of this book, is characteristic.[7]

It was in this literary atmosphere of sermons about the New World, its future and its religion, sermons preached by puritans, Puritans, and High-Church Anglicans, that our first American sermon appeared in print. It reflects in content the New World environment and atmosphere of missionary enthusiasm in which it was written. It is from the pen of Alexander Whitaker, puritan friend of William Crashaw, and it shows the same spirit (though not the form) the later sermon of Donne displays. It was sent to Crashaw in a letter or as a letter in sermon form, dedicated to Sir Thomas Smith, then treasurer of the Virginia Company, on July 28, 1612. It appeared in print, with a dedication-introduction by Crashaw, in London in 1613. Its author, minister at Henrico in Virginia, has been discussed in the preceding chapter as an example of the puritanically inclined Anglican who was inspired personally by missionary zeal. He urged any clergy who rebelled against surplice or subscription to come to Virginia and labor with him, for there such matters went unregarded.[8]

Whitaker's sermon, like his two surviving letters, reveals him as a moderate puritan. His attitude toward doctrine and formalism or liturgy is essentially that which from his time to ours has dominated the Episcopal Church in Virginia and usually throughout the South. But it is a literary as well as a religious work best understood so far as form is concerned in the light of its models and the compositional practice of the period. And it is a historical work of considerable value for its observations on the Indians.

It is significant that Whitaker's sermon, unlike that of his friend Crashaw, is written more in the style of that earlier fellow Cantabrigean, William Perkins, than of his contemporary John Donne. That is, it is in the plain, pithy tradition of composition prevalent at Cambridge in Whitaker's time, a tradition which remained in Virginia and southern Anglican preaching as long as it did in New England Puritan discourse.

Presbyterian Historical Society, Philadelphia

Samuel Davies—poet, pamphleteer, educator, pulpit orator, hymnwriter

Courtesy of Charleston *Evening Post, The News and Cour*

St. James, Goose Creek, South Carolina, completed 1719

This plain style of Whitaker's sermon is only one of several styles distinguishable in the preaching of this dominant seventeenth- and eighteenth-century literary genre. In the seventeenth century there were basically five forms or styles, all considerably overlapping; some developed early in the period and some late, though all were distinguishable to some degree in the preaching at the beginning of the next century. Preachers and their preaching of the seventeenth century have been labeled usually, according to groups with which associated, as (1) the Anglo-Catholics, including Donne; (2) the other Anglicans to 1660, including Jeremy Taylor; (3) the non-Anglicans to 1660; (4) the Cambridge Platonists and Latitudinarians; and (5) those of the Restoration with Reformed Style.[9] The first two of these are complex in grammar and often embroidered in language, though with emphasis upon different elements of composition. The latter three represent relatively plain styles. Though in their respective generations preachers of all these styles had approximately the same general educational and theological background, their styles differed individually a great deal. And their personal creeds did not necessarily determine the style they employed. Perry Miller argues that the first generation of American Puritans developed a plain style, admittedly parallel to the plain style in England, showing as it evolved peculiarly American characteristics. He repeatedly contrasts it with what he calls the Anglican style, by implication something derived in the early years from Donne and Jeremy Taylor, with an elaboration and complexity of form totally unlike the Puritan.[10] He sees it continued with modifications in the jeremiad of the later seventeenth century, and Heimert demonstrates that it is the basic style of the Calvinist preachers such as Jonathan Edwards and the revivalists, continuing among Calvinist preachers at least to the Revolution, though admittedly new influences were changing its shape.[11] Heimert does not stress or even especially consider contrasts in form with the usual Anglican sermon, for he is primarily interested in contrasts of another kind—between Calvinism and Arminianism. Other writers both before and since Miller often seem to have taken for granted that New England had a plain style unique at least in America, a form that shaped the later evangelical preaching into our national period, a style generally followed today in all America. One point noted above is that this plain style was by no means confined to New England or to nonconformists in general. It began in the southern colonies with its first Anglican ministers and was their principal form of expression, if one is to judge by extant examples, all through the colonial period.

The first great theological influence on Whitaker when a student at Cambridge was the sermons and thought of William Perkins and his followers.[12] Perkins' works were the most popular sermons of the time, and they were to remain so for generations.[13] Perkins may be called the model, not the founder, of the plain-style school of preaching. St. Augustine and Peter Ramus in their treatises of the sermon as rhetoric were among his own models and sources,[14] the former probably for function and the latter for form and function. Perkins' sermon examples and his "The Art of Prophecying," the latter a preaching manual, had a permanent influence on the puritan sermon for their Calvinism as well as for style and purpose.

Perry Miller has given a descriptive definition for the "Puritan sermon," as it appears in Cotton and earlier in Perkins, which is acceptable for the southern sermon as long as it is for the New England. Preceding it is a description of the sermon as it was delivered by Andrewes and Donne, a form of discourse he simply labels "the Anglican sermon."

> The Puritan sermon quotes the text and "opens" it as briefly as possible, expounding circumstances and context, explaining its grammatical meanings, reducing its tropes and schemata to prose, and setting forth its logical implications; the sermon then proclaims in a flat, indicative sentence the "doctrine" contained in the text or logically deduced from it, and proceeds to the first reason or proof. Reason follows reason, with no other transition than a period and a number; after the last proof is stated there follow the uses or applications, also in numbered sequence, and the sermon ends when there is nothing more to be said. . . . [T]he Puritan begins with a reading of the text, states the reasons in an order determined by logic, and the uses in an order determined by the kinds of persons in the throng who need to be exhorted or reproved, and stops without flourish or resounding climax. Hence it was accurately described in contemporaneous terms as "plain," and the Puritan aesthetic led Puritans to the conclusion that because a sermon was plain it was profitable. . . . Sermon style [by the middle of the century] was not a matter of taste and preference, it was a party badge.[15]

If the last sentence were true for Maryland and Virginia in 1650, and one must doubt that it was, it was certainly not true for the southern colonies half a century later, when sermons by Calvinists and Arminians, Tories, Whigs, Jacobites, High and Low Anglican Churchmen, Presbyterians, and Baptists employed the form with much the same modifications that appeared in New England.

Miller, sometimes admittedly, is oversimplifying in describing the sermon. There was among the Puritans who usually employed the plain style some "witty" preaching of the kind of Donne and Andrewes, with elaborate and twisted conceits and a plenitude of imagery. There was occasionally the appeal to the Jewish Rabbins, as Donne had made. There was some of the ornate prose of Jeremy Taylor and many of his homely metaphors woven into the plain style, or at least appearing in the same sermon with it. Richard Baxter and the Scots supplied some of the models for particular American sermons, and their styles in general were plain, though they and their American counterparts varied widely in the degree of emotionalism they displayed. But in the latter half of the seventeenth century the precise plain "scientific" prose, said to have grown out of the necessity of explaining clearly the investigations of members of the Royal Society, came to be felt by both Anglican and Puritan preacher, and its influence in the next century may have been considerable.

An Anglican like Joseph Glanvill, writing before 1681 on preaching, championed a plain style which had the support of the other great churchmen of the time like Bishop Burnet and Archbishop Tillotson (of whom more below). This was a style reformed and hammered into a new logical plainness, for only thus, it was felt, would a sermon—or other literary prose—reach the public for which it was intended.

The particular audience or congregation might determine the subject and content of the pulpit oration. Jonathan Edwards' sermons have been classified in this way in four general groups: disciplinary, pastoral, doctrinal, and occasional,[16] of course all overlapping. Again these are appropriate for southern colonial discourses. The disciplinary depicted depravity and the horrors of eternal perdition, warned against the backslidings of parishioners, and urged repentance and conversion. These qualities or themes are especially characteristic of the evangelical Calvinism of the eighteenth century, as we shall see. The pastoral are concerned with the duties and privileges of religion, often beautifully meditative, and addressed to the needs of regular attendants or communicants. The doctrinal interpret the preacher's faith and concentrate on Bible exegesis. And naturally the occasional celebrate thanksgivings, calamities, funerals, and marriages. The latter three are categories into which the work of most American Protestant divines between 1607 and 1763, of all denominations, may be divided. The largest number of surviving printed southern sermons are occasional, though during the Great Awakening the evangelical and evangelical-polemical became frequent. The surviving manuscript sermons may fall under any of the four categories.

Whitaker undoubtedly preached sermons of each kind to those first Anglo-Americans. But the one printed surviving sermon is not addressed to his local congregation but to the Virginia Company of London and perhaps to all the Protestant English world. It is basically Calvinist, evangelical, and of course occasional. Even in vocabulary it is Calvinist; and providence, predestination, original sin, and the covenants are expressed or implied. Crashaw's introduction states that Whitaker never intended it for publication, else "he would otherwise have adorned it" with evidences of his learning in Latin and Greek, the Church Fathers, and biblical glossaries. Perhaps this is true, and Whitaker merely intended that it should be read before the Virginia Company; but the Dedication to Sir Thomas Smith and the implied audience-reader addressed would suggest that its author at least *hoped* it would be printed. For this sermon belongs with those of Symonds and Donne as pious propaganda for the plantation reaching beyond the Company itself, in this case an unashamed begging for funds, stores, and men to make the undertaking prosperous.

Whitaker preached from Ecclesiastes 2:1 "Cast thy bread upon the waters." He begins by mentioning his *hearers* (not his *readers*), evidence only that it was intended for oral delivery *first* before the Company. He follows almost exactly the formula Perry Miller gives, explaining circumstances and context and the various meanings of terms like *bread* and *waters* in the plainest prose. Then he states the five points he intends to make concerning "Liberalitie," one expanded "reason" following another with little transition. His second point concerns the desperate need and obligation to Christianize the Indians, and in making it he gives a remarkably objective description of these people and their way of life, especially of the diabolical qualities in their religion. Like the New England Puritans, he relies primarily on the Bible for his arguments. By page twenty he is through the four points of his "doctrine" and goes on to the "application," the situation in Virginia, which has several subdivisions. For the last six pages, presumably to incite the interest of his audience, he gives a biological and topographical description of the colony—its rivers, fauna, and flora; above all he emphasizes its natural material abundance. He closes with a paragraph of mild exhortation.

Though one might think from this outline that the last pages spoil the logic of his argument, they really are an amplification of his "application," for the point is that the New World will eventually return sevenfold the bread of "charity" cast upon the waters. Such was the result when the art of Master Perkins was infused with the missionary spirit and the exciting marvels of men and beasts of the western hemisphere. It is theological principally by implication, as already suggested. It is logically organized and reasoned.

Though Whitaker probably did not preach to his parishioners at Henrico of red men and trees and animals they might see for themselves, he surely followed the form he here employs. Not another sermon for the next half or three-quarters of a century is known to survive from the southern colonies. But from this example, what one knows of the education and temper of the clergy, of the kind of religious reading of clergy and laity, as well as of the texts of eighteenth-century sermons preached by elderly men educated and having begun their work in the preceding century, one has bases for concluding that Whitaker's was close to the form of sermon heard in Virginia and Maryland for several generations after he was gone.

Before proceeding to later sermons one should note the sorts of religious books the southern colonial had in his library, for they certainly parallel in nature and form what he heard in church. Ample evidence is offered in the preceding chapter that the seventeenth-century Anglican clergy in the Chesapeake Bay colonies were probably Low-Churchmen. Just as positively one may assume that their parishioners were, for from the inventories of books in wills and from the titles mentioned in letters and other places, it is quite evident that the private libraries of both clergy and laity were in the beginning largely puritan and that the later seventeenth-century divines most frequently represented were puritan, Low-Church, or Royal Society stylists and thinkers.

A study of books present in Virginia before the dissolution of the Company in 1624, as observed in an earlier chapter, points out that most of them were both religious and puritan.[17] In the cargo of the ship *Margaret*, along with two copies each of the Bible and the Book of Common Prayer, went three copies of puritan Lewis Bayley's *The Practise of Piety*, a compendium of puritan sermons preached at Evesham which had reached its twenty-fifth edition by 1630 and fifty-ninth by 1735 and remained popular in the southern colonies throughout the colonial period.[18] In 1620/1621 one plantation owner bought, among many other books, *The Works of G. Babington* (Bishop of Worcester), a complete edition having appeared in 1615. Babington, a middle-of-the-road Anglican preacher, included among his voluminous writings many expository dialogues and other vade mecums in a relatively plain style. His works appear again later in many southern libraries. In the same early collection was "Smyth of doctrines," apparently a short title for one of the seventeen editions of puritan Henry Smith's *Collected Sermons* published between 1591 and 1622.

In January 1621 books presented to the new college at Henrico included St. Augustine's *De Civitate Dei* and "Master *Perkins* his workes." Both titles have strong puritan or Puritan connections. As Perry Miller says, "One might demonstrate that [St. Augustine] exerted the greatest single influence upon Puritan thought next to that of the Bible itself, in reality a greater one than did John Calvin."[19] William Perkins, Whitaker's fellow collegian and master architect of the puritan sermon, has been noted above. As in the case of Bayley, his works appeared in most southern libraries, lay and clerical, of the seventeenth century.[20] In the second volume of his collected works was "The Art of Prophecying," his previously mentioned preaching manual used alike by Puritans, puritans, and Anglicans in New England and Virginia.[21] Another author long used and approved by Puritans was Zacharias Ursinus, sometime student under Calvin, whose *Catechisme* had been published in English at Oxford in 1591. An "unknoune person" had in August 1623 donated for the use of Virginia churches that might need them three large Bibles, two Books of Common Prayer, and "Ursinaes Cathechisme." Exactly what volumes Whitaker, Bucke, Robert Hunt, and other clergy had with them is not known, but their libraries referred to in the records must have contained all these and many more.

As the years went on, the collections of books seem to have increased about in proportion to the population, though one can estimate fairly only when titles are listed. If a minister's 1635 library inventory is typical, the clergy owned personally impressive collections of theological works, including biblical commentaries, several works of St. Augustine, Erasmus, Hooker, the Church Fathers, Greek Testaments, books on the Sacrament, Tremellius, popular later Jacobean preacher Byfield, Calvin, Ursinus, Quintilian, Keckermann, and numerous other volumes of sermons.[22] In Maryland in 1654 and 1656 volumes of sermons as well as *The Practise of Piety* were among the books of churchmen.[23]

The great libraries of laymen analyzed by Louis B. Wright contained much the same sort of material, later libraries of course adding new and current titles. Some of the authors or titles mentioned above appeared in the middle and later part of the century. Not all of them were Puritan, but neither were all the theological works in the library of a Cotton Mather. A word should be said about a few of the sermons. Richard Baxter, "tainted" as he was with dissent, was popular in Virginia Anglican libraries. His *Christian Directory; or, A Sermon on Practical Theology* (1673) and the *Saints' Everlasting Rest* (1650) were in many libraries such as Ralph Wormeley's and John and Robert Carter's. He was still popular in South Carolina in 1747 and 1763.[24] The titles are a mixture of strongly Anglican, strongly Puritan, puritan, and middle-of-the-road or conciliatory. Parson Lewis Latané, of French Huguenot origin but an orthodox Church of England minister educated at Oxford, as late as 1732 owned Donne's sermons, along with many others, and the works of John Calvin.[25] With his sermons appeared religious tracts and a number of works on the art of sermon composition, as those of Perkins and Keckermann.

The most popular preacher of them all was Archbishop John Tillotson (1630–1694), whose works appear in from one to fourteen volumes in nearly every southern colony, as frequently in lay as in clerical collections. He was easily the most widely read British preacher after his writings began to appear in print about 1661. Beginning as a Puritan and educated at Puritan Cambridge, he was always considerably in debt for form and some ideas to his Calvinist father-in-law, Bishop Wilkins, another great preacher well represented in southern libraries. But partly under Chillingworth's guidance Tillotson departed completely from the Calvinism Wilkins retained.[26]

Before the Great Awakening Tillotson was read and approved by moderates even among the Puritans and other nonconformists, and after that by the rational and liberal preachers of New England.[27] Certainly the later New Englanders read him. But his gentle tolerance of most things other than transubstantiation and predestination and atheism, his latitudinarianism and his plain style, made him a favorite model for southern colonial preachers and favorite reading matter in their parishioners' homes. Tillotson was renowned for converting the Earl of Shrewsbury from Catholicism, for his championing of natural *and* revealed religion, for his rationalism, and for his hostility to enthusiasm. All of these except the first were conducive to making him anathema to the later George Whitefield, but for the forty or fifty years before the American Awakening his sermons were read widely in the southern colonies by all who could read. He continued as a favorite with Anglicans after the revival began. One may safely say that the most frequently found single religious title in the southern library, except for the Bible and possibly *The Whole Duty of Man*, to the end of the colonial period, was Tillotson.

Part of the key to Tillotson's popularity is contained in what seemed to some contemporaries the contradictions in his beliefs and actions: partly because he was a personal friend of his sovereigns William and Mary, he was accused by the Jacobites of trying to make the Anglican church Presbyterian; but there was his concomitant firm and unequivocal stand against Calvinism and predestination (he frequently disputed irresistible grace with the Calvinists) and his genuinely sincere crusade against Roman Catholicism and atheism. One biographer sees his religion as far from idealistic, as an appeal to "our best interest," our selfishness.[28] He was a relatively liberal thinker. He used Locke and sensationalism to put transubstantiation to rout. He did not believe in using the Church Fathers or other "authority" to support commonplaces, though clearly he was well versed in patristic literature. He has never been considered a great argumentative thinker, but he was able to do much to turn late seventeenth-century atheism into a sort of Christian deism. It is his prose-style-plus-emphasis which is his great accomplishment. For before him in his century the English pulpit wooed men toward Puritanism. With him it wooed them away from it.

His was a plain style descended from Perkins, but a style which had suffered alterations under the influence of the Royal Society and its precept and example of a precise and accurate vehicle for ideas. In Tillotson's hands the sermon became an essay, expanded from notes beforehand into complete form, memorized in its entirety, and presented without reference to manuscript. Perhaps his discourses were too obviously organized, a fault common to Puritan and Anglican before him. The conceit was almost non-existent in his work, the few images homely and unsophisticated, though there is occasionally a rhetorical passage.

He did not originate modern English prose, though Dryden acknowledged his debt to him. He shared in its creation with Cowley, Temple, Dryden, Bishop Wilkins (his father-in-law), and the earlier puritan preachers. Addison and Steele owed much to him, and thus so may have the colonial American newspaper essay. Eighteenth-century textbooks and manuals for schoolboys or scholars included examples from him. Benjamin Franklin and Noah Webster are among the later Americans who extracted or pointed to his sermons as models of English prose.

This all too inadequate survey of Tillotson has been intruded here in order to emphasize what will become obvious to anyone who will read the extant body of southern colonial sermons before Whitefield and Davies. Most of them were Anglican, and most of them share Tillotson's rationalism and his plain style. Even the few Presbyterian sermons from the period resemble his in form. They share with his the occasional rhetorical flourish or impassioned tone. If their content differs, it was because their American composers were following his example, and that of his predecessors and confreres, in fitting proper words to proper audiences. Some individuals go beyond him in a display of learning, but they are few. For great or solemn occasions the colonial sometimes heightened tone or rhetoric, or tone with rhetoric, as he did. When the Great Awakening came in the 1730s, Presbyterian and Anglican, Arminian and Calvinist, evangelical and rationalist, had a plain and strong and clearly outlined frame on which to stretch their materials. John Locke has been called America's philosopher, for he has ruled our ways of thinking. Though Tillotson's realm was not so large or his reign so long as Locke's, this Anglican prelate may be called colonial America's theological stylist. He began to influence the sermonic segment of American literature even before Locke became our model and arbiter in philosophical and political matters.

Ironically enough, the only known surviving Anglican sermon other than Whitaker's from the seventeenth-century South is somewhat stiffer and more ostentatious than Tillotson's work usually was. It was preached and written out by Deuel Pead (d. 1727), like Tillotson a Cambridge man though of a younger generation, admitted pensioner to Trinity in 1664 just as Tillotson was beginning to achieve his fame.[29] Pead came first to Maryland, served in Anne Arundel County about 1682, and preached before the Maryland Assembly October 14, 1683.[30] This is the first recorded occasional sermon by Pead, who was later to preach on special events before British congregations of all kinds, including members of Parliament and the King himself.

Pead remained in Maryland only a very brief time after preaching to that colony's Assembly, for the vestry book of Christ Church, Middlesex County, Virginia, records that by November he had been persuaded to become the minister of that parish.[31] Bishop Meade was under the impression that churchwarden Major-General Robert Smith had brought him straight from England in 1683. What probably happened was that Smith had met Pead in England and soon after the clergyman came to Maryland persuaded him to move to Christ Church Parish. As noted in the preceding chapter, the vestry of this parish was perhaps at the time the most distinguished, and perhaps the most affluent, in British America, including a Skipwith, a Chicheley, Beverleys, Wormeleys, Robinsons, and other leaders of the colony, one a baronet and another a knight. Though never inducted, Pead served faithfully and well for seven years. Here a son and two daughters were born. To the parish or glebe he gave his livestock and other material possessions when he departed for England about 1690.

Feeling that too little attention was paid to the Holy Communion, Pead began at Christ Church a monthly series of Saturday afternoon sermons which would be preparatory to the Lord's Supper to be celebrated the next day, services through which parents and children and "servants" (meaning slaves largely) would be guided to an understanding of its significance. This sermon was in a sense a development from Whitaker's Saturday catechizing or instructing, but it was more formal than that.

Pead probably returned to England at the suggestion of John Holles, Earl of Clare and by 1694 Duke of Newcastle, who became his lifelong patron. In 1691 Pead was appointed "Minister" of St. James's, Clerkenwell, London, a position he held until his death. In the same year he became chaplain to Holles and in 1707 was further rewarded with a rectorship in Essex. From 1694 through 1709 Pead preached and published —sometimes with dedications to Holles, once to King William—an interesting series of sermons on historical and state subjects and occasions, interspersed with others on strictly moral and spiritual themes. Then, as he had been earlier in Virginia, he was a staunch supporter of the status quo, now William instead of James II. There was nothing strange or inconsistent in his turning his support to William and Mary and Anne rather than continuing to acknowledge the Catholic Stuarts, for like most Anglicans his loyalty was to established authority.

In other words, Virginia had as a rural clergyman for a number of years a man later to become one of the more popular ecclesiastical commentators upon and eulogists of the last of the reigning Stuarts. He preached sermons on the deaths of Queen Mary and of King William. He preached a thanksgiving sermon in 1706 for the victories of Marlborough, another on William's escape from assassination in 1696, another on the union of England and Scotland in 1707, one against Louis XIV and Pope Clement XI in 1709, another on the "Dreadful Storm of Wind" in 1704, and one on James Woosencraft, "The Converted Sinner," in 1701. There were also more purely doctrinal and moral sermons considered worth printing, such as "Jesus is God" (1694) and "The Wicked Man's Misery" (1699).[32] Pead shows a remarkable change of pace, or change of style, reflecting subject and occasion. "The Wicked Man's Misery" is as plain and un-adorned as any Puritan prose, or as Tillotson at his plainest." Jesus is God," more doctrinal though aimed at Everyman, is full of scriptural references, erudite discussions of etymology, and Hebrew phrases, none qualities entirely eschewed by users of the plain style. In "Sheba's Conspiracy" (1696), dedicated to William III, Pead learnedly explicates Old Testament history, discusses contemporary political doctrines, and argues persuasively and lengthily in a loyalist sermon. Elsewhere Popery and Socinianism, biblical history, classical history and myth, medieval history, Amsterdam and London as sinks of sin, are among many subjects considered. The classics are quoted liberally. Pead is never ponderous and always logical, not a great preacher but a superior one. And, one might add, his English sermons lack the stiffness of the lone American specimen of his art which survives.

There is plenty of evidence in the Assembly records of Maryland, Virginia, and the Carolinas in the later seventeenth century that occasional sermons were sent, at the request of the auditors and at their expense, back to England to be printed, though copies have not yet been found. This one was forwarded by Virginia Governor Lord Effingham on May 10, 1686, to William Blathwayt, astute secretary of the Lords of Trade: "For here hath been a Cockney Feast. It was, and is annually to be the 23 of April [anniversary of James II's accession]. There was a very handsome appearance for this place. I have sent you the sermon that was preached at James Towne on that occasion." And the governor goes on to describe bonfires, gun salutes, drinking of toasts to King and Queen, and the desire to take men's minds from other things, perhaps the fear of a Roman Catholic insurrection.[33]

How the unpublished manuscript made its way to the Bodleian Library cannot now be traced, but there it is.[34] Why Pead was chosen as the anniversary speaker, since he lived some distance from Jamestown, one may guess. His sermon before the Maryland Assembly would suggest that he was already known as an able preacher, and his own parish probably agreed with Maryland as to his ability. Then the sponsors of the feast, the "Loyal Society of Citizens born in and about London and inhabiting in Virginia," probably recognized Pead as a fellow Cockney (most Londoners then were born within sound of Bow Bells), for we know he attended Westminster School, and in the body of the sermon he suggests that he grew up, and perhaps was born, in London.

But to his sermon. It is neither long nor labored. Its prevailing imagery is nautical, either because of the speaker's own preference and experience or because he knew his congregation could appreciate the terms more readily than the more learned flowers of rhetoric. Pead himself had been a chaplain in the British Navy in 1671.[35] All his hearers were perforce familiar with salty terms, either as professional sailors or as passengers. For Pead as for others, it was an easy passage from the saline to the sublime, still employing the language of the sea in lofty conceptual figures from the King James version of the Bible. Yet the roughness of style, the hastiness apparent in sentence form and general manuscript state, suggest that the author had to send off his manuscript without opportunity to polish. Indeed, in his Dedication to Lord Howard of Effingham, Pead is frank to state that he hopes his reputation as preacher and author will not suffer too much from this manuscript sent off hurriedly under compulsion, for he knows it is rough work. This is no mock-modesty, as his tone plainly shows.

This "Sermon Preached at James City in Virginia"[36] is not in the plain style of Perkins and the Puritans or of Tillotson and the Royal Society. Nor does it follow the metaphysical tradition of Donne or the ornate embroidered disquisition of Jeremy Taylor. The form is conventional, with quotation of text, brief opening historical and grammatical explication, points and application and conclusion. But its outlines are not the harsh enumerations of other Anglican and Puritan preachers. There are no obvious divisions and subdivisions. The transitions are graceful and barely discernible. It is a logical or rational sermon, for one point leads to another. The iteration and reiteration of the text in whole or in part, Psalms 122:6, "Pray for the Peace of Jerusalem / They shall prosper that love thee," reminds the auditor of this particular occasion and the plea for political harmony the preacher is emphasizing.

Pead quotes the Bible in Hebrew, the Jewish Rabbins like Kimhi, and numerous verses from the English Bible; he refers to ancient and contemporary history, including the rebellion of the Duke of Monmouth and the Earl of Shaftesbury and its relation to London and Virginia; and he cites holy living and piety as the means to individual and political happiness and harmony. Figures of speech, including various kinds of imagery other than the nautical already mentioned, are fairly frequent. His allusions indeed seem too learned for a congregation of middle or lower-class Londoners, but one must recall that he was addressing the governor and many colonial officials and probably a number of the educated from "in and about the city."

What significance the sermon possesses seems principally in subject and purpose rather than form. The political sermon came to be a popular American literary exercise, especially on this subject of harmony and loyalty. In some sense it represents the combination of piety and politics (though not trade) just as do the sermons of Copland and Price and Donne. It has nothing of the missionary spirit of Whitaker's more moving and interesting sermon, and it gives little inkling as to the kind of doctrinal or pastoral sermon Pead probably addressed to his Christ Church parishioners. "Jesus is God" or "The Wicked Man's Misery" among his later sermons are probably more nearly representative or suggestive of the weekly pious fare the Beverleys and Wormeleys and humbler folk received.

So much for seventeenth-century southern sermons known to be extant. Presbyterian Francis Makemie was preaching on the Eastern Shore of Virginia and Maryland in the 1690s, and a tract of 1694 and a sermon of 1707 of his do survive, both considered below. Parson Waugh of Stafford County, Virginia, a vehement Whig, preached highly seditious and inflammatory sermons in the 1680s, but what they contained and what their form was can only be guessed.[37] A former Virginia clergyman about 1685 preached in Westminster Abbey "Trade before Religion," a diatribe against English merchant traffic in slaves,[38] to be commented upon later in connection with the author's religious tracts. The Reverend Stephen Fouace gave a Thanksgiving Sermon before the Virginia General Assembly on April 8, 1692, which that body voted to have printed, and later another sermon before the Assembly in 1693.[39] There are also recorded notices of memorial and other sermons before this Virginia legislature. Though Commissary Blair did not publish the first edition of his sermons until 1722, some of those printed may have been preached during his fifteen years in the Virginia colony before 1700.

For Maryland there remain the record of Pead's 1683 sermon before the Assembly, of puritan Governor William Joseph's "sermon" before the same body in 1689,[40] and of two locally printed sermons of the Reverend Peregrine Coney of 1694 and 1696. Coney,[41] personal friend and chaplain of Governor Nicholson, preached both sermons before the governor and Assembly and had them printed by William and Dinah Nuthead respectively, the first at St. Mary's and the second at Annapolis. No copy of either is known to be extant. The 1696 sermon, on May 7, was a solemn thanksgiving for His Majesty's success and safe arrival. Then there was the Presbyterian or Puritan Reverend Charles Nicholett (Nicolet), who in 1669 preached before the General Assembly a sermon considered by that body too political and actually seditious. Nicholett was fined forty pounds of tobacco and censured, and he soon after withdrew to New England. Of North or South Carolina sermons by Anglicans, Presbyterians, or Baptists, though there is a record of preaching, none seems to have survived.

The Quakers, though they technically did not preach formal sermons, in their testimonies addressed to Meetings of Friends in Maryland, Virginia, and North Carolina, and in the debates they frequently engaged in with Anglican or Presbyterian clergy, were doing something very close to preaching. The journals of Fox, Edmundson, and Burnyeat in the later seventeenth-century South indicate little or nothing of what they said or how it was presented. But Thomas Story, in his *Journal* of the same period (published in 1747), did give long excerpts and sometimes perhaps fairly exact and complete transcriptions of his testimonies and his debates. To other Friends he expanded upon doctrine and belief on such matters as Baptism and Grace and Spirit. The debates were longer and more lively. In Virginia, for example, he "disputed" in a biblical text with an Anglican French-born clergyman James Burtell, and others named George Walker, James Wallace, and Andrew Monro, among several. He names at least two Maryland clergymen with whom he engaged in theological argument. The Inner Light, Water Baptism, and Unpardonable Sin were favorite subjects. Story disputed shrewdly and at times eloquently. Most of his experience in the upper South (which included a small section of North Carolina) took place in the very last years of the seventeenth century. It should be noted that his arguments with southern Anglican clergymen differ not at all from those he had then and later with New England Puritan divines.[42]

Thus the primary evidence is scarce for the form and content of the seventeenth-century southern sermon. But the secondary evidence as to sermons in libraries and of sermons preached is considerable. And then in the earlier eighteenth century the numerous extant discourses preached by clergymen trained in the preceding century, most of whom had actually begun preaching well before 1700, will afford further evidence of the nature of the seventeenth-century southern religious discourse.

THE EIGHTEENTH-CENTURY SERMON

Eighteenth-century southern sermons survive in printed pamphlets and collections, in manuscript fragments, single works, and bound volumes, and in printed books primarily devoted to other things, such as family history or colonial architecture. Represented among them are all the forms which appeared in the colonies in the seventeenth century and one or two new or at least altered types which came into being with the Great Awakening. Most of those printed before 1738 as individual pamphlets were preached upon public occasions. The manuscript sermons are, with occasional exceptions, pastoral and doctrinal. Those in printed collections may represent all the purposes for which their New England contemporary Jonathan Edwards used the sermon.

The occasional sermon may be for a funeral, a day of thanksgiving or fasting, the meeting of the legislative assembly, the annual gathering of such organizations as the Masons or the Scots Club, the accession of a monarch, the founding of a school, or the dedication of a new church. There were also strong diatribes against Roman Catholics, atheists, and free-thinkers; homely moral or ethical disquisitions against gambling, fraud, and wealth; pleas for Christianizing the slaves and for education; and discourses on the sacraments of Baptism and the Holy Communion. From the Great Awakening to the Stamp Act, that is, from 1738/1739 to 1763, the same occasions incited sermons and the same subjects were used as before. But new forms and relatively new subjects appeared, for the French and Indian War was in progress, and the evangelicals and the rationalist-conservatives in some instances made their sermons doctrinal polemics. Though the modified jeremiad of New England, with its lamentation and prophecy of dire consequences of wickedness in an evil age was present in the South earlier in the century, it appeared most frequently during the Great Awakening. A wide range of subjects from patriotism to an unconverted ministry offered themselves to all sorts of clergy. Though the sermon in the last generation of the colonial period was frequently an impassioned polemic, it is interesting to observe that many of the best discourses of the evangelicals are not controversial, and that on the whole the Anglican clergy continued to go about their business of teaching the good and pious life to their flocks as if there was no such thing as the great revival going on around them. This is especially evident in almost all the dozens of manuscript sermons surviving in the Maryland Diocesan Library.

THE EARLY PREACHERS

What is still one of the earliest extant examples of southern printing in this country, if not the earliest, is fittingly the first southern sermon of the new century, Maryland Commissary Bray's *The Necessity of an Early Religion Being a Sermon Preach'd the 5th of May before the Honourable*

Assembly of Maryland, printed in Annapolis in 1700 by Thomas Reading.[43] It was preached before this colonial legislature, less than two months after Bray's arrival in the colony, from Ecclesiastes 12:1, "Remember now thy Creator in the days of thy youth, while the evil days come not, nor the years draw nigh, when thou shalt say I have no pleasure in them." Though addressed to all, it refers particularly to the work the clergy must do in the province, and why. In other words, it is Bray's inaugural. His introduction speaks of the double duty to train children and adults in religion. The first of his two points is explication to show "wherein the duty consists, and what it is to Remember our Creator," and the second concerns what motivations should make remembrance of the Creator advantageous to the young. Under explication he delineates the attributes of God, His Creation, and His Providence for Man's Redemption. Reiteration of the terms of the text keeps the principal objective constantly in view. Under the second heading, motivation, he turns to "the beloved Disciple *John*" as a model, and goes on easily from one argument to another. On the fourteenth page of his twenty he again enumerates, this time in three parts, the dangers of delay in becoming pious Christians. How should one remember the Creator?

> Study to know him in his Nature and Attributes, in his works of Creation, Providence, and of Grace, and in those Excellent and Glorious Laws he has given us. . . . *Remember him* as a discerner of the Thoughts and Intents of your Hearts. . . . Remember him as now sitting in Heaven, and Registering up in a Book all your Words. . . . Remember him next as a Holy and Righteous Judge that Eternally hates Sin and will infallibly punish it, if not Repented of. . . . Lastly, remember him as an infinitely good and gracious Governour that will Recompence all your pains, and watchfulness, and diligence in serving him, with Rewards ten thousand times beyond the merits of your deservings.[44]

On the last page, in a restrained though fervent conclusion, building his clauses around the oft-repeated word *Vain,* he warns the unrepentant sinner, and he breaks off with a final paragraph of rhetoric reporting the joys of Judgment Day for the pious. Quietly eloquent the sermon is, beautifully organized in exclamations, rhetorical and real questions, and reiterated words. There are no learned allusions to ancient languages or literatures, no multitude of marginal biblical sources, no elaborate figures or images. It *is* the plain and reasoned style of a natural evangelical, for this preacher was the great founder of three national or international missionary societies. It is less doctrinal than most of Jonathan Edwards' sermons. It is less rhetorical than the later Presbyterian Samuel Davies' pulpit oratory. But the sermon reminds one of both, as it reminds one of Tillotson and the tradition of reasoned eloquence of the Anglican church.

Most other American Anglicans of Bray's time did not possess his abilities as a speaker, but on the whole this one surviving sermon from his American period is a fair model of and for the southern clerical discourse for the next generation or longer.

Other sermons during the subsequent decade are, with one exception, known only by author and title or by the furor they created. Bray's brother commissary in Virginia, James Blair, had in 1702 preached a funeral sermon on the death of King William. Blair claimed that his commendation of the mildness and gentleness of the King's reign caused the Virginia governor, now Francis Nicholson, to consider it a reflection on himself "for his furious and mad way of government." Nicholson in turn claimed that Blair had gravely reflected upon the late James II, and that Blair was not sending an accurate copy of the sermon to the Archbishop of Canterbury, to whom both were writing.[45] One would give much to find *any* draft of the sermon.

Two years later in South Carolina the Reverend Edward Marston, rector of St. Philip's and from all accounts a born troublemaker, reflected severely on the acts of the General Assembly and was ordered on October 10 to bring to that body the notes preached on Acts 18:17 on October 1 and notes on another sermon. He flatly refused, telling his congregation he was not accountable to the Assembly. Two other clergymen, both nonconformists, Archibald Stobo and William Screven, testified that Marston had said nothing about the Fifth Commandment prejudical to the Assembly. Marston apparently had supported dissenters against the move for establishment, but he was persona non grata to so many people for so long that it is difficult even to guess just what his discourses contained.[46]

Also in 1704 two Maryland clergymen, preaching at the opening of St. Anne's Church, Annapolis, on September 24, had their sermons printed by Thomas Reading. These men were Thomas Cockshutt, rector of All Saints in Calvert County, and Dr. James Wooton of Westminster, Maryland, later chaplain of the provincial Assembly.[47] Our earliest word of Anglican or other formal preaching in eighteenth-century North Carolina occurs in the Reverend James Adams' letter to the S.P.G. of June 10, 1708, in which he states that he has "preached some preparatory sermons to the Lord's Supper," as others before and after him were to do.[48] In October 1710 the Maryland lower house recorded its thanks for sermons to Edward Butler and James Hindman, but what they preached on is not mentioned.[49]

One Anglican sermon other than Bray's does remain from this first decade, and it is worth commenting upon for several reasons. First and foremost, its author was George Keith (c. 1638–1716), Scot and formerly a famous Quaker preacher and writer. His apostasy from the Society of Friends in 1700 and immediate ordination in the Anglican church was a long-remembered event in ecclesiastical history. In 1702 he returned as an S.P.G. missionary to America, where in earlier years he had been a co-laborer and friend of Fox and Penn. He was immensely successful in bringing American Quakers back to the English church. In Massachusetts in broad Scots dialect he called out to some "in the queen's name" to return to "good old mother church." In Maryland he was especially effective among the Presbyterians. In the two Chesapeake Bay colonies he preached from April through July 1703 and was back in the area in April–June 1704, when near Kicketan (Kecoughtan, today Hampton) he visited his daughter and son-in-law, grandparents of George Wythe, Signer of the Declaration of Independence.

Further, it is of some interest that this is the only surviving colonial-southern published work of a prolific theological writer whose titles fill twenty-three pages of a catalogue of books by Friends. His best-known work, his *Journal,* like the similar writings of his former co-religionists Edmundson, Fox, and later Woolman, is frequently quoted.[50] Among his discourses in Virginia, Maryland, and North Carolina are a thanksgiving sermon at Kecoughtan in 1703 on Psalm 18, a sermon at Captain Sanders' in North Carolina from Romans 1:16, another at Kent-Island in Maryland on I Corinthians 3:11, 12; and another at Kecoughtan from Acts 20:21. The evidence of his journal (kept only in his Anglican missionary years) and other sources is that he preached usually from notes. The great modern Quaker Rufus Jones praises his excellent style, earnest spirit, clearness of thought, and moderation of temper: "Had he died in 1690, [his works] would have ranked high as Quaker classics."[51]

The Power of the Gospel in the Conversion of Sinners in a Sermon Preach'd at Annapolis in Maryland . . . July the 4th . . . , M D.CCIII, was printed and sold by the Thomas Reading mentioned above. Preaching from I Thessalonians 1:5, "For our Gospel came not unto you in Word only, but also in Power and in the Holy Ghost, and in much Assurance, &c.," Keith gives a defense of and exhortation upon the orthodox Anglican and Trinitarian way in Christianity. In structure the sermon is normal plain style, beginning with explanations and background of the text and proceeding to points to be explicated. There are a few references to "chief Authors," but no learned marginal comments. He does refer to and translate Greek words or phrases.

Keith discusses Pauline meaning for the term *Gospel* and from thence goes into the theme of conversion of sinners through the sincerity of gospel doctrine as *preached.* He points out how the principles of Natural Religion come from our own reason, itself enlightened by the Father of Lights. Important as Natural Religion is, Revealed Religion affords us far more noble motives to incite us to obedience. He almost incidentally refutes the Quaker doctrine of the Inner Light or Power as means to conversion. His conclusion "by way of application" is evangelical or missionary, and he exhorts his listeners or readers to find their new conversion to a full profession of Christianity in the "Power and Form" of the Church of England.

If there had been more clergy and more laity within the southern colonial church with Keith's power of conviction and persuasion and evangelical spirit, dissent would surely not have gained the dominance it attained in the next half-century. For after Keith, with all due regard to Blair's aggressiveness and the sincere piety of scores of Anglican clerics, the Church of England lacked militancy. Even in Commissary Garden at mid-century there was only the desperately cornered kind of rebuttal to dissent when it was too late. Keith's sermon was effective in a number of ways in his own time. Today it stands as an excellent example of what the S.P.G. and Anglican church might have done had there been more missionary preachers like Keith.

An erstwhile opponent of Keith was the author of one other printed sermon surviving from this decade. This was Virginia-Maryland Presbyterian Francis Makemie, who in March 1706/7 preached a sermon in New York which was printed in Boston. It may be considered southern because of its author's citizenship in the Chesapeake Bay region and his constant affiliation with that region. As Makemie tells us in his dedication, this was the sermon which caused his imprisonment in New York during a missionary visit. It was originally intended as two discourses but was here telescoped into one. The imprisonment by Governor Lord Cornbury was on grounds more arbitrary than any ever employed in Virginia—the alleged disturbance of the Church of England and teaching of pernicious doctrine. Makemie challenges anyone to find in the sermon evidence to support these allegations. He calls it a practical and plain sermon, in "the New Mode of Preaching," and may mean by the latter simply that it is a *printed* defense. *A Good Conversation: A Sermon Preached at the City of New-York January 19th 1706* . . . was printed in 1707.[52] On the title page appear two scriptural quotations having to do with persecution, and the Latin "Preces et lachrymæ sunt arma Ecclesiæ." The dedication declares the work to be both defense and persuasion, evidence of innocence and attempt to save souls. Makemie discusses two divisions of the text from Psalms 50:23, the enduring *promise* to show the Salvation of God, and the sort of person who will receive this Salvation. Considerable explication of terms is followed by amplification of points, principally through scores of biblical references. "Well Ordered Conversation" he will not call the Meritorious Cause or the Efficacious Procuring Cause, for to do so would be to assert "down-right *Popish Merit*, in derogation to *Free Grace*, and the efficacious Merits of our Redeemer."[53] Gifts of Grace, the Renewing Spirit of God, Covenant-Relation to God, Regeneration, Repentance, and Civil Order are some of the doctrines or subjects covered. After thirty pages he turns to *"Obstructions and Impediments,"* discussing five, and in the final pages gives Application and Exhortation.

Makemie is correct in claiming that his sermon contains nothing against the Church of England or civil establishment. It is dull and, as the author was aware, entirely too long. It touches upon or implies Calvinist doctrines with the same apparent inherent contradictions the rationalists before and after were never able to accept. It is a pastoral and doctrinal and not really an evangelical sermon, but in it are elements or principles the New Light Presbyterians were to support strongly a generation later. The Presbyterians of Great Britain, both in the English Westminster Assembly and in Scotland, had been committed to an established church. Here in the American colonies south and west of New England in Makemie's time they were beginning their turn in the opposite direction. Though Makemie champions toleration in his *Narrative*, it is in this sermon that he most emphasizes the principle. Samuel Davies was in many respects his heir in representing the Presbyterian move toward religious liberty.

The second decade of the century is most voluminously represented in the forty-eight surviving manuscript sermons of the Reverend Robert Paxton (or Packston) of "Keckatoun on James River," presumably Kecoughtan, or Hampton, where Keith's daughter lived. Existing records do not connect him with the parish, known after 1621 as Elizabeth City, but there are a great many gaps in these records. A few entries in surviving documents indicate that he was one of the abler preachers in Virginia. He was licensed for the colonies on October 21, 1709, probably when he was ready to sail for Virginia. The Bruton Parish, Williamsburg, vestry book lists him as being asked to preach at that church on December 17, 1710, and a year later (November 18) William Byrd II notes in his diary that at the same church "Mr. Paxton gave us a sermon that was very good."[54] Most of the rest of what we know of the man personally is a note written in the first half of the Paxton manuscript (Harvard-Houghton Library, MS. Am. 1561): "Fourtie eight sermons preached by Mr. Robert Paxton preacher of the Gospel in Virginia who lived four years in Kickatoun upon the River James and died the 25th March 1714 and ordered these sermons (being written with his own hand) to be sent to his father John Paxton parish schoolm[aste]r and precentor at Humby in Scotland."[55] In the clergyman's clear and perpendicular hand appear a group of what are probably, in subject and general form at least, fairly typical pastoral and doctrinal sermons preached to a village and rural congregation over a period of years. Of the four dozen, one is a fast sermon, at least three are on the Sacrament and others on the Crucifixion and Passion, one each on the Incarnation, Christ the Redeemer, the Nature of Christ ("Of the Son of God"), the Holy Ghost, and the Gospel Light. Addressed to the individual are sermons on imitating God, Repentance, living a good life, blameless living, moderation, Godliness making happy, Anger, Humility, Patience, and Walking Circumspectly. Along with these are the Soul's Rest in Christ, the Soul's Loss and Gain, Salvation, the Burden of Sin, and Love. Since Kecoughtan was a seaport, the sermon "Of Sea Dangers" was particularly appropriate.

The first sermon in Paxton's manuscript book, "The Son of God," from I John 5:5, "Who is he that overcometh the world, but he that believeth that Jesus is the Son of God," in subject and form anticipates somewhat the pulpit oratory of the Presbyterian Davies. Paxton follows the plain style and organization, with scriptural quotation as his primary "proof." There is no Latin or Greek, no elaborate imagery, no allusion to patristic writing. He preaches straight Protestant Christianity, emphasizing Jesus as the Son of God and our only Redeemer, and explaining why we should and must adore him. Except for its minimizing of the doctrines of Grace and Covenant, this might have been preached in Jonathan Edwards' or Samuel Davies' pulpit. It is quiet, moderately eloquent, well reasoned. And the second sermon, "The Resurrection of Christ," from Acts 2:32, is very much like it in tone and temper.

"Of Salvation," with text from Titus 2:11, "For the grace of God that bringeth salvation hath appeared to all men," is interesting to compare with Calvinist sermons for its definitions and explanation of *Grace* and of *Salvation.* Grace, says Paxton, sometimes "denotes favour and kindnes," but the grace of God does sometimes "signify a certain inward working of the spirit," and in a more restrained sense "is frequently set to signifie the gospell of Christ as here so stiled because the terms and priviledges of that Salvation tendered by it are the effect." He then explains Original Sin, and adds the perhaps un-Calvinist suggestion that God has not left us helpless in this weak and miserable state. That grace does not bring salvation to all men is not because it is insufficient but because they do not accept "of its office." And he uses the same comments as do the Calvinists, from St. Paul, to arrive at opposite conclusions. The New Covenant was the command to declare unto all men their chance for salvation:

> [Divine justice being fully satisfied or repaired by Christ's Redemption] that generall sentence of condemnation passed upon all the sons of Adam is suspended and a foundation is layed for the shewing mercy and granting pardon, In respect whereunto

The performances of our Savior bringeth Salvation to all men, as having in the behalf of man transacted and ratified a new Covenant very necessary for and very conducible to the Salvation of man[kind] whereby Salvation is made attainable and is really tendered unto all upon feasible and equal conditions, whereof if any man, however stained or loaded with the guilt of most heinous transgressions, If he do embrace the overtures of the grace of God discovered in the gospell, and consent to [comp]ly to the terms propounded therein, that is, if he sincerely believe, seriously repent and return to the hearty desires and earnest resolutions to serve him, God is ready to dispense mercy and pardon. . . . A Merciful Creator, who would have all men to be saved [if they] deny Ungodliness and Worldly lusts and . . . live soberly righteous and godly in this present world.

The next sermon, "Living the good life" (Titus 2:14) appeals through an eloquent explanation of Christ's sacrifice for man. "Of Moderation" (Philippians 4:5) is another pastoral disciplinary discourse on a favorite philosophy of the Virginia colonial gentleman, who frequently spoke of the Golden Mean, or the Horatian or Aristotelian Mean. The world, the flesh, and the devil against holiness and piety, this world versus the next, are the considerations which should govern men as they act out this little life.

Paxton's parishioners in a litigious age must have noted with interest and curiosity the title of a sermon "Of Justice and Equity" (Luke 6:31, "And as ye would that men should do to you, do ye also to them likewise"). "Religion may be fitly divided into piety and Justice," Paxton begins, and then he continues in a remarkably able survey of the effect of religion on governors and governed and in promoting universal love. The law of equity is the Golden Rule, in the light of nature and of Christ. "Of the burden of Sin" (Matthew 11:28, "Come unto me all ye that labour and are heavy ladened, and I will give you rest") is a discourse of sweet reasonableness, with a tranquility of tone not every colonial sermon possesses.

Probably most significant is what Paxton has to say of the Sacrament, on which he preached more than once, perhaps like some of his predecessors and successors on the Saturday afternoon or evening before the Communion Service, or perhaps on the preceding Sunday. "Of the Lords Supper," preached from Acts 2:42, "And they continued steadfastly in the apostles' doctrine and fellowship, and in breaking of bread, and in prayers,"[56] is a discourse upon the nature of Sacraments in general, explaining the name, meaning, parts, efficacy, number, and necessity of them. He begins with Roman meanings and uses of the term and proceeds to our Christian meaning, an outward sign of an inward and spiritual grace. Grace, covenant, and salvation are all involved in the Christian sacrament, which is more than mere ceremony, and should bring inward and spiritual grace to each participant. Baptism and the Lord's Supper as the two essential sacraments are as necessary to salvation as avoidance of guilt, and grace and salvation depend largely upon the ordinances of God. Such is his clear and reasonable exposition of a principal doctrine and requirement of the church.

Thus the four-year term of the young minister's career in the province of Virginia may be measured by his careful, plain, sincere, eminently reasonable, and quietly pious discourses. Most of his sermons are short. He never wanders from his subject. William Byrd, who had listened to the great contemporary London preachers and read their predecessors, was showing good judgment in being pleased with the sermon he heard at Williamsburg on a November Sunday morning in 1711.

THE LATER COLONIAL ANGLICANS

William Byrd's own parish priest, the Huguenot Peter Fontaine (1691–1757), has left one example of the sort of sermon Byrd may have heard at Westover from 1720 until his death in 1744, though it is an occasional rather than a pastoral or doctrinal discourse. Fontaine, educated at Trinity College, Dublin (where among other things, Byrd drily remarks, he learned to darn socks), was Byrd's bowling and billiard companion, his guest many times, and chaplain of the expedition of 1728 described in Byrd's *Secret History of the Dividing Line* and *History of the Dividing Line*. In his diaries Byrd records their frequent meetings and sometimes a comment upon the Sunday sermon. Most often he simply listened, once he had heard the sermon before, but several times it was "a good sermon." One evening at Westover the two spent the entire time conversing in French. Fontaine was clearly a lover of good wine and good food. But also, besides his sermons, record of his ardent and arduous efforts to baptize and Christianize the frontiersmen along the route of the Dividing Line affords evidence of his awareness of the religious needs of the colony.

Fontaine's surviving sermon was composed for a family thanksgiving, celebrated annually, for their rescue when attacked by French privateers in the south of Ireland. It was preached before a congregation of Fontaines, Maurys, and other interrelated Anglo- and Irish-Huguenot families on the first of June, the anniversary of the deliverance, in this case in 1723. A descendant, Ann Maury, published it in 1853 from the original manuscript.[57]

It is an entirely Anglican, orthodox, plain-style sermon preached from Romans 15:6, "That ye may with one mind and one mouth glorify God, even the Father of our Lord Jesus Christ." Along with the amplification of his points, Fontaine alludes to the Christian heroism of "our parent," who was persecuted, imprisoned, and in hiding for his Protestant faith, and he pays equal tribute to "our mother," who fled hand in hand with their father from "the pestilential breath of the whore of Babylon" to Britain, and then across "the great and wide ocean," when "the Lord placedst their feet on dry land in a place of safety." Like the early Puritan ministers of New England, he reminded his hearers that they must never forget the Lord's blessings, "the remarkable deliverances which have been performed in favor of our family."

Mildly eloquent, this sermon does not measure up to the several of Robert Paxton, though it is manifestly unfair to judge any preacher by one sermon. There is none of the Calvinism here which sometimes crops up in other Huguenots' sermons even when they have become Anglicans. The Fontaines and their tribe, the very people here addressed, and their descendants, have had a distinguished place in southern and in American history. But William Byrd may have hit the parson off pretty accurately, allowing for the exaggeration of caricature, when in the *Secret History* he tagged him as Dr. Humdrum.

Almost as frequently as he heard Fontaine, William Byrd listened to James Blair, the Bishop of London's commissary, first in Jamestown and later in Williamsburg. In the two earlier of the three fragments of his diaries remaining, Byrd records hearing Dr. Blair some fifteen times, and in the old age of both of them in 1739–1741 he often went to the commissary's house and had chocolate or coffee *and prayers* with his fellow member of the Council. Byrd heard Blair preach on several special occasions, such as Good Friday, the assizes, and a funeral. The funeral sermon in 1710 was for the Reverend Mr. Solomon Whateley, "which he did very well." The assize sermon, December 11, 1711, "was very indifferent." On the Good Friday discourse the diarist makes no comment. But in one other instance he records "a very indifferent sermon" and in three "a good sermon." As for subjects, Byrd notes two, "the world spirit" (December 3, 1710), and "about peace" (May 1, 1720).[58]

From the nature of his office Blair had to preach on many special occasions, as the 1702 funeral sermon on King William noted above. On August 29, 1705, at a meeting of the clergy of Virginia, he preached on Matthew 11:29 ("Take my yoke upon you, and learn of me; for I am meek and lowly in heart: and ye shall find rest unto your souls"). The majority of the clergy, who did not like Blair, considered "Mr. Com[missa]ry's Sermon on Meekness and *Power*" as really a slightly disguised threat or "overaweing" sermon not at all on meekness.[59] And they mention another sermon preached to them on Luke 10:16 ("He that despiseth you despiseth me") and still others of a like threatening nature.[60]

In April 1719 the scholarly Reverend Hugh Jones, finding fault with the "doctrine" of Blair's discourse at the convention of the clergy, "desired Mr. Commissary to print it. He excusing himself as never having appeared in Print. . . . he would transmit a copy of it to my Lord Bishop of London." This last the clergy insisted upon. Governor Spotswood, with whom Blair was always at odds, wrote on April 9 concerning this same sermon that it so reflected on the Royal Government that he demanded forewith a copy in writing. This Blair sent him, but wrangling over the commissary's alleged practices continued.[61] From other knowledge we have of Blair there can be no doubt that he might have used the sermon, as he used men and circumstances, to further his own ends—or what he might have called the church's ends.[62]

Though, as he avows, he may never have ventured into print in sermon form by 1719, within three years a group of his sermons were published, the first edition in five stout volumes. These discourses, the most voluminous surviving in printed form from any southern colonial Anglican, are significant of the man, of his church, and of religious literature in America. The title, *Our Saviours Divine Sermon on the Mount, Contain'd in the Vth, VIth, and VIIth Chapters of St. Matthew's Gospel, Explain'd and the Practice of it Recommended in diverse Sermons and Discourses . . . To which is Prefix'd, A Paraphrase On the whole Sermon on the Mount . . .* London . . . MDCCXXII, indicates that the subject matter may be restricted, as to a certain extent it is.[63] That it went through a second edition in four volumes prepared for the press in 1732 but not published until 1740, with an additional dedication (of 1732) and a preface (of 1739) by the eminent theologian Daniel Waterland, would indicate in itself a certain degree or kind of popularity, a fact Dr. Waterland also vouches for. Blair and/or his friends and successors such as Commissaries William and Thomas Dawson did prepare for publication a collection of Blair's miscellaneous sermons, which would presumably reveal much more of the man's mind and doctrine, but the arrival of the manuscript copy in London is the last we know of it.[64]

Thus as a sermon writer Blair must stand upon this related series of discourses he chose himself for publication. Undoubtedly they were preached to his congregation at Bruton Parish Church and perhaps some of them earlier to the people at Jamestown and Henrico. One must recall that he was educated in the seventeenth and not the eighteenth century and that his theological background was that of the Church of Scotland as well as of the Church of England. This Scottish-English combination was significant. Even more than Tillotson and Glanvill and Blair's other English models, the Scottish Episcopalians placed a high value on the private use of the Bible and pointed their discourses to Christ as Saviour. The Scots were never as far from Calvinism in some respects as were the English Episcopalians, though Blair's only demonstrated agreements with the Calvinists were the same as those of most Anglicans. Usually he attempted, somewhat dramatically, to confute Calvinist doctrine.

The Bruton Parish congregation should also be kept in mind. Though in legislative season it was crowded with the elite, usually the educated planters of the province, even then, and at all other times, its regular communicants were small and great farmers, artisans, a few college professors, shopkeepers, and occasionally even members of itinerant companies of actors. When he held a convention, Blair might preach on a fairly elevated plane to an assemblage of university-educated clergy. But from Sunday to Sunday he had to address himself to the barely literate as well as to the middle and upper classes. That the preacher was well aware of this reality is shown in the sermons themselves and in the dedications and other introductory matter.

In the dedication of the first edition to John, Lord Bishop of London, Blair notes that in Virginia one does not have to preach against deists, atheists, Arians, or Socinians as one did in the mother country:

> Yet we find Work enough . . . to encounter the usual Corruptions of Mankind, Ignorance, Inconsideration, practical Unbelief, Impenitence, Impiety, Worldly-Mindedness, and other common Immoralities. For which Reason, the Practical Part of Religion being the chief Part of our Pastoral Care, I was easily inclined to fix my Meditations on our Saviour's Divine Sermon on the Mount.[65]

In the dedication to the intended edition of 1732 to Edmund, Lord Bishop of London, Blair notes that the executors of Dr. Bray, to whom he had transferred his rights, intended this new edition. In his own preface, Blair declares that these sermons were designed "for a plain Country Auditory, without any thoughts of publishing them to the World" and that "the chief Thing I have aimed at, and hope in some measure to have attained, is a just and true Explication of the literal Sense of the *Words*, and the giving of right Notions of the Christian Duties therein described, with a serious Recommendation to the Practice of them."[66]

The Reverend Doctor Waterland, who wrote a new preface dated 1739 for the second edition, himself a distinguished Anglican theological writer opposed to extreme latitudinarian ideas, was also suspicious of mysticism and philosophy in religion and rested his defense of Christianity entirely on external evidence.[67] How congenial Blair's words were to him is evident in what he says of the commissary's sermons:

> A Man bred in the *Schools*, or conversant only with Books, may be able to write *Systems*, or to discuss *Points*, in a clear and accurate Manner; But that and more is required in an *able Guide*, a compleat *practical*

Divine, who undertakes to bring down the most important Truths to the Level of a *popular Audience;* to adopt them properly to *Times, Persons and Circumstances;* to guard them against *latent* Prejudices, and *secret* Subterfuges; and lastly, to inforce them with a becoming Earnestness, and with all the prudent Ways of Insinuation and Address. A Person must have some Knowledge of *Men,* besides That of *Books,* to succeed well here; and must have a *practical Sagacity* (which nothing but the Grace of God, joined with Recollection and wise Observation, can bring) to be able to represent Christian truths to the Life. . . .

[O]ur Author has, in my Opinion, very aptly joined the *Commentator, Preacher* and *Casuist* all in one; And I cannot but approve the *Example* he has himself given, and the *Model* he has so handsomely recommended to others. . . . It is extremely proper, that the Text and the *Sermon* should not appear Strangers to each other, but rather as near Kindred. . . . One Particular I cannot forbear to take notice of (which an attentive Reader may often observe in the Course of these *Sermons*) how happy a Talent the Author had in deciding Points of great Moment, in a very *few* and *plain* Words, but the Result of *deep Consideration,* and discovering a great *Compass* of *Thought.*[68]

Blair certainly had a sense of organization. Beginning with Matthew 5:1 and going through 7:29, the sermons form a coherent body of work. Sermon I of Volume I (Matthew 5:1) is on the scope, design, and occasion for the series. Sermon II (same text) is concerned with the audience whom he addresses, "By *Disciples* are meant *all* Christians." Sermon III continues the topic, with an appendix attacking a "late great author" who does not interpret "Disciples" as Blair does. Straight through the Beatitudes and other "doctrines" Blair goes, often having several sermons on one verse. The form, as already noted, is essentially Tillotsonian plain style with perhaps a Scottish tinge, but the latter more in emphases than in form. In the last sermon of the final volume Blair refers to his prologue and epilogue as though the whole series was perhaps a morality play.

The peroration or exhortation or simply conclusion of Volume I, Sermon XI (Matthew 5:8, "Blessed are the pure in heart"), is characteristic of his diction and thinking:

I shall conclude with a short Exhortation to all to study this Character of a true Member of *Christ's* Kingdom, that is, of a true *Christian, Purity of Heart;* a most rare Virtue in this corrupt Generation, in which men are so far from it that they have shaken off all Modesty, which is the outward Garb and Appearance of it, and think it a Point of genteel good Breeding to glory in their Excesses, as to the Contrary Vice. It is no wonder we have so little true Knowledge of God, and so little Sense and Experience of divine Things, when we neglect so much of the best Means of attaining it, the purifying our Hearts.[69]

Moral law, the meaning of the seventh commandment, the great sin of perjury, the Christian doctrine concerning divorces, common swearing, are subjects concerned with behavior. Of the love of enemies, of Christian perfection, of vainglory in good works, of sincerity and secrecy in prayers, Heaven and holiness as our particular care, false hope of heaven, are more abstract in concept but treated just as practically.

As Bishop Meade has noted, Blair does not "enter fully into some doctrines of the gospel, though he recognizes them sufficiently to show that he held them according to what may be termed the moderate Arminian scheme."[70] Blair objects to the argument of "the learned Calvin" in several places (e.g., II, Sermon I, pp. 12–13). He protests against conversion by "Fire and Faggot" or any other means of persecution or coercion. In common with most preachers of his time, Puritan or Anglican, he suggests that "we suit our Mind to our Fortune, nor ambitiously struggle after higher things than we find the divine Providence has cut out for us."[71] Sermon V of Volume III is on secret or private prayer, a favorite topic of the period, as one can see from slightly later Maryland sermons and from a sermon of James Maury of Virginia (see below), who uses many lines of Blair's sermon verbatim, and without acknowledgment, though both possibly may have been employing a common source.[72] Blair declares his belief that God does not bestow equal measures of Grace upon all, and he speaks of "an inward Light of the Mind and Conscience, which is to direct the moral Part of our Actions." He hardly needed to observe, as he does, that "Moral preaching is good Christian Preaching."

His Greek and Latin are unobtrusive but frequently present, and he quotes French more than once. Style and belief are well represented together in Volume III, Sermon XI (Matthew 6:10, "Thy Will be done on Earth as it is in Heaven"):

All this may be said of future events, which are entirely in God's Hand, and we know nothing at all of them, but in general depend on God's wisdom, Power and Goodness. But then there are some particular Events, for which we have something more to depend upon, than this general, implicit, but ignorant Faith; namely, where God has by Prediction, or Promise, or by a Train of Providences, or by some other manifest opening of the Scene discovered somewhat more clearly what he is about; then as his Will and Design opens up more and more, we have greater Encouragement to strike in with it, and to say, *Thy Will be done.* For though God's Designs in general are dark, and the Footsteps of his Providence hard to be perceived, like that of the Way of a Ship in the Sea, which makes but a slender Impression, and which is soon worn out; yet when he has long held a steady Course, so that it is plain what Port he steers for; as his Designs open more and more, there is a great Beauty in them, and his Providence shall be more explicitly complied with.[73]

Bishop Meade gives Blair's sermons restrained praise, commending the author's straightforward condemnation of the sins he saw around him, and his denunciation of Romanism. Moses C. Tyler, calling Blair the actual founder of "intellectual culture" in Virginia, approved the sermons for several qualities. He sees a great range of topics, an elaborately graceful organization, and a "moderate, judicious, charitable, catholic" quality of mind and a smooth and simple style directed toward practical results. He admits Blair is not brilliant, merely practical and effective. Another nineteenth-century critic echoes both Dr. Waterland and Tyler.[74]

Add to these remarks the fact that Blair shows no sense of humor, and we almost have him as the preacher of *these* sermons. But something should be said of his use of rhetorical devices, for like other exponents and practitioners of the plain style from Perkins to Tillotson, and in America from Shepard to Edwards, he did employ them. As one writer explains, in moderation Blair uses analogies, parables, and figures of speech, "all of which reflect his understanding of Christ's purpose in using similitudes."[75] He employs imagery not to make complex suggestions of ideas, but rather in the prosaic fashion of one-for-one parallels between objects and ideas in the minds of his hearers. Three of his sermons are constructed around a simple analogy, and he uses fossil metaphor (metaphor "in fossil stage long before the seventeenth century") as did Shepard and Edwards and most other preachers born in or near the seventeenth century. And through parables of his own invention and figures of speech there is a more or less direct emotional appeal to his auditors. A favorite is the "reward" image. Most of his allusions, like his footnotes, are biblical. He does invent some beast images, and like Pead and Shepard and a host of others before him, he employs the imagery of the sea for all sorts of purposes. Much of the latter is biblical, as was that of the Puritans. But Blair and his parishioners had made sea voyages, he and many of his vestry more than once, and they lived but a few miles from the tidal rivers bordering the Atlantic coast of America. Therefore in more ways than one, "For what port are you bound?," the Church as "a leaky ship," the voyage of life, and the good-tempered shipmaster must have appealed sensorily to these hardy transplanted Englishmen. Blair's employment of images in linguistic functions in combinations of the practical and emotional make his work a contradiction of Alan Heimert's claim that colonial non-Puritan theologians used images more for ornamentation than for functional value,[76] as they are another proof that the Anglican could employ the plain style as frequently and as effectively as could the Puritan.

From Blair in 1722 to James Horrocks in 1763 is not a great length of time, and the Anglican sermon in Virginia continued in some ways as Blair and even the earlier Paxton left it. The great events of the French and

Indian War and of the Awakening, however, affected it at times, though never so much as they did the Presbyterian or other dissenting sermons. There are odds and ends of fragments and records of sermons in Virginia, such as arrangements for two endowed memorial sermons to be preached in perpetuity; a set of anonymous sermon outlines for 1729; a portion of a funeral sermon preached on Robert Carter in May 1732 at Nomini Hall; the latter part of a sermon preached to a convention of the clergy, probably by one of the Dawsons, between 1732 and 1740; and part of a confirmation sermon probably by Commissary Thomas Dawson in 1751, another good plain-style doctrinal discourse.[77] Then there is the request of the General Assembly that Commissary Thomas Dawson print the sermon preached before them on Acts 22:28, on October 30, 1754.[78] Two sermons preached at Curles, Richmond, Deep Run, and other places in 1752 and 1759 almost surely were composed by the Reverend Miles Selden, minister of Henrico Parish, 1751–1785. The first, on "The Decay of Christianity," employs a more impassioned rhetoric than Blair's but just as simple an organization. Of the second, "A Thanksgiving Sermon," only four pages survive.

In the same collection is a fast sermon by John Moncure of Overwharton Parish, Stafford County, dated July 28, 1756, one of the many preached throughout the colonies in moments of desperate crisis in the War.[79] In his twenty-one pages Moncure, preaching from I Kings 21:29, devotes almost two-thirds of his space to the situation of Ahab, and the preacher's "application" to his time is a modified jeremiad. For he demonstrates the wickedness which has brought the war upon the people of America and prophesies further "Judgments" unless they mend their evil ways. In conclusion, he calls for a fast and a searching of souls. This is perhaps the most impassioned Anglican rhetoric to come down to us from colonial Virginia. It is hortatory, as was that of the evangelicals. It does not employ learned references, for it is essentially biblical. Moncure was a Huguenot, by way of Scotland, which fact may account for something of his tone. What he preaches is Presbyterian damnation, but also salvation through repentance.

Two clergymen have left in print or manuscript several sermons each and other writing which give them rank as literary figures. The earlier of the two was the Reverend William Stith, graduate of Oxford, author of a history of early Virginia, and president of the College of William and Mary from 1752 until his death in 1755. He is mentioned elsewhere in several connections in this study. He was certainly one of the ablest of the Virginians of the generation before the Revolution.

Stith had been master of the William and Mary Grammar School in 1731 and subsequently minister of Henrico Parish (being succeeded there by Selden). Though he attained the presidency of the college, he never succeeded in his other ambition, to be the Bishop of London's commissary. His connections in Williamsburg through his uncle Sir John Randolph were powerful, though not likely to emphasize his religious orthodoxy. But Stith was an able preacher, and his three extant printed sermons were delivered at the official request of the House of Burgesses before the General Assembly.[80]

A Sermon, Preached before the General Assembly at Williamsburg, March 2, 1745–6[81] appeared while he was rector of Henrico Parish. In his dedication to the speaker and gentlemen of the house, he acknowledges that he was never a great admirer of "State-Sermons," but he believes that on the present occasion something is demanded. He preached from Mark 12:17, "Render to Cesar the things, that are Cesar's; and to God the things, that are God's." For a man who did not believe in state sermons, Stith launched into a remarkably perceptive analysis of the relation between rulers, people, and biblical injunction. The Bible did not, as some people claimed, rivet "the Shackles of Mankind" and prove that kings held their crowns immediately from God by absolute and "indefeasible" title. His first point in the "Prosecution of this Discourse" is along these lines; his second concerns the character of the English Constitution and government; the third, the potential dismal consequences of the present attempt of the French against our rightful king and church; and the fourth, a few "inferences" of duty and instruction. Throughout his first section he uses the Bible and Roman history to prove that Christian doctrine in no way supports tyranny. Here as later he shows himself Lockean. The "proofs" of the second point are even more Lockean, the material of the third strongly anti-Jacobite. The application is that it is the duty of every man to resist Pope and Pretender, and the conclusion calls upon everybody to search his own heart for the evil of his ways and then turn to God. It was an effectively reasoned political sermon of the Whig stamp.

The Sinfulness and pernicious Nature of Gaming. A Sermon Preached before the General Assembly of Virginia: At Williamsburg, March 1st, 1752[82] was a pastoral rather than a political discourse. Stith says it was written "for the Instruction and Admonition of my own Parish." It was used now because it fitted the present circumstances of "our Country, and more necessary to be insisted on." The text, Exodus 20:17, "Thou shalt not covet," is of course part of the Tenth Commandment. Stith says he is speaking of a particular kind of coveting which devours lands and houses, manservants and maidservants, oxen and asses, and everything else. This is the sin of gaming, which was a major evil of the day; the preacher observes that it was not beneath the dignity of the Burgesses to hear a sermon on the subject. In participating in what was once an innocent pastime, man sins against his neighbor, his country, his family, himself, and God. It is the most virulent of the reigning evils among his country-men, and he must speak against it.

This down-to-earth, frank, straightforward assault on an evil other clergymen, notably some Marylanders, also attacked was highly ap-proved by Stith's theological opponent Samuel Davies, who mentions it it a tract he wrote in reply to Stith's third printed sermon. Like Blair, Stith was concerning himself with present needs. It is more specific than any of Blair's sermons and therefore perhaps even more effective.

It was Stith's third sermon, however, which provoked controversy, for it is doctrinal. *The Nature and Extent of Christ's Redemption. A Sermon Preached before the General Assembly of Virginia. At Williamsburg, November 11th, 1753*[83] was delivered after he became president of the college. The dedication is to Sir George Lyttelton, Bart. (1709–1773),[84] author of the *Observations on the Conversion and Apostleship of St. Paul* (1747), which, Stith says, is "one of the neatest, clearest, and most con-vincing Defenses of the Christian Religion, that our Age hath produced." The following discourse was written, Stith avers, to the same purpose "of wiping off from the Gospel the Stain of Cruelty and Injustice." Accord-ing to the preface he does not remember ever having read earlier Locke's *Treatise of the Reasonableness of Christianity*, which he now finds his sermon in some respects resembles, but that if he had done so it was twenty-five years before when he was in the university. At the same time he confesses himself a studious reader of Locke's works in general.

Stith begins with the long text from Matthew 7:13, 14, "Enter ye in at the strait Gate, for wide is the Gate, and broad is the Way that leadeth to Destruction, and many there be which go in thereat: Because strait is the Gate, and narrow is the Way, which leadeth unto Life, and few there be, that find it." These words, terrible at first reading, must be studied carefully. In quoting "a late Author from our Press" (Samuel Davies) Stith poses that author's question, "Is it not certain, that the most of Man-kind perish? And to hope the contrary, however natural it is to be a gen-erous Soul, is blasphemously to hope, that God will be a Liar."[85] Again there is the plain style and the well-reasoned argument—this time a doc-trine and an argument, however, which many of his fellow-Anglicans considered theologically ultra liberal, and his Presbyterian brethren considered almost if not actually heresy. For Stith argues that it was the Jews only of whom Christ was speaking when he said only a small frac-tion shall be saved. First Stith considers the sense of the words of the texts; next he compares them with other texts thought to have the same meaning of condemning the greater part of mankind; and third and finally he shows that Christ actually did come to save the *whole world*

(I John 2:2). Though the discourse itself is in plain enough language, Stith buttresses his arguments with passages of the original Greek, the Church Fathers, and modern writers such as Limborch and Locke. The fourth section, in which he argues that as *Redeemer* Christ came to save the majority of mankind, including the heathen who have never heard his word (for "It is shocking to right Reason, and contrary to Principles of common Sense" that they should be held to impossibilities). This he supports from St. Paul, as he does the whole matter of the wideness of redemption, from the same authoritative statements the Calvinists used to attempt to prove the opposite. This sermon was written, Stith summarizes, "To vindicate God's Ways to Man,—to clear up and explain to human Reason his righteous Methods of Grace and Salvation." Stith is not to be misunderstood as saying Salvation is a trifling affair easily obtained. Man must work for it. His design was only to explain "the Sense of these Scriptures; and to shew, that they by no means contain a Denunciation of eternal perdition against *the most of Mankind*."[86]

Stith had not for nothing read Locke, attended Oxford, and listened to his uncle Sir John Randolph, "the Christian deist." Though accused of deism (perhaps because of this sermon), Stith never goes beyond Arminian Christianity, or Lockean Christianity, in his interpretation of the Scripture in the light of reason and common sense. Christianity had to be a reasonable religion if men were to live by it—so he felt. His great Calvinist contemporary Davies, like some of his fellow Anglicans, would have agreed only by giving "reasonable" an entirely contrary definition. Actually Davies answers the sermon in a tract discussed below. In this sermon Stith represents the extreme expression of Christianity as common-sense reason, and yet not a disintegration into deism. One can see the path straight from this rational Christianity, however, to the optimistic deism of Stith's cousin Thomas Jefferson and many another who sat in the Assembly in 1753 or later in the Continental Congress.

The ablest among Stith's Anglican clerical contemporaries in Virginia, in both literature and theology, was one of those Irish-Huguenots, born in Dublin, who had arrived in Virginia with his parents when he was a small boy. This was the Reverend James Maury, most of his life connected with Fredericksville Parish in Louisa and Albemarle counties, and somewhat notorious in the great test case of "The Parson's Cause," in which Patrick Henry made his political and oratorical debut.[87] This patriarch of a great American family was an able essayist on several subjects (including pieces in the *Virginia Gazette*, which possibly may be connected with his name); especially was he a pioneer thinker and performer in education, for he operated a boarding school and wrote what is today a frequently quoted treatise on education.[88] His letters on public and private affairs and persons are as valuable as his essays. Jonathan Boucher, the Loyalist parson and writer, thought Maury had "the command of a fine style. . . . [He wrote] with propriety, force, and elegance."[89] Among his pupils were Thomas Jefferson, Bishop James Madison, and Dabney Carr.

Unlike Stith, Maury was an entirely Virginia-educated product. The ailing James Blair, not long before he died, wrote (1741–1742) for this "ingenious young man" a letter of introduction to the Bishop of London, complimenting Maury's diligence and mastery of Greek and Latin and systems of philosophy and divinity. Blair remarked that the small Maury looked younger than he was, but that at twenty-four he was ready to be ordained. And like the later Bishop Meade, Blair observed that home-bred William and Mary graduates made Virginia's best clergymen.[90]

A number of sermons by Maury from what was apparently originally a sermon book somewhat like Robert Paxton's survive in the Alderman Library of the University of Virginia. One sermon-tract, printed in 1771 after its author's death in 1770, was probably written a year or two after 1763. The manuscript sermons included a funeral discourse, two on prayer, one addressed to children, one on happiness and tranquillity in religion, another on the Flesh versus the Spirit, and one on the righteousness of God, among others. The manuscripts are a series of working texts, for passages are much marked though and revised. These sermons employ the usual plain style with its clear organization, some marginal scriptural references, and some references to contemporary authors. Maury also had the habit of many of his brethren of giving the dates and places when and where each sermon was preached.[91]

Twice in 1750 he preached from Ephesians 6:1, 2, 3, "Children, obey your Parents in the Lord. . . . Honour thy Father and Mother," reflecting the schoolmaster and the psychologist as well as the clergyman. The style is entirely suitable for the parents but by modern standards is stiff and perhaps too erudite for children.

The first of two sermons on prayer (Matthew 5:6, "But thou, when thou prayest, enter into thy Closet; and, when thou hast shut the Door, pray to thy Father, which is in secret; and thy Father, which seeth in secret, shall reward thee openly") is one of Maury's best. He explicates at length the text itself. On page six, in explanation or definition of terms, he explains the original Greek meaning of the word rendered *Closet* in exactly the phrases used by Commissary Blair in his sermon on the same topic, and goes on in Blair's words for about three paragraphs. The rest of the sermon seems completely original, however, and more lively than Blair's. Maury strikes severely at enthusiastic effusions and extemporaneous harangues such as are being delivered to unruly and senseless mobs.

All his points are well taken, and his concluding strong additional attack on revival meetings would indicate that this sermon was prepared for and aimed directly at the proponents of the Great Awakening.[92] The second sermon, less polemical, considers the manner of preparations for prayerful devotion.

"The Flesh and the Spirit" presents the usual contrast between "Reason and Passion, or the Spirit and the Flesh," in the same style.[93] One discourse on happiness and tranquillity in religion, the second of two preached on this subject, employs Psalm 37:37, as its text. It is in the Tillotsonian or Stithian vein, not the Calvinist.[94] His funeral sermon (Ecclesiastes 12:1, "Remember now thy Creator") was originally preached at the service for Miss [Sithe?] Quarles on December 23, 1748, but he used it at least seven more times before September 1759, presumably in similar situations. This is in effect a pastoral sermon, not emotional, really serene and admonitory. The first of two discourses on Matthew 6:33 ("But seeke ye first the Kingdom of God and his Righteousness, and all these Things shall be added unto you") shows (pp. 9–10) how anti-Calvinist Maury was, for he promises that sincere prayer for forgiveness, or true repentance, will bring full pardon. A sermon not quite surely Maury's (but included in manuscripts with his)[95] on Matthew 6:10 (a clause of the Lord's Prayer) is in his style, with a fine philosophical ending after a logical development. "The Character and Divinity of Christ" (John 3:2) emphasizes Christianity as a complete system and as a natural system of religion. He refers to the "caviller" Lord Bolingbroke as being convinced by the "evidence."[96] A later Maury sermon on prayer bases its argument on both Reason and the Gospel.[97] Another doctrinal and pastoral sermon, on the Ascension, is curiously rational, for Maury goes so far as to say that the Ascension is "undoubtedly figurative," for God is a spirit and consequently has no bodily parts. Then there is an anti-slavery fragment. Such in bare outline are the themes and spiritual philosophy of the sermons of this Virginia-bred clergyman who may be considered as able as any Anglican parson of the colonial period. One might remember that Thomas Jefferson felt the force of this mind before he did those of his professors at William and Mary.[98]

A sermon of thanksgiving "Upon the Peace," preached at Petsworth in Gloucester County in 1763 and printed at Williamsburg in that year, is a suitable climax, finale, and summary for the colonial Anglican sermon in Virginia. It was delivered by James Horrocks, a youthful M.A. of Trinity College, Cambridge, master of the Grammar School of William and Mary, soon to become president of the college and within five years commissary, and perhaps the last aspirant for a Virginia bishopric before the Revolution.[99] It is a gathering of some favorite Anglican themes, for it touches upon masters and slaves, gambling, squandering of patrimony, and the love of peace. Dedicated to Governor Francis Fauquier, "a friend of liberty," it warns that civil liberty must be restrained through obedience to law, but not before it relates that liberty rhetorically to the New World Paradise.

> Oh Liberty! Thou art the Author of every good and perfect Gift, the inexhaustible Fountain, from whence all Blessings flow. Without thee, what avails the Sweetness of Climate, or the most delightful Situation in the World? what avail all the Riches of Nature, the various Production of the Earth, the Mine bringing forth a thousand Treasures, the Olive and the Vine blooming upon the Mountains, if Tyranny usurps the happy Plains, and proud Oppression deforms the gay-smiling face of nature.[100]

Though Horrocks is still within the frame of the plain style, here present is the eighteenth-century parliamentary oratory, which in a few years was to leave its mark in the printed political rhetoric of both England and America. In other words, as in New England and among the southern nonconformists, pulpit oratory had evolved or in some respects revolved or returned to Andrewes and Symonds. Sublimity had touched the Anglican style.

The mid-eighteenth century in Maryland, that province's golden age in essay and verse, also produced a number of remarkable sermons by well-educated and astonishingly versatile clergymen. Most of these preachers had connections with the famous Tuesday Club of Annapolis. Henry Addison (d. 1789), a native of Maryland connected by blood or marriage with most of the leading families of the colony, was the brother-in-law of Dr. Alexander Hamilton, secretary of the club. A graduate of Queen's College, Oxford, as were so many of his Virginia contemporaries, he was a frequent visitor at the Tuesday Club. His parish was in Prince George's County, St. John's, Piscataway.[101] Thomas Bacon (d. 1768), musician (composer and instrumentalist), compiler of the laws of Maryland, founder of free schools, brother of shipping merchant Sir Anthony Bacon of London, was a native of the Isle of Man. In the Tuesday Club he was Signor Lardini, the official musician and composer of most of the club's favorite songs.[102]

William Brogden (1710–1770), another native of Maryland, former student at Trinity College, Dublin, schoolmaster as well as clergyman, a scholar and ardent reader (he left a valuable library), had a parish in Anne Arundel County and a large plantation nearby.[103] Thomas Chase (1700–1779), born in England and a graduate of Cambridge, was one of the "Baltimore Bards," "Bard Bavius" of the Tuesday Club "History."

He was the father of a future signer of the Declaration of Independence and associate justice of the United States Supreme Court.[104] He held parishes in Somerset and Baltimore counties. Thomas Cradock (d. 1770), brother of the Archbishop of Dublin, was also educated at Cambridge, held a parish near Chase and was the other of the "Baltimore Bards" of the Tuesday Club. A fairly prolific author, besides his sermons he published a version of the Psalms discussed in a later chapter.[105] Musician, poet, and schoolmaster, he was an able preacher. John Gordon (d. 1790), educated at Queen's College, Oxford, and rector of St. Anne's, Annapolis, was a strong Whig and a member of the Tuesday Club.[106] James Sterling (1701?–1763), born in Ireland and educated at Trinity College, Dublin, was a playwright, poet, satirist, friend of Swift and others of the great on both sides of the Atlantic, was minister at St. Paul's, Kent County, and collector of customs for the port of Chester.[107] These men left a body of manuscript and printed sermons, most of them collected more than a century ago by the Reverend Ethan Allen for the Maryland Diocesan Library, the largest assemblage by far of colonial southern sermons known to exist.[108]

Two isolated sermons preceded them in 1726–1727 and 1738, among the extant manuscripts supposed or proved to be Anglican sermons. The first, a funeral sermon on Ecclesiastes 4:2 ("Wherefore I praise the dead which are already dead, more than the living which are yet alive"), may be the earliest surviving sermon of a minister permanently settled in Maryland (as Bray and Keith mentioned above were not). It was preached on the death of Thomas Bordley by the Reverend John Humphreys (d. 1739), graduate of Dublin and rector of St. Anne's, Annapolis, 1725–1739.[109]

Beginning with observations on man's mortality and the conqueror worm, Humphreys continues with a woeful picture of earth's miseries, original depravity and "its invincible argument against the felicity of human life," and the vanities of that life. Manhood stands between birth and death "like a parenthesis of woe." Homer calls man a leaf, Pindar a dream of a shadow, and a sacred author says his life is "but a vapor." Finally Humphreys pays tribute to the deceased as a great and true son of the Church of England. Though the hortatory and poetic are here, this is still in the plain style unweighted by heavy learning or elaborate conceits.

The anonymous 1738 sermon, preached in both Virginia and Maryland, is a "Serious advise . . . To the atheisticall free Thinkers of the northren nik in Virginia and Mary Land," written in a crabbed and nearly illegible hand with illiterate but phonetic spelling.[110] It may not even be Anglican; certainly its tone is more that of the dissenting revivalists of the period in its hell-fire and lost-soul exhortations. It is not especially Calvinist in doctrine, except perhaps by implication, and it is less literate than any known Presbyterian sermon of the period. It came probably either from an uneducated Baptist or one of the few uneducated Anglicans who were complained of frequently to the Bishop of London. More than any sermon of Whitefield, Davies, Josiah Smith, or Edwards it is in the nineteenth-century brimstone-and-perdition tradition. That it may have been preached as early as 1738 in communities which included some educated and sophisticated men who were probably deists is worth noting. But it may have been addressed to other elements of Potomac River society.

One should observe that the sermons which have survived of the seven or so mid-eighteenth-century Maryland parsons just introduced and about to be discussed lack polemical quality, as far as the Great Awakening is concerned, and usually reveal, as noted previously, an apparent lack of awareness by their authors of the revival going on all about them. These clergymen preached for state and other special occasions, on doctrine, and on morals. They were concerned with salvation and redemption, but usually in a rational and Arminian fashion. But they could preach with fervor from strong conviction, as on the question of Christianizing slaves and their masters' duty in the matter.

Henry Addison, if one is to judge by his one known extant manuscript sermon, used the plain style, culminating his discourse with a light figurative embroidery. His text, Hebrews 2:3, "How shall we escape so great salvation?"[111] is developed in simple diction with few allusions, an explanation of the Old Testament meaning of salvation, and presentation of two aspects of Christian salvation in three divisions. The sermon is undated, probably having been written about 1760.

That true son of the Enlightenment Thomas Bacon printed at least eight sermons between 1748 and 1753, all on subjects close to his heart but of varying effect on ours. The first six were on the old question of conversion of the Negro, the question by no means solved in his time. In *Two Sermons, Preached to a Congregation of Black Slaves at the Parish Church of S.P. in the Province of Maryland. By an American Pastor . . . London . . . M. D CC. XLIX,*[112] he addressed the Negroes but printed the sermons for white readers on both sides of the Atlantic. In the first, he somewhat bluntly tells his auditors that one objection of white men has been "that your being baptized only makes you more proud and saucy," the early but very real objection noted in Chapter V.[113] But he tells his "dear Black Brethren and Sisters . . . that their God is no respecter of persons" and that, though their bodies are not their own, their souls are. He develops his discourse in three simple points as to why they should serve

God, what service God expects from them, and what sort of reward they may expect to receive. Masters and mistresses are "God's Overseers," and he quotes scripture in support. In the second sermon (Ephesians 6:8, "Knowing that whatsoever good thing any man doeth, the same shall he receive of the Lord, whether *he* be bond or free") he outlines the duty or behavior they owe their fellow servants and themselves and the rewards of fulfillment of that duty.

In *Four Sermons upon the Great and Indispensible Duty of all Christian Masters and Mistresses To Bring Up Their Slaves in the Knowledge and Fear of God . . . Preached at the Parish Church of St Peter in Talbot County, in the Province of Maryland . . . London . . . M. D CC. L.,*[114] he addresses his parishioners in a dedication as well as in the four sermons. You must acknowledge, he tells them, "Blacks or Negro's to be the same species with [yourselves, and] that they have human Souls." Differences in complexion afford no solid argument. The four sermons, all preached from Colossians 4:1 ("Masters, give unto your servants that which is just and equal, knowing that ye also have a master in heaven") are based on one principle, the "indispensible Obligation" of every owner to bring his slaves to the knowledge and fear of Almighty God. Instead of taking up a number of points in each sermon, he employs a separate discourse for each of four. He outlines all the current objections, practical and allegedly moral, and answers them with force and eloquence, and he spells out the exact measures masters should take to help their slaves, such as encouragement to attend service and catechizing, appearing as sponsors in baptism, and employing catechists who can and will instruct the slaves in their own quarters.

Like many other Anglican clergy of the time, Bacon was a Mason, and like other clergymen, he preached to his Order on one of its anniversaries. His subject was brotherly love of a somewhat different sort or application from that presented in the preceding six sermons, but there can be no doubt of the sincerity in his use of the occasion to proclaim human brotherhood in Christ. *A Sermon, Preached at Annapolis, in Maryland, before a Society of Free and Accepted Masons In the Parish Church of St. Anne, June 25th, 1753 . . . Annapolis . . . M D CCLIII,* has long been known by title, but as recently as 1922 no copy had been examined in our time. One now has turned up in the Library of the Grand Lodge, A.F. & A.M. of Massachusetts, in Boston.[115] Dedicated to Bacon's friend Dr. Alexander Hamilton, master, and to the two wardens and brothers and fellows, it was printed with a notice of request for publication signed by Jonas Green, secretary. Green and Hamilton, the two leading members of the Tuesday Club, indicate at least a tenuous connection between the organizations. The sermon, on I John 4:21, on loving one's brother, is a warmly affectionate discourse, unmistakably anti-Calvinist in the matter of Free Will, and emphasizing the Christian quality of brotherly love. It does not fail to note and condemn the covetousness, gaming, and other sins to which the Annapolis brethren may have been inclined. It is the least formal of Bacon's extant sermons, without enumerated divisions; but it is also clearly addressed to a more educated and homogeneous congregation than he had in his parish church.

A Sermon, Preached at the Parish Church of St. Peter's in Talbot County, Maryland: On Sunday the 14th of October 1750. For the Benefit of the Charity Working School to be set up in the said Parish, for the Maintenance and Education of the Orphans and Other Poor Children and Negroes . . . London . . . M. D CC. LI,[116] to which proposals, rules, and a subscription roll were attached, was naturally designed by Bacon to attract financial and other assistance in Great Britain as well as throughout the Chesapeake Bay region. It was dedicated to seven Maryland subscribers, and there is evidence in the *Virginia Gazette, Maryland Gazette*, and Dawson Papers that he solicited and obtained financial assistance in Virginia and perhaps in Pennsylvania. Preaching from Galatians 6:10, he exhorts his reader-hearers to "do Good unto all Men: especially unto them who are of the Household of Faith." Reasoned and eloquent, the scriptural gloss and "proof" are followed by a condensed history of British charity schools. He argues for both black and white, for he has found almost as many neglected among the latter as the former. He defines *charity* in many ways. Any one of his several definitions is characteristic of author and style:

> In its *Nature* it is pure and disinterested, remote from all Hopes or Views of worldly Return, or Recompence from the Persons we relieve:—We are to *do Good and Lend, hoping for nothing again.*—In its Extent it is unlimited and universal; and though it requires that an especial Regard be had to our *Fellow Christians*, it is confined to no Persons, Countries, or Places,—but takes in all Mankind;—*Strangers*, as well as *Friends*,—the *Evil* and *Unthankful*, as well as the *Good* and *Grateful*.—It has no other Measure than the Love of God to us, who gave *his only begotten Son*; and the Love of our Saviour, who laid down his life for us, even whilst *we were* his *Enemies*.—It reaches not only to the Good of the Soul, but also to such Assistance as may be necessary for the Supply of the bodily Wants of our fellow Creatures.—And the absolute *Necessity* for practising this Duty, is the very same with that of being Christians;—. . . . *By this shall all Men know that ye are my Disciples, if ye have Love one to another.*[117]

William Brogden's commonplace books, many pages being made up of tracts and sermons, repose in the Maryland Diocesan Library. But at least two of his sermons also were printed. Three or more years before Bacon he preached before the Masons *Freedom and Love. A Sermon ... in the Parish Church of St. Anne, in the City of Annapolis, on Wednesday the 27th of December, 1749 .... Annapolis ... M D CC L.*[118] Like Bacon's, it is dedicated to Dr. Alexander Hamilton and other officers and brothers of the lodge. His text, Galatians 5:13, "For Brethren, ye have been called unto Liberty; only use not Liberty for an Occasion to the Flesh, but by love serve one another," was to be used in a more famous sermon by New England liberal Jonathan Mayhew a little later for a somewhat different purpose. Brogden's approach is rational: Man is endowed by Nature with a desire for liberty which must not be allowed to degenerate into libertinism. By Nature alone, man is a slave, propelled by the tyranny of disorderly appetites and disorderly dispositions. But also by the light of Nature he discovers a God, who through Right Reason leads him to moral and positive liberty. Brogden agrees with the Puritans that man has liberty to do good, to *love* through benevolence and beneficence. With all this he believes "Free Masonry" agrees, and the preacher precedes his benediction with the appropriate prayer:

> May it please our almighty Lord, to establish us with Grace in the Truth of his holy Gospel; and to strengthen us in the inner Man; to raise us all from the Death of Sin, and Bondage of Pollution, to the Life of Righteousness and true Holiness: That we may be lively Temples of the *Holy Ghost*, founded on Jesus, the true *Corner Stone*; and finally pass through the Grave, and Gate of Death, to a joyful Resurrection, through the same Jesus Christ our Lord.

References are made a number of times to Brogden's sermons against Popery, but of them only one of 1755 has been preserved in print, and even that had been lost to view as recently as 1922.[119] *Popish Zeal Inconvenient to Mankind, and unsuitable to the Law of Christ. A Sermon, Preached in St. Barnabas Church, Queen-Anne Parish: On the Fifth of November 1754. ... Annapolis ... M D CC LV,* is a combined sermon against the Roman Church (primarily as represented by the Jacobite and French-Indian threats) and thanksgiving for deliverance therefrom. Preached from Galatians 4:17, 18, it begins with an interesting address to any Roman priests who may read it. Brogden notes that he has recently preached a sermon contrasting the Roman and Reformed religious: in a sense this present sermon is a companion piece. His contentions are buttressed by long and learned notes on European history, including that of the Jesuits and other Catholic orders. His attack is directed at the unscrupulous means to conversion and persuasion employed by the Roman

Church—the Gunpowder Plot, English Catholics, and the Inquisition. He quotes Archbishop Tillotson, a fellow anti-Romanist. He concludes with a patriotic review of British opposition to Rome from Henry VIII to the present, with an exhortation to live the Christian life according to the church his parishioners profess. This is an able "historical" and argumentative sermon demonstrating the continued or revived awareness of Roman Catholic aggressiveness in North America.

Thomas Chase, rector in Somerset County on the Eastern Shore and in Baltimore County, is represented in the Maryland Diocesan Library by a considerable number of manuscript sermons and fragments of sermons. They include a wedding sermon, Ecclesiastes 4:9, "Two are better than one," and sermons on doctrine, blasphemy, morals, and fear of the Lord. In 1750 he preached on "Religious Retirement" or "Prayer" from Matthew 14:23, fairly close in purpose and doctrine to the sermons by Blair and Maury on private prayer, though from a different text. It is a reasoned discourse in the plain style. Chase records at the end that he preached it twelve times in all between 1750 and 1774, usually at St. Paul's, Baltimore, but once in Annapolis. Another sermon of 1751, from Malachi 3:6, is concerned with God's immutability. Man's changeableness is contrasted with this attribute of the Divine, but the emphasis of the sermon is on Mercy as a quality of God's immutability.[120] This is perhaps an orthodox Anglican call to repentance, worth contrasting with the emotional exhortations of the revivalists of the period.

Hymn writer, secular poet, classicist, schoolmaster, and preacher, Thomas Cradock was, like Bacon, a true son of the Enlightenment. *Two Sermons, with a Preface shewing the Author's Reason for Publishing Them* ... (Annapolis , ... 1747),[121] dated the sermons 1745 and 1746 respectively. The first, "Innocent Mirth not inconsistent with Religion. A Sermon Preach'd April 23d, 1745, in St. Paul's Church," from Proverbs 17:22, also survives in manuscript, of which more below. The second, a longer discourse, "A Sermon Preach'd at St. Thomas's Church, on the Day set apart by his Excellency the Governor and his Council, to give God Thanks for the Conquest of the Rebels ... ," is another of the thanksgiving sermons for British and Protestant victory such as have been noted earlier in this chapter. It is a good example of the Anglican occasional discourse.

The short sermon from Proverbs 17:22, "A merry heart doth good like a medicine," which might be called "The Merry Sermon," is unlike any other known existing religious writing from the colonial period. If it were not so genuinely Christian in context, one might suspect it might have come from the revelers—or a wanton gospeler—at the Merry

749

Mount of Thomas Morton in New England a century before, at least as Hawthorne suggests in two stories that the gospeler thought and spoke. Its tone is joy; its argument, that the good man should have a merry and cheerful heart. For man was born to be sociable:

> When he's wholly absorbed in himself and looks with an evil eye on every thing hearty and sociable[?] can that soul promote harmony that has no harmony in itself: will the violin please the ear with its voice, when its strings are broken? or who can say the haut boy joins the concert when in the hands of an unskillful player? No, the morose surly unchearful man can never answer the end of his creation: he can never be a good man, nor the good christian, the good neighbor or the good friend; he may say what he will but if he has not a merry heart, he wants a very great characteristic of the humane mind. And pray what are the good things of this world given us for? to enjoy and possess them in a rational manner: not to abuse them indeed: but to use them like men cheerfully, gracefully, as our servants, to furnish to us the comforts of life. . . . [on such festivals among heathen and christian nations] 'twas then they crown'd themselves with the choicest flowers and enriched their bodies with the most elegant perfumes, then did the skillful artist string most ravishingly his lute and the heavenly voice exerted itself in chanting forth most melodiously the praises of its country—then the jocund youth and sportful fair joined in the sprightly dance together and moved to the measures of the sounding instrument.[122]

Thus in the tone and spirit of an older England did Cradock's short sermon celebrate Britain's victories over an ancient foe and St. George's Day. In his conclusion the preacher urges that joy be seasoned with prudence, as proper to every Christian. This is one of the most delightful and happiest prose essays of British America.

But these sermons of thanksgiving and celebration represent only one phase of this man's pulpit oratory. Some time before 1763 (for he became paralyzed in that year), on the occasion of the founding of an academy, Cradock preached in Philadelphia one of the major colonial discourses on "The advantages of a learned and liberal education," taking as his point of departure Acts 26:24, 25, "And as he thus spake for himself, Festus said with a loud voice, Paul, thou are beside thyself; much learning doth make thee mad. But he said, I am not mad, most noble Festus."[123]

This is really a religio-educational essay. Cradock begins by observing that "a very ignorant man cannot well be a good man," and proceeds to prove his thesis rationally, with Festus as an example of ignorance and that of Paul strongly in favor of a learned life. Cicero, Solomon, the Greeks, Egyptians, and Chaldeans are cited as proponents of learning. The

Lacedaemonians had, with their disdain of learning, a long history of tyrants. The glory of Athens, its influence in softening the wild Romans, the Augustan age, the Church Fathers, especially Lactantius and St. Augustine, are all involved in his argument. Great Britain itself is his last great example before he turns to Philadelphia's new academy, which will be an ornament and a comfort to the city and to America.

Cradock felt so deeply about the debased character and behavior of so many of his fellow clergy that in 1753 he preached a courageous sermon on the subject, a discourse he clearly intended to be printed.[124] He begins by admitting to his "Audience of all Ranks" that his subject is a very uncommon one, and he claims their indulgence, for he speaks from conviction and necessity. His text is Titus 1:5, "For this cause left I thee in Crete, that thou shoud'st set in order the things that are wanting and ordain elders in ev'ry city, as I have appointed thee." He had hoped some more venerable brother clergyman would take up this matter, but none had done so (he had been in Maryland almost ten years). As his text suggests, the duties and character demanded of the clergy are clear. Incidentally, he mentions[125] how much a resident bishop would help in these matters, and how the Bishop of London had been thwarted when he attempted to have one consecrated. Cradock names unhappily staffed parishes, though he refrains from naming the unworthy incumbents.[126] He makes four points, that men are under no apprehension of being called to account, that wicked men attempt to get into clerical office because they know they will not be called to account, that the condition of persons whose welfare depends upon such clergy is very bad, and that unless the case is well managed against these weak and evil men there will be great harm in aspersions from the Anglicans' enemies, the Papists and dissenters. Incidentally, he strikes an ecumenical note in observing that he has cause to rejoice that all branches of the Christian Church seem to be growing closer together.

Cradock makes few if any specific charges, though he alludes to failure to hold services and perform sacraments and bad examples in personal conduct. If a personal element is involved here, there is no sign of it. As Cradock says, he speaks from the clearest conviction with a good conscience, with no personal motive but the good of the Church of England in Maryland his great concern. Much complaint, and more specific complaint, of this sort of thing is recorded in letters from the clergy to the S.P.G. and to the Bishop of London, but this is apparently the only existent southern Anglican colonial *sermon* on the quality of the clergy and its remedy.

Two other pastoral sermons on moral matters probably exemplify the

CARL A. RUDISILL LIBRARY
LENOIR RHYNE COLLEGE

sort of discourse Cradock must usually have given. One of them is concerned with wealth (with some emphasis on the sin of gambling), the other with fraud.[127] That on fraud, from I Thessalonians 4:6, is developed under three points concerning the extent, the object, and the occasion and circumstances of committing the fraud. The application points out the injuries to ourselves and to others, including the helpless, and to God. As for him who has defrauded, he should at once repent and make full restitution; for those who have not, the temptation should be shunned. This is a simple, short, and homely sermon. The second discourse, on Proverbs 13:11, is more clearly concerned with the ethics of acquiring wealth, how it may be legitimately obtained by a good Christian, what means he may pursue, and what unlawful and indirect ways must be shunned. Cradock stresses gradation, every man in his appointed rank in the great scale of creation and of society. Various abilities bring various rewards. He concludes this rational discourse with the application that all must mortify in themselves all inordinate desires and lay up for themselves treasures in Heaven.

That these two pastoral sermons came close to the end of his active career in 1763, when he was ill and disabled, seems likely. They are reasonable and clear, but neither has the force, literary grace, or eloquence of the others here mentioned. They appear to indicate a definite diminution of powers.

John Gordon, rector of St. Anne's in Annapolis and subsequently of St. Michael's in Talbot County, a member of the Tuesday Club, has left two published and at least two manuscript sermons.[128] The first of the latter, from Job 5:6, 7, undated but probably preached any time between 1745 and 1790, is concerned with the afflictions of man and the humility and desire to repent that they should teach us. Moderately eloquent, smooth, scriptural, clearly sophisticated but without learned embroidery, it is a good pastoral sermon. The second, on Hebrews 13:14, has the ancient emphasis on man's frailty and on this life as but a voyage from one unknown to another. Life is short and unhappy, but there is a future state of rewards and punishments, and, one may add, it is here hardly a Calvinist state.

In his two printed occasional sermons Gordon shows two things about himself, that he was a Whig and that he was a Mason. *A Sermon Preach'd before His Excellency Thomas Bladen, Esq.; Governor of Maryland, at the Parish Church of St. Anne. . . . On the Day of Public Thanksgiving to Almighty God, for suppressing the late Unnatural Rebellion . . .* Annapolis . . . M D CCXLVI[129] was dedicated to the governor. In his preface Gordon hails the victory over the secular arm of Popery, the spiritual argument long ago having been silenced by the voice of reason. He preached from Exodus 14:13, of the salvation the Lord has wrought for the Chosen People in freeing them from the Egyptians. Gordon goes into the horrors of Popish persecution and slavery, using various Protestant "historical sources" and reinforcing them with long documentary notes not included in an oral delivery. A long series of apostrophes and exhortations on liberty, Christian and civil, anticipate nineteenth-century Fourth of July oratory in its spread-eagle qualities. Almost effusively patriotic, though plain enough in diction, it is about as near as most Maryland Anglicans came to the evangelical spirit around them.

Like other Masonic brethren, Gordon addressed the Annapolis lodge on June 25, 1750, after he had become rector of St. Michael's on the Eastern Shore. His *Brotherly Love Explain'd and Enforced. A Sermon Preached before the Society of Free and Accepted Masons in the Parish Church of St. Anne's .... Annapolis ... MDCCL*[130] is like the two others noted above dedicated to Dr. Hamilton and others of the brotherhood. Brotherly love, tolerance ("embrace whom we cannot convert"), mercy, are his points for discussion. Application to the Masonic brotherhood is obvious: they believe in being free, and they believe in human love.

Far more eloquent than Gordon was that quondam playwright and present poet, essayist, and revenue officer the Reverend James Sterling, rector of St. Paul's Parish, Kent County. Two editions, one of Annapolis and one of London, survive of his *Zeal against the Enemies of our Country pathetically recommended: In a remarkable Sermon, Preached before His Excellency the Governor of Maryland and Both Houses of Assembly. ... December 13, 1754*, printed in Maryland and Great Britain in 1755.[131] It is prefaced by an unusual prayer, strongly resembling the Anglican liturgy in its cadences, but petitioning "Prosper the Arms of these confederated Colonies for their mutual and common Safety: Humble in Europe and America the hostile Aggressors and Disturbers of England's Peace." It includes much more on undissoluble union. From Galatians 4:18, "It is a good thing to be zealously affected always in a good thing," Sterling launches into his discourse with brief preliminary. He explains the purport of his text, demonstrates from history, Jewish particularly, the rise and fall of states and of the arts and sciences, and by way of application calls for enforcement of the doctrine of the text by all interested in the welfare of their country. Sterling was apparently a natural dramatic, even melodramatic, orator. Jewish history is a horrendous example of indifference and division; modern Dutch is another. Then he soars into a panegyric on artists and statesmen who made the classical world.

The application is a stirring call for volunteers to fight with soldiers from other colonies against a common enemy. He warns of the insidious plans of the French, and he points out the French and Indian slaughter of the Virginia forces:

> The Reason of their Kings is publish'd from the Mouths of their Cannons; and where their Clergy fail, Dragoons most powerfully convert. . . . Turn over the Pages of your shining Annals, and while you read of what has been done in the Fields of *Cressy*, *Poictiers*, *Agencourt* and *Blenheim*, tell your bounding Hearts the same Blood enriches your own Veins, and ensures approaching Victory! Ye Sons of the *Reformation*, confirm'd by the Death of so many bright Martyrs, guard your holy Religion from *Papal* Persecution, Idolatry, *Irish* Massacres, Gun-Powder-Treasons, and worse than *Smithfield* Fires!

All this addressed to the members of the General Assembly! They were to raise the funds, and probably the troops. But this is the one southern Anglican recruiting sermon of the French and Indian War which survives for comparison with the two or three by the great Virginia Presbyterian, Samuel Davies. Davies addressed the potential soldiers, Sterling their political representatives. The two clergymen make some of the same appeals to history. Davies is eloquent and persuasive; Sterling is eloquent and histrionic and perhaps persuasive. In their contrast they parallel as orators in some ways the later Richard Henry Lee and Patrick Henry, called the Cicero and Demosthenes of Virginia, for the ancients as well as Perkins and Tillotson and sublimity were here in this mid-eighteenth-century world of war and emotion.[132]

One wishes that the perceptive Hugh Jones' only known printed sermon, *A Protest against Popery* (Annapolis, 1745),[133] had survived, for it would be interesting to see whether he was as effective as preacher as he was as historian. But there is to be noticed one more Maryland Anglican sermon of the period, preached on Good Friday in 1763 by the Reverend Thomas Pread (Read),[134] from I Corinthians 2:2, "I determined not to know any thing among you, save Jesus Christ, and him crucified." The dignity of Christ's person, the nature of his sufferings, and the merits and efficacy of his sacrifice and atonement are the points for amplification and application. It is perhaps symptomatic in this age of reason that the preacher feels he must emphasize that belief in the redemption and belief in morality are equal in value. Another plain style sermon is thus far from Calvinist.

The one surviving North Carolina Anglican specimen of pulpit oratory was printed. *To [sic] Sermon, Preached in Christ-Church, in Newbern, in North-Carolina, December the 27th, 1755, Era of Masonry, 5755, Before the Ancient and Honourable Society of Free and Accepted Masons. . . . By Michael Smith, B.A., Newbern . . . M DCCLVII,*[135] is dedicated like the

Maryland discourses to the master and brethren of the local lodge. Smith preached from Proverbs 27:6, "Faithful are the Wounds of a Friend; but the Kisses of an Enemy are deceitful." Like others concerned with brotherly love, this sermon contrasts man in an isolated and a social state, and the common bond of humanity and natural friendship: "Two *Americans*, tho' born [in] different Provinces, meeting in *Africa*, will think their being *Americans* a sufficient Reason for the[ir] uniting their Hands and Hearts." In reason and eloquence it is not the equal of the Maryland sermons. Smith also the same year received the thanks of the General Assembly of his colony (on October 7) for a sermon preached before them the day before.[136] Two other sermons printed respectively in 1761 and 1763, by a Mr. Camp and by James Reid, the second on the subject of public schools, were probably the best North Carolina sermons of the colonial period,[137] but no copies are known to be extant, and the quality of the sermons can be guessed only from their contemporary reputation.

Though the letters and contemporary reputations of South Carolina early-eighteenth-century Anglican clergymen would suggest that they were effective preachers, their sermons have not survived. Numerous as are the letters of Gideon Johnston and Francis LeJau, for example, there remains no sample of their pulpit oratory. Actually as many dissenting sermons as Anglican—or more—preached in South Carolina remain extant, if one counts Whitefield as a dissenter and assumes that certain sermons he preached all through America were delivered in that province. Even without Whitefield the noted Josiah Smith and a few other nonconformists appeared in print more frequently than did the two leading Anglican clergymen of the mid-century, and with approximately the same number of sermons.

The two Church of England parsons who published a number of sermons were Commissary Alexander Garden and the Reverend Samuel Quincy of Charleston. Garden appeared in print over a period of years, and Quincy gathered his score of discourses into one collection. From 1719 until 1755 Garden preached and published on a variety of subjects, though most of his well-known pamphlets were directed against revivalism, the "Methodists," or Whitefield personally. The personal and doctrinal controversy between Garden and Whitefield has been touched upon in the preceding chapter and will be again in connection with religious tracts later in this chapter. The sermons show that intellectually and oratorically, for an upper-class auditory, Whitefield met in Garden a worthy adversary. In *Regeneration and the Testimony of the Spirit. Being the Substance of Two Sermons Lately preached in the Parish Church of St. Philip, Charles-Town, South-Carolina. Occasioned by some erroneous Notions of certain*

Men who call themselves Methodists. . . (Charleston, 1740; Boston, 1741),[138] Garden's text might well have been one chosen by Whitefield himself: Romans 8:6, "The Spirit itself beareth witness with our spirit, that we are the children of God." Garden's parishioners are reminded in his dedication that they recently heard these two short discourses within the "enchanting sound" of Whitefield's voice. The sermon plunges immediately into an attack on "Enthusiasts" and their claims of a particular Regeneration and New Birth. After explication of the text, Garden gives his own position, supporting it with references to recent printed rational arguments. Here and elsewhere he proceeds on the basis that he is fighting a cyclical religious phenomenon that has appeared many times before, as in the latter seventeenth-century, and that its attractions must be warned against once again. His argument is rational, and punning: "Beware therefore, my Brethren, of such Pretensions;—of the old Story over again! . . . Suffer not your *Passions to be moved*, but as your *Minds are instructed;* And run not away with the agreeable Voice of the *Preacher* in your Ears, for the *Soundness of his Doctrine* in your Understandings."

This otherwise effective discourse is marred for the modern reader by its occasional inappropriate, or at least jarring, sarcasm, a quality more pronounced in Garden's polemical tracts. His arguments are conventional and sound enough: Regeneration is not, and cannot be, the work of a moment, and there is the basic contradiction of Calvinist Predestination and Salvation through instantaneous Rebirth. In conclusion, he couples Cromwellian Puritans and Methodist Enthusiasts as those who have brought desolation to the heavenly and earthly kingdoms.

Garden was a Scot. His assistant minister, Samuel Quincy, was probably an Oxford graduate of English origin. Ordained by the Bishop of Carlisle in 1730, he had been an S.P.G. missionary in Georgia before he moved to South Carolina. He left Charleston in 1749, carrying with him subscriptions for an edition of his sermons which he had printed in Boston the next year.[139] An abler writer and perhaps an abler pulpit preacher than his ecclesiastical superior, Quincy published in *Twenty Sermons On the following Subjects*[140] an extended series of reasoned and eloquent attacks on Whitefield and enthusiasm, and included with them a number of effective pastoral and general doctrinal sermons. I and II are on "Christianity a Rational Religion" and "The Characteristicks of True Religion"; VIII, "The great danger of Neglecting Salvation"; XVII, "The Nature and Necessity of Regeneration"; and XX, "The Danger of Wilful Error," the last preached at a visitation of the clergy in 1745. Of the rest, XI is a funeral sermon on Robert Betham, formerly of Queen's College, Oxford; XII he preached in the time of pestilential fever; V was in preparation for the Holy Communion, and others are concerned with immortality of the soul, the vanity of human life, and moral behavior (evil-speaking, avoiding offense, doing good for evil, and bearing affliction).

Sermon I, "Christianity a Rational Religion," is from I Corinthians 10:15, "I speak as to wise men: judge ye what I say." After a long explication of St. Paul's circumstances when making this statement, Quincy comments on his announced subject: "Indeed all the Doctrines of Christianity are not equally clear and perspicuous; but they are according to their Importance, and nothing is prepared to our Belief that is contrary to the Sense and Reason of Mankind. Where any Thing is delivered to us in a doubtful and undeterminate Sense, we have no Warrant to fix a determinate Meaning to such Things." This particularly applies to doctrines dependent wholly upon Revelation, "which are discoverable by the light of Nature. . . . For if they are not contradictory to Reason, much more if they carry in them a high Probability of Truth, we have all the Reason we can require to admit them as true." The truth is, man possesses very inadequate notions of God and another world, but this does not mean we lay aside our belief in them. But our ignorance in various points should cause us to suspend judgment. Here he hits directly at the vitals of the arbitrary interpretations of Whitefield and certain others of the New Lights. These "erroneous men" serve themselves by denying the use of reason.

Though Heimert's assertion that Quincy was the first confidently to express the belief that "Christianity [is] a Rational Religion" may be open to some doubt, he is one of the abler exemplars of the "negative reaction" to the revival.[141] In "The Nature and Necessity of Regeneration" is the Anglican and rationalist explication of the doctrine. Quincy makes three points in interpreting "To be born of the spirit," mentions the different mistaken explanations which have been advanced, and finally declares that being born of the Spirit "in the plain Sense and Meaning" is necessary for salvation. His amplifications and explanation are eminently reasonable within a Christian context, and he includes some sound psychological observations or explanations of the "violent Perturbations of Mind" shown so often by the enthusiasts. The sober, *rational* Christian embraces his religion after duly weighing and considering proofs and arguments. The enthusiast embraces it without reason or examination.

Quincy is perhaps with Stith the most effective of the southern Anglican preachers who directly opposed the Great Revival. His weapon is reasonableness. He did not feel the necessity or the desirability of sneering or making sarcastic remarks about the individual or general characteristics of the evangelicals. A shrewd observer of men and doctrines, he wrote and spoke from rational conviction without rancor. Corruption and degeneracy, he believed, spring from failure to exercise the reason, which of itself frees us from "the Bondage of Superstition, Ignorance, and Prejudice."

Carl Becker saw Quincy's rational and philosophical arguments as representing one of the sources of the ideas preparatory to the Declaration of Independence.

DISSENTERS AND THE GREAT AWAKENING

As pointed out in the preceding chapter, not all nonconformist clergymen were in agreement with the principles, doctrines, and actions of the Great Revival. No Maryland dissenting minister of the period of any conviction has left a known sermon. But for Virginia, the Carolinas, and Georgia there are extant many polemical and often distinguished discourses. Most of these are evangelical or revivalist, but some on the conservative side offer their testimony also. Most on both sides are Presbyterian, but even before 1763 several Baptist contributions were of some significance.

In Virginia, in the Shenandoah Valley and in Amelia in the south central region, Old Side Presbyterians were established early in the eighteenth century. Because of the invasion of their regions by New Side preachers such as William Tennent and Samuel Blair and because they were with the Anglicans charged with being "an unconverted ministry," their clergy spoke so strongly and bitterly that there was for some fifteen years a split in their church. A good example is John Craig, an Old Sider and M.A. of Edinburgh, who preached for nearly thirty years at the Tinkling Spring Church in the Valley. His own style was plain, strenuous, and Calvinist. He did not approve of the hell-fire, thunder, and terror of his enthusiast brethren.[142] At least one specimen of his pulpit oratory survives, a "short" final sermon (8,000 words) preached at Tinkling Spring in 1764.[143] It is in the tradition of the New England Puritans and older Presbyterians in its emphasis on the Covenant of Grace and Christ the mediator. For these had been his topics for over twenty-five years, Craig reminded his congregation.

His ally in middle Virginia, John Thomson, a Scot and M.A. of Glasgow, had arrived in Delaware in 1715, served in Pennsylvania and Maryland, and then continued on into Virginia. He lived in the Buffaloe community, then a part of Amelia County, from 1744 to 1750 and visited and lived and preached in other parts of Virginia and North Carolina, dying in the latter colony in 1753.[144] He published other writings and in 1741 a sermon and tract to be discussed later. Both the latter, though they were written in his Pennsylvania or Maryland pastorate, are worth noting because they represent the Calvinist Old Side point of view he championed in three southern colonies. *The Doctrine of Convictions set in a clear Light, or an Examination and Confutation of several Errors relating to Conversion.*

Being the Substance of a Sermon Preached by the Author to his own and a Neighbouring Congregation, with some Enlargements ... (Philadelphia, 1741) is a direct reply to the unusual stir "of late" produced by Gilbert Tennent's charges of unconverted ministers.[145] The explication is short, the doctrine longer, for it is an examination of the doctrine of the New Side clergy. It is opposed to preparatory convictions (the compilers of the Westminster Confession found none); it admits the necessity of true Grace but differs from the New Side in its definition. This eighty pages of plain style is principally reasoning along conservative Calvinist lines.

Though Tennent and Blair are others of the New Light Log College group who invited themselves to Virginia in the early stages of the revival, the official missionary of the New Castle Presbytery was the Irish-born John Roan, a product of the Log College and a schoolmaster as well as preacher of some eminence. He was sent to Virginia, particularly to the Hanover County people in 1744 and remained several months into 1745. He caught fire before one large gathering and poured forth invectives against anything and everything not New Light. Dissenter Joshua Morris noted that "A perfidious wretch deposed he had [heard] Mr. Roan utter blasphemous expressions in his sermons." His reviling of the established church finally brought the law against him, and on April 19, 1745, he was "presented" by the Grand Jury of the colony for his preaching in the house of Joshua Morris in James City County:

> "At church you pray to the Devil"—and "That your good works damn you, and carry you to hell,"—"That all your ministers preach false doctrine, and that they, and all who follow them, are going to hell," and "The church is the house of the Devil,"—that when your ministers receive their orders they swear that it is the spirit of God that moves them to it, but it is the spirit of the Devil, and no good can proceed out of their mouth.[146]

Roan soon returned to Pennsylvania. As a master of invective he was surpassed by Gilbert Tennent and Samuel Finley, the latter of whom held forth on the Pennsylvania-Maryland boundary at Nottingham for his seventeen most active years.[147]

In North Carolina in 1764 Jacob Ker, licensed by the Presbytery of New Brunswick some time early in 1763, preached on one of Samuel Davies' famous topics, "The One Thing Needful," in a good plain-style sermon, very different in content from but similar in spirit to Davies'.[148] But this was late in the first Great Revival. Earlier, in South Carolina there were distinguished supporters of the Awakening, men who like the Pennsylvanians found themselves opposed by the conservative Old Siders in their midst. They were Presbyterian and Independent and Baptist.

759

When Whitefield preached or awaited a ship in Charleston, he persuaded a group of dissenting ministers of several denominations to unite in holding a weekly lecture to encourage and instruct their converts. The first of these lectures was a sermon by a Baptist from an Ashley River congregation, the Reverend Isaac Chanler.[149] *New Converts exhorted to cleave to the Lord. A Sermon on Acts. XI:23 Preach'd July 30, 1740, at a Wednesday Evening-Lecture in Charlestown* (Boston, 1740)[150] begins with a brief introduction on Whitefield, tracing the history of his great work in "these parts." Typically evangelical, the sermon is a presentation of Whitefield's Calvinist doctrine of Grace in the context of Justification and Regeneration. Addressed to young people, it is in plain style, far from polished even in its plainness, as far as language is concerned. Another Baptist, Oliver Hart, has left us no sermons but a number of sermon outlines and an extensive diary.[151] In the latter Hart mentions preaching on July 17, 1757, to Colonel Boquet's regiment of soldiers in Nightingale's pasture, a not uncommon practice of Anglican and dissenter alike. His sermon outlines (1754–1765), all with texts from Timothy, are concerned with such subjects as "Christ the Mediator," for which there is a full outline and even one completely written portion. All these indicate a plain style, a well-organized argument of the orthodox variety, and an evangelical though not controversial tone. These two men show that urban Baptist ministers of the mid-eighteenth century were as well educated as their Anglican and Presbyterian brethren, and perhaps as evangelical as the latter.

South Carolina dissenters, like Virginia New Light Presbyterians, were strongly patriotic. Not all their sermons are strictly doctrinal or polemical. In the "Old Meeting House" in Charleston on September 14, 1744, in the midst of dire peril from the French and Indians and on a government-proclaimed fast day, Israel [or John] Evans, preached on *National Ingratitude Lamented: Being the Substance of a Sermon,*[152] from Isaiah 1:3. As was proper at such a time of danger and tribulation, the preacher's discourse was a mild jeremiad, pointing out the people's sins and warning of the dire consequences of ingratitude and impenitence.

In Georgia, at least for brief periods during these years, were two if not three of the great preachers of the Christian world, for here were John and Charles Wesley and George Whitefield. Charles Wesley's stay seems to have left little impression, for he was not then an active preacher. Through his hymns he has become part of the American religious heritage. John Wesley's Georgia years are still being disputed by biographers and theologians over whether they were pre-evangelical and really pre-Methodist or actually a significant stage in his development toward Aldersgate and his revivalism. In Georgia Wesley frequently preached without notes on portions of Scripture, as on the Sermon on the Mount (February

26, 1737). On June 24, 1737, he preached before the local Masonic lodge in the appropriate Anglican manner.[153] On February 20, 1736, he had discoursed at Savannah from I Corinthians 13:3, "Though I bestow all my goods to feed the poor, and give my body to be burned, and have not love, it profiteth me nothing."[154] This discourse "On Love" is a normally organized plain-style sermon, only gently evangelical in its purport. It is eloquent, and the reader even now seems to feel the power-in-wraps with which Wesley preached. Its touching account of his father's deathbed anticipates the emotional appeal of his later English sermons. Perhaps more significant were the complaints by Georgia planters that his preaching and prayer meetings were impelling the lower classes to improper acts at improper times, acts which hurt the prosperity of the colony.[155] But Wesley's tremendous impression on America was to come in later years, even after his own lifetime, through his followers and his writing. His brand of Arminian revivalism was not to triumph in America until the second Awakening, in a later generation.

Not so with their friend and fellow Oxonian George Whitefield, who disregarded the disillusioned John Wesley's advice and came on to Georgia anyway. Technically or theoretically he was Wesley's successor in Savannah, although at the time he was only in deacon's orders. From the moment of his setting foot on the American strand, perhaps inspired by the ghosts of Pilgrims, Puritans, and Presbyterians (some quite lively ghosts), Whitefield began to differ from the Wesleys. His Calvinism grew stronger as theirs disappeared entirely. Perry Miller, and especially Alan Heimert in the two books here frequently referred to, have discussed the kind of reconciliation, or fusing, of apparent opposites of the predestinarianism and covenant of Grace of Calvinism with the emotional calls for repentance of such revivalists as Whitefield, and the matter is discussed briefly in the preceding chapter. The paradox and the contradiction are yet with us. But here is space only for concern with a few of Whitefield's American, especially southern, sermons which illustrate the polemicist and the peculiar sort of Calvinist he was.

In the collected and even individually published discourses of the Great Awakener it is often impossible to tell whether or not he ever preached a particular sermon in Georgia or some other southern colony. His habit was to use sermons more than once. He might give Boston as the place in which a certain sermon was preached (especially if he published it in that city), though actually he might have given it a dozen or a score of times between Savannah and New England. In a few instances he does indicate, or his editor indicates, that a sermon was prepared for Georgia or other southern congregations.

The Eternity of Hell Torments, acknowledged as *A Sermon Preached at Savannah in Georgia*[156] in 1738, is from Matthew 25:46, "These shall go away into Everlasting Punishment." It is hortatory, of course, but it argues of man's future punishment or salvation on the familiar Calvinist grounds; and except near the conclusion, when Whitefield gives the imagined meditation of the wretched or wicked in dramatic form and beseeches "ye *Christians* of a Lukewarm Laodicean Spirit" to reconsider, it is pretty dull reading. Not even the warm promise to the repentant arouses response in the *reader*. Whitefield's voice and oral delivery must have been his great assets. *Thankfulness for Mercies received a necessary Duty. A Sermon Preached on board the Whitaker, At Anchor near Savannah in Georgia on Sunday May the 17th, 1738* (London, 1738),[157] from Psalm 107:30, 31, is a pastoral sermon, spoken to his friends and parishioners in Georgia. With some fervor the great preacher warns them of dangers ahead and of the need of prayer and repentance. It is not doctrinal.

A third sermon, printed after he had preached it a second time in London, *The Great Duty of Family Religion: A Sermon Preached at the Parish Church of Saint Vedast, Foster Lane* (London, 1738),[158] is dedicated to the Inhabitants of Savannah, Georgia, who had received it with attention and joy. Upon the text from Joshua 24:15, "As for Me and my House, we will serve the Lord," it is the fairly usual plea from the clergy, including the Anglicans, for a return to household prayer and meditation. Though there is emphasis on fallen man and Free Grace in the conclusion, this sermon should have been well received by Anglican parishioners anywhere.

He must also have preached to the Georgians and other southern colonials *The Duty and Interest of Early Piety* (Boston, 1739),[159] with the text from Ecclesiastes 12:1 that Commissary Bray had used in 1700, a familiar and favorite Anglican subject. It is in part addressed to the younger members of his audience, but all should note his definition of religion, not outward profession or baptism, "but a thorough, real, inward Change of Nature, wrought in us by the powerful Operative of the Holy Ghost, convey'd to and nourish'd in our Hearts, by a Constant use of all the Means of Grace, evidenc'd by a good Life, and bringing forth the Fruits of the Spirit." His arguments are not strong rationally, nor are they emotionally appealing on the printed page. One other sermon of 1739, this early period, should be noted; for it is among his most famous: *The Almost Christian. A Sermon Preach'd to a Numerous Congregation in England. . . . To which is added, A Poem on his Design for Georgia* (reprinted Boston, 1739).[160] Though the title implies first printing in England, it became one of his best known everywhere and almost certainly was preached throughout the southern colonies. From Acts 26:28, "Almost thou persuadest me to be a Christian," Whitefield defines "An *Al-*

most Christian [as] one of the most hurtful Creatures in the World: He is a *Wolf in Sheep's Clothing*; He is one of those false Prophets our Blessed Lord bids us beware of in his Sermon on the Mount." The pre-Romantic poem which follows, "To the Rev. Mr. Whitefield, / On his Design for Georgia," must have been written before his first setting out, for it mentions that "Westley" will be waiting on the shore to receive him. The sermon is much more rhetorical, more complex in sentence structure, than those apparently intended primarily for the colonies. In its continuously flowing cadences the reader catches a little of that golden torrent which rushed from the great revivalist's lips.

Several of his collections, from ten *Sermons on Various Subjects* (London, 1739) through the dozens of others into the nineteenth century, certainly contain many preached from Maryland to Georgia. Undoubtedly many times he spoke extemporaneously, at others from notes now lost, though some publishers of his sermons advertise that they were taken down verbatim in shorthand from his pulpit delivery. Among the sermons are several of pastoral quality and purpose such as those for Georgia, many doctrinal, many polemical, many hortatory, along with combinations of these in form and intent. In the South, though he spent little time in North Carolina, Whitefield must have preached many or most of them in Annapolis, Hanover, Williamsburg, Charleston, and smaller places near them.

The southern gazettes, official or semiofficial organs of government, are remarkably impartial in their publications of Whitefield and anti-Whitefield materials. Most or all of their printers, who were also booksellers, printed or reprinted Whitefield sermons, tracts, letters, and journals and offered them for sale along with those of his opponents.[161] Southern colonials were reminded of him after he was dead by a waxwork likeness on display in Charleston and by the steady stream of his discourses pouring from the presses. His spoken and written word left an impression on the southern religious mind and manner, perhaps more permanently than on the northern, where Unitarianism, Roman Catholicism, and other nonevangelical attitudes were soon to turn New England and some of the middle states largely away from all he represented. It was the South and the new West which after a pause continued in new Awakenings, with several significant alterations, the ideas of the Great Awakener.

Among Whitefield's staunchest and ablest supporters in the colonies was the South Carolina-born and Harvard-educated Josiah Smith (1704–1781),[162] Presbyterian and perhaps later Independent minister of churches at Cainhoy and Charleston in his native province. Grandson of Landgrave Thomas Smith and son of Dr. Thomas Smith, a graduate of Edinburgh, Josiah was probably induced to go to Harvard by his Smith cousins who had settled in Boston. He was ordained in Boston on July 11, 1726, by Benjamin Colman, Cotton Mather, and other leading Puritan ministers. His first two sermons preached there were printed, one of them given at the time of his ordination, with a preface by Colman, who praised the great ability, humility, and modesty of the young man who had just then gone to Bermuda, and from whom great things were expected. By the spring of 1727 Josiah and his family had returned to South Carolina, where he settled as pastor of the Presbyterian church at Cainhoy, about twelve miles from Charleston. Though there were New England Puritans in the neighborhood, Smith found the dissenting interest declining, its condition deplorable when compared with that of the paradise of Puritanism, New England. Early in his career he was impolitic or untactful enough to tell his congregation that New England excelled Carolina in government, virtue, justice, religion, education, charity, and even loyalty to the Crown.[163] He soon joined New England-born Nathan Basset(t), minister of the Congregational or Independent Church in Charleston, in dispute and rebellion against the Scottish Presbyterian element which was attempting to enforce theological uniformity on the Congregational-Presbyterian churches, uniformity such as subscription to the Westminister Confession. Smith stood for the right of individual judgment and published a sermon on *Humane Impositions Proved Unscriptural, or, The Divine Right of Private Judgment* (Boston, 1729). He was answered by the Scottish leader, the Reverend Hugh Fisher, in *A Preservative from Damnable Errors* (n.p., 1730). Smith's rejoinder, *The Divine Right of Private Judgment Vindicated* (Boston, 1730), insisted he was no Arminian, but his declaration before the Presbytery that he adhered to all but three non-essential articles of the Confession was not accepted by the majority. The controversy went on in an exchange of sermons and letters.[164] Smith kept his pipeline to Boston wide open, and for the rest of his life many of his sermons and tracts were printed there, where, one suspects, these early discourses particularly excited more *general* interest than in South Carolina—except among the nonconformists. When the Scots seceded from the joint church in Charleston, Smith accepted a call to become his friend Bassett's colleague there. This was in 1734. When Bassett died four years later, Smith became the senior minister of a prosperous parish. Among his other interests was the conversion of the Negro, though he did not go as far as his New England friends in recognizing their equality with the white man.[165] As his reputation grew, he made friends abroad as well as in the colonies. One of his correspondents was Isaac Watts, the great hymn writer. When Whitefield arrived in 1739/40, Smith was ready to throw open the doors of his church to him, though southern Old Side Presbyterians and important conservative Congregational New England churches did not do so, among other reasons because of what they considered the "indignity" of his ardent preaching. Actually Whitefield had to rely on Smith and Chanler, as has been noted, *only after* he had so insulted and outraged Commissary Garden and the Church of England that they could no longer condone or accept him.[166]

But long before this, Josiah Smith was a widely known preacher, for his sermons had been published and distributed in both Massachusetts and South Carolina. He was most prolific.[167] For forty years, 1729 to 1769, new sermons and new editions appeared, the last of them in Charleston but as late as 1757 in Boston. One sermon at least was published in Philadelphia and Glasgow, and one work in Edinburgh and London.

Humane Impositions, his third known printed sermon,[168] from John 17:8, "I have given them the words which thou gavest me," is a direct challenge to Old Side dissenters: "If Christians have not a Right to Examine all Doctrines by the Scriptures, I would ask, What use the Scriptures are to them? ... I am far from pretending to exalt Reason above Revelation. But Reason is absolutely necessary to improve Revelation to its proper end." It is curious that Smith's argument is that of many Anglican clergy inclined to Latitudinarianism, for he was not. Especially was this true among those replying to Smith's friend Whitefield, who denied that any but his own interpretation of doctrine was possibly valid. It is no wonder that at the time (though it was a decade before Whitefield) Smith was declared heretic and Arminian.

Two other sermons on the subject by Smith are in the same vein, one the already mentioned *The Divine Right of Private Judgment Vindicated* and *No New Thing to be Slander'd* (Boston, 1730), the opposite point of view from that taken by Presbyterian Hugh Fisher in *A Preservative from Damnable Errors* (Boston, 1730) and in *The Divine Right of Private Judgment, Set in a True Light* (Boston, 1731). Meanwhile, or during the same period, Smith had printed in Boston four of his pastoral sermons preached before his congregation at Cainhoy. *The Duty of Parents, to instruct their Children* .... 1727 (published 1730) has a familiar subject.[169] *The Greatest Sufferers not always the Greatest Sinners. A Sermon Delivered in Charlestown ... South-Carolina, February 4th, 1727, 8 ... Occasioned by the Terrible Earthquake in New-England* (Boston, 1730)[170] is the defense of New England as the cradle and capital of piety and all goodness and a reminder to Carolinians that their own sins might better deserve such an earthquake in their vicinity. *Solomon's Caution against the Cup ... Delivered at Cainhoy ... March 30, 1729* (Boston 1730)[171] uses the familiar text from Proverbs 23:31, 32. In his vehemence on the subject of temperance Smith outdoes any of his known Church of England contemporaries. *The Young Man Warn'd: or, Solomon's Counsel to his Son . . . Cainhoy . . .* 1729 (Boston, 1730),[172] from Proverbs 1:10, is addressed to both parents and children. These pastoral and moral sermons must have been peculiarly appealing from a young man in his twenties, of a prominent family, an exponent of the right to think and the duty of the sober and pious life, for "Religion is the proper business of every Man's life." As one might expect, these are conventionally organized, plain-style sermons. They are mildly Calvinist, very mildly hortatory.

Before the advent of Whitefield, Smith had printed at least two other sermons. One, an ordination discourse for the Reverend John Osgood to the Congregational church at Dorchester S.C., *The Character and Duty of Minister and People . . . Delivered March 24, 1736* (Charleston, [S.C.], 1736), is a sound exposition with little doctrinal content.[173] The other, *Sacred to the Memory . . . of Nathan Basset* (Boston, 1739; Charleston, 1773),[174] was his tribute to his friend and colleague.

By far Smith's most famous sermon was on *The Character, Preaching, etc. Of the Reverend Mr. George Whitefield . . . Preach'd in Charlestown . . . March 26th . . .* 1740 (Boston, 1740),[175] with prefaces by Dr. Colman and Mr. Cooper. It appeared in later separate editions in Philadelphia and Glasgow in 1740 and 1741[176] and in 1785 as an introduction to *Fifteen Sermons Preached on Various Important Subjects by George Whitefield, To which is Prefix'd . . . .* [177]

Thus early a nonconformist clergyman known for his independence of thought strongly supported the controversial evangelist. This sermon, Heimert believes, "forestalled criticism of Whitefield and even served to stimulate a desire [in the North] to hear this 'prince of pulpit orators.' "[178] Preaching from Job 32:17, "I said, I will answer also my part, I also will shew mine opinion," Smith declares "My design from this text, is to shew my impartial opinion of that Son of Thunder, who has lately graced and warmed this desk; and would have been an ornament, I think, to the best pulpit in the province." The allusion to "the best pulpit in the province" may be sarcastic. The "impartial" quality of the testimony may be dubious, but the argument is strong if the reader is a Calvinist. For Smith discusses with approbation Whitefield's ideas of Original Sin, Justification by Faith alone, and Regeneration. When he says, "True religion is an inward thing, a thing of the heart," Calvinists and Anglicans might agree, up to a certain point, but the emotional quality Smith had come to admire caused the conservatives in both groups to draw back. Smith's description of Whitefield's manner of preaching, at any rate, was enough to attract the curious to hear the evangelist:

Many thought, *He spoke as never man spoke*, before him. So charmed were people with his manner of address, that they shut up their shops, forgot their secular business, and laid aside their schemes for the world; and the oftener he preached, the keener he seemed to put upon their desires of hearing him again! How awfully, with what thunder and sound did he discharge the artillery of Heaven upon us? And yet, how could he soften and melt even a soldier of Ulysses, with the love and mercy of God! . . . So methinks (if you will forgive the figure) saint Paul would look and speak in a pulpit.[179]

From this time on Smith's sermons in subject and manner are more hortatory, though he never approaches Whitefield in this quality. In *The Burning of Sodom . . . Preach'd at Charlestown, South Carolina, after a most Terrible Fire* on November 18, 1740 (Boston, 1741) and in a later sermon on the same subject included in his *Sermons on Several Important Subjects* (Boston, 1757)[180] he uses his own community's catastrophe for mild jeremiads, reminding the people of the vices prevailing among them but not saying that the catastrophe had occurred as a direct result of those sins. *Jesus Persecuted in His Disciples* (Boston, 1745), *A Zeal of God Encourag'd* (Boston, 1745), *The Church of Ephesus Arraign'd* (Charleston, 1768), *The Broken Heart Revived . . . 1773* (2nd ed., Charleston, 1773), and *St. Paul's Victory and Triumph* (Charleston, 1774), suggest even in their titles that he belonged with the evangelicals the rest of his life. He also preached a number of funeral sermons on parishioners and fellow clergymen, undoubtedly drawing most attention with *Success a Great Proof of St. Paul's Fidelity. Sacred to the Memory of . . . George Whitefield* (Charleston, 1770).[181]

In 1749 Smith became partially paralyzed and could never afterward articulate clearly, but once a month until the Revolution his patient and affectionate congregation continued to listen to scarcely intelligible oral presentations, some of which they could read afterwards without difficulty in print. He died in 1781 in exile in Philadelphia (for his zealous Whiggism), and it is not surprising that his mortal remains were deposited beside those of Samuel Finley and Gilbert Tennent, his peers among the major figures of the Great Revival. Unlike the Tennents especially, Smith was never bitter or vindictive, even in his polemical tracts and letters noted in the concluding section of this chapter.

If Whitefield was the Anglo-American St. Paul in the pulpit, he was rivaled by another apostle, Samuel Davies, "the Apostle of Virginia," American born and bred, perhaps the greatest colonial pulpit orator. His ministry has been considered in the preceding chapter, and his ability as a writer of tracts will be noted in the concluding section of this chapter. By education and conviction a New Light Presbyterian, he began his Virginia labors with the support of the Pennsylvania leaders of the revival and through occasional visitations by Whitefield himself. Davies came upon the scene long after Josiah Smith and left it long before, but his renown as preacher and the popularity of the multi-volumed editions of his sermons for a full century attest to his having been the greater mind and forensic talent.[182]

Curiously little until the last few years has been written on Davies' sermons, which, with the possible exception of those of Jonathan Edwards, were until our Civil War the most popular colonial religious discourses in print. Between 1766 and 1864 nineteen or more editions or reprintings of Davies' *Sermons on Important Subjects* appeared.[183] The eighty-two homilies of the nineteenth-century editions are almost all the sermons ever published by this Presbyterian, who died at thirty-seven. Sprague in *Annals of the American Pulpit* devotes two or three pages to the sermons, little of it criticism; only W.H. Foote (*Sketches of Virginia*) among nineteenth-century American religious historians gives serious, extensive attention to these discourses. Quite recently Heimert and Miller have included Davies in their anthology *The Great Awakening*, though no sermon is given or excerpted. In Heimert's *Religion and the American Mind from the Great Awakening to the Revolution*,[184] however, appears the most extensive and incisive attention ever devoted to Davies' ideas, themes, doctrine, and style. In four or five of Heimert's ten chapters Davies is quoted or paraphrased or interpreted more than perhaps any figure other than Jonathan Edwards. Even more than Edwards', it is clear, Davies' sermons are representative of the prevailing thought among the evangelicals of the Great Awakening. To see his sermons in full and proper perspective from an intellectual, theological, and literary point of view would, however, probably require a separate book as long as Heimert's.[185] Heimert has set him properly in almost every instance, but almost always the emphasis or the point of reference is to the revivalist movement and its characteristic ideas or theological and intellectual background, not to Davies' own. Thus even from this major study no unified conception of the man's pulpit orations can be drawn. The titles of the chapters in which Davies appears most frequently do, however, suggest strongly Heimert's interests and Davies as representative of them: "The Work of Redemption," "The Beauty and Good Tendency of Union," "The Danger of an Unconverted Ministry," and "The Wisdom of God in the Permission of Sin."

The majority of even the printed sermons were written under the pressure of pastoral and evangelical duties in Virginia, and most of the few remaining were written during his brief tenure as president of Princeton. Many in the collected editions bear the date of their first delivery, and the dates of many others can be determined by looking at them in their individually issued pamphlet form. Davies apparently had an extensive library and certainly a sound classical education. His sermons were composed with care; he declares that he spent at least four days in preparatory hard study before writing each of them. This may seem incredible for a man who was frequently journeying from place to place, but this very situation meant that he could use them more than once, as almost all his contemporaries did.

Unlike his friend Whitefield, Davies was a graceful and commanding figure. And unlike Whitefield (if we may believe many contemporaries), he had dignity. Those who heard him at the beginning and at the end of his ministry testify to a "venerable" appearance, though one recalls that he died at thirty-seven. The charming and melodious voice must have rivaled Whitefield's. One must remember that he was a poet, not only employing a cadenced rhythm in much of his prose but composing appropriate hymns to match most of his sermons.[186] Other poets, particularly those whose themes were religious or moral, he quotes frequently. Among his favorites were Milton, George Herbert, Pope, and pre-Romantics like Edward Young and James Thomson. One may add the nonconformist hymn writers like Watts and Doddridge. From this poetic imagination comes some of the sublimity of style, the majesty of imagery, which was to continue to develop in Anglo-American literature. It has been said that he and his fellow Calvinists developed a peculiarly American form of sublimity in religious ideas and their expression. One should say rather that Davies, who more than any other southern or American colonial revivalist employs the sublime, is the heir of the great English pre-Romantic artists and one of the forerunners of the later American full-blown literary and theological Romantics of the Charles G. Finney variety. Davies did show in sermons and poems and tracts forensic and doctrinal qualities distinctively influenced by his American environment.

Like Josiah Smith, Davies was no bigot, though he was probably a stricter Calvinist than Smith. Like other Calvinists of the Great Awakening, he emphasized some articles of the Westminster Confession and ignored others. Among his sermons those which are pastoral and doctrinal are as eloquent as those prepared for special or great occasions.

One acute commentator, W.H. Foote, observes that a first reading sometimes gives the impression that Davies is dealing too much in mere words, but that when we catch his spirit we see that passages formerly considered verbose are in reality meditations, pausings for breath before proceeding to new points. He gives scant space to controversial doctrine, and in the sermons he is not the inexorable logician he could sometimes be in his tracts. Like a good lawyer (and Davies once acted as his own attorney in

pleading the case of the dissenters before the General Court of Virginia),
he mixes facts, principles, and feelings, not always in order, but always to
good effect. That is, he was constantly aware of the sort of persons to whom
he spoke, the time, and the place. A sermon prepared for a particular occasion in America, his diary tells us, he simply could not deliver in England.
It did not fit the occasion.[187] An earnest preacher, he was never as boisterous
or vitriolic as his friends the Tennents and Blair.

Perhaps recently the evangelical interest in an impending millenium
has been stressed too strongly, for in the hundreds of sermons of the southern colonies it is not one of the explicitly major considerations, though
implicitly it may have lain behind much of the work of redemption.[188] The
emphasis in most sermons is on redemption, not because of the imminency
of a millenial period, but for the sake of God and the individual human
soul. Davies did voice his conviction that the French and Indian War
would determine whether the great age of "slaying the witnesses," the fall
of Babylon, was upon mankind.[189] But obviously, and here one aspect of
Davies' Americanism becomes explicit, the future of mankind is hinged
upon what happens on this continent. One of his most poetic paragraphs
hails the approach of that "happy period," as though all is determined in
the right direction. Allied to much of this was the hope and sometimes
belief, which has been shown in the thought of a few other southern evangelicals (and their opponents the Anglican and conservative Old Siders),
that Christianity will be unified, a vision whose beauty provoked or invoked
famous passages from Cotton Mather and Jonathan Edwards. It is in some
ways responsible for the definition Edwards developed of virtue as "love
to being in general" and called forth from preachers like Davies paeans of
praise of the divine love—not neoplatonic divine beauty. It is a Calvinist
love, for God as parent also dispenses justice. But in his famous sermon
"God is Love" Davies stresses this happier side of Calvinist Christianity in
a prose rhythm which, in the hands and minds of listeners like the young
Patrick Henry, was to form the mainstream of secular political expression:

> Love is a gentle, pleasing theme, the noblest passion of the human breast,
> and the fairest ornament of the rational nature. Love is the cement of
> society, and the source of social happiness; and without it the great
> community of the rational universe would dissolve, and men and angels
> would turn savages, and roam apart in barbarous solitude. . . . Love is the
> softener and polisher of human minds, and transforms barbarians into
> men. . . .
> *God is love;* not only lovely and loving but love itself; pure, unmixed
> love, nothing but love; love in his nature and in his operations; the object,
> source, and quintessence of all love.[190]

More vital to Davies than the millenium was eschatology, which is his major concern in such sermons as "The General Resurrection" and "The Universal Judgment."[191] The first words of the former indicate not only his theology, but his intellectual descent from or kinship with certain seventeenth-century worthies and eighteenth-century graveyard poets like Edward Young and Robert Blair, and his anticipation of William Cullen Bryant:

> Ever since sin entered the world and death by sin this earth has been a vast grave-yard, or burying-ground, for her children. . . . The earth has been arched with graves, the last lodging of mortals, and the bottom of the ocean paved with the bones of men. . . . And how many generations have succeeded one another in the long run of near six thousand years! . . . The greatest number of mankind beyond comparison are sleeping under ground. There lies beauty mouldering in the dust, rotting into stench, and loathsomeness, and feeding the vilest worms. . . . There lie the wise and learned, as rotten, as helpless as the fool. . . .
> And shall they lie there always? Shall this body, this curious work-manship of Heaven, so wonderfully and fearfully made, always lie in ruins, and never be repaired?[192]

From these sombre questions Davies turns to the warm love and glory of the Resurrection, with the proper warning to the sinner. In another major sermon, "The One Thing Needful," the preacher asks and answers the question, "For what are we placed in this world? . . . we are placed here to prepare us for the grand business of immortality, the state of our maturity, and to qualify us to live forever." The text, Luke 10:41, 42, is Christ's admonition to Martha that she has forgotten the one thing needful, "the salvation of the soul."[193]

Davies shared with other evangelicals the feeling that the conservative ministry was "unconverted," though he seems not to have used the word: "I must speak out in the present situation of my country, however unwilling I am to touch the sacred character. O Virginia! thy prophets, thy ministers, have ruined thee. I speak not of all."[194] And he proceeds to arraign the established clergy principally for neglect. In another sermon, he is direct even in his title, "The Love of Souls, a Necessary Qualification for the Ministerial Office,"[195] in content an amplification of what he had touched upon in the earlier sermon.

Among Davies' pastoral sermons were at least five preparatory to the celebration of the Lord's Supper, and for several if not all of them he composed appropriate hymns.[196] Others were on "Salvation through Grace," "The Nature of Justification, and the Nature and Concern of Faith in It," and "Grace."[197] He preached on the "Necessity and Excellence of a Family Religion."[198] A dozen were extremely hortatory, ringing the changes on Sin, Death, and Resurrection many more times.[199] In one of them he used the spider figure made famous by Jonathan Edwards and employed by Thomas Shepard before Edwards. Davies' version is worth comparing with Edwards': "Consider your present dangerous situation. You hang over the pit of destruction by the slender thread of life, held up only by the hand of an angry God, as we hold a spider, or some poisonous insect, over a fire, ready to throw it in. You are ripe for destruction."[200]

Four stately funeral sermons are among his most moving. "Saints Saved with Difficulty, and the Certain Perdition of Sinners," "Indifference to Life Urg'd, from Its Shortness and Vanity," "Life and Immortality Revealed in the Gospel," and "The Certainty of Death: A Funeral Sermon" were preached in 1756, 1759, 1756, and 1758 respectively.[201] They are also among his most learned, allusive, and figurative, especially "Indifference to Life Urg'd." But they are also among his most hortatory and persuasive, urging the sinner, in view of such a prospect, to repent while he may. And naturally they are also strongly doctrinal. Each is a kind of personal jeremiad, or something akin to that favorite earlier Calvinist form of oral discourse.

Other occasional sermons employ his usual imagery, cadenced prose, and Calvinist sublimity. Two ordination sermons, two New Year's discourses, a somewhat different sort of funeral oration on the death of George II, sermons in time of sickness and earthquake, on Christmas Day, on thanksgiving for victory or fast for defeat, and a last "Apostolic Valediction" are among them.[202] "The Duty of Masters to Their Servants" (Lynchburg, Va., 1809) was on a subject dear to him as it was to other Presbyterians and Anglicans noted above, the conversion of the Negro.[203] Davies' sermons in general are said to have attracted many slaves, and on some occasions there were as many blacks as whites in his congregation.[204]

Even "A Sermon on the New Year," with the text from Jeremiah 28:16, "This year thou shalt die," was a practical and persuasive plea to his students at Princeton to heed the call of God. It was also prophetic, for in the year it was preached, 1761, Davies did die. He employs "This year you may die" as a sort of incantation, repeating it again and again with his usual cadences. "The Religious Improvement of the Late Earthquakes," preached in Hanover County on June 19, 1756, is one of the evangelical comments on the catastrophes of 1755. The terrible grandeur of the power of the natural forces is sublime, and so Davies expresses it. But the sermon is also a jeremiad addressed to Virginia as the prophets had addressed the Hebrews and Jerusalem. The fascination with storm and turbulence Davies displays in so many of his poems is also here evident, and he quotes at length a graphic description from his favorite Edward Young's *Night Thoughts*. He concludes the sermon with one of his own best-known hymns beginning "How great, how terrible that God, / Who shakes creation with his nod!" and concluding "When lightenings blaze from pole to pole!"

One of the most moving of his discourses was his farewell to his congregation at Hanover, "with whom I fully expected to live and die." He reviews his life and work among them, the emergency and need at Princeton, and his own reluctance until circumstances forced him to accept the call to its presidency. He urges them to continue to progress. "Among you I have spent the prime of my life; among you I have labored and toiled in the delightful work of saving your souls." He bids two farewells, one to the penitent and one to the impenitent:

> FAREWELL, ye saints of the living God, ye "few names even in HAN-OVER, that have not defiled your garments." Ye shall *farewell* indeed. That God, whose the earth is, and the fulness thereof; that God, who makes angels happy. . . . He will guide you through the intricacies of this life, and then receive you into glory. . . .
>
> Shall I say, FAREWELL, impenitent sinners? Alas! you cannot *farewell*, however heartily I wish it. . . . Flee, flee, all of you, from the wrath to come. . . . Farewell—"finally, brethren, farewell; be perfect, be of good comfort, be of one mind, live in peace, and the God of love and peace shall be with you."—which may God grant for Christ's sake. *Amen.*[205]

But Davies and the revivalist Presbyterians were of the church militant, and that this militancy should in an age of war assume or direct itself somewhat to secular aims was inevitable. Heimert has shown how the evangelicals as a whole entered into this struggle against the French and Indians and Popery with such zeal that some finally felt they had gone too far. Even Davies had to remind his flock that the *Church Militant* was more impressive than the armies of the British King, and this especially after his most famous sermons urging his listeners to serve their country along with their God.[206] But meanwhile he had become the colony's best recruiting officer and orator in a series of sermons reprinted in this country and in Great Britain many times. "On the Defeat of General Braddock, Going to Fort Duquesne" (Hanover, July 20, 1755), "Religion and Patriotism the Constituents of Good Soldiers" (Hanover, August 17, 1755, to Captain Overton's company of volunteers), "The Crisis" (Hanover, October 28, 1758), and "The Curse of Cowardice" (Hanover, May 8, 1758, to a militia muster) are among the great religious orations in the English language. And they are of such stuff as the pious Christian Patrick Henry and the free-thinking Thomas Paine spun their persuasive eloquence, especially when liberty or death was the theme in a time which tried men's souls.[207]

The first of the four, in the time of Braddock's tragic defeat, the text naturally from Isaiah 22:12–14, begins in the woe of the jeremiad:

> And, O Virginia! O my country! shall I not lament for thee? Thou art a valley of vision, favored with the light of revelation from heaven, and the gospel of Jesus: thou hast long been the region of peace and tranquillity; the land of ease, plenty, and liberty. But what do I now see? What do I now hear? I see thy brazen skies, thy parched soil, thy withering fields, thy hopeless springs, and thy scanty harvests. Methinks I also hear the sound of the trumpet, and see garments rolled in blood. . . . And shall I not weep for thee, O my country?[208]

In a calmer tone he comments on the recent calamities and then points to two causes of the present danger—the sins of the land, and its security and inactivity in times past. He points out that strangers say Hanover is the county distinguished for religion and morals. If so, alas, what can be said for the rest? Deism, infidelity, unconverted clergy have ruined Virginia.[209] But, he urges, put yourselves in an attitude of defense, observe your orders, never submit to "French tyranny and Popish superstition." You Negroes among my hearers must be aware of what a French victory would mean. Among other things, you would have to pray in Latin, which you understand not a word of! But in conclusion he offers words of hope and warnings against overconfidence, with an exhortation to prayer.

The other sermons in this group are better oratory and better logic. "Religion and Patriotism the Constituents of a Good Soldier," from II Samuel 1:12, begins by reviewing the scene more calmly, with a warning of the Popish tyranny and slavery and massacre which lurk on the frontier. Davies quotes a passage on courage from Addison's *The Campaign*. Here occurs his famous footnote on Providence's having preserved the youth Colonel Washington "for some important service to his country."[210] Much of this discourse is a mixture of common-sense advice and eloquent encouragement: "And Virginians! Britons! Christians! Protestants! if these names have any import or energy, will you not strike home in such a cause." Sin has brought upon us this ravaged country, but all is not lost.[211]

"The Crisis: or, The Uncertain Doom of Kingdoms at Particular Times" was indeed written in times that try men's souls. Repentance is necessary. The comparison with great Nineveh is not per se apt, but Davies makes it so. And here he brings in the "millenarian vision" that whatever the military outcome, there will be a new Heaven and a new earth.[212] For man can and must repent.

"The Curse of Cowardice," from Jeremiah 48:10, is perhaps the most famous of the group. Like "Religion and Patriotism," it was a direct recruiting sermon. Beginning with a meditation upon the blessings of peace, the preacher refers to those who prevent it and the outrages they have committed. He reminds his auditors why they are present—that at this very moment "some miserable Briton or Virginian may be passing through a tedious process of experiments in the infernal art of torture." "Such . . . is the present state of our country: it bleeds in a thousand veins; and without timely remedy the wound will prove mortal . . . and cursed is he who, having no ties sufficiently strong to confine him at home, *keepeth his sword from blood.*"[213]

Here he wishes he had the "all-prevailing force of Demosthenes' oratory —but I recall my wish that I may correct it. Oh! for the influence of the Lord of armies, the God of battles, the Author of true courage and every heroic virtue, to fire you into patriots and soldiers this moment!"[214] And like other evangelicals in 1775 after Davies lay in his grave, he invokes upon those who hold back without cause "the curse of Meroz" (Judges 5:23), who came not "to the help of the Lord against the mighty."[215] His hearers must carry with them into the conflict a determination to do eternal battle against sin in all its forms—"quit you like men, be strong."[216]

Militant Presbyterian who took delight and fear in nature's as well as man's mighty upheavals, Davies, even at his sternest, most denunciatory and most imprecatory, gives his reader today a feeling of the serene confidence he had in his cause. With the beautiful voice his contemporaries testify he possessed, he must indeed have seemed to young Patrick Henry a Christian Demosthenes. Perhaps no other American pulpit orator before the Civil War was so genuinely enjoyed by so many who heard him or read his words. The Baptist and Methodist later phases of the Great Awakening produced some able preachers, but there was no Davies among them. From his alternately epigrammatic and incantatory phrases, the vigor and vision of his patriotism, may well have sprung that native American oratory, strongest still—too often in debased form—in the South in which he labored.

THE RELIGIOUS TRACT

More difficult to classify or to pigeonhole than the sermon is the religious tract. Any prose essay primarily concerned with explicating or arguing such religious matters as the state of the church, a doctrine or set of doctrines, the validity of church organization or practice, the rightness or wrongness of an individual's ideas (and all these overlap) may be called a religious tract—provided it was not prepared for oral delivery before a congregation. But questions still remain. Are the essay-explanations of the exploration and settlement in the New World by Hakluyt and Purchas religious tracts? Would the chapters or appendices of colonial histories concerned with the state of the church by such clerics as Hugh Jones, William Stith, or James Blair be considered religious tracts? Are the contemporaneously published letters of individual clergy to English prelates or the S.P.G., when they present or argue a certain point, to be called tracts? Are the journals of the great Quakers Fox and Edmundson and Story and Woolman or of the revivalist Whitefield in reality tracts because of their authors' purposes in writing and their publishers' in printing them? Are the letters to editors of British and American newspapers and magazines, or the essays in those periodicals, tracts if they deal with religious subjects? In a broad sense, all are religious tracts if their purpose is to persuade, whatever polemical or explicatory or narrative form they assume.

But this brings us face to face with enormous masses of material which cannot possibly be mentioned, much less commented upon, here. Most of the space will have to be spent on the separately printed books or pamphlets, usually the latter, designed to advance a particular point at a particular time. That they will not tell the whole story of religious and theological controversy especially is obvious, and this results in some inevitable distortion of the picture of an age or movement. Bernard Bailyn's and Merrill Jensen's recent anthologies of pre-Revolutionary political pamphlets are made up in one instance entirely and in the other almost entirely of these separately printed pamphlets, despite the fact that equally able, and at times vastly superior, arguments appeared only in the pages of the colonial gazettes. The essays on liberty and taxation and kindred matters in the *Virginia Gazette*, for example, for the fifteen years before the Revolution may be the very finest political literature of the period before 1790. The Whitefield controversy is discussed perhaps as well, and with more vitriol, in the pages of the *South-Carolina Gazette* in some essays as in the separate imprints of Chanler, Garden, Croswell, and Smith. But in the narrower sense the journal pieces were not tracts.

In a few instances will be considered the religious essay never printed in its own day, but possibly read fairly widely in manuscript, which has been preserved to us in original form or in a recent printing. The ramifications and details of movements and individual actions behind any of these colonial tracts is often lost to us. Their general rather than specific significance or emphasis is usually all we can now follow. But it is hoped that the writings here considered offer a representative picture of southern thinking on major theological and religious questions of the period.

THE SEVENTEENTH CENTURY

The intent of the homiletic discourse is often exactly that of the tractarian. Thus Alexander Whitaker's sermon with William Crashaw's preface together constitute a strong plea for aid to the plantations for religious reasons, as do Whitaker's letters to Crashaw, Smith, and Gouge. In Father Andrew White's 1633–1635 accounts of Maryland one might discern Roman Catholic propaganda.[217] But they are only obliquely and implicitly doctrinaire. The annual *Letters* of the English Province of the Society of Jesus (e.g., excerpts for 1634, 1638, 1639, 1640, 1642, 1656, and 1681)[218] are naturally concerned with the activities of the members of their order in Maryland, their trials, tribulations, and triumphs, but they are more religious "present states" than tracts aimed to impress an adversary or the public.

The only other work printed in English for the Chesapeake Bay colonies before the 1653–1657 troubles in Maryland was definitely a tract, by a Jesuit, a plea for enacting appropriate laws so that Roman Catholics might sell estates in England and remove to and settle in Maryland. *A Moderate and Safe Expedient To remove Jealousies and Feares of any danger, or prejudice to this State, by the Roman Catholicks of this Kingdome, And to mitigate the censure of too much severity towards them. With a great advantage of Honour and Profit to this State and Nation* was originally printed in 1646.[219] Then in Maryland (of course printed in Great Britain) came the flurry of religio-political pamphlets between 1653 and 1658 attacking or defending Lord Baltimore, his governor, puritan William Stone, acting governor Thomas Green(e), and the Roman Catholics. Mixed up in the matter was a royal governor appointed by Charles II (in exile), when it was represented to that sovereign that Lord Baltimore had in his colony sold out to the Puritans. The new governor was captured by Parliament on his way down the Channel. Greene during his brief tenure had followed Virginia governor Berkeley in a proclamation of Charles as ruler. This proclamation Lord Baltimore, who was in a dangerous and delicate situation anyway, had Stone recall. But the harm had been done, and the Proprietor was attacked on all sides. His old enemy Claiborne, long a royalist, now saw his opportunity and applied to Parliament for a commission to reduce both the colonies to obedience.

The Lord Baltemore's Case, Concerning the Province of Maryland (London, 1653) is entirely political and legal, an answer to Claiborne's allegations, and includes Charles II's commission for the new governor who never arrived. In 1655 appeared an answer, *Virginia and Maryland, Or, The Lord Baltamore's printed Case, uncased and answered* (London). It naturally concerns in part the "battle" on the Severn between the Puritans and the Proprietary forces under Governor Stone.[220] All this paralleled, with a peculiar American twist, what was happening in England. *Virginia and Maryland* is a rejoinder reviewing events and the legal action, or illegal action, behind them.

In 1655 also appeared at least three other tracts, all closer to the religious side of this political dispute. Leonard Strong's *Babylon's Fall in Maryland: a Fair Warning to Lord Baltamore...* (printed for the author, n.p.) was by a Puritan from Providence (later Annapolis), a Puritan settlement also mentioned in the preceding chapter, and a commission appointed by Parliament to preserve peace and administer justice. This highly partisan account conflicts with the next to be mentioned in its fixing of the responsibility for the recent strife and in the numbers slain. *A Just and Cleere Refutation of a False and Scandalous Pamphlet Entituled Babylons Fall in Maryland ...* (London) by John Langford, "Gentleman, servant to Lord Baltemore," is a refutation, but not an entirely clear one. Involved is Captain Roger Heamans of an armed merchantman at anchor in the river when the conflict took place. Strong's and Langford's accounts contradict each other as to the reasons for Heamans' support of the Puritans.

Roger Heamans entered the lists with *An Additional brief Narrative Of a late Bloody Design Against the Protestants in Ann Arundel County, and Severn, in Maryland in the County of Virginia ...* (London). In good gospel language Heamans avers that "He hath seen the plotting of the Wicked, and the Deliverance of the Innocent."[221] John Hammond, author of *Leah and Rachel, or, the Two Fruitful Sisters Virginia and Mary-Land* (1656) replied in about the same year, 1656, in a pro-Baltimore pamphlet *Hammond versus Heamans, Or, an answer To an audacious Pamphlet, published by an impudent Fellow, named Roger Heamans* (London, n.d.).[222] Hammond, who in his better-known work is a conciliator, here speaks bitingly of those "blood-sucking Sectaries, who mention God in their lips, but in their hearts are far from him." This is the best-written pamphlet of the lot, employing documents and personal knowledge to great advantage. It flays the Puritans for ingratitude, hypocrisy, and broken promises. The situation and the events certainly had their comic aspects. If Ebenezer Cook had come along two generations earlier, he might have made a trenchant satire or a mocking burlesque of both literary and military contestants. It is significant that the only dissenter-Anglican literary campaign in the southern colonies of the seventeenth century should have been so strongly infused with economics and politics.

But other dissenters and churchmen were concerned with the Chesapeake world. Two who were much interested had never been in the New World at all. Lionel Gatford, staunch Anglican clergyman, appealed to Cromwell to save the souls of the Virginians in *Publick Good Without Private In-*

terest (London, 1657). His unreliable opinions as to the causes of the sad state of affairs in Virginia are presented with vehemence. With equal vehemence Quaker writer Francis Howgill in *The Deceiver of the Nations Discovered: and His Cruelty Made Manifest* (London, 1660) insisted that intolerance existed in Maryland and outlined the sufferings of the inhabitants of that colony.

Far more interesting and reliable than either of these is a Virginia Anglican's tract, R[oger] G[reen]'s *Virginia's Cure: or an Advisive Narrative Concerning Virginia. Discovering the true Ground of that Churches Unhappiness, and the only true Remedy* ... (London, 1662).[223] Roger Green, the presumed author, was a Cambridge M.A. who had officiated in Nansemond County and perhaps at Jamestown. The plea, addressed to the Bishop of London, reports the alarming state of religion in a colony of straggling farms along the river banks. The author asks his lordship to persuade the King of the absolute necessity of building towns in each county, and schools to go with them. To finance the operation, he suggests that appeals be made for charity in every parish church in Great Britain. Among the other suggestions are the interesting ones that planters with many servants be required to build houses in the towns to which these servants may repair on Saturday afternoons for catechizing and remain over night for the Sabbath services; and that young candidates for Holy Orders be given "Virginia Fellowships" at the two English universities, the holding of which will oblige them to occupy parishes in the colony for seven years after graduation and ordination. He suggests further means of raising funds, the most obvious being import duties in England on each hogshead of tobacco. Only one of his suggestions seems to have been fully followed: that needy ministers setting out for the colony be allowed £20 for transportation and outfitting. He also insists that one of the cities be made the seat for the bishop who must be sent over.

R.G.'s point is a good one, at least from the clerical point of view. Straggling communities prevented attendance at divine services, or afforded an excuse for absence. Such communities also meant no schools, and the writer observes that in his time no Virginia boy will be educated enough to enter a profession. Then there was the Indian question: if the red men saw the whites as godless and blasphemous, they themselves would never be converted.

Virginia's Cure was neither the first nor the last work that urged establishment of towns as a remedy for the colony's ills, but perhaps the only one to urge it as a religious remedy. Later in the century tobacco planters and their factors and the General Assembly had laws enacted for towns and laid them out, though for another century they never prospered. But they had the example of old and New England to show that urban centers made for a homogeneous, cultivated, and (Green thought) God-fearing people. This well-written pamphlet, not so visionary as it seems at first glance, was one of the few printed expressions to come from seventeenth-century Anglicans presumably in the "missionary" field.

Morgan Godwyn, son of an archdeacon and grandson and great grandson of bishops,[224] graduate of Christ Church, Oxford, served as minister near Williamsburg in York County and for several years in Stafford before returning to England. He may have gone to the Barbadoes for a short time, but most of his career was spent at home after he left Virginia. Godwyn never lost interest in Virginia, for he wrote concerning it and the other colonies' religious state at least three times between 1680 and 1708, and preached at Westminster Abbey in 1685, "Trade preferr'd before Religion and Christ," a sermon on the plantations.[225]

His three tracts consider the same problems R.G. does, but his primary aim is something else. *The Negro's and Indians Advocate, Suing for their Admission into the Church: or a Persuasive to the Instructing and Baptizing of the Negro's and Indians in our Plantations. . . . To which is added, A brief Account of the Religion in Virginia* (London, 1680) is dedicated to the Archbishop of Canterbury,[226] and its plea is directed to him. Godwyn sees the state of religion in the colonies much as R.G. does, but his main theme is that the Negroes and red natives "have naturally an equal Right with other Men, to the Exercise and Privileges of Religion." Brydon thinks[227] that here may have been raised for the first time the question of the civil status of the Negro child after baptism. At any rate, Godwyn states flatly that Christianity by its very professions and nature must promote the religious education and conversion of the black and red men. Perhaps equally interesting is the tractarian letter attached, written to Sir William Berkeley after or about 1667 and possibly just as Godwyn was leaving Virginia. After praise of the governor as the tutor who has raised the colony from childhood until "now almost grown Adult, needing no assistance from, but rather to afford some to her Mother Country,"[228] Godwyn joins R.G. in pointing out that "contempt of religion [that] brings any pious eye to tears." It is caused by the vestries' power of "*hiring* (that is the usual word there)," and the scattering of the inhabitants so that they do not attend church services. He professes to prefer in many respects the new fruitful and pleasant land to old England, but he adds a list of abuses of the church, culminating in the clergy's being entirely at "the Mercy of the People," which cause him to leave the colony. It is strictly an Anglican clergyman's point of view, albeit a fair one, of conditions in the late 1660s, not in the 1680s.

A year later, in *A Supplement to the Negro's & Indians Advocate: or, Some Further Considerations and Proposals . . .* (London, 1681)[229]

Godwyn returns to his major theme. Here he answers the planters' objections—those discussed in the preceding chapter and referred to in some eighteenth-century sermons noted above in this chapter—and reports various incidents of cruelty in the treatment of Negroes. Virginia he believes treats its Negroes somewhat more humanely than do other colonies, and there is some evidence to suggest that he is here directing his remarks primarily to the Barbadians. He denies the Negroes' alleged stupidity, actually finding them most ingenious, and he denies that they are at all averse to becoming Christians.

Twenty years after he handed it to a friend, another set of observations by Godwyn was published. *Some Proposals Towards Promoting the Propagation of the Gospel in Our American Plantations. Humbly Offered in a Letter to Mr. Nelson* ... (London, 1708)[230] observes in its preface that conditions in the colonies are probably better now than when Godwyn was there. This pamphlet repeats some of the earlier charges, and the editor or commentator pleads for a bishop or bishops in the colonies. This last was admittedly the reason for the publication at this time.

The quarter century of the Quakers' golden age in North Carolina and great missionary effort in Virginia and Maryland was in a sense marked by tractarian zeal, but usually in the form of journals or diaries which were, like the greatest of Quaker journals published almost a century later, designed to reach and comfort or convince a reading public. Chief among them are *A True Believer's Testimony of the Work of True Faith* (London, 1661), dated from Maryland and recounting George Rofe's experience in the two Chesapeake colonies; *The Life & Death, Travels and Sufferings of Robert Widders* (London, 1688), which contains several references to the author's journeys in Maryland; *Truth Exalted in the Writings of that Eminent and Faithful Servant, John Burnyeat* (London, 1691), which contains a journal of travels, essays, and/or sermons especially referring to Maryland; George Fox, *A Journal or Historical Account* (London, 1694), which describes his journeys and Meetings in America in company with Burnyeat and Widders; *A Journal of the Life of Thomas Story* ... (London, 1747, etc.), containing texts of his "convincements" and debates as well as visits; and William Edmundson, whose *Journal* (London, 1715) in its American portions falls within the seventeenth century and who like Fox and others included Virginia, Maryland, and North Carolina in his itinerary. Not printed until the nineteenth century is "An Humble Expostulation ... of the People Called Quakers" presented to the Maryland Assembly in 1695. The essay argues, for one thing, that in neighboring Pennsylvania the Friends are allowed to enjoy liberty without swearing to various oaths of loyalty.[231]

Political, but with strong religious implications, was Maryland's earliest extant printed work, *The Address of the Representatives of their Majestyes Protestant Subjects, in the Proviunce of Mary-Land Assembled. To the King's most Excellent Majesty* (St. Mary's, 1689),[232] a broadside, probably by John Coode, quondam Anglican clergyman and tempestuous political and religious leader. Extant only in the London edition is *The Declaration of the Protestant Reasons and Motives for the Present Appearing in Arms of their Majesties Protestant Subjects in the Province of Maryland* (1689),[233] another strongly Protestant tract by a group of members of the Assembly.

Francis Makemie and George Keith, in the days when the latter was still a Quaker, engaged in a pamphlet duel concerning the Presbyterian catechism. *An Answer to George Keith's Libel on a Catechism* (Boston, 1694) was recommended by Increase Mather and other Puritans.[234] Many proclamations and memorials regarding religion in Maryland were not published until the nineteenth or twentieth century. A good representative of these is "The Present State of the Protesant Religion in Maryland. . . . A Memorial Representing the Present Case of the Church in Maryland," a 1700 statement of the reasons why the Church of England should be established and a survey of the parishes and clergy.[235] Fewer have appeared for Virginia, probably because American copies were destroyed in three early wars on her soil and because the few surviving copies in British repositories have not yet been printed.

Seventeenth-century pamphleteering on religious subjects or ecclesiastical government seems to have been confined then, in the southern colonies, to the Chesapeake Bay region. Except for the two known items from the Nuthead press in Maryland, all that was printed contemporaneously appeared in London. Obscure and controversial points of doctrine such as engaged Roger Williams and John Cotton and a dozen other Puritans were not discussed in printed form in Virginia and Maryland, partly because there was less interest in them and partly because polemical treatises, to circulate widely, would have to be printed in England. By the time the printed form reached the colonial reader, the whole issue at stake could have become out of date or the potential reader could have lost interest. Perhaps the Quakers and, toward the last, the Presbyterians did circulate tracts in manuscript (as Makemie's pamphlet just mentioned). Perhaps the absence of printing facilities caused the facile or even potentially profound writer to turn to the art of satire, for in this form he might wage effective warfare and circulate his concise message in doggerel or heroic couplet by hand. Even the clergy at the end of the century were doing this, and on through 1763 poetic satire continued to be a favorite vehicle for attacking anything. Though a generation before 1763 both Virginia and

Maryland had their printing presses and their gazettes, the argumentative essay and the prose satire were appearing in the latter—provided they did not go too far in offending the colonial government.

THE EIGHTEENTH CENTURY

Though all through the first quarter of the eighteenth century Maryland (alone among the southern colonies) had a press, there remain no evidences that it printed religious tracts. Just as Dr. Bray's was the first printed eighteenth-century southern sermon, so some of his tracts of the same period stand first among their kind of expression in the century. Such examples as "The Present State of the Protestant Religion in Maryland" and "A Letter, to such as have contributed toward the propagating Christian knowledge in the Plantations,"[236] are hardly controversial, however, but were written to support the cause of the S.P.G. in Maryland. Both of them and others proposing parochial libraries were protested in "An Answer to a Letter from Dr. Bray," by Joseph Wyeth,[237] apparently a Quaker. Bray is accused of hurting or destroying the religious liberty of the people of Maryland, and former Quaker George Keith is given a roasting as a man of "an unstable mind." [238] There is no indication that any of these tracts were printed in America.

Printed in England by an Englishman but based on materials assembled or written in South Carolina by John Ash and Joseph Boone, representatives of that colony in London, was a famous pamphlet. For Daniel Defoe in his *Party-Tyranny* (1705) used these colonial gentlemen's works as a basis for his pamphlet on civil liberty, which was among other things a plea for dissenters. Later, in "Queries upon the Foregoing Act," Defoe continued to defend Carolina liberty, and expanded the "Queries" in 1706 into *The Case of the Protestant Dissenters in Carolina.*[239] About the same time George Keith, the former Quaker and present Anglican missionary whose sermon is discussed above, published *A Journal of Travels from New-Hampshire to Caratuck on the Continent of North-America* (London, 1706), [240] in form somewhat in the tradition of the Quaker journal but with his experiences shaped into propaganda for the Anglican cause. One other Maryland tract, Commissary Jacob Henderson's *The Case of the Clergy in Maryland* (Annapolis, 1730?), is a religio-economic essay protesting against the "Act for Improving the Staple of Tobacco," which would deprive the clergy of some one-fourth of their income. The dispute represented was roughly analogous to that springing from the Two-Penny Act in Virginia a full generation later.[241]

By the time of Henderson the southern presses were beginning to print or reprint doctrinal or controversial religious essays. William Parks at Williamsburg in 1733 reprinted the popular work of Charles Leslie, *A Short and Easie Method with the Deists*, the eighth edition from the original London edition having appeared in Boston in 1723. But most tracts, including catechisms, were printed in England and distributed by the S.P.G. or sold by the provincial printers in their bookshops. The colonials did print some locally written materials of some significance, but most of these did not appear before 1740, when the Great Awakening was well under way. In one manner or another they were usually connected with the Great Revival.

Presbyterian Old Sider John Thomson, noted above, published two pamphlets at least partially springing from the revivalist controversy within his own church. Heimert observes that a work of his is the one exception to the otherwise uniformly ill-tempered satire and personal abuse in Old Side literature. This work—and one of the two pamphlets just mentioned —is *The Government of the Church of England, and the Authority of Church Judicatories established on a Scripture Foundation: And the Spirit of rash judging arraigned and condemned, Or the Matter of Difference between the Synod of Philadelphia and the Protesting Brethren justly and fairly stated* ... (Philadelphia, 1741); it is probably a product of his Maryland ministry. For 111 pages he addresses the "Candid and Christian Reader" on the validity of the Westminster Confession and on how Tennent and Blair violate it, on Whitefield's unfair and heterodox argument against *The Whole Duty of Man*, and on the *lack* of basic disagreement between the Anglican and Presbyterian churches. This is a classic statement of the conservative Presbyterian position on the Revival. In this gesture of brotherhood toward the Church of England he anticipates the second pamphlet, his Virginia-composed *An Explication of the Shorter Catechism by the Assembly of Divines Called the Westminster Assembly* (Williamsburg, 1749), in an appendix of which he compares the Thirty-Nine Articles with Presbyterian doctrine and finds only four on which the two churches do not agree. Thomson appears inclined to be ecumenical or at least conciliatory, and he clearly wished to avoid clashes between Christian groups on the frontier, where all needed their strength for a common cause.

In 1749 in South Carolina a scholarly Baptist minister, Henry Heywood, published *Two Catechisms by Way of Question and Answer; each divided into Two Parts. Designated for the Instruction of Children of the Christian Brethren ... commonly known by the name of General Baptists.*[242] Though the Quakers in South Carolina by mid-century were "a poor handful," there was among them a most effective religious writer. This was Sophia Hume, a native of the colony and granddaughter of the more famous Mary Fisher of Boston.[243] She was a person of some education who

784

had undergone an unusual religious experience. In *An Exhortation to the Inhabitants of the Province of South-Carolina, To bring their Deeds to the Light of Christ, in their own Consciences. . . . In which is Inserted, Some Account of the Author's Experience in the Important Matter of Religion . . .* (orig. ed., Philadelphia, 1748),[244] she accuses her countrymen of looking upon her, after her six years' absence, as despicable because of her religion and appearance. Her voyage to her native place she believes to be in accordance with the will of God. She speaks out against worldly apparel, music in churches, the theater, fairy tales, histories of Tom Thumb and other frivolities, and the liturgy.[245] In conclusion she calls upon the South Carolinians to become as children again and the Chosen People of God. They should remember that *all mankind* have a measure of the Light or Spirit or Grace of God. Thus salvation is "a matter of personal obedience." She gives her own experience, which has so wrought upon her that she had to return to her native place to bring her "friends and neighbours" to God. A companion piece, undated, is *A Caution to Such as Observe Things and Times . . . an Address to Magistrates.*[246] Rather naive by modern religious standards is Sophia Hume, but her earnestness and sometimes awkward eloquence indicate something of how the Quaker appealed to his fellowmen, in oral discourse or in tract.

Equally earnest was Samuel Bownas, another itinerant and famous Quaker whose *Account of the Life, Travels, and Christian Experience in the Work of the Ministry of Samuel Bownas* was published in 1756.[247] His preface to the reader declares, "The following Sheets exhibit to thy Perusal a *plain Man's* plain and undisguised Account of his own Progress in Religion," thus pointing another Quaker autobiography in the direction of the tract. From 1702 he traveled extensively in America, in Maryland and especially in Virginia. He is one of the few Quakers not afraid to express a sense of humor in his writings:

> I was in Company with the Governor of *Virginia,* at our Friend *Richard John's* House, upon the West Cliffs in Maryland, for we both lodged there one Night, and I heard that he had been studious in a Book against Friends, called *the Snake,* and Friends greatly desired he might have the Answer called *the Switch,* but knew not how to be so free with him as to offer it to him.[248]

One more Quaker tract from the South should be noted, Thomas Nicholson's *An Epistle to Friends in Great Britain,* dated from Little River in North Carolina in 1762[249] and probably sent to the author's Yearly Meeting at home in England. It is a brief four-page exhortation to hold fast to the faith.

Southern colonial Lutheran tracts are hard to come by. But Pastor Jaspar

Stoever of Virginia, while on a visit to Europe in 1737 to raise funds for his co-religionists, published at Hannover in Germany a short treatise relating the religious history of his congregation and pleading for assistance. The whole tract is now available in English.[250]

From North Carolina in 1758 came Anglican Alexander Stewart's *The Validity of Infant Baptism*, printed by James Davis at the colony's own press at New Bern.[251] He takes up point by point the objections of the Antipaedobaptists, or Anabaptists, "the most industrious and prevalent sectaries in this part of the world." The Bible, the Church Fathers, Roman history, and plain reasoning are employed in this little treatise. The arguments are familiar, the assumed and declared strength of the Baptists and the insistence on their adult immersion at this date perhaps a little surprising.

Hugh Bryan of South Carolina, mentioned in the previous chapter for his part in the conversion of slaves, was a wealthy, pious, and undoubtedly mentally unsound Presbyterian layman.[252] His Negro school was conducted for a time by the Reverend William Hutson, a former actor whose wife, Mary Hutson, was a pious and sentimental enthusiast. In London in 1760 John Conder and Thomas Gibbons, important dissenters, edited for their fellow nonconformists in both hemispheres *Living Christianity Delineated in the diaries and letters of two eminently pious persons lately deceased; viz. Mr. Hugh Bryan and Mrs. Mary Hutson, both of South Carolina.*[253] The two British worthies shaped these southern colonial materials into an effective "testimonial-to-grace" tract, and incidentally give some biographical information. Bryan's boyhood captivity among the Indians, his reading Bishop Beveridge's volume of meditations, a number of his letters of the 1739–1740 period, and his diary for 1751 are facts and materials all worked into what purports to be a mystical or semi-mystical experience in his being drawn toward God. These two South Carolina Presbyterian ministers testify to the saintliness of Mrs. Hutson, using extracts from her diary and some of her letters to show her religious concern. Her letters are in the style of Pamela's in Richardson's novel—and of certain later Sunday school literature. "A Meditation by Mrs. Hutson on the Soul's Entrance into Glory" (p. 158) and "Some Account of Mrs. Mary Hutson, in her Departing Moments" (pp. 160–162) by their very titles indicate the quality of the religion delineated.

The Swiss-German tracts or reports on the Georgia colony, in the German language, are just beginning to appear in English translation. Most are largely reports on the country and the state of toleration of their religion, but some are genuinely pietistic discourses.[254] Among them are the Urlsperger Tracts, 1735–1740, collections now in the University of Georgia Library, including accounts of Indians, diaries of Bolzius and Gronau, sermons, and other materials. Most of the published work of John Joachim Zubly, who lived and wrote in South Carolina and Georgia, appeared after 1763, but two of his sermons were published at Germantown in 1747 and 1749. His large compendium-tract, *The Real Christian's Hope in Death; or, An Account of the edifying Behaviour of several Persons of Piety in their Last Moments* (Germantown, 1746) is one of his few publications in English within the colonial period.[255] Rather curiously, the Presbyterian Swiss-born editor has a recommendatory preface by Richard Clarke, rector of St. Philip's in Charleston. The 187-page book is a collection of harrowing—or peaceful—death scenes arranged chronologically from the death of the Swiss John Jacob Ulrick to that of "C.L.P." (the last and others translated from the German), with footnote meditations by the author-editor, all the "scenes" European and clearly intended for Lutheran or nonconformist consumption. The translating, presumably by Zubly, is very effective. This is one of the curious by-products of American revivalism, connecting it with European movements and with the sentimentalism of the period in all forms of literature.

The Reverend Richard Clarke, just mentioned, himself published in 1759 an extremely eccentric tract, *The Prophetic Numbers of Daniel and John Calculated, In Order to shew the Time, When the Day of Judgment For this First Age of the Gospel, is to be expected: And the Setting up of the Millenial Kingdom of Jehovah and his Christ* (orig. ed. Charles-Town, S.C.; reprinted Boston),[256] indicating among other things that the nonconformists were not the only believers in an approaching millenium. Clarke had resigned the rectorship of St. Philip's and had gone to London. There he republished the work and published another of similar import. Apparently he was admired as a preacher; he is said to have composed his sermons (and perhaps tracts) "under the impressions of Music, of which he was passionately fond." Dalcho calls him a Universalist tinctured with the doctrines of Jacob Behmen.[257] In any case, this was an interesting man to have in the pulpit of the colony's leading Anglican church.

Perhaps the most voluminous religious work to appear in colonial South Carolina was Baptist clergyman Isaac Chanler's *Doctrines of Glorious Grace Unfolded, defended, and practically improved . . . and the Methods of divine Sovereignty . . .* (Boston, 1744).[258] Chanler, already noticed as friend and champion of Whitefield, here considers certain of the Thirty-Nine Articles of the Church of England, in "Of Original Sin," "Of Predestination and Election," "Of particular Redemption," "Of Effectual Calling," and "Of Perseverance." To these he adds an appendix on the Socinianism he sees in the work of James Foster, and points out how near Arminianism appears to Socinianism in that work. This is probably South Carolina's first theological treatise, but it is clearly tractarian in motive.[259]

Chanler's work is an ambitious attempt to prove that the Thirty-Nine Articles are Calvinist, and in doing so to support Whitefield against the local and other Anglicans who interpret them differently. Each of the subject headings mentioned above is for an unnumbered separate essay. Yet there is a unity in the whole, suggested in the general title and strongly argued in the Introduction, which is a summarized statement of these Calvinist doctrines. The reader will note that these are the particular Calvinist doctrines stressed by Whitefield, not all the major tenets of the Genevan's theology. The thinking is clear enough, though too frequently supported by pages of quotation from other Calvinists. Chanler concludes his longest section, "Of Predestination and Election" (more than two hundred pages) with the verses of three of Isaac Watts' hymns. The whole work is quiet, firm, within its premises well argued and proved, and worthy of further study as a major treatise of the Calvinist side of the Awakening.

One tractarian of North Carolina, first Anglican, then Presbyterian, then Quaker, and finally excommunicated by the last, was the author of three pamphlets, only the first of which falls within the colonial time period and is a genuinely religious exposition. This is *Some Remarks on Religion, with the Author's Experience in the Pursuit thereof, For the Consideration of All People, Being the real Truth of what happened, Simply delivered: without the help of School-Words or Dress of Learning* (Philadelphia, 1761),[260] by Hermon Husband. The author, bearing in some respects the stamp of the radicalism of the Revolution, is in his two later pamphlets (1770 and 1771) directly concerned with political events of the period after 1763, especially the Regulator movement, which had strong religious associations. In fact, all his political activities appear to have had religious backgrounds. *Some Remarks* is perhaps our best extant example of the emotional experiences of a southern eighteenth-century intellectual, a man who groped as long and earnestly as did Jonathan Edwards, though without the latter's apparent success. Despite its relative simplicity of diction and revelation of feeling, *Some Remarks* deserves comparison with other American literature of the inner life, including Edwards' *Personal Narrative*, of which in many ways it is suggestive.

Spiritual experiences Husband had. "Yet my Soul longed for his Presence, nor could it be satisfied without him." He concludes that through the Quaker meetings he has had intimations of that Immortality he worships and wishes to unite himself with. Hermon Husband alone is testimony of the strength of introspection and rationalized emotionalism in the eighteenth-century South. He thinks and he feels his God.

The Great Awakening evoked more heated controversy than Thomson or Chanler represents. The intensity of feeling of Old Side Presbyterians and most Anglicans on the one hand and evangelical Presbyterians, Independents, and Baptists on the other resulted in polemic and reasoned argument from many quarters. Some of the replies or attacks were in sermons or sermon-tracts on the order of the mild Thomson's, with greater vehemence. But men like Whitefield and his allies produced and provoked real tracts supporting or attacking Whitefield's position. Here in some instances regional lines were crossed, for Commissary Garden and Josiah Smith of South Carolina and Andrew Croswell of Connecticut engaged in a sort of three-cornered controversy, some of it in sermons and some in tracts.

One will recall that on Whitefield's first visit to Charleston, when he was in deacon's orders, he had been treated courteously by Garden and invited to preach in his pulpit. When Whitefield returned for a second visit, he seemed a different man, attacking the "unconverted ministry," *The Whole Duty of Man*, Archbishop Tillotson's works, treatment of the Negro, and a variety of doctrines accepted and practiced by the Anglicans. This led in 1740 to Garden's *Six Letters to the Rev. Mr. George Whitefield* (2nd ed., Boston, 1740).[261] Garden felt that as the Bishop of London's and his church's representative, he must speak. His sermons have been noted. But in the *Six Letters* he produced a vitriolic tract made up of epistolary exchanges. His first letter is courteous enough, but Whitefield's reply is curt and defiant. From then on Garden lets loose. The first three letters concern Justification. The doctrinal argument is fairly usual and commonplace, but Garden gets in some sharp digs at Whitefield's apparent inconsistencies. The fourth concerns "The Case between Mr. Whitefield and Dr. Stebbing stated, &c.," and Regeneration. The fifth, on Tillotson's works and *The Whole Duty of Man*, is more sarcastic than persuasive. The last is also on Tillotson and on the Negroes, the latter in relation to Whitefield's letter to the inhabitants of the southern colonies as to their religious treatment or ill-treatment of slaves. In the last matter Garden was on firm ground, for he himself had a better program than Whitefield's vague suggestion on catechizing.

Six Letters is not a happy performance. One might say Garden descends to Whitefield's level, or below it, for he refers to "your Mountebank way" and makes other personally insulting remarks. An angry man writing without sufficient deliberation, he probably did the Anglican cause as much harm as good. But his attack was read from Boston to Savannah. At this point Andrew Croswell of Connecticut, a Calvinist but not a New Light, decided to enter the lists against Garden in defense of Whitefield. He was the first New Englander to reply, in *An Answer to the Rev. Mr. Garden's First Three Letters to the Rev. Mr. Whitefield. With Appendix concerning Mr. Garden's Treatment of Mr. Whitefield* (Boston, 1741).[262]

Garden's rejoinder is *The Doctrine of Justification According to the Scriptures, and the Articles, and Homilies of the Church of England, explained and vindicated, in a Letter to Mr. A. Croswell, of Groton, in New England. Being a Reply to the said Mr. Croswell's Answer to Mr. Garden's three first Letters to Mr. Whitefield, With a Postscript* (Charleston, 1742).[263] His first pages are devoted to satiric "Notes" on Croswell's *Answer*, ridicule of the allegedly fumbling replies of the Calvinist being the principal weapon employed. Large sections of Croswell's letter are quoted with concluding comment. In a postscript, Garden half apologizes for his vitriol, observing that "evil Communications corrupt good Manners."

In both tracts Garden considers Wesley and Whitefield as one in doctrine, when actually they were already going off in opposite directions. Garden sneers once at Wesley's new Moravian notions, but otherwise he seems to consider all Methodists or Wesleyans as Calvinists. On the whole Garden's doctrine and argument are simply those of the Church of England in his time, rational and—he would have demurred at the adjective—Arminian. The tone and style, to have come from a dignified and devoted churchman who had done a great deal for the Christian cause in the colonies over which he had jurisdiction, are the surprising qualities of the work. It is the major example (there are several minor ones in the gazettes) of the extremes to which the emotions induced by the Great Revival led the otherwise self-controlled and dignified. The pamphlets were read in England as well as America, and Garden's two remain a significant contribution to the Whitefieldian controversy.

The other remarkable southern tracts of the period of the Awakening are those of Samuel Davies. They are as often concerned with religious toleration in Virginia as with Calvinist or evangelical doctrine. Though Davies is rightly known first as a preacher and then as a poet, he is also one of the more effective prose pamphleteers of his generation.

Davies' letters to the Virginia officials and to dissenters in England are almost religious tracts in themselves. For example, the extract surviving of a letter to Dr. Philip Doddridge of October 2, 1750, which Doddridge sent on in part to the Bishop of London, is at once a survey of the Presbyterian situation in middle Virginia and an indirect plea that the Act of Toleration include Davies' congregations and brother preachers, or his denomination throughout the colony. The bishop was impressed: Davies' point was "fairly stated." [264] Largely on this letter as basis there grew a correspondence of some years' duration.[265]

But even earlier Davies had replied to attacks on his New Side Presbyterians. Old Side John Caldwell's *Impartial Trial of the Spirit operating in this part of the world*, originally published in Boston in 1742, was brought out in a new edition in 1747,[266] with a preface by the Reverend Patrick

Henry (uncle of the patriot), Anglican rector at Hanover. Caldwell's book attacks the preaching of terror, the emphasis on "experience," the uneducated ministry of the New Lights, the doctrine of witnessing the spirit's conversion, and New Light intolerance, among other matters. Davies felt that he should answer it, since it was aimed straight at him and his congregations. His reply was *The Impartial Trial, impartially Tried and convicted of Partiality* (Williamsburg, 1748). He answered both Henry's preface and Caldwell's text. On Caldwell Davies launches a sharp personal attack, "proving" among other things that the Old Light minister was an imposter. The argument is on sound rational grounds, based on the facts of New Light history and belief, and showing some study of the effects of mental states on bodily disorders. He is more convincing than his two opponents. Doubtless he won with those really willing to be "impartial." He himself was living proof against the charge of an uneducated ministry. In his *Appendix proving the Right of the Synod of New York to the Religious Liberties and Inemunities allowed to the Protestant Dissenters* he argues that, if other nonconformists such as Quakers and Old Side Presbyterians are entitled to the benefits of the Act of Toleration, so are his people. If the law does not extend to the colony at all (an English and colonial official interpretation), then his people cannot be considered culpable. The *Appendix* is even better argued than the longer tract to which it is attached.

There is some evidence that Davies, like most of his contemporaries, possessed the power of sarcasm or satire. Lampooned by "Artemas," he replied in "A Pill for Artemas." It is unfortunate that both these tracts appear to have been lost: only a little information on their content and style remains.[267] Best known of his pamphlets, however, is *The State of Religion among the Protestant Dissenters in Virginia: In a Letter to the Rev. Mr. Joseph Bellamy of Bethlem, in New-England* (Boston, 1751),[268] a sober survey and argument read and reprinted under varying titles on both sides of the Atlantic.[269] Here Davies points out the favorable attitude of ex-Governor Gooch, the opposition in the General Assembly to granting licenses for preaching or for meeting houses, the number of communicants in his congregation, the situation of the Negroes and the number he has baptized, the aid received from the synod, and other data to prove his group's sincerity and right to legitimate existence. At this time and until he left for Princeton, Davies fought for religious toleration, especially with his New Side Presbyterians in mind, on the ground that the old British Act of Toleration applied in the colony and to his people. This King's Attorney General Peyton Randolph refused to allow. While Davies was in England and Scotland, he tried to stir dissenters there into aiding him, but almost all they were able to offer, as one commentator remarks, was sympathy. Davies withdrew from the field with this battle undecided, but he left the weapons and ammunition which Randolph's cousin Thomas Jefferson and the latter's friend James Madison could employ to good and final advantage a few years later. The *Letter to Dr. Bellamy*, as it was frequently called, was certainly one of the major documents in the colonial fight for religious freedom.

But it is in a tract published first in the twentieth century that the reader follows the cerebrations of Davies' mind at their best. This manuscript was prepared for publication by its author but for several reasons was never printed in his time. It is doctrinal, it is denominational, it is effectively logical, and it is theological literature of significance. *Charity and Truth United: Or, The Way of the Multitude Exposed: in Six Letters to the Rev. Mr. William Stith, A.M. . . . In Answer to Some Passages in His Sermon Entitled, 'The Nature & Extent of Christ's Redemption'. . . . In which is also contained a Survey of the moral Character of Mankind in all Ages; an Inquiry into the Nature of true Religion & Virtue; & a Vindication of the Divine Perfections in the Infliction of future Punishments*[270] is only a part of its title. But it indicates that the work was begun as an answer to Stith's sermon discussed above, in which the president of William and Mary had argued quite forcefully the Arminian position on Good Works and their relation to Justification and Salvation, declaring that he believed the majority of mankind would be saved but that he could not pretend (though others did) to say exactly how many would merit salvation.

Stith's is a kindly, latitudinarian, rational sermon which probably sat well with the majority of his auditors of the General Assembly, though not necessarily with all his readers. It was a learned sermon. In it, near the beginning, Stith cites and again at the end alludes to Davies' *Impartial Trial, impartially Tried*, with its statements that most of mankind shall perish. In other words, Stith's is an anti-Calvinist, anti-New Light, and anti-Davies sermon, though without vehemence or vulgarity or vinegar.

Stith's discourse, delivered in November 1753, was published early the next year (New Style), and Davies' answer is dated on the final page July 4, 1755. Thus the Presbyterian set out almost at once to answer the Anglican. In an introductory note Davies says he was circulating it among friends for critical comments when the news of Braddock's defeat came. Therefore he thought it unseasonable then to publish. Meanwhile President Stith died, and the author thought its publication would be an insult to the memory of the dead, a man Davies clearly admired. The manuscript was preserved, however, having been sent to England in 1760 to a friend, and through the granddaughter of this friend it was secured and brought back to America to the Presbyterian Historical Society in 1853. Only as recently as 1941 this most logical, theological, and literary of Davies' prose tracts appeared in print.

The "six-letter" idea, common enough as a form in the period, still may have been suggested by Garden's *Six Letters* against Whitefield. The divisions are as natural as those explicating the text or applying the doctrines of a sermon. But Davies' sermons are poetic prose or prose poetry. They are not always entirely and obviously logical, even when they have a unified emotional effect. Here is presented a different side of this Presbyterian mind. Whatever eloquence is here is distinctly prose eloquence, the result of down-to-earth reasoning. The learning is considerably greater than that ever displayed in his sermons—Davies' own translations of Greek and Latin texts, scores of references to philosophers from Plato to Bolingbroke, to historians, Church Fathers, theologians of the Renaissance like Grotius and St. Thomas More, and nonconformists of his own time like Doddridge. All are used to bolster his argument. Biblical references appear on every page. One has only to grant Davies' Calvinist premises, as one does for Jonathan Edwards, to be quite convinced. If one does not, he can still admire the marshaling of facts and words.

Davies declares that he has "travelled a little in the World" (a great deal for that day) and has observed men and their failure to seek for salvation. He pretends to no intuitive insight into the motivations of men, but is convinced by his reason and the Bible, the arbitrary Calvinist interpretation (or its rationale) of the latter being his mighty bulwark. He may or may not be departing from old-style Calvinism in his statement, "I grant that none shall perish, but by their own willful fault." [271] He declines to pass upon other questions, such as that of infant damnation.[272] Like other dissenters, he delights in quoting to an Anglican what some English bishop has written on a certain doctrine, something which seems to contradict one of his opponent's points. Davies fails to share Stith's conviction of the salvation of the heathen who have never heard the Gospel, for they cannot be proved to be pious and Davies doubts that they are. And again he uses the Thirty-Nine Articles against Stith's proposals, another procedure in which dissenters delighted.

In Letter Three, Davies drops the epistolary style and addresses his readers directly. He never returns to the earlier form. He calls what he writes "a popular Address"; though it is certainly not a sermon, it is hortatory. Who shall be excluded from Heaven, and why? Who shall enter Heaven, and what are the prerequisites of eternal life? With Chillingworth, he insists here as he has in his sermons, that "The Bible, the Bible is the religion of Protestants." So he runs the gamut of biblically induced questions about the potential heir to salvation.

In his sixth and final letter Davies anticipates and attempts to challenge the observation that, if so few are to be chosen, religion is "a gloomy & melancholy Thing" destructive of the happiness of human life.[273] His own

793

religion was a serene and happy one, and he attempts to show that Calvinist religion can be so for all. But he goes into a curious series of inductions and deductions, climaxed by his laying down a position as probable: "That tho' the great Number of Mankind be miserable, yet the far greater Part of the intelligent Creation will be holy and happy forever: or, that the miserable Part of the Creation may bear no greater a proportion to the happy, than the Number of Criminals executed in a Government, bears to the rest of the subjects."[274] One notes "intelligent Creation," which Davies describes as composed of beings throughout a universe we as yet do not know, and the Angels themselves. Thus mankind may form the criminal element of "intelligent Creation." He has no doubt that Mars, Venus, Jupiter, and Saturn are as well peopled as the Earth, and he implies that their inhabitants may be much more virtuous. The eighteenth-century theory of "plenitude" is here implicit. And the pre-Romantic sublime is almost explicit. Thus he concludes that, though the greatest part of mankind is sinful and unhappy, this is not at all the situation for intelligent beings of a thousand worlds. These are suppositions, he allows, but suppositions based on reason.

He concludes by way of a summary and a defense of his doctrine of Predestination as neither unjust nor inconsistent with the human will nor horror-inspiring. It is a crystal-clear statement of a position few moderns can accept and perhaps even fewer view objectively.

Thus in *Charity and Truth United* and the sermon which provoked it two of the best colonial southern minds participated in a theological controversy as serious as any ever fought out in New England. Such disputations are infrequent in southern intellectual history, primarily because too few felt the need of writing controversially on religious matters.

The last group of pamphlets to be considered as theological or religious literature are perhaps more nearly political. But one of the major participants was a clergyman, the difference of opinion grew out of an act the clergy considered as directed against them, and the whole matter is a bringing into the open forum of the press the ever-present conflict between the people and the established clergy. Many have said that the outcome marks the first great victory of the people in the cause of religious liberty. For the conflict was there, and had been since the earlier seventeenth century, despite the personal friendship and blood kinships of clergy and laity. But it is more than the culmination of a historic struggle. It is one of the first battles in the political campaigns preceding he American War for Independence, and it took place in the oldest colony, Virginia.

The imposition of the Pistole Fee by Governor Dinwiddie and the literary consequences therefrom are matters discussed in Chapter IX. Needful to consider here are the "Two-Penny Act" and "The Parsons' Cause," the joint source of polemics between lay and clerical leaders. The controversy grew out of economic measures made necessary because of Virginia's responsibilities and debts from the French and Indian War and the conditions of growth and the value of tobacco on the world market. In 1748, 1755, and 1758 the Assembly had to pass laws that for the ensuing twelve months all debts formerly payable in tobacco might be paid in cash at two pence per pound. This was no new thing in Virginia, but in 1758 John Camm and other prominent clergy protested it on the ground that it constituted an infringement of the rights of the clergy, who were the only sufferers of any great loss of income thereby.

Brydon blames this "revolt" of the clergy on the group educated at Oxford (Queen's College especially) already noted, who, he claims, had only British notions of the church in mind and paid no attention to the peculiar needs of the colony.[275] After the Act of 1755 these clergy and their allies wrote two petitions of protest to the Bishop of London. The two together drew only seventeen signers out of seventy clergy in the colony. The Two-Penny Act of 1758 was enacted with the same limitation as the previous one, that it would terminate after a year. Thus the Assembly could leave in force a law which would have been implemented in all its phases before the King had a chance to veto it. This was a clear evasion of the King's prerogative and was based upon a theory of government of Colonel Richard Bland, burgess from Prince George County, who later published his "principle" in his second tract against Camm. His argument was that in times of emergency the General Assembly was justified in passing and the governor in signing any act necessary. The college clergy, faculty members who also in most instances were ministers with parishes, were roused to vigorous action after the passage of the 1758 law, for in that year there was a scarcity of tobacco. Though the commissary refused to call a convention, Camm and his associates did so. About thirty-five met in Williamsburg in November 1758. Camm was sent to England with an appeal to the King.

Behind all this lay the decay of the Anglican establishment and the rise of dissent, the unwillingness of Anglican laymen to go beyond "practical" and "sensible" religion, and some previous clergy-laity cases which aggravated a bad situation.[276] And behind it all lay the old tradition of an independent vestry. The Tory faculty at William and Mary got into deep trouble with the General Assembly. Camm, an able member of that faculty, took with him to London a legally correct "Representation" of the clergy which described the 1748 and other acts fixing salaries (including the Two-Penny Act) and accused the governor and Assembly of breaking contracts between vestries and ministers. One able historian believes that the basis of the immediate trouble lay in the Tory English-trained ministers' refusal or inability to adapt themselves to vestry control of parishes. A great amount of correspondence between the governor in Virginia and Board of Trade in England, and factional essays within the colony, presented the situation from various angles.

Camm succeeded in getting the Bishop of London on his side. His Lordship wrote a letter to the Board of Trade full of misinformation and misrepresentation of Virginia events, at least according to Virginia historians.[277] The King formally disallowed the acts and appointed Camm as official messenger to deliver this proclamation and another communication to governor Fauquier at Williamsburg. Camm did not hurry to return but did advise his fellow clergy in Virginia to sue for back salary due. When he did return, he discovered that in all these lawsuits against vestries the Virginia courts (except in the case of James Maury) reported the suit to governor and Council without acting or before acting. According to long precedent a disallowance by the King had the effect of law only from the time it was formally presented to the governor (it did not reach Fauquier until June 1760). County juries rendered their decisions therefore in favor of defendant vestries. Appeals were made to the General Court, and then to the Privy Council in England. So the matter might have ended.

When Camm finally delivered his two official documents to the governor, he was reprimanded severely for misrepresenting affairs to authorities in England and was ordered out of the governor's mansion. The governor's indignation spread to others, and the pamphlet warfare began between the Reverend John Camm on one side and Colonel Richard Bland of Prince George County and Colonel Landon Carter of Richmond County on the other. The pamphlets were widely read throughout Virginia and neighboring colonies and have been read by Anglo-American historians ever since.

Landon Carter, whose recently published diary[278] is a classic of colonial southern literature, called himself in later years the first mover for liberty in the colonies. His editor mentions a prodigious number of works on liberty and kindred subjects as his. He had already opposed the Pistole Fee. Now he opened the Parsons' Cause—Two-Penny paper war with *A Letter to a Gentleman in London, from Virginia*, and *A Letter to the Right Reverend Father in God, the Lord B——p of L——n*, both dated from Williamsburg in 1759.[279] As he always did, Carter wrote in a tone of high resentment of the bishop's interference and charge that the Assembly had encouraged dissent and was guilty of disloyalty.[280] Colonel Richard Bland, called affectionately and half-facetiously by Thomas Jefferson "the wisest man South of the James River," antiquary, historian, parliamentarian, pamphleteer, and poet, had a considerable part in many phases of the Two-

Penny and Stamp Act reactions.[281] He entered the lists on Carter's side with *A Letter to the Clergy of Virginia* (Williamsburg, 1760),[282] a survey of the situation with emphasis on the rights of Englishmen, but also directly answering the bishop's letter to the Board of Trade. Bland was an abler penman than Carter, though he never wrote as much, and he refuted paragraph after paragraph of the bishop's unfortunate communication. In referring to royal prerogative, he states that the welfare of the people is the first law of any land and must take precedence. He ends with a warm defense of Governor Fauquier.

Camm's visit to the governor here intervened, and soon afterward Fauquier urged Colonel Carter to appear again in print. Before he did so, the General Assembly had drawn up a temperate "Representation."[283] Meanwhile from April 1759 the series of lawsuits on the part of the clergy continued. One of the ablest clergyman in the colony, the Reverend James Maury, whose sermons have been noted above, had instituted suit in Hanover April 1, 1762. The trial in December 1763 was memorable for young Patrick Henry's great debut as an orator and the token award of one penny damages.

While such cases continued, John Camm replied to his opponents in *A Single and Distinct View of the Act, Vulgarly entitled, the Two-Penny Act: containing An Account of it's beneficial and wholesome Effects in York-Hampton Parish. In which is exhibited a Specimen of Col. Landon Carter's Justice and Charity; as well as of Col. Richard Bland's Salus Populi* (Annapolis, 1763).[284] Answering the challenge of Bland that he give an open justification of the clergy's complaint, and including letters such as Landon Carter's of June 16, 1762, Camm shows himself as able in forensic debate, and as savage, as his opponents. Like the two colonels, Camm advances good reasons in precedent, history, law, and economic need. He refuses to accept Bland's and Carter's analyses of the general economic condition of Virginia at the time.

Bland promptly offered rebuttal in the *Virginia Gazette* of October 28, 1763, and Camm replied in another letter of "Observations."[285] Carter reentered the fray with *The Rector Detected, Being a Just Defence of the Two penny Act, Against the artful Misrepresentations of the Reverend John Camm* ... (Williamsburg, 1764), dated from Sabine Hall in October 1763. He added another point to Bland's on the precedence of public welfare over royal prerogative; that is, that a prince should be more than willing to suspend anything to favor his people provided his own royal right or that of other subjects was not affected. And he mounted a vigorous attack.[286]

Camm returned with *A Review of the Rector Detected; Or the Colonel Reconnoitred* (Williamsburg, 1764),[287] a strong but not quite outrageous refutation, in part page by page, of *The Rector Detected*. Punning, pseudo-Latin derivations for words, and all shades of satire and sarcasm are employed. There are hot words, and a judge is quoted as saying the King "had forfeited the allegiance of the people of Virginia" for disallowing their act. To the Tory author, and perhaps in the cold light of history to many another, this was treason. Eventually Camm appealed to the Privy Council when the General Court ruled against him, and the General Assembly sent its agent a bundle of documents for use by the lawyers for Virginia in defending its stand.

As far as the tracts and our interests in this chapter are concerned, the paper war ended with a pamphlet by Bland just as all these preparations for a legal showdown were being made. This was *The Colonel Dismounted or the Rector Vindicated in a Letter Addressed to His Reverence: Containing a Dissertation upon the Constitution of the Colony* (Williamsburg, 1764), signed "Common Sense."[288] It is generally agreed that this is the most effective and best written product of the controversy. It goes far beyond the others in its confrontation of the basic issues of the constitutionalism involved in the case. Here Bland's years as student of and participant in government (at this time he had been a burgess for twenty-two years) and in previous political controversy served as background for a great document.

The free and constitutional rights of Englishmen, American Englishmen, was his theme, and no British parliament could deprive them of those rights. Laws on internal policy must be with their own consent. Taxes respecting an internal problem are arbitrary and may be opposed.

Bland begins in a facetious tone, addressing "Your Reverence" again and again and reviewing mockingly the previous episodes or acts in the drama. Then he has "the Colonel" open a conference discussion of the ideas presented in pamphlets such as the *Single and Distinct View* and *Letter to the Clergy*, pretending to take them as the opposite of what was intended. He comes gradually to serious refutation of Camm, still keeping to the quasi-dialogue form and to the rights of Englishmen: "Under an English government all men are born free, are only subject to laws made with their own consent, and cannot be deprived of the benefit of those laws without a transgression of them."[289]

The three appendices, earlier letters of the controversy—the first by Bland and the other two by Camm—should be read, as Bailyn points out, as prefaces to the pamphlet, and read in the order in which they were written (III, I, II) to enable the reader to see the more scurrilous tone or level of the preceding controversy. In its mock inversion of roles, *The Colonel Dismounted* continues the satire but on a more sophisticated level.[290] In the southern colonies as in England it was an age in which the literary satire was the guardian of the public weal. *The Colonel Dismounted*, aside from the real significance of its content, is one of the most ingenious and polished examples of the genre produced in this country before the Revolution.

Bland, who resembles his contemporary Davies in his knowledge of the classics and of earlier and contemporary English literature, added to this knowledge a thorough acquaintance with the great writers on jurisprudence and theory of government. He employed history and fact for his major arguments. His last works (known only by subject) indicate something of his versatility—a study of land tenure in Virginia, a treatise on baptism written to refute the Quakers, and probably a tract on the American episcopate. And this does not count essays still unidentified in the *Virginia Gazette* and other periodicals, and essays in issues of that *Gazette* now missing. He was yet to write *An Inquiry into the Rights of the British Colonies* (1766), but *The Colonel Dismounted* is usually considered the abler work.

Thus the southern colonial religious pamphlet, which may have begun in the shorter tracts embedded in Hakluyt and Purchas or in missionary calls to come over and help us, and continued in sectarian and doctrinal controversy and advice on the Negro and Indian, culminated before the Revolution in a basically political review and advocacy of the rights of freeborn men. It is worth noting that the New England religious tract developed along somewhat different lines but also came to the Revolution as a consideration of the rights of the individual in the New World. In coming at long last to morality, liberty, and politics this southern and the northern controversial or explicatory pamphlet still retained many of the qualities or colorations of the religious and theological arguments from which it had sprung. In later generations it would return to religion and theology, then often in their relation to social movements with or without the tinge of politics.

Few southern colonials except certain Presbyterians went to bed after chewing a morsel of Calvin as had New Englanders such as Cotton Mather. But many of them must have taken with them to their couches the problem of the relation of religious belief to government, to conversion of the heathen around them, and to the proper functions of a Christian laity and clergy. Not so often as the Cottons and Mathers of New England did they rise the next morning to put pen to paper to express their cogitations. But more than has been noticed by literary or religious historians, a number of them did write religious tracts for their times. Only incidentally and occasionally do these reach the level of literature, but they remain, with the sermon, as significant records of the southern forms of puritanism and rationalism, of the independent spirit of the southern colonial congregation whether Anglican or nonconformist, and of the various individual and occasional problems of southern colonials. Few would deny that all these have had their parts in the development of the American mind.

CHAPTER SEVEN

Science and Technology, Including Agriculture

CONTENTS

—◆—

Introduction   805

First Fruits of the Wilderness: The Bowers of Arcadia   811

Resident and Visiting Scientists: The Advent of the Royal
    Society and Its Aftermath, Primarily in Life Sciences   818
    Principally Botanical   821
        The Later Seventeenth Century to 1710   822
        The Eighteenth Century to 1764   844
    Zoology   865
        Ornithology   866
        Entomology   869
        Animals, Including the Vertebrates, Molluscs,
          and Crustacea   870
        Ethnology   874

Other Aspects of Natural Philosophy, Primarily Physical   875
    Geology, Seismology, and Paleontology   875
    Meteorology, Climatology, and Astronomy   882
    Chemistry and Electricity   889

Geography, Surveying, and Cartography   893
    Roanoke and Jamestown   893
    The Middle and Later Seventeenth Century   896
    The Early Eighteenth Century   900
    The Later Eighteenth Century to 1764   903

Medicine   906
    Physicians, Surgeons, and Apothecaries   907
        The Seventeenth Century   908
        The Eighteenth Century   915
    Diseases and Epidemics   928
    Treatment, Including Surgery and Research   935
    Materia Medica   936

Agriculture, Theory and Practice   937
    Early Cultivation and Systems of Farming,
       Including Refertilizing   939
    The Staples: Tobacco, Rice, Indigo, with
       Hemp and Grain   946
    Horticulture: Science and Art, and the
       Literature of Colonial Agrarianism   954

Technological Industry   961
    Farm Related   965
    Community Related   971

Bibliography   1073

Notes   1085

~~~ The People wherewith you plant, ought to be
Gard'ners, Plowmen, Labourers, Smiths, Carpenters, Joiners,
Fishermen, Fowlers, with some few Apothecaries, Surgeons,
Cooks, and Bakers. In a Countrey of Plantation, first look upon
what kind of Victual the Countrey yields of it self to hand;
as Chesnuts, Wallnuts, Pine-Apples, Olives, Dates, Plumbs,
Cherries, Wild-honey, and the like, and make us of them. Then
consider what Victual, or esculent Things there are, which
grow speedily, and within the Year. . . . Iron is a brave
Commodity where Wood aboundeth. . . . Growing silk. . . .
Pitch and Tar. . . . But moil not too much under Ground; for
the Hope of Mines is very uncertain.

—FRANCIS BACON, "An Essay on Plantations"

All over the Country, is interspers'd here and there, a surprizing
Variety of curious Plants and Flowers. They have a sort of
Briar . . . . There's the Snake-Root. . . . a great Antidote in all
Pestilential Distempers. . . . There's the Rattle-Snake-Root. . . .
The *James-Town* Weed. . . .

Of spontaneous Flowers they have an unknown Variety:
The finest Crown Imperial in the World; the Cardinal-Flower,
so much extoll'd for its Scarlet Colour, is almost in every
Branch. . . . And a Thousand others, not yet known to *English*
Herbalists. Almost all the Year round the Levels and Vales
are beautified with Flowers of one Kind or other, which make
their Woods as fragrant as a Garden.

—ROBERT BEVERLEY, *The History and Present State of Virginia*,
ed. L. B. Wright (Chapel Hill, 1947), pp. 138–40, 298

In general I rise at five o'Clock in the morning, read till seven, then take a walk in the garden or field, see that the Servants are at their respective business, then to breakfast. . . .

I have got no further than the first volume of Virgil but was agreeably disapointed to find my self instructed in agriculture as well as entertained by his charming penn; for I am pursuaded tho' he wrote in and for Italy, it will in many instances suit Carolina. I had never perused those books before. . . . But the calm and pleasing diction of pastoral and gardening agreeably presented themselves. . . . The majestick pine imperceptibly puts on a fresher green; the young mirtle joining its fragrance to that of the Jasmin of golden hue perfumes all the woods and regales the rural wander[er] with its sweets; the daisys, the honeysuckles and a thousand nameless beauties of the woods invite you to partake the pleasures the country affords.

. . . I intend then to connect in my grove the solemnity (not the solidity) of summer or autumn with the cheerfulness and pleasures of spring, for it shall be filled with all kind of flowers, as well wild as Garden flowers, with seats of Comomil and here and there a fruit tree—oranges, nectrons, Plumbs, &c. &c.

—From a letter c. 1742 in *Letterbook of Eliza Lucas Pinckney, 1739–1762*, ed. Elise Pinckney (Chapel Hill, 1972), pp. 34–36

IT WAS THE FORTUNE of the southern colonial to live in the first great age of modern science and to be directly affected by that greatest of European corporations of the curious, the Royal Society of London. Indeed the settler in turn affected the outlook and the body of knowledge the Royal Society represented, and some of the Virginians and South Carolinians and others here to be discussed were themselves Fellows, officially inducted participants, in this congress of searchers for truth and thereby improvement of their world. A generation or two later those Britishers most anxious to apply acquired knowledge to immediate practical utility, through contrived processing or manufacturing, formed the Royal Society of Arts (arts in the sense of crafts and acquired skills), and in this too the southern settler had a part.

Scientific curiosity displayed itself in the southern British colonies simultaneously with their first settlement, and even elementary forms of technology appeared within a few years of first landfall. Science remained throughout the period basically utilitarian. When it was indulged in for its own sake, it was nearly or actually as much art as it was what today we call pure science. Technology was even more overwhelmingly utilitarian in purpose, though in several notable crafts technology developed into genuine art, and in a few instances one may argue that an art grew into a science or a technological process.

As in his religion or his books or his education, the colonial, like his friend or colleague left behind in Europe, had centuries of Old World development behind his scientific knowledge. Study and understanding of man's environment had developed slowly during the Middle Ages, but from the beginnings of the Italian Renaissance to the culmination of the English flowering in the age of Elizabeth and James the pace of investigation accelerated enormously, and it was to culminate, or, as far as England was concerned, to proceed on rational observation and experimentation in the chartering in 1662 of the Royal Society just mentioned. Raleigh and Dee and Bacon and the Tradescants had been among those of the previous generation who had prepared the way, and Robert Boyle, Christopher Wren, and John Evelyn (and one American, John Winthrop) had part in forming the organization.

But this is getting ahead of the story, for "curious gentlemen" standing on New World soil or back at home in Britain found that in the beginning they had to depend on their Spanish, Portuguese, and French predecessors, especially the first of these, for guidance and useful description of a continent and hemisphere they did not know. Gonzalo Fernandez de Oviedo y Valdes (1478–1557), José de Acosta (1539?–1600), Francisca Hernandez (fl. 1615), Nicolas Bautista Monardes (c. 1493–1588), and Peter Martyr (1459–1526), several of whom are mentioned earlier in this study as historians of Spanish America who had visited the New World or had published primary documents, showed considerable interest in all phases of the environment of the Western Hemisphere, from climate and topography to fauna and flora.[1] To be sure, climate and topography as well as fauna and flora were usually of tropical or subtropical regions as opposed to the temperate zone of British settlement. But the Spanish and French had reconnoitered a considerable portion of the area which was to be the territory composing the southern colonies, and they had settlements in East and West Florida, immediately adjacent to Georgia and the Carolinas. It was they who recorded, usually in Latin and sometimes in Spanish and French, the strange qualities of what seemed to many a new garden of Paradise, based in rich soil producing delectable fruits, odoriferous flowers and trees, and new and unknown animals, birds, and insects. Though the exact species recorded or described by the Latins was not always to be found in the southeastern mainland British colonies, quite often it was, and if not, something similar and identifiable as closely related was located by the early English settlers. Yet well into the eighteenth century and even since, these early Gallo-Iberian descriptions of New World products and soils and climate were used as starting points and guides for the curious gentleman from and of Great Britain. Furthermore, three of the foremost English naturalists who explored the West Indies—Sir Hans Sloane, Dr. William Houstoun, and Mark Catesby—had affiliations, direct and indirect, with their fellow collectors and observers in the English mainland colonies.

George Sandys in the 1620s and 1630s and William Byrd II a full century later actually owned and showed their familiarity with Acosta and Martyr and most of the rest, as did many other colonists. But the reliance of the curious or the enterprising, of those who sought exotic plants for exchange or for utility as materia medica, or who planned cities, surveyed boundaries, established factories or furnaces, or built or fashioned pottery or furniture, was naturally more directly on the patterns and models, and usually the active encouragement, of men and societies of similar interests in Great Britain itself. The relationship between American collector, artisan, or industrialist and English scientist and technological promotional organization was a complex and sometimes paradoxical one. Usually the resident of the United Kingdom, furnished with new and strange materials by the colonist, would classify and organize and report to his colleagues and take most of the credit for them. Or the London collector might be as relatively generous as Sloane and Petiver and Collinson and John Ray in naming the donors in their reports and yet take most of the credit, or at any rate receive it. Despite Sloane's personal expedition to the West Indies and the resulting natural history of the area he explored, it remains a question whether his contemporary renown and his abiding fame may not rest in large part on the strenuous labors of his friends and correspondents in the American garden of plant and animal life.

Yet the fact is obvious from the surviving letters, lists, and *horti sicci* in British repositories, not to mention the early American plants or their descendants still very much alive in British gardens, that without home encouragement by exchange of plants, persistent inquiries, and some financial support the remarkable record of the study of natural philosophy which is one of the more obvious facets of the southern colonial mind would never have been made. Though relatively only a handful of colonial Americans themselves organized or classified or theorized inductively or deductively on their discoveries or experiments in the natural world, until Benjamin Franklin most of these (with the exception of a Josselyn and a Winthrop and a Dudley and a Colden) were residents of the area from Maryland to Florida. The southern colonials' agrarian way of life and the early stage of development in natural and physical science at that time, their climate and vegetation, and their inquiring minds were among the elements which are represented by a Banister, two John Claytons, a Mitchell, a Catesby, a Lawson, a Garden, and a few score others who survive in that peculiar kind of immortality, the names of species and genera of plants, animals, and insects.

Medicine, the simple and complex crafts, mining, metal refining, spinning, and a dozen more forms of technology also derived in pattern or model largely from Great Britain, though French Huguenots and German Palatines or Moravian Brethren sometimes brought their own techniques. But these European processes were greatly altered or at least modified by the new environment, far more than were those for gathering or even theorizing on living things or on stones or soils. Climate, labor supply, simple know-how, and above all imperial regulations designed to curb large-scale industry in the colonies were factors in producing fairly radical differences. Southern plantation industries such as weaving, brewing, and coopering had their parallels in many British manors, but colonial wineries and silk-weaving, never genuinely successful but often tried, had no real British counterparts. Brickmaking, coopering, sawmills, furniture and upholstery work, and paper and wind mills did have British counterparts, but there were in the South for most of them new conditions which affected the work and its results as well as the form of the relatively simple machinery employed. Glassmaking was the earliest of American manufactures, but it is significant that the skilled craftsmen who labored at it were Polish or German or Italian. Iron mining and even blast furnaces were almost as old as the Virginia colony, but the British imperial policy of licensing certain colonial manufacture caused the owners of blast furnaces, throughout the colonial period, to be restricted to the making of raw-material pig iron or, if they went on to the manufacture of andirons and pots or more sophisticated utensils for local consumption, to defy authority or manage to have their activities winked at by colonial administrations. And though most provincial governors, especially in the long view of history the abler ones such as Spotswood of Virginia, Dobbs of North Carolina, and Sharpe of Maryland, were dedicated imperialists believing strongly in Crown prerogative, these same men pleaded again and again that their colonies be allowed to develop much more manufacturing and thus technology, on the apparently logical ground that in the eighteenth century British industry could not supply colonial demand.

Other phases of technology too owed pattern and inspiration to European models, perhaps fewer of them entirely British than most of those just noted. These included cartography, an art-craft-technique which by 1763 was represented by several dozen significant, accurate, and beautifully engraved (usually in England) maps by southern colonials. Contrary to generally held popular and even historical opinion, towns of the southern mainland sprang not from mushroomlike growths but from the careful geometrical pattern-plats modeled on those of cities of Great Britain and western Europe. And from Jamestown, and perhaps Roanoke Island, to the forts of the Chesapeake and the Savannah and the Ashley-Cooper, on to those on the Cherokee frontier, able engineers adapted European defenses to the terrain and the materials available with startlingly similar resemblances and results.

Technology and industry, though they never held the degree of importance in the southern area that they did in New England, were a definite consideration of the southern mind from 1607 on. George Sandys landed at Jamestown in 1621 with instructions to found or encourage at least half a dozen kinds of industry, from iron and glass furnaces to shipbuilding. Edward Digges a few years later was engaged in silk manufacture, among other technologies. And at the end of the colonial period the union, or balance, of agrarianism and technology shows a sort of culmination in the farm-and-industry plans of Thomas Jefferson, who manufactured nails not only for himself but for his neighbors and was a beginner in producing many homecrafts and agricultural tools. The development of the textile industry in the South in the nineteenth and twentieth centuries did not all come about because factories moved south to obtain cheap labor; some of it was inherent as a natural and necessary concomitant of the agrarian system. Admittedly technology in the southern colonies was on the whole, certainly on a large scale, incidental to other things, but before the Revolution the southern mind was aware of its necessity and the consequent implications for the future.

Finally, one should recall the native red man's effect on the white settler's methods in agriculture and the very crops the settler grew, and the adaptation of the aboriginal's methods in making certain kinds of pottery, fishing gear, boats, and other things. Two of the staples of agriculture and a means of the planter's wealth and health were discovered in the New World—tobacco and maize, or Indian corn. The colonists' cultivation of corn would for a century or two follow the native method. The Indians' use of certain plants as medicine affected the search for new botanical varieties and indirectly resulted in some of the papers published in the *Philosophical Transactions* of the Royal Society. And the red man was, along with the black servant, a favorite subject or material for the early ethnologist.

FIRST FRUITS OF THE WILDERNESS:
THE BOWERS OF ARCADIA

The literature of promotion, discovery, and history should be kept in mind as one reads the present chapter, for much of the record of science and technology in the southern colonies is preserved in those writings. Especially is this true for natural history, the semiamateur study of aspects of nature which has developed into modern natural science. Though it is always difficult and often impossible to separate the serious professional scientist from his equally enthusiastic and perhaps well-educated collaborator who devoted the major portion of his time to other matters, what the two together accomplished in the colonial South is of some significance in the long history of man's attempt to understand and cope with his environment.

In Great Britain, as often on the continent, the natural historian evolved from the professional collector, the individual of varying degrees of formal training who sometimes through personal interest but more often as representative of an organization such as a museum or public garden, frequently a wealthy merchant or professional man, and most often a nobleman or prince or sovereign, gathered anything and everything in which the *curious* (the word soon came to mean *investigative*) mind would be interested or by which it might be amused. The Tudor and Stuart kings and many of their subjects such as the famous Lord Arundel of James I's time were avid collectors of a wide variety of objects, from buried Grecian marbles or the Black Prince's gauntlets to rare animals and birds and fishes from all parts of the globe. These personages in high places employed knowledgeable agents, often men who had traveled extensively or had a wide range of contacts throughout the Renaissance world. It was men of this latter group who were the forerunners of the professional scientists, for they perforce had to learn a great deal about all manner of things before they developed the intelligent discrimination necessary to separate the genuine or the genuinely rare from the spurious or well known. Many of these men, after serving a limited apprenticeship or even half a lifetime in gathering for others, set up their own collections. Two of the latter were the elder and younger John Tradescant; their private harvest (they were also agents for royalty and nobility) of rarities through the machinations of one Elias Ashmole became the nucleus of the Ashmolean Museum at Oxford, rightly the *Musaeum Tradescantium*, the latter being the title of the little book of 1656 cataloguing their "ark" of curiosities. Another, a century later, was the physician Sir Hans Sloane, Bart., whose natural history collections became the British Museum. Both the Tradescants and Sloane were intimately connected in their labors with the southern colonies, though for the moment only the former concern us.

Herbals, herbaria, and gardens were palpable evidences of the enormous proliferation of interest in plant life which came with the discoveries of new lands and of new plants in old lands. The interest sprang from several quarters, such as the developing medical science which searched for new plants as healing drugs, the needs of western Europe for new sources for ship's stores (timber, pitch, and tar), the developing appetite for exotic fruits and vegetables, and merchant and upper-class desire to develop gardens in which herbs and flowers and shrubs and trees from all parts of the world might be arranged in precise but complex geometrical patterns or scattered in artful-artless profusion in a simulated natural garden. By the eighteenth century the ornamental gardens were definitely stylized, though in the seventeenth there seems to have been more emphasis on variety than arrangement—with some notable exceptions. The elaborate herbals, springing originally from manuals of "physick" plants, gradually became scientific books in our sense, carefully classifying. They presented illustrations and verbal descriptions which to begin with were again records of "physick gardens," which might be cultivated by the same curious gentleman who had an ornamental and kitchen garden (the latter two or the three often blended).

John Gerard (1545–1612), whose herbal is recorded as present in southern colonial libraries, was the sort of professional botanical collector who worked for Queen Elizabeth's Secretary of State Burghley in what seem to have been royal or public gardens and created for himself his private garden. His *Herball, or Generall History of Plants* (London, 1597) contained 1,800 woodcuts. It was replete with errors, but it remained a standard reference book or manual for the botanist on both sides of the Atlantic for many generations, happily in several editions corrected and to some extent rewritten. And other English gardeners wrote similar works or translated and adapted French or Dutch or Italian books for English use.[2]

Of the prominent British collectors perhaps the most significant for America and the South in his official capacity was John Tradescant the Younger (1608–1662). He and the elder John (d. 1658), probably of Cornish origin, attracted such patrons as Robert Cecil, Earl of Salisbury (1563?–1612), and the King and Queen. The two, as their catalogue shows, had traveled extensively in Europe and North Africa, and the younger, as recent evidence suggests rather conclusively, had made expeditions to Virginia more than once. The garden and museum of natural history they set up at Lambeth, the latter known as "Tradescant's Ark," were by the 1630s among the sights of London. Two lists survive of the museum-garden's contents, both recently printed or reprinted. The first, a 1634 garden list of plants of John the Elder, is not of as great general interest as the little *Musaeum Tradescantium* (originally London, 1656), which lists the "Collection of Rarities Preserved at South-Lambeth neer London." The ark contained fifteen varieties of objects or specimens, from birds and fishes and insects through minerals, mechanical contrivances, weapons, costumes, utensils, coins, and medals, with an elaborate catalogue of trees and shrubs and plants, and in conclusion a list of "Benefactors." The last is a long roll of names beginning with the King and Queen, the Duke of Buckingham, the Archbishop of Canterbury, the Earl of Salisbury, many other noblemen and women, and dozens of knights, doctors, military officers, merchants, and simple gentlemen.

But the contents of this museum include the first known formal exhibit of objects from the southern mainland colonies, along with much else "from Virginia, Bermudas, Newfoundland, Binney, the Amazon, and the East Indies, . . . All Manner of Rare Beasts, Fowls and Birds, Shells, Furs, and Stone . . . ,"[3] these objects being but the beginning of a list which included thirty kinds of Indian tobacco pipes; bows, arrows, darts, quivers, and tomahawks; robes of bearskin or feathers and one of shells said to have belonged to Powhatan himself. The catalogue from Virginia included three sorts of hummingbirds, a redwing blackbird, redbirds and bluebirds; muskrats and wildcats and spiders and flying squirrels and rattlesnakes; and semiprecious stones, shells, pillows, cradles, and "an Indian little round table." But it was the gathering and propagation of a multitude of new plants from the Chesapeake Bay region which was most impressive. The younger Tradsecant is given credit for introducing to England the tulip tree (*Liriodendron tulipifera*), the swamp maple (*Acer rubrum*), the hackberry (*Celtis occidentalis*), the sycamore (*Platanus occidentalis*), and the black walnut (*Juglans nigra*), and perhaps was responsible for several others.

Mea Allen presents strong argument for John the Younger's presence in Virginia in 1637, 1642, and 1654, and the probability that he was also there in 1632. Long before the earliest of these dates, not later than 1624/1625, this Tradescant or his father, probably the latter, was corresponding with George Sandys, treasurer in Virginia. And one may be sure that learned traveler-poet who supplied to the Lambeth museum little Egyptian idols from his wanderings in the Mediterranean region a decade earlier was writing about curiosities he had found or might find in the Chesapeake area.[4] It may have been this curious son of an Archbishop of York who was responsible for "Powhatan's robe," still on display at the

Ashmolean, as well as various kinds of implements and fauna and flora, but there were many more persons connected with Virginia who also might have supplied all sorts of things before the younger Tradescant ever visited the New World, perhaps Governors Yeardley and especially Wyatt, John Pory, or others of the learned and philosophical observant men who lived in the colony between 1612 and 1630.

But in some respects this is again getting ahead of the story. More than a generation before Sandys and Wyatt arrived in Virginia there had been at least two intelligent observers, one of great learning and the other of remarkable observational and artistic gifts, who had at least described in words or painted in watercolors dozens of the marvels of the New World with which this chapter is concerned—fish, animals, birds, plants, red men's agriculture and primitive technology, geography, and geology. These men—Thomas Hariot and John White—and their work have been considered at length earlier, but it should be pointed out here that White drew and colored maps and plats of towns and fortifications, made magnificent paintings of Indians at sport or labor or ritual and of beautiful and strange plants and animals including the amphibians, and drew some remarkable topographical sketches of the newfound land. Master Hariot's *A briefe and true report*, our first extensive treatise on American natural history and agricultural potential with promotional overtones, has also been mentioned earlier in other contexts. Hariot mentions metals, soils, timber, and other commodities. Though the Roanoke Island settlement was gone before 1590 and a new beginning in peopling was made some distance away at Jamestown, southern history, scientific and otherwise, begins in North Carolina. Not only did White and Hariot make an attempt: their work, through deBry's engravings of White's work and the several editions of Hariot's report, was never lost. Clearly the founders of Jamestown and its resident chroniclers, Smith and Strachey and Percy, knew, absorbed, and employed the 1585–1590 pictorial and verbal record of their southern colonial predecessors. In other words, the work of the Englishmen on the Carolina dunes marked the beginning of an unbroken and distinguished tradition of interest in and investigation of natural environment, its nature, its uses, and its implications which the southern settler would continue to develop. All was not lost with CROATAN.[5]

Captain John Smith (1580–1631), who in many respects took up the account of English America where Hariot and White left off, was a historian and promoter and an observer of the Indians. In both aspects of his accounts he comments on natural history and other scientific matters. His writings, from *A Map of Virginia* (1612) through *The Generall Historie of Virginia, New England, and the Summer Isles* (1624), reveal him as an able geologist, geographer, and cartographer as well as ethnologist, and

in a more amateur way as a natural historian. The *Map of Virginia* was remarkable in many ways, and as a guide for topographical, geographical, and
cartographical analysis it was to affect European ideas of Anglo-America.
Glass and iron manufacturing began in Smith's time, though their production was undertaken more seriously later.[6] He relied on Hariot quite closely,
as already suggested, for his accounts of flora and fauna, though he certainly
added a few personal observations. Perhaps not quite so obviously promotion writing as Hariot's, Smith's work in its scientific observations is directed
even more toward the utilitarian, the ship's stores from the forests, the profitable fisheries, the animals in relation to the fur trade, and the metals,
soil, and rock useful in brickmaking, glasswork, and iron refining. But his
description of the opossum (an animal Hariot does not describe though he
may mention it under another Indian name) was the first of a long line of
delineations and anatomizings of this curious little beast through the rest
of the colonial period, investigations recorded in print in such prestigious
publications as the *Philosophical Transactions* of the Royal Society. Perhaps
more than Hariot he records elements of the southern environment which
might fascinate the curious. Even the detailed ethnological descriptions of
the red man appear to be designed more to satisfy European curiosity than
to calm the fears of the potential colonist.

William Strachey (1572–1621), one-time student at Cambridge, secretary to Governor Lord de la Warr (1610–1611), poet and chronicler-
historian, owed much to Smith and perhaps even more to Hariot and
older chroniclers.[7] But like Smith he has a great deal to say from direct
observation and study, especially in his accounts of the red men and his
apparently highly original Indian vocabulary. His accounts of coastline
formation and fossil remains go beyond Smith toward modern thinking
on geology, and he reports Dr. Bohun's experiments with native plants
for medicinal purposes and the physician's making of wine from wild
grapes.

In letters, annual reports of the state of the colonies, lists of "Virginia"
plants in English gardens, and other scattered data there is considerable
evidence that the British amateur and professional scientists between Sandys
and Tradescant and the formation of the Royal Society in 1662 were gathering southern American objects of many kinds and that the colonists were
continuing their activity and experiment in technology, the latter especially
of the household or individual-plantation variety. Medicine and technology
will be considered at greater length below. Here one can only glance at
somewhat scattered suggestions of varied interests and applied theory beginning in Sandys' time, about 1620.

For in 1620 there was great evidence of interest in commodity, especially
through agriculture. John Bonoeil's *Observations to be Followed ... {for}*

Silkworms . . . (London, 1620) was written with the potential Virginia grower in mind. In fact, the earliest writing on any crops in Virginia seems to have been on silk production, and that writing came long before 1620.[8] All during the period before 1662 men like Edward Williams and Samuel Hartlib, encouraged by John Ferrar and his daughter Virginia, were writing of sericulture for the benefit of the Virginians, and there is abundant evidence of at least sporadic if not continuous interest in the cultivation of the mulberry tree and the silkworm. The cultivation of tobacco for the European market was of even greater interest and was written about from John Rolfe's time. Both crops were intelligently and at least for a time successfully grown and developed by Edward Digges of Bellfield near Yorktown, the quality of whose tobacco was so high it was called the E-Dees, and some of whose correspondence regarding his experiments in agriculture was published in the *Philosophical Transactions* and elsewhere.[9] In 1650 Williams gave "A valuation of commodities growing and to be had in Virginia in 1621, which thirty years later, have improved from one-half to treble." His list is revelatory of the variety of southern colonial processing and the raw materials which were treated. Iron, crystal rock, and other minerals appear to have been quarried or gathered and shipped in bulk as ore or ballast, though iron and alum at least were being refined from this time, as will be shown. Ship's stores, such as pitch, tar, turpentine, and masts, had to be prepared from American trees and plants. Oils were extracted from rapeseed, walnuts, and linseed. Furs had to be dressed and cured. Potash, salt, alum, aniseed, saffron, and a dozen other products necessarily went through some stages of refinement from their natural state before they could be shipped abroad. Williams wrote primarily about the commodities native to or prepared in Carolina, but without exception save possibly sugar all of them might also have been found or grown in the Chesapeake area. Thus in the first half century of settlement, the southern colonist was not only clearing and cultivating soil; he was producing crops with European market value and refining other natural resources for the same purpose, altogether, despite the growing concentration on tobacco production, employing numerous techniques and requiring sharp observation and clear comprehension of what might be found in the wilderness or Arcadia around him.

In 1656 John Hammond's *Leah and Rachel, or, the Two Fruitful Sisters Virginia and Mary-Land* . . . (London) concentrated on the Bay area. His book has been noticed as a promotion pamphlet, but its description of natural and cultivated products of the region reflects growing population and increased awareness of mineral, animal, and plant resources. Hammond points out the emphasis on orchards and gardens, principally planted in European fruits and flowers but in the latter mingling the native with the imported. Though he sees Indian and English corn and tobacco as the staple agricultural commodities, he predicts that, as the European mulberry tree grows up, tobacco will be neglected and silk and flax will become the two major crops and industries (in their curing or preparation and subsequent weaving).[10]

Medicine and medical men before the Restoration of Charles II and the chartering of the Royal Society will be discussed briefly in the section on medicine. But the medical man in Virginia in the 1630s was already gathering plants, partly out of curiosity but undoubtedly largely for their potential as physic. About 1634 the English naturalist Parkinson noted that "*George Gibbes* Chirurgion of Bathe" had brought back from Virginia the seeds of various plants, including the "Aster Virginens lutens alter minor" and other new varieties tentatively named with the word *Americanum* or more frequently *Virginiana* or *Virgianum* appended to the Latin label.[11] In the Bodleian Library, in a good state of preservation, there remains a *hortus siccus* (or a collection of dried flowers and plants) brought from Virginia in the decade of the 1650s. And in 1661, soon after his return, Charles II received from Edward Digges a present of Virginia silk. Meanwhile before 1650 some unnamed Virginian sent to a friend in England a little note describing again that perennial curiosity the opossum; one Daniel Hoare sent probably to a friend at Oxford a careful drawing and description of parhelia of the sun he had observed at "Blonte Point in James River" in February 1648; and Samuel Maverick of Massachusetts, after a year's residence in Virginia, carried back to New England a large collection of shells, bones, and stones from the bank of the James River, found when a well was dug.[12] But not all products of scientific curiosity or craftsmanship were exported. Wine and glass and ironware were produced for provincial consumption. English gardens were almost surely imitated at Jamestown in its first decade, and certainly tobacco was planted even in its streets. Among the more prominent residents (as far as the records go) was George Menifie (Menifee), who had come to Virginia in 1625, was a burgess by 1629, and by 1634 had on his estate "Littletown" in James City County a large garden, "contain[ing] fruits of Holland and roses of Provence."[13]

Thus there is evidence in the oldest colony that the attitude toward science and technology developing in England in the first six decades of the seventeenth century had a parallel among the Englishmen who had ventured to the North American continent. They were ready to take their part in the experimental and theoretical projects of the Royal Society and in the technical explorations and inventions of the Royal Society of Arts. It is perhaps worth emphasizing that at least three Virginians, including Edward Digges, were represented in the first volume of the *Philosophical Trans-*

actions of the Royal Society in 1665 and that in the same volume was included an essay on how to kill rattlesnakes in the colony. Settlers in their first century contributed materials and observations in many areas. Of pure mathematical or other abstract speculation they contributed nothing in print, but Daniel Hoare's astronomical drawing is only one of several evidences that Newton and Boyle, and their predecessors of the earliest Stuart reigns, influenced and shaped some of the thinking and the conclusions from observations done in the South Atlantic area.

RESIDENT AND VISITING SCIENTISTS: THE ADVENT OF THE ROYAL SOCIETY AND ITS AFTERMATH, PRIMARILY IN LIFE SCIENCES

The Royal Society, taking shape in 1660 and chartered in 1662, was probably the first formal organization of scientists in the western world. With the year 1662, one historian has remarked, the modern world began. If so, there had been a long period of gestation before birth, both on the European continent and in Great Britain. Toward the close of the sixteenth century loosely organized groups had for a time existed in Italy, France, and England. The London Royal College of Physicians founded in 1518 had for many years been merely a licensing body. Francis Bacon, rebelling against the rigid restrictions of medieval scholastic philosophy, envisioned in several of his books a new sort of scientific cerebration, necessary if the discoveries in the New World were to have their full potential effect on European thinking. He urged extended efforts in experimental research, a development of the combined empirical and rational faculties of men in his era and continuing steadily into the future. Facts had to be ascertained precisely, which meant a vast amount of spadework, followed by a continuous progress of related inductive knowledge and conclusions drawn therefrom. All this would have to be supported financially through a nationally endowed or sponsored institution.

His plans met opposition and obstacle, for Stuart kings and then Commonwealth claimed that no funds could be found for such a program, and entrenched university Aristotelians opposed the whole concept long after Bacon's time. One Oxford experimental club, formed in 1648, did attempt to implement Bacon's ideas. It included such future great men as physician-chemist Robert Boyle, political economist and statistician William Petty, astronomer-architect Christopher Wren, and the later Bishop Wilkins, all together about thirty men of unusual talents. As the Commonwealth tottered, the club dispersed, but several of its prominent members had by 1659–1660 joined with Londoners such as diarist-gardener John

Evelyn and Scottish statesman-philosopher Sir Robert Moray (who had Virginia connections) and several of the professors at Gresham College to meet periodically and discuss natural philosophy and witness certain experiments. Though there may be some dispute about whether these groups were the nuclei or moving spirits in the founding of the Royal Society, the fact is that a little while after the Restoration of the monarchy, a group interested in the new science met at Gresham College. In the chair was Dr. Wilkins; the date was November 28, 1660. A college for the promoting of "Physico-Mathematicall Experimental Learning" was proposed, and they (about a dozen men) agreed on weekly meetings and an admission fee. Forty-one others were invited to join with them. In fact if not in formal recognition, the society was under way. The King's approval, organization and rules, the name "Royal Society" suggested by John Evelyn, and the 1662 royal charter followed in order. Statutes declare the intention of the group to examine all systems and theories, experiments and histories natural, mathematical, and mechanical, and many other matters to compile "a Compleat system of Solid Philosophy." Members were to experiment and collect natural objects and curiosities, among other activities, and to read and discuss letters and other reports from all parts of the world. The society was a self-governing and self-perpetuating body. New members were elected upon nomination of old members. Objectives, the society's records indicate, were broadly Baconian, and as in the great philosopher's own ideas there is a strong element of utilitarianism. It was perhaps this last element which induced and produced most of the remarkable collaboration to come from the British colonies of North America.[14]

The net the society wished to fling out to collect objects for study was planned to be worldwide, and to a limited extent it was, for British ships were then roaming the seven seas. Actually it never successfully penetrated the Spanish and Portuguese empires, despite friendly overtures of various kinds, including offers of exchange. Obviously botanical, zoological, and geological specimens, and data on meteorology, particularly of their respective domains in the New World, would have been of advantage to both. French cooperation was somewhat better, but never what the society wished. Materials from the Mediterranean came fairly easily, though the coverage of the area was spotty, and the objects from Asia or Africa were in most respects even more haphazard, though there was enough from China, botanical especially, to prepare the way for some interesting and significant comparisons.

Foreign correspondence with interested persons was to be, along with the activity of ship captains and traveling British scientists, a chief means of observation and of collecting. Fellows of the society sent abroad to represent their government or trade were expected to be highly useful and often were. The correspondence between outsiders and individual members of the society was equally as important as official communications: such letters were frequently read before the Fellows and often printed in the *Philosophical Transactions*. Though there were many genuinely foreign Fellows throughout the world, one gets the distinct impression that by far the most active participants or contributors outside the British Isles were the colonial Fellows of the West Indies and more often of the mainland possessions. Undoubtedly the existence of the society, the official encouragement of its officers, and the private encouragement of individual members, incited and sustained a great interest in and enthusiasm for the experimental approach among colonials.

Stearns gives what may be considered an impressive checklist of colonial Fellows from 1661 to 1783. Actually on examination it is not nearly so impressive as he thinks, for of the fifty-odd members, at least seventeen or eighteen resided outside the mainland colonies, ten were royal governors, and several (as Sir Alexander Cuming) paid only a fleeting visit to America. John Winthrop (1606–1676), who was in England from 1661 to 1663 in an attempt to secure a royal charter for Connecticut, was one of the original Fellows. The next mainland colonial, William Byrd II, was elected in 1696 when he too was a resident of London. Of the royal governors several southern ones, such as Henry Ellis of Georgia and Francis Nicholson and Francis Fauquier of Virginia, had something to contribute from their own observations. Dr. Houstoun, attributed to Georgia, actually never set foot in that colony, though he was authorized by Georgia Trustees to gather plants in the West Indies for the Savannah gardens or as potential provincial crops. Mark Catesby, not included in the lists of colonial Fellows by Stearns, Sachse, or Denny,[15] actually spent far more years in the colonies than at least half the "Colonial Fellows" listed, and certainly secured his election by the work he did in and concerning the South Atlantic region. Dozens of men (and some women) from the southern provinces alone highly deserved the recognition membership would have accorded them, as will be indicated, for their scientific labors and even publication in the *Philosophical Transactions* but never attained it, in contrast with the eminent, such as two Calvert governors, Governor Hunter of New York, and William Penn, members or Fellows like other Britishers whose social or political prestige would be useful to the society. Dr. Arthur Lee of Virginia, elected in 1766, was despite his medical education at Edinburgh primarily a political writer. Among those elected principally for their actual work in the New World, Doctors John Mitchell and Alexander Garden, of Virginia and South Carolina respectively, were with Benjamin Franklin and the John Winthrop mentioned above among the most genuinely deserving of those who did receive the accolade. Shryock perhaps to the contrary, at least half a dozen southern colonists on their merits deserved election ahead of Cotton Mather, and certainly ahead of William Brattle and Harvard President Leverett of Massachusetts. Though perhaps there is insufficient evidence to generalize dogmatically, New England and middle colony scientific observation and experiment appear to have been predominantly physico-astronomical-electrical (Josselyn and the Bartrams and Colden excepted) while the southern was natural history and ethnology and meteorology (especially climatology), as far as contributions to the Royal Society are concerned.

Raymond P. Stearns gives New England priority over the southern colonies in the chronological record of its interest in the new science through the Royal Society, primarily through John Winthrop, the sole original colonial member because he happened to be in England at the time. He shows that Winthrop read the first paper by a colonial, on the process of making tar from the knots of pitch pines, and later papers on tree planting and on maize, or Indian corn. In the Northeast this first generation of modern scientists—John Josselyn, Samuel Sewall, and Increase Mather, for example—concentrated on physical phenomena, except for Josselyn, the one non-Puritan among them, who recorded observations in natural history. Thus Stearns goes along with certain other historians who declare the New England Puritans as by nature receptive to the new science, though other writers take the opposite point of view regarding the seventeenth-century northeastern mind.[16]

PRINCIPALLY BOTANICAL

As in the pre-Royal Society and pre-Restoration period, the first southern colonials continued from 1662 to show a many-sided interest in science, though predominantly in natural history and agriculture, perhaps in the former partly because there was much fauna and flora to be found and examined in their region. But even in the decade of the founding of the Royal Society Virginians were describing for the scientists in London such varied matters as unusual weather conditions including storms, a comet, plants, minerals, serpents, and the now-familiar problems of tobacco and silk culture. Ironically for those who consider science inherent in Puritanism, it is worth noting that a great deal of investigation and the encouragement of collecting and experimentation in seventeenth-century America came from several prominent Anglicans, among them Henry Compton (1632–1713), Bishop of London, who with his gardener, George London, created a garden of exotic (largely American) plants, and from other American clergy or southern laymen corresponding with English bishops, deans, and other clerics concerning experiments and collection of specimens. And the place of individual Quakers as developers and promoters of natural history in its Anglo-American phase is obvious wherever one looks. If one agrees that the New England mind was receptive to the new science, he must upon the evidence agree that southern and middle-colony Anglican minds, abetted by Quakers, were equally receptive, though their emphases may have been different. That Winthrop and a few other Puritans performed more experiments in physics and chemistry than did perhaps any southern colonial save the first John Clayton may perhaps be best explained by the existence of Harvard College's experimental apparatus, gathered before a permanent southern college was founded. As far as technical processing is concerned, there seems to have been in this post-advent period about as much carried on in the South Atlantic area as in the middle and northern colonies, despite the latter's obvious advantage of settlement in towns.

The Later Seventeenth Century to 1710

The first case in point is Edward Digges, the silk and tobacco cultivator already mentioned, who was in London in 1669 and clearly had been in intimate contact with several members of the Royal Society. As he returned to Virginia in that year he carried with him a set of "Directions and Inquiries Concerning Virginia," twenty-four instructions-queries which remind one of those which more than a century later inspired Thomas Jefferson's *Notes on the State of Virginia*.[17] The list in its comprehensiveness is suggestive of the aims of the society and what it thought—or hoped—Digges himself might do or get others to do. First was needed a detailed history of the Virginia plantation. The second urgent necessity was a "perfect account" of the history of tobacco including its "physical" uses, and an explanation by the Reverend Alexander Moray of Mockjack [or Mobjack] Bay of the new Sweet-Scented variety. Several of Moray's letters to the society were published, including at least one printed (in extract) in Volume I of the *Philosophical Transactions* along with communications from Virginia by Digges and Captain Silas Taylor. The third of the instructions was that Anglican clergyman Moray be consulted on the progress of "Silkwork."[18] Other queries or requests were concerned with experimentation in rice, coffee, olives, and vines; with gathering samples of various sorts of earth presumably for use in pottery or porcelain manufacture; investigation of stones, minerals, iron ore, and possible encouragement of iron mills. Attempts should be made, it was suggested, to discover hot baths for medicinal use, the headsprings of the navigable rivers, the preparation of various kinds of silk grass; to discover (and give the uses of) native plants such as *Wichacan, Pocone,* and *Chincombe-tree* (chinquapin); to find oak, cypress, pine for ship's stores and to determine the possible suitability of hemp planting; to supply samples of grasses, berries, herbs, and animals of all kinds. The society wanted to know whether the native inhabitants of the northern Chesapeake Bay region were gigantic in stature, and those of the eastern portion dwarfish, "as hath been reported." Other questions were asked about the expertise of the red men in hunting, swimming, fishing, and diving; of the state of Virginia towns, cattle, tillage, and pasture, kitchen gardens and orchards, potash manufacture; of the influence of clearings (destruction of forests) on the health of the inhabitants; and of compass readings, ocean tides and currents, charts of changes in wind and weather, of meteors and comets and thunder and lightning, of samples of sea water of different degrees of latitude. One of the more interesting requests was "to make a good Map of Virginia, and especially of the coast thereof, with the Longitude, Latitude, and to sound the depth near the Coast in ye shallow places, roads etc."

Obviously this was a large order, and there remains no evidence that a busy man such as Digges, however much he may have been interested, did gather or could have gathered the answers to this comprehensive questionnaire on environment, agriculture, and technology. That the society thought he could, and that in 1669 probably he himself thought he might, is evidence that there were thus early in Virginia men of perhaps as diverse interests as Digges and Moray. Digges had only another five years to live. Perhaps he did assemble many of the answers. The observables, and the agricultural and technical products asked for had actually almost all been touched upon, at least, by Hariot, Smith, and Strachey, among others. In one sense Digges was merely being asked to bring information on Virginia up to date, but the slant of the questions and the drift of the reasoning behind them represent a new experimental approach to observables and to processes. The later historians Beverley and Jones were in many ways supplying more than an answer to the first request for a history, for the two of them together discussed matter and method of land, agriculture, and red natives. Others drew maps, though not for some time were the cartographers to indicate all that the society wished to ascertain about headsprings of rivers or the depths and contours of the tidal shelf.

Moray, who may have had a copy of the inquiries, was an active experimenter in rice and French barley, and offered to attempt to grow coffee if seeds were furnished. Tobacco and silk interested him, but a more urgent need was a set of directions on how to make "common white salt," very much a necessity. His letter of February 1665 read before the society March 28, 1666, is a long epistle[19] to his kinsman Sir Robert Moray discussing many of the things just mentioned, and in addition recommending new settlements in what was to be the Carolinas, referring to his fighting on the King's side at Worcester, and rhapsodizing on the paradisiacal state in which he lived. His sentence is often quoted: "Could a publick good, consist with a hermetick condi[ti]on, I should prefere it before all others, but the nixt to it which is the settling in a wilderness of milk and honey: non can know the sweetness of it: but he that tasts it: one ocular inspection, one aromatick smel of our woods: one hearing of the consert of our birds in those woods would affect them more than a 1000 reported stories let the authors be never so readible." And Moray concludes by promising to do his best with the queries directed to him (of course an earlier set). Meanwhile he again, as in his last letter, recommends his friend and parishioner Colonel Willes [Willis], who would be able to satisfy Sir Robert regarding some of "those phylosophick speculations." Thus Willis was a third curious gentleman in this small compass with Digges and Moray. Moray disappears from the epistolary exchanges after 1668, either by returning to Great Britain or, as seems more likely, succumbing to the diseases which might occur even in the odoriferous forests of the Chesapeake area.

There are names and tantalizing glimpses of other scientific-minded southern colonials in the decade. Thomas Glover, who lived in Virginia several years, described a terrible storm of 1667 and strange fish and wild fowl and towering mountains, as well as the usual soils, trees, and medicinal roots in a long "Account of Virginia" published much later—in 1676 in the *Philosophical Transactions*.[20] Glover's is probably the most complete account of its length for Virginia during the seventeenth century. In it and in John Lederer's later accounts of the exploration of 1669–1670 is mentioned an able mathematician and surveyor, Colonel John Catlett, a man of learning, piety, and scientific interests who, long before Lederer, planned an expedition west of the mountains. The provincial and county records show him in Sittingborne Parish, Rappahannock County, by 1650, having migrated from Sittingborne Parish in Kent. By 1665 he was presiding justice of the old Rappahannock County court. He is said to have been killed by Indians while serving with the militia against them soon after his return from the last Lederer expedition. One learns most about him personally from a letter of April 1, 1664, to his kinsman Thomas Catlett at Hollingborne in Kent. He bewails the news that so many godly ministers have been turned out of their places, he outlines the dangers of border warfare and a possible rebellion of "servants" (probably white at this early date) which was discovered and thwarted, and he notes with reverence and wonder the working of God's Providence in these and other matters. Yet he scorns the folk belief in astrological signs foretelling what would happen. Catlett made "an almanack and discourse of the vanity and uncertainty of judicial astrology" which won him praise and favor from

Governor Berkeley and the secretary of state when he presented copies to them. The ancestor of United States President James Madison, Catlett in his breadth of interests was a worthy progenitor of his much-better-known descendant.[21]

The secretary of state in Virginia under Berkeley, Thomas Ludwell (1628–1678), by 1666 was writing to Lord Arlington of the Board of Trade and Lord Clarendon and Lord Berkeley of Stratton on such subjects as the organization of government in Virginia (by counties, parishes, courts, officers, militia, etc.), the fear of proprietary government, tobacco problems, the exploring expedition of 1669–1670, and the conjectures as to the proximity of the western sea. He described the prodigious storm of hail as large as turkey eggs and the havoc among men and animals created thereby. This was in April 1667. He follows it with a vivid description of the "dreadful hurricane" of August 27 of that year, in which at least ten thousand houses were blown down and every plantation crop ruined. Though he gives no indication of having been trained in scientific observation, in his several letters Ludwell supplies a great deal of meteorological and agricultural information and shows a considerable interest in geography and topography. He was a curious gentleman and a fairly good example of the colonial southern political leader's half-deliberate, half-inadvertent part in exploring and depicting his environment.[22]

Ludwell describes for the benefit of the London official or other economically and politically interested parties. The next two observers of consequence were collecting, describing, experimenting, and speculating for other scientists or industrialists or for themselves: the first John Clayton and John Banister. Clayton (1657–1725) remained in the colony for only two years, 1684–1686, ostensibly sent as minister for the Jamestown parish but surely also to make scientific observations. He wrote about Virginia from the colony and for many years thereafter from England and Ireland, and his later experiments with steam and gas heating had some relation to his stay in the colony. His case affords positive evidence of a mind in the seventeenth-century southern area which went far beyond mere collection and description. He sought for reasons, was properly skeptical of hearsay and folklore, and displayed his experimental proclivities from this early period of his life, in the colony especially in agriculture.[23] He appears to have absorbed an enthusiasm for science while he was at Merton College, Oxford, under the master who was perhaps a kinsman, Sir Thomas Clayton. He may have received an M.D. degree as well as the B.A. and M.A. (1682) of which there is positive record. In 1687 he appears to refer to a series of experiments he had carried on during the two years between receiving his M.A. and his departure for Virginia,[24] especially with the "Digester," the prototype of the modern pressure cooker. Clayton, who corresponded with the eminent scientist Robert Boyle from Virginia in 1684, described these earlier experiments to that gentleman after he returned from America. In the 1682–1684 period he had made investigations of some medical significance regarding the specific gravities of liquids such as urine and with the burning of coal gas for illumination.

On the voyage to Virginia, Clayton kept up his observation-experimentation, some of which he later reported to the Royal Society. Marine animals, ocean currents, and the self-designed speaking trumpet used in locating a dangerous leak were the objects of his attention and in the last instance the result. In Virginia he boarded with a family he never identified, on a plantation near Jamestown, a situation which induced or at least encouraged his agricultural experimentation. He offered suggestions on how to drain swamps to produce rich and productive fields, on the proper care of livestock, and on an improved method of preparing tobacco seedbeds. And he demonstrated by draining at least one swamp and producing under his method five times as many usable tobacco seedlings in a given plot of ground as had ever been done before.

Clayton clearly had set out for Virginia with the intention of doing a great deal in science. He included in his supplies specially blown glasses for making studies of specific gravities, microscopes, barometers, thermometers, and chemical instruments. All these were lost when the ship carrying them, a companion vessel to his own, went down on the crossing. Years after, when he continued to discuss the Chesapeake region, he had to rely on his memory and a few notes. He had listened carefully to many persons and made many inspections and explorations for himself. He collected fauna and flora—he mentions three hundred herbs he had gathered. His bad luck continued in England when his bird collections were thrown out (while he was ill) because of their odor!

Clayton came to know well many of the leading persons of both Chesapeake colonies. One, for example, was William Digges of Maryland, son of the Edward mentioned above and deputy governor of that province, whose wife was the stepdaughter of the third Lord Baltimore. The wife's brother Nicholas Sewall provided an instance of luminescence reported to Boyle. In Virginia, Clayton was on intimate terms with Governor Lord Effingham and Secretary of State Nicholas Spencer, onetime acting governor; William Sherwood, wealthy planter and political figure mentioned elsewhere in this book; Ralph Wormeley; and especially John Banister, fellow-naturalist and probably rector of a neighboring parish of Charles City County. At this time Banister was well along with his *Catalogus Plantarum in Virginia Observatarum*, of which more later. Then there was William Byrd I, probably Clayton's most congenial friend, from whom the parson learned a great deal about Virginia, historically and environmentally, and perhaps about the Batts and Fallam 1671 expedition already mentioned in other chapters and its exploration of the Appalachians. Somehow he was able to copy the original journal kept by the party, a narrative he recognized as an important document, one which in our time has been published several times.[25]

On Clayton's return to England he came to know personally many eminent scientists, including several with whom he had already corresponded, and in 1688 he was elected a Fellow of the Royal Society. Even before this friends had been urging him to report his observations on Virginia, a task he at first declined because of the loss of the instruments and books which might have enabled him to keep more accurate records. But eventually he agreed, and by 1688 he began a series of letters to the society presenting his observations of the Chesapeake country. The Glorious Revolution interrupted the communications but in 1693 they were resumed and completed. More of this in a moment.

While he was in Virginia, Clayton had corresponded with a number of people, though only a few letters survive. One of April 24, 1684, to a "Doctor of Physick" contains along with medical observations Clayton's shrewd (and already quoted) analysis of colonial Virginia mental character and interest. His letter of June 23, 1684, introducing himself to the great Robert Boyle, enclosing the Sewall story of electricity in the wearing apparel of Maryland's ladies, mentions William Digges and describes the American firefly. In 1687 after his return to England, in a lengthy epistle Clayton answered some of Boyle's queries concerning the Digester and the nature of air, gas, and water under peculiar conditions. Clayton's later experiments in these and other kindred matters are recorded in papers read before the Royal Society and in some instances printed in the *Philosophical Transactions*. Among them is the relation of a significant experiment of illuminating with coal gas, a process of which Clayton seems to have been the inventor or discoverer, and of steam and nitrous particles in the air, apparently unrelated to his Virginia stay except as it shows the quality of mind of the writer and suggests that he may well have performed similar experiments in Virginia.

The earliest of the letters concerning Virginia, written in 1687, did not reach the Royal Society in time to be published with the others in the 1690s, though it was published in the *Philosophical Transactions* in 1739. It is a letter to Dr. Nehemiah Grew (1641–1712), noted plant anatomist and Fellow, on "The Aborigines of the Country."[26] It remains one of the valuable comments on the red men, especially on their medical practices. The second epistle, written on May 12, 1688, when Clayton was rector of Crofton at Wakefield in Yorkshire, was concerned with the observer's meteorological observations in Virginia, where "The Air and Temperature

... is much governed by Winds," actually an astonishing feat of recall, for the abundant detail and conclusions could hardly have come from a few outline notes, which were apparently all Clayton had. His so-called "Second Letter" (actually third) is concerned with the waters in and about Virginia, from ocean and bays and rivers to springs, and their effect on the human constitution. Here he shows his interest in specific gravity and laments the loss of his glass vessels which prevents his experiments in America from being conclusive. Fossils he had seen in banks or been shown by Banister, the nitrous qualities of tobacco, and an extended description of tobacco culture are also in this paper. Next was read his copy of the narrative of the Batts and Fallam expedition in its attempt to discover the South Sea. This was followed by a severely critical account of English colonial agricultural methods. The growing of wheat, his experiment with draining a swamp, more on tobacco culture, the condition and situation of Jamestown in relation to soil and crop development, and cattle are among his topics here. "Of the Birds" is a separate paper, in which he identified many varieties and describes the mockingbird in some detail, the latter with a discussion of the relation of its anatomical structure to its peculiar abilities in singing.

Observations on natural history continue in his next paper, on snakes and vipers, elk and deer, the opossum, rabbits and squirrels and muskrats, bats and wildcats, bears and beavers, wolves and foxes, frogs and tortoises. Included is a consideration of possible cures for snake or viper venom, especially of remedies of various sorts for rattlesnake bite.[27] This essay is followed by an unusual discussion of air, water, and steam, a paper read before the Royal Society at the same occasion as that on the beasts of Virginia but concerned with the method and results of the experiments employing one of "Mr. Papine's new Digesters,"[28] really a continuation and elaboration of his pre-Virginia experimentation. Two other brief essays apparently by him, on fossil alum and "China Varnish," were sent to the society.[29]

Clayton was not merely a persistent and imaginative observer and experimenter: he wrote well. Lively anecdote and vivid description and striking archaic similes are among the qualities which make him one of the more readable of the early colonial scientists. He was versatile and observant of detail. If his instruments had got to Virginia with him, a genuine beginning of scientific experimentation in the physical sciences as well as the natural might have begun in the South generations before they were. And if he had brought back the fauna, flora, soils, and stones he collected, much more of the Chesapeake Bay environment would have, or might have, become widely known in the seventeenth century.

As it happened, a fellow laborer in Virginia, as well educated, and in natural history and ethnology at least as discerning and imaginative, overshadowed Clayton in his actual collections, correspondence, and observations. The Reverend John Banister, although he has descendants living in Virginia and the United States today, might have been largely forgotten but for the publication of his most important extant work by famous English botanists in their own large works and the preservation of correspondence in the *Philosophical Transactions.* In addition, a few botanists through the centuries have recognized the value of his specimens reposing in the British Museum as part of the Sloane Collection, and in recent years it has been discovered that both Robert Beverley's and John Oldmixon's accounts of Virginia owe much to Banister's until recently unpublished work. Besides this, Stearns' study of Banister and his contributions and *John Banister and His Natural History* by Joseph and Nesta Ewan have demonstrated this clerical scientist's significance in the story of colonial intellectual development.[30]

John Banister (1650–1692), born in Gloucestershire and educated at Magdalen College, Oxford (M.A., 1674), where he was clerk and chaplain 1674–1678, probably became interested in natural history through such men as Robert Morison, Robert Plot, and Bishop Henry Compton. It was perhaps in these years that Banister gathered his first great "Herbarium Siccum" of plants in the Oxford Physic Garden and the surrounding fields,[31] a work appropriated by Plot in his *Natural History of Oxfordshire.* When Banister sailed for Virginia in 1678 via the West Indies, he was apparently subsidized in his scientific pursuits by a circle of English patrons, most of them Fellows of the Royal Society. He may also have been officially a "missionary" clergyman for the Church of England, though direct evidence of this possibility has not come to light. His resources were slender—no such instruments as Clayton set out with—and he had to beg his patrons for brown paper and even a good microscope. He did have a useful library. In Virginia his principal financial and intellectual resource was William Byrd I, but he married a prosperous widow in 1688 and left children who were to remain friends of the second William Byrd and whose children in turn were prominent in later generations. Banister's life was short, for in 1692 he was accidentally shot by a hunter as he gathered specimens along a river bank. He was mourned especially in England by such naturalists as Martin Lister, a personal friend, who wondered whether a successor in any way comparable could be found for the pioneer naturalist. For a number of decades no one could be found.

Banister's papers, though apparently ordered to be sealed and sent to the Bishop of London, in some part found their way into the collections of Sir Hans Sloane and thus into the British Museum. Others were treated carelessly and unsystematically by James Petiver. And some are in the Fulham Palace Papers of the Library at Lambeth, for which all of them were probably intended. Martin Lister had shells and drawings which came to the Ashmolean Museum with other items in 1683, and various persons possessed some of his drawings and specimens.[32] Of his written works, several have survived in more than one copy in Great Britain or in Virginia. Banister himself published nothing, but several of his letters appeared in the *Philosophical Transactions*, and various other documents were printed during or soon after his lifetime. The Ewans have edited all they could find, including his drawings in the Sloane Collection, and published them together in their recent handsome volume. The state of many manuscripts indicates that Banister prepared them with publication in mind.

Probably his earliest Virginia-composed work is his letter to Dr. Robert Morison of April 6, 1679, written from William Byrd I's home at "The Falls" at present-day Richmond. This long epistle begins with a recital of Indian troubles and proceeds to the nature of the country, agriculture, types of grain and vegetables, and of course tobacco. It goes on into the fur trade, mentioning beaver, otter, fox, wildcat, raccoon, and deer. Then it proceeds to lists of other mammals, birds, fish, nuts, fruits, and flowers, though the writer acknowledges that he cannot identify many plants he sees, blaming his inability on the want of the proper books, which almost surely had not then been compiled. He plans to go to Indian towns and learn something of their living customs and their knowledge of plants as medicines. He concludes with a description of their sweating houses or steam baths. In other words, in this one letter Banister outlines or suggests the lines of inquiry he plans to follow.

Banister probably did not know as many of the eminent and powerful as did his friend Clayton, but he seems to have been fairly intimate at least with William Byrd I, Theodorick Bland, and probably Commissary Blair and Governor Nicholson. There is no evidence of officially designated missionaries to either Indians or backwoodsmen in Banister's time, though his going among the Indians may have had such a declared purpose as conversion. It seems probable that he was rector of Bermuda Hundred, a small parish near the junction of the Appomattox and the James, a position which would have allowed him great freedom of movement and of time for his scientific pursuits.[33] When the first plans for the College of William and Mary were being formalized, the Virginia Assembly appointed Blair and Banister as the two clergymen among those gentlemen who were to be founders or first trustees of the said college, an act in itself seeming to indicate recognition of Banister's learning and educational experience. He did not live to see the formal charter or the matriculation of the first students.

As he collected, Banister taught himself to draw, and there remain many depictions of plants with instructions for the engravers written on the sheets, another proof of his intention of publishing. In a letter of about 1685 to an unidentified English botanist[34] he expresses his amazement at the strange and myriad aspects of nature around him, and he mentions John Ray's request for specimens and perhaps suggestion of a catalogue. Banister proposed to send annually to Ray and other members of the Royal Society plants, roots, seeds, and drawings. His observations on insects collected in 1680, published in the *Philosophical Transactions* much later (1701), present another phase of his activity. The manuscripts representing this work in the Sloane Collection are mixed with others—Latin descriptions of Virginia plants, long discussions of fossil marine animals and shells, stones, vegetables, and other aspects of nature.

Petiver published some bits of Banister's insect-plant work in the *Philosophical Transactions* and other media, and engravings of his molluscs were printed in Martin Lister's *Historia sive Synopsis Methodica Conchyliorum* (1685–1692). But the turmoil of the Glorious Revolution prevented the publication of his "Natural History of Virginia," the plans for which he outlined in a letter of about May 5, 1688.[35] What Banister described was a comprehensive survey of his Chesapeake environment which would have included much more, though with somewhat differing emphases, than the work Edward Digges had been asked to do in answer to set queries. His outline shows the influence of English studies such as Plot's *Natural History of Oxfordshire* and Ray's *Methodus plantarum nova* (1682), the latter perhaps in its revised form as the *Historia plantarum* of 1686–1704, along with the cataloguing systems of Morison and others. But he knew that he was indeed dealing with a new world, and he planned elaborate exposition of its peculiar properties. When he died in 1692 several parts of his projected work were ready for the press, though other sections were represented by notes or *horti sicci.*

Though some of Banister's materials remained in Virginia and were probably destroyed decades later when the family home on Hatcher's Run burned, some were gathered up and dispatched to Bishop Compton by colonial officials.[36] In addition to the publication of some of Banister's work by Petiver and Lister noted above, a few rewritten and systematized descriptions by Bobart appeared in Volume III of Morison's *Plantarum Historiae* (Oxford, 1699). Leonard Plukenet included about eighty Banister figures of plants in his *Phytographia: sive, Stirpium Illustriorum et Minus Cognitorum Icones* (1691–1696); John Ray recognized Banister's contributions to the flora of Virginia, published additional new species and seed lists, and noticed further Banister materials successively in the three volumes of his *Historia plantarum*; recently recognized has been the unacknowledged use of Banister manuscripts on water and soil and natives, sometimes verbatim, in Robert Beverley's (1705) and John Oldmixon's (1708) histories mentioned above. The list of natural history borrowers goes on well into the eighteenth century, among them Dillenius, Sherard, Doody, Linnaeus, and a few other Continentals. After his discoveries in the West Indies, Dr. William Houstoun, to be noticed further later, gave the generic name of *Banisteria* to many seeds, and plants were grown from them by Philip Miller, gardener of the Chelsea Physic Garden, who published an account of these plants in the seventh edition of his *Gardener's Dictionary* (1759). Linnaeus adopted the name in his *Genera Plantarum* and *Species Plantarum*, through which *Banisteria* is still identified as a tropical and subtropical genus of several species. His collections themselves meanwhile enriched the gardens of England public and private with flowering dogwood, willow oak, chinquapin, red oak, and sweet bay, among other exotic trees. All together it is estimated that Banister sent 340 species of plants, 100 insects, 20 molluscs, and some fossils and stones to his English patrons. Probably about two-thirds of these were new species. He drew sketches of about 80 plants and some of molluscs and insects. His references to birds are inferior to Clayton's, but a well-known historian of our early science avers that "no other field naturalist had contributed as much, and so well, to the natural history of Virginia, or to any other British colony in America." [37]

But this is not quite all the story. The writings per se deserve some attention, for they show an acute mind at work on problems of a new area for investigation. The five extant manuscripts of Banister's plant catalogue are indicative of his efforts and accomplishments and even his own opinions of them. The collated edition of this plant catalogue recently published by the Ewans gives his materials and ideas appropriate background and framing.[38] The same scholars have edited his work on molluscs, fossils, and stones, and "The Insect and Arachnid Catalogue" which show Banister as the first intelligent observer of molluscs and insects in North America.[39] The molluscs are also considered with fossils and stones—in other words, as geology. Since Hariot's time southern colonists as well as European savants had puzzled over the origin of fossils, as their ancestors had done. In America there were also stones and soils to become excited about, particularly if one considered their possible practical uses. Banister's specimens, drawings, and descriptions were possibly sources for Lister and Linnaeus, as his plants were.[40]

Perhaps the general intellectual historian will be most interested, however, in the manuscripts, incomplete and somewhat unpolished as at least one of them is, of the two planned major works, or parts of the same major work, segments of which Banister probably felt he had almost ready for the printer when he died. These are the "General Natural History" and the account "Of the Natives." Both may have been in some sense answers to queries such as Robert Boyle had suggested long before, to questions such as Digges carried back to Virginia with him. Similar queries had been included in the "Instructions" to governors and other officials of the earlist British colonies at Roanoke and Jamestown, and were probably modeled in part on Spanish and Portuguese procedures in investigating the nature of their New World provinces. Again we are indebted to the Ewans for magnificently edited and collated printings of the two works. The natural history is brief and fragmentary, almost outline in form, though Beverley was able to use some of it word for word. It adds little data to that Banister gave his friends in his lists and letters and specimens, though fresh glimpses of the hummingbird and of nature's abundance are presented. And "Of the Natives" is a significant document in the long history of our written observation of the red man. Banister wrote well, so well that able historians such as the two mentioned, Beverley and Oldmixon, used him extensively, the former adding some detail from his own observation and reading.

John Banister was the right man in the right place at almost the right time. Despite the disruptions of the Bloodless Revolution and his own lack of equipment, but for his untimely death at forty-two he would probably have given us what he planned and his English friends of the Royal Society and the Temple Coffee House Botany Club wanted, a comprehensive natural history of the Chesapeake world, itself representative of English America, its environmental qualities of climate, geography, mineralogy, fauna, flora, and native inhabitants. As it was, no such work appeared for any mainland colony throughout the colonial period. Only after independence did Jefferson, in his *Notes on the State of Virginia*, prepare the first relatively inclusive account of what was ostensibly the story for one colony but was indeed representative and to some extent inclusive of all British America.

Virginia activity in natural history even for the seventeenth century did not end with the death of Banister. For the next decade plants and seeds and other curiosities and brief observations went to the Royal Society, to Sloane, Petiver, and others. It is often difficult to be sure whether the person from whom Sloane, for example, received them was but the transmitter in England or the original source in Virginia. One set of 1693–1701 Sloane folios lists seeds from Sir Robert Southwell and Mr. and Mrs. London, who were certainly not in Virginia, but it also includes seeds "from Virginny" from Mr. Thomson, Mr. L[u?]nda, and Mr. Byrd, and others sent from the colony by the governor's order. Another 1694 list is of "Trees from Virginia received from Charles Hartgill . . . and sons sent to Esqr Blathwait," with the outside inscription "For Mr Doody."[41] And on April

12, 1697, Nicholas Moreau in Virginia wrote of the new land to the Bishop of Lichfield and to the Archbishop of Canterbury. To the former, Moreau gave a fairly detailed account of Indian medicine, including the uses of snakeroot, and a cure for intermittent fever; to the Primate, the colonist expatiated further on the red men, mentioning his more detailed account of them sent to My Lord of Lichfield.[42] Thus, though English collectors could find no substitute for Banister, interest in Virginia natural history continued on both sides of the Atlantic.

In seventeenth-century Maryland there is something of physicians and medicine rather early after the first settlement but little information of activity in natural history until the arrival of the Reverend Hugh Jones, the earliest of the four of that name in this Chesapeake province. Jones, who died in 1702 in his thirty-first year, was probably sent to Maryland by Bishop Compton, ostensibly as an S.P.G. missionary, in an attempt to fill Banister's place as a scientific correspondent with the Temple Coffee House Botany Club and the Royal Society. William Byrd II, elected F.R.S. in 1696, assisted then and later in efforts to secure a missionary scientist. Jones was to all appearances a good choice, for he was a young man of Glouces-ter Hall, Oxford, who had served as deputy at the Ashmolean Museum. He was hurriedly ordained and shipped off with the idea of becoming chaplain to Governor Nicholson (then in Maryland), though it was soon realized that he was too young (or immature) for this ecclesiastical post. He did spend the first five weeks in the colony in 1696 with the governor, and then settled as minister of Christ Church in Calvert County.

Members of the Temple Coffee House Botany Club, men such as Petiver, Doody, Sloane, and Ayrey, saw to it that Jones went to Maryland with proper equipment for collecting fauna and flora, a thermometer (broken on the voyage) for weather observations, and requests for specimens. Ar-riving in August 1696, he immediately began gathering materials, and by March of 1697 he sent letters and two boxes of specimens to some of the individuals just named: one containing trees, plants, seeds, and berries to Doody and Ayrey, one with fossils, shells, and insects to Petiver. These gentlemen in turn brightened Jones' colonial environment with bottles of beer, a Cheshire cheese, medicine, and news sheets. To assist in his collect-ing, they added more brown paper (for mounting and preparing speci-mens), wide-mouthed bottles, and spirits for preserving fauna and flora. There was even a little quarreling among the club because Jones favored some but not others with Chesapeake country materials. Jones continued to supply his friends and supporters until he became ill in 1700: he sent at least one more box in 1701, and died a little more than a year afterward.

There are letters from Jones to Petiver, Doody, Ayrey, and Benjamin

Woodroffe (the master of Gloucester Hall) between 1699 and 1701 describing voyage and province and the specimens he was shipping to them. In whole or in part, his letters appeared several times in the *Philosophical Transactions* in 1698–1699, and others survive in the Sloane Collection of the British Museum, the Ashmolean at Oxford, and the Royal Society's various manuscript archives. Of the extant early letters one of the most interesting is that to Dr. Woodroffe, which contains a good capsule account of the topography and political organization of the Chesapeake Bay province, its trees and their uses, songsters including the mockingbird and reptiles including the rattlesnake, climate, food and drink, varieties of religious faiths including some cutting remarks against the Quakers, the striking lack of towns and artisans, the plan for the new capital at Annapolis drawn by Governor Nicholson, and finally the vanishing red man.

Soon it was realized that Jones, an able and indefatigable field collector, was by no means an adequate replacement for John Banister. He gathered specimens but failed to describe the places where he found them, leaving all matters of classification and nomenclature to the English recipients. He published nothing himself and apparently did not even write down catalogues of what he had gathered. Despite a few real discoveries among his collections, they are at best disappointing. Had Jones lived twenty more years, perhaps the flow of instructions coming in monthly epistles from Petiver and others would have made their impression, and he might have become a systematic natural philosopher.[43]

Contemporary with Hugh Jones was William Vernon (d. 1706) of Peterhouse College, Cambridge, who sailed for Maryland in January 1698 under the direct sponsorship of the Royal Society and with the intention of claiming an "allowance" offered by Governor Nicholson, presumably to be chaplain and scientist-in-residence. Vernon came with the aim of remaining several years, but some misunderstanding between him and Nicholson, perhaps inspired by jealousies among members of the Royal Society, impelled him to return by the end of the year. Vernon had gone on the understanding that he would receive the allowance from the governor and £25 per annum from the society. That he worked primarily in Maryland was natural and probably a matter of indifference to the society, for the fauna and flora were exactly those of Virginia which Banister had investigated with such conspicuous success.

Short as his stay was, Vernon gathered copiously for the Royal Society, his friends, and himself. In July of 1698 he wrote to Sloane from Annapolis that he had specimens for him and for others on which he would lecture every Friday night at the meeting of the "Honourable Club." Vernon presented Nicholson with two quires of plants which were passed on to Secretary William Blathwayt of the Board of Trade and the Plantations. These specimens and the others for his sponsors and for himself made his reputation. He was invited to undertake a similar visit to the Canaries, but he was never able to do so.

Despite this generally good impression, John Ray was disappointed in the imperfections of Vernon's collections; here again was no Banister. A third man in Maryland, who arrived in March 1698 and proved to be no more meticulous than Vernon, was the Saxon physician Dr. David Krieg (d. *c.* 1712), skilled in drawing and natural history. Accompanied by "Isaak the Butterfly Boy" (apparently a subordinate who ran errands and chased butterflies), Krieg arrived with letters of introduction from major English naturalists, gathered every conceivable kind of living thing, practiced medicine a little, and returned to Europe (England) by November. Elected an F.R.S. in January 1699, by May of that year he accepted a position as physician to a nobleman in Riga. His specimens were carefully studied by Petiver and Ray and others, who complained of his carelessness as they had of Jones' and Vernon's.

Little more is known of Maryland scientific investigation in the era before 1706 or 1710. Sloane in 1697 exhibited before the Royal Society "The Tongue of a Pastinaca Marina . . . Lately Dug up in Mary-Land," published under this title in the *Philosophical Transactions* (XIX, no. 232 [Sept., 1697], 674–676). A rather interesting anonymous "Narrative of a Voyage to Maryland, 1705–1706" preserved in a British Museum Sloane manuscript (2291, f. 1) presents details of a voyage from Plymouth apparently to the Eastern Shore, for it contains many references to Richard Bennett of Wye and mentions Sweatman's Ordinary "upon the Eastern Shore," along with all the details of the natural environment. On March 26, 1706, a Stephen Bordley, almost surely the clergyman (d. 1709), wrote to Petiver offering his services in collecting, though he admitted his present ignorance of procedures. No reply remains, and for a time the story of natural history in Maryland ends. Despite the inducements of Nicholson and the Temple Coffee House Botany Club it had by no means even approached in value the work done in Virginia.[44]

Except for the Roanoke voyagers, about the only depiction of natural history from North Carolina before 1700 is Samuel Wilson's *An Account of the Province of Carolina* (London, 1682). Wilson includes brief accounts of North and South Carolina, mentioning both the Albemarle and Ashley River settlements. His presentation of animals and plants is of the seen and the unseen, all of it clearly promotional. John Lawson was in both Carolinas as early as 1701, though his published work and influence came a little later and will be considered after a look at the South Carolinians.[45]

From 1669 in South Carolina there are a number of manifestations of scientific interest, such as the records of Dr. Henry Woodward, who lived

Courtesy of Dr. T. Dabney Wellford and The Virginia Historical Society

Landon Carter (1710–1778) of Sabine Hall in Virginia

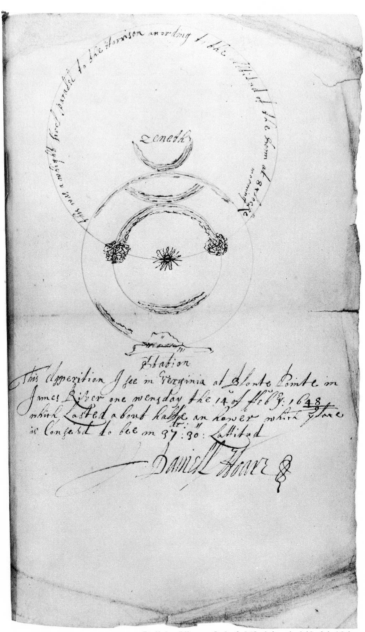

Bodleian Library, Oxford, MS. Ashmole 242, fol. 126 r

The earliest known astronomical observation sent from the
southern colonies to Great Britain

and traveled among the Indians from Port Royal inland in the 1660s and 1670s. In 1674 he sent to the Earl of Shaftesbury "A Faithful Relation of my Westoe Voyage," which in the past century has been printed at least twice.[46] Though quite concise, the account offers the future searcher clues to location and types of trees, soils, animals and furs, Indians, and even something on topography. If the date given for a letter to Shaftesbury by Joseph Dalton from Charleston dated January 20, 1672, is accurate, then the Proprietor had at least two years before been informed by Woodward of the nature of the country, the crop possibilities including silk culture and mulberry trees, and other matters interesting to natural historians and to agricultural technologists.[47] By May 18, 1680, another Charlestonian, one N. Mathews, had addressed to a friend or relative in Scotland a description of the town and the medicinal plants in the neighborhood. These latter he had discovered through Indians, who made efficacious remedies of many kinds from them. Mathews expresses a wish repeated in many other southern colonial epistles: that he "should be glad to see here some ingenious Gentleman—who hath good knowledge of Simples and knows how to find out the phisicall value of all things."[48] Undoubtedly this wish, perhaps for a collector with less obviously practical purposes in mind, appeared many times between Mathews and William Byrd II, who repeats its substance. As here indicated, the ostensible reason for such collecting was materia medica, but the result of its implementation in the eighteenth century was to enlarge tremendously the boundaries of botany and zoology and allied disciplines per se and the use of native plants and animals in many other practical ways.

Two years later a young Oxonian, Thomas Newe, wrote from Charleston to his father, then Butler of Exeter College, three letters which taken together reveal much of the natural environment, including his observation of a comet. Most significant in the present connection, however, is a request for "the best herbalist for Physical Plants in as small a Volume as you can get." Newe goes on to indicate his own personal interest in studying useful South Carolina flora. There is no indication of direct European encouragement from such collectors as Petiver and Sir Hans Sloane.[49]

Though there are several general descriptions of South Carolina topography, geography, and living organisms in the next decade and a half, medicine is the only science which appears frequently in the record, and then generally as physicians are referred to. In 1695 "Some Observations made upon the Herb Cassiny; imported from Carolina showing its admirable virtues in Curing the Small Pox. Written by a Physician to Esq: Boyle in London" by a John Peachie was addressed to England, though as early as 1678 Daniel Cox had described the herb's effects.[50] By 1698 several members of the Temple Coffee House Botany Club had become aware of the potential treasures to be derived from South Carolina, and Petiver and Lister began a correspondence and exchange with Robert Steevens of Goose Creek in that year. In the next two years Petiver received animals and plants which he could include in his *Musei Petiverani ...* (1695–1703). Between 1700 and 1704 he had among his Carolina correspondents and collectors a number of educated colonists whose enthusiastic letters now repose among the Sloane manuscripts in the British Museum.

Among them was Edmund Bohun, Jr. (1672–1734), son of the chief justice of South Carolina for 1698–1699 and a young man who may have botanized with Petiver on a business trip to England in 1699. Bohun was a merchant-planter of Charleston from 1699 to 1702 or 1703. On April 20, 1700, Robert Ellis, another of the Carolina group, wrote that he was living with Bohun and that they were most industrious in their collecting for Petiver. Ellis mentions sending by Captain Taylor two volumes of plants, a book of butterflies, a box of insects and several parcels of shells. Ellis was still at it in 1704. Bohun frequently carried his collections in person on his business trips to England, if one may judge by his letter to Petiver of April 28, 1701.[51] Ellis was still writing and collecting as late as April 25, 1704.

In a late letter Ellis mentions his work with George Francklyn (Francklin or Franklin), a physician-apothecary who had known Petiver and other naturalists before he left England about 1700. Francklyn like Bohun may have gone back and forth to London, for Ellis' 1704 letter mentions his having just sailed for England, though Francklyn's last recorded letter was written from Downton in Wiltshire (it still concerns matters botanical) and the 1704 journey may have been a permanent move back to Great Britain. It is said that on his voyage home he was taken by the French, which may have meant, as it did in other instances, that many plant-animal-fossil collections which accompanied him were ruined or destroyed. Associated with these three were first Robert Rutherford, a ship's surgeon, and then William Halsteed, a ship's captain (also referred to as Major Halsteed, probably because he was a Carolina planter as well as a seaman). On May 1, 1700, Halsteed wrote that he had just seen Bohun and Ellis and that like them he was sending Petiver a fine collection. Rutherford brought home some now unidentified plants but was chiefly useful as a contact man and encourager of the resident collectors of the group just mentioned.[52]

Thus the London botanists at the turn of the century had in Charleston a group with great enthusiasm who collected, probably largely on their own plantations throughout the area, and who for a five- or six-year period kept a steady stream of specimens flowing toward London. They did not work haphazardly, for they were supplied with books of directions, the ever-necessary brown paper, and other equipment. Those just mentioned persuaded others to cooperate, for their enthusiasm seems to have been contagious. Ellis and Bohun, for example, in visiting Sir Nathaniel Johnson's Silk Hope plantation, persuaded that gentleman to exchange with Petiver, much to the profit of the former governor's garden as well as the London collections. Halsteed seems to have been the intermediary who secured the interest and services of the Reverend Joseph Lord and Madame Hannah Williams, and a little later (in 1706) of Daniel Henchman. These latter three were mutually acquainted and could inform and encourage each other, and they carried on for many years after their first mentors had passed from the Carolina scene.

Joseph Lord (1672–1748) of Dorchester was discoursing at length to Petiver from January 6, 1701/2, principally on zoology but also on plants. He had more useful guides on animals than on plants, though he refers to *Gerard's Herbal* and owned Culpeper's *English Physician*, which described herbs. Lord, a native of Massachusetts and a Harvard graduate of 1691, had studied under advocates of the new science and went first to Charleston as a missionary before he settled in what must have been the more congenial one-time Puritan community of Dorchester twenty miles away. Preceding the 1701/2 letter were five quires of dried plants, which Petiver acknowledged and reciprocated with books and papers on natural history. Lord continued his long letters and boxes of all manner of curiosities through 1711, when he heard through Madame Williams that Petiver was dead. The correspondence itself is a mine of information, with analysis and speculation by the writer.[53]

When Petiver requested more abundant specimens of Carolina fauna, Lord, who claimed he never got very far from home, referred the London naturalist to his nearest neighbor, Daniel Henchman (1677–1709), another former Harvard student who had been dismissed before graduation for stealing a silver spoon. In South Carolina Henchman served Governor Johnson as an Indian agent and boasted in the one letter Petiver received (he claimed there had been three others previously) that he had traveled between 500 and 600 miles beyond the farthest English westward outpost. His long, boastful letter relates his ambitious plan to write a "Medicus Occidentalis," that he had perfected a map of the country, and that he hoped Petiver would be his patron. Petiver read his letter before the Royal Society on December 18, 1706, and encouraged Henchman to send specimens of all kinds. When he had received nothing by 1708, Petiver wrote again and sent a gift of dried English plants "as a Pattern." Upon inquiry he learned of Henchman's death in 1709. He was never able to locate or have shipped to him the perhaps imaginary collections of which Henchman had written.[54]

Madame Hannah Williams sent a collection of butterflies to Petiver by

Halsteed as early as 1701, and a cordial correspondence ensued which was carried on for several years. An attempt to renew it was made as late as 1713 when her son called on Petiver in London. She sent principally insects, snakes, shells, plants, and Indian items, including herbs and medicines. Petiver sent her his printed directions for collecting and preserving specimens, newssheets, his own printed works, catalogues, and drugs from his apothecary shop. The exchange seems to have dwindled because of the difficulties of communication during "Queen Anne's War" and because Mrs. Williams had the premature report of Petiver's death mentioned above. There is no evidence that she resumed the exchange after her son's 1713 visit.[55]

The only other scientist who is known to have corresponded with Petiver from the Carolinas before 1710 is John Lawson, one of the notable contributors of scientific data from the southern colonies. His major work, *A New Voyage to Carolina* (London, 1709), was of course a result of his observations from 1700 until his return to London for a visit in 1708/9. It may have been the Charleston group just mentioned, people Lawson surely met when he landed in that city in 1700, which brought Petiver and the most notable of North Carolina scientific observers into correspondence. But as has been recently suggested, Lawson may have come to both Carolinas with the backing of the London scientific group, primarily to gather specimens for them.

Lawson and his 1709 book have been considered, the natural history and kindred sections excepted, at some length in Chapter II. Lefler and Stearns are inclined to believe that Lawson was a Londoner who had been trained as an apothecary and came in that way to know James Petiver, and that Petiver and his friends commissioned Lawson to go to the Carolinas as their agent in collecting animals, plants, butterflies and other insects, seashells and other curiosities.[56] Lawson had sailed for America in May 1700, and after a fortnight in New York went on the same ship to Charleston in South Carolina. What he did in the southern seaport before he began his circuitous exploratory excursion to North Carolina in December 1700 is unknown, except that he made the acquaintance of Bohun and Ellis and Halsteed and perhaps others of Petiver's correspondents and probably learned in more detail what the London collector wanted. In his first extant letter to Petiver of April 12, 1701, from Bath County in North Carolina, he mentions an earlier one he had written from "Albemarl County," and he promises to begin collecting, especially the desired seashore items, at once.[57] The letter can be read as a new agreement in answer to Petiver's "advertising" for assistance, but it seems more nearly a request for further details on a previously-agreed-upon excursion and collection, though in 1709 Petiver wrote to William London the gardener that he had "lately obtained an Acquaintance with one Mr. Lawson Surveyor General of Carolina" whose "Natural History of Carolina" [*A New Voyage to Carolina*] had recently been printed. This 1709 communication seems to say that the two had not previously met, but it may have been Petiver's way of keeping London from knowing that Lawson had been supplying him from Carolina for years.

Whatever Lawson collected for the English apothecary between 1701 and his visit to England in 1708/9 remains obscure, for the plants from Carolina remaining in the Sloane Herbarium and labeled as from Lawson to Petiver appear to be of the 1710–1711 period.[58] In the years before 1708 Lawson was an exceedingly busy man, planning and founding cities, negotiating with the Indians, and probably carrying on some private trade. In the letter of 1701 he refers to a journal he had sent to Petiver, which may have been the account of his event-filled "thousand mile" journey from Charleston to the Neuse River. He early began surveying in North Carolina and in April 1708 seems to have been appointed surveyor-general to succeed Moseley.[59] On the long 1700–1701 trek Lawson noted all phases of his environment, including topography, climate, fauna and flora, and geology, among the other matters, for he discusses all these in his natural-history section of the 1709 book. Whether he had found time to collect or not, he had absorbed a great deal. Also, in the preface to *A New Voyage*, Lawson declares that he had spent most of his eight previous years in the northern Carolina province in traveling. As an educated and observant student of nature he must have seen most of the things and the land he describes in the section of his book bearing the caption "The Natural History of Carolina." Most of this chapter, and his other sections for that matter, appears to be original. The principal historian of horticulture in America declares that this "is the most accurate and detailed of the early natural histories of America, and is written in a fascinating style."[60] Some of it indubitably was drawn from earlier chronicles such as Smith's, but in the main Lawson's sprightly or poetic descriptions are his own. Hedrick, the authority just quoted, may, however, be giving Lawson a little too much credit for accuracy.

"The Natural History" is simply packed with data on indigenous plants and on plants brought from Europe or the Orient and domesticated in Carolina. The author compares or contrasts all these with European species or growths. He begins with a detailed presentation of trees, vines, shrubs, and wildflowers. Oaks and their uses take up two pages. Varieties familiar to every southern American today, such as the dogwood and laurel and chinquapin, are described for European readers totally unfamiliar with them. Wild grapes, American mulberries, persimmons, huckleberries, and purple raspberries are among the fruits Lawson has seen in the woods. Even the sugar maple, which he admits grows only toward the mountains and to the north, is mentioned along with Indian methods of tapping. Later he gives a list of sorts of English apples which thrive in his area, and along with them pears, quinces, peaches, figs, and cherries.

Lawson pauses in his verbal pictorial to explain why the European grape should be cultivated in Carolina, and then turns to animals he has seen. Though he may have seen the buffalo and actually eaten this beef, he acknowledges that its "chief Haunt" is the Mississippi basin, and gives a few details from books or hearsay. Bears, panthers, wildcats, wolves, tigers (he claims he has seen one), skunks, otters, beavers, muskrats, opossums, minks, a variety of rabbits and deer and squirrels, rodents, and insects are all here. In the last category he places alligators, a dozen varieties of snakes, and lizards. He tells good stories of alligators, including one which built its nest under his house and roared so loudly that the building shook and his dog was dazed. Nor could he resist even more elaborate tales of rattlesnakes and dozens of other reptiles. His bird list is especially interesting, for it is one of the most complete for the whole first century of Carolina settlement. From "Baltimore bird" to catbird and "Whippoo Will" today's American will recognize our present feathered songsters. Lawson devotes a long paragraph to describing the bald eagle and its habits. He claims two varieties of mockingbirds.

His fishes are divided into three groups. The first, to be found in the salt and fresh waters of Carolina, range from whales to swordfish to eels and herring. The freshwater fish include sturgeon and catfish; the shellfish, crabs, oysters, clams, shrimp, crawfish, and mussels, among others. Unusual specimens are presented in some detail, including size and usefulness to man. He goes on for pages on varieties of the finny tribe, suggesting his intimate acquaintance with them in salt surf or inland white rapids.

Thus his published natural history, informative as it is, could not have been of much use to the Temple Coffee House Botany Club except as a whetter of curiosity and of desire for specimens. Lawson is often credulous (though never so much so as Josselyn in New England) and yet he corrected many previous misapprehensions regarding American plant and animal life. His bird lists were larger than if not so discriminating as John Clayton's, and he was definitely conscious of distinct differences in the fauna of Europe and America. His sympathetic descriptions of the red men are said to be still useful to anthropologists.[61] His book appeared too late to attract the first great British natural history circle of Plukenet, the younger Bobart, and Ray. And it was to be overshadowed in the next generation, at least as far as natural history is concerned, by Mark Catesby's great volumes.

Yet it was in Lawson's last two years in Carolina, before he was executed by the red men he had befriended, that he really seriously undertook what he had promised Petiver to do years before. At least as far as there is record his scientific collecting came in these last years. Lawson had returned to America in 1709/10 with a group of Swiss and Palatines whom he attempted to settle at New Bern and nearby. Though Petiver tried to spur him into activity by sending on March 14, 1709/10, various medicines, a *Hortus Siccus* of English plants, and some tracts on natural history, Lawson did not find time to do much for the London group for some months. Meanwhile, on January 11, 1709/10, just as he left England, he had thanked Petiver for Ray's book on physic and useful medicines and had promised at the same time that he would supply monthly reports with collections. From the Neuse River in Carolina he wrote on December 30, 1710, that he was at last actively at work and had already sent a small box of specimens by way of Kecoughtan in Virginia to Petiver and a Mr. Fettiplace Rolley, and that he was continuing to collect for them and for Mr. London. Lawson states that the specimens were in four vials with a preservative liquor and/or in brown paper. Insects, fossils, plants, and acorns were among them. He found that birds lost their color in their plumage if preserved in the aforementioned liquor and that a spirits-preservative he himself had made was somewhat better.

Most of the letter is a series of seven or eight resolves (five numbered) as to what he himself will do from then on. The list reads somewhat like the printed instructions or the letters of request the English group of naturalists had been sending abroad to correspondent-collectors for over a generation. The first item concerns the plants and seeds he will gather, the second the animals, the third birds, the fourth fishes, the fifth insects, the sixth fossils and minerals and soils, and the others matters of agriculture, climate, and topography. This is an intelligent and imaginative program but one hardly within the realm of possibility for a man in Lawson's situation.

On July 24, 1711, within two months of his death, Lawson wrote from Virginia once more to Petiver, excusing himself now because of the troubled times (Indian uprisings, perhaps) but stating that he was sending with the Carolina governor's lady a book of plants admittedly badly packed. He said he had many more at his home on the Neuse but that he had not been there since the previous January. Apparently these last plant specimens were collected in Virginia. So ends the story of the scientific endeavors of the last of the gifted collectors of what may be called the Old Colonial Era, or the first century of settlement in the southern area.[62] Lawson's natural history, despite its lack of formal scientific format, was perhaps more valuable to contemporary and later naturalists than were his fragmentary and badly preserved specimens. Yet he was not well informed in the latest scientific methods or literature, and therefore his book is a classic for reasons other than the natural-history section.

The Eighteenth Century to 1764

There was no completely barren period for natural historians in the southern colonies between 1710 and the work and publication of the first major figures of eighteenth-century collecting and writing, partly because Mark Catesby (1683–1749) arrived about a year after Lawson's death and partly because there were several other interested individuals. But in many respects Lawson seems to conclude the first thrust of English activity. Catesby and his contemporaries seem to represent a new era. These were formally or self-trained field workers who could write up their own findings and in some instances illustrate with watercolor drawings of a quality not before present in America. Amateurs of course continued, and without their support British collections and the records of the Royal Society would not be nearly so rich as they are in the specimens of South Atlantic nature. In this era the gentlemen with curiosity and the professional or semiprofessional naturalists were in constant communication, more than ever each group aiding the other and becoming at times indistinguishable.

One of the amateurs, William Byrd II (1674–1744), second native Fellow of the society, has been called "the most constant link between the Royal Society and Virginia during the first half of the eighteenth century."[63] Byrd was in England sporadically about half of his entire life, and from at least the 1690s on he was supplying data and specimens (rattlesnakes, opossums, ginseng, snakeroot, etc.) by shipment or personal presentation, and was corresponding with Sir Hans Sloane and others of the London coterie concerning many phases of his native colonial environment. Byrd was perhaps the most persistent colonial in urging Sloane and the society to send a natural philosopher to the Chesapeake Bay area to observe and record plant and animal life, the former especially with the not unusual idea of finding new materia medica for the European world. Byrd also had communications from Petiver, who was a vital link between the seventeenth-century naturalists and the new group centered now in Sloane. Although Byrd's interests were basically utilitarian in this area, he enjoyed beautiful plants and strange animals per se, though not so much as did his brother-in-law Robert Beverley II, whose delight in gardens and attendant birds and bees will be noticed again below. In personal and semipublic letters to members of the Royal Society, in his two Dividing Line histories, and in his diary the master of Westover exhibits his interest in the potentials of native flora and fauna and what may be done with imported

European plants and animals. Snakeroot, ginseng, and ipecac he found growing around him, and he strongly urged their medicinal use. Then there were agricultural uses for several native plants. Without formal scientific training and too varied in his interests to spend the time necessary to acquire it for himself, he remained "a backward student of experimental science," though he dissected muskrats and experimented widely in hemp, vineyards, and orchards. He was credulous of miracle cures from local plants, as were many of his medically trained contemporaries. He has been called a seventeenth-century virtuoso rather than an eighteenth-century scientist. If this be true, so were others who taken more seriously as scientists than he, and whether true or no his encouragement of investigators more thoroughly trained than he aided materially the progress or development of natural history during the latter half of the colonial era.

Of the dedicated individuals he assisted and entertained and employed to advise him one was a major naturalist of the period before 1764, a man called by his biographers "the colonial Audubon," an appellation which fails to do full justice to his several abilities and publications. This was Mark Catesby (1683–1749), born in Essex in England, and first coming to America in 1712 perhaps as escort to his sister Mrs. William Cocke, wife of the Virginia secretary of state who had arrived two years earlier. Within a week of his reaching Williamsburg, Catesby met William Byrd. With the active cooperation of Byrd, Cocke, and Governor Spotswood himself, Catesby almost immediately began botanizing and frequently was a guest at Westover, where he advised the owner how to lay out and plant his garden. Fortunately, the naturalist appears in several pages of Byrd's diary, which gives the most intimate and detailed account now known of the reserved scientist.[64]

Probably Catesby was educated in one of the better sort of grammar schools discussed in Chapter III. His biographers believe that through certain family connections he came to know John Ray and his friend Samuel Dale and was encouraged by them in the study of botany if not other branches of natural history.[65] In the preface to his major work Catesby mentions that during the Virginia years (1712–1719) he sent to his friend Dale dried and living plants and certain observations on the country. Some of these specimens went to Dr. William Sherard, who was in a sense Ray's successor as the principal botanist of the age. Catesby also sent seeds and plants to Thomas Fairchild, prominent Hoxton nurseryman, and by 1715 Petiver was publishing accounts of Catesby's discoveries in Virginia. Besides his friend Byrd, Catesby was horticultural adviser to John Custis and Thomas Jones, the latter of whom married his niece, Elizabeth Cocke. He traveled widely in Tidewater Virginia and on to the mountains, and during his years in the province made a voyage to Bermuda and Jamaica, where he gathered seeds, supplementing Sloane's collections from Jamaica. In October 1719 Dale wrote to Sherard that Catesby was back in Virginia with "about 70 specimens of which half are new." Soon Catesby, returned to England, was well known to Sherard, Sloane, and others of the Royal Society. And through this group Governor Francis Nicholson in 1720, then on his way to his new post in South Carolina, made an offer to subsidize Mr. Catesby in observing "the Rarities of that Country for the uses and purposes of the Society." Others contributed, and after a delay of more than a year Catesby sailed for South Carolina to begin his labors, which were to result in one of the great achievements in natural history in the colonial period in mainland North America.

Reaching Charleston in May 1722, Catesby spent three busy years in the colony collecting specimens and making notes, drawings, and watercolors of the natural products of the area from North Carolina boundaries south across the later Georgia into Florida and westward into the Piedmont. At times on his field trips he had the assistance of a Negro boy and of Indians, and in Charleston among others Governor Robert Johnson and Dr. Thomas Cooper helped him to prepare and to organize the really enormous collections of fauna and flora he shipped to his English friends and even to a few continental ones. Sloane and Sherard, Dillenius and Dale, Fairchild and Collinson, and Sir Robert Walpole were among the literally dozens who enriched their gardens and their areas of knowledge through their representative in the lower southern colonies. The collections included a great range from seeds and plants and mosses and shells through reptiles and fish and birds to Indian tools and weapons. His observations on topography, geology, climate, and agriculture, with figures of living animals and plants, often in color, were made for his later use. He visited certain places several times in order to observe plants at various stages of growth. Much of what he sent his friends was new.

In 1725 Catesby sailed to the Bahamas and continued his investigations there. By 1726 he was back in London, his collecting days concluded, though he was to continue to receive items from friends in the colonies. His funds for various reasons had dried up, or their sources had, and for a time he wondered whether he would be able to publish the great book he planned. To cut costs, he resolved to do much of the illustration himself, and learned from a French artisan how to etch copper plates. He was then able to prepare his own delineations, and apparently he already knew how to hand-color them. Collinson lent him money, and he found what was for him doubly profitable employment in the nursery-botanical gardens of two friends at Hoxton and at Fulham. There he earned enough to live on and at the same time to watch his American plants come to flower or fruition.

The book took shape slowly but surely, as his friends Sherard and Dillenius helped with the Latin names for plant specimens, and he was able to follow Ray, Willughby, and Sloane in identifying certain birds, fishes, and animals. Fossils he learned from Burnet and Woodward, and unfortunately subscribed to their theory of origin and distribution in relation to the biblical Great Deluge. By the spring of 1729 the first portion of the book, containing twenty plates, was completed, and he presented a copy to the Royal Society. Succeeding parts were presented through November 1732, when the first volume was completed. Six months later Catesby was himself an F.R.S. The second volume likewise appeared in small installments and was not completed until December 1743, and the Appendix as late as April 1747. In its final form the work had 166 "Encouragers" or sponsors, from Queen Caroline and other princes and princesses, ambassadors, peers of the realm, bishops, and Sir Hans Sloane to other members of the Royal Society. Significantly the volumes had a number of colonial supporters, including six governors and Proprietors, William Byrd II, John Randolph, and Benjamin Whitaker of Virginia, Alexander Hume and Alexander Skene of South Carolina, John Bartram of Pennsylvania, and Colin Campbell of Jamaica.

The *Natural History of Carolina, Florida, and the Bahama Islands* was indeed, as two contemporaries characterized it, a noble and splendid work. There were more than 200 colored plates picturing 143 birds, 171 plants, 46 fish, 9 quadrupeds, 33 amphibia, 31 insects, a map of the area represented, an account of the area's history, topography, climate, soils, botany, zoology, and agriculture, the red natives (much indebted to Lawson), and at least one item of technology—pitch and tar manufacture. His early observations in Virginia are frequently referred to or used as illustrations in the book. The text was printed in parallel columns of French and English. The strongest points are the collections of the new and unknown. Though his coloring is uneven, the elements of the drawings are ingeniously posed. He perhaps inaugurated, and at least perfected, the method later used by Wilson and Audubon of combining birds, beasts, and plants in a single plate, thus presenting correct ecological settings for his specimens. His birds are his finest studies.

Catesby contributed nothing toward systematic classification, though some of his nomenclature has persisted through all the Linnaean binomial system and its subsequent refinements. The book was for its kind enormously popular, being pirated on the Continent and published in whole or in part in German, Latin, Dutch, and French. Linnaeus used it extensively, despite his alterations in nomenclature, especially on fauna. Linnaeus' own work in flora and Thomas Walter's *Flora Caroliniana* (1788) superseded it in certain respects a generation later.[66]

Catesby published three other things. An essay on "Birds of Passage" appeared in both the *Philosophical Transactions* and (in part) in the *Gentleman's Magazine* in 1747–1748. He did the plate for Christopher Gray's one-sheet *Catalogue of American Trees and Shrubs That Will Endure the Climate of England* (1737). Under two slightly differing titles in 1763 and 1767, years after his death, appeared his second most important work, *Hortus Britanno-Americanus . . .*, which he completed in 1749 just before he died. The eighty-five shrubs and trees, illustrated by smaller copies of the plates in the *Natural History*, have new descriptions, a few errors in the *Natural History* are corrected, and the emphasis here is on the plants' potential usefulness on the English market. In other words, it appears to be an adaptation and addition-edition intended as an advertisement-promotion piece.

Many of Catesby's drawings, paintings, and collections are extant in such places as the Oxford herbaria and the British Museum. Many unpublished drawings and paintings of American species lie among the Sloane manuscripts. His name and his work came to be known over most of western Europe, thanks to his patrons in London, long before he returned from his researches in the southern British provinces. He later corresponded with Dutch and Russian savants and with Linnaeus. Of the major American naturalists of his time he corresponded with John Bartram and also exchanged information with General Oglethorpe of Georgia. More significantly the largest number of his American friends were Virginians, including the leading gardeners and botanists of their day—William Byrd II, John Custis, John Clayton II, Sir John Randolph, and Dr. John Mitchell—men who, with the exception of Randolph, are today placed in the major or first rank of curious colonials. This affiliation with Virginians in friendship and intellectual communication and blood is, as mentioned above, often reflected in his major writing. Thus the *Natural History*, despite the limiting and limited area suggested by the rest of its title, is the first great environmental study of the whole range of the southeastern colonies by a man who spent his active working years in the area and learned from his human provincial contemporaries as well as from or concerning their fields and forests. And Catesby himself with his English friends drew into the active brotherhood of eighteenth-century scientists a number of American colonials, especially his southern friends and John Bartram, who would widen the realms of knowledge by communication with each other as well as with the London circle.

There is considerable evidence that during Catesby's stay in Virginia and his writing years in London the Chesapeake region supplied him and others, such as the Quaker Peter Collinson, with all sorts of materials. Marylanders as well as Virginians were interested. In 1730 schoolmaster and poet Richard Lewis of Annapolis reported to Collinson and the Royal Society on observations of the aurora borealis and in 1732 on other celestial phenomena, an earthquake, and a "Fly Tree," the leaves of which with a sac containing insects and their grubs he forwarded to Collinson. Lewis' final contribution in 1733 was accompanied by two insects identified by Sir Hans Sloane as two mantises, probably our praying mantis.[67] On June 3, 1736, Dr. Richard Hill of Londontown, Maryland, replied to an inquiry from Royal Society Secretary Mortimer regarding the efficacy of the Jerusalem oak and the throatwort as remedies. Hill believed that at least the former relieved not in itself but because of or through the glass of spirits in which it was administered. Andrew Scott of the same province sent to Sloane through Dr. Massey (1678?–1743) in 1736 a collection of thirty-six plants, and in a letter to Sloane of August 6, 1739, he mentions sending plants to Lord Petre (1713–1742) and offers more to Sloane. In 1733 the Quaker Gilbert Falconer of Kent County had written a long letter to Secretary Mortimer regarding the Jerusalem oak and throatwort, which inspired the further inquiry from Mortimer to Dr. Hill just noted. Sloane had another correspondent in Maryland in Edward Lloyd of Wye River, who had seen Sloane's collections in London and in 1740 reported in a letter the great pearls to be found in Chesapeake Bay oysters.[68] Along with two pearls Lloyd sent other indigenous Maryland products, such as the Psalms of David and the Lord's Prayer in Arabic "done perfectly" by a slave in his neighborhood.

After these men only three others of that province communicated with the Royal Society, all of them in 1749–1752 and principally concerning medicine. One, Richard Brooke, visiting the Society, told of a phenomenon in Maryland on May 3, 1749, of three concentric rings around the sun. He presented a strange insect and the proboscis of an amphibious creature killed by an Indian beyond the mountains. Later he sent in other communications on the weather and diseases. The *Maryland Gazette* of Jonas Green carried a number of essays on natural phenomena and medicine, but only those concerning the latter seem to have originated in the province.

In natural history investigation during Catesby's visit and throughout his lifetime Virginia was much more active than Maryland. John Custis, Sir John Randolph and his brother Isham and later John Randolph, Jr., the second John Clayton, Byrd, Catesby's niece Mrs. Jones, Thomas Booth (of Stafford County), Dr. John Mitchell, Dr. John Symmer, and a few others wrote of fauna and flora and often sent specimens (frequently in exchange for British or Oriental seeds or plants). Some were merely obliging English naturalists, such as Catesby's niece, who on March 1, 1729/30, received a letter from her uncle informing her that he was sending uncolored the first section of the *Natural History*, and that he needed Virginia cones, acorns, and seeds of all kinds, especially a large quantity of poplar and cypress.[69] On September 20 (*c.* 1732–1737) Symmer, a neighbor of Clayton, wrote to Sloane that he was sending by means of William Nelson a gift box of specimen products which included insects, worms, a snake, a rattlesnake's rattle, bones, and minerals. In 1737 Symmer acknowledged a reply from Sloane and mentioned a small piece of a curiosity he was sending in the care of a divinity student. A list of the curiosities, some medical, including a human skull, which Symmer sent about this time, is in the Sloane manuscripts. Symmer and other physicians who manifested an interest in plant life per se and for medical purposes were, as Blanton indicates, in considerable number in eighteenth-century Virginia.[70] In 1735 a Robert Bristow of a Virginia family, writing from London to his attorney Thomas Booth in Stafford County, requested a parcel of cedar or fir cones, some Virginia black walnuts with their rinds, and any other varieties of trees Booth thought might be worth cultivating or propagating in England, noting that he had some of the cones Booth had sent years before. Bristow desired them for his own place in the country. This single letter is indicative of the widespread interest in southern flora of people who were not naturalists and carries the implicit suggestion that such items were frequently being sent to Great Britain.[71]

Colorful Sir John Randolph and sturdy Isham Randolph were only incidentally interested in fauna and flora from the Royal Society's point of view, but both made definite contributions of collections and of information. Custis, an eminent horticulturist, did his best to supply all sorts of things to British friends and correspondents who were not necessarily gardeners, floral or herbal. Custis' correspondence (printed a generation ago) with English and American brethren of the garden spade and the more general naturalists Collinson, Catesby, Bartram, and dozens of others, shows that the colonial supplied, to Collinson especially, much besides seeds, bulbs, and plants for decoration or the herb bed. His letters are a mine of information on what he received in return as well as of the specific items he sent abroad. Collinson asks for chinquapins, thanks Custis for his account of the opossum and discusses its anatomy, tells of the "newly discovered" love apple or "Tomiato" (tomato), and thanks him for the hummingbird nest.[72] Isham Randolph, sea captain and planter and friend of William Byrd II and many of the British scientists (and incidentally grandfather of Thomas Jefferson) was never so successful a man as his brother Sir John, but he seems to have drawn friends and to have displayed throughout his life a genuine curiosity about American nature. He is significant as an intermediary, messenger, and conversationalist on Virginia subjects during his frequent visits to London, and there is evidence that British naturalists respected his abilities and were most grateful for his services. Collinson recommended to John Bartram that on the latter's southern collecting tour he make Isham's house his headquarters from which to operate while he was in Virginia.[73] Sir John Randolph, who lived in Williamsburg, seems to have had a garden and, like his brother, to have supplied English friends and acquaintances with American plants.[74] How active a collector he was is unknown, for his letters and other manuscripts have largely disappeared, but he was also a planter of diverse agricultural pursuits, and it is more than probable that his interest in his environment was one of the incitements to horticultural interests displayed by his son John, Jr., the loyalist and friend of Jefferson. As it is, Sir John Randolph as scientist remains a shadowy suggestion, though a strong one, from the few details known of him personally and the Enlightenment curiosity evidenced by his library about the world in which he lived.[75] John Randolph, Jr., brother of the patriot Peyton, was to produce the only book on horticulture written and published in the southern colonies. His work will be considered with that of other gardeners.

Two major Virginia naturalists of the period before 1763 remain to be noticed. One of them, a second John Clayton (1694–1773), has a growing fame as his botanical work is being rediscovered. British born, he came to Virginia probably or at least possibly in his childhood, though his education was in the homeland. After his schooling he lived in Virginia, rarely stepping outside its boundaries during the rest of his long life. He was a county official and self-taught scientist. In contrast was his friend Dr. John Mitchell (1711–1768), native Virginian educated at Edinburgh, trained in botany by the well-known Professor Charles Alston of Edinburgh, and eminent not only as a botanist but as a zoologist, physician and medical theorist, cartographer, agriculturist, historian, and anthropologist. In 1745/6 Mitchell gave up a lucrative practice in Urbanna on the Rappahannock to remove to London. In England he became an active F.R.S., a mapmaker whose work was to be the basis for land settlements in peace treaties two generations after his death, a historian of North America, and a scientist who continued to develop his interest in southern American environment. Both Clayton and Mitchell were to influence directly European—not simply British—thinking on New World natural history from Catesby's time to at least the end of the eighteenth century. They corresponded with other Americans, with the major English and Scottish naturalists, and with Gronovius at Leyden and Linnaeus at Uppsala. Each had one or more plants named after him. When Peter Collinson was called upon to name the competent Linnaean botanists in America, he cited Clayton, Colden of New York, and Mitchell.

Hindle, who thinks that Pennsylvania was ahead of the rest of the colonies in developing naturalists and seedsmen (a doubtful conclusion from the evidence), admits that "the best systematic treatise on American botany was the result of the industry of a Virginian."[76] This was of course the Gronovius-Clayton *Flora Virginica* (Leyden, 1739–1743, 1762), which the most recent investigators indicate was much more Clayton's than earlier historians of science knew: that is, that the colonial was far more than the mere collector of specimens which the Dutch scholar systematized and published, and that Clayton had ready as a second edition a version much superior to that published by the son (of the original collaborator), Laurens Gronovius.[77]

John Clayton, whose English family were prominent gentry or minor nobility, soldiers and lawyers, had possibly come to the Chesapeake area with his father about 1705, by which date the latter was secretary of state for newly appointed Lieutenant-Governor Edward Nott. The future botanist would thus have been eleven when he reached Williamsburg, or he may have remained in England longer and attended Eton. By 1713 his father had been recommended by the new Lieutenant-Governor Spotswood as attorney-general, a position the elder Clayton was to hold for the remainder of his life. The father was, as his son became, a personal friend of William Byrd II and John Custis and Mark Catesby. The botanist's amount and place of formal education is not definitely known, though in 1735 he mentioned his once fluent Latin and he was held by his contemporaries as a very learned man. His recent biographers suggest that about 1707 he may have been sent back to Eton, which his brother Thomas later attended for two years before entering Cambridge. Clayton is referred to as Doctor by Thomas Jefferson and Laurens Gronovius; yet most of his Virginia friends referred to him as Mr. Clayton or Captain Clayton or even the "Honourable." That he had indeed medical training of one of the sorts discussed in Chapter III above is entirely possible, but it seems more likely that in some fashion or degree he studied law. The office he held throughout his life from at least as early as 1720, clerk of the county court of Gloucester, would certainly have required some knowledge of legal procedure.

Actually the modest clerkship of the county court seemed to suit its holder exactly, for it gave him enough time to roam the fields in search of flora as well as to become a prosperous planter. Probably inspired by Catesby, he developed his own botanical garden and talked and corresponded with Byrd. Soon he was introduced by Catesby to the great Leyden naturalist Gronovius, and probably to Collinson. At any rate, the last put him in touch with John Bartram. In 1729 Clayton sent to a Londoner, Mr. Pole, a "Box of Natural Rarities" which were to be passed on to the Royal Society.[78] To Catesby he sent many plants, some of which were passed on in turn to Gronovius, who made Linnaeus acquainted with them. Incidentally, outside the field of botany there are only three known Clayton observations, one of them the description of the whippoorwill.[79]

By 1735 Clayton was sending to Gronovius large quantities of dried plants for identification, and he still continued his shipments even after he learned to distinguish most of the specimens himself. In the late 1730s he sent to Holland "A Catalogue of Plants, Fruits, and Trees Native to Virginia." After considerable revision, some unjustified, and the regularizing of the descriptions and classifications in accordance with Linnaeus' system (Clayton had used John Ray's), Gronovius published in 1739 the *Flora Virginica Exhibens Plantas Quas V.C. Johannes Clayton in Virginia Observarit atque Collegit . . .* [by] Joh. Fred. Gronovius (Leyden). Without Clayton's knowledge or consent, the Dutch naturalist thus published the book in his own name, though he does acknowledge Clayton's work in his title and preliminary pages. There is no evidence of resentment on Clayton's part: actually the book incited him to renewed efforts to master the Linnaean system and to supplement his collection. Linnaeus recognized the colonial Virginian's accomplishments by naming the charming American wildflower, the spring beauty, the *Claytonia*. In 1743 a second part of *Flora Virginica* was published by Gronovius with a nearly identical title page from new specimens supplied by Clayton.[80] In the same year the first short-lived American Philosophical Society (of Philadelphia) invited Clayton and Mitchell of Virginia to be corresponding members.[81]

By 1740 Clayton was speaking with authority and Gronovius quoted his observations to correct Linnaeus. During the rest of his life Clayton continued his observations, ranging farther and farther afield, even into the Great Valley. In 1755 he and Bartram appeared in the London *Gentleman's Magazine* (XXV, 407–408) in "Some Remarks Made on Dr. Alston's Dissertation on the Sexes of Plants by two celebrated botanists of North America, both dated June 10, 1755." In April 1758 John Ellis wrote to Linnaeus that "Mr. Clayton of Virginia has lately sent Mr. Collinson his Flora Virginica greatly enlarged and improved. Mr. Collinson has put it in my hands to look it over: It is to be published immediately as soon as the Plates can be got ready which Mr. Ehret has undertaken to do."[82] Gronovius had himself since 1743 been working with Clayton on a new edition, which presumably Clayton had given up hope of completing with his European collaborator. In the fall of 1761 two editions appear to have been ready for the press, the Dutch version having been completed by Gronovius' son Laurens, who dated the introduction to his second edition January 1, 1762. The Gronovius (plus Clayton) edition was, as far as one may now judge by the fragments of Clayton's own mentioned above, vastly inferior to what the colonial himself alone had prepared, but it was in print, and what happened to Ehret's drawings and the major portion of Clayton's manuscript one does not know. A copy of it—or at least a number of his papers—was in family hands in Virginia for many years, some of it was destroyed with clerks' records in New Kent County in a fire in 1787, and more perhaps lost by descendants in Virginia in the next century.[83]

Clayton lived on for more than a decade after the second Gronovius edition of his work appeared in 1762. They were busy years. In 1760 John Bartram had visited the Virginian, and the talk and intellectual exchange had been good. The communication continued by mail for years—until at least 1765. In 1768 Clayton's old friend Collinson, though he died that year, was advising the son, Dr. Thomas Clayton, reminding the younger man of the great part his father had played in intellectual history by exerting his "Genius." In 1773 Clayton became president of the newly founded Virginia philosophical society for promoting all sorts of knowledge. The young vice-president was future Governor John Page, Jefferson's lifelong friend, who was later to write of John Clayton as both scientist and man.[84] In 1774 Clayton was dead.

Benjamin Smith Barton, himself a noted naturalist, wrote in 1805 that Clayton had supplied "the best foundation of our knowledge of the plants of a considerable part of the tract of country now called the United States," and Gronovius had remarked to Linnaeus as early as 1739 that "Clayton, if not unmatched, is at least the most distinguished foreign resident [among naturalists of his time]."[85] During his own life and since, John Clayton has been recognized throughout the western world as a major botanist, much of whose work is still useful. Other naturalists of Europe and America named at least eight plants for him, and in the latter half of the twentieth century he is still being honored for his work.[86] Through Linnaeus he was elected to the very selective Swedish Academy of Sciences. Thomas Jefferson refers to Clayton's plants many times in his *Garden Book* and *Notes on the State of Virginia*, and in the latter added after one list, "There is an infinitude of other plants and flowers, for an enumeration and description of which I must refer to the Flora Virginica of our great botanist Dr. Clayton. . . . This accurate observer . . . passed a long life in exploring and describing its plants, and is supposed to have enlarged the botanical catalogue as much as almost any man who has lived."[87] Though circumstances never brought Clayton the public recognition which would probably have come had all his writings been published, there is enough evidence to prove that he was a creative and critical scientist as well as a collector. He combined in his activity three characteristic southern colonial interests—politics, agriculture. and natural environment—with his personal emphasis on the last. He inspired in his younger Virginia contemporaries, especially of the 1773 Williamsburg philosophical society and their friends, an interest, though certainly a more limited one, in the plants of his beloved colony. John Page, St. George Tucker, Thomas Jefferson, Francis Gilmer, and others of the next two generations of Virginians continued to collect, observe, and experiment with southern flora during a period necessarily dominated by the stirring events of the Revolution and the War of 1812, politics on a larger scale, the development of jurisprudence and general education, and other elements in the building of a state and nation. Every one of those mentioned and many others remained amateur scientists all their lives, and as late as 1815 Gilmer was botanizing from the Peaks of Otter in Virginia to the hills of northern Georgia.

Dr. John Mitchell, Clayton's close friend and fellow naturalist, has not yet in our day received all the attention he deserves. Until quite recently there was no full-length study of him as there is of Clayton. Generally his varied intellectual interests have been treated much more unevenly in scattered essays, of course partially because they are unusually varied.[88] Perhaps no more widely learned than Clayton, Mitchell did have a formal scientific education at Edinburgh, and his interests, some of which are noted above, embraced medicine (including research on yellow fever), zoology, climatology, cartography, history and anthropology, electricity, physiology, chemistry, and agriculture, in all of which areas he wrote something, in many instances something quite significant.

Within very recent years it has been proved conclusively that Mitchell was a native Virginian, son of an affluent planter and merchant of Lancaster County, though even since the proof appeared such historians as Stearns have failed to note the evidence and assert that because Mitchell seemed to have a low opinion of the colonies and left them for good in 1745/6, he was not a colonial born.[89] Actually, ill-health more than hunger for more congenial intellectual surroundings than his friend Clayton could offer him seems to have determined the permanent removal to Great Britain. Before that, Mitchell carried on his medical practice from Urbanna in Middlesex County and wrote on all manner of subjects from his observations in the Chesapeake Bay area. Even then he took a sort of American or national imperial attitude, usually considering the colonies as a whole, especially when he was describing something he had discovered or experimented with in only one or two of them. Naturally his illustrations are usually from Virginia. In his last twenty-two years in England he continued to write on southern colonial agriculture and national agriculture, to map North America, and to compose histories of the British possessions along the Atlantic coast. In other words, throughout his life Mitchell remained very much an American and southern colonial son of almost every phase of the Enlightenment.

As a naturalist Mitchell was most of all a botanist. As early as October 4,

1738, upon hearing that his old teacher at Edinburgh, Dr. Charles Alston, had been promoted to a professorship in the Scottish university, Mitchell wrote a long letter describing his botanical activities and expounding his theories, and thanking Alston for having incited his interest in the subject.[90] He also enclosed seeds for the university botanical garden. His references to other scientists indicate that he had in his library[91] many volumes on plants, from John Ray's *Historia Plantarum* (1688), which included Banister's catalogue, on through Catesby, Parkinson, Dillenius (Oxford professor of botany), Linnaeus, and many other European naturalists. Apparently even a year or more earlier he had been in correspondence with Collinson and knew something of what was going on in Great Britain and had already sent "hundreds" of plants to Dillenius at Oxford. In the same year, 1738, the first of his known writings to be published, "Dissertatio brevis de principiis Botanicum et Zoologorum" was dedicated to Sir Hans Sloane, and in 1741 his "Nova Plantarum Genera" to Peter Collinson. Without their dedications they appeared in print in 1748 (and again in 1769) in Volume VIII of the Nuremberg *Acta Physico-Medica Academiae ... Leopoldina ... Ephemerides ...* (Appendix, pp. 178–202). With the "Nova Genera" Mitchell in 1741 shipped 560 plants, twenty-five of which he believed were new. He seems to have been mistaken in four, and descriptions of eleven others were anticipated in print before his work appeared; but he still receives credit as the discoverer of ten. Mitchell's work in the "Dissertatio" was the first colonial American plant taxonomy, a genuine effort to classify according to newer systems. His proposal, unlike Linnaeus' "sexual system," was based on genetic relationships as established by breeding experiments. Like other naturalists of his time, including other physicians, he was vitally interested in the medicinal qualities of various plants, especially the snakeroot.

Historians are generally agreed that Mitchell's pioneer work in plant classification, his own modification of Ray, Linnaeus, and others of his time, is his most important contribution to botany. He collected plants until he left Virginia and had more of them shipped to him in London after that date. His interest in plants in his post-American period was primarily economic or utilitarian in the modern sense, as witnessed in his 1748 paper before the Royal Society soon after his election to that body, "An Account of the Preparation and Uses of the Various Kinds of Pot-ash." [92]

In 1746, on his voyage to Great Britain, a Spanish ship had overtaken his and confiscated his baggage, which included, he said, more than a thousand specimens of various curiosities. They were eventually recovered through France, but all the botanical items were ruined. After making some excursions to Scotland in search of plants and placing a few orders with John Bartram, Mitchell became too absorbed in other matters to devote a great deal of attention to what had been a favorite avocation which had given him much of his reputation as a scientist. Although he had less opportunity for botanizing in England, he did become closely associated with Lord Bute and the Duke of Argyll, both avid botanists, and assisted Lord Bute in establishing the Royal Botanic Garden.

As noted above, almost surely Mitchell removed to England in 1746 primarily for reasons of health. Tidewater Virginia in his time had a number of epidemics and a great variety of disease and other physical infirmities. He may literally have worked himself into a decline, for the parish and county records show that he prescribed for and attended scores of the parish poor as well as his private patients. Then the good intellectual company of his neighbors John Clayton and William Byrd and John Custis and an occasional John Bartram was not enough to satisfy the restless as well as inquiring mind.

Besides medical research and theory, to be noticed later, Mitchell amused himself, and sought some ecological truths, in his delvings into other areas of science. Zoology and kindred subjects had always gone hand in hand with botany. The opossum, an animal of perennial interest from at least Captain John Smith's time, had attracted the attention of the Royal Society as early as 1698 and again in 1704. In 1741 Mitchell sent to Collinson a paper, "An Account of the Male and Female Opossum," which was read to the Society on February 1, 1742/3. It created such a favorable impression in London that the society asked two eminent physicians to comment upon it. They did so, and requested that the author report further on the subject. Thus a paper by Dr. Mitchell of July 8, 1745, "Farther Observations on the opposum," was read to the society on March 20, 1745/6, laying to rest the old stories passed on by Lawson and Byrd, among others, that the foetus grew from the mammae by describing the discovery that it was delivered from the womb by a passage then unknown in other animals. The detailed description forms one of the better zoological essays emanating from any of the American colonies.

Mitchell dedicated one of his works to Sir Hans Sloane concerning medicinal plants in Virginia, though it was never published. It is of interest that the colonial physician was one of only two men nominated to head the British Museum when it was first established, although many scientifically inclined Englishmen sought the post.[93]

Renaissance and Enlightenment scholars had been interested in the problem of color in the human race, an interest that the southerner Samuel Stanhope Smith of Princeton was to manifest in 1788. Between Smith and the first two American investigators of the subject, John Josselyn and William Douglas, came Mitchell, whose curiosity was spurred by a prize offered by the scientific academy of Bordeaux upon the causes of complexion of

Negroes. Too late for the competition, Mitchell's "An Essay upon the Causes of the different Colours of People in different Climates" was sent to Collinson from Urbanna and read in parts at several Royal Society meetings, finally appearing in the *Philosophical Transactions* (XLIII, no. 424 [1744], 102–150). He argued that color came from climate and differences in way of life and structure of skins, altogether in seven verbosely expressed propositions. Though his ideas are outmoded by Mendelian and Darwinian research and laws, his logic is still impressive.

In the five late books presumably his, in at least two or three instances on historical and politico-economic subjects, Mitchell (or the author) has constant reference to American flora and sometimes fauna, and if the *American Husbandry* (2 vols., London, 1775) is indeed his, he thus continued even after death to have some say about American plants. Lyman Carrier argues that the section of the 1748 edition of John Harris' *Voyages and Travels* (2 vols., London, 1744–1748) on the English in America, *A New and Complete History of the British Empire in America* (3 vols., London, 1756), *The Contest in America between Great Britain and France by an Impartial Hand* (London, 1757), and *The Present State of Great Britain and North America* (London, 1767) have in content, phrase, and attitude exactly the same qualities as *American Husbandry*, and that all are clearly Mitchell's. The Berkeleys, however, do not believe *American Husbandry* or the Harris material to be Mitchell's. The physician's research in climatology, electricity, chemistry, and medicine belong in other areas below, as does what is generally considered his most distinguished and significant contribution to eighteenth-century science, his map of North America, though Stearns prefers his taxonomy. Mitchell's work is tinged, though not tainted, by an imaginative utilitarianism which in natural history turned him to the medicinal and genetic and in history and cartography toward a realistic yet creative imperialism. He wanted to build his heavenly city on North American ground for the use and benefit of the British empire. Personal ambition is also obvious in much of what he wrote. Yet, despite or because of it all, he ranks with the major colonial men of science of his day.

North Carolina's almost sole contributor to science between Lawson and the Revolution, so far as is now apparent, was Dr. John Brickell (fl. 1731), author of *The Natural History of North Carolina* (Dublin, 1737). This famous or infamous history, which went through several Dublin editions and has influenced European impressions of Carolina over many years, is by most scholars felt to be a shameless plagiarizing of Lawson and other earlier accounts. This it is indeed, in whole sections, but there also seem to be some additions of Brickell's own in the section

on birds, beasts, and plants. This physician, who lived at Edenton, seems
to have made excursions into what is now Tennessee and almost surely
made some observations of fauna and flora as he traveled, for he was
known as a naturalist—of sorts. Though the title of the volume is something of a misnomer, for its most significant portions are those concerned
with social and economic conditions, the author called it a "compendious"
collection. The general and derivative characteristics of the book have been
pointed out in Chapter I. It remains only to repeat here that Brickell did
add to Lawson and other sources in every category of natural history,
sometimes accurately but frequently using examples to develop some
bizarre theory of his own. Like Mitchell, he was interested in the medicinal
uses of plants. Undoubtedly other North Carolina physicians were interested in plants for the same reasons, though there is little evidence of
collection or attempt to communicate to London any findings. Educated
nonprofessionals such as the last royal governor of our period, Arthur
Dobbs, did show among other scientific interests—almost all utilitarian—some desire to know North Carolina plant and animal life. The
books in Dobbs' library (see Chapter IV) in themselves indicate something
of this desire. Dobbs is apparently the discoverer of the Venus's-flytrap,
as letters of his in April 1759 and January 1760 indicate. He describes
the plant in some detail and notes that it grows in latitude 34° but not
in 35°.[94]

The early turn-of-the-century South Carolinians who communicated
with and collected for London naturalists, especially for the Royal Society
group, have been touched upon, and the greatest of all "pure" scientists
of the later period, Mark Catesby, has been discussed with the Virginia
group because his labors in North America began in the Chesapeake
provinces. But long before the *Natural History of Carolina* the minor
collectors just referred to had made the Temple Coffee House Botany
Club and the Royal Society conscious that South Carolina and its surrounding areas was a rich field for natural historians. In Catesby's time
and on down to 1764, the end of the period, there were more or less permanently resident Carolinians, some of them natives, who carried on investigations in the field individually or in cooperation with friends, and
there was a steady flow of specimens sent by them to the London group.
Like the Virginia naturalists of the Tidewater, these residents formed a
Charleston scientific community. Since most of them lived in the seaport capital or spent a portion of each year there, they could and did form
a closer group, especially in discussion of intellectual matters, than the
Chesapeake planters scattered on plantations along different rivers ever
did. Since Charleston was a seaport with relatively easy access to northern

ports, they had contacts with the middle colonies and especially with New England much more than Virginia had, as the mention of the Massachusetts Harvard men among their earliest group has already suggested. But they also had frequent direct communication with Great Britain, and among them were a large group of European-educated men, usually but not entirely in law and medicine, as earlier indicated. Of the mid-eighteenth-century naturalists, almost without exception the major collectors and experimenters were physicians, including the first Carolinian (probably first native American) to receive an M.D. degree from Edinburgh (John Moultrie) and the first native American to receive an M.D. from the continental medical center at Leyden (William Bull). Other physicians who have to be taken into account for interests outside or only bordering on their profession are Thomas Dale, Lionel Chalmers, Thomas Cooper, and Alexander Garden, though not all were naturalists. Scottish intellectual and educational influences were quite pronounced in this group, setting them somewhat apart from the Virginians, who were (despite Mitchell's Edinburgh education) largely English in orientation and origin. Related in some of their interests to these men were the horticulturist-agriculturists who also sent seeds, insects, plants, and animals to Great Britain, among them Henry Laurens, Eliza Lucas Pinckney, William Middleton, Mrs. Martha Logan (who was the author of an early American book on gardening), William Young (who had a Charleston nursery and worked with Garden), and Governor Robert Johnson. Among these Garden, Gregg, and Laurens corresponded with Linnaeus, and many more with Collinson and Sloane and other Britons. Linnaeus' letters show that John Gregg sent him a "kidney-shaped Sea-pen" and had sent Lord Hillsborough many plants.[95]

William Bull (1710–1791) soon forsook medicine for politics and was for several years acting governor of South Carolina. His continued interest in science is shown, however, in official records, for in 1742 he was corresponding with Collinson, to whom he sent botanical information on the colony. He entertained and aided Catesby, as has been noted. Dr. Thomas Dale (1699–1750), nephew of Samuel Dale, English botanist and physician, is said to have been a graduate of Leyden. A classical scholar and translator, active politician, and controversial physician, he was also an indefatigable collector of botanical specimens, some of which during his lifetime went to his uncle and to William Sherard. After his death his collection of South Carolina plants was sent to Johann Fredericus Gronovius in Leyden.[96] His belletristic writing will be noted in a later chapter.

Henry Laurens and his wife, primarily gardeners, were also interested in trees and plants for agricultural and other uses, leaning much more toward the European import than the American export. A Mary Dering was writing and shipping to Sir Hans Sloane in 1728 and 1729, and a year earlier a D. Standish was apologizing for sending in one lot nothing more than ore and petrified wood, suggesting that he was another who was concerned with natural history. Eliza Lucas Pinckney and people such as the two Laurenses, Thomas Jenner, and Henry Yonge were not really botanists or zoologists, but in their horticultural and agricultural and even paleontological work all connected in one way or another with American plants and animals.[97] Even agricultural crop parasites or insects were of considerable interest per se to the Royal Society, and the cochineal or indigo-producing insect was an agricultural element in itself worthy of continued investigation. In the last years of the period, men such as the former merchant the Reverend Charles Woodmason and Dr. Alexander Garden wrote to the Royal Society of Arts concerning useful plants and other products of the country, such as potash and rice, and in so doing at least touched upon natural history.[98]

As a naturalist at least, and perhaps as a physician, Dr. Garden (1730–1791), born in Aberdeen and often confused with his South Carolina contemporary the Anglican Commissary of the same name, was the most versatile and indefatigable. He studied medicine at Marischal College, Aberdeen, and at the University of Edinburgh. Professors in each institution, James Gordon of Aberdeen and Charles Alston of Edinburgh, inspired in him his lifelong interest in botany. Unable to pay the fees at Edinburgh for a medical degree, in 1752 Garden departed for Charleston, where he began almost simultaneously his careers in the practice of medicine and in investigation in natural history.[99]

About ten days after he set foot in South Carolina, where he was for two years assistant to a Dr. William Rose of Prince William Parish, he shipped a parcel of "pink root" or *Spigelia marilandica* L., a popular worm medicine then and now, to Dr. Rutherford of Edinburgh. In the following January he sent a description of the plant to Dr. Alston. In the same period his fellow Carolina physician Dr. John Lining published his observations on the virtues of the root in the Edinburgh *Essays and Observations, Physical and Literary* (I [1754], 386–389).[100] Garden's own more detailed essay went to Dr. Whytt of Edinburgh in 1757 and much later, in 1771, it appeared as "An Account of the Indian Pink by Alex. Garden M.D. . . ." in *Essays and Observations* (III [1771], 145–153).

Meanwhile, the slaves appeared to Garden to know more natural history—from direct experience—than did their masters, with the exception of Dr. Bull, or at least so Garden said. To publicize his own discoveries and experiments and to keep up with the latest developments in the life sciences and kindred subjects, he began to develop a widespread correspondence with English and Scottish naturalists and later with men of similar interests in other colonies. Inclined to be tubercular, in 1754 he took a summer trip north in hope of thus regaining his health. It was a momentous journey, for on his excursion he became acquainted personally with Cadwallader Colden in New York and John and William Bartram and Benjamin Franklin in Philadelphia and John Clayton in Virginia. He also saw the latest books by Linnaeus (Bull had earlier ones in Charleston) in Colden's library and was at once excited by the new system as he then came to understand it. He also read many other new books and imparted to these northern gentlemen the information he already had about the Royal Society of Arts and its program. He returned to Charleston refreshed in mind and body.

Soon afterward Garden succeeded to the elderly Dr. Lining's practice. Though urged by British Dr. John Huxham (1692–1768) to study the medical qualities of plants, Garden declined, for he saw in botany a science in its own right. Jane Colden in New York, John Ellis (1710?–1776) in London (his principal English encourager), Henry Baker of the Royal Society of Arts, Linnaeus, Gronovius, and others received his letters on Carolina plants. He urged Carolina planters to try new agricultural methods recommended by the Royal Society of Arts. In 1755 he made a journey with Governor Glen to Saluda in Cherokee hill country, keeping a journal of his expedition now unfortunately lost. Evidently Ellis mentioned membership in the Royal Society, and the cautious and thrifty Scot came to the fore in Garden as he inquired about the fees. When he found he could not be admitted as a "foreign" member with minimum fees, he stated emphatically that he would not pay to any society such an amount. Many years were to pass before he did become a Fellow on Ellis' nomination.

While Garden's medical practice grew and he occasionally experimented in matters related to his profession, he made plain to contemporaries on both sides of the Atlantic that he considered himself first of all a scientist. He refused to be a paid collector of specimens, as were his friends the Bartrams. The hundreds or thousands of rarities he sent to Europeans went to those who might appreciate them, though of course he always hoped for comment and even argument. His circle of correspondence continued to widen as he sent with his letters to older friends shells, seeds, and insects. He was in 1755 elected as the first American member to the Royal Society of Arts (or Premium Society), which sought to encourage all utilitarian technologies and applied natural and physical sciences.[101] Garden was in the spirit of the society in writing on the condition of slaves, on improved economy in rice production, and in advocating horse-powered threshing machines and grape and cotton and silkworm culture, as well as in discussing hemp and potash. He began to complain in the same year (1755) that his practice was preventing his going on botanical excursions, but he was accomplishing something in the area. He wrote Linnaeus that he had learned more about plants during his one year of using the latter's classification system than he had in three when he employed other methods of identification.

Garden was often critical of others' work, sometimes unduly so. He saw a recent natural history of Jamaica as better than that prepared by the "pompous . . . and illiterate Botanist Sir Hans Sloane," and he was frequently unfairly severe, modern specialists suggest, in his comments on "Catesby's blunders" in depicting leaf detail and the color of fish.[102] This caustic severity is one of the several evidences of a prickly nature and of a man who could be unduly jealous of others who had achieved fame in his favorite area of research.

Garden not only collected and corresponded. He described plants, disagreed with Linnaeus in the identification of a plant and won his point, suggested that certain new plants be named in honor of friends, contributed to Clayton's own now-lost second edition of *Flora Virginica*, described Halley's comet in 1759, and participated in the fight against local epidemics, especially smallpox, in his writing and experiment. In amphibiology he was making some exciting discoveries of a "Mud Iguana" (*Siren lacertina*), of which he sent specimens to Linnaeus and Ellis. The latter, after he found Linnaeus believed it to be a new genus, gave a paper, "An Account of an Amphibious Bipes," before the Royal Society (*Philosophical Transactions*, LXV [1766], 191–192). Several other essays were written on this discovery. He examined and had sketches made of ususual turtles, shipped a collection of birds to England, and insects such as fireflies, fishes, lizards, and alligators, and by 1769 was corresponding with the noted zoologist Thomas Pennant (1726–1798), F.R.S.[103]

By 1765 Garden was considering retirement from his medical practice and by 1771 had purchased a plantation of 1689 acres in St. James' Parish, Goose Creek, fifteen miles from Charleston. His health was deteriorating, but he continued to collect and to send natural-history specimens to his friends in Great Britain, to Linnaeus, and to the younger Gronovius. He sent an exciting account of the electric eel through John Ellis to the Royal Society, a communication presented February 23, 1775, his last important one from Charleston. As the war came, Garden, with close ties to both sides, attempted to maintain a neutral position. But after Yorktown he was banished and his property confiscated. In London in 1783 he finally signed the register of the Royal Society and took part in its deliberations. He died in 1791.

No southern colonial, with the possible exception of Dr. Mitchell, received more recognition abroad and in the colonies than did Dr. Alexander Garden. In America he was a corresponding member of the revived American Philosophical Society (1769) and the American Society for Promoting and Propagating Useful Knowledge (1768). He was elected to the Edinburgh Society (1760) and the Swedish Royal Society (1763) as well as to the Royal Society and the Royal Society of Arts, the latter two at least already mentioned. "A species of eternity" for Garden, as the Berkeleys quote Collinson as having called it, came when Linnaeus officially named the Cape jessamine the *Gardenia*. The Latin appellation appeared in the *Species Plantarum* of 1762, and the plant has been so distinguished ever since. His specimens survive in the British Museum, the Oxford collections, and the Uppsala gardens and museum. Though natural history, especially botany, was his great love, he did much in many other areas, some to be noted briefly below. As already suggested, his bent was utilitarian, though he himself insisted frequently that plants should be studied for themselves and not as materia medica (as he had been taught at Aberdeen and Edinburgh). He impressed with his knowledge not only Cadwallader and Jane Colden and the Bartrams and Benjamin Franklin in America, but also European scientists of a dozen countries. He was almost the only American scientist who could and did disagree with a major European in a field and won his argument. This he did more than once with Linnaeus, at a time when Cadwallader Colden and his theories on gravity were being crushed by European criticism. Garden's usefulness to other scientists, another way of measuring his place, is undoubted. Between 1898 and 1958, for example, Gunther and Wheeler and Wilkins used his specimens and directions in lectures and studies of plants, fishes, and shells. The South Carolina historian Edward McCrady, in calling Garden "the most famous physician of colonial times," was undoubtedly referring to his combined reputation as medical practitioner and general scientist in his own day. Yet his influence on intellectual or general history in the eighteenth century is not equal to that of John Mitchell or on botany to that of John Clayton.[104]

Except for what visiting naturalists such as the Bartrams and a few South Carolinians may have found and commented upon in Georgia in the colonial period, there is little evidence of collecting and observation of plants or animals or shells in that province. Agriculture, including silkworm culture, the Trustees' public experimental garden in Savannah, and materia medica searched for by a few physicians did, however, occupy or attract the attention of a number of these first Georgians, and all these interests involved some use of the corpus of knowledge of natural history and of its methodology. A competent botanist, Dr. William Houstoun, had been engaged by the Trustees to seek out in the West Indies plants (useful certainly) to be tried out in the Savannah garden, but neither the man himself nor his successor as botanical collector, Dr. Robert Millar, ever reached continental America. The well-educated and perceptive William Gerard De Brahm, surveyor-general of the Southern Department, designer of forts and other buildings in South Carolina and Georgia, and historian (through his *Report of the General Survey in the Southern District of North America*), certainly did observe and note or describe trees, climate, all sorts of shrubs ornamental or strange or useful, and scores of other geographical or topographical matters on South Carolina, Georgia, and East Florida. And recently Professor Joseph Ewan has discovered an article published in 1756 in the *Hamburges Magazin* entitled (translated) "Report and Remarks on the Plant Kingdom in Georgia by a Preacher of the Ebenezer Colony, 1752." The author, as Ewan indicates, was almost surely J.M. Bolzius, who wrote with the assistance of the physician J. Andrew Zwiffler. This was the first local flora for Georgia. That this first report came from a German settlement and was printed in German is significant of the intellectual curiosity and education of the Salzburgers.[105] One of Georgia's early governors, Henry Ellis (1721–1806), F.R.S., naturalist, and geographer, sent reports occasionally to the Royal Society via his relative John Ellis. Governor Ellis' materials, however, were primarily discussion of or observations on the Georgia weather. He did attempt to import new seeds and plants to improve the economy. Ellis departed from the colony in 1761 and carried on marine research in the Mediterranean until he died at Naples. Though his predecessor Oglethorpe had also been interested in plants and animals from a utilitarian point of view, it was Catesby and the Bartrams who as visitors recorded what is now known of colonial Georgia fauna and flora and the impressions these living things made on the first generation of Europeans who saw them.

ZOOLOGY

Although from time to time the interest of individual southern colonists and of the Royal Society and British individuals on aspects of nature other than botany have been touched upon, a little more should be noted about some of them. Concerned as southern naturalists were with flora, their study of plants was usually accompanied by observation of other living elements of their environment. Their zoological interests, for example, are indicated in the communications to the Royal Society, the manuscripts and books of Catesby and Mitchell and many others, and the boxes of specimens sent to Great Britain.

Ornithology

In the late seventeenth and the whole eighteenth century, the southern naturalist was almost as much impressed by birds as he was by plants. One recalls that from the time of John White feathered creatures had been drawn or painted and that they were described by all the men who had made observations on plants—Hariot, Smith, Strachey, and the mid-seventeenth-century promotion pamphleteers. Actually these men had been preceded in this pastime of bird-watching and description by the field naturalists of New Spain such as Oviedo and a dozen others.[106] With the founding of the Royal Society had come bird work in England, including colored drawings. John Ray (1627–1705) and Francis Willughby (1635–1672), the former already mentioned as a pioneer in botany, the latter especially addicted to zoological investigation, were among the active ornithologists. In New England Winthrop and Josselyn included feathered types in their observations and specimens. In London Dr. Martin Lister (1638–1712) was gathering information on birds from his southern colonial correspondents in Virginia, Maryland, and South Carolina, including curious persons such as Joseph Lord and Madame Hannah Williams mentioned above.

Willughby, called a founder of modern ornithology, had published posthumously by his friends his *Ornithologia* (English edition annotated and edited by Ray, 3 vols., London, 1678) which includes among other illustrations the "Virginia Nightingale," which is our American cardinal. Thus this first book of scientific ornithology in Europe contained southern American birds.

In Virginia, the elder naturalist named John Clayton was the first southern colonial to give an authoritative ornithological observation. His essay "Of the Birds [of Virginia]" (*Philosophical Transactions*, XVII [1693], 988–999)[107] is the most extensive surviving description of bird life of the era in the South Atlantic area. Later in England he was to join Dr. Allen Moulin in making anatomical studies of birds. American ornithologists are still impressed by the number of birds they are able to identify from his descriptions. Clayton's contemporary and brother clergyman John Banister scattered through his plant catalogue and insect-and-arachnid catalogue references to a number of southern birds, and in his fragmentary "Natural History" he describes turkey-buzzards, humming-birds, geese, ducks, and other waterfowl. Banister's surviving papers, however, indicate no detailed observation of birds approaching Clayton's.

John Lawson, on the other hand, includes more extensive lists of birds than any earlier traveler, naming some fifty-six land varieties besides extra "sorts" under various groupings and also noting fifty-three waterfowl. Though he did not live to do it, the surveyor-explorer planned "a strict collection" of all the living things of the region, naming birds specifically along with other creatures and plants. Brickell used Lawson's bird descriptions, adding particularly to those related to medicinal uses of the feathered tribe. Lawson's listings and descriptions in "Birds of Carolina" in *A New Voyage*[108] indicated a careful, systematic, and relatively comprehensive coverage. Included are various local anecdotes regarding habits and habitats. Some of the birds he describes no longer may be found in Carolina: thus his observations are significant in many ways. As he admits, he describes often from memory, and his descriptions are therefore uneven. But since his book went through three English and two German editions between 1709 and 1722 he gave the early eighteenth-century European world a knowledge of South Atlantic American birds it had never had before.

Mark Catesby, often called the founder of American ornithology, has been discussed in some detail above. In his illustrations the birds are even parts of three-subject pictures with plants and mammals or other vertebrates. *The Natural History of Carolina, Florida, and the Bahama Islands* includes among its 200 colored plates 113 birds against accurate natural backgrounds.[109] Seventy-one of Catesby's list were used by Linnaeus as the bases of his descriptions. Catesby seems to have adapted the general pattern of the Ray-Willughby *Ornithology* for this portion of the *Natural History*, and its Latin designations for most birds. Measurements, calls, and folklore concerning various types are among the useful and entertaining aspects of this section of the *Natural History*. Some backgrounds and postures are awkward or inaccurate, but on the whole he was amazingly true to what is known today.

In addition to the plates in the *Natural History* and the lists and descriptions there is in the British Museum a volume of "Bibliotheca Sloaniana" containing drawings by Catesby of twelve birds, fishes, shells, and molluscs, with some fish and amphibious creatures. Catesby's "Of Birds of Passage" was published, after delivery before the Royal Society, in the *Philosophical Transactions* and the *Gentleman's Magazine*,[110] the latter an extract from the former. They are of interest because they show Catesby's theories of the causes and method of migration. Catesby himself admitted that his study was based on rational conclusions unsupported by actual observation. This essay was an outgrowth of his work for the birds of the *Natural History*. Based on assumptions of the uniformity of climate of the same degree of latitude, it is of course quite faulty, and in another generation it was superseded. Perhaps the Enlightenment passion for symmetry had misled him, as his biographers remark, yet it was superior to the explanations of any of his contemporaries.

Despite his enormous contributions to other phases of natural history, Catesby's most important work, historians of science agree, is in ornithology. He presented for Europeans of his own day a comprehensive, detailed, and illustrated body of material on the birds of the South Atlantic British colonies. One ornithologist, Witmer Stone, wrote in 1929 that the *Natural History* "forms the basis of the ornithology not only of the Southern States, but of the whole of North America."[111] The account of birds' migratory habits makes his statement true, at least for eastern North America.

After Catesby, for the remaining decades of the colonial period most of the work on American birds was done from Great Britain and the European continent by men such as George Edwards and Eleazar Albin. Albin's *Natural History of Birds* (1731) depicted and listed several species of southern American birds, including our cardinal. Edwards' *The Natural History of Uncommon Birds* (4 vols., 1743–1751) contains many American varieties, some forty-odd in Volumes I and II and many more in Volume III. Of these a great proportion are southern, or are found in the South. In his later *Gleanings of Natural History* (1758–1764) Edwards notes others, such as the Maryland yellowthroat. Undoubtedly many of his specimens and descriptions came through his friend Sir Hans Sloane from southern naturalists previously mentioned. Other naturalists better known as botanists, as Linnaeus and Thomas Pennant, included birds in their writings, and several of these fowls are southern. There is an interesting Pennant plate of Baltimore orioles at nest.[112] As already noted, the major Virginia botanist John Clayton the younger contributed a description of the whippoorwill to Catesby's *Natural History*. Alexander Garden sent many birds and other zoological specimens to Thomas Pennant, including the chuck-will's-widow. Pennant cited Garden's contributions frequently in his *Arctic Zoology* (London, 1784–1785) including snakes, fish, and other animals. He also named the black-crowned night heron the "Gardenian Heron" in his honor.[113] And the minor collectors already mentioned frequently included in their shipments from the Chesapeake colonies or the Carolinas some ornithological specimens. Men like William Byrd II and John Custis were interested in hummingbirds, especially in their flower gardens. But with Catesby the distinctive southern published contributions to American ornithology concluded.

From the reign of James I through that of George III Britons at home were curious about and delighted with the exotic birds of their colonies. From kings to merchants and country gentlemen, they were eager to possess living cardinals, blue birds, mockingbirds, hummingbirds, and many of the other varieties described by travelers and promoters. Hardly a ship sailed for London from the Chesapeake or from Charleston which

Virginia State Library

Alexander Spotswood, colonial governor of Virginia

Sᵗ. John   Tradescant Senᵗ.

Ashmolean Museum, Oxf

John Tradescant the Elder, first known collector of American flora and fauna

did not carry caged songsters, usually the more highly colored ones. Though many died en route, enough survived for laymen and scientists to wish to know more of the native habitats of their pets. The rarer and more delicate birds, incidentally, usually reached Britain only as preserved specimens. The ornithologists who described or drew or painted the objects of their studies produced popular books, for though American birds never throve in Britain as did American plants, they interested men and women equally as much as did trees and flowers.[114]

Entomology

As anyone who has lived in the southeastern United States knows, multitudes of native insects from ants and cockroaches and rhinoceros beetles to beautiful moths and butterflies and painful and dangerous chigoes (chiggers) and ticks and spiders still infest the region. Happily, mosquitoes have become a little rarer. But the earliest chroniclers and explorers wrote of these insects, and British naturalists sought specimens of all varieties. An imported insect, the cochineal, was used in eighteenth-century South Carolina as the basis of a wealth-producing agricultural industry, at least for a time, and the Europeans were anxious to examine this little bright red creature too. American bees are mentioned at least from Oviedo's time. After the advent of the Royal Society, many of the letters exchanged between southern colonial collectors and Petiver, Collinson, Sloane, and others mention insects and arachnids.

His own correspondence and the published works of English friends such as Petiver mention the work of John Banister, the man who, George Browne Goode says in his *Beginnings of Natural History in America,* was the first to observe intelligently the insects and molluscs of North America.[115] In 1680 Banister sent Petiver fifty-two species of insects and observations upon them, later communicated to the Royal Society. Linnaeus used some few "Virginia" species, all he had, in *Systema Natura.* Recently the Ewans have collated and published the three surviving portions of Banister's "Collectio Insectorum, atque Aliarum Rerum Naturalium in Virginia . . ." (1680–1692) with very useful notes. From wasps through cicadas ("We call them here dry flys"), on through grasshoppers and mantises to ants and glowworms to beetles to species today classified as arachnids. This is not only a creditable first American effort: it is a perspicacious and critical organization and listing still useful.

The first Reverend Hugh Jones of Maryland had sent insects, along with other things, to Petiver before 1698, but as noted above he did little or nothing to identify them as to place or habitat or to classify them in other ways. Vernon and Krieg in the same period in Maryland did similar work in entomology, Richard Lewis about 1732/3 described a mulberry tree which apparently bred "flies" in its leaves, and Richard Brooke in 1752 presented to the Royal Society an undescribed insect. As in other phases of natural history, however, the province of Maryland did little to advance knowledge of colonial insect life.

In Virginia most of the contributions to entomology after Banister for decades were quite minor, usually scattered offerings of specimens. The Sloane manuscripts show the rhinoceros beetle arriving in London in 1701 with other Virginia curiosities. But South Carolina, with a much warmer climate and a greater number of insects, was more helpful. The Nathaniel Johnson-Joseph Lord group at the beginning of the eighteenth century did a good deal of insect gathering. Lord included butterflies among his curiosities. In North Carolina, John Lawson included some insects and in his set of resolutions vowed to study their breeding places, food, and other pertinent matters regarding them.[116] He asked for vials and pins in which and with which to preserve them. In *A New Voyage to Carolina* he lists alligators, vipers, lizards, turtles, and snakes, and he calls beetles, butterflies, grasshoppers, locusts, and moths, "Reptiles, or smaller Insects." Obviously he was not an entomologist.

Mark Catesby included genuine insects in both text and illustrations of his *Natural History of Carolina*, e.g., some beautiful butterflies in full color. Actually in the plates the insect is usually, as might be expected, an appendage of plants and birds or beasts. But Linnaeus used a few of his descriptions. South Carolina contributions to entomology might well include Garden's collections of insects sent to Henry Baker and the Royal Society of Arts, and a description of the praying mantis in Latin, with a drawing by De Brahm. Garden also sent an account of the cochineal insect to Baker for the society and performed experiments to ascertain the effect on humans of eating the fruit of the prickly pear, on which the insects feed. John Ellis asked Garden for an account of the cochineal insect and read his reply to the Royal Society. It was published in their *Transactions* in 1762.[117] Thus most of the work in entomology done by British naturalists on American specimens from the southern colonies had to come from scattered sources, including John Bartram after his long excursion through the area.

Animals, Including the Vertebrates, Molluscs, and Crustacea

The Spanish had preceded the English in writing of the strange animals of America as they had of other matters. And Thomas Hariot and John White between them described and painted fur-bearing mammals such as bears, martens, wildcats, skunks, and deer, as well as molluscs, fish, and crustaceans, and various kinds of reptiles. In animals especially the interests of the writer and the artist did not entirely coincide. The surviving White drawings and paintings seem to concentrate on various sorts of fish, crustaceans, and reptiles, and a variety of birds and insects, while Hariot describes southern deer and rabbits, muskrats and probably raccoons, opossums, squirrels, and other vertebrates more than he does the animals White depicts.[118] From Jamestown various colonists such as George Percy and Francis Perkins wrote of whales and swordfish and tortoises seen on the voyage over or of local birds being sent to England as presents. These never matched Captain John Smith's descriptions, however, for in his *Map of Virginia* appear scores of animals which repeat and supplement Hariot's rather scanty list. He identifies by names still used a number of beasts Hariot had been content with vaguely describing. Like his predecessor, Smith had an eye for commodity and therefore emphasizes fur-bearing mammals including beaver and otter, weasels, and opossums.[119] By 1620 colonists were boasting that European cattle and horses were larger and more prolific in Virginia, and one declared that deer produced two or three fawns at a birth.[120] In the next half century promotion pamphlets continued to mention fascinating animals, though except for the birds there is little indication that these animals were being shipped to Great Britain alive or preserved—except as cured pelts for the fur trade.

The Reverend John Clayton wrote a letter on the "Beasts of Virginia," in which he discusses English cattle and horses domesticated or running wild in Virginia, sheep, deer, elk, hogs, raccoons, opossums, rabbits and other wild creatures also mentioned by his predecessors. He describes how beavers build their houses, the bellowing of huge frogs and the pack-horse bell-jingle sound made by a smaller variety, the rattlesnake and its bite and cures, and something of other sorts of reptiles. Though the good parson appears somewhat too credulous, he had observed a great deal himself, and many of the secondhand accounts of bites, cures, and poisons shed light on the daily life and beliefs of colonists of varying degrees of formal education.[121]

John Banister, if one must judge by his surviving papers and preserved specimens, was more interested in almost every other phase of his American environment than he was in the beasts. Crustacea, principally crabs and crayfish, and parasitic worm shells possibly from within oysters, and some molluscs certainly caught his attention. He also has a bit to say of the beaver and the other fur-bearers, of the sweet flesh of the deer, of squirrels and porpoises, and of the never-neglected opossum. The sturgeon, shad, herring, rock, perch, and other fish he has observed in fresh water. But as far as extant evidence goes, Banister never looked on beasts or on crustacea with the critical scientific eye with which he examined birds, plants, red natives, and even molluscs. It is hard to believe that a scientist of the Enlightenment's beginning with these other interests would have neglected to collect and attempt to classify these living things as well. Perhaps studies by him of more animals will yet be discovered. He seems to have shipped a great variety of specimens. Apparently he gathered molluscs such as oysters and mussels for Sherard, Lister and others, and he is said to have been the first man in North America to observe molluscs scientifically, though fossil shells were sent from Maryland before his work arrived from Virginia.[122]

William Byrd has much to say of animals in his histories of the Dividing Line, especially of bear and wild turkey, though he is much more concerned with plants and birds. In 1715 he arrived in England with gifts for the Royal Society, including "the bones of the penis of a Bear and of a Raccoon." Much earlier, in 1697, he presented a rattlesnake and an opossum. The latter was dissected, and the anatomical drawings made of the work were published in the *Philosophical Transactions*. Petiver and Sloane asked Byrd to collect animals along with other rarities, but the result appears to have been only token compliance with their requests. Meantime Catesby had begun work in Virginia and the more southerly colonies, doing a great deal more with reptiles and fur-bearing animals as well as birds than the master of Westover ever did. Intent on a relatively complete natural history of the southeastern colonies, Catesby was of necessity interested in all forms of life. As an ichthyologist, he produced only a little, principally some rather stiff pictures of fish and descriptions of them. He dealt with molluscs only in an introductory section. His crabs are from the West Indies. Turtles and snakes were more interesting and varied and perhaps better drawn. And he tried to dispel myths which had grown up around herpetology—as of the certain cures for snakebites. He denied that the tail of the water moccasin was as deadly as its head. Linnaeus, however, mistrusted Catesby's snakes and preferred Dr. Alexander Garden's testimony concerning these now familiar reptiles. But alligators, lizards, and frogs are also all in the *Natural History*.

Of the relatively minor groups in the great history the mammals are most important. Catesby originally may not have planned to include mammals in the book, but the volumes appeared with a skunk, squirrels of several varieties (including flying squirrels), foxes, rabbits, even a crudely drawn bison (buffalo) and a fairly good description of the beast. Catesby's biographers conclude that his work with zoophytes is really prescientific and thus has been largely unused. About the same thing may be said of his mammals, though his fishes and reptiles have received considerable attention and were employed or borrowed by later scientists,[123] despite Linnaeus' misgivings.

Among other eighteenth-century Virginia collectors only a few seem really concerned with classification and description of animals, and even then it is usually the snake, the opossum, and sometimes the frog which were shipped to Britain or described. Dr. John Symmer of Gloucester County was by 1736 sending snakes and their rattles among his "medical curiosities."[124] John Mitchell's principal contribution to zoology was his study of the opossum presented to the Royal Society in 1742/3 and 1745/6, anatomical studies already noted. Perhaps his long essay on the different colors of the human skin noted above may be classed under zoology.[125] And John Custis in his letters to Collinson argues as had others against the old myth of rattlesnakes charming birds.[126]

Of the major Virginia historians of the eighteenth century—indeed of the period between Smith and Strachey and Jefferson—only Robert Beverley devotes considerable attention to animal life. His Chapter V, "Of the Fish," mentions or describes dozens of varieties from whales to bass and herring, and includes various crustacea and molluscs with them. In the same section he gives a vivid account of Indian methods in fishing, from spearing to netting or weirs or, in the case of the sturgeon, clapping a noose over the tail. For good measure he pictures American fish hawks seizing their prey and then the bald eagles taking them from the hawks, giving one eyewitness account. The succeeding chapter discusses wild fowl and hunted game and describes in detail the birth of a young opossum (an explanation Mitchell disproved). Thus in *The History and Present State of Virginia* (1705) a learned author who is not really a naturalist by interest or observation preserves some useful details of real and imagined animal life early in the eighteenth century. That he draws from Smith and others a century earlier indicates among other things that wild life of stream and forest had changed little in that period. Beverley buttresses his points taken from earlier chroniclers by anecdotes from his own experience.[127]

Except for Alexander Garden, whose discovery of the mud iguana noticed above was exciting and fresh, relatively few published anything significant on southern American zoology before Jefferson and his circle. This does not mean that nothing was written and published, for the Royal Society's printed papers show scores of small items on American fish, amphibia, molluscs, mammals, birds, and other forms, but that the Royal Society naturalist from its foundation in 1662 was usually much more interested in plant life, partly because its potential usefulness—as commodity—was more apparent. Thus a Buffon in France might form his theories of the inferiority of animal life in the New World partially for lack of evidence —evidence against his theory which the later President Jefferson went to great expense and trouble to supply him. The southern colonial in 1764 ate fish and game, sold or sewed hides and furs, and watched rather idly the beaver building dams or the opossum carrying its young as no other mammal he knew did. Only with the administration of Thomas Jefferson and his Lewis and Clark expedition and the opening of the West did all forms of zoology become of interest to many educated men in America. Only birds and to a much lesser extent fish had received any degree of curious attention from southern settlers—or scientists.

Ethnology

From his first sight of the red man in North America, the European had begun to compare him primarily with the whites of Europe, occasionally with the oriental Mongol, and sometimes with the black African. From Roanoke and Jamestown the English settler attempted to explain the Indians as a separate race or as a branch of a hitherto unknown race. The old theories of Carthaginian, Phoenician, Welsh, Hebrew, and other possible origins have been considered at some length in Chapter II. Welsh or Hebrew origin was the favorite explanation of the earliest settlers, and one or the other was advanced seriously by various scholarly writers down to the Revolution. James Adair between 1760 and 1775, one recalls, wrote a long book comparing the southern tribes and tribesmen with the lost tribes of Israel in an impressive series of parallels from religious ritual through government and physical appearance. No historian ignored the subject completely, though most expressed no great interest in the matter.

John Mitchell, as has been indicated, devoted a long and rational argument to prove that skin color was determined by climate, and he was followed in the national period by others with similar or slightly differing arguments. The debates and theorizing as to Hebrew lost-tribe origins continues to our own day, and despite the proof-by-experience advanced by certain twentieth-century theory holders, the most comprehensive argument in literary form so far produced is that of the southern Indian trader James Adair.

Ethnology and anthropology throughout the colonial period from Massachusetts to Georgia were mixed with religion, especially fundamentalism and Calvinism, or so-called Calvinism. Even some of the major members of the Royal Society wrote books on the relationship, declaring in most instances that anatomical structure and modes of living of all races were not incompatible with the Scripture taken literally. The titles of several of the books by John Ray and others mentioned in Chapter IV are evidence that the southern colonial reader was quite familiar with the arguments of the orthodox or would-be orthodox regarding the origin and nature of men of every hue and stage of civilization. The ethnological and anthropological studies issued by the United States government for almost a century now nearly always begin with the accounts of the red man recorded by the southern colonial settlers. And some of them, such as certain of Mooney's studies of the Cherokees, really get little beyond what was known even by semiliterate Indian traders in 1764. Ethnology and anthropology are by no means new in the southeastern area. Red, white, and black stayed at the upper surface of the southerners' consciousness.

OTHER ASPECTS OF NATURAL PHILOSOPHY, PRIMARILY PHYSICAL

As every extant evidence from general history, promotion literature, and scientific record would indicate, the southern colonial's interest in his natural environment was centered primarily in flora and then in fauna. As collector, classifier, and namer (labeler) in these areas he has an important place in the history of science. But botany and zoology inspired kindred interests such as geology, climatology, meteorology, and paleontology, and in the latter decades of the period, following in part the examples of their British kin and in part the examples set by such colonials as Benjamin Franklin and John Winthrop, they displayed a moderate enthusiasm for the kindred areas of chemistry, astronomy, and electricity. As in natural history, the southern mind was often interested in these matters for purely practical reasons, but the physician or planter who measured temperature or recorded wind velocity or observed parhelion or comet frequently lost sight of the economic usefulness of his subject-object and became immersed in his pursuit for what today we would perhaps call pure intellectual delight or delight in advancing the frontiers of human knowledge. If the colonial had been personally questioned on this thing or that, he would almost surely have declared its *usefulness*. But as noted in this and preceding chapters, to the son of the Enlightenment through and especially including Thomas Jefferson, the term was almost all-embracing, for it was even "useful" if it stimulated or enriched or ornamented the mind per se.

GEOLOGY, SEISMOLOGY, AND PALEONTOLOGY

From Thomas Hariot on, geology, including the nature and formation of soils, minerals, metals, and precious stones, and their significance, was recorded and commented upon. The example had been set by the Spaniards, for Oviedo, Monardes, and Acosta contain much on iron and its value, gold mines, metals of all kinds, and earth formations. At least the former two Iberian observers were pre-Copernican in their concept of the earth in relation to sun and planets and therefore origins. Hariot shows that he knew Monardes and perhaps had his book with him on Roanoke Island, yet the Oxford scholar, with the assistance of his mineral man (probably a Thomas

875

Vaughan) and even perhaps the harsh methods of Ralph Lane in extracting information from the red men, made an accurate geological map of the region. It was of course part of *A briefe and true report* published separately in 1588 and in deBry (in four languages) in 1590. The essay was, as already mentioned, ostensibly promotional. The uses to be made of alum, iron, copper, and other metals are mentioned and emphasized along with their location. The "mineral man," apparently a combination of geologist, mining engineer, assayer, and refiner and in this case the earliest Englishman of this profession in the United States, probably supplied many of the details and some of the analyses.

Hariot's report is a succinct summary of the essential geological features of the region he and Lane and Vaughan explored. There was a wide, flat coastal region without stones, a distinct fall line with hard crystalline rocks which extended an unknown distance west, a whitish clay useful as medicine, a multiplicity of types of rock including a hard, durable stone, iron in some of the rocky ground, copper which had some silver in it some distance inland, and an excellent and plentiful clay for brickmaking. He seems to imply also that he recognized fossil shells in the sediments of the coastal plain.[128]

At Jamestown Captain John Smith made observations of metals, rocks, soils, and kindred matters which reveal him as a competent geologist, perhaps even more observant than Hariot, though he lacked the latter's university training. He scorned the gold seekers among his fellows, though he admitted the presence of a small quantity of metal. But he carefully denied any appreciable amount of any precious metals; iron ore and its possibilities were more to his liking. Like Hariot, he was able to distinguish the coastal plain and the piedmont. He noted that crystalline stones had worked down from the mountains and that there were other "glistering tinctures from metals in various soils." "The vesture of the earth in most places doth manifestly prove the nature of the soile to be lusty and very rich," he averred, and went on to describe "*terra sigillata* ... bole Armoniac ... black sandy mould ... fuller's earth ... marl," and even "a fat slimy clay ... [and] a very barren gravell."[129] His kindred topographical descriptions will be noted below. Yet in proportion to the recital of events in the development of the colony and relationships with the Indians all the geological information taken together is small indeed.

William Strachey, as has been shown, borrowed at least one-third of his first book of the *Historie of Travell into Virginia Britania* from Smith's *A Map of Virginia.* In fact, geological descriptions (e.g., *Historie*, p. 34) seem mere outright thefts or paraphrases from Smith, and other parts seem straight out of Purchas or Hariot. Yet he follows one section directly from Smith with a fairly detailed and presumably original observation concerning tidewater or lowland as opposed to piedmont, of fossils in the modern sense of former living organisms, which Hariot or Smith apparently did not comprehend:

> All the Low-Land, of South and North *Virginia*, is conjectured to have bene naturally gayned out of the Sea; for the Sea through his impetuous, and vast revolution (who knowes not), swayinge upon every Coast, in some places wyns, and in other places looseth ... banckes of Oysters and Scallopps, which ly unopened, and thick together, as if there had been their naturall Bed, before the Sea left them. .... Moreover, the Mould and sword of the earth is not 2. foot deep all along neare the Sea, and that which is, comes only by the grasse and leaves of Trees, and such rubbish, rotting upon yt in continuance of tyme; for in digging but a fathome or 2. we commonly find quick sand, againe under the crust of the Surface, we fyne not any stones, quarryes nor rocks (except nere the high-Land).[130]

Between 1626 and the organization of the Royal Society, little of geology and kindred subjects appears in print save scattered remarks in promotional pamphlets. In the 1630s the younger Tradescant seems to have brought back some mineral samples with his other curiosities from Virginia. But with the formation of the Royal Society, English natural philosophers began to prepare the way for more enlightened work in the American area. Dr. Martin Lister (1638–1712) in his *Historiae Animalium Angliae Tres Tractatus: Unus de Araneis, alter de Cochleis tum terrestribus tum fluviatilibus; tertius de Cochleis Marina . . .* (1678–1681) has systematic descriptions of fossils, among other things. And more important, he published in the *Philosophical Transactions* (XIII, no. 164 [1684], 739–746) a proposal for a geological map. He showed a considerable knowledge of living and fossil conchylia, though he was reluctant to identify the fossils with living animals. Actually he never accepted John Ray's opinion that "petrified shells" and "Stones figured like Plants" had ever been living specimens.

In 1676 Thomas Glover, formerly a chirurgeon in Virginia (from at least 1667) sent to the Royal Society a communication describing the province's topography, hinting at precious stones, and declaring iron ore was sufficient for iron works. He mentioned a stone which Sir Henry Chicheley had found in a river's bed and had placed in a ring. Earlier, in 1669–1672, John Lederer had described soils east of the Appalachians and declared that in them are "daily discoveries of fish-shells three fathoms deep in the earth ... these parts are supposed some Ages past to have lain under the sea." The Reverend Alexander Moray sent c. 1666–1668 to his kinsman Sir Robert Moray stones, minerals, and metals, though he had been disappointed in his collecting.[131]

The first John Clayton did much more. He wrote to the society of the many petrifying waters to be found in Virginia and commented on the vast quantities of oyster shells in the earth, so thick and extensive that they seemed to form a vein of rock. Others less petrified could be burned to make lime. He gives theories of their origin and descriptions of other shell banks, and of perfect teeth and ribs petrified, probably of a whale, all found in the hills beyond the falls of the James River. Some of these and similar huge bones had been shown him by Banister.[132]

Then Clayton turns to soils and the particular adaptability of certain types to crops such as tobacco and the problems of keeping soils fertile, a matter to be discussed further hereafter. His lost microscopes and chemical instruments he was sure would have assisted him in determining effects of soils on tobacco. Later in another letter he comments on the good marl to be found in various places among "some breakes of Hills" and of proper mixtures of lime of oyster shells with cold clay soils for agricultural purposes. In the latter paper he comments on the abundance of iron ore, clay, rocks at the fall line, and some black lead the Indians brought to Colonel Byrd, and he concludes this discussion with hearsay from Colonel Nicholas Spencer of "vitriolick or alluminous earths" on the banks of the Potomac.[133]

Clayton's friend John Banister declared he could say little of Virginia minerals "because the colonists seldom break the earth any further than with the plow or hoe." Yet he listed a number of fossil remains from far beneath the surface or showing in exposed rock. He seems to have found a kind of fossil clam, sea urchin spines, and either whale or mastodon skeletons far inland.[134] Twenty or thirty miles above the freshes of the James River he found petrified oysters, scallops, and bones with teeth (perhaps fossil sharks'), and he made some drawing of Miocene fossils.

William Byrd I, patron and friend of Clayton and Banister, spent a great deal of his time searching for minerals and fossils and shipping them to England for identification, probably the former because he was searching for useful iron, copper, or other metals.[135] His son-in-law Robert Beverley II in the History and Present State of Virginia has a chapter "Of the Earths, and Soil," in Book II. Though he relies in part on earlier writers such as Smith, this first native historian convinces his reader that he knows most of what he says from his own observations. From various sources pointed out in earlier chapters of this study one is aware that he lived much of his life with nature and that he accompanied the Spotswood expedition into the Valley of Virginia. Beverley finds three kinds of land—in lower tidewater, upper tidewater or piedmont, and heads of rivers. Each has its peculiar agricultural virtues or advantages, and concomitant disadvantages. The types of trees and shrubs thriving in each locality are named and the nature of the soils themselves explained. The upper piedmont, or heads-of-rivers, land he finds most varied, including rich lowland and meadows, even

878

swamps from which grow enormous trees, useful fuller's earth, clays, marls, coal for firing, stone for building or paving, and pebbles. He points out that lying travelers have written that there are no stones in all the country. Mineral earths, including iron and lead, are plentiful and various, and he mentions the iron ore and works at Falling Creek (of which more below) as they were before the 1622 massacre. He quotes Purchas and Whitaker and refers to Indian lore for stories of gold mines and crystal rock. And he keeps returning to the false tales of the flatness of all Virginia, referring to hills, ridges, mounts, and the actual mountains of the Piedmont and Appalachians. Five waterfalls and springs abound in the upcountry. In this topographical-geological survey Beverley indicates what the educated colonist of 1705 knew of these features of his province.[136]

Meanwhile the first Reverend Hugh Jones, sent in 1696 to succeed Banister, arrived in Maryland. In March 1697 he was shipping boxes including fossils and stones to such people as Petiver and Dr. John Woodward (1665–1728), F.R.S. In the four years allotted to him in the New World Jones shipped soils as well as shells and fossils and wrote of them to his old mentor Dr. Woodroffe (printed in extracts in the *Philosophical Transactions*). Petiver felt Jones' strongest quality was his knowledge of fossils,[137] though in geology and paleontology as in other areas Jones did no writing. His friends and contemporaries Vernon and Krieg in Maryland shipped a few fossils along with their other materials, but the source of the Maryland mandibles of a "Pastinaca marina" exhibited by Sloane to the society in 1697 remains unknown.[138]

William Byrd II shared with his parent a primarily practical curiosity about minerals and other matters of soil. He was especially interested in iron ore and the possibility of processing it, yet he was genuinely curious in a non-utilitarian sense too when he asked Sir Hans Sloane for samples of minerals he might compare with those around him for purposes of identification. The reply that he would have to send his specimens to the society where they could be examined by experts did not bother him. He made at least one general observation, "We have several mines and Minerals in this country, which for want of men of skil rest quietly in their beds."[139]

In the Carolinas, especially South Carolina, the turn-of-the-century group of naturalists contributed besides fauna and flora some shells and fossils. Joseph Lord was especially active in this collecting. In North Carolina, John Lawson's sweeping coverage in *A New Voyage to Carolina* had much to say of the fertility of the soil, and of free-stone and marble in certain areas. Not until 1710, however, did Lawson spell out what he hoped to do in this area. He planned to investigate "Fossils as Earths, shells, stones, Mettals, Minerals, stratas, paints, Phisicall Earths, where & when found & what subterranean matters are yet discovered & wt. methods has been heretofore taken to discover & work mines of all sorts." [140]

Mark Catesby included in his Carolina collecting at least shells and soil. He did something in paleontology, showing himself to be a diluvialist strongly influenced by Thomas Burnet's *Theory of the Earth* and John Woodward's *Essay Towards a Natural Theory of the Earth*. He refers to the fossils discovered at his niece's home in Virginia, where, when a seventy-foot well was dug, a "Bed of Glossopetrae, one of which was sent me," was found. He continues, "All Parts of Virginia abound in Fossill Shells of various Kinds, which in *stratum* lie imbedded a great Depth in the Earth, in the Banks of Rivers and other Places, among which are frequently found the Vertibras and other Bones of Sea Animals." He also recognized that the bones of the mammoth and elephant were similar, for he so commented on the teeth dug up at Stono in Carolina. This is believed to be the earliest identification of the mammoth and perhaps of a vertebrate fossil in America.

"Of the Soil of Carolina" in the *Natural History* includes most of Catesby's observations and even speculations concerning the geological character of the region. He distinguishes the coastal plain, several soil types by what grows best on them, and a genuine sense of the interrelationship of plants and soil. Considering his scant opportunity for observation, his account of the mountains is good though his sense of their geographical location is fuzzy.[141] Almost as much as his flora-fauna work, Catesby's geology is significant.

Though John Symmer of Virginia in 1736–1737 sent some stones and minerals to Sloane, the last really significant commentator on geology before 1764 is the already frequently mentioned Dr. Alexander Garden of Charleston in South Carolina. John Bartram in 1756 proposed to his southern friend an idea for a geological map quite similar to that planned by Dr. Martin Lister in 1684. Even before this, Garden had been collecting minerals with Bartram and Colden in the Catskills and also with Governor Glen on their inland expedition in 1755, and had shipped mineral specimens to several persons in England, including some from Indian country. From Nicholas Crisp of the Royal Society of Arts he received instructions on methods of assaying. Though circumstances prevented much more work in geology, he did send overseas clay samples from the New Windsor or Savannah Bluff; in turn the recipient sent him samples to use in comparisons.

Seismism, earthquake phenomena, might be included in a later section of this chapter, though it seems essentially a geological science. The southern colonies never felt the impact of the great "shakes" recorded in New England, at least as far as the records go. The extant descriptions are all of the eighteenth century, and even then they are frequently newspaper accounts of quakes in areas outside the region. The first located report of a southern colonial earthquake is that of poet-educator Richard Lewis of Maryland to the Royal Society of October 27, 1732, through Collinson. It is also one of the most detailed.

> On Tuesday 5th Sepr Last abt. Eleven in the morning an Earthquake was felt in Divers places in Maryland the most particular account I have heard of It was From Mr Chew. It shook his House for some time, & stop'd the Pendulum on his Clock. during its continuance a rumbling noise was heard in the air & many people who did not feel the shaking as well as those who did complained of a dizziness in their Heads, & sickness at their Stomachs, att the same time I have been Credibly informed It was felt in Pensilvania & New England but I have not heard weather It extended to North or South Carolina[142]

The 1737 Philadelphia earthquake aroused wide interest in Virginia, and the *Virginia Gazette* of 1738 in three January issues carried a series of articles in explanation of this natural phenomenon. There were several suggestions as to causes, with the conclusion that they were all uncertain.[143] Other newspapers carried similar essays and later notices of the widespread 1755 quake. The correspondence of Henry Laurens, for example, includes several letters from January 1756 on noting the effects of this 1755 so-called Lisbon earthquake, which were felt in tides as far away as the West Indies and Bermuda.[144] In March 1756 the *Maryland Gazette* printed "A Meditation upon Earthquakes, lately published in English" and on May 20 and 27 printed essays on the Lisbon earthquake.

Perhaps because the area never felt earthquakes directly as New England did, its scientists or news reporters or theologians never paid the attention to seismism or seismology as did the colonial Massachusetts men. As early as 1638 Josselyn had speculated concerning their origin, and Paul Dudley and Benjamin Colman studied and reported on them up through the tremors of 1727. Soon after the Lisbon earthquake of 1755, New England experienced a lesser one of its own, so terrifying that John Winthrop read a lecture at Harvard on earthquakes, and the aged Reverend Thomas Prince published a sermon on earthquakes as tokens of God's displeasure (with an appendix on electricity as a secondary cause). Winthrop added an appendix to his lecture when it was printed denying Prince's contention. So it went until the English Reverend John Michell in 1760 published his "Conjectures," the beginning of modern scientific seismology. There may be more in the southern colonies' gazettes (most of them as yet unindexed) than is now known to indicate the area's interest in the subject, but so far a fairly thorough examination of the newspapers shows little evidence of particular interest in the subject from North Carolina to Georgia.

The *Virginia Gazette*, which is well indexed, carries between 1737 and 1778 at least 150 separate notices of or essays on earthquakes in all parts of the world, including New England, Delaware, and Lisbon. It records some tremors in Virginia itself in the 1770s, and one sermon printed in 1756 was preached in Hanover County by the Presbyterian Samuel Davies on the 1755 earthquakes. The sermon, in the tradition of the Great Awakening, concludes with one of Davies' most frequently quoted and sung hymns, beginning "How great, how terrible that God, / Who shakes creation with his nod!" The rest is a versified depiction of a geological phenomenon mixed with doctrinal innate depravity.[145]

There is little if any evidence that the parsons of the established church showed more than the normal interest of rational men in natural phenomena. Dr. Archibald Spencer, Franklin's mentor in electricity but an Anglican cleric in Maryland and Virginia, wrote with approval to Bishop Sherlock in 1750 that he had heard the governor of one of the provinces say at his own table that he did not believe earthquakes to be threatenings from the Almighty, though Spencer seemed to agree that Sherlock had properly used this natural phenomenon to stir the consciences of hardened sinners. Spencer had the reputation among his Anglican brethren of being a deist, probably meaning a rationalist.[146]

METEOROLOGY, CLIMATOLOGY, AND ASTRONOMY

New World atmosphere, heat, and winds were commented upon by the same scientist scholars who wrote of other phases of the western environment. They also noted new positions of stars and phenomena of appearance of the sun and moon in certain seasons under peculiar conditions. Acosta especially went into some detail to prove by American conditions that the Ptolemaic was the correct view of the universe. Since he was widely read, his ideas remained influential with some men for many decades. But each new discovery or published detail of air, wind, temperature, and heavens chipped away at his theory.

Thomas Hariot betrayed an old fashioned idea of climate in his belief that the same plants grew in the same parallels of latitude everywhere in the world. George Percy's principal contribution to New World meteorological observation was concerned with the blazing star he saw following a storm. John Smith in his *Map of Virginia* describes the climate, insisting that the temperature of the country agreed well with English constitutions, though the summer was as hot as Spain and the winter as cold as France or

England. He notes the seasons and the cool breezes which make the summer heat bearable, along with frost, fog, winds, rain, and the great amount of thunder and lightning.[147] Thunderstorms, more frequent and violent than the Briton knew at home, were to be subjects for comment in themselves and later in their relation to electricity. Thomas Glover in 1673 described a wind storm he had endured in 1667.

As early as 1648 one Daniel Hoare [?] sent to someone at Oxford a clear yet complex drawing of two parhelia (sun dogs), bearing the explanation "This Apperition I see in Verginia at Blonte Pointe in James River one wensday the 14th of ffebEy: 1648/9 which Lasted about halfe an hower which ye [fixe?] is Cons[id]erd to bee in 37dr:30″ Lattitud." In 1667 another brief note arrived at Oxford describing "A Comet," which "apped ye 26 of Febr like unto a Javlin it reached d[own?] from ye Horizon to be 15 & 16 degrees. It appd about sun set & continued about 5 or 6 houres at a tyme. It appd not . . . above 6 or 7 dayes."[148] These two observers remain unknown, but in 1667 Thomas Ludwell, secretary for the Virginia colony, wrote to Lord Berkeley of Stratton, brother of the governor of Virginia, and to Lord Arlington of strange natural events in the colony. To Arlington he gave an account of a recent expedition beyond the mountains, where every morning a great fog rose in the air and remained until ten o'clock. This phenomenon, Ludwell suggested, might mean a great sea or river to the west. To Lord Berkeley Ludwell wrote of "a most prodigious Storm, of hail many of them as big as Turkey eggs which destroyed most of our young Mast and fruit," broke all the glass windows, and flooded all the creeks and bays. The damage, according to his story, was catastrophic.[149] And then in 1669 there were the "Directions" for Edward Digges; one direction concerned tides and their relation to the moon's age and a request that he keep a register of all changes of wind and weather by day and night, the direction from which the wind blew, and all snows and hurricanes. This was not a suggestion Digges could possibly have had time to follow.

The first significant southern colonial critical observer of these matters of climate was the Reverend John Clayton, who having lost his instruments on the voyage over, wrote the essay "Of the Aire," which is the most comprehensive published in the seventeenth century on Virginia climatology and meteorology, though it was done primarily from memory. He compares seasons, winds, and temperatures with the British climate, and observes the effect on the sick of different temperatures in rooms. He presents in detail the fearful qualities of thunder and lightning and one personal anecdote concerning the terror these phenomena induced and the fatal effect of lightning on one man who sat in a window smoking his pipe. Most interesting is his anticipation of Benjamin Franklin's fascination with the antics of lightning. He also gives several examples of mighty primeval oaks struck and even stripped of bark by lightning. He theorizes as to possible causes of both thunder and lightning, including saturated air and wind motion and meteors as possible influences. He classifies as "meteors" the gossamer cobwebs and flickering lights over marshes (thought now to be caused by methane combustion). It is a thoughtful and rational presentation of phenomena, with some logical speculation as to their origins.[150]

Meanwhile John Seller of London had in 1684 and 1685 published *An Almanack for the Provinces of Virginia and Maryland*.[151] The locally published *Virginia and Maryland Almanack* survives in a William Parks issue of 1732, and in 1733 Theophilus Grew began his Maryland almanacs. The 1732 issue was produced by John Warner, philomath, surveyor of King George County, Virginia. Warner had been associated with a 1729 Maryland almanac also published by Parks and continued to compose for Parks until about 1743. Throughout the period in most of the southern colonies, as soon as there was a printer, the almanac was likely to appear under local auspices. Before that there might be one from England, or in the Chesapeake provinces from Philadelphia. Usually considered as the poor or semiliterate man's reading matter, it was much more than that. From the humblest literate yeoman to George Washington, colonists read it, followed its directions, and wrote marginalia in it. Though it served many purposes, naturally its chief function was prognostication of the weather. The Virginia almanac, a fairly typical one, contained a calendar of sun risings and settings, a list of eclipses of the sun and moon for the year, risings and settings of seven stars, items concerning politics, agriculture, roads, medical cures, history, recipes, and lists of all sorts of things. It was the layman's meteorological guide. Since almanacs received hard use, and newspapers which might advertise new annual issues began late in the South, evidence on and of provincial almanacs is fragmentary, but enough of them survive to show that by the late seventeenth century the simplest farmer was probably conscious of and curious about comets, eclipses, and forecasts of the weather. Through these little annuals in the eighteenth century meteorology was everyman's science.

Perhaps the philomaths who composed the almanacs got some of their information, or suggestions for procedure, from local observers such as the Reverend John Clayton or the first Reverend Hugh Jones (who made observations on climate in his letters back home). The Maryland-Virginia historian Hugh Jones published in London in 1753 *The Panchrometer, or Universal Georgian Calendar. . . . Also the Reasons, Rules, and Uses of Octavo Computation.* The book is really a series of essays expounding the author's theory of a "natural calendar" in part based on Scripture. His plan for regularizing the year's length is certainly his own. In all, the hundred-page book indicates hard thinking and observation, but far too little sense of the practical; it is logical within its limits.[152]

The learned Richard Lewis who commented to Collinson two years later on an earthquake was in December 1730 informing his London friend of the aurora borealis and sun spots seen the previous October, phenomena never before observed "in this Quarter." His detailed description begins with the faint red in the sky at six at night and the developing colors as the night advanced. He supports his own observation with that of Dr. Samuel Chew of Maidstone, who had for some days observed the same thing at morning and evening.[153] And in 1752 visitor Dr. Richard Brooke described to the Royal Society an observation made in Maryland in May 1749 of three concentric circles around the sun.[154] By this time the golden age of the province's intellectual activity was in full swing, centering in Annapolis. The meteorological investigations represent one of its lesser manifestations, for other forms of expression and investigation are more impressive than the scientific.

A generation before Dr. Brooke, John Lawson in Carolina was noting and publishing, along with his natural history, various comments on climate and weather in his province. "As for the climate, we enjoy a very wholsome and serene Sky, and a pure and thin Air, the Sun seldom missing to give us his daily blessing" is a summary hardly disagreeing with William Byrd II's disparaging remarks about Carolinians, who were indolent because of plenty and a warm sun. Although this is in his *New Voyage* of 1709, in his 1710 resolves Lawson included his plan to plot the weather for each day and month in relation to growing things. He comments that in this year 1710 the winter has been as mild as an English May or June.[155]

Catesby's *Natural History* contains a section "Of the Air of Carolina," a careful though nonstatistical study. He considers hurricanes, the relation of climate to plants, and the moderating effects of water—especially the sea—which allow figs and oranges to grow near the coast but not inland. Despite some inconsistencies, the climatological observations are useful backgrounds for his more elaborate discussions of growing organisms.[156]

While Catesby was working and writing, others were also measuring and recording, perhaps in matters of weather more carefully than he. His friend William Byrd II wrote to Sloane in 1741 asking for a reflecting telescope, barometers, and thermometers, partly for the use of his son, who was beginning to study natural philosophy.[157] The second John Clayton before 1752 found space amid his botany to describe to Collinson what he calls the smoky weather as a presage of drought. Clayton concludes that it does not arise, as some colonists believe, from tar-pitch fires in forests or from Indians burning off land, but from natural causes of interaction of water and heat with profoundly calm weather, especially in swampy or moist wooded areas. The manuscript also contains a discussion of whirlwinds and horizontal lightning, Collinson notes in publishing extracts from the letter in the *Gentleman's Magazine* (June 1752, pp. 262–263), but the recipient publishes none of the details.[158]

Farther south others were recording the weather. Governor Henry Ellis, F.R.S., of Georgia, sent reports to the Royal Society about his province via his kinsman John Ellis. For accounts or recordings of extraordinary heat he went about the streets of Savannah or the forest trails with a thermometer dangling from a chain attached to his umbrella. He noted that the heat was far greater in summer than he had ever experienced in equatorial Africa and commented on the relation of weather character to plant growth.[159] Ellis observed scientific curiosities all over the world, and his Georgia communications to London were not among the least of his original contributions to knowledge.

Dr. Alexander Garden from his arrival in South Carolina suffered from the heat, especially since the year 1752 supposedly set new records of one hundred degrees in the shade and 126 degrees in the sun. In 1757–1759 he sent meteorological journals to Stephen Hales in Great Britain and exchanged weather data with Governor Ellis of Georgia. From Ellis he received a copy of a plan for assuaging the summer heat by underground cool pipes bringing air to the rooms of the house in a striking anticipation of the air-conditioner or the heat pump. In 1775 Garden was seriously ill, probably one reason why he read his friend William Gerard De Brahm's "Essay on the Balance and Counter Balance of the Atmosphere." Long after he returned to Britain, in 1784, he supplied much of the material for the "Climate of North America," a part of the supplement (1787) to his friend Thomas Pennant's *Arctic Zoology*. In a kindred area of interest Garden had as early as 1759 sent Henry Baker of the Royal Society an account of Halley's Comet as it appeared over Charleston in April and May of that year. There is no mention of instruments. Garden related the comet's declination and path.[160]

Two of Garden's Carolina contemporaries were at least equally as interested in weather phenomena as he was. The elder was Dr. John Lining (1708–1760), for a time Garden's partner in the practice of medicine. Lining searched for the causes of Carolina diseases and epidemics, undertook over a long period "statical experiments" on himself from 1740, and by 1742–1743 saw his observations on them published by the Royal Society (*Philosophical Transactions* of 1742–1743). These investigations were a curious mixture of medicine, meteorology, and other disciplines, and in the end they were disappointing. But along with his measurements of his own metabolic procedures, Lining began in April 1737, with the use of a barometer, a thermometer, and a hygroscope, to record weather conditions.

Though Lining was unable to correlate weather and disease or weather and health, his observations were made known through the Royal Society and appeared in Governor Glen's *A Description of South Carolina* (1761). They included a record of daily temperatures, barometric pressures, rainfall, and winds.[161]

Slightly younger than Lining was Dr. Lionel Chalmers (1715–1777), also at one time a professional partner of Lining. In some respects Chalmers' climatological-medical studies were an outgrowth of Lining's earlier work, though Chalmers was an able scientist in his own right. The latter began his meteorological observation and records in 1750, later published an *An Account of the Weather and Diseases of South Carolina*. His *Essay on Fevers* appeared in Charleston in 1767, in London in 1768, and in German at Riga in 1773, etc., and he published other essays in the *American Magazine* and the *Pennsylvania Chronicle*. His annual meteorological records of Charleston were presented to the Royal Society from time to time. He differed from Lining in his findings, in that he gave no weight to barometric readings or humidity. His weather observations were written in the traditional form of earlier general descriptions of the province. In exactness, he is compared unfavorably with Lining, but in other areas yet to be considered he was at least as highly respected as his elder contemporary.[162]

The scientific work of these and several other Charleston physicians between 1725 and 1775 is remarkable, especially considering the handicaps under which they labored. George Milligen-Johnston's *A Short Description of the Province of South-Carolina, with an Account of the Air, Weather, and Diseases of Charles-Town* (London, 1770), written in 1763, is another example of the union of meteorology and medicine in the southern colony. All this was a part of the long-postulated relationship of diseases and environment which was being undertaken by the first John Clayton in Virginia, Cadwallader Colden in New York, and William Douglas in New England.[163]

In Williamsburg as in Charleston there was in the mid-eighteenth century meteorological interest, perhaps not so overwhelmingly confined to medical men as in South Carolina. In his diary of 1751 and later John Blair, nephew of Commissary James Blair, recorded among other things his meteorological observations. In his more extensive journal-diary of 1752–1778 Landon Carter of Sabine Hall entered his observations on comets (which brought rain), the aurora borealis (which brought drought), sun dogs (which brought rain), night rainbows, and the Transit of Venus in 1769. Weather was a cause of illness, and it manifested its directions by various signs such as rainbows, lightning, hurricanes, and lunar phases. He observed storms, thaws, whirlwinds, heat flashes, and other meteorological phenomena scores of times, usually as an educated man who as a farmer was reluctant to give up popular beliefs about the significance of the unusual in the air or heavens. He sometimes gives scientific interpretations, as those from the Royal Soceity, as explanations, and his detail is precise and almost surely accurate.[164]

Dr. John Mitchell's versatile mind showed some interest, though not a major one, in climatology. In his late work *The Present State of Great Britain and North America* (1767) he set forth his idea that Englishmen should have settled in the lower Mississippi valley rather than on the Atlantic coast. He cites Catesby and Lining among others whose meteorological observations show that the south Atlantic area is unfit for Europeans. In a footnote he finds three factors producing the cold of North America. It is evident that his meteorology was shaped by his unhappy personal experience with his native Virginia climate and by his political conviction that the French must be driven from North America. Westward the course of empire was in his opinion only for the British.[165]

One of the most curious of late colonial Virginia governors was Francis Fauquier, F.R.S., friend of Jefferson and John Page and through them linking the scientific thought of the colonial era with that of the first national period. One of Fauquier's papers on a Virginia hailstorm appeared in the *Philosophical Transactions* (L, pt. 2 [1759], pp. 1746–1747). After the governor's death his son wrote on May 31, 1770, to Robert Carter requesting his father's microscope, camera obscura, and solar microscope, along with two fiddles and gold medals and a case of painting bottles.[166] Williamsburg and the college under such a governor must have been stimulating to the young red-haired musician from Albemarle who was throughout his life to measure and keep record of the meteorology (including temperature and humidity) of his places of residence.

Leading to more ambitious and comprehensive meteorological observations in the young republic were Fauquier's two young friends and their friends. John Page, poet and wealthy planter of Gloucester County, was interested in all phases of the world he lived in. Over many years he kept weather diaries and reported his observations to the American Philosophical Society in Philadelphia. He was one of the two southern colonials known to have shown a marked interest in the famous 1769 Transit of Venus. Though Page's observations were fairly good considering his lack of proper equipment (he used perspective glasses), he himself complained bitterly that the College of William and Mary did not use its very excellent apparatus to observe the Transit.[167] From the roof of the mansion Rosewell he spent hours and months watching the celestial bodies through a telescope.

Thomas Jefferson, in his garden and farm books, his personal correspondence, and his *Notes on the State of Virginia* displayed an enormous interest over a long lifetime in climate and meteorology. For years and years he kept daily and seasonal temperature readings at Williamsburg and Monticello which he compared with those of other persons in Virginia and the middle states. His chapter on "Climate" in the *Notes* considers rainfall, winds, growing seasons, temperatures, frosts, and other phenomena. He concluded from his own readings that the American climate was becoming more moderate. One historian of science calls him the pioneer and leader in early national meteorological investigation. His "Weather Memorandum Book" was kept from 1776 to 1820. He conducted with his friend James Madison, President of William and Mary (and later Bishop), a series of simultaneous weather observations at Williamsburg and Monticello during 1722–1775. He led American observers in informing Europeans, and he notified both his fellow countrymen and Europeans that he hoped for accurate and complete records of conditions for every state. His intimacy with the Williamsburg group of the 1760s had prepared him to become a significant meteorologist. Thus the southern colonial observer of his own climate made his way into the national era.[168]

CHEMISTRY AND ELECTRICITY

Every colonial pharmacist and physician had to be a chemist, and in the later decades of the colonial era physicians were among those who experimented with electricity. One doctor in Virginia in 1620, Mr. Russell, is also referred to as "Acmunist and Chimist," and his experiments with artificial wine suggest that the latter appellation was quite proper. Also clergy and planters and merchants were interested in these matters. And in the one southern institution of higher learning came the earliest American academic recognition of the physical sciences when William and Mary offered some instruction in chemistry, and the institution remained a pioneer through the eighteenth century in several physical sciences including electricity.[169] Actual professorships of chemistry came only well after 1763, and electricity remained largely in the hands of nonacademic investigators.

Chemistry throughout the colonial period was primarily in the hands of apothecaries. There is still some dispute as to whether early chemist-pharmacists might in some instances have been practicing physicians, but by the mid-eighteenth century it is clear that many "doctors," with or without M.D. degrees, also conducted apothecary shops. They dealt entirely with drugs and compounds, imported or made locally. Along with some interested laymen, they experimented with soil chemistry, or fertilizers, or with dyes and preservatives and similar useful products.[170] Dr. John Mitchell showed some interest in chemistry per se and as a necessary procedure in his profession, but he left very little to indicate any extensive experimentation. A few gentlemen over a period of years published essays in such journals as the *Virginia Gazette* which show a mild interest in and comprehension of matters chemical.[171]

Though activity in chemistry is hard to locate, work in electricity by the second third of the eighteenth century was being done from Boston to Charleston or Savannah, itinerants lectured on the subject and gave appropriate demonstrations, and the colonial newspapers carried interesting items concerning its origin, nature, perils or dangers, and practical uses, the last being in the colonial period primarily speculation. Dr. Archibald Spencer, onetime practicing physician and later Anglican clergyman who spent the last years of his life in Virginia and Maryland was, as mentioned above, the medium through whom electricity was introduced to Benjamin Franklin. Spencer was in Boston in 1743 giving lectures and demonstrations when Franklin came to know him and to become interested in the science, an interest which would of course become one of his major claims to fame. For Franklin soon went far beyond this early mentor.

But meanwhile from 1743 to 1751 Spencer, a Scot probably from Edinburgh, was lecturing along the Atlantic seaboard. In the latter year he was ordained—after he had tried unsuccessfully for the professorship of mathematics at William and Mary. On his Virginia tour he visited Dr. John Mitchell, whom he had probably met earlier in Philadelphia. At least one Virginia cleric of influence thought Spencer was a deist and so advised the Bishop of London, Dr. Edmund Gibson. But Gibson died, and Thomas Sherlock, who succeeded him, ordained Spencer, who was licensed for Virginia in 1749, arrived there in 1750, and went immediately on to Maryland.

In Annapolis Spencer was at first cordially received by such fellow Scots as Dr. Alexander Hamilton, who saw to it that the lecturer-parson was invited to the meetings of the Tuesday Club. Its minutes or "Records" and "History" indicate that Spencer soon rubbed the Maryland group the wrong way, a fact perhaps suggested by his club appellation "Dr. Rhubarb." Though he continued to be unpopular with a number of people, he was rector of All Hallows in Anne Arundel County in 1751, and in 1755 he was elected member of another famous group, the Ancient South River Club. He died in 1760.[172] Franklin himself purchased his electrical apparatus.

An abler scientist than Spencer, if one may judge from current accounts including Franklin's, was Ebenezer Kinnersley (1711–1778). English born and Philadelphia bred, he became a Baptist minister. He was a conservative during the Great Awakening, however, and his lack of enthusiasm for evangelism and his independent rationalism resulted in his unemployment—ecclesiastically— though his church continued to regard him as among its more distinguished members. About 1745 he became associated with Franklin in electrical experiments. The 1749 *Maryland Gazette* shows him on tour in that year as a lecturer on the new science. He also was a guest of the Tuesday Club, in his case on May 16 and June 13, 1749. His lectures appear to have been joint productions with Franklin, and Kinnersley became one of the leading scientific lecturers of colonial America. Franklin's first identification of lightning and electricity was in a letter to Kinnersley of April 1749 with a copy to Dr. John Mitchell. The experiments drawn up by Franklin and delivered by Kinnersley are advertised in the *Maryland Gazette* at least three times in May 1749. Their reception was all the speaker-demonstrator could have wished for.

Kinnersley's lecture tours seem to have been confined to the Chesapeake Bay region, though the *South-Carolina Gazette* for May 28, 1750, gave a syllabus of them, probably taken from the *Gentleman's Magazine*. Kinnersley and Franklin both corresponded with Dr. Lining of Charleston concerning the South Carolinian's experiments. The *Maryland Gazette* and indirectly the *Virginia Gazette* (from lost issues quoted elsewhere) indicate that Kinnersley's lectures in the two provinces were a great success. Though later he had a remarkable and even distinguished career in Philadelphia, in this period in the South he was known for his writing and speaking on this favorite subject, for he was quoted in newspapers and studied carefully in his experiments by a few southern colonials who attempted to proceed from where he left off.[173]

The extant issues of the *Virginia Gazette* indicate that at least up to and during the Revolution colonists of that province were much interested in the subject popularized by Franklin and Kinnersley. In 1752, soon after the former's experiments had been widely publicized, the *Gazette* carried five essays relating to electricity. They were based on news from Paris and Bologna in two instances in October and November, and in three others from Europe in a December issue. The lightning-rod idea announced by Franklin in 1753 resulted in five essays from 1755 through 1772 on this subject. There were other articles on medical uses of electricity to cure paralysis, deafness, toothache, and other disorders or diseases. Only two essays in the *Virginia Gazette*, both by John Winthrop, attempted to explain the nature of electricity.[174]

Charleston, the southern colonies' one real city, was naturally a center of interest in electricity. The *South-Carolina Gazette* from at least as early as October 31, 1748, carried advertisement of experiments and lectures on the subject by Samuel Dömjén, one of Franklin's students, who notified the public that he would appear on Wednesday and Friday weekly at Blythe's Tavern and would give private demonstrations upon request. Dömjén had traveled through Maryland, Virginia, and the Carolinas on the way to Charleston, probably lecturing all the way. In 1753 Dr. Lining's own kite experiment repeated Franklin's and was described in the *Gentleman's Magazine* for September and in the *South-Carolina Gazette* of July 30. Lining's reply to a question regarding the cause of death of a scientist who was examining his apparatus during a thunderstorm was published in the *Philosophical Transactions* of the Royal Society (XLVIII, pt. 2 [1754], 757). More of the physician's work is discussed in the *Gazette* of July 31, 1755. Lining corresponded with Franklin and carried on his work in this area almost up to his death in 1760.[175]

South Carolinians continued their interest in electricity. Even Pennsylvanian Lewis Evans, to be considered later here as a cartographer, bought an apparatus and gave a course of lectures on natural science and electricity all the way south to Charleston. In the *South-Carolina Gazette*, essays and advertisements of lectures on electricity appeared in 1760, 1765, and 1767.

In 1775 Dr. Garden was showing a marked interest in at least one form of electricity, appropriately that related to a living organism, the electric eel. Garden gave the most detailed description of the creature in his time, published in the *Philosophical Transactions* (LXV [1775], 102–110) in the form of a letter to John Ellis.[176]

Long after he had left Virginia, Dr. John Mitchell published in the *Philosophical Transactions* (LI, pt. 1 [1759], 390–393) "A Letter . . . Concerning the Force of Electrical Cohesion," perhaps in part the result of his contact ten years earlier with Spencer and Franklin in Philadelphia and in Virginia. But in this essay he dealt with experiments of Robert Symmer, a fellow member of the Royal Society, with which he had assisted. Robert Symmer was a brother of Dr. John Symmer, whom Mitchell had known in Virginia. Mitchell also read before the Royal Society Franklin's 1749 "The Sameness of Lightning and Electricity" and is said to have had the audacity or malice to write the author that it was "laughed at by the connoisseurs."[177] Franklin did not charge his friend Mitchell with either audacity or impudence for this intelligence.

Thus southern colonists made a few contributions to the new science of electricity, and the frequency with which they printed essays on the subject drawn from reports from various parts of Europe and America indicate their very considerable interest in this anticipation of a new day in science and technology. In both chemistry and electricity the trend, notable in Benjamin Franklin, was as in other areas toward the utilitarian. Directed conduction of lightning might prevent fires and deaths; proper application might procure new relief from pain and illness. So chemistry tended to become agricultural and medicinal. Yet these colonial Americans, auditors and spectators and lecturers and inventors of instruments, were to a very considerable extent merely *curious* in the sense of the Enlightenment, often enjoying these new wonders of nature for themselves alone.

GEOGRAPHY, SURVEYING, AND CARTOGRAPHY

The three areas of geography, surveying, and cartography are closely related and, like other scientific disciplines, overlap. These three constantly overlap. They were employed in promotion literature, in land acquisition, in determining boundaries. At its best, and at its most colorful, cartography approaches art. They all range from imaginative science, utilitarian or otherwise, to almost pure technology. They were practiced or studied or produced in every southern province. They were important tools and areas of investigation to every British empire builder.

Geography, or the study of it along with other things, had resulted in the discovery of the New World. Once the hemisphere was known, Spanish investigators already mentioned such as Oviedo and Acosta depicted and explained the significance of its geography as they knew it. Since much of the interior and portions of the east and west coastlines remained unexplored until the eighteenth century, geographical descriptions, charts, and maps were hazy, often inaccurate, often mythical. The share the southern British colonial had in geographical discovery and description has already been suggested in Chapter I and elsewhere. His contributions to American cartography began at Roanoke Island and continue steadily to the threshold of the Revolution. Some are mere sketches or hasty drawings; others represent perhaps the most skilled workmanship of the colonial period. In order to know where they were and what they possessed the settlers had to survey their region and their individual tracts of land, for both economic and political reasons. Too little is known of the history of surveying, and even that little can only be touched upon here, but one should always remember that the sciences of geography and cartography were dependent upon it. And as William P. Cumming reminds us in *The Southeast in Early Maps*, a chronological study of cartography is really a study of initial misconceptions and their gradual correction through three centuries.

ROANOKE AND JAMESTOWN

As early as 1582 instructions for a proposal of a Gilbert-Raleigh colony in America included information for a Thomas Bavin, who was to act as surveyor and painter as in the 1585–1588 period John White did.[178] The dials, compasses, paper and ink and black lead, among other things with which Bavin was to supply himself, were surely much the same as those White actually carried, though some of them and additional instruments or tools may have been in Hariot's equipment, for the two prepared the map in cooperation. The surveyor-cartographer White was to make "cardes" [maps] of four sheets of paper royal with appropriate "signs" thereon as he went about the unknown region attended by men who carried the writing material and instruments.[179] By 1585 the English (exact persons unknown) had made a sketch map of Virginia, the earliest English map of North America known to have been based on direct observation. It shows Chesapeake Bay and the Roanoke Island area, and it may have been based on White-Hariot preliminary sketches. Hariot had sailed as scientific consultant and surveyor (in the general sense) of everything he saw, but he was also a most useful adviser if not partner in White's mapmaking. White's first definitely identified map is the detailed 1585 drawing of eastern North America from Cape Fear to Chesapeake Bay, the major contemporary configuration of the coastline in the late seventeenth century, and the source for names of places and locations of villages.[180] In 1585 White also mapped North America from Florida to Chesapeake Bay, this time employing information from John Dee's 1580 map, Spanish and French sources, and mere conjecture. DeBry's engraved map based on a now lost variant of the first 1585 representation of the area has names and spellings of doubtful validity. Quinn conjectures that alterations (in the form of additional inlets) may have come after White revisited the region in 1587.[181] As William P. Cumming has demonstrated so beautifully and carefully, there were actually, at least for the southeast below the second Virginia, eighteen maps drawn by French, Spanish, and English surveyor-cartographers before 1600, and between 1600 and 1607 a number of non-English maps before the first British settlements in the region were founded. Among them were the Mercator-Hondius map of 1606, one of the most beautiful ever made. Most of them use the White 1590 work along with other early charts.

But maps presenting large areas were not all White left. Intriguing are his watercolor sketch of the camp of the Englishmen on St. John's Island in 1585 and the beautiful diagram-drawing of the fort on the same island. Among the engravings in deBry's *America* are "The Englishmen's Arrival in Virginia," a topographical sketch, and "The Town of Secota." The colors of the two 1585 maps in watercolor bring out contrasts between sea and shore, concepts of natural history, and something of the English heraldry which was to appear in later colonial maps. With the White-Hariot drawings and paintings, the colonial southern tradition of interesting and significant cartography, based on generally sound principles of geography and precise surveying (at least in spots) was off to an auspicious start. The colonial mapmaker or his European contemporary never got entirely away from these qualities in depicting the North American coastline.[182]

Maps from the first full generation at Jamestown are equally distinguished and certainly as influential in later North American cartography, though one misses the glowing colors of John White. What is perhaps the earliest "draughte of Virginia" is a multicolored (in green, red, and brown inks) quite interesting drawing of the area around Jamestown, including the Chesapeake, Hampton Roads, the James and York and Pamunkey rivers and branches thereof, the English town and a number of Indian villages. The extant "copy" of 1608 is believed to be from the original enclosed in June 1607 by "Robert Tindall, Gunner, to Prince Henry," the heir apparent.[183] Though topographical details and even names for many places are lacking, the coastal contours are in general quite accurate, especially in view of the short space of time in which Tindall, later a ship's captain and surely at this time knowledgeable in navigation, had in which to explore rivers and bays and inlets. The so-called Zuñiga map, discovered in the Spanish archives by Alexander Brown, presumably is a copy of a sketch sent by Smith from Jamestown in 1608. Crudely drawn, probably because Smith like Tindall had had little time for exploration, it contains despite distortions much useful information, including a dotted line showing Smith's captivity trail December–January 1607/1608, and a number of annotations worth careful examination.[184]

As noted in Chapter I, Captain John Smith's 1612 *A Map of Virginia* is a valuable historical and promotional account. Perhaps its most important feature, however, is the engraved map itself, to today's reader the most familiar of all examples of seventeenth-century Virginia cartography. It was also the greatest influence on early map making. "Virginia Discovered and Discribed by Captayn John Smith Graven by William Hole" was made according to the instructions issued in 1606 by the London Council for Virginia to discover whether the James River rose out of mountains or lakes. Smith had begun exploration of the whole Chesapeake Bay area in June 1608 and concluded it in September. He then sent a draft of the map to London with an accompanying letter. This was probably the original draft for the first printing of *A Map of Virginia*, and it was probably the same drawing he sent a copy of to Henry Hudson for use on the latter's third voyage. Then Smith continued his explorations. He and not Tindall appears to have given the names of capes and rivers and islands which have survived.

The first edition of *A Map of Virginia* appeared without the map, which had been published previously some time in 1612. Oriented west, 16″ x 12½″, with a scale of leagues and half leagues of 15 to 68 mm., it gives latitude from 36° to 41° north. The four major rivers are named Powhatan, Pamunk, Tappahanock, and Patomeck, respectively. Two illustrations show Powhatan's home (interior) on the upper left, and on the right margin a large Indian with a bow, features of almost every copy of the first engraving. The map appears not only in Smith's 1612 *Map of Virginia* but in his 1624 *Generall Historie* and in the 1625 Purchas *His Pilgrimes*, with some changes in succeeding issues, as additions of Smith's arms, new place names, all together in eleven states. Its importance can scarcely be overemphasized.[185]

Smith's map distinguishes coastal plain and piedmont as Hariot had done in Carolina and it shows landfalls mariners might recognize. It assumes that Virginia is no island, and it indicates a great deal of topographical detail, together with hundreds of names of places and native tribes as well as the few English settlements and many other markings. The geological and natural-history data which appeared in the printed text could be fitted into the map. Its location of Indian tribes is our sole source for this sort of information for the period. All the intricate features of the coast are fully developed. Anglo-American geography was established.

THE MIDDLE AND LATER SEVENTEENTH CENTURY

Although there are a number of maps including Virginia before the establishment of Maryland, no one of them is known to have been drawn by a colonist or explorer or based on observation after Captain Smith. Smith's 1612 engraving had of course included much of what was to be the other Chesapeake colony, ten of the little houses representing Indian towns falling within the limits of Maryland. Trees, probably intended to indicate size and character of forest growth, also show some fifty-eight localities or varieties of woodland.

The first map probably based on fresh observations of the new province of Maryland appeared in *A Relation of Maryland* (London, 1635) and was labeled "Noua Terrae-Mariae tabula." The cartographer appears to have used Smith, if at all, purely from memory, though his map has some names and features in common with the 1612 engraving and its derivatives. But there are many changes and additions.[186] In the next few years to mid-century, other Virginia-Maryland maps appeared, usually and perhaps always derived from Smith and earlier continental European engravings. In 1651 appeared a curious item perhaps drawn by a woman, Virginia Ferrar of Little Gidding, whose family had been connected with Virginia since 1619 or 1620 but who had as far as is known never visited the New World. Some sources give her father, John Ferrar, as compiler. Entitled "Old Virginia and New," the chart is a combination of fact and fiction covering an area from Cape Fear to Cape Cod, vaguely following deBry and Smith and showing the China Sea just west of the Blue

Ridge. The collection of data came in fact from persons who had visited the region, and the map (in five states) was published with a promotion pamphlet, "Virginia . . . Richly Valued: More especially the Southern Parts."[187]

Perhaps drawn from notes made in America is the vellum manuscript map by Nicholas Comberford, "The South Part of Virginia Now the North Part of Carolina," drawn in 1657 with the latter part of the title in a later hand. The territory depicted extends from Cape Henry to Cape Fear (the present Cape Lookout) and shows the inland features for a short distance. It differs in many ways from preceding maps, for it shows English names which survive in present-day nomenclature. Topography is more accurate and more detailed. The survey for it was probably made during a 1656 expedition. Unfortunately it was never published. Though it was not drawn by a colonial (Comberford was a well-known London mapmaker), it was surely based on new materials and perhaps on an American-drawn rough draft.

The next Carolina cartograph, also still in manuscript, was drawn in 1662 by a colonial American, William Hilton (a New England explorer who later wrote a promotion-discovery pamphlet) and his fellow townsman, Nicholas Shapley. It is a rough outline sketch on paper of the exploration of the Cape Fear region, and appears to be a copy entirely in John Locke's hand from an original now lost. In 1666 Horne's *A Brief Description of the Province of Carolina on the Coasts of Floreda . . .* (London) contained as frontispiece "a most accurate Map of the Whole Province." Probably based on Shapley's 1662 outlines, much new information perhaps from Horne's later voyage has been added. It may have been the work of Horne himself. There are also 1670 and 1671 charts of coastal areas or the Ashley River section of Carolina of some historical interest but not special importance, though the 1671 Ashley-Cooper rivers map is beautifully drawn and apparently was used for one or more engravings.[188]

In the Chesapeake Bay area there were interesting maps in 1666 and 1670 and 1672. George Alsop's rollicking promotion-description, *A Character of the Province of Maryland* (London, 1666), discussed in Chapter I, contains a map apparently prepared by this colonial who had returned to England. It is said to have been based on "experimental knowledge of the country, and not from [an] imaginary superstition." It does not correspond with either the Smith or the 1635 *Relation of Maryland* map. Carelessly done with resultant distortions, it includes new views of Indian costume and hairdress and various wild animals. Mountains and rivers are out of proportion, but many Maryland streams are given their modern names for the first time.

The exploration-route map appearing in *The Discoveries of John Lederer . . . 1669 . . . 1670* (London, 1672) covers the whole territory traversed by Lederer in his three expeditions in Virginia and North Carolina. Its new information on a cartographically barren region was quickly adopted by Ogilby and others. It seems likely that the learned German physician drew at least the rough draft himself at the time or immediately after his journeys.

Last of the three great maps of Virginia to appear in the seventeenth century is Augustine Herrman's *Virginia and Maryland. As it is Planted and Inhabited this present year 1670. Surveyed and Exactly Drawne by the Only Labour and Endeavor of Augustin Herrman Bohemensis. W. Faithorne Sculpt.*, published in London in 1673. This map engraved in four great sheets has been reproduced in full facsimile from the John Carter Brown copy, but it is so valuable and rare that the Library of Congress had no copy until it recently arranged an exchange with the Bibliothèque Nationale of Paris. There is no change from Smith in the essential topography of Virginia, but English names have supplanted the old Indian ones, and the spread of plantations along the banks of the Chesapeake and the great rivers has produced hundreds of names and locations of these groups and of numerous Virginia counties which had come into existence. It extends a short distance into Carolina. Beautifully drawn and engraved, it is the result of "probably the best surveying in the colonies during the seventeenth century," though as Cumming points out it is not superior in scope and detail to the slightly later map by Surveyor General Mathews of South Carolina. With deBry's of 1590 and Smith's of 1608–1612, this is one of the most influential maps upon the cartography of Virginia.[189]

In 1675–1676 appeared John Speed's *Theatre of the Empire of Great Britain* (London) containing verbal descriptions and maps of various colonies. Though apparently none of the cartography is directly the work of colonists, the sometimes exquisitely drawn and colored maps published during Bacon's Rebellion are valuable as both works of art and records based directly on colonial observations. In 1675 an addendum to Speed's *Theatre* contained (opposite page 250) a small map of Carolina which largely follows Ogilby's empire map and Lederer. In 1676 in another addendum the *Theatre* contained a map with "A New Description of Carolina" based largely on the Lederer work. And in the 1676 *Theatre* proper appears "A Map of Virginia and Maryland," perhaps the handsomest of the lot, on the versos of pages 43 and 44. This engraving shows indebtedness to Herrman and to Smith. The recent full-color facsimile is a thing of real beauty and cartographic interest.

There are literally dozens of other maps, printed and manuscript, still in existence for the remainder of the seventeenth century and listed by Cumming, Swem, and Mathews for the Carolinas, Virginia, and Maryland respectively. Their sources go back to Spanish charts and come up to sketches such as Lederer's (before it was printed). During the last two decades of the century the best map by a colonial is "A Plat of the Province of Carolina in North America. The South part actually Surveyed by Mr. Maurice Mathews," a colored manuscript reposing in the British Museum. A derivative of Mathews', the 1711 Crisp map, forms with Herrman's a cartographical survey from Maryland to Florida unrivaled by any of the middle and northern colonies. Mathews' work is almost blank for the interior of the country, but it shows the correct directions of river flow and the location of the Appalachians and of roads about Charleston and even "Savana Towne and fort."[190]

During the course of the century travelers and settlers' reports and promotion pamphlets had supplied a great amount of geographical and topographical detail which the cartographers, especially those compiling from multiple secondary sources, had been able to incorporate into their drawings. Thomas Glover of Virginia (noted above in other chapters), a chirurgeon, is an example of one who supplied to the Royal Society much geographical data, not all accurate. John Clayton's essay "Of Water" began with a precise description of the location of the colony of Virginia between Cape Henry and Cape Charles, and of Chesapeake Bay and the great rivers emptying into it. And one recalls that he supplied the Royal Society with a copy of the journal of the Batts-Wood-Fallam expedition beyond the mountains in 1688 and what they thought they saw. The journal excited great speculation as to the geography of the interior of North America. Then the first Hugh Jones of Maryland in 1698/9 sent a general and fairly accurate description of that province. More significant is the reconnaissance survey of both Carolinas in 1700–1709 incorporated into *A New Voyage to Carolina* by Lawson. Here is the work of a professional surveyor-engineer who drew plans for Bath and New Bern and for de Graffenreid's Swiss colony as late as 1710. The 1700–1701 journal incorporated into *A New Voyage* was in itself of great use to geographers, locating rivers, Indian tribes and trails and trading paths, swamps, pine forests, and barrens. He follows the diurnal record with a formal description, geographical and topographical, of the coastline—harbors, inlets, bays, latitude, and again rivers and creeks.[191] Then by 1710 the southern colonists had explored, surveyed, and recorded matters of latitude, coastal contours, bodies of water, settlements, even shires and counties all along the shore, and in general they knew the southwest-northeast direction of the Appalachians and had some solid knowledge of certain features of the land beyond the mountains. They had prepared the way for the development of knowledge of geography and of the science-art of cartography. The misconceptions incorporated into their surveys and maps and descriptions would gradually be chipped away as men trained in more recent techniques in surveying and map making and observation took over the continuing quest for knowledge of the area.

THE EARLY EIGHTEENTH CENTURY

Though engraved or printed maps usually had to be published after completion in England, the southern colonist did a great deal of surveying and drawing. Some of what he did remained in manuscript in London or in the colonies. The Lords of Trade and the Plantation frequently requested charts or maps of coastlines, harbors, or specific areas, and the results received from the Chesapeake colonies and the Carolinas in many instances still repose in the British Museum or the Public Record Office or among the personal papers of some official. Typical of the early published plans of localities is Edward Crisp's *A Plan of Charles Town* engraved by James Akin in London in 1704. One never published for fairly obvious reasons is "Mr. Robert Beverley's Acct of Lamhatty," a twelve by ten-and-half inch map of 1707. The drawing traces the journey made by a Creek Indian who had escaped from the Shawnees in the Virginia Blue Ridge mountains. It is interesting in locating Indian villages which Lamhatty named and marked on the map. Then there is a 1708 manuscript plan of the town of Low Wickham in North Carolina reposing in the archives of that state.[192]

The best-known maps of the period are those printed in atlases and geographical or imperial histories, as the many maps of H. Moll and R. Morden and their fellow cartographers in London. But perhaps the most accurate and potentially useful of the engraved maps made in the first quarter of the eighteenth century is that of Edward Crisp already mentioned, the 1711 *A Compleat Description of Carolina . . .*, based in part on Mathews and Thomas Nairne and taking up the southern coast where Herrman's map leaves off, as mentioned above, in such an accurate plotting of coast and inland that the two together were to be sources for many maps for the next thirty years. An equally popular engraving, unfortunately far less accurate, compiled by Johann B. Homann in 1714, is "Virginia Marylandia et Carolina in America Septentrionali Britannorum . . . Norumbergae," first appearing in Homann's *Atlas Novus* of that year and in later atlases throughout the century. In Sir William Keith's *History of the British Plantations in America* appeared a new map of 1738 dedicated to Lord Fairfax. It is most original in respect to northern Virginia and appears to have been drawn just as the first settlers moved into the Valley.

Garrulus Carolinensis.
The Chatterer.

Frutex Corni folijs &c.

Colonial Williamsburg Photograph

"The Chatterer," engraving by Mark Catesby for his *Natural History of Carolina . . .*

South Carolina Medical Association

Dr. Lionel Chalmers, eighteenth-century Charleston physician and scientific writer. A portrait by Jeremiah Theus, from Joseph I. Waring, *History of Medicine in South Carolina,* 1964

Fairfax Harrison believes it is the work of Jacob Stover, early Valley "land grabber," or was drawn from notes submitted by Stover. It could well represent a manuscript map now missing from the Public Record Office.[193]

Baron de, or von, Graffenreid, Swiss partner of John Lawson and acquaintance of the Byrd family in Virginia, left behind him three manuscript maps of North Carolina dated 1716 which were in this century published by the German-American Historical Society in Philadelphia and edited by A. B. Faust. Though Graffenreid seems to have used as outline an earlier printed map, he added new names of islands and inlets along the coast in MS. A. In the B and C manuscripts appear "plans" of the Neuse and Trent rivers and houses and towns. Eccentric Sir Robert Montgomery's "Plan representing the Form of Setling the Districts, or County Divisions in the Margravate of Azilia" (1717), mentioned in Chapter II and elsewhere, is a map of the abortive utopia planned for what became Georgia territory. It is included in Montgomery's printed *A Discourse Concerning the design'd Establishment of a New Colony to the South of Carolina, In the Most delightful Country of the Universe* (London, 1717). The next year the new edition of Lawson, now entitled *A History of Carolina*, carried a new and entirely different map from that in earlier editions of his work. It shows Lederer's Lake, Savanna, and Desert, actually a retrospective map.[194]

In 1721 there were at least four manuscript sketches or plans of South Carolina and even present-day Georgia cities, rivers, and harbors, including one of the fort at Charleston, of which more below. The Public Record Office in London contains many such plats or drawings of the next few years, evidently ordered from colonial officials by the Board of Trade. Among them are plans of the boundary line of Virginia-North Carolina run in the year 1728, the history of which is told so entertainingly in Byrd's double masterpiece. There are also surveys of Byrd's North Carolina land made by his friend Mayo in 1733, Byrd's first map of Richmond dated 1737, and a plan of the Potomac River of the same year. Then there is William Mayo's map of the Northern Neck of Virginia surveyed for the commissioners (including Byrd) for the settlement of Lord Fairfax's boundaries in 1737.

In 1735 a captain in the merchant service between London and Virginia drew the first large map of the Chesapeake area since Herrman's. This was Walter Hoxton, who dedicated it to the London merchants trading in Virginia and Maryland. The maker states that his original section is distinguished by a shading within the line from the outer part of the coast. The rest is based on an old map. The author's evidence indicates that he personally explored from Cape Henry to Newport News and Back River in Virginia on to the fall line of the Potomac. Hoxton is a

Maryland name, and one may be fairly sure that this cartographer and his descendants owned land there. That is, this seems to be a colonist-drawn map.

In 1738 there were perhaps two colonially produced maps of Virginia, and in 1742 a survey of the Rapidan River. In 1745 three English-printed cartographs of the two Chesapeake colonies appeared in editions of *The English Pilot*, but the year 1747 marks the beginning of the final and greatest period of Virginia-Maryland pre-Revolutionary cartography.[195]

Meanwhile in the Carolinas a number of maps of significant use to contemporaries were drawn but never published. Three of these of 1724 depict the territory of the southeastern Indians, and all three are deer-skin-shaped, with the originals in the Public Record Office or the British Museum. Then there is a manuscript plat of "Charles Town" (as it grew it was diagrammed frequently) about 1725, and a pencil-and-ink drawing of the Cherokee Traders' Path from Charleston to the Congaree in 1730. Catesby in his *Natural History* (1731) gives a map of Carolina, Florida, and the Bahamas, which makes use of a 1722 predecessor.[196] Then begin the Georgia charts, the first drawn in Great Britain from South Carolina sources, as the map in *Some Account of the Designs of the Trustees for Establishing the Colony of Georgia in America* (London, 1732). Within the year there were others. South Carolina plans of cities, such as Beaufort in 1733, continued. There is also the great 1733 Henry Popple map of the British Empire in North America, based on many earlier sources and not evidencing the skill of Mitchell or Evans (see below), but yet a map of great influence on subsequent charts of the region. Far more interesting, especially because of its colonial origin, is the chart of North Carolina by Edward Moseley of that province, dedicated to Governor Johnston, and printed in London in 1733. This rare map gives a great many names of settlers and their locations along the sounds and rivers. It is the first known approach in North Carolina cartography to the detailed survey made by Mathews in the Charleston area fifty years earlier, or by Herrman in Virginia and Maryland earlier still. Moseley attempts to portray the interior, but the paucity of information is still obvious. Technically this should have been a fairly accurate map, for Moseley had been surveyor general for the colony as early as 1710 and had been a commissioner of the Dividing Line with William Byrd II in 1728/9. There are suggestions that he did several other maps, though they have not been located.[197] Almost as interesting is the copperplate for an engraving of "Virginia Pars Carolinae Pars" (the dividing line) ordered by Byrd in 1737 for his proposed publication of the "History of the Dividing Line" in 1738. The plate remains in the Bodleian Library (Rawlinson, Copperplate No. 29), one of the definite proofs that Byrd intended publication of his manuscript. Through 1746 the manuscript and printed maps continued, but for the Carolinas there was little of real significance. Most were designed to satisfy the curiosity of the European, a few to meet the demands of the Board of Trade, and very few indeed to meet the needs of colonists or explorers or traders.

THE LATER EIGHTEENTH CENTURY TO 1764

The two and a half decades from 1747 to 1770 were for southern colonial cartography most significant and even distinguished, for the settlers themselves produced in this country or during visits to London several of the most useful and detailed maps so far to appear on America. Most of them came from professional surveyors or engineers, such as Joshua Fry and Peter Jefferson and William Gerard De Brahm, and others from soldiers and other explorers. The influence of these maps, or of some of them, was to affect American political history well into the nineteenth century, and most of them were to be used in one way or another by later cartographers.

Chronologically they may be said to begin with the manuscript survey maps of 1747 made by Peter Jefferson and Robert Brooke, of the Northern Neck of Virginia. With two other surveyors they had been authorized to recheck the survey of 1736–1737, and their work was approved by William Fairfax, Joshua Fry, William Beverley, and two other officials.[198] Cumming describes 1749 manuscripts of "A Plan of the Line between Virginia and North Carolina, from Peters Creek to Steep Rock Creek, ran in the Year of our Lord 1749" by Joshua Fry, Peter Jefferson, and two others, which represents ninety miles of survey used in the later Fry-Jefferson map and adding to the 1728 survey. A manuscript (cloth) of the same year joins the previously surveyed section to this one by six pieces pasted together.[199] Thus there is ample visual evidence that Joshua Fry, formerly William and Mary professor of mathematics, and his neighbor in Albemarle County, Peter Jefferson, had become Virginia's leading surveyors. Naturally they were selected as the "most proper and best qualified" persons to draw a map of the inhabited part of Virginia, a project which had been urged in the legislature for years. Colonels Fry and Jefferson may have completed their map by the summer of 1751 but its receipt was not acknowledged in England until March 1752. The first edition was probably struck off in 1753/1754. It was corrected and supplemented in a 1755 issue of four plates (in two states), and it appeared with a new imprint about 1761 and 1775. French versions were c. 1757, 1776 (in two states), c. 1793 (in two states), and another version of 1777. Derivates from it include the Mitchell map (to be discussed below), the Washington Journal Map, and a famous French map of North America.[200] This now extremely rare and historically and intrinsically valuable map is one of the major geographical compositions of colonial British North America.

Other historically eminent figures of the Chesapeake area also were in some way connected with maps, usually as drafters. George Washington, himself a surveyor remembered for his work for Lord Fairfax, may have drawn some of the early sketches of the western country which were bases for such charts as the 1754 *London Magazine* "Map of the Western Parts of the Colony of Virginia." Thomas Cresap of Maryland, well-known settler of western Maryland, did indeed draw in 1754 a map of the sources of the Potomac, the draft placed in the hands of Governor Sharpe in the early part of June of that year. In 1755 Lewis Evans, Welsh-born, already famed as a cartographer in his own colony, drew or completed *A General Map of the Middle British Colonies, in America* which included Virginia and Maryland. Printed in London to be sold there by Dodsley and in Philadelphia by the author, it was based largely on actual surveys, of a high order of workmanship, and the most ambitious project and performance of its kind undertaken in America up to that time. It was a significant event in the history of colonial graphic arts, especially since it was often sold in a fully colored state. Fry and Jefferson's map was the chief source for Virginia, as Hoxton's was for Maryland.[201] The Evans map was widely used throughout Europe for many years to illustrate the situation of the contending forces in the Revolution.

Also in 1755 was completed and published native Virginian Dr. John Mitchell's *A Map of the British and French Dominions in North America* (London) covering the coast from southern Labrador to Florida and Texas. Despite its considerable topographical detail drawn from such reliable sources as the Fry-Jefferson, Barnwell 1722 manuscript, and other regional charts, its aim was primarily political, showing the boundaries (as the English claimed them) of the various divisions of the country. The bibliographical history of this large and comprehensive engraving is as complex as its influence. It was used as the basic map in the framing of the 1783 treaty of peace between the new United States and Great Britain and in several later boundary disputes.[202]

In the Carolinas and Georgia of this period there was a most prolific cartographer, the aforementioned gifted engineer William Gerard De Brahm(1717–1799). He arrived with Salzburgers in Georgia in 1751, and in 1754 was a surveyor for the colony. Three years later he had completed surveys in South Carolina and Georgia which he published (in 1757) as *A Map of South Carolina and a Part of Georgia* (London). It went through several editions in itself and was the basis for other 1773 and 1775 maps and the 1780 edition (with more detail on western South Carolina). It had been based on surveys by the author himself and by his fellow surveyors Bull, Bryan, and Gascoigne. His plats or plans for cities and forts and other geographical units are well represented in illustrations for his recently printed *Report*. With De Brahm's work southern cartography definitely got away from the amateur or semiprofessional into the professional.[203] From 1755 to 1770, from the Carolinas through East Florida, he executed his engineering surveys and maps during a long and remarkable career, presumably the only one of its kind in the southern colonies. He returned to Europe some time in the 1760s, was back in the colonies briefly in 1775–1776, and then as a Loyalist left for England again. Back in Charleston in 1784, he tried to retrieve some family fortunes. Again in England in 1788–1789, he settled in Philadelphia in 1791, where he lived out the remainder of a long life. Dying in 1799, as a Quaker he was interred in the Friends Burying Ground.

Another soldier, for De Brahm was technically that at times, was Lieutenant Henry Timberlake of Virginia, whose description of the Cherokees from 1762 is discussed earlier. Accompanying his printed *Memoirs* (London, 1765) is "A Draught of the Cherokee Country. On the West Side of the Twenty four Mountains, commonly called Over the Hills." This well-drawn map shows the Tennessee River, Fort Loudoun, the abandoned Virginia fort, the chief Indian towns, and a list of the principal men of each town. Mountains, creeks, rivers, paths, and other features make it a valuable topographical chart of a small territory.[204] The last Virginia map of the period, published seven years after 1763, is by John Henry, father of the more famous Patrick. Henry in 1766 petitioned the legislature for assistance in having it engraved, giving several reasons why it was needed. Several times the Assembly rejected his proposal for help in surveying roads preparatory to final drafting. But the petitions of 1766, 1768, and 1769 indicated to the Virginia burgesses that it was a detailed map he had in mind and that he had as early as 1768 a large number of individual subscriptions but insufficient to warrant publication. Nevertheless it was engraved in London by Thomas Jeffreys and published in 1770 under the title *A New and Accurate Map of Virginia Wherein Most of the Counties Are Laid Down from Actual Surveys—with a Concise Account of the Number of Inhabitants, the Trade, Soil, and Produce of that Province*. Despite the ambitious plan and comprehensive gazetteer quality of Henry's work, it did not really challenge the Fry-Jefferson map as the definitive cartographic delineation of the province, though it has its useful and updated features.[205]

From Thomas Hariot to De Brahm and Henry, for almost two colonial centuries the cartographic representations of the Southeast from Maryland to Florida are impressive, according to the specialists more impressive than those done for any other part of British North America. They sprang from a combination of exploration by intellectual observers who recorded geographical and topographical features; of surveying by self-trained individuals of the George Washington and Peter Jefferson variety or by university mathematicians such as Joshua Fry and William Mayo or the engineer-genius De Brahm; and of fairly skillful draftsmanship by the colonials combined with more or less skilled and ingenious engravers in London. Many of the extant manuscript maps indicate considerable artistic and drafting skill in the color, figures, and coastal outlines.

Upon these as a basis were drawn the first great maps of the early national period: the 1786 outline of Virginia by Thomas Jefferson included in his *Notes*, inspired by the Fry-Jefferson map and enhanced by the author's own observations and genius; the 1807 *Map of Virginia* by Bishop James Madison; the 1778 Hutchins map to accompany Hutchins' *Topographical Description of Virginia, Pennsylvania, Maryland, and North Carolina*; and similar work for the more southerly states. Even the maps of the Lewis and Clark expedition to the Pacific, charts of segments or sections of the area and of the whole continent from the Mississippi to the west coast, the final map called "a major contribution to the geographic knowledge of Western North America," are but more recent examples of the combination of curiosity and observation and graphic ingenuity of the southern colonial explorer.[206] Perhaps this southern cartographic genius culminates in the great ocean charts of a son of the Huguenots, Matthew Fontaine Maury.

MEDICINE

As shown earlier and later in this book, medicine and various kinds of medical practitioners affected directly almost every element of life in the southern colonies. The practitioners were among the earliest naturalists, and for the last full century of the colonial period perhaps a majority of the students and collectors of fauna and flora were physicians. Mineralogy, meteorology, and electricity they studied for professional purposes and to satisfy their natural curiosity. They listened to the Indians and tried red man's remedies from native plants or his methods of surgery, and professionally they attempted to cope with diseases both in individual cases and in epidemics which they did not understand and often were unable even to identify.

As noted in Chapter III especially, those who practiced medicine were of many levels of training and economic and social standing. Some of those who prescribed for their friends and neighbors were not professionals, but planters such as John Custis and William Byrd II or clergymen such as John Banister or the first John Clayton. Those who were called "doctor" more often than not combined with a medical practice a career in agriculture or politics or even sometimes in law or military service.

Obviously, in a strange new world subject to local diseases for which he had no immunity and to intensified danger form Old World diseases he brought with him in a dormant state, the southern colonist was throughout the period in desperate need of medicine and of medical advice. In addition, the average colonist's life of relative isolation rendered it almost impossible for him to secure any professional advice or therapy available in the village centers or even in the rural area if the distance of the physician's domicile from his own abode was considerable. Thus except in certain infrequent situations for short periods no adequate medical service was available to most southern colonists.

It was not available for at least two other good reasons: the science of medicine itself had not in Europe advanced very far until the last half-century of the period, when the work at Leyden and Edinburgh began to make itself felt; and there were simply far too few men with the normal training of the period who were willing to venture into the unknown America. Those who did come tended to cluster in centers such as Annapolis and Williamsburg and Charleston, so much so that in the two smaller of these towns provincial governors wrote to Britain that no new or additional physicians could make a living in them. Governor William Gooch in the second quarter of the eighteenth century wrote that only one physician in Williamsburg was earning an adequate income. He was indeed the best trained man of his profession, but any or all the others were sorely needed in rural counties. Unless a physician was also an Indian trader—and a few were—he rarely would actually risk his life on the western frontier.

PHYSICIANS, SURGEONS, AND APOTHECARIES

Yet as early as Jamestown and perhaps as early as Roanoke Island there were practitioners of the medical arts among the southern settlers. In 1584–1585 in (anonymous) notes for Raleigh's voyage, there is this direction: "Then I would haue a phistien as well for the healthe of the souldier as to discouer the simpels of earbs plants trees roothes and stons." Ralph Lane speaks of "our Appotocaryes" and "our Physycyan" in 1585, but it is believed that no surgeons or apothecaries from Grenville's fleet remained over the winter in the New World. John White's narrative of the 1590 voyage to Virginia does mention the drowning at Roanoke of "Hance the Surgion."[207] And in Jamestown there were a number of apothecaries and physicians of various kinds.

The Seventeenth Century

The joint-stock Virginia Company of London first chartered in 1606 numbered among its members several prominent physicians, including Dr. Theodore Gulstone, Dr. Leonard Poe, Dr. Thomas Winston, and Dr. John Woodall, along with at least six others. Woodall was the author of *The Chirurgion's Mate* (1612), a popular book in seventeenth-century Virginia libraries. These men with the officials of the Company saw to it that the first group of settlers included surgeons or chirurgeons: Thomas Wotton, gentleman, and William Wilkinson. And "the first [additional] supply" included Dr. Walter Russell, gentleman, and two apothecaries, Thomas Feld (Field) and John Harford. Thus by 1608 the relatively small number of settlers had among them representatives of all the major branches of the medical arts—if these representatives lived long enough to be together.[208] Though throughout the seventeenth century and most of the next the duties of the three sorts of medical men overlapped, there are interesting distinctions in training and social status, as just suggested.

Though some of this matter has been touched upon in Chapter III, it seems best at this point to attempt to define or characterize the types of medical men who came to the southern colonies in the seventeenth and eighteenth centuries. Toward the end of the period, and in certain instances throughout the colonial era, many of these men had two or three different functions, or played two or three different parts. Highest in the social scale and best educated at least in formal fashion were the physicians. This elite group was organized in 1518 as the College of Physicians. Although it has been shown that they were often apprenticed at the beginning of their careers, they usually acquired university training and, increasingly as time went on, degrees. Whatever the training or degree, they were usually referred to as "doctor," though in the early years and in certain colonial localities not always so. They practiced largely among the upper classes (or upon their servants), but they were hardly general practitioners in today's sense—more nearly internists. Theoretically they would not work with their hands as did surgeons or engage in trade as did apothecaries.

Surgeons had been incorporated in 1461 in the British Company of Barber-Surgeons, but as has been pointed out by American historians, from Jamestown on the two trades or professions seem to have been entirely separated in the southern colonies and actually probably in all the colonies. Yet in these centuries surgeons rarely held university degrees but were trained by apprenticeship and hospital instruction. Hence to this day in Great Britain, and usually at that time in America, a surgeon was merely "mister." They were concerned with structural emergencies, skin diseases, and superficial growths, matters in some sense peripheral to the art of medicine. Though their services were required by persons of all social levels, their professional status was inferior to that of physician. Of the two first Jamestown surgeons, however, as noted above, one was listed socially as a gentleman and one somewhere below that social status. In these instances and others the qualifying "gentleman" after the surname may have meant just that in the British sense, that the men so designated came from families of the social status so suggested.

Apothecaries also lacked the professional and usually the social standing of physicians. They were trained by apprenticeship and sometimes in hospital wards, though their London Society as in the case of the surgeons provided some instruction. It was only a short step from compounding drugs to prescribing them, however, and as early as the middle sixteenth century they were becoming general practitioners for the masses. Not too far removed as modern parallels are the activities of military hospital corpsmen or the paramedics of civilian life. By 1617 they had separated from their affiliation with the Grocers Guild because they considered themselves professional men: thus the *Master, Wardens, and Society of the Art and Mystery of the Apothecaries of London*. Over the next half-century they waged war with the physicians, who in 1632 managed to get a law passed forbidding apothecaries from selling medicine without a prescription, but by 1665 the apothecaries were again encroaching on the practice of physicians. By the end of the seventeenth century the physicians had set up their own dispensaries for delivering medicine to the poor, in direct competition or rivalry with the apothecaries. One result was the famous poem of Dr. Samuel Garth called "The Dispensary," which went through two editions. Suits and countersuits, recriminations and disputes, marked the relationship between the two groups for another half-century, but by 1627 the Society of Apothecaries had offered training in botany and by 1753 added courses in materia medica.

In many of the southern libraries mentioned in Chapter IV were the *Pharmacopoeia Londoniensis* or the *Edinburgh Pharmacopoeia*, both published by the Royal College of Physicians, though in the case of one revised edition of the former the apothecaries were invited to assist in making it as free from errors as possible. The dispensatories, medical manuals sponsored largely by the apothecaries, were in most southern libraries of any size, including those of physicians and planters who fancied their knowledge of medicine was sufficient for them to treat family and servants and friends for many ailments. Between 1718 and 1736 John

Quincy's *A Complete English Dispensatory* went through ten editions, and John Wesley's *Primitive Physic* had a long life in many editions to the middle of the nineteenth century.

In the later eighteenth century in both the colonies and Great Britain, as the well-qualified apothecary engaged more and more in general practice, the chemist or druggist took over most of his old business. In the South Atlantic provinces, it is possible that the first Dr. George Gilmer of Williamsburg, who is called an apprentice-trained physician (though he went to Edinburgh University for some further training), was actually a well-qualified apothecary who knew he could handle a physician's practice and went back to school to legitimize his status. He continued to operate an apothecary shop for some years in the Virginia capital, as did his son and grandson, who were fully trained as physicians at Edinburgh. So other Maryland and South Carolina "doctors" as often as not operated apothecary shops or at least dispensatories.[209] There also came to exist at least in the future United States a group called surgeon-apothecaries, men closer to being old-fashioned general practitioners than anything else.

But to return to Jamestown. "Mr. Thomas Wotton our Chirurgion generall" evidently cared for the wounded and diseased among the first settlers, but he disappears from view by 1609. He was the gentleman. The second chirurgeon or surgeon was Will Wilkinson, concerning whom nothing more is known. But when the first supply of 120 settlers arrived in January 1608 it included Dr. Walter Russell, physician; Post Ginnat, chirurgeon; and two apothecaries. Russell, the first real physician of British America, almost immediately performed valuable service in his treatment of Captain Smith after the latter was poisoned by a stingray. Russell was also one of the authors of the accounts in *A Map of Virginia*, especially of this one concerning the treatment—a printed comment marking him as the first physician writing of medical treatment in the English New World colonies. Of the chirurgeon and two apothecaries nothing more is known.

Smith himself was capable of the field soldier's sort of medicine, and specified in his *Sea Grammar* the duties of a surgeon. At Jamestown he treated successfully a badly burned Indian,[210] but when he himself was badly burned by a gunpowder explosion, he preferred to return to England for treatment.

Many months after Smith's departure from America, Virginia's first officially designated governor, Lord de la Warr, arrived accompanied by Dr. Lawrence Bohun, doctor of physic, said to have been trained in the Netherlands. Appointed by the Virginia Company of London specifically for service in the colonies, Bohun among other things set up the first botanical garden in Virginia. The garden may have been inspired by the dire necessity for drugs, for letters back to London at this time pleaded that empty medicine chests must be replenished. Though Bohun left Virginia with the governor in 1611 when the latter was ill with scurvy, he returned to the colony or attempted to do so several years later, with some three hundred colonists. He also attempted to import fruit trees and seed and to use local American trees or their sap for medicinal purposes. He died bravely in a sea fight with the Spaniards in the West Indies probably as he was returning to Virginia from England in 1621. Councilor and optimistic supporter of the colony, he was certainly the most colorful and probably the most useful of the medical men under the Virginia Company's charter.[211] Here in the first generation was a physician-researcher who experimented with several things which might improve treatment or cure illness.

Bohun was probably a Leyden or Utrecht M.D. His successor, Dr. John Pott, was an M.A. of one of the English universities, a learned man in the ancient languages who was to pursue his professional and somewhat turbulent political career in the colony until his death about 1642. He had been appointed physician-general in 1621 and had in that year accompanied Governor Sir Francis Wyatt to Jamestown. He had been recommended as well trained in both chirurgery and physic; that is, he was thus early combining two of the once separate medical disciplines. Court records are full of his personal disagreements with other settlers and of his acquisition of lands, including a plantation on the site of the later Williamsburg. Richard Townshend, Pott's apprentice, later had a highly creditable career in medicine in the colony. Pott's apothecary is listed among those killed in the 1622 massacre.

There are records of Pott's skill in epidemical diseases and in curing individual ailments. (From his time on patients were hospitalized quite frequently in the homes of their physicians, though the first public hospital for the sick, Mount Malado, had been established near or in the new town of Henrico in 1611.) In 1628/1629 Pott was for a year acting governor of the colony. Later a ringleader in rebellion against Governor Harvey and on trial for murder and rustling other men's livestock, he seems to have escaped all punishment and probably died soon after he had seen his first colonial chief of state, Sir Francis Wyatt, restored to the governorship for 1639/1640 or 1641. Even when Harvey had him arrested and presumably convicted, that governor begged for Pott's life on the ground that no one else was skilled in epidemical diseases. This career merits further study.[212]

The apprentice Richard Townshend, who was supposed to have been trained under Pott technically merely as an apothecary, had to sue to get the instruction agreed upon. This was in 1626. By 1628 Townshend had been free of indenture for two years and was already a member of the House of Burgesses—while Pott was acting governor. Later a councilor and wealthy landowner, Townshend was frequently in England on business. He was dead before 1652, and not much record remains of his practice of his profession. A usually forgotten man, at least as a physician, is Captain William Norton, described by Captain John Smith as an "industrious Gentleman, adorned with many good qualities besides Physicke and Chirurgery, which for the publike good he freely imported to all gratis, but most bountifully to the poore." Another obscure figure is "Master Cloyburne the Surgian," who had arrived with Wyatt and Pott in 1621. About this time too came Mousnier de la Montague, Walloon or French, and parson-physician Robert Pawlett (arrived 1621 and elected to the Council the same year). Several others in the days of the Company died or left early. The evidence points to at least a reasonable ratio of medically trained to lay colonists in the period to 1624.[213]

Throughout the century legislative and judicial records, and the statutes themselves, are filled with references to Virginia medical men, to alleged exorbitant fees, to unqualified practitioners, to "miracle-cures" by trained physicians or Negro slaves or Indians. Dr. Blanton has long chapters on epidemic diseases, medical education, simples and therapy, medical practice, woman and medicine, and much on the physicians' private and public lives and vocations and avocations other than medicine. Some of these have been discussed in this and preceding chapters and more will be considered below. His long list of physicians of the century ranges from a multitude of names simply rescued from the records of death or a single activity to those of physician-parsons John Banister and John Clayton, longtime practitioners Edmond Helder and the elder Daniel Parke, German explorer Dr. John Lederer, Presbyterian-founding-father-physician Francis Makemie, and silkworm man Dr. Richard Russell. All these men seem to have been practicing doctors of physic or surgeons, though certainly many must have had apothecary shops in addition.[214] As already noted, some of them in the latter half of the century contributed to the *Philosophical Transactions* of the Royal Society or are represented in manuscripts in the files of that organization or in the British Museum. Their recorded contributions to medical knowledge are negligible. Inadequately trained as many of them were, most of them probably did their best to alleviate suffering. As the century drew to a close, the ratio of medical men to the total population is difficult to determine. Ships' surgeons and others with some training might increase the ratio without increasing the degree of service to population, for many of them became and remained planters or merchants, at the time apparently much more profitable occupations.

Maryland medicine in the seventeenth century somewhat parallels Virginia's, as do so many other phases of that colony's history. In the smaller Chesapeake province as in the larger no real medical license was required, though in 1676 a Dr. Edward Husbands of Calvert County was forbidden to practice on suspicion of poisoning several members of the Assembly. A Dr. John Stansby of Baltimore County, a member of the legislative body, was a prosecutor. According to one of the few medical historians who have diligently searched the archives, there were probably more persons practicing medicine in Maryland with totally inadequate training than in Virginia—at least judging by the examples he gives. That is, there may have been more quacks, a group flourishing for various reasons in every American colony. Obviously too many who styled themselves "doctor" had only apprentice training within the colony. In a few instances indentured servants educated in some form of medicine were hired out to practice.

As in Virginia and Great Britain, the practitioners in Maryland were of several social levels. The onetime barber-surgeon, in this province again probably purely surgeon, often rose in social and political status as well as professional and was called "doctor." University-trained physicians were scarce: two were George Binks and Dr. George Hack, the latter of both Virginia and Maryland. There were a few German and French physicians, with what training we know not. Ships' surgeons settled in the colony and in a few cases practiced their profession. Their education, of course, was largely or entirely through apprenticeship and possibly hospital practice. Some of the chirurgeons had "of London" placed after their names. Many were referred to as "Mister," as in England.

Sometimes as in Virginia, women, especially wives of medical men, acted as nurses. Occasionally these same women practiced medicine, as county and court records bear witness. And nearly all obstetrical work was left to midwives. Record of their care and charges is fairly frequent.

One list, based on thousands of miscellaneous records, shows the names of about one hundred seventeenth-century Maryland practitioners of medicine, though there were surely dozens more. Most of the hundred if professionally identified at all are called "chirurgeon," with sometimes "and apothecary" added to the first designation. Many were county sheriffs, colonels of militia, clerks of county courts, burgesses or even acting governors, councilors, and several clergy (as Francis Makemie). As late as 1693 only two apothecaries as such are listed in the province. Evidently most of the chirurgeons also prepared and sold drugs. There is one 1709 list of specific medicines in the inventory of Zechariah Allen, a Baltimore County apothecary. John Briscoe, one of the original settlers, is said to be the first Maryland physician, but no record of his training has been found.[215]

For North Carolina there appears to be no medical history, or history of practice, for the seventeenth century. It seems highly likely, however, that the province into which John Lawson trekked from Charleston in South Carolina in 1701 had had some medical practitioners during the preceding century. In early South Carolina the first settlers had heard of Indian remedies before they arrived and by 1680 if not before were writing home about native treatments, many of them discussed in Chapter II above. When they founded Charleston in 1670 they brought with them current knowledge of medicine and almost surely some persons trained in medicine. Certainly they brought with them instructions to search diligently for American herbs "whose Medicinal Vertues were rare and admirable."

Stephen Bull, an early colonist of lower Carolina, wrote in 1670 that many persons had "feaver and Ague" of the "seasoning" variety, and soon after Governor Joseph West that "Here is wanting among us a good Doctor, and a chest of good medicines." Yet most newcomers, including the two just named, were impressed by what they considered the healthfulness of the climate. The settlement grew rapidly, and by 1684 there was a serious epidemic of what may have been malaria. In the subsequent years many new arrivals died, and others on the way over. There were probably from the beginning medical men of some sort but probably as West may have been suggesting no fully qualified doctor of physic. News of epidemics during the rest of the seventeenth century, according to some historians, directly affected colonization.[216]

As in the Chesapeake colonies' records, little more about the medical men who filtered in remains than their names and their nonprofessional activities. Dr. Henry Woodward is best remembered as the trader-explorer among the Westoes mentioned in preceding chapters. A Dr. Will Scrivener, deputy for Lord Berkeley, came in 1670 and died in 1671. Dr. Thomas Smyth (Smith), Landgrave, left his instruments of chirurgery and half his medicines to his son George. In 1678 Doctors William Clarke and Peter Bodett arrived. Clarke, who styled himself "Chirurgeon" in his will, may have been the first real practitioner of the town. Joseph Blake and James Williams were surgeons. A Dr. Charles Burnham, New England Quaker, was prominent in politics even though his spelling and grammar do not mark him as a learned man. Dr. John Hardy was remembered or recorded as a property owner and sued Governor Colleton "For Phisick and as a phisitian," a suit which in the end appeared to prove Hardy the debtor.

An apothecary of good reputation, Mr. Charasse, was in the colony by 1684, one of the ten medical men (including several of those mentioned in the paragraph above) who were on hand during the epidemic of 1684. Though there is no evidence of systematic medical activity before 1700, the legal and legislative records tell something of drugs for the poor and sick and of developing public interest in health and disease. An act of 1685 provided for cleaning of streets and lots as a sanitary measure; another of 1698 concerned open privies, slaughter houses, and sheep pens, all of which had to be removed from the town proper. At the end of the century in 1696 Dr. Isaac Porcher, Huguenot refugee and ancestor of a more famous physician, had settled on the Santee, later removing to Goose Creek. Council records of 1692 indicate that another Huguenot chirurgeon, John Thomas, was paid for performing the first known autopsy in South Carolina. Antoine Cordes, like Porcher, was said to be a doctor of the University of Paris, though they are generally referred to as surgeons.

The names of a dozen other physicians and apothecaries appear in the county and provincial papers of this period. As in the more northern colonies, there is little or no evidence that in this first generation of the colony medical men made contributions to the knowledge of the health of mankind in America,[217] yet the story of the second and third quarters of the eighteenth century is quite another matter.

The Eighteenth Century

Medicine in itself in the southern colonies of the eighteenth century is an interesting story of research, experimentation, and some discovery. It includes firsts in both surgery and internal medicine and a quite voluminous literature published largely in British or European continental journals and books. Several medical practitioners from Maryland to the newly founded Georgia became well known or even famous in peripheral areas of science. And the ocean traffic in physicians increased many fold, both of young Britishers and a few others coming to practice in the South Atlantic area and of native young southern colonials crossing to Edinburgh and Leyden and other great medical centers to be trained and in some instances to receive the degree of doctor of medicine.

Most of the eighteenth-century apothecaries came straight from such centers as London, but some had learned their profession through apprenticeship in other parts of Britain, in the colonies of which they were natives or in a few instances on the continent. In the American South, as already pointed out, the distinction between chirurgeon and apothecary and general practitioner in physic continued to be very thin or to be blurred.

A comprehensive history of early Maryland medicine remains to be written, as it does for North Carolina and Georgia. For some knowledge of the interesting Maryland physicians of the mid-eighteenth century, for example, one must scour the pages of the *Maryland Gazette* and the *Pennsylvania Gazette* and the court and county and province legislative records as well as British publications of Edinburgh and London. Among the more distinguished within and without the profession were Gustavus Brown (1689–1765), Alexander Hamilton (1712–1756), Henry Stevenson

(1721–1814), and Adam Thomson (d. 1767), three of them Scots and the other Scotch-Irish. In addition, there were the men known primarily through notices or advertisements in the *Maryland Gazette* or mentioned in local records: Dr. George Walker, A.M., of Anne Arundel County, who arrived in 1720 from England; Dr. George Buchanan, chirurgeon, who arrived from Scotland in 1723, died in 1750, and in the time between recorded several land purchases and pushed through Baltimore health ordinances; John Stevenson, brother of Henry, who arrived with the latter from Ireland in 1745; Dr. William Lyon, who in 1746 established Baltimore's first drugstore; Dr. Swinton, surgeon, killed at Braddock's defeat; and several others, including Dr. Josiah Middlemore (d. 1755), Dr. Charles Frederick Wiesenthal (arrived from Germany 1755), and a Mrs. Hughes and Mrs. Littig, in 1752 midwives respectively to the English and the Germans.[218]

The *Maryland Gazette*'s advertisements offered Virginian John Tennent's *Every Man His Own Doctor; Or, The Poor Planter's Physician* (1734), of which more below; a declaration of a Mr. Torres that he could cure cancer (1745); rattlesnake root and its uses (1746); and the services of an old Negro with medical secrets. Essays appeared on the most timely topic of smallpox inoculation, on effects of a bite from a viper, on a hospital for the poor and insane, and on hydrophobia. Then there were the notices of the lectures of Dr. Archibald Spencer on electricity, which included a good deal on the potentialities if not actualities of the "newly discovered" form of energy to bodily health or healing.

At midcentury smallpox continued, as it had long been, a major prevalent disease in the English-speaking world. In America there had been epidemics, in one of which the future father of his country, who resided in the Chesapeake area, was facially marked for life. The care and possible cure or prevention of the disease was a lively topic in all the colonies. Cotton Mather in New England had been an American pioneer in experimentation and publication of his results. The medical communities in Annapolis and Baltimore shared with their city neighbors in Philadelphia active investigation of its causes and possible prevention. Particularly involved were Alexander Hamilton and Adam Thomson.

Hamilton, M.D., of Edinburgh University, where his father had been principal, and educated also in the pharmacy of David Knox, surgeon, had followed his elder brother Dr. John Hamilton to Maryland in 1739. Almost immediately he became a leading physician of the colony and with Jonas Green a leading spirit in the Tuesday Club of Annapolis. He is best remembered in his belletristic capacity, but he also made a contribution to the recorded history of medicine in America. On visits to Philadelphia and points north he came to know other physicians from New England through

Pennsylvania, and in Philadelphia he exchanged views with Doctors Phineas and Thomas Bond of that city and with Dr. John Mitchell of Virginia. He was particularly intimate with his fellow Scot and fellow Marylander Adam Thomson. They were both poets, but they also had similar views of inoculation for smallpox and both wrote on the subject. In November 1750 Dr. Thomson delivered a lecture in Philadelphia on the preparation of the body for inoculation in which he attacked mere empiricism in medicine and emphasized the necessity for theory and principles. When the discourse was published, several Philadelphia physicians objected to it. Essays against its ideas appeared in the *Pennsylvania Journal* in 1750 and 1751, and in the latter year the well-known Dr. John Kearsley published an all-out attack in *A Letter to a Friend, containing remarks on a discourse proposing a preparation of the body for the small-pox* . . . (Philadelphia, 1751). Among other matters of the regimen in preparing the body for smallpox Thomson proposed that legislatures appoint suitable examining bodies for those who wished to practice medicine. Hamilton wrote *A Defence of Dr. Thomson's Discourse* . . . (Philadelphia, 1751) dated from Annapolis, April 27, 1751, in the form of a letter, probably to Dr. Phineas Bond. Hamilton's is an able assemblage of the facts—and arguments—for Thomson's proposal, which was by no means startlingly original. Hamilton criticizes by reasoning and satire. From the modern point of view, something may be said for both sides, but in and for their own time Thomson and Hamilton had the better medical argument. Though it is probable that both the Maryland Scots wrote and published on medicine elsewhere as they did on belles lettres, this pair of papers on inoculation is their well-known scientific contribution.[219]

Dr. Henry Stevenson is remembered as a physician who operated in his own house near Baltimore in 1768–1776 and 1786–1800. He had been called by 1765 "the most successful inoculator in America." Besides the citizens of Baltimore, he inoculated scores in the rural counties throughout his part of Maryland. He was to live long enough to assist in organizing in 1799 the Medical and Chirurgical Faculty of Maryland. Charles Frederick Wiesenthal, though most of his career comes after 1763, was in practice in Baltimore by 1755 and remained there for thirty-four years. At some time in his career he erected buildings for a medical school and dissecting room on his back lots and also in 1788 helped to form a medical society. In the Revolutionary War generation there were a number of prominent Maryland practitioners who helped to prepare Baltimore to be the great teaching and practicing medical center it was to become in another two or three generations.

One other Maryland physician-parson, Dr. Archibald Spencer, already mentioned in connection with his lectures and experiments in electricity, should be recalled. Along with his reputation as a scientific lecturer he was known to some of the eminent physicians of his time "as a most judicious and experienced Physician and Man-midwife." He practiced medicine in Philadelphia before he took orders and removed to Maryland. Almost surely, like other less qualified parsons, he had some medical practice during his later years. When he died in 1760 his books on physic and anatomy were still in his library. He discussed most aspects of science not only with Benjamin Franklin but with medical men such as Alexander Hamilton, John Mitchell, Thomas Moffatt, Lloyd Zachary, Richard Mead, Phineas Bond, Cadwallader Colden, and Dr. Thomas Cadwallader, leading figures on both sides of the Atlantic.[220]

Partly because of the colony's rapidly increasing population, the story of medicine in Virginia in the eighteenth century is much fuller than it was for the seventeenth. In character, however, medicine in the new century was not greatly different from what it had been earlier. Most physicians-surgeons-apothecaries had been trained in Great Britain, and quacks had become even more numerous. In the latter half of the century more colonials went to British and continental medical schools, and a beginning of medical societies and hospitals in the modern sense was made, though most of both of these came in the South after 1763. More and more able men throughout the colonies entered the medical profession, and experience with widespread epidemic diseases brought more intense study of them. As the mid-eighteenth century has been called the Chesapeake colonies' golden age in wealth and power and even in intellectual pursuits (and the same holds generally true for colonial South Carolina), so medicine to at least a degree measured up to the other elements of the society. But by then the urban centers such as Philadelphia and New York were beginning to demonstrate a capacity for medical training and research impossible in the agrarian southern colonies.

Medicine, the department around which the European medical schools were built, presented a variety of theories of cause and effect. At the beginning of the century the most popular ideas, especially in Great Britain, were those of Thomas Sydenham, whose books were in most southern libraries of any size, as were those of his successor in influence, Hermann Boerhaave. Later Virginia and Carolina youths in many instances studied under William Cullen at Edinburgh and heard his theory of "solidism" (concerning the "solid" parts of the body, especially nerves), though some of them preferred the theory of John Brown of the same university, who classified all disease as constitutional or local, sthenic or asthenic.[221] The eighteenth-century Virginia colonial doctor seems to have been better educated and possessed of more intelligent or informed clientele than his predecessor, but he was still handicapped by his devotion to theory. In practice or therapy he had apparently advanced little, for he continued to sweat, purge, and bleed his patients—notoriously including George Washington —as his earliest predecessors in the Virginia colonies had done. Yet there were a number of able physicians within the professional limitations of their time.

The chirurgeon of the seventeenth century was fast disappearing, though his appellation was used by various sorts of practitioners in medicine for some years. After the Revolution he had virtually disappeared even in name. But British surgery was at a low ebb in the earlier part of the century, and the training of surgeons who came to America was little better than it had been in the seventeenth century. There were a few notable exceptions in the later century. William Baynham, born in Caroline County the son of a physician, apprenticed first to Dr. Thomas Walker of Castle Hill and then a student at St. Thomas' Hospital in London with further study at Cambridge, practiced in London most successfully for a time but returned to Virginia in 1785. As a practitioner of surgery and medicine he was sought after throughout the states. He wrote and demonstrated on a number of matters including injections and made models for anatomical museums. His reputation was international, and he was appreciated in his native Virginia. But his work really comes after the period under study. There are a dozen other late eighteenth-century figures of almost as great reputation and talents. Among the abler men within the colonial period were Colonel Jesse Brown (d. 1771), Southampton County surgeon, John Symmer and two Thomas Claytons of Gloucester, smallpox specialist John Daglgleish of Norfolk, and Jean Pasteur, Geneva-trained surgeon who settled in Williamsburg about 1700 and was succeeded by an even more successful son.

Obstetrics made two major advances in the century, the use of forceps and of men midwives. In America European-trained John Moultrie of South Carolina and William Shippen of Pennsylvania raised the dignity of obstetrics in this country, and by the last third of the century their influence together with that of others is evident in Virginia practice. The *Virginia Gazette* notes a number of male midwives usually with the prefix of "Doctor." Female midwives took more than ever to newspaper advertising to keep any town practice, though undoubtedly they were employed frequently in rural districts.

Medical fees had been a subject for Virginia legislation since the midseventeenth century, and in 1736 another act for regulating them was passed.[222] Pharmacy was changing, though many old habits lingered on. As an independent profession it did not receive the support of American physicians until after the Revolution. In Virginia the apothecaries trained in Britain were preferred to those who had been apprenticed locally. In the colony as in England and Scotland, however, an established physician or surgeon took several apprentices in pharmacy. Some went on to medical schools in Europe in order to become full-fledged doctors, and a few were trained further in medicine under local physicians of eminence. Late in the century Theodorick Bland and other Virginians educated at Edinburgh proclaimed that hereafter they would not degrade their profession by mingling the trade of apothecary or surgeon with it, proof in itself of what was quite usual in their native colony. As Dr. George Gilmer and others had done earlier in Williamsburg, Dr. Hugh Mercer and his partner-physicians in Fredericksburg opened their own apothecary shop in the 1760s. Many advertised their medical wares in the *Virginia Gazette*, as did William Heath in 1752. Many alleged that they prepared their own compounds from mixtures of native and imported materials. Persimmon, sassafras, "red root," and other native plants went into one remedy. Patent medicines, usually from England, were sold by apothecaries and merchants despite the protests of most physicians.

There is a considerable list of apothecary shops in Williamsburg alone. One of the earliest was that of Thomas Wharton (d. 1746), who had among his patients Randolphs, Bollings, and Ludwells. Prominent Dr. George Gilmer, Sr., already mentioned, had established his practice as early as 1731 and with his shop and patients became a prosperous man. Dr. Peter Hay had a shop from 1744 to 1766 "adjoining the Market-Place." Others found the competition in pharmacy in the capital village as keen as that in medicine and moved into the country or into more remote villages.[223]

The best account of a physician's problems in Williamsburg is to be found in the "journal" that Dr. John de Sequeyra, quite eminent local physician, kept between 1745 and 1781. Incidentally, Jefferson credited him with the introduction of the tomato into Virginia. His actual record is an account of the diseases common in Virginia in the period. Intermittent fevers, pleurisy, pneumonia, worm fevers in children, scarlet fever, smallpox, dysentery, violent colds, inflammatory fevers, quinsy, whooping cough, measles, distempers of the breast, mumps, and contagious fevers are among those he notes before 1764, with often a mention of the method of treatment (purging, etc.) or the drugs used. Of course he and most of his contemporaries were often mistaken in their diagnoses or identifications. Usually the disease was prevalent; sometimes it was epidemic.[224]

Attention has already been given to the fact that many southern colonial physicians, including Virginians, wrote on many phases of science other than medicine. Yet the science most frequently represented in articles in the *Virginia Gazette* is medicine—usually in articles on smallpox—and not always written by local practitioners. There are in addition advertisements of many cures by quacks or sometimes by men who apparently had some sort of formal medical training. The latter especially were often itinerants, though one stayed for a long time at Yorktown. Another advertising "French Doctor" said he was living in Norfolk. There are notices of newly discovered cures, frequently through such means as medicinal springs or the Seneca rattlesnake root, the latter of which William Byrd II believed in firmly.

Four essays on this efficacy of the snakeroot appeared in the *Virginia Gazette* during 1738 by "John Tennent, Practitioner in Medicine," the most prolific medical writer of the colonial South. He had already published two essays in the *Gazette* in 1736 and 1737. He and his ideas seem to have met with considerable opposition in his own colony and then and later in the other American provinces and in Great Britain. Yet he was defended by Dr. Thomas Bond, at the time (1739) writing from Paris originally to the *Pennsylvania Gazette* in an essay reprinted in other colonies. Other persons wrote on Joanna Stephens and her cure for stones (1739) and on the cure-all pills and powders of Joshua Ward of England (1737). In 1766 a series of four letters proposing a cure for cancer appeared, with consequent denunciations. There are later essays on "fevers," including yellow fever and whooping cough. Descriptions of cures for snake bite appeared in 1739 and 1755 and for deaf-and-dumb persons in 1752. A scattering of essays on European medicine appeared between 1737 and 1771.

The matter of inoculation for smallpox, as already noticed in consideration of Maryland, was discussed in all the American colonies. Cotton Mather's method of 1721 used successfully by a South Carolina physician in 1738 (see below) helped to bring its general acceptance. It was really variolation, a primitive form of inoculation which in turn led to vaccination. At any rate, disputes as to its efficacy continued to rage, and the *Virginia Gazette* of 1767–1772 contains dozens of separate discussions, though there were at least six from 1737 to 1766, when an essay on smallpox from the August 1736 *Gentleman's Magazine* was reprinted. The first mention of inoculation in the *Virginia Gazette* of October 1737 tells of its successful use by a group of Philadelphia physicians, including Kearsley, Cadwallader, Shippen, and Bond. In 1739 a news notice of the continuance of smallpox in South Carolina was printed with information as to the passage of a bill prohibiting inoculation within two miles of Charleston. The outbreak of the disease in 1752 resulted in an essay by "R.W." tracing its history and strongly advocating inoculation.[225]

The prolific medical writer John Tennent noted just above made himself well known in all the southern colonies and in Great Britain. He was a controversial figure, and his enemies or the enemies of his theories considered him a mere charlatan, but his friends believed he was a great benefactor of humanity. Tennent came to Virginia as a young man, probably in 1725, and settled in Spotsylvania County near Fredericksburg. In 1736 William Parks published in Williamsburg Tennent's *Essay on Pleurisy*, and the controversy on Seneca snakeroot was begun in print. Governor Gooch and William Byrd II believed in his theory regarding the uses of the Indian medicine, and he managed to get Sir Hans Sloane, Dr. Richard Mead, and the French physician Jussieu interested. Tennent soon was in England to advertise his great panacea. He persuaded three major British physicians to recommend him for the degree of doctor of physic from Edinburgh (which he did not receive), and he returned to Virginia waving these credentials. In the colony he managed to get £100 from the House of Burgesses in recognition of his publicizing his boon to mankind, but in 1739 he was back in England, where his career ended in debt and disgrace. Sir Hans Sloane did rescue him from debtors' prison, though what happened afterward is obscure.

But Tennent's list of titles is imposing. The household manual *Every Man His Own Physician; Or, The Poor Planter's Physician* (second edition, Parks, Williamsburg, 1734), found in many colonial libraries, is believed to have been his. Benjamin Franklin printed three editions in Philadelphia in 1734, 1736, and 1737. The 1736 *Essay on Pleurisy* is generally conceded to be his chief work. In 1738 *An Epistle to Dr. Richard Mead, Concerning the Epidemical Diseases of Virginia, Particularly, a Pleurisy, and Peripneumony* (Edinburgh) again shows the surprising efficacy of snakeroot. *A Reprieve from Death in Two Physical Chapters* in London in 1741 is concerned with the cure of epidemic fevers in the West Indies; *Physical Enquiries* (London, 1742) considers the effects on the constitution of change of climate; about the same time appeared *The Case of John Tennent* (London, 1743), a brief defense of his personal conduct in London and an account of his search for a cure for annually returning diseases in Virginia; and finally came his *Physical Disquisitions: demonstrating the real causes of the blood's morbid rarefaction and stagnation* (London, 1745). Tennent was paranoid, overly enthusiastic, and probably insufficiently trained even by the standards of his own day, but his writings and practice created more than a ripple in the medical waters of his time.

John Mitchell, among his varied writings, managed to publish one significant piece in the area of his vocation. Even then it appeared without his consent. Ironically enough, it gives him a place in important American medical literature. In 1737, when he had visited Philadelphia in search of health, he showed Benjamin Franklin his manuscript account of the yellow fever epidemics in Virginia in that year. Franklin had a copy made so that Colden could see it and some time later asked Mitchell's permission to print it. Mitchell's reply shows how little he thought of the state of American medicine, and pointed out that eminent Scottish physicians had urged him to enlarge it into what might be a definitive study before publishing. He had, he declared, gathered more materials over several years which were not yet in shape to include. Franklin eventually gave a copy to Benjamin Rush, who followed its suggestions in the Philadelphia epidemic of 1793. The Pennsylvanian, who eventually was the means of the essay's being published, believed the method saved many thousand lives.[226] Mitchell also long thought of writing a natural and medical history of North America and went so far as to question Cadwallader Colden and others about various sections of the Atlantic area, but he had too many interests to allow him to focus properly on this one.

Though there were dozens of physicians of ability in Virginia in the eighteenth century to 1764, it is characteristic of the state of medical knowledge in the colonies that it is not for their medical work that the greatest men among them are remembered. John Clayton, John Banister, and John Mitchell appear frequently in the annals of the period because of what they did in natural history; Hugh Mercer, Arthur Lee, Theodorick Bland, and Walter Jones, of the mid-century generation, remain men of mark for their distinguished careers in army, diplomacy, and politics, often after the Revolution.[227] Among those born one and two decades later than these, Virginia was to produce several medical men of at least national reputation in their profession.

Again in the eighteenth century there is very little on North Carolina physicians, though a few names appear. Doctors Armand John De Rosset, John Brickell, Martin Kalberlahn, and Ephraim Brevard are familiar names to most students of the history of the province, but little is known of their medical activities. Governor Thomas Burke, a physician, is remembered for his early practice on the Eastern Shore of Virginia, his literary quarrels and poetic satire in both Virginia and North Carolina, and his legal and political and military careers in the latter colony. Yet he did not reach North Carolina until the last year of the period, 1763.

But in South Carolina there was remarkable medical investigation, debate, and publication. Charleston in this as in other areas was unusual in the South and even in the British colonies as a whole. A prosperous agriculture and flourishing trade in a city of rapidly expanding intellectual and aesthetic as well as hedonistic interest attracted a steady flow of immigrants throughout the eighteenth century. Since the attractive features were accompanied by a subtropical climate and a considerable proportion of swampland which resulted in many varieties of fevers and other afflictions, physicians were in unusual demand. They came, perhaps not so much to make the environment salubrious as to make good livings or fortunes for themselves. In provincial and county records, local pamphlet publications, the *South-Carolina Gazette*, and sophisticated or learned journals of England and Scotland their writings are referred to or printed. In provincial newspapers such as the *Gazette* are also essays copied from English or European journals, often on epidemics rampant in various parts of the world, notes of new cures, names and notices of recently arrived physicians, a few midwives' advertisements, and comments on hospitals for various diseases or people, as several of 1749–1764 "for sick Negroes." Charleston physicians translated and published useful medical treatises from Latin or French. Most of the city's weather observers between 1670 and 1871 were physicians anxious to ascertain possible effects of temperature and moisture on individual health or in precipitating epidemics. Botany was most often materia medica to be tested on human guinea pigs. A steady flow of almanacs tells of the nostrums of the period, such as Negro Caesar's cure for poison or Howard's for yaws, and Tennent's *Every Man His Own Doctor* was apparently as popular in Charleston as in the Chesapeake country. In 1755 a faculty of physic was organized to support and protect the privileges and dignity of the profession and to investigate the question of proper fees.

The greatest long-range problem of the South Carolina physician was the epidemics of yellow fever, smallpox, measles, whooping cough, bloody flux, malaria, and other diseases which debilitated or decimated the white, black, and red populations. It was principally but not entirely on these that he wrote, and the matter of disease and epidemic will be looked at in a moment. As in Maryland, many of the major physician-researchers were transplanted Scots. For example, Dr. John Lining (1708–1760), born in Lanarkshire and one of the most distinguished and earliest of these men, has already been mentioned for his work in meteorology and a number of metabolic ("statical") experiments performed upon himself and the results published in the *Philosophical Transactions* of the Royal Society in 1742–1743 (LII: 491–509) and 1744–1745 (LIII: 318–330). He published a general table of his observations in Dr. Chalmers' *Account of the Weather and Diseases of South Carolina* noted above. His paper on yellow fever was published in the Edinburgh *Essays and Observations, Physical and Literary, read before a Society of Physicians* (1756), II, 370–395, and separately in Philadelphia in 1799. "Of the anthelmintic Virtues of the Root of the Indian Pink" had been extolled in the same journal ([1754], I, 386–389). His love of botany and interest in electricity have already been touched upon. He has been called, possibly with some exaggeration, the most versatile scientist of colonial America.

William Bull (1710–1791), scion of a major South Carolina family, is principally remembered medically as the first American-born student to graduate in the profession abroad, as he did at Leyden. As a student of the great Boerhaave, Bull had a fine reputation as a medical scholar. On his return to America, however, he immediately entered politics and rose to be lieutenant governor of the province. He sent communications concerning botany to Peter Collinson, and he suggested legislation to regulate the practice of physic in South Carolina. He was a member of the committee appointed to attempt to prevent the spread of contagious distemper (epidemics). For his medical brethren he was a good man to have at court.

Born about 1700 were three active physicians, Thomas Dale, James Kilpatrick (later Kirkpatrick), and John Moultrie, the latter two Irish or Scottish-born and educated. Dale (d. 1750), son of an English apothecary and a graduate of Leyden, arrived in South Carolina in 1725 and soon became prominent in social, medical, and literary activity. He translated many useful medical works from Latin, and his fine collection of local plants was sent after his death to Gronovius in Leyden. He was also judge and poet, and in medicine is remembered principally for his pamphlets debating with Dr. Kilpatrick the proper manner for smallpox inoculation. His medical equipment and library were substantial. Among his 2,273 books were 325 "Medicinal Anatomical & Botanical" and others related.

James Kilpatrick (he changed the spelling to Kirkpatrick when he removed to England) was born in County Carlow, Ireland, about 1700 and came to Carolina probably as early as 1718, though his name is first recorded in 1724. He seems to have been educated at Edinburgh. Perhaps the death of his young son from smallpox in 1738 led to his special interest in preventive measures. He had the rest of his family inoculated by the method he thereafter promoted, consisting of the use of a healthy person and a virus attenuated by passage from person to person: that is, by using the pus from an inoculated person rather than from a natural case of the disease. The 1738 epidemic was a severe and widespread one made worse by a bad epidemic of whooping cough. The following year yellow fever (or what was taken for it) took its toll. Among Kilpatrick's newspaper and journal and separately printed essays on inoculation, the separate pamphlets created the greatest general American and European attention. In a list of twenty-three probably the best were *A Full and Clear Reply to Doctor T. Dale* (Charleston and London, 1739), *An Essay on*

*Inoculation occasioned by the Smallpox being brought into South Caro-
lina in 1738* (London, 1743), *A letter to the real and genuine Pierce
Dod from Dod Pierce* (London, 1746), *The Analysis of Inoculation* (3
editions in London, 1754–1761, and in German, French, and Dutch,
1756, 1757, 1755), and *Some Reflections on the Causes and Circumstances that may retard or prevent the Putrefaction of Dead Bodies* (London, 1751). He was off to London in 1742, where after changing the
spelling of his name he may have proceeded to the degree of M.D. He
became famous. His work in belles lettres will be considered later. His
South Carolina experiments and observations, never really appreciated in
the colony, were the bases of his later distinction throughout Europe.

John Moultrie the elder was Scottish born and probably first reached
Charleston in his capacity of ship's surgeon in the British navy about
1728. He is said to have studied at Edinburgh as his son did later, but
of his medical education there is no sure evidence. He lived until 1771,
a most prominent figure in all phases of South Carolina life, and president of the Faculty of Physic. His local reputation was very high indeed,
especially for the accuracy of his diagnoses. He may have been the first
physician in America to specialize in obstetrics. Apparently he was too
busy to publish more than scattered and so far unidentified pieces in
provincial newspapers. His son, the first native American to graduate in
medicine at Edinburgh, published only a little more than his father (according to present evidence), but he maintained the family reputation for
intelligent and learned diagnosis and treatment.[228]

Perhaps equally as able as Lining was Dr. Lionel Chalmers (1715–
1777), Scottish born and educated, probably receiving his training at
St. Andrews. He arrived in Charleston about 1737 and found the four
active physicians just discussed (Bull was of course not one of them) on
the ground before him. He struggled for a time, but after his marriage
to Martha Logan in 1739 he seems to have become firmly established.
He was one of those who also had an apothecary business, in his case in
partnership with two other men, until 1754. Chalmers began his own
meteorological observations in 1750, as noted above with the account of
his accomplishment in the area in books and essays. His 1754 "Of the
Opisthotonos and the Tetanus" was published by Dr. John Fothergill in
Medical Observations and Inquiries by a Society of Physicians in London,
I (London, 1758).[229] The degree of M.D. was conferred by St. Andrews
in 1756 partly as a result of his distinguished publication. He continued
to write, as his aforementioned internationally known essay on fevers
and essays on apoplexy, the dry belly-ache, catarrhal peripneumony, and
catarrhal consumption. As early as 1771 Cullen of Edinburgh was speak-

ing of him in his lectures. He was highly respected throughout the medical world.

Slightly younger but contemporary with these men was the botanist-physician Dr. Alexander Garden (1728–1791), already commented upon at some length in other scientific connections. Waring refers to him as "The Reluctant Physician," as perhaps in a sense he was, for he was intensely interested in investigation of fauna and flora per se as well as per utile. In 1754 he sent to his old professor Charles Alston of Edinburgh his six-step proposed investigation of alleged poisoning by slaves in South Carolina, an interesting medical approach. During 1760 he studied smallpox epidemics carefully and used his Maryland-Pennsylvania friend Dr. Adam Thomson's approach to inoculation. He considered his own particular form of this treatment highly successful. He trained several apprentices who became distinguished physicians in their own right. Four of these went on to Edinburgh, where they dedicated their theses to Dr. Garden. Meanwhile he had assumed responsibility for the health of the parish poor, in itself a complete career had he allowed it to be. His two published writings directly related to medicine are plant-related, on certain uses of the pinkroot and of the ashes of tobacco. One may sum up his contribution to medicine in his colony by saying that he set the example for an investigative-research approach to all professional problems. His name alone brought Charleston medicine and science to the attention of the western world.[230]

Georgia's colonial medical history naturally is brief. Even so, there were some significant activities and some physicians who should be noted because of the kind of work they did. Among the promoters of the colony were two prominent British physicians, Dr. Hans Sloane and the Rev. Dr. Stephen Hales. One of the first and continued activities of the colonial generation of settlers was to ship to England consignments of "bear's oil," snakeroot, rattlesnakeroot, chinaroot, sassafras, sumac, and other medicinal products of southern North America. As in South Carolina, fevers and bloody fluxes seem to have been in the beginning the principal scourges, with some later smallpox which swept away whole tribes of Indians. All sorts of patent medicines were in supplies sent by the Trustees, for even eminent physicians frequently recommended them.

Among the first physicians were regimental surgeons who arrived with the troops. A friend of Oglethorpe who may not have begun with any direct military connections was Captain and Doctor Noble Jones, who received the now historic tract of Wormsloe, Isle of Hope, and who was the ancestor of other prominent Georgia medical men. Dr. Jones was the original surveyor of the colony and was always politically active. He trained his son, the perhaps even better known Noble Wymberley Jones, a distinguished physician and Revolutionary patriot. The first active practitioner in Georgia appears to have been Dr. Samuel Nuñez Ribiero, a Jewish escapee from the Inquisition in Lisbon. He performed valuable service before he removed to South Carolina in 1740.

In his journal of March 1734 Bolzius mentions the Salzburgers' apothecary-surgeon Andrew Zwiffler, whose name occurs in the records several later times. Many other physicians and surgeons who were also pharmacists are listed before 1764 in Savannah and the German-Swiss communities, including other Salzburgers, a few British M.D.'s, and one Connecticut-born Yale graduate. There was also the rebellious planter and satirist Dr. Patrick Tailfer, of whom more later. In the town of Augusta there were physicians as early as 1759, when Dr. Thomas Ford was paid for treating the Indians. The first autopsy known to have been performed in this now historic medical community was in 1766 by Dr. Andrew Johnston.

Two other aspects of Georgia colonial medical history are mentioned elsewhere in other connections: the Trustees' Botanical Garden, which included materia medica, and John Wesley's enormously popular *Primitive Physic* (1747), the latter seeming to grow in part at least from the great clergyman's experience during his brief sojourn in the colony as rector in Savannah and technically as missionary. The Salzburger reports now being published tell us a great deal about the problems of the sick in early Georgia and of apothecary Zwiffler's valiant—and appreciated—efforts in behalf of his co-religionists. These reports should some day be incorporated into a comprehensive history of Georgia medicine, as should a thorough study of its early hospitals and attempts to cope with various epidemics.[231]

DISEASES AND EPIDEMICS

In this and preceding chapters, as Chaper II, on the red man, the problems and facts of diseases and epidemics have been touched upon. In the relatively few contemporary descriptions of the actual health situations in the southern colonies from Jamestown to 1764, no clear or satisfactory clinical picture of diseases emerges. Colonial promoters were reluctant to advertise even in their own newspapers the dangerous features of their environment; the medical practitioners as far as one may judge today from the contemporary evidence as often as not diagnosed or identified ailments incorrectly, and few if any province-wide statistics were kept.

Yet there does exist a considerable body of material which indicates that disease reached epidemic proportions sporadically, and for brief groups of years seasonally, in all the southern colonies. Historians of medicine are still trying to determine causes and nature of these widespread illnesses and their effect on the economic and social and political life of individual provinces. Most agree that they played a tragic role in the story of the colonies, but whether or not the epidemics affected colonization appreciably they disagree upon.[232]

Of the 105 original settlers at Jamestown more than half died the first summer, and of the total number arriving before 1624 six-sevenths died. Percy and Smith among their contemporaries and the later William Stith have commented on this "Great Mortality," though all three blame it to a great extent on "mere famine." Percy's "scorbutical dropsies" and "cruel diseases with swellings" may have arisen from the meager diets; in other words, they were deficiency diseases. Scurvy is referred to on a number of occasions, Lord de la Warr himself being a victim of it. Diarrhea during starvation did not, as Dr. Blanton points out, imply necessarily epidemic dysentery, though later in that first century dysentery and "burning fevers" (typhoid?) were among the major health hazards. Certain fevers were referred to in all the southern colonies as "seasoning," and whether or not they were malaria or typhoid or either of these and/or other ills is still a disputed question. Incidentally, it is probable that Mount Malado, the first free hospital of British America constructed at Henrico in 1611, was a direct and practical response to widespread illness which seemed at the time to be epidemic.

Blanton is probably right in believing that food deficiencies were the principal cause of death in Virginia throughout the seventeenth century and therefore a principal impediment to the growth of population. Alexander Brown and Mary N. Stanard point to swarms of mosquitoes and stagnant pools as indicating malaria, but Blanton presents good evidence that the disease was not a major factor in Virginia's first century and that it definitely was not a major cause of the great mortality in the first two decades at Jamestown. Malaria in Virginia and elsewhere in America appears to have been a man-made disease, perhaps primarily the result of carriers from Africa and Europe; for it was not epidemic until potential bearers arrived steadily in great numbers and created in what once was forest the stagnant pools for the breeding of the *anopheles* mosquito.

The plague, one may recall, was prevalent in London and England at the time Jamestown was settled. A few rather dubious references are made to a "contagious disease called the plague" treated by colonial physicians. There is no contemporary record of yellow fever in Virginia in the first century. It was to come there and elsewhere with the accelerated slave trade in the eighteenth. Some winter epidemics occurred, basically respiratory, but whether pneumonia, pleurisy, or influenza is uncertain.

Smallpox and measles, frequently confused, were epidemic in the seventeenth century. They wiped out whole tribes of non-immune Indians, as already suggested, and were serious but not decimating among the whites. One may conclude that wars and famine, lack of women, and a high rate of infant mortality were greater factors in keeping down Virginia's population during this century than were contagious diseases epidemic or isolated.[233]

Even less than in the seventeenth century were eighteenth-century diseases in epidemic proportion a major factor in Virginia's growth or general health. There were cases in considerable numbers sometimes called epidemics, but often the disease was incorrectly identified, according to modern historians of medicine. For this second century there are many informal records of disease which do not tell much save that in letters and conversation Virginians were showing that they were highly conscious of the existence of certain contagious diseases among themselves and in neighboring provinces. Fithian the tutor writes (August 12, 1773) that the conversation at the dining table "was on the Disorders which seem to be growing to be epidemical Fevers, Agues, Fluxes—A gloomy train." As already noted, local gazettes and imported British journals presented accounts of outbreaks of various diseases in many parts of the world. From 1700 to 1764 occasional days of fasting and prayer were set aside by governors in hope that the Almighty would aid the afflicted.

Yellow fever received much attention, for the morbidity it had created in other colonies and areas of the world had made Virginians highly conscious of its existence. Few grasped at the time that it was peculiarly a disease of the American Atlantic seaboard usually occurring in ports visited by large numbers of ships from the Barbadoes. The earliest recorded epidemics are of 1737 and 1741/1742 and were described by Dr. John Mitchell in his classic essay already mentioned several times. Mitchell's practice in the seaboard area gave him access to many supposed cases. The remainder of those in the century occurred after 1763.

The history of Mitchell's essay written in the 1740s and finally published by Dr. Benjamin Rush in 1805 in the Philadelphia Medical Museum has been reviewed just above. One must admire Mitchell for opposing exsanguination and other strenuous therapies of the day, even if his explanations now fail to impress. Dr. Gordon W. Jones, an able historian of medicine now living close to Mitchell's one-time American residence, has recently reexamined the evidence and decided that the Virginians did not suffer from yellow fever in 1737, on the grounds that the season was wrong, it was contagious, children survived, etc. Dr. Jones decides that it was probably typhus or relapsing fever, of which he describes the symptoms. The Berkeleys give reasons for its having been Weil's disease.[234] Smallpox, the other more clearly identified disease (though still confused with measles) with appalling morbidity and mortality, was feared the world over, though as has been observed it was so nearly universal in seventeenth-century England that certain immunities had been built up. Variolation, or inoculation, discussed already in connection with individual physicians, had been used successfully in this country early in the eighteenth century by Cotton Mather and Zabdiel Boylston and certain southern colonials. Its efficacy was disputed, however, and aroused the controversy noted above in the Chesapeake colonies and in South Carolina.

There are a few scattered examples of inoculation before 1768, far fewer than in Carolina, for no great champion or advocate such as Kilpatrick in Charleston or Thomson in Maryland was there. Actually, though much talked about, smallpox was never so prevalent in Virginia as in the crowded northern cities or the port of Charleston. Little is heard of it before 1747 when the town of Williamsburg passed a law fining any white inhabitant who should receive or harbor a Negro infected with the smallpox. In 1752 in the *Virginia Gazette* appeared a locally authored essay advocating inoculation, for the disease was then relatively widespread there. In 1759 smallpox appeared in Winchester, near the frontier, and there are other notices of it in 1760 and 1766. A Williamsburg epidemic occurred in 1768, causing a reenactment of the 1747 law. But as suggested above, the disease in Virginia is to be remembered primarily as an inadvertent means of well-nigh annihilating the red man. In one epidemic on the Eastern Shore, for example, the total population of Indians was cut in half.

Malaria was the third major eighteenth-century disease in Virginia. Its presence at various times and places was often noted, though modern medical historians are skeptical of proper identification in many instances. The intermittent or remitting fevers, they point out, may or may not have been malaria. There are a dozen other possibilities. Dysentery also is hard to pinpoint, though the "flux" or "bloody flux" was a dreaded and often mortal distemper. Diarrhea might have a number of causes. The flux debilitated the British army at Wills Creek in the French and Indian War, it killed William Fitzhugh in 1701, and many another person prominent or obscure died from some sort of dysentery during the century. Every Virginia doctor was aware that certain drugs and other remedies and regimens helped alleviate here and elsewhere.[235] Tennent's "Universal specific," the snakeroot, was aimed at, among other ailments, pleurisy in epidemic proportions.

Maryland's diseases were exactly those of its neighbor on the Chesapeake, with perhaps a little more emphasis on and possibly prevalence of syphilis (known as country duties or French pox). Scurvy, dropsy, flux, griping of the guts, fever, boils, sores, and seasoning may have been the result of varying combinations of conditions or more rarely of contagion. The "seasoning" which afflicted newcomers may have been, as Dr. Blanton suggests, typhoid rather than malaria. "Cures" varied from traditional European remedies to Indian plants.

Epidemics are recorded in Maryland, as the great distemper in the Delaware area in 1657/1658, and a more widespread one in 1663 (it caused the adjournment of the provincial court). Some sort of epidemic disease in 1697/1698 caused people to flock for cures to the Cool Springs of St. Mary's County. A group of houses provided by the province have been called collectively the second public hospital in the colonies. In the eighteenth century Dr. Adam Thomson's writing and practice of preparation for inoculation and the subsequent literary dispute have been commented upon. The work of Doctors Alexander Hamilton and Henry Stevenson in smallpox inoculation or in publicity regarding it has also been noted. Annapolis, with its relatively easy accessibility to Philadelphia, was at least as much as Williamsburg a center for the practice of medicine and promulgation of ideas on diseases, epidemics, and treatments.[236]

As with physicians, almost nothing has been written on North Carolina diseases. John Lawson gives some idea of the state of health in the 1700–1709 period in *A New Voyage to Carolina*. The surveyor-general mentions vaguely several sicknesses and distempers among de Graffenreid's Swiss colonists, the devastating effects of smallpox among the Indian tribes and their suicidal attempts at remedies, their infection with syphilis, and their medicinal cures for all manner of diseases and injuries, the children's colic and their freedom from rickets, and native longevity attributable to their freedom from tuberculosis. In a 1710 letter he notes the spotted fever, fluxes, and dropsy, which Palatines had brought with them in their ship and which had killed about half of them. He blames the crowded conditions aboard ship for the death rate. On the whole (remember that *A New Voyage* was a promotion book) Lawson found North Carolina a salubrious area.[237]

Governor Arthur Dobbs half a century later indicates in his reports to the Board of Trade that North Carolina was afflicted by the same sorts of seasonal diseases suffered to the north and south of it, pointing out at one period that the province had "been very sickly with Agues and intermittent fevers by a long dry season . . . [and that] one third of the members of the Council and Assembly [were] laid up from time to time."[238] These annual or seasonal reports contain no record of widespread diseases, though North Carolina shared to some extent the outbreak of epidemics which afflicted the Chesapeake colonies and South Carolina at varying times. Lack of a really accessible seaport undoubtedly

Their rype corne.

Their greene corne

Corne newly sprong

Their sitting at meate

The place of solemne prayer

The house wherin the Tombe of their Herounds standeth.

SECOTON.

A Ceremony in their prayers wth strange iesturs and songs dansing abowt posts carued on the topps lyke mens faces.

Copyright by the Trustees of the British Museum

"Village of Secoton," the John White drawing of the 1580s adapted by Theodor deBry for *Historia Americae*

Washington-Custis-Lee Collection, Washington and Lee University/Virg

John Custis IV ("Tulip" Custis), botanist

kept down the spread of foreign diseases found frequently in Virginia and the Charleston neighborhood.

South Carolina has left more records and certainly had for white and black and red populations more diseases. For most of the period Charleston as the busiest port south of Philadelphia was a gateway through which a number of African and European diseases entered and then spread. Yet seventeenth-century settlers died at Beaufort and Charleston (in the 1680s) of what then appeared to be native contagions in epidemic proportion, though Waring and Blanton seem to disagree as to whether some of the fatalities were from malaria.[239] At any rate, the Proprietors consequently ordered the provincial courts to be adjourned during the summer months. About all that medical men could do during the first thirty years of the colony was to treat individuals and recommend sanitary laws and practices.

Smallpox was active in 1697 and became widespread among the Indians in 1698, with results similar to those in other southern colonies. When the government wrote in 1698 that two or three hundred persons had died from the disease the number probably did not include red men. An Act of 1698 concerned the importation of communicable diseases, with provisions for inspection and quarantine. The smallpox epidemic affecting Carolina in 1698/1699 was probably that which had begun in Virginia in 1696 and had spread southward through the Indians. Also in 1699 yellow fever struck Charleston at the same time it did Philadelphia. A letter from Mrs. Afra Coming of March 6, 1698/1699, describes the smallpox epidemic in graphic terms, and another describes the yellow fever, though it is admitted that the latter has not been definitely diagnosed.[240] In 1700 smallpox reappeared, in 1706 yellow fever in virulent form, an influenza in 1709, and "pleurisies" in 1711 and 1712. "The Malignant Fever" of 1711 caused three or four funerals a day in Charleston. A new Act of 1712 was designed to protect the city and province from "disease coming from the sea."[241] Meanwhile hospitals had been constructed. Dysentery, smallpox, malignant fever, pleurisy or influenza continued to afflict the colony to the end of the Proprietary period.

All these diseases continued sporadically under the royal government: for example, smallpox mildly in 1732 and perhaps in 1737. Then began the great work of inoculation, with Dr. Kilpatrick as the principal local advocate; he claimed in the *South Carolina Gazette* in 1738 that he had inoculated eight hundred persons, and in his *Essay on Inoculation* he described his method.[242] Dr. Dale's opposition to Kilpatrick's mode was expressed in newspaper essays and pamphlets as noted above. Their writings are discussed at some length by Waring.

933

The unfortunate year 1738 also produced a severe epidemic of whooping cough, perhaps the first major outbreak in the colonies. But this year also saw Dr. Lining begin his meteorological and metabolic experiments which would at least lead to real advances in preventive medicine. In 1743 an epidemic throat disease appeared, in 1745 the mumps, and in 1747 the measles, all probably worse among the Indians than the blacks or whites. In 1748 yellow fever was back, in 1749 whooping cough, and in the next few years yellow fever and smallpox again. By 1750 two hospitals in Charleston were caring for the ill.

In 1760 a further important step against smallpox was taken by the building of a hospital where the inoculated might be watched and nursed and those ill from the disease cared for. The numbers inoculated soared. Then from this time to the Revolution the writings of Chalmers, Garden, and others here mentioned on the diseases of the Charleston area appeared in various parts of the world. South Carolina continued to have the unenviable distinction of having the most widespread and virulent epidemics among the southern colonies, but also the enviable distinction of possessing an unusually able group of physicians who took some important steps toward prevention and identification.

A book-length study has been made by St. Julian Ravenel Childs of *Malaria and Colonization in the Carolina Low Country, 1526–1696*, in which the author has studied statistics and accounts from 1670 to the end of the century, with attention to the relative morbidity of servants and masters, of different sections and times, of legislation, of Charleston as a health center in relation to the rest of the colony. He finds that society influenced disease more than disease influenced society, and that the Carolina boom of 1682–1684 subsided for economic and environmental reasons rather than from unhealthiness or disease. He concludes that malaria, at any rate, did not materially affect the development of the colony.

As already intimated, some of these epidemics connected at least with South Carolina (though they may have come in from the north) were a more effective means of exterminating the red man and removing the principal obstacle to expansion than treaties or wars. In one outbreak, it is estimated, half the Cherokee population died, and it is known that Catawbas, Creeks, and Choctaws were among the many tribes seriously affected.[243]

Georgia's history is much as South Carolina's on epidemics, though relatively in miniature. Fevers of several kinds, dropsies, smallpox, and the rest of the known diseases affected the people of the colony because of their constant intercourse with South Carolina. The fact that despite their towns of Frederica, Ebenezer, and Savannah they lived in comparative isolation may have prevented or mitigated severe epidemics. But after a few years Georgia's proximity to and later adoption of incoming Carolina slaves constituted a constant threat to health. In 1758 there was a severe outbreak of smallpox in Augusta from June to October repeated again in 1759 and 1772.[244]

As far as can now be determined, there was little diphtheria or scarlet fever in the colonial South. Sore throat distempers, as quinsy, are reported from Virginia in 1686 and late in the century in South Carolina. More than one historian of medicine has agreed with Dr. Gordon W. Jones, mentioned above, that alleged yellow fever, such as that described by John Mitchell, was really something else; Duffy guesses that it was dengue (relatively mild). Malaria probably came later than earlier historians have surmised. Two facts stand out in the story of southern colonial diseases and epidemics. First, from mumps to smallpox they obliterated or decimated whole tribes from Jamestown's early decades to the Augusta Treaty of 1763 and thus profoundly affected the course of western expansion. Second, South Carolina was the location of the most frequent and virulent epidemics from 1670 on, and of a group of physicians who distinguished themselves and their profession by experimenting and publishing their attempts to combat them. Eighteenth-century Carolina medical writing is among the most interesting and historically significant literature of the southern colonies.[245]

TREATMENT, INCLUDING SURGERY AND RESEARCH

The treatment of the injured and the ill, which must involve surgery and research, has to some extent been discussed in the chapter on the red man and in the present chapter above. It is a huge subject on which not very much has been done, primarily a few essays and parts of the fine volume on South Carolina by Waring and the several on Virginia by Blanton. There were some interesting improvised surgical activities and some lay and professional research in cures and treatment and prevention. The journals or diaries of a William Byrd II or a Landon Carter indicate some of them. The drugs administered have been incidentally mentioned, especially in connection with apothecaries and their shops. Provincial and county records, the archives and publications of professional societies in Edinburgh or the London Royal Society or the Royal Society of Arts, and the archives of the Society for the Propagation of the Gospel in Foreign Parts, offer the future student of southern medicine rich sources, and there are others in innumerable letters or letterbook correspondence. The professional or lay treatment of the patient was normally according to the

935

rules and directions given in the British-published manuals and textbooks of surgery and medicine, and the manuscript and printed primary materials or records of treatment should be studied along with these volumes known to have been in southern libraries.

MATERIA MEDICA

Almost all the indigenously American part of materia medica has been discussed at least indirectly in the consideration of botany and botanists. The subject is also touched upon in the brief section on apothecaries and their wares. Though the substance and form of drugs changed appreciably over the almost two centuries of the period, the chemist's or apothecary's shop in the colonial town usually carried the latest patent medicines and locally compounded or imported drugs such as are listed and discussed in Harold B. Gill's *The Apothecary in Colonial Virginia* (Williamsburg and Charlottesville, 1972) and in Waring's and Blanton's histories of southern provincial medicine. Some southern surgeon-apothecaries "invented" new compounds growing out of their experience. Often they used herbs and minerals derived from the red men and found in their own colonies. In the later years of the colonial period physicians and apothecaries followed closely what was being done in making new compounds at Edinburgh or Leyden or Uppsala. Slightly earlier the colonial botanical pharmacists had learned a great deal of the medicinal value of various plants from their English apothecary correspondents such as Petiver and Parkinson. In turn they had told their English friends of the potential therapeutic qualities of many plants, as has been pointed out. John Custis, William Byrd II, and Mark Catesby were among the laymen who recommended to physicians such as Sir Hans Sloane or London apothecaries the American variety of ginseng, the Seneca snakeroot, ipecac, and other New World plants. Naturally, professional or semiprofessional medical men such as John Banister, John Clayton I, Alexander Garden, or John Tennent might commend or recommend with even greater confidence. Perhaps William Byrd II in a letter to Sir Hans Sloane summed up the attitude toward native materia medica:

> The Truth of it is, Our Woods abound with so many useful Plants, that woud you do as much good after you are dead, as you do while you are alive, You must improve the scheme of Dr. Radcliff, and bequeath in Your Will an Exhibition for one or more Plantery Physicians, whose Travels should be confined to . . . the New World only, where Nature seems to be more in her youth, and to come later and fresher out of her Creators hands.[246]

AGRICULTURE, THEORY AND PRACTICE

English America, as every record and description indicates, was not even at the beginning believed to be a treasure house of mineral wealth. It would be useful to Great Britain primarily as a land of living wild flora and fauna and as a great and rich wood and farm land which would supply the food and other materials essential in the developing of a prosperous kingdom. Concomitant with and part of these ideas or ideals or aims was the theory of almost inexhaustible virgin land and of a pastoral world in which Englishmen might relive a version of the golden age. Pastoralism implied some sort of paradise; and a quest for an Eden, though usually a fairly practical, working one, was implicit in the British ideal.[247] Chapter I of this study has discussed some of the early manifestations of these concepts, and Chapter II has considered some aspects of primitivism.

As suggested above in various contexts, almost every colony began with the policy of importing potential small-scale farmers, who would be allotted fifty acres per individual, or possibly up to five hundred. The proprietary colonies of Maryland and the Carolinas did not begin exactly that way, but the large areas allotted to original proprietors, and in the Carolinas to Landgraves and Cassiques, were in turn broken up by sale or lease into tracts of modest acreage. Later of course the economic life of the southern colonies came to be based considerably on great landholdings, slave labor, and the accelerated production of exportable staples. Yet even in the South the small farmers far outnumbered the great planters and did so to the American Civil War and after. The southern colonist was usually, therefore, except for the professional men and public officials who served him, a farmer of some kind. Even the physician or lawyer or merchant or sailor was almost sure to own and till some soil. And the urban classes of Charleston, with the possible exception of a few artisans and clergy, had roots deep in the land in that they owned and cultivated plantations. America, and more intensely the southern colonies throughout their history, was thus basically agrarian, with elements of the pastoral ideal in both theory and practice. The life of the mind was inextricably bound into the life of the body and its physical surroundings. Dirt farmer or great landowner, the settler looked at weather and soil, seeds and livestock, crops and taxes, and his small-scale trade industries and his architecture with the eye of the agrarian, an eye varying in its perception and selective quality according to his social and economic and mental status or development.

937

Even a lifelong urbanite such as Benjamin Franklin thought as his constituents urban or rural did, as a farmer, and so did the lawyers of Charleston or the physicians of Annapolis or Williamsburg. The colonial farmers have been characterized as of necessity self-reliant, narrow and extremely provincial in their outlook, generously and imaginatively optimistic as the pastoral idealist would naturally be, and possessed of a profound and abiding faith in work of some sort—mixed with a certain hedonism. Yet the more fortunate economically had traveled to Europe or at least kept up with the latest books and events of the western world and were by no means provincial in outlook. After 1763 the large planter persuaded his less opulent brethren to follow him into pan-American union, something the small farmer did because he knew that fundamentally the great landowner's interests were his and that therefore he must trust his more opulent neighbor. Despite warnings from among themselves that they were rapidly depleting their source of wealth—rich topsoil—and that a single economic style—tobacco or rice or indigo—would lead to ruin, these men remained throughout the colonial era optimistic. They believed they had solved some of their problems by moving on to new lands in the west. Certain of the sons of the soil were wastrels, as there are in any class or time or society— from the yeoman's son who became a smuggler or a petty criminal to a William Byrd III who gambled away a great patrimony earned in one generation and at least preserved in the next. But overwhelmingly, from professional men to public officials, they seem to have taken for granted, with Thomas Jefferson, that at least in several senses those who tilled the soil were the chosen people of God. Tilling the soil meant work, and in the South more than the North it meant outdoor work all the year round. Perhaps the never-ending labors of the southern farm produced the reaction or counterpart or concomitant, that strong love of recreation, that hedonism which W. J. Cash sees as a major element of southern character.

It has often been pointed out that the majority of southern settlers came from rural England, Ireland, Scotland, Switzerland, the Palatinate, or France. Yet a substantial number were from metropolitan areas: in 1686, for example, so many natives of the city of London were in the vicinity of Jamestown that a Cockney feast and commemorative sermon for them were prepared. And there is considerable evidence that clergy, physicians, and lawyers often came from such cities as London and Edinburgh and Dublin. Then there was another sort of characteristic case, as that of Bedfordshire-born William Fitzhugh, who for twenty years toward the close of the seventeenth century wrote frequently to close relatives of his name in Bedfordshire and in London. All these Fitzhughs seem to have originated in the country or county town, or were at most one generation removed from it. And on record are many instances of Londoners, whatever their backgrounds, quickly adapting themselves to crop cultivation, clearing land and rearing livestock.

EARLY CULTIVATION AND SYSTEMS OF FARMING, INCLUDING REFERTILIZING

In practice southern agriculture of the colonial period had two sources —Indian methods and materials of planting and harvesting, and European methods and seeds the settlers brought with them or learned of from imported manuals. Many of the herbals and other books on plant growth have been noted in Chapter IV and Indian planting has been mentioned in Chapters I and II. But something more should be said, especially of the latter.

As early as Arthur Barlowe's "Discourse of the First Voyage" to Raleigh's Virginia in 1584–1585 there is an account of Algonkian fruits and vegetables, the sowing and harvesting and growing seasons, and the fertile soil. The Indian method of planting maize, or corn, is dealt with briefly, as is the colonists' experience in planting English peas, which are alleged to have grown fourteen inches high in ten days. A little later Thomas Hariot in *A briefe and true report* devoted a great proportion of his account to the native agriculture, going into more details on their vegetables. He tells of his group's experience with sugar cane and citrus, which they had hoped would thrive. Noting that his readers may know of other commodities capable of being grown in Virginia, he himself describes native plants and their potential as food, clothing, and export goods. Maize in its varieties and uses, kidney beans, another smaller bean or pea, pumpkins and melons and gourds, sunflowers and oraches, are mentioned. He believed the red men used no fertilizer whatever and describes the planting of corn and beans or other seeds in hills about a yard or more apart. Then he devotes three paragraphs to what Spaniards call tobacco. Finally there are the John White drawings with accompanying descriptions of the growing corn and tobacco and the watchman seated under a cover in the cornfield so that he may frighten off birds which otherwise would consume all the grain.[248]

John Smith mentions and often expatiates on the same native crops as well as on wild berries and fruits and other nutritious plants. Gabriel Archer, Francis Magnel, and George Percy also note native fruits, nuts, beans, and other wild or cultivated foods. Archer emphasizes Indian methods of cultivation and the rich soil. Smith has much incidental material concerning Indian cultivated plants in *A True Relation*, but in *A Map of Virginia* gives considerably more. "Of their Planted fruits in Virginia and how they use them," a section of *A Map*, explains the aboriginal division of the agricultural year into five seasons with a harvest period from September to the middle of November, in which there were great feasts and sacrifices. The planting of corn in hills, four grains with two of beans in each, is almost identical with Hariot's account of the procedure, though Smith gives the depth of the hole for planting and points out that women and children do the weeding. Hariot noted crude spades and hoes in use, but Smith says the holes were made with a stick.

Smith describes also the growing and appearance of corn and ways of cooking varieties of dishes from it, and the cultivation of pumpkins, gourds, and fruit of the passion vine. Then he turns to other phases of agriculture, as livestock and soil fertility. He mentions tobacco almost incidentally and gives nothing like the detail Hariot and White earlier presented concerning its appearance, and practically nothing of its cultivation. There are the well-known references to Smith's having to force his gentlemen to work, but presumably neither he nor they did much cultivation of native plants. To anticipate the winter season they made attempts to farm English style, though details remain generally vague. In *The Generall Historie* he did say more, and in one place or another points out the potential value of ship's stores from the forests to be gathered as ground is cleared, and he anticipated later methods of revitalizing wornout soil. Though Smith's strong advocacy of Indian methods of planting native food crops was expedient, the habits thus acquired by colonial farmers may have slowed or set back European methods of cultivation quite considerably.[249]

As in so many other matters, William Strachey in his *Historie of Travell into Virginia Britania* owes much of his discussion of the agricultural methods of colonist and Indian to Smith or to Hariot, though again he adds interesting details from personal observation, making some comparison between Indian cooking and that of the ancient Greeks. Corn and beans are grown as Smith and Hariot described. Chapter X is devoted to native products, including ship's stores, fruits, herbs, animals, fish, and even metals and minerals. He emphasizes wild grape and the wine Dr. Bohun and others made from them, "full as good as your French-British wyne." He rightly saw native Virginia tobacco as poor, by no means equal to that of the West Indies. West Indian seed may have been introduced in his time or just after in 1610–1611, rather than a little later with John Rolfe, who experimented with the imported seed. The plentiful seafood and wild fruits he mentions explain only in part the slowness of the colonists in settling down to the hard work of farming English fashion.[250]

From these days under the Virginia Company of London to 1763, during the latter years especially in the half-cleared fields of the frontier, the agricultural lessons of planting in hills (later in Tidewater they learned of fish as fertilizer with the corn and beans in each hill), of burning off land, of girdling trees, and of turning over the ground with hoes or other small hand implements instead of with plows, were learned too well in the South. These practices, especially the last, seem to have been in part responsible for the rapidly expanding import trade in blacks from Africa, who could work in the hot fields with the hoe as the white could not and the Indian men would not be persuaded or forced to. But from the beginning, or almost from the beginning, the southern colonist had the great agricultural manuals of his time. Anthony Fitzherbert's *Boke of Husbandrie* (1523 and many later editions), Sir Hugh Platt's *Flora's Paradise* or *The Garden of Eden* (1608 and later), and Thomas Tusser's *A Hundreth Good Points of Husbandrie* . . . (1557, etc.) were books he might have read in Britain, and for two centuries in America he could get new revised and updated editions of these standard works on English farming. Contemporary with the early settlers, and included in their libraries with the older works, were Gervase Markham's *Way to Get Wealth* (1631), an anthology of treatises on farming; Gabriel Platte's *Treatise on Husbandry* (1636, etc.); Walter Blythe's (Blith's) *English Improver, or a New Survey of Husbandry* . . . (1649); Samuel Hartlib's several works on husbandry and silkworms (from 1645); and the two argumentative agricultural works of Sir Richard Weston (about 1646), perhaps the ancestor of the man of the same name publishing book after book on practical husbandry toward the end of the eighteenth century. Of the seventeenth-century experts on agriculture, Hartlib seems to have had the most to say about American colonial farming and farm-product processing. But Markham's translation of Estienne and Liebault's *Maison Rustique; or, The Country Farm* (1616), written on the planning and management of great French estates, was popular in the South. Copies of it turn up in several libraries, including John Carter's.

Following orders or instructions or suggestions from the Virginia Company and then from the King and his Board of Trade and the Plantations, Virginia and all later southern colonies through Georgia tried to cultivate the grape and the silkworm. The efforts were spurred by wishful thinking, some half-knowledge of conditions, and a little sporadic temporary success. Viniculture was attempted at Jamestown and for the next two centuries with a few tantalizingly interesting results, as Robert Beverley II's wines. The colonists experimented with vines from abroad and with the native wild grape. Sericulture, or silkworm and silk production with mulberry trees' foliage as food for the worms, was an even more persistently sought-after production. The Spaniards long before the English had thought silk growing a possibility, but the British colonies had what seemed distinct advantages: they had an indigenous mulberry tree which seemed suited for worms, and the latitude was the same as that of China or Persia.

In 1621 the Virginia Company sent over a pinnace primarily to carry silkworm "seed" from Italy, France, and Spain. In the same year they decided to concentrate on the seed from Valencia, said to be the hardiest. Within a few months European mulberry trees as well as silkworm seed had been planted or set out and seemed to be thriving. The King himself was much interested. Actually sericulture had been attempted as early as 1608–1609. It was obviously at once an industry and an agricultural pursuit, and its apparent possibilities were used in promotion. It was tried again in 1613, and some Virginia-grown silk was carried by Rolfe to England. By 1616 a specially trained servant of John Bonoeil, a silkworm keeper of James I, went to Virginia and spent six years. Moderately successful results grew from this well-organized effort. A silkworm house was built, and under Sir Edwin Sandys' administration, beginning in 1618, there was considerable interest in the project. Even the first General Assembly of 1619 attempted to aid the undertaking by legislation.

The promotion and the hope continued. New books on sericulture were composed with Virginia in mind, and *Observations to be followed,* the first unit of a sizable body of seventeenth-century silkworm literature, was completed and published and copies were sent to America in 1621. Before 1621 silk was the great hope of government and farmers alike, and glowing reports continued to that date. After the 1622 massacre George Sandys, director of industry, required that every plantation impale two acres of ground, employ two men in vineyard work, and build a two-story silkworm house. More seed came in and various prominent planters devoted themselves to the cocoons.

After the dissolution of the Company in 1624 interest in silk continued. Governors and Assemblies took steps to discipline imported French growers, and in 1639 Sir Francis Wyatt was ordered to see that white mulberry trees by planted. Gradually the Virginia settlers had come to realize the complex problems such as the three greatly differing varieties of mulberry trees, of which the American variety was the least suitable for silkworms. Meanwhile such men as Ralph Hamor in 1615 and Edward Williams in 1650 in their books or tracts reported on the Virginia undertaking. By 1665 a Major Thomas Walker was said to have planted seventy thousand trees (almost surely imported) in two years.

English persons interested in the Virginia silk spurred on the settlers, especially by writing books and pamphlets and even a few verses on the subject. Virginia Ferrar, William Edwards, and Samuel Hartlib were among those ardent promoters. One of the prominent colonists to go in for sericulture was the aforementioned Edward Digges, who lived near Yorktown, governor of the colony during the Commonwealth period. His fine tobacco marked "E.D." was equalled only by his silk. He imported Armenian and Turkish workmen, raised some worms successfully, and taught his fellow colonists how to wind silk. He was supported enthusiastically after the Commonwealth period by returned royal governor Berkeley, who in 1668 sent Charles II a present of silk, which the monarch ordered to be made into bed furniture for his own use. But Berkeley could never get the skilled workers he requested, and by 1672 the work had languished. In 1676 Thomas Glover in his "Account of Virginia" noted somewhat prematurely that the only living part of the project was a few mulberry trees. Historians continued at times to mention silk, and individuals and governments of other colonies encouraged silk production, evidently believing that their climate and growing conditions were more suitable than Virginia's.

Sporadic encouragement for both grape and silk culture had come through subsidies. A few skilled workers came though never nearly enough. But these seventeenth-century attempts to adapt outside agricultural products to New World conditions show quite definitely that southern colonists, and their governments in America and in England, did not give in to the tobacco or other so-called one-crop systems without a real struggle to diversify. Englishmen at home hoped as much as the colonists that these two valuable and popular importations into Great Britain might be produced on British soil. It was, within the limitations of contemporary knowledge, an intelligent and even imaginative attempt to improve the human condition with what were in large part luxuries.[251]

About 1688 John Banister included in his manuscript natural history of Virginia much indirect and some direct information about Virginia farm cultivation and crops. Concerning corn he tells a great deal, of the many ways of preparing it, of the several varieties, and of the soils in which it thrives best. By his time the white colonists had improved somewhat on Indian methods of planting and weeding and had invented a hoe-harrow, called a brake-harrow, of which Banister intended to enclose a drawing. And by this time the settler had learned the nutritive qualities of more native plants and was enlarging his acreage devoted to English imported root vegetables, herbs, and fruits. Banister compares the vegetables and melons he knows with those Hariot noted, and he gives three paragraphs to tobacco—the two principal varieties, the topping necessary during growth, the sowing, and the curing. He says much of the sweet potato but almost surely did not know the white or Andean potato. His notations indicate that the variety of crops in Virginia had enlarged greatly during the century and that the farmer was developing his own way of cultivating the native corn and tobacco. He also implies that concentration on and over-production of tobacco would deplete or impoverish the soil and prevent young colonists from learning some important other things about agriculture,[252] a warning given by others years earlier and repeated for generations after him.

The Reverend John Clayton's interest in improving agricultural conditions in Virginia by draining swamps, enriching soils, and improving the quality of the tobacco leaf has been in part noted already. In planting tobacco he advocated steeping the seed in an infusion of manure and mixing it with ashes, methods a nineteenth-century agriculturist states were still used in his time, the mixing with ashes being practiced by all planters. Clayton has something to say on the use of maize as fodder for cattle and on the much greater yield of English wheat per acre in America than in Britain. He was distinctly disappointed in what he considered the slovenliness or unimaginativeness of his fellow colonists in their cultivation of the soil.[253] His own experiments and ideas set or anticipated methods at once more practical and more ingenious.

The parson's contemporaries Hartwell, Blair, and Chilton in *The Present State of Virginia, and the College* (1727, written 1697) devote part of a chapter to "Cultivation" in Virginia, giving a pessimistic picture of land worn out by overplanting both corn and tobacco and of the barren old fields which result, of uneconomical hoeing instead of plowing as the method of cultivation, and of the craze to plant only tobacco. The two lawyers and the Bishop of London's Commissary were or had been planters and knew whereof they spoke, but the persistent desire for quick cash (or its equivalent), a now venerable American tradition or trait, prevented their warnings or those of others from being heeded save by a few thoughtful farmers—and then in later generations.[254]

Robert Beverley's concluding chapter in his 1705 *History and Present State of Virginia* is concerned with indigenous important "natural products" and with the advantages of husbandry. He writes at length of some favorite aspects of cultivation, as apple and peach orchards, plums, cherries, nectarines, and his own grapevines. He avows that every sort of English grain thrives in the Chesapeake area; that rice does well; that flax, hemp, cotton, and silk have flourished; that livestock become fat; that there are great fertile fields in swamps to be had for the draining, and that there are a thousand other kindred advantages the country affords. He depicts, as recent writers have pointed out, a potential paradise, but he concludes by suggesting that his province (and by implication the surrounding colonies) are by no means an Eden, for the "slothful indolence of [his] countrymen" prevents a full realization of an actual earthly ideal. He hopes that his book may rouse them from their lethargy.[255]

Parson Hugh Jones, scientist and whilom professor at William and Mary, has his say about Chesapeake Bay agriculture in several different chapters of his *Present State of Virginia.* He adds some useful details not in Beverley or unemphasized there, such as the life of Negro slaves, wasteful methods of clearing land, the worm fences which protect corn planted in hills, more on methods of cultivation during the growing season, the fine quality of wool and hams and bacon. Later he has something on the profitableness of silkworms and mulberry trees, though he handles this rather naïvely. Then he, like some other historians, elaborates on methods of procuring tracts of land, a promotion feature essential to the would-be agriculturist. Jones is not the pessimist and the cynic Beverley at times is, nor is he the prophet of future agricultural woe other contemporary commentators are.[256]

In Maryland both half-satiric prose narrator George Alsop in *A Character of the Province of Mary-Land* (1666) and savage poetic satirist Ebenezer Cook in *The Sot-Weed Factor* (1708) tell stories of the indolence and slothful ways of living of tobacco planters great and small. John Hammond earlier in *Leah and Rachel* gives a favorable sketch and implications as to Maryland's agriculture and sees a steady improvement in cultivation and manner of living in both Virginia and Maryland. On the threshold of the Revolution minor official William Eddis wrote to Britain of the rather dreary farms in the back country or frontier but at the same time recorded his realization of the almost unlimited agricultural potential of the country. He also took space to explain the mechanics of the land-tenure or ownership system for all the provinces of America, of fees, of quit-rents, warrants of escheat, the land-office, and other features or bases of the farming system. He elaborates on the basic three-step system of warrant-certificate-patent and of the resulting complications which drove many people to large landholders or speculators (including companies) for their land.[257]

In every one of the provinces the function of indentured servants and of slaves in the cultivation of the soil is touched upon in all sorts of communications—governors' annual reports, private letters, and such histories or promotion pieces as those mentioned above. The early Chesapeake writers say more of indentured servants and farm workers than do the Carolinians. George Alsop and Hugh Jones considered that, though the bond servants were lazy, undependable, sometimes even criminal, most were useful to their owners and to themselves. Seventeenth-century Virginians such as William Fitzhugh saw the black slave as difficult to procure and apparently used white servants in most farm duties, though by Landon Carter's time a century later the situation had changed markedly. That South Carolina planters could and did have profitable plantations is evident from the 1775 *American Husbandry,* possibly but not probably by the aforementioned Virginian Dr. John Mitchell (and at least compiled from other known work of his), which gives tables of initial investments, labor and other expenses, and calculations for the ensuing twelve years. "Plenty of good land free from taxes, cheapness of labour, and dearness of product sold, [together] with cheapness of that consumed" gave the Carolinian planter enormous advantages over his British counterpart.

Dozens of other aspects of the agriculture of the southern colonies John Lawson, Eliza Lucas Pinckney, George Milligen-Johnston, the Salzburgers in Georgia, and numbers of provincial governors comment upon for the planters and the house officials. In every colony, within a few short years of settlement, and naturally varying with the depth and quality of the topsoil, there was the great question of revitalization of wornout land. The planter either moved on to new land or studied ancient and modern works on fertilizer and rotation of crops, or experimented himself (as the Reverend John Clayton suggested he do). To some extent every planter made the attempt to reconcile his crop or seed to his soil. Carters, Blands, Randolphs, Pinckneys, Dulanys, and small farmers in varying degrees all tried a variety of innovative combinations.

But before the end of the eighteenth century men such as John Beale Bordley and Thomas Jefferson began to appear in print on agriculture, and there were scores of newspaper essays by working planters writing under pseudonyms, as Landon Carter and Henry Laurens. And there was the remarkable book *The Present State of Great Britain and North America* (London, 1767), by native Virginian John Mitchell, which showed some understanding of almost every phase of South Atlantic agriculture, from land tenure to labor to suitable crops to fertilization.[258] Again southern cerebration seems to have been applied to a practical problem of environment rather than to abstract theological doctrine.

THE STAPLES: TOBACCO, RICE, INDIGO, WITH HEMP AND GRAIN

In a certain sense southern colonial agriculture was diversified through all the years of its history, for every farmer attempted to grow plants and livestock which would feed him and his family. Thus Indian corn was to be seen on every plantation from Maryland to Georgia, for the grower used it as food for himself and his family, including servants and slaves, and for much of his livestock. A very small amount was exported or sold to townspeople, though usually the latter had their own garden patches which included it. The same was true of orchards, pumpkins-gourds-melons, leafy and root vegetables, and anything else that would supply the dining table with variety. Grains were also raised primarily for stock or brewing. The average southern colonial plantation of fifty or fifty thousand acres (the latter never in one continuous plot) would present to the visitor's eye first a considerable percentage of forest or woods (first-growth or springing up in old fields), acres of corn and English wheat and some oats and barley and later lucerne, orchards or at least some fruit trees, and smaller areas of vegetables, besides the kitchen-flower garden, and a large expanse of the money crop, or export or sale crop. For as in every other agricultural economy, the southern planter sought for at least one money crop or what would stand for money or credit with London merchants, provincial or parish levies (including those which paid the clergyman), or local trade or purchase.

Virginia and Maryland with upper North Carolina found such a crop quite early, a crop around which centered economic and political and even theological controversies, all of which were contributing factors leading to the American struggle for independence. Lower North Carolina, all of South Carolina to the middle of the Piedmont, and later Georgia tried and found at various times and places different money crops, most notably rice and indigo, and to a lesser extent hemp, with cotton beginning to be a major crop at the end of the period. The more southern colonies grew some tobacco but never on the scale or with the results in the Chesapeake provinces. As the author of *American Husbandry* pointed out, the "noxious weed" grew from Quebec to the West Indies but was profitable only in Maryland, Virginia, and North Carolina.

The first "commodity" crop of the southern colonies was therefore tobacco. As noted by Strachey and others, native Algonkian-area tobacco was bitter and inferior in leaf-plant structure, and almost surely by 1610–1611 Virginia planters were importing the much superior West Indian or Central American varieties, usually calling it "Spanish tobacco," later distinguishing two major varieties, Oroonoko and Sweet-Scented. The finer quality may indeed have arrived with John Rolfe about 1610, when he reached Jamestown via Bermuda and shipwreck. By 1612 was planted *Nicotiana tabacum*, the larger of the Spanish-American varieties, and "never was a marriage of soil and seed more fruitful."[259]

Yet there were problems. Probably as early as 1565 Sir John Hawkins had brought the plant to England from Florida, Drake brought more in 1586, and by 1604 its consumption was so extensive that James I wrote his *Counter Blast*. Yet six years later the value of the import was £60,000. As Lord Sackville's papers indicate, in the 1614–1617 period after Virginia and Bermuda had begun production and shipment, the combined value of their crop and Spanish import was enormous.[260] By then, despite the warnings and protests of the Virginia Company, the plant was everywhere in English Virginia, grown even in the streets of Jamestown.

Exactly where Rolfe got his seed or plants remains unknown, but as early as 1615 (written in 1614) Ralph Hamor gives full credit for the improved variety's importation and development in Virginia to Rolfe, "who first tooke the pains to make the triall therof," partly because he liked it and partly because he wished to find a "commodity," or money crop, to help the Company investors. In 1616, Rolfe himself, in *A True Relation*, notes that even by that date Governor Dale had to curb production, for the weed was so profitable many were planting it and nothing else. Dale required that every farmer who planted tobacco must plant for himself and every manservant at least two acres of corn.[261] This restriction Rolfe quite clearly approved. By 1617, after some further cross-breeding and other experimentation, Virginia had produced a superior variety which was exported in the weight of twenty thousand pounds. Every plantation from Shirley Hundred west was growing it. The production was an early triumph over official policy of government of all kinds. It became a craze, and one reason for the half-successful (from the red man's point of view) 1622 massacre was that the planters had given the Indians weapons with which to hunt game for food while the English grew tobacco.

Frequent legislative or executive attempts were made to reduce the amount of tobacco grown. But planters moved on west in search of new rich tobacco land, and along each of the great rivers emptying into the Bay there were plantations with warehouses, wharves, and other facilities for growing and curing and exporting. Maryland colonists began almost at once after first settlement to grow tobacco, and acts to regulate crops and exports are among the colony's early legislative enactments, though most of the major regulatory measures came in the eighteenth century, especially the Tobacco Inspection Laws local and British, which resulted in a spate of essays for several years in the *Maryland Gazette* from 1746/ 1747 on through 1763. Maryland began by concentrating on Oroonoko and grew little Sweet-Scented, but as in Virginia even by the latter half of the seventeenth century there was overproduction and individual and governmental attempts were made to curb production and manipulate price. The British interference by tax or regulation met with strong opposition in some quarters of the Chesapeake colonies, and the whole tobacco industry was a major factor in the economic and political protests and rebellions leading to the open break between homeland and colonies.

Meanwhile Virginia tobacco production first pursued a northerly direction toward the Potomac until about 1720 and after that date showed a thrust westward. Commercial production above the fall line came about 1720 and by the end of the colonial period was at the foot of the Blue Ridge. From 1764 until the Revolution the major expansion to the south took place. Gradually Piedmont replaced Tidewater as the great tobacco belt, and so it remains today in Maryland, Virginia, and North Carolina, though it has also spread into mountain valleys and beyond them into Kentucky and Tennessee. The plantbed-cleared-land-hoeing-topping- suckering-harvesting-curing methods are described at length in many places, and the processes continue much as in the colonial period, except that by 1800 the plow had to a great extent replaced the hoe. Curing has been by air and fire. Oroonoko (Oronoco, etc., spelled at least three or four ways), a large, porous, strong tobacco, grew well in moderately rich soils and areas possessed of certain chemical properties; but it never brought the prices that Sweet-Scented did, which required a somewhat different and richer soil. The parson who was paid in tobacco was always grateful if he had a Sweet-Scented parish. From these two major varieties developed other subspecies.

Transportation was naturally a major problem. William Fitzhugh's letters tell something of it, and the cartouche of the Fry-Jefferson map illustrates shipment. Transportation in the Chesapeake Bay country was principally by water, often from the Tidewater planter's own wharf aboard the Britain-bound ship. The tobacco was packed in great casks or hogsheads and rolled or carried in wagons or carts to the wharves. Piedmont Chesapeake and all North Carolina tobacco were disadvantaged in this matter until long after our period, though the planters developed various ways of getting their product to market. Regular tobacco trails or roads developed, as from the Roanoke Valley to Petersburg, or flat-bottomed boats were used on the upper reaches of the rivers to get the hogsheads to the wharves.

After some sad experiences at both ends (grower and buyer) from spoiled, poor-quality, dirt-filled, and other inferior tobacco, inspection laws had to be passed, the first in Virginia as early as 1619. But new situations arose, sometimes large-scale resistance to phases of regulation, and the question of tobacco inspection fills many pages of the legislative records of the three tobacco colonies. After the newspapers were established in the eighteenth century, it was as already noted an ever-recurring subject for debate. The laws were often quite complex and far-reaching, required costly enforcement procedures, and had frequently to be amended almost immediately after they went into effect. The 1730 inspection law was, with a few changes, the basic Virginia code for the remainder of the period. Warehouses, inspectors, types of casks and other containers, destruction of inferior product, appeals, stamped approvals, weights and other matters were covered.[262] Warehouses and production and prices and amount of exports, local tobacco rebellions and cutting, are all phases of the story of this great staple of the upper southern coastal colonies.

In the history of any state or nation, no other crop or resource ever played a more significant role than tobacco did in colonial Virginia, Maryland, and, toward the end of the period, North Carolina. It affected social, political, and economic life in ways which cannot be here pointed out. In the beginning it was not a major factor in the importation of slaves; in fact, its first flourishing came almost entirely through the use of white indentured servants (and of course small landowners themselves) in its cultivation. But it did encourage importation of African labor, which would be found even more profitable farther south with other staples. It affected urbanization: many of the towns of the three-colony and later three-state area are direct outgrowths of the warehouse-inspection stations located where they now stand: for example, Richmond, Petersburg, and Danville in Virginia.

There is an enormous literature on tobacco alone, as the Arents Collection of the New York Public Library bears witness. Even for the colonial period it is imposing, going back to the earliest Spanish explorers. The historian-explorers touched upon in this and other chapters comment upon it, some approvingly, and some bewailing its omnipresence. William Byrd's *A Discourse Concerning the Plague* (1721) includes considerable reference to it, Ebenezer Cook's versions of *The Sot-Weed Factor* are poetic satires concerned directly with the society tobacco had brought into being, and dozens more pieces in verse and prose berate or celebrate the golden weed. Jefferson in his *Notes on the State of Virginia* and the author of the *Present State* are among the later agricultural theorists who examine the whole tobacco culture relatively dispassionately.

The author of *American Husbandry* considered rice the grand staple of South Carolina, for as he saw it the Charleston golden age from perhaps 1730 to 1775 was based on a rice economy. Before the earlier date the planters of the Carolinas had grown both rice and indigo with only fair success, though recent investigators believe that the seed from which the great South Carolina crop was to develop was imported from Madagascar possibly as early as 1685. Yet rice was probably not profitable in South Carolina until 1710 and not really the great commodity until about twenty years later. Between 1735 and 1739 it was grown extensively in southeastern North Carolina with some success until in the latter year a summer drought destroyed the crop. It was still being grown in the Cape Fear region long after the colonial period was over, but it was never so successful as to make an appreciable element of the colonial North Carolina population immensely wealthy. Later in the early 1760s in Georgia the engineer De Brahm provided tables of expenses in developing a rice plantation in such detail as to suggest that it was then a major element in that province's agricultural economy, though he may have been suggesting that there was much low land to be cleared and converted into rice fields. The Georgia Salzburgers as early as 1734 were cultivating rice in their low-lying ground, though their first crop was not very successful because of drought. Rice seems not to have been successful in Georgia until black slave labor was introduced, but it was almost from the beginning of the colony a crop, and many Georgians such as the Salzburgers were kept from starvation throughout the whole of the first generation by being supplied with edible rice, possibly grain grown in Carolina.[263]

In South Carolina rice was on everyone's lips and in everyone's letters, even in provincial laws. In 1720 rice became legal tender in South Carolina as tobacco had long been in the colonies to the north. Merchants such as Henry Laurens from 1746 well into the 1760s could hardly compose a personal or business letter which did not comment on the state of the commodity or on transactions related to the grain. Even Eliza Lucas Pinckney, plantation mistress usually remembered for her intense interest in another crop, often mentions her rice production, including comments on droughts which in certain years spoiled the harvest as it had in regions to the north and south of the Carolina Low Country. For some years the economy largely based upon it seems to have been sounder than the Chesapeake tobacco economy ever was. Colonial rice had a European as well as a British market which it could reach, and perhaps for that reason, and the fact that the colony had in Charleston a merchant class capable of handling the commodity, Carolina planters seem never to have become as deeply indebted to London or other British factors as were the Chesapeake tobacco growers. Rice alone, and certainly when combined with indigo, may account for the astonishing number of young South Carolinians affluent enough to receive general or legal or medical education abroad during the twenty-five years just before the Revolution.[264]

Indigo, as noted above, had been tried early in the two Carolinas and at the time had not proved profitable. Like rice, it was a money crop before the end of the seventeenth century. But despite the instructions in 1690 allowing it to be accepted for quitrents and a special 1694 act for encouragement of growing both the plant and the insect which together produced this valuable dyestuff, its development as a major crop was slow. When the War of Jenkins' Ear separated Carolina from its rice outlets or established markets, a substitute export was badly needed. The story of Colonel George Lucas' sending seed of *Indigofera tinctoria* from the West Indies to his daughter Eliza (Mrs. Pinckney) is well known. It is at once the success story of a woman entrepreneur and planter and of the rapid development of a major crop. By 1740 Eliza was experimenting with it and working indefatigably to overcome one obstacle after another. The 1741 crop was small but produced "20 weight" of indigo. A mixture of new seed from the West Indies with that of the previous crop was the basis for the 1742 harvest, but not until 1744 was it shown conclusively that the indigo from her Wappoo plantation was of promising quality. Most of the 1744 crop was saved for seed and generously given to a great number of people. Others who successfully planted a 1745 indigo crop can be identified by their seed advertisements in the *South-Carolina Gazette*. Indigo culture spread quickly, and the blue-dye cakes established credit in London banking houses for many South Carolinians. In 1747 more than 135,000 pounds were produced, and good seasons soon produced at least a million. It had become the new staple, not in the colonial period displacing rice, but taking a place alongside it. Mrs. Pinckney's interest is evident in her letters throughout the period of experiment and establishment of production. In his business letters Henry Laurens wrote of it as much as he did of rice, and that is to say a great deal. Christopher Gadsden showed it was still a Carolina staple in his newspaper essays of 1769 and long after the period of this study, 1784. Governor James Glen's *A Description of South Carolina* (1761) describes the varieties and suggests that rice and indigo be grown on the same plantation, for the two are produced at different seasons. And Dr. George Milligen-Johnston in *A Short Description . . . of South-Carolina* (1770, written 1763) remarks that during his day in the province indigo was cultivated with great success, and near the end of his book he devotes a chapter to describing the whole process, from soil and seed to the drying house for the small, square cakes. *De Brahm's Report* (1760s), in the South Carolina section, declares that indigo is an excellent crop in either Up Country or Low Country and that one field has been known to produce three full crops "of that Culture." *American Husbandry*, using Glen's and perhaps Milligen-Johnston's accounts, gives several pages to the cultivation of this second of the grand staples of Carolina.[265]

Indigo was tried in Georgia too, but of the three great money crops South Carolina in the decades before 1776 was the leading producer of two, and Virginia and Maryland of the other. As we have seen, all the colonies grew Indian corn primarily for provincial consumption, and although some was shipped abroad it did not in the colonial period become a significant item of export. Wheat flour was beginning to be made from local grain for at least a century before the Revolution in all the colonies, perhaps most successfully in the Chesapeake area. There was some export of flour before 1776. Flax was grown and spun on many farms but almost always for local use. Hemp, as an item of naval stores, was also grown sporadically in all the southern provinces. William Byrd II wrote of its potential uses and suitability to his lands, so did other planters in every colony. It was grown and sold sufficiently to have been a fairly important item in agricultural economy. It was encouraged for years by bounties from Britain, but it never became an export of first importance. Contrary to popular belief, cotton remained a minor crop with small export value throughout the colonial period. A few other naval stores may well be classified under technology and manufacturing rather than agriculture and will be noted below.

The southern colonial farmer grew then tobacco, indigo, and rice, and occasionally wheat, as cash crops. He was of necessity vitally concerned with them, but the journals and letters of a William Fitzhugh, a William Byrd II, a Landon Carter, and those anonymous and pseudonymous essayists in the provincial gazettes indicate that the planter was always at least considering diversification, which he professed to believe would improve the economy in general and enrich his personal way of living, or himself. He wrote of pests, especially weevils and other insects which threatened many kinds of crops, he understood that he held or would soon hold wornout or impoverished land, and he proposed all sorts of remedies for the situation. But there is little evidence that he practiced what he preached as to revitalization of soil: he most frequently followed the course noted—moving his tobacco or other staple on to new lands. His sons thought harder and wrote longer and more significantly of their agrarian problems, partially because in their time suitable new lands were harder to come by. And some of the latter did implement the sound farming procedures their fathers knew and neglected. There were experimental and practical colonial farmers who attempted to vary or to obliterate the tyranny of a single or double grand style, men like Landon Carter and George Washington and some of the Carrolls and Bordleys and Dulanys of Maryland. Dr. Mitchell fully understood the importance of new land west of the coastal plain and its place in future agricultural development. There is little clue to what the small or middling farmer, who was in the numerical majority by a great deal, thought or tried to do about the crop system. He was not and probably never had the chance to be articulate in print, though the newspapers were open to him within the usual limits. His sons between 1790 and 1830 were to join their more opulent neighbors in agricultural societies for the improvement of soil, crops, and livestock. The southern colonial farmer was hampered by his own greed, by the practical necessity of a cash crop, and by British monopoly. He did adapt British and continental and Indian farming methods in his large-scale staple production, however, and probably more than any other kind of American showed by his example how the huge open spaces of the Mississippi basin might become the breadbasket of a great nation and for a time of the whole world. For his grand staples proved that imported seeds and plants could be acclimated and that crops on a grand scale might be produced in America as they had not been in Europe. And then he suggested by a variety of examples how they might be transported to market.

HORTICULTURE: SCIENCE AND ART, AND THE LITERATURE OF COLONIAL AGRARIANISM

The colonial garden has already been mentioned, primarily in relation to botany and agriculture. One form of it, the tree-shrub-flower garden, will be discussed at some length in the next chapter, on the fine arts. Yet there is no way to separate completely the useful or practical plot of intensively cultivated ground from the artistic. Herbs and even vegetables, especially the latter if they were leafy, were often part of the symmetrical pattern of growing things fenced or walled off within close range of the plantation center, its manor house. But there were plots of ground devoted entirely to food plants, perhaps occasionally combined with medicinal. And there were orchards, protected or confined plantings of fruit trees usually grown from seed or slips brought from the Old World. These kitchen gardens, orchards, and later nut groves were, as one learns from ground plans of early South Atlantic estates, as much a part of the comprehensive artistic plan as were box-bordered beds of flowers, English yews, and American shade trees. In somewhat reduced form the modest farmhouses, particularly in the older settled districts, were also surrounded in graceful patterns by useful and ornamental living things.

In this chapter these gardens planted to feed or clothe or quench the thirst of the colonial southern settler should be considered briefly. To intelligent and educated men such as Laurens or the Middletons or Dulanys or Byrds or Custises, they offered challenges in ingenuity as well as patient and careful experimentation in planting and cultivation. English in appearance as most of them were, they contained scores and perhaps hundreds of New World plants. Long before Columbus, Peruvians and other Central and South Americans had developed into edible forms a number of native plants which by the time of British settlement had been carried as far north as Canada. Though the North American red man was far behind his southern kin in adapting and domesticating the wild root or fruit, he did do something in supplying himself with convenient food supplies other than maize. His use of the gourd, sweet potato, pumpkin, and melon may have been learned in slow degrees from Mexico and below. The Indian that the first southern settlers met along the Atlantic seaboard was so well supplied with seafood and wild animals that he did not have to look very hard or long for vegetable sustenance.

954

Fruit he found wild in abundance. Yet the seventeenth-century colonists observed gardens adjacent to aboriginal villages, and even the earliest mention the variety of domesticated vegetables presented to them. White's Secota painting-engraving shows tobacco and corn as the principal crops within the village itself or just outside, but there are also obviously sun-flowers with edible seed and pumpkins and perhaps melons. White's drawing shows symmetrical patterns, squares and circles and other shapes conforming in part to land contours.

From the seventeenth century to Thoreau's time the Cherokees had the reputation of being the best of Indian husbandmen. Their vegetables and fruits were so abundant that some horticultural historians have felt that they must have been largely vegetarian. The Spanish and French Jesuits long before Roanoke and Jamestown had taught these red men and others how to grow apples and especially peaches and vegetables, partly European and partly Central American. Tomatoes, native to the Andes, had been eaten on the southern continent by whites as early as 1583 and were probably eaten by North American Indians long before Collinson described them to Custis in a 1742/1743 letter and Jefferson made them a matter of printed record in his *Notes on the State of Virginia.* They were not a part of kitchen gardens in the colonial South, though their relative the white potato became so fairly late. Nor was sweet corn planted near the residences until the national period.

European peas and native and European beans under various names were cultivated by the early whites. Though African in origin, water-melons were being grown by Indians from the Gulf to Canada by 1607. When the Jamestown settler arrived with his own assortment of seed (at first quite meager) he found among his red neighbors the edible plants mentioned, varieties he would cultivate in his own garden. No doubt visitors such as John Tradescant the younger as well as resident expert horticulturists such as George Thorpe of the college property or Edward Digges of the York River plantation within a few years, perhaps months, of arrival were planting for food.

Men like John Smith emphasized the variety of fruit trees they expected to grow in America, which they rightly judged to be a natural orchard. Apples, pears, apricots, figs, and peaches at first did not thrive, but by the second half of the century a large planter such as William Fitzhugh had 2,500 apple trees enclosed with a locust fence. Though this con-stitutes more than a kitchen orchard, with his large staff Fitzhugh felt he must make large quantities of cider. There were lesser and greater orchards, their fruit used for alcoholic beverages or eating raw or cooked. Often the planter combined beauty and convenience and even manufacture by planting edible mulberry trees which afforded shade and lived long close to his house, or these or other useful trees in his kitchen garden or flower garden. The promotion literature of both centuries is filled with references to kitchen gardens in which English parsnips, carrots, turnips, and radishes were grown beside indigenously American melons and pumpkins. Beverley believed that the abundance of peaches among the Indians proved that fruit to be a native of America, and so did botanists a century later. Virginians usually grafted trees, as did the middle and northern colonists.[266]

Maryland's horticultural history is much the same as Virginia's with perhaps an even greater emphasis on apples for cider. Ornamental gardens were as frequent, especially among the upper classes. Trees on manor-house grounds in both colonies were usually native. Maryland's Labadists were gardeners of note, producing both the useful and the ornamental, though the latter came to an end in 1722. Ornamental gardens were not, as is frequently stated, confined to the upper classes until the mid-eighteenth century. Probably an analysis of the value of the property of those who owned Miller's *Gardener's Dictionary* (fourth ed., 1754) in this and the other southern colonies would suggest strongly that the middling classes also went in for household gardening, ornamental and practical.[267]

Perhaps the cradle of European gardening in America is, as Hedrick states, the region from north central Florida through Georgia into South Carolina, for to that area the Spanish and French brought Old World fruits and other plants earlier than 1600. South Carolina or North Carolina gardens in general are described by Robert Horne in 1666, by Thomas Ashe in 1682, and by dozens later. John Lawson naturally tells most about North Carolina, including Indian peach orchards, varieties of cherries, and even the wild plum and its possibilities. Besides indigo and rice, Eliza Lucas Pinckney was noted for the trees, flowers, shrubs, and vegetables she had under cultivation. Perhaps the best-known of South Carolina gardens, to be discussed in more detail in the next chapter, was at Crowfield on Goose Creek. The property passed into the hands of the Middleton family in 1722, and the great garden they developed is described by Eliza Pinckney on a 1742 visit. The Drayton family's Magnolia Gardens (perhaps going back to 1671) are also well known today, though not for food plants any more than the Middleton acres.[268]

American Husbandry devotes considerable space to the South Carolina fruits and vegetables grown in the later eighteenth century but says little about enclosed horticultural areas save the incidental mention of kitchen gardens which contained "every sort of useful plant that is commonly cultivated in England." At the same time, the author observes that "garden-stuff" grows better to the north. By the end of the colonial period kitchen gardens and orchards were frequent in the Charleston area, however, if one may judge by such advertisements of seeds and plants as appeared in the *South-Carolina Gazette* and *South Carolina American and General Gazette.*

Savannah was laid out as a city with small gardens, probably primarily for the kitchen, adjacent to each dwelling and with a large public garden just outside the urban center. The Trustees planned an extensive botanical garden to be filled as soon as possible with West Indian useful plants and a few ornamentals, which Dr. William Houstoun and then Robert Millar were commissioned to collect. The garden was to have one section set out in mulberry trees for silkworms, another in rare medicinal plants (Millar's idea), and another in vineyards. It was a ten-acre plot on Yamacraw Bluff, one corner of it including an old Indian mound, and in the area there were several sorts of soil. The acreage was fenced and apparently laid off in squares, with orange trees planted along the cross walks. The northern part was for the time left as a grove of native hickory, live oak, ash, bay, sassafras, and magnolia. Figs, pomegranates, and olives from the warmest parts of Europe were tried, as well as West Indian coconuts, coffee, and cotton, with East Indian bamboo.

Houstoun and Millar gathered throughout the Caribbean whatever they thought might thrive in Georgia. Neither of them ever reached Georgia in person, but many of their plants and others from various parts of the world did arrive, including bamboo seed and bamboo plants, vine cuttings from France, and olive trees from Venice. Von Reck recorded in 1734 that the nursery was already thriving, but in 1738 a severe frost blighted the young orange trees and damaged the vines and mulberry leaves. The garden languished, despite the importation of a group of indentured servants to tend it, for these laborers turned out to be lazy, obstinate, and dissatisfied. Conditions gradually became worse as olive trees failed to become fruitful. By 1740 the experimentation in new plants was principally carried on by individuals, and the public garden had become merely a nursery for white mulberry trees to be furnished gratis to all planters who desired them. In this form the garden seems to have survived until 1747 or 1748. De Brahm in 1751 found only a few olive and fruit trees as testimonials of the effort. Though viniculture and sericulture continued in private hands and were officially encouraged, they too in the end failed. Yet the Trustees Garden as the first major agricultural experiment station in America had been well organized and at first well conducted. It is representative of the at least sporadic agricultural experimentation which has survived in the South.[269] Change of government, insufficient skilled labor, failures in experiments because of cold and drought, and above all the drying up of funds brought it to an end.

One of the more interesting intellectual and even literary features of useful gardening in the southern colonies was the agrarian manual read and sometimes written by the settler. Several of the manuals studied by literate farmers had been first published in the sixteenth and early seventeenth centuries (see Chapter IV). In the eighteenth century these were still appearing in new editions, but the two most popular by English writers were Jethro Tull's *Horse-Hoeing Husbandry* (London, 1731–1733, etc.) and the various editions of the aforementioned Philip Miller's *Kalendar* (London, 1732, etc.) and his famous *Gardener's Dictionary* (London, 1724, etc.), the latter writer's work full of allusions to southern plants and planters and botanists from Tradescant, Banister, Clayton, Catesby, to Dale. Tull was most concerned, however, with large-scale planting. He invented a machine drill and advocated hoeing as the principal means of cultivation of growing crops. He was an agricultural bible to George Washington and Thomas Jefferson, though they also relied on more recent British writers such as Bradley and Young and Sinclair.[270] Jefferson quotes Miller as to season and time for planting particular things, sometimes showing no consideration of differences in English and Virginia climate.

But just before the colonial period concluded and immediately after its conclusion appeared the first of a number of significant horticultural manuals written by southern colonials. The several almanacs already mentioned may have relied on actual American observation for their tables for planting, cultivating, and harvesting, though some authors in the New World provinces preferred to draw on such books as Miller's *Kalendar* and *Dictionary* for their prognostications or directions. One of the earliest American garden manuals was included in *Tobler's Almanac* in South Carolina in 1752, written "by a lady of this province." This "calendar" was probably the work of Mrs. George Logan, born Martha Daniel, whose father was one of the margraves of the colony's first decades. John Bartram met her in Charleston in 1760 and praised her garden and arranged an exchange of seed. She died in 1779, and her calendar is said to have been issued in pamphlet form after that date. Later *The Palladium of Knowledge by Mrs. Logan for the Year of Our Lord 1798* (Charleston, 1798) appeared. She discussed ornamental gardens but devoted most of her space to the useful. Undoubtedly most of her knowledge, and probably most of her writing, came before 1764.

And one must not forget the already frequently mentioned great book on colonial agriculture, *American Husbandry*, which from internal evidence appears to have been written by a southern colonial. The volume is at its best, its most perceptive, in considering the problems and features of southern gardening as well as general farming from Maryland through South Carolina and Georgia. Perhaps to throw the reader off the track as to immediate authorship, there are constant allusions to or quotations from earlier writings by John Mitchell. The writer discusses tobacco with the assurance possible only to one who knows whereof he speaks. In most respects the book is the summation of southern colonial thinking on agriculture before the Revolution. It does not agree with some colonial expression as to the place of agriculture in the American economy, for the author quotes Mitchell in support of the frequent London or home argument that the "Colonies should live by their agriculture without either Manufactures or Trade, but what is confined to the Mother Country." The book, one repeats, may have been Mitchell's in essence, but it was printed from an incomplete manuscript after Mitchell's death when the colony-home government struggle was reaching its height. The editor of the book as it exists was probably shaping the materials a bit as British propaganda.[271]

The original issue of an early Virginia calendar, surviving only in manuscript, was by Williamsburg gardener Joseph Prentice. The parts that survive cover 1775 and 1784–1788, though it may well have begun in the colonial period. Probably written between 1758 and 1764 was *A Treatise on Gardening*, usually identified as the work of John Randolph, Jr. (1727–1784), son of Sir John and brother of Peyton and close friend of Jefferson. Most of his life a resident of Williamsburg, he was well acquainted with the Virginia climate. The author is most interested in kitchen gardening, and delineates in detail treatment of plants, especially vegetables in various soils. Of course he discusses proper times and ways of planting and reaping. A recent editor of *A Treatise* is inclined to date it not later than 1765 or earlier than 1758, on internal evidence. The first edition was probably published about 1770, and presumably notes and bits were added in the subsequent edition before the third (printed in 1816 and 1826). Potatoes receive little attention, cauliflower considerable. Lettuce, parsley, chives, artichokes, horseradish, gooseberries, peppers, and red rishes are among other garden produce considered. The book concludes with a planting-growing-harvesting calendar. There are references to earlier Virginians, especially historians who discuss vegetables, and to Miller and Bradley, the author's British authorities.[272]

There were other gardeners' manuals in the 1780s, as South Carolinian Robert Squibb's, and many more in the first national period. The most widely respected southern writer on this subject of husbandry was John

Beale Bordley (1727–1804), scion of a prominent Maryland family, at least five of whose books and pamphlets were in Jefferson's great collection. He was more concerned with large-scale farming and rotation of crops than with gardens, but he was concerned with horticulture too. His books were published in the 1780s and 1790s, but their roots lie in the 1760s and 1770s. He anticipates the great group who wrote on southern agrarian problems, such as James Greenway on wornout lands (1793), Joseph Doddridge on the culture of bees (1813), Jacquelin Ambler on lucerne (1808?), G.W.P. Custis on sheep-breeding (1808), Richard Mason on farriery (1811), and James M. Garnett, William Tatham, and Thomas Marshall on various aspects of husbandry and gardening. Some of the most ingenious farmers wrote little if at all on agriculture or gardening— John H. Cocke, Joseph C. Cabell, and Thomas Mann Randolph. Jefferson himself had a great deal to say on most aspects of growing plants, though more in letters and journals than anywhere else. But there was a culmination of agricultural experimentation in the eighteenth century in the writings of John Taylor (1753–1824) of Caroline, such as his *Arator* (Georgetown, D.C., 1813), John Frederick Binns (c. 1761–1813) in *A Treatise on Practical Farming* (Frederick, Md., 1803), and Edmund Ruffin (1794–1865), in his *Essay on Calcareous Manures*, at least two of them American classics appearing in many editions. The last has been called by a government expert as recently as 1895 "the most thorough piece of work on a special agricultural subject ever published in the English language." Yet Ruffin was but answering once more the southern lowland challenge of wornout lands with which his fellow provincials had been struggling since the mid-seventeenth century.

The southern kitchen garden presented many of the problems the writers on general agrarian questions discussed. But this garden, as its reconstruction at Williamsburg and on solitary estates demonstrates so vividly and often so beautifully, was an integral part of the mansion-group planning. Then the frontiersman was even more likely than the planter in the older areas to be a kitchen gardener, for he had for the sake of convenience and protection from marauders to keep his living food stocks in compact form close to his dwelling. In the upper Piedmont and the mountain valleys he, like his Tidewater forebears, adapted European plants to the strange terrain and mixed them with native vegetables and fruits grown in part by Indian methods.

One repeats that the colonist was often wasteful and lazy as well as greedy, and only toward the end of the period was he fully conscious of what he was doing to himself and his children. Yet from the time of William Byrd I, in the person of the Reverend John Clayton, on to the nineteenth century agrarian scientists, experimentation went on in soil revitalization, cultivating, rotation of crops, and other problems of heat, drought, moisture, and cold. In provincial print all this was first suggested in essays in the gazettes signed "Agricola" or "Arator" or other appropriate pseudonym, articles written by thoughtful farmer-statesmen such as the Maryland Dulanys and Ogles and Bordleys, Virginia Carters and Byrds and Blands, and Carolina Laurenses or Glens or Middletons or Manigaults or Pinckneys. The experimentation and newspaper essays led to writing in book or pamphlet and on into the remarkable age of agrarian theory represented in print by the papers of the Georgia Salzburgers, the Carolina planters, and above all the Chesapeake Bay area gentleman farmers in the two generations after the War for Independence.[273]

TECHNOLOGICAL INDUSTRY

Several of the subjects already considered in this chapter are at least in part representative of technology, such as silkworm and tobacco and indigo preparation. Most of those technological processes so far mentioned are related to agriculture, and they and others usually a part of agrarian practice will be noted in varying detail here. Other technical operations, such as mining and shipbuilding, may or may not be related to urban centers. Brickmaking and bricklaying, blacksmithing, pewtering, carpentry, cooperage, and a dozen other trades or crafts might be practiced in rural or in town situations. So might glassmaking, brewing, and pottery manufacture. Usually in the village or town or city environment were printing, clockmaking, and instrument making or repair, upholstering, and dozens of other crafts most profitable where a number of persons came together, at least periodically.

Contrary to much popular and even professional historical belief, from the settlement at Jamestown on to the 1760s there were deliberate and organized attempts at manufacture throughout the southern colonies. As the seventeenth century slipped into the eighteenth the manufacturing and industrial craftsmanship in the South Atlantic area fell much behind that of New England, New York, and Pennsylvania. The relative failure of southern colonial technology resulted from a number of causes, but except in one or two unusual instances, the failure was not directly the result of Great Britain's prohibition in order to protect home technical enterprise, though there can be no doubt that the British government discouraged what it considered potential competition. Yet the Virginia Company of London and then the Board of Trade and the Plantations advertised for and sent over skilled craftsmen in several fields. Perhaps unfortunately for southern colonial economy, these workmen and their projects were seldom if ever really successful. Indigo processing, which appears to have been a prosperous semi-industry up to the outbreak of hostilities in 1775–1776, was perhaps more of a self-developed manufactury (with the help of the West Indies) than a transplated European one.

The transit of technology from the Old World to the New is yet to be explained in a comprehensive and chronological survey which considers most of the factors. For New England, manufacturing and trading sprang in part from the scarcity of land (limited by the six Indian nations) and from a climate and soil less adapted to agriculture than was the South, in part from the developing Puritan-Yankee habit of mind, and in part from the semi-independence of the region for many decades, which meant a freedom from actual or implied prohibition from London. Then, possibly because the Yankee inventive genius and ingenuity were applied to projects which the home government felt offered little competition and because the British government recognized by the end of the seventeenth century that northern urban centers had developed and had to have scores of artisans to manufacture commodities, northern industries were at least tolerated. One repeats that the Anglo-American colonies were indeed agrarian, all of them, but some were less so than others. What southern technology there was grew from factors suggested or pointed out in other chapters of this book, education and reading and geography and promotion literature and Indians and fine arts and even religion as well as agrarian situations, shaping its forms and determining its peculiar manifestations.

The contours of the southern coastline, the nature of southern soils and minerals, the needs of the large and the small plantation were among several facts and factors that produced small-scale manufacturing, some mining, shipbuilding, and what might be called domestic industry. From John Smith to Henry Laurens or Landon Carter the southern colonist employed and often trained artisans and frequently planned manufactury (which did not always come into being). For the upper- and middle-class planter was by necessity a small-scale manufacturer, in a few rare instances an inventor, and frequently a promoter of means to power—water, wind, animal, even steam. This aspect of his occupation and mental processes was in the first national period to reach a modest climax in Jefferson's plantation naileries and his mould-board plow and in Cyrus McCormick's threshing machines. But the cerebrations of the southern settler were never exercised on technology to the extent the mental exercises of middle-colony or New England contemporary were.

Early Jamestown, a capitalistic enterprise organized as a communal plantation, was founded by men who may have been a little unrealistic about what as settlers they would find in the New World but realistic enough to discover in a few short months—if they had not already known it before first planting—that there should and must be skilled tradesmen or craftsmen present if the "nation" they were establishing was to stand. Perhaps the officials of the Virginia Company knew in 1606 that too large a percentage of the first planters were "gentlemen"—whether adventurous young sons of the Renaissance or simply remittance men does not really matter—but could do nothing about that disproportionate segment of their passengers because of internal and external pressures. There were thirty-six gentlemen (including the Council), a surgeon, and four boys. The twelve laborers, who would delve and carry and chop, were all too few by any sort of administrative plan. But not quite so bad was the proportion of skilled technologists, as we may call them, four carpenters, a blacksmith, a barber, a sailor (for pinnaces), two bricklayers, a mason, and a drummer, 105 in all including the surgeon. The first supply of 120 contained twenty-nine gentlemen (including Dr. Russell and a new councilor), twenty-one laborers, six tailors (clothes were becoming ragged), two apothecaries, a surgeon, a cooper, a tobacco-pipe maker, a blacksmith, and a jeweler, a refiner, two goldsmiths, a gunner, and a perfumer, besides "divers others." The proportion in this second group was better, though the metallurgist-perfumers were to look for what was not found and needed blacksmiths remained scarce. The next supply included besides Mistress Forest and her maid Anne Burras, only eleven laborers, twenty-eight gentlemen (including two councilors), and fourteen tradesmen or craftsmen, without specification of the last group's particular skills, seventy in all. Besides the tradesmen were eight Dutchmen and Poles, or eight Germans and a number of Poles, evidently skilled in glass or other industry. The unspecified group included some soldiers, with a sergeant, as Smith tells us in recounting explorations. The third supply arrived in rather imposing number, but their roll call is omitted from Smith's account.[274]

Surviving letters from the resident Council in Virginia and the Company's Council in London show cognizance of the dire need for artisans and laborers. Laborers of course remained in demand as British colonial agriculture developed, and the indentured servant and the African slave were attempts to supply the demand of the middle and large plantations. Though the supplies of agrarian labor were in certain senses never adequate in an expanding country, one may judge from the documents of the Virginia Company and the Board of Trade and the Plantations under the Crown that the constant and urgent need was for skilled men. Later in the seventeenth century William Fitzhugh and William Byrd I looked for both kinds, and the great planters of the eighteenth century never found enough of either, though they began to show more and more need for specialists, including trained gardeners and masons and housebuilders, and as merchant-planters for their town interests sought craftsmen who could manufacture.

In the period under the Company, there is a paucity of documentary evidence between 1612 and 1619. For this and the remainder of the Company's period Kingsbury has included in her *Records* all she could find. In May 1618 a list of men to be sent to the colony included four carpenters, two sawyers, a bricklayer with his tools, and twenty-eight husbandmen and laboring men, along with iron tools and a grindstone for their use. A list of 1619 men and provisions gives principally numbers, but there are tenants for governor's, college's, Company's, and minister's glebe land, and "Boyes to make Apprentices for those Tenants," presumably implication that the tenants were skilled specialists. In the same annual accounting it is noted that there are Poles to make pitch and tar and that silkworkers and "skilfull Vignerons" and sawmill builders are among the newcomers.

The first meeting of the General Assembly in the same year, 1619, petitioned the Company to send skilled workmen for the erection of the college buildings. The instructions given governors de la Warr, Argall, and Yeardley are copied into the record. Significant is the order that all skilled tradesmen who arrived after the departure of Sir Thomas Dale "shall worke at their trades for any other man" and be paid justly. The Virginia Company's broadside "Note" of January 1620 of what had been sent during the preceding year includes listings of three "principall men" to be masters of the ironworks, three for the saltworks including a Frenchman from Rochelle, four "Dutchmen" from Hamburg to erect sawmills, eight French "Vignerons" from "Languedock" who were also skillful in breeding silkworms and making silk, together with trained English silkmen. Most comprehensive and illuminating is the list of June 22, 1620, of artisans the Company much desired for public and perhaps private or semiprivate projects in Virginia. It lists thirty-two sorts of trades or skills, including those of husbandmen and gardeners (notice the distinction), brewers, bakers, sawyers, carpenters, joiners, shipwrights, boatwrights, plowwrights, millwrights, masons, turners, smiths and coopers of all sorts, weavers, tanners, potters, fowlers, fishermen, fishhook-makers, netmakers, shoemakers, ropemakers, tilemakers, edge-tool makers, brickmakers, bricklayers, hemp and flax dressers, limeburners, leather dressers, and ironworkers, miners, and vignerons. Glassmen are not mentioned, but sixteen Italians for making beads and other articles at the glassworks were brought over by May 1622. By then experiments in cotton, indigo, silk, saltworks, and other agricultural-commercial technologies were well under way. The massacre of 1621/1622 (the 1622 list given above was made before the news reached England) destroyed entirely some of the installations for these experiments, but in a surprisingly short time most of these and others were again in operation. The glassworks erected by Captain Norton and George Sandys (the second attempt at this industry) finally ceased operation, but as resident treasurer Sandys explained it, more because of the viciousness, dissatisfaction, and laziness of the Italian artisans than from Indian alarms.[275]

Nor was this merely a period of public enterprise. Through his long residence in the colony and the perquisities of his various offices, including the governorship, Sir George Yeardley had amassed a comfortable estate. He was commended by the London Council for putting up a windmill on his own property and experimenting with that and other things useful for himself and as examples to others in the colony. The official or public enterprises under the Company, sericulture and viniculture, have been noted above, with at least the implication that they also became private enterprises. Iron mining and manufacture, and glass manufacture, public and private, will be discussed below. The instructions to governors as to encouragement of skilled workmen such as coopers, potters, brewers, furniture makers and cabinetmakers read as though the Company was subsidizing them in their trades but with the implication at least that their labors would be private enterprises, with the profit going directly to the artisans. The brickmakers and bricklayers were probably at first public employees building foundations for houses and sometimes chimneys and walls and perhaps gun emplacements within Jamestown and Henrico. But as officials and private gentlemen began to acquire fairly extensive acreage and build dwelling houses thereon, the same men or their former apprentices must have worked for individuals or as individuals. So with their successors in Virginia or other southern colonies, who may or may not have come under some sort of governmental sponsorship—in the end they worked for themselves or someone who hired them. But perhaps the simplest way to consider southern industry-technology from Jamestown to the Augusta Indian Treaty of 1763 is to look at it as either farm related or community related.

FARM RELATED

As the larger farms and plantations developed during the later seventeenth and the eighteenth centuries, each became a miniature center of industry, manufacturing a number of things usually for individual household or agricultural use but sometimes for both the makers and their neighbors. These do not include the silk-processing buildings and tools, the tobacco curing, or usually the indigo processing, all of which were for export directly or through provincial merchants. Though silk production, as already suggested, never amounted to a great deal, at least from Virginian Edward

Digges in the mid-seventeenth century to the Georgia Salzburgers some silk was spun and exported. Digges and many others had their spinning done on their estates, but by the 1760s the Georgia Germans were sending their cocoons each spring to a "Filatur" in Savannah, where the manufacturing was done, though the last reels were shipped to England by the Ebenezer colonists in 1772.[276] Many a colonist from the Susquehannah to Florida died believing that silk would eventually become a cash staple on his plantation. But there simply never were any silk nabobs, or the equivalent of later dollar millionaires, from this industry as there were from the more purely agricultural raising and processing of tobacco or rice or even indigo. Nor did viniculture ever produce or result in enough wine or brandy beyond what was consumed on the farm to be sold profitably, though experimenters such as Governor William Berkeley and Robert Beverley evidently gave bottles or casks to neighbors and entertained their guests with the produce of their own wineries.

Fruits and grains or their products such as malt were the materials for brewed, distilled, or otherwise fermented liquors which were considered by most colonists the only really healthful drinks. The malt liquors, ale and beer, many wines, and gin and rum were often imported, especially the rum which usually came from the West Indies via New England ships or was made in New England. The malster worked in brewing in the earliest Virginia community manufactures, and brewing continued to be carried on throughout the colonial era in Williamsburg and other later towns such as Fredericksburg.[277] So in other colonies. But also from malt made with native barley or imported many an estate owner made his own beer or ale for his household and even for his field servants. The middling and lower classes also did some brewing of a beverage from dried Indian corn or a dozen other native plants as a substitute for malt. In county records there are many references to private brewhouses, as Francis Page's, Edmund Scarborough's, and a Mr. Bushard's, all in seventeenth-century Virginia. In 1705 Robert Beverley, in remarking that the colonists' "Small-drink" was wine, water, beer, and milk, mentions that the richer sort brewed their small beer from malt straight from England and that their own excellent barley was not used for want of malt houses. He adds that the poorer sort make their beer from molasses and bran or maize and persimmons or other local products. In South Carolina Henry Laurens wrote to a Philadelphia merchant for three hundred bushels of the best barley malt, which one of his customers was going to use in setting up a brewery, though whether the drink would be for public sale or private or plantation consumption is not made evident. Others had made beer in South Carolina long before. John Lawson mentions that there was plenty of "distillation" from malt and fruits, presumably on the larger estates he knew.[278] Late in the period

Governor Glen of South Carolina writes of beer as a commodity reexported from Charleston, not made in the colony. Bridenbaugh points out that German settlers everywhere in the South as well as elsewhere planted barley from which brewing malt was made, and county and newspaper records as well as letterbooks bear him out. Martin Bolzius, answering in 1734 the questionnaire from Germany, remarks that his fellow colonists were cooking for themselves a "healthy beer . . . out of syrup, Indian corn, and hops," and that therefore a professional brewer was not yet needed among the Salzburgers. By 1740 the Georgians generally, however, seem to have been brewing from barley malt.[279]

In the 1760s in Virginia lawyer-entrepreneur John Mercer, whose fine library is noted in Chapter IV and his mansion and other buildings in a chapter below, had fallen upon hard times and thought of recouping his fortunes by establishing a brewery at Marlborough, his great estate. This would have been of course plantation-connected and yet a community project in that he would sell to all who would buy. He purchased forty Negroes to grow the grain and hired a Scottish brewer to be in charge of the malt house. The product was so bad that of a schooner load sent to Norfolk in 1765 only two casks were sold. The *Virginia Gazette* of April 10, 1766, carries a long advertisement of the Marlborough brewery, offering strong beer, porter, and ale. But the whole project ended in miserable failure. Mercer was a brilliant, able, and imaginative lawyer and a fairly efficient general planter who knew too little about brewing to make it a success.[280] His attempt is incidentally a classic example of the truth that only a thin or invisible line separated plantation and community manufactury.

Other members of the upper classes also tried their hands at making beer, principally or entirely for home use. Landon Carter, who throughout his life experimented with crops and with plantation industry, tried his hand at this potable. Though his earliest direct reference to brewing is of 1770, he mentions that he is trying it as he had many times in the past. From his barley he made malt by a family recipe sent by an old brewer from Weymouth years before and brewed it with molasses, which "made a fine table drink." In 1777 he was still attempting what he had made years before at his father's.[281]

Carter's account indicates that beer was not his ordinary drink, and Bolzius in Georgia had remarked that most colonists preferred a beverage easier to come by. This was frequently the West Indian–New England rum, which might be drunk in diluted form with water or in various forms of punch, which usually included citrus fruit when the latter was obtainable. But the average planter did make his own beverage. There were private and perhaps semipublic wineries as early as 1612 or 1620. The costly experiments in viniculture from then to the very end of the period, with imported French or Italian vignerons and grapevine slips and with attempts to adapt the native wild grapes such as scuppernong or fox were never consistently successful, though at times governors and other officials boasted of delicious native wines. The industry was encouraged for at least two kindred reasons—it did not rival established British manufactures, and it would enable the British to be independent of Franco-Italian wine supplies.[282]

There are at least two examples of relative success by private gentlemen, the two experimenters noted above, or on private estates. One was that of Governor Sir William Berkeley, who in 1663 was making his own wine from grapes grown at Green Spring. When he offered to send a hogshead of Virginia wine to an English friend, he observed that the yield from his own planting of the year before had been as good wine "as ever came out of Italy." From several accounts including his *History* already mentioned, Robert Beverley was an even more successful producer of wines from his own American vineyards. He served them to the members of Spotswood's tramontane expedition and carried quantities along with the party, which he himself joined. Young Huguenot British officer John Fontaine in his 1715 journal describes the vineyards and tells the story of a wager Beverley made that he could produce in one year seven hundred gallons of good wine. Fontaine noted that Beverley had caves and a wine press, according to Spanish methods, and had among other vines several French varieties. In his 1705 *History* Beverley himself points out why he thinks previous attempts at wine making in Virginia and Carolina have failed. He considers Berkeley's ultimate failure to have been the result of carelessness in his vineyards. He sees the earlier 1622 massacre as the means of destruction of a promising viniculture nursed by Frenchmen.[283]

Despite these experiments with domestic wines, the average planter who could afford wine at all seems to have been content to import it from Europe, usually through his British factor. From the Jamestown period on, sack and claret and dozens of other varieties, along with north European aquavitae, came in on ships which took the Chesapeake planter's tobacco in place of the European potables and edibles they carried. The letters of merchants in all the southern colonies mention hundreds of times the acquisition of cases or casks of wine, as do the letters of the planters who ordered for themselves. The Virginia Byrds and Carters and Randolphs on the great rivers usually procured quantities straight from Europe, as did some later Carolina and Georgia planters. But in the Chesapeake country and the Carolinas and Georgia there were middlemen, especially the merchants of Annapolis and Baltimore and Oxford, of Williamsburg and Norfolk, of Wilmington, of Charleston, and of Savannah, who ordered in large quantity and sold retail.

But the southern colonists of all classes were likely to use as their daily table beverage a mild alcoholic drink manufactured from fruits grown on their own farms or in some instances found growing wild. The most popular of these was cider, at first imported and then made in the plantation cider mill from the planters' own apples. In 1686 William Fitzhugh's 2,500 apple trees, most of them grafted and enclosed by a locust fence, were cultivated largely to provide this beverage. He hoped to have some cider beyond household needs which he might offer for sale. Later he wished to send to an English friend samples of his product but declared his cider inferior to that of a certain shire of the homeland. When John Mercer's estates were sold in 1771, there were cider presses at each plantation and a cider mill at Marlborough. Hugh Jones in the 1720s said that every planter made cider which, if aged, was "not much inferior to that of Herefordshire" and a little later in the same book declares it superior to that of the same English county, his native place. Though apples were grown in South Carolina and Georgia, other fruits were grown more successfully in those provinces. In 1762 Henry Laurens was ordering from his English agents sixty dozen bottles of beer and forty dozen of cider, which might indicate Charleston and South Carolina preference for the English products.[284]

Pears were made into perry on a large scale in most of the provinces. Peaches were made into a mild drink and into peach brandy, apparently in all the colonies from Maryland to Georgia, for both Indians and whites had peach orchards from the earliest years of the period, as has been noted. In the inventories of scores of planters stills are included which might have been used for peach or other fruit brandies and later for corn or bourbon whiskey. Landon Carter mentions several times his own stills and brandy and once recalls that his father, Robert "King" Carter, had large orchards and "made abundance of cider and [peach] brandy," and he notes that he himself distills "low wines" (from Peach Mobby) into a very good brandy. Carter lent or rented his stills to neighbors, evidence that plenty of fruit but not a great deal of apparatus was available. The Salzburgers' first fruit in Georgia, 1734 to 1736, was the peach from Indian-grown or wild trees. They mention brandy too, but not as a native product in those first years, though it certainly did become one later.[285]

A multitude of other plantation industries grew out of local needs. Carpenters were in great demand from the beginning for building anything from a hogpen to a house. At first most were indentured, but on the middle and larger plantations there were soon trained black slaves who could do even some fine cabinet work and in a few exceptional cases interior wood carving. Allied to the carpenter was the cooper, declared to have been the busiest artisan of the colonial South. If he was an independent individual he often worked in the cities and sometimes for wages on the plantations. Most plantation coopers, like the first carpenters, were probably originally indentured and again were succeeded in part by blacks trained by the skilled whites. The cooper, who made casks and kegs for beverages and hogsheads and barrels for corn, tar, turpentine, flour, and above all rice and indigo and tobacco, was indispensable. Almost everything shipped out had to go in the containers he manufactured. Cooperage on a large-scale plantation or a single-owner group of plantations was in itself a fairly extensive industry and certainly the largest southern craft in number employed. In some instances planters bought their kegs and barrels from town manufacturers, but more frequently the plantation "household" made tubs, coolers, casks, kegs, butter-churns, pails, ships' buckets, and other rounded wooden receptacles.

As late as 1774 Robert Carter of Nomini Hall had a Scottish cooper retained at an annual salary, and at that late date there were many other white indentured servants working at the trade in Virginia and Maryland. John Carter, Jr., and Ralph Wormeley in Virginia in the early eighteenth century both had Negro coopers, as did Robert "King" Carter in 1732 and Richard Chapman in 1739. In the lower South white artisans were sent at first, though after slavery was introduced in Georgia blacks were trained in the craft. Even greater numbers of coopers were needed in South Carolina and Georgia than in upper Carolina and the Chesapeake settlements. Bridenbaugh estimates that black coopers were used almost exclusively in the rice and indigo plantations of the lower colonies.[286] In this as in other crafts, however, the majority of southern artisans throughout the colonial period were probably white.

Though immigrant cordwainers found few to buy quality shoes, since those who could afford them preferred to import, the shoemaker who could fashion leather shoes was to be found on almost every plantation. Like coopers and others mentioned, in the early years he was usually a white indentured servant and later a hired free white craftsman or a Negro slave. The farm shoemaker cobbled for all the slaves, his fellow servants, and even for the master's family when they needed rough footgear or required repairs on imported boots, shoes, or slippers. In 1737 Isham Randolph exchanged the remainder of an indenture for 250 pairs of shoes for his slaves. By the end of the period probably more than his fellows in most crafts, the farm-related shoemaker was frequently black. But since this was one craft in which journeyman cordwainers or shoemakers could and did make a decent living and there was after 1750 considerable demand for trained cobblers along the frontier and in the Piedmont, the white traveling cobbler became a familiar sight in at least those regions.

Many plantations had among their hired hands or indentured servants weavers, silk and hamp and flax spinners, blacksmiths, and tinsmiths, all of them artisans representing trades also practiced for the merchant-industrialists or general public in the towns. Again blacksmiths and other metalworkers, and a few spinners and weavers, were eventually trained among the slaves. The imported white spinner or weaver might come from any European country. Some masters encouraged blacks in learning a trade so that these slaves might buy their freedom with what they earned within or without the owners' households, but though instances are often cited, they were the exceptions. Relatively few actually worked their way to freedom.[287]

COMMUNITY RELATED

Though few were the towns of the colonial South in the seventeenth century, in the eighteenth they had multiplied quite considerably. Capital villages such as Annapolis, Williamsburg, Brunswick or New Bern or Edenton or Wilmington, Charleston, and Savannah had grown into fair-sized towns supporting many sorts of trades. Along the fall line or on inlets from the sea were villages in which artisans could support themselves, sometimes quite well: at Patuxent and Oxford and Baltimore in Maryland, Fredericksburg and Falmouth and Petersburg and Richmond in Virginia, Beaufort and Bath in North Carolina, Beaufort and George-town and Orangeburg and Dorchester among others in South Carolina, and Frederica and Augusta and Ebenezer in Georgia. Inland beyond the falls or dotted along the coasts were other specialized communities engaged in making tar and pitch, mining, or smelting iron and other metals. In the tiny town of Chuckatuck within thirty miles of Jamestown lived about 1675 Joseph Copeland, as far as is known English America's first pewterer.[288] Iron mining and smelting and manufacturing and a few other enterprises were privately owned industries, sometimes by an individual and sometimes by a company, the latter flourishing here and there for a time in certain areas.

The first attempts at manufacture were made under the Virginia Company of London, both at Jamestown and up the river at Falling Creek near today's Richmond. These were in glassmaking and iron mining and smelting. Hakluyt and others urged potential colonists before 1590 to develop mines and industry which would augment rather than supplant British products, and to manufacture or process materials not found in

Great Britain or not suitable to the climate, exactly paralleling the aims in agriculture. The conditions for glass manufacture seemed suitable in Virginia, and the shipment of iron ore and pig iron to the colonies soon possessing both from local sources and local processing seemed uneconomical, though the British iron industry always kept a wary eye on its New World (much of it southern) counterpart. There were other reasons for these two, both of which have continued or been "revived" frequently in the United States to the present time, though the southern colonies were not for long a center of glass manufacture.

Because of the furnace built within a mile of Jamestown in 1608 for glassmaking, this manufacture has been called America's first industry. Glass was manufactured in Great Britain, but not nearly enough to supply the demand, and few Englishmen were skilled in the craft. Captain Newport's rapid survey of natural resources in the Jamestown vicinity convinced the Virginia Company stockholders that here might be a feasible undertaking which would yield quick profit. By the summer of 1608 among those sailing for the colony were "eight Dutchmen and Poles," the former almost surely Germans. A glasshouse was erected "with all offices and furnaces thereto belonging," as William Strachey notes. Later that year when Newport returned to England he carried samples of trials made in glass, besides soap-ashes, pitch, and tar. Our other glimpses of this first manufacturing experiment are indirect, as Smith's story of a fight with an Indian near the glasshouse, and mention of a second "trial" made in the spring. The Dutchmen seem to have given trouble from the first, and they may have contributed little to the project save in the actual erection of the glasshouse. The Poles were probably the glassmakers, though they may have employed the German methods of the time.

This venture must have come to an end in the fall of 1609 when Smith returned to England and the great starving time was upon the colonists. When relief came with Lord de la Warr in 1610, there is no evidence of the revival or survival of the glass factory. In 1621, when English glass manufacture was booming but still not adequate, Company Treasurer Sir Edwin Sandys decided to give glass another try in the colony. A Captain Norton offered to go to Virginia with skilled workmen and manufacture useful commodities as well as beads for trade with the Indians. This time a group of six Italians, perhaps from Murrano, were the glassmakers. Everything went wrong: a storm blew the glasshouse down, the Indian massacre temporarily shut it down, and Norton died. George Sandys, local treasurer and director of industry, was determined to revive it, even sending to Europe for sand the workers said they needed. But the workers fell sick and wanted to go home, and Sandys believed they deliberately cracked the furnace. In 1624, perhaps partially in preparation for his own return to England the next year, he gave up. His comment about the workmen was that a more damned crew Hell never vomited.

In the last few decades the site of one of these two glasshouses has been examined. Ivor Noël Hume and other reputable archaeologists feel that it is probably the 1608–1609 furnace and building, primarily from the type of glass drippings they have found there. Hume does not believe that the second furnace ever manufactured glass beads for trade, though he admits that in the 1920s and 1930s beads were often found in the woods near Jamestown and that many of these survive today. J.C. Harrington excavated the site referred to in 1948 and has written his own account of what he found. None of the original glass objects are large enough to indicate for what they were used. The reconstructed glass factory is today turning out receptacles such as were used at the time in the same sort of glass as was found on the site. If anything was manufactured before 1625, it would most likely have been bottles and bull's-eye window glass and perhaps drinking glasses. At least there were two valiant attempts to establish what would in later hands become a great industry.[289]

In his excavations at Green Spring, the site of Sir William Berkeley's mansion and household industries, Hume finds evidence of what may have been glassmaking there in 1666. These include two pieces marked and dated "Aug. 6, 1666" from a glass-lined brick trough. The find is of great interest but affords no real clue as to its purpose. Hume conjectures that Berkeley, knowing of the previous experiments at Jamestown, attempted to manufacture bottles to contain the wine he was making from his own grapes. There were glasshouses at the time in New Amsterdam: why not in Virginia? A century later John Mercer advertised in the *Virginia Gazette* of April 18, 1766, that if encouraged sufficiently he would set up a glasshouse for making bottles. He had in mind personal use of them in connection with his proposed brewery, but he would also sell bottles. Fortunately, however, for his already precarious financial situation, the encouragement was not forthcoming. The middle states, especially New York and New Jersey and Pennsylvania, were to develop this industry begun in Virginia.[290]

The second community or capitalistic manufacture, iron, was more successful than glass. The ore of the Appalachians from Pennsylvania to Georgia, from the spurs of which the first iron came, is still being used. The Virginia colonists, heeding the instructions of the Company, sought for and found iron ore in the very first year. There seem to have been crude smelting furnaces at Jamestown, really earth ovens, in which iron was smelted by fires fed by logs and charcoal. Though the order to search for iron had been given for much the same reason as the order to manufacture glass—that Britain needed more than it had—there was a difference: iron was to be shipped home as ore or pig iron, and the final shaping was to be done there. This was the official British trade policy through most or all of the colonial period, though the Board of Trade and other officials came especially in the eighteenth century to wink at colonial manufacture of fairly simple utensils and tools for home use. Raw or finished, iron was expected to be a major product of the colonies, and at the beginning in the Chesapeake colonies.

According to the explorers and the metallurgists who accompanied them, there appeared to be plenty of iron ore in the first colony, even far east of the Appalachian deposits. In 1609 Newport carried some of the ore (Smith had previously sent samples) to the mother country, where it yielded sixteen or seventeen tons of iron from an indeterminate quantity of ore and was pronounced of excellent quality. In the colony some time before 1610, as Francis Magnel testified, the English had iron mills or manufactures.[291] In 1619 the Company decided to invest a sum given for the education of Indian children in an iron manufactury, which would bring a maximum income for the purpose and promote the economic welfare of the colonists. They looked to the iron found in Smith's time, principally that in the Falling Creek area up the James River, near the fall line, on the south side of the stream.

But as early as 1609 there were millwrights, iron miners, "iron finers," "iron founders," "Hammermen for Iron," "Edge tole makers for Iron Worke," "Colliers for charcole," and "Wood cutters." This is indicative that from the very first, or at the very first, the English intended that their Virginia ironworks would have a blast furnace, a refinery, and a chafery. As indicated above, the old and simple process for producing wrought iron in crude earth ovens may have been used. These ovens may have been for making bar iron for shipment rather than for smelting. At any rate, blacksmiths in Virginia by 1607 and 1608 were working at forges, as they testify, and in 1955 a forge area was definitely identified at Jamestown.

Though the records of the early iron manufactures are scarce, some do exist. In 1619 along with provisions sent to Virginia were 150 persons to set up ironworks there, for the iron seemed extraordinarily good, primarily at Falling Creek. Captain Blewett, who was to be director, died soon after his arrival, but his "people" made some progress. The men from Warwickshire and Staffordshire who arrived in 1619 and later were trained ironworkers. Others came later. Despite discouragements of various kinds, in 1620 the Company sent three "principall men" to be in charge. In 1621 it was asserted that the ironworks were the great hope and expectation of the adventurers and that £4,000 had already been spent on erecting the works in the colony. In 1621 also John Berkeley offered to go over and take charge of the project. His list of twenty work-men he should carry with him is indicative of what he intended to do, a staff appropriate to the combination of furnace, refinery, forge, and chafery. Berkeley set up his own men and furnaces and forge at the Falling Creek site and wrote home sanguine letters about his prospects. Subsequent re-ports from his superior, George Sandys, and from Berkeley himself con-tinued to be optimistic.

Then came the 1622 massacre. Twenty-seven people at Falling Creek were killed, including Berkeley. The ironworks were demolished, the machinery was broken, and the tools were scattered. At first it was de-cided that this was merely delay, that the project would go on, but the dissolution of the Company and the general economic instability of the colony saw its end in 1623.

Though Spotswood almost a century later was to be the next significant producer of iron, mining of the ore and concomitant smelting and prepara-tion were urged in the years between. Ore was sent to England in 1628, and in 1630 Harvey visited the works and sent home some samples. In 1634 Sir John Zouch and his son came to Virginia resolved to reestablish the works at Falling Creek. In 1693 William Byrd I, who had acquired the Falling Creek property, gave some attention to a reestablishment. Beverley reports that this Byrd, his father-in-law, drilled in search of rich veins of ore, both iron and lead. The Falling Creek site is said to have had a new iron-works in 1749, when Archibald Cary came to own the property, and his forge could be clearly identified as recently as 1876. A note in J.F.D. Smyth's *A Tour of the United States of America* (London, 1784, I, 28–29) asserts that the valuable mills and ironworks were set fire to and destroyed in 1781 by an expedition under Benedict Arnold.

There is abundant evidence of waterpower resources as well as iron in the Falling Creek area, and building stone for the necessary housing. Twentieth-century excavations on the site bear out historical records of the blast furnace and some of the iron products. Handmade axes, nails, and spikes were among the locally salable products. Slag, a wharf, stone bases for furnaces, old heavy timbers, charcoal, ore, lumps of iron also were found. The Falling Creek seventeenth-century cast iron, made in a different way from what was used a century later, is naturally of different texture from the later product. Hatch and Gregory, in their illuminating essay on the subject, discuss in detail the blast furnace, the refinery, and the chafery at Falling Creek, the process of manufacture, and the trained artisans of sev-eral kinds employed in the work, altogether a fascinating story.[292]

The statutes of the remainder of the seventeenth century indicate that not only iron but at times implements forged by smiths were exported from the Virginia colony. Sporadically the settlers were specifically forbidden to export, probably at periods when British iron manufacturers felt they had more than sufficient amounts from within the homeland. But in the first third of the eighteenth century, in both Virginia and Maryland, a number of mines and furnaces were operating, and at least some of the simpler utensils were being made, ostensibly to be sold only within the colonies. In Virginia alone in this period at least four different mine-furnaces were operating, some of which continued for a long time thereafter. And in Maryland the Principio works opened in 1715, together with their lineal descendants all the way to Wheeling, represented a continuous living industry.[293] Of the latter more in a moment.

William Byrd I's interest in developing the Falling Creek iron property had not amounted to anything. It took the influence and the strategic planning of a colonial governor to get the industry going again in Virginia. This official was Alexander Spotswood, who arrived in the colony in 1710. The "Tubal Cain of Virginia," as William Byrd II dubbed him, with a fairly usual mixture of public and private interest, became almost immediately concerned in provincial economy. Byrd among others was then, as he was twenty years later, hoping to revive the iron industry near the falls. In association with a few other gentlemen, he approached Spotswood with a plan, which the governor received with favor. It was hoped that the Burgesses would subsidize it for a time as a public welfare project, and that the Board of Trade would approve. Neither happened, and for some years nothing more was done about manufacturing on this spot. But some time before 1713 Spotswood, in a survey of the frontier, discovered or at least became aware of valuable iron deposits in the wilderness above the falls of the Rappahannock. Undiscouraged by his previous official rebuffs, the governor persuaded a group of Virginia associates to undertake the development of iron as a private industrial business venture. They hoped for approval and even financial aid from the Queen, especially since in the beginning they stressed the streaks of silver (which turned out to be negligible) in the same ore.

Through a combination of circumstances which may or may not have been accidental a group of skilled German and Swiss Protestant miners and ironworkers were secured. The workers arrived in April 1714 through a transaction made by their agent, the Baron de Graffenreid, and Colonel Nathaniel Blakiston, the Virginia agent in London. Carefully maneuvering in case the Queen's full consent had not been obtained, Spotswood established the miners on the Rapidan as a frontier buffer, alleging or implying that their development of the iron industry was but a secondary consideration. The settlement was named Germanna, and the House of Burgesses, in recognition of the Germans' service as a border guard, exempted them from levies for seven years and established the parish of

St. George for their benefit. Thus they were settled only twelve miles from the ore deposits. Though Spotswood was cautious about the matter as he waited the new king's consent, the governor had at least eleven of the Germans at work by March 1716. It was 1718 before he reported to London that iron mines had been discovered near the Rappahannock by the Germans.

With his partners Thomas Jones, merchant, and Robert Beverley II, the planter historian, he bought up enormous tracts of land in the vicinity. The Mine Tract, including fifteen thousand acres patented in 1719, eventually came into Spotwood's sole possession. His first German Swiss were replaced by about seventy Palatine Germans who arrived as indentured servants. Gradually he had bought out his partners and before 1723 had built the Tubal furnace a few miles below the confluence of the Rapidan and the Rappahannock. In that year his industry had become the talk of Virginia. He was manufacturing not only pig iron for export but casting chimney backs, dog irons, and cooking utensils for colonial consumption. Twenty tons of pig iron went in that same year to Bristol as ballast, and a few years later he declared that his product was in great demand among the ironmasters of Great Britain. After his retirement from the governorship he had built a mansion at Germanna and established his household there so that he might personally supervise his major business. He did not marry until 1724 while on a visit to Britain, where he remained until 1730. Though his ironworks had suffered during his absence, he soon got things going again, eventually using blacks, both men and women, in the undertaking.

During the decade before his death in 1740 Spotswood was involved at various times in three furnaces. He was a partner in the Fredericksville or Chiswell Furnace twenty-five miles southwest of Fredericksburg. Besides his Tubal works, he set up a shipping point on the lower Rappahannock, where he had a third establishment, an air furnace, on Massaponax plantation. He showed it to William Byrd in 1732 soon after its completion. The profits of the Spotswood works were said to be very considerable as late as 1759. In 1739, the year before his death, he offered to lease the Tubal works. His proposals or stipulations for the proposed transaction survive and have recently been printed in facsimile. The terms emphasize various factors of ironmaking in America.[294]

Even larger than Spotswood's works was the manufactury at the aforementioned Principio furnace and its affiliates from about 1715. The parent forge was in Cecil County in Maryland, and the company formed to develop it were principally Englishmen. By 1751 investors had acquired or built two additional furnaces in Baltimore County and the Accokeek furnace, owned in part and managed by Augustine Washington, father of George,

977

in King George County, Virginia. This last was one of the four principal pre-Revolutionary Virginia ironworks. This Maryland-Virginia company turned out the same sorts of pig iron and manufactured items for provincial consumption as did the Spotswood plants. The Baltimore Iron Works, organized by Charles Carroll and Daniel Carroll of Duddington with some of the Dulanys, Taskers, and Robert Carter of Nomini Hall as later partners, was established on the Patapsco in 1731 with an investment of £3,500. It was a flourishing industry, each of five proprietors in 1765 drawing an annual profit of £500 from its products. In the 1770s Carter had considerable income from his shares, for he shipped bar iron to Great Britain and to Virginia ports. After the Revolution Carter continued to sell in Great Britain and paid the tuition for his two sons at college in Rhode Island in iron. Finally in 1787 he sold his share for £20,000.

The manner of operation of the Baltimore plant is worth observing. Each stockholder contributed to the expenses in food and Negroes. A resident manager supervised the forges and mining and notified the owners when the quantity of iron was made. Sometimes, as in Carter's case, they sent for the iron in their own vessels. From his own iron Carter manufactured various articles in his smith shop at Nomini Hall—axes, hoes, plows, ten-penny nails, and other useful agricultural or household implements.[295]

The most detailed picture of the iron manufacture of the 1730s in Virginia and Maryland is William Byrd II's "A Progress to the Mines in the Year 1732." The master of Westover had become enormously interested in the possibilities of developing his inherited iron deposits, the old Falling Creek property which had been part of his father's home estate. Byrd had been interested since at least 1710, as his diary shows, and at that time as has been noted Spotswood had encouraged him in what may have been the semipublic project. The initiative and perhaps even the idea seem originally to have been Byrd's and may have suggested development of other iron projects to Spotswood.

"A Progress to the Mines" is one of Byrd's more objective narratives. Based as are his others on daily journals, it is the story of his visits to several mines, forges, and furnaces to learn what he could about iron manufacture and to decide whether he should undertake it himself. First he inspected the Spotswood-Chiswell mine, after he had renewed an old acquaintance with Charles Chiswell and his wife and absorbed all his host could impart in a few hours about ore analysis, the distance a furnace could be from water carriage, the transportation problems at the mines and furnace, the problem of sufficient wood for charcoal, the number of slaves necessary to carry on all the business of an ironworks, and how much it would take to feed them. Other matters, such as skilled colliers and firemen and cost of transportation to England, were discussed. Then he and

Chiswell traveled to the Fredericksville mines (some miles from Chiswell's home and mills), where he learned a great deal more firsthand about mines and furnaces and charcoal, sow iron, and pig iron. He was told that as yet there were four furnaces but no forge in Virginia, but a good forge at the head of the bay in Maryland.

From Chiswell, Byrd traveled on to Spotswood and Germanna. Here the former governor lived up to his reputation as the Tubal Cain of the province by giving Byrd a series of lectures on his own projects and on the American iron industry in general, including capital investment and labor needed and a hundred other things. Later Byrd visited the mines twelve or thirteen miles from Germanna with his old friend and watched the process of ore excavation (by gunpowder) and other steps preparatory to firing or transporting. After a few days Byrd proceeded to the Accokeek mines of Augustine Washington mentioned above. Again the reader gets a fairly detailed description, including the methods of firing the furnace. Byrd met the Gloucestershiremen who had built this and the Fredericksville furnace. The technical aspects of Spotswood's air furnace are outlined, and the process of melting sow iron to be cast into chimneys, andirons, fenders, plates for hearths, skillets, and other necessities is discussed. Despite all of Byrd's obvious interest, he did not go into the business on a large scale. He probably realized from this journey that the finances and mechanical complexities of the industry were too much for him, especially with his multitude of other interests, despite the fact that what he had seen was clearly profitable.[296]

Other Chesapeake area iron industry should be noted. One was a Valley of Virginia operation near Winchester at Cedar Creek which preceded 1763, was bought out in 1767 by Isaac Zane, Jr., and was operated as the Marlboro Iron Works. By 1771 it was producing bar iron and castings, besides kettles, pots, other kitchen utensils, and farming implements. Soon a second furnace was erected by Zane near Stephensburg, and before the Revolution he was shipping his product from Falmouth on the Rappahannock to England. Originally a Philadelphia Quaker, Zane lived on a magnificent twenty-thousand-acre iron plantation in a stone house surrounded by most of the comforts and luxuries of his age. It was he, incidentally, who was to purchase the Byrd library and dispose of most of it in a Philadelphia sale. Zane is a good example of the frontier-capitalist-planter-industrialist of the colonial South.[297] His letters are indicative of his temper and that of his class and occupation.

Another Virginia iron manufacturer was Archibald Cary of Ampthill, who operated his works at the old Falling Creek site. This was at mid-eighteenth century, and the project failed to prosper. James Hunter of Falmouth, on the other hand, operated a highly successful manufactury.

The Fry and Jefferson map shows Holt's Forge on a branch of the Chicka-hominy, though today there is no evidence of an iron furnace there save one of 1770 operated by William Holt and Francis Jerdone. This latter was probably Providence Forge, which was in operation until 1782 or 1784. And there was at least one other Valley of Virginia forge or furnace in Augusta County in 1760 owned by a John Miller.

The state of the iron industry alone is indicative that the southern colo-nial had an eye for business, by no means disdained participation in large-scale industry, and certainly was technologically curious and so far as one can tell from his records quite perceptive of the principles of manufacturing in the new age just dawning. Chiswell, Spotswood, Zane, and Washington knew what they were doing, and their potential co-industrialist Byrd seems to have understood and appreciated both their problems and their successes.

At the end of the colonial period there emerged in the Chesapeake area another major industry akin to the land-related crafts, and like other later industry growing out of them—flour and grain milling. Though there were gristmills for Indian corn and wheat flour throughout the South, especially in the upper colonies, they were designed to supply the owner and possibly a few neighbors. In the 1760s John Ballendine of the Northern Neck con-structed a merchant mill at the Falls of the Potomac, which was said to have been the equal in equipment and product of any in America. A wharf and a crane, a three-and-a-half-story building containing a mill, two pairs of stones, bolting mills, fans for blowing away chaff, with a staff of four men and two boys, ground out fifty thousand bushels of wheat per year. Adjoining were a large bakery, granaries, a retailing store, and a stone residence for the miller.[298] Forty-odd years later Augustus John Foster of the British legation in Washington observed that flour exported from Alexandria was the finest of the American continent, and that a Scottish baker there produced a good quality of biscuit.[299]

Shipbuilding was a colonial industry from Massachusetts to Charles-ton. In the southern colonies it began at Jamestown, where small craft for navigating the Bay and the many rivers became a necessity. The first were built before 1611, and by 1613 small ships or sloops to carry grain were being constructed. The Warwick faction of the Company declared in 1619 that in the earlier years barges, shallops, pinnaces, and frigates had been made in the colony. Under Sir Edwin Sandys there were more ambitious naval projects, and skilled workmen were sent over to cooperate with iron and sawmill workers in getting forest and metal materials and putting the vessels together. After the revocation of the Company charter in 1624, the industry appears to have fallen into complete decay, though in the 1632–

1650 period there are many evidences of boat and pinnace building. Construction of larger vessels was recommended and encouraged, and after 1661 bounties were given persons who would construct vessels large enough to make sea voyages. There are several evidences of tobacco and other cargo ships having been built in the colony during the seventeenth century, though shipbuilding never became a major activity.[300]

In the eighteenth century a shipyard at Point Comfort turned out an unknown number of vessels and repaired others. Norfolk gradually became a shipbuilding center as it became a busy port. Scows, schooners, sloops, brigs, and other ships were built. After 1763, at the beginning of the Revolution, shipbuilding boomed.

Maryland, later to become famous for the Baltimore clipper, was by the 1730s at latest building boats and ships at various places, with a principal yard on the Patapsco near Baltimore. Maryland oak proved to be especially suitable for shipbuilding. By 1729 poet Richard Lewis was celebrating in verse the large ship the *Maryland-Merchant*, built at Annapolis. Before 1752, probably at the Baltimore yard, was built the *British Merchant*, which carried a burden of one thousand hogsheads and stayed in the Virginia trade for thirty-six years. A painting of a Maryland shipyard owned by Richard Spencer hangs over a fireplace of "Spencer Hall," presumably painted some time before the Revolution.

Though the actual Baltimore clipper appeared after the Revolution, the type is mentioned as early as 1730, with the first newspaper reference in 1746. Apparently it was at first sloop-rigged and gradually came to be schooner-rigged. The Maryland-Virginia builders were specialists in fast ships, and "Virginia-built" became a name for Chesapeake Bay–built products. Thus, according to a principal authority on sailing ships, the upper southern colonies during the colonial period were the most prominent American constructors of useful commercial vessels. One should add that Maryland, like Virginia, built fishing and oystering and pilot boats, and that along the southern coasts small craft were turned out by more or less skilled craftsmen. Yankee ingenuity—if by that is meant New England ingenuity—appears to have been used in copying rather than inventing the fast American sailing vessel.

By 1740 Charleston had a large shipyard, three others were nearby, and there was another at Beaufort. Twenty-four square-rigged vessels were built in the area between 1740 and 1779. Georgia began building ships by 1741, and like the Carolinians found the live oak an excellent material for hull and deck.[301]

Though bricks were occasionally brought as ballast from the mother country, in all the southern area soil was found, at least in spots, suitable for brickmaking. As already shown, brickmakers and bricklayers were among the earliest artisans imported at Jamestown, and they continued to be imported, or trained through apprenticeship, throughout the colonial era. Though the planters often had bricks made by their own men at home, all the capital towns had brickyards and brickmakers, and journeymen were employed by master builders or architects. No more ingenious or handsome examples of colonial craft survive than the brickwork one may still see in private mansions, churches, and public buildings. But one should remember that the bricks were also used for other purposes, as walls and foundations and chimneys for humbler farmers or for the great planter who preferred a frame dwelling or began with one.

Pottery was also as old as Jamestown, where a kiln site was uncovered in 1955 with all sorts of products nearby. The kiln was in operation at least from 1625 to 1650—crude, utilitarian, lead-glazed earthenware being its principal product. Captain William Rogers later had a kiln at Yorktown, and almost contemporary with the Jamestown works was Sir William Berkeley's kiln at Green Spring (probably 1660–1680), and the Challis site nearby discovered in 1961 has yielded most interesting objects of great sophistication and delicacy, probably from a period ending about 1730. There were, as archaeologists have assured us, dozens if not scores of potteries in colonial Virginia.[302]

In North Carolina the Moravians at Betharaba were the best-known colonial potters, bringing their artisans from among their own brethren in Pennsylvania. They set up a kiln in the 1750s but fired nothing of importance until after the very end of the colonial period. Then they became famous for their special kind of brown earthenware, though they made other things, including tiles.[303] In Maryland, potters advertised their wares in the *Gazette* of July 29 and November 29, 1746, and of September 2, 1756, among other times. In 1770 John Bartram advertised in the *South-Carolina Gazette* that he was making "what is called Queen's Ware," and undoubtedly there were potters who did cruder utilitarian work before this late date.

Andrew Duché, born in Pennsylvania about 1709, established with two servants in Savannah in 1731 a "Potter's Trade." The Earl of Egmont sent him samples of Chinese porcelain to serve as models, and Colonel Stephens' report of 1740 shows that the pottery works using local clay were successful and that they were exporting to neighboring provinces. In 1743 Duché was in England and for some years he was in Virginia before he returned to Philadelphia. He owned a lot in Norfolk and probably lived in that town. The Virginia episode may have been between Georgia and England, for he showed influential people in the mother country samples of Virginia clay and of fine porcelain he made from it.

The evidence suggests that Duché invented a process of making porcelain from American kaolin while he was in Georgia. If so, he seems to have been the first native American successfully to make porcelain on this continent. It may have been Virginia clay he was using in Georgia, for he testified in England that his earth was found in the back country of Virginia, perhaps among the Cherokees, as he searched for mines. His story is a little hazy, but there seems no doubt that he manufactured porcelain at an early date.[304]

Gold and silver smiths advertised in the provincial southern gazettes throughout the eighteenth century, especially before the Revolution. Several of them manufactured, but that which has been identified by mark has not usually proved distinguished. Many of them found their trade so small that they also worked in other areas—as tavern keepers, shoemakers, peruke makers. Several offered liquor in the silver tankards or goblets they made, as did John Chalmers of Annapolis about 1754. He had been preceded in Maryland by silversmiths from 1715. James Inch of Annapolis combined cooperage and watch repair with his silver work, and he was a fine craftsman. Charleston, South Carolina, had according to the museum of that city at least fifty-two silversmiths, though again little remains of their work. John Paul Grimké, a London-trained craftsman, had to abandon his work and open a shop offering imported English baubles and repair services. A Brewington made a silver porringer about 1711/1712. In 1703 Nicholas de Longuemara was making knives and forks and an admiralty seal. There are in the records silversmiths named Dupuy, Perroneau, Gowdey, Petrie, Pitts, Sarrazin, Stoutenburgh, Vanall, and others who manufactured. In the last thirty years of the century there were more craftsmen in South Carolina who produced beautiful silver work than in all the colony's previous history.

Fifteen men are known to have worked as silversmiths in Williamsburg in the period 1699–1780. In that capital town was the house of John Coke, who worked in both precious metals and left for modern archaeologists many mementoes of his trade. Gold and silver drippings and the stones used to polish the metals are among the finds. His predecessor John Brodnax had in 1719 left, among other articles in a considerable estate, silver porringers, castors, a vinegar pot, a snuff box, and a silver-hilted sword. A communion service of about 1725 at St. Paul's Church, Edenton, North Carolina, labelled "A.K.," has been ascribed to Alexander Kern of Williamsburg. The evidence suggests, however, that very little flat silver or vessels were ever made in Williamsburg, probably because as in other things the planter preferred the London product.[305]

Virginia, especially the Tidewater area, has been the most thoroughly excavated of the provincial inhabited regions. A little silver has been found at estates such as Rosewell or in an Isle of Wight field. The largest hoard, unearthed by accident, has been that in a Nansemond County field in 1961, an amazing collection of colonial salvers and tankards and a cruet stand. All the items have the initials, however, of London silversmiths between 1768 and 1773 and were not provincial products.[306]

Names of thirty-four silversmiths appear in eighteenth-century North Carolina records, none of them in Edenton. Surviving business records of 1761–1762 show that a Thomas Agnis was making specific silver articles in Edenton. Spoons of various sizes were among them. Georgia's Savannah silversmiths are in evidence within the colonial period but no products of their works seem to be known.[307]

Cabinetmaking, noted in passing several times, when not distinguished was at least competent in the southern capital towns, particularly Annapolis, Williamsburg, and Charleston. In the last, Charles Warham, who moved there in 1734, seems to have been the pioneer furniture maker. Later came Josiah Claypoole of Pennsylvania. Two Carolina artisans reversed the usual trend and moved north to Philadelphia. But men such as Claypoole and Jonathan Badger were real artist-artisans. Gerard Hopkins of Philadelphia rose to prosperity in the trade in Baltimore.[308]

Maryland, close to Philadelphia, seems to have possessed a number of watch and clock makers who came to the Chesapeake province from Pennsylvania. William Faris, Thomas Sinnott, and Thomas Martin were one group that settled in Annapolis and two journeyman watchmakers from London opened a shop in Baltimore. Benjamin Chandlee (1723–1791) of a well-known family of instrument makers from London also opened a shop in Baltimore. Benjamin Chandlee, Jr. (1746–1821), just after the colonial period moved to Virginia and eventually opened a brass foundry and shop in Winchester, where he produced clocks, surveying compasses, sundials, apothecary and money scales, telescopes, and other instruments which mark him as one of the finest craftsmen of eighteenth-century America. There were a number of other able instrument makers slightly later in the Chesapeake colonies.[309]

Though Annapolis, Williamsburg, Norfolk, Wilmington, Savannah, even Charleston had scores of types of craftsmen, Bridenbaugh was unable to give by name one distinguished artisan of the southern area, though in the next chapter the reader is able to identify several who were half artists, half artisans. Hartwell-Blair-Chilton, as has been seen, pointed out that by 1697 even in the towns of the South there was little opportunity for an able craftsman to make a good living from his trade. The planter almost always preferred British products. The seventeenth-century and even eighteenth-century silver in use in Virginia, the fine furniture, hangings, carriages, house decorations, and a dozen other amenities of civilization were brought in by ship. Yet there is in Charleston and in the Chesapeake colonies still remaining in private families furniture and other cabinet work, and here and there copper pieces and pottery and other kindred forms, which show expert craftsmanship or artistic merit and were made locally.

But printing did thrive, including in Virginia a concomitant paper mill, once it had a substantial footing. From Parks' *Maryland Gazette* of 1727 to the *Georgia Gazette* of 1763, the newspaper was a thriving business, as already noted in a preceding chapter, and the handsomest books from pre-1764 colonial America were issued by southern presses. In 1744 near Williamsburg, with the financial support of Benjamin Franklin, Parks set up the first southern paper mill, an event which elicited a poem of jocular tone from Joseph Dumbleton. In both Virginia and Maryland, sometimes with special fonts of type, Parks and his successors published some memorable and several distinguished books, presumably with the aid of capable journeyman printers. How much help the first printers of the Carolinas and Georgia had is still difficult to judge, for they frequently advertised in their own and other newspapers for journeymen and apprentices. Along with printing and papermills went bookbinding, almost but not quite always carried on in the printing shops. Thanks to research conducted at Williamsburg, a great deal is known about this leather craft in Virginia and Maryland. Probably the first bookbinder of colonial America was Jone Hill of Lower Norfolk County in Virginia in 1647, formerly a craftsman at Oxford in England. The next known southern binders come years later, after William Parks was established in Maryland and Virginia, and they and their lineal successors carried on well into the national period. In the two fragmentary surviving *Virginia Gazette* daybooks, almost every prominent name of the years covered appears as a patron of the craft. Among the scores having books bound and decorated were Littleton Tazewell, Wilson Cary, John Randolph, Jr., Dr. William Dawson, the Reverend Thomas Dawson, William Nelson, Robert Carter Nicholas, our old friend John Mercer (a frequent patron), John Clayton, George Wythe, William Byrd II, Peyton Randolph, Governor Francis Fauquier, Robert Bolling, Jr., and Thomas Jefferson. The ornaments and stamping and leathers which went into some quite creditable covers may still be seen.[310]

The colonial crafts especially come close to or overlapped the fine arts, and in the next chapter on the fine arts there will be mentioned even more artisans who were also artists, or assisted true artists, in a variety of areas from metalwork to architecture and building. These overlapping intents, skills and geniuses, and occupations occurred in both North and South. One of the hybrid skills in which the southern colonies attained distinction is engineering, which most scholars would place under technology but which in the hands and minds of some forgotten men, or remembered ones such as De Brahm, really became art, as does the cartography done by the same men. Canals, dams, fortifications, public buildings, towns, in fact or on paper, were creations of ingenious minds which combined scientific principles with imagination. At Roanoke Island, Jamestown, New Bern, Edenton, Charleston, Savannah, Frederica and Ebenezer, among dozens of other towns living or dead, were carefully laid out streets, squares, parks, gardens, with drawings or plats to indicate the original concept. Scores of these plans, drawn or painted, are extant, from John White through De Brahm with Governor Nicholson of Maryland-Virginia between with his ingeniously laid out capital towns for the two colonies.

What did a string of coastal agricultural provinces in a temperate climate merging into the subtropical accomplish in science and technology in less than two centuries? In natural philosophy or science they did a great deal, leaving the names of pioneer naturalists and their regions permanently in the records of botany most of all, but of zoology and geology as well. Their professional and amateur meteorologists gathered still useful data. In surveying they were more than reasonably adept and left their mark in great maps of areas or of the whole of British America as reminders of their accuracy of observation and skill as civil engineers. In medicine came no startling experiments or discoveries but such a body of well-grounded speculation and printed evidence that they stood on a part with their northern colleagues in the years before 1764. In astronomy, electricity, and chemistry they showed some interest but not sufficient to rival the Boston and Philadelphia groups.

Southern colonial agriculture at this distance seems at first to present an exasperating and frustrating picture, for today one is likely to feel that much might have been done which was not. Actually the failures subside or fade into the background when one looks at the accomplishments: from a primitive stick-and-hoe adaptation of native cultivation into a moderate and large-scale, carefully organized plantation operation which was actually or potentially powerful and for a time lucrative. There were experiments in fertilizing and in horticulture, though in the former not nearly enough. The staples, the money crops, were at times so profitable many believed they always would be and gambled with poor soil and bad weather to the point of disaster. But at the end of the period, despite some debts to merchants in Britain, the southern agriculturist was financially and occupationally in a golden age—or at least he lived as though he were.

The southern farmer has been accused of living for the day, of not looking forward to the future. Yet great planter or small farmer kept his eye on fertile lands to the west which might replace his own rapidly deteriorating acres. Like William Fitzhugh, many prepared for eventualities. A William Byrd III did not, though his father and grandfather did.

Technology when it was farm-related was probably equal to its British rural counterpart. In community or urban or cooperative settings it did not measure up to what was being done in the mother country. In mining for metal and processing it, in printing, in tar and soap-ash manufacture, men showed intelligence, resource, and ingenuity. Though the middle states eventually took over the principal southern large-scale industries, in the colonial period, especially in the Chesapeake region, certain industries got their American start and continued for several generations.

A look at southern colonial technology and science reveals that in these areas the settlers were alert, persistent, and often ingenious. Agriculture was the principal science and caused directly or indirectly much of the technological achievement but by no means all of it. And the southern botanist and cartographer were without superiors on the continent, perhaps indeed without equals. The regional colonial mind was above all conscious of its physical environment.

Slavery by 1720 or 1730 was affecting appreciably the physical energies and perhaps dulling the mental energies of the southern white, but in most instances he ignored slavery's deleterious implications and demanded, particularly in the deeper South, more and more black labor. Slavery was omnipresent, it was a powerful force, and yet on the cultural surface it is curiously inconspicuous as one examines the period. In science and technology, the black was but one of several implements or elements to keep the agricultural and industrial machine moving.

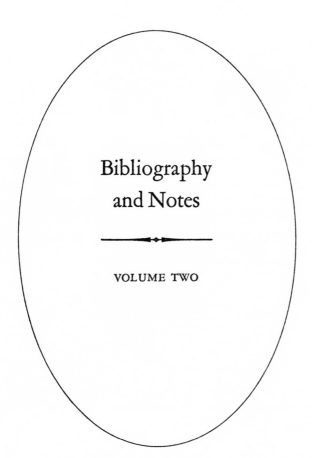

Bibliography
and Notes

VOLUME TWO

Chapter Four: Books, Libraries, Reading, and Printing

Bibliography

Manuscript sources have been used here more frequently than in preceding chapters, for the majority of inventories of books from personal estates still lie in county records of the former coastal colonies, though at least photographic copies have been gathered in state archives and libraries. Many others lie in state and local historical society collections, in university libraries, or in private hands. Some of these have been abstracted or printed in part, but my own research in the state and historical society collections, and the assertions of their directors, convince me that in no instance have more than a fraction of the book lists been published. My first researches consisted in following leads from various oral and printed suggestions. My second round of visits to manuscript repositories has usually followed suggestions made in printed studies or certain documents listed below. Some of my most significant materials were suggested by directors and archivists who knew much better than I possibly could what their collections included. I am indebted to them and to curators of provincial materials in the universities of the southern region and in the historical societies. Many suggestions and photographic materials came by mail long after I had been convinced that I had all that it was possible for one person to gather in one lifetime.

There are manuscript materials other than book lists which reveal much about colonial reading. In the Duke University Library Manuscript Division is a collection of papers, notes, and drafts by Alice Mary Baldwin on "The Reading of Women in the Colonies before 1750." Especially in university and historical society collections but also in state libraries and archives are letters and bills of lading which indicate what books people were buying or reading. A number of unpublished doctoral dissertations, generally more easily available in several photographic forms than other manuscript materials, are included here with the printed sources.

Since it would be quite difficult to give a list of general printed sources in any order of priority in time or importance, they are probably best listed loosely usually by general subject. The studies of books, libraries, and reading in the colonies as a whole and then in the individual colonies are given first, followed each time by the major histories of colonial printing and provincial printing. A useful collection of essays covering all these areas is Hellmut Lehmann-Haupt et al., eds., *The Book in America: A History of the Making, the Selling, and the Collecting of Books in the United States* (New York, 1951).

The vogue and influence of a number of European writers in the colonies is studied in several books and essays: Mary-Margaret H. Barr, *Voltaire in America, 1744–1800* (Baltimore, 1941), despite the inclusive dates of its title of little use for the period before 1764; R.S. Boys, "The English Poetical Miscellany in Colonial America," *SP*, XLII (1945), 114–130; Leon Howard, "Early American Copies of Milton," *Hunt. Lib. Bull.*, no. 7 (April, 1935), 169–179, and George F. Sensabaugh, *Milton in Early America* (Princeton, 1964); Howard M. Jones, *America and French Culture, 1750–1848* (Chapel Hill, 1927); Edward A. Richards, *Hudibras in the Burlesque Tradition* (New York, 1938), touching slightly on the subject of this chapter; Paul M. Spurlin, *Montesquieu in America, 1760–1801* (Baton Rouge, 1940), and *Rousseau in America, 1760–1809* (University, Ala., 1969), both late for this study; Edwin E. Willoughby, "The Reading of Shakespeare in Colonial America," *PBSA*, XXXI (1932), 45–56; and George B. Watts, "Marmontel's Vogue in America," *MLN*, LXIX (1954), 267–269.

Other studies concentrate more specifically on politico-philosophical relationships: John Dunn, "The Politics of Locke in England and America in the Eighteenth Century," in *John Locke: Problems and Perspectives*, ed. John W. Yolton (Cambridge, Eng., 1969), pp. 45–80; Fredric M. Litto, "Addison's *Cato* in the Colonies," *WMQ* (3), XXIII (1966), 431–449; H. Trevor Colbourn, *The Lamp of Experience: Whig History and the Intellectual Origins of the American Revolution* (Chapel Hill, 1965); and Caroline Robbins, *The Eighteenth-Century Commonwealthman: Studies in the Transmission, Development, and Circumstance of English Liberal Thought from the Restoration of Charles II until the War with the Thirteen Colonies* (Cambridge, Mass., 1961).

Other books are more general, usually, some concerned with intellectual climate, some with collecting and libraries, some with reading. Generally suggestive but including entirely too little on the subject under discussion is Walter M. Whitehill et al., *The Arts in Early American History: Needs and Opportunities for Study* (Chapel Hill, 1965). Many of the studies of books in America contain only a passing or perfunctory reference to the southern colonies, though for reasons mentioned in the text of this chapter those concerned with parochial or church libraries usually have much to say of the South. Of varying degrees of usefulness are Carl R. Cannon, *American Book Collectors and Collecting from Colonial Times to the Present* (New York, 1941); J.T. Hurst, "Parochial Libraries of the Colonial Period," *Am. Soc. Church Hist. Papers*, II (1890), 46–49; Thomas B. Keyes, "The Colonial Library and the Development of Sectional Differences in the American Colonies," *Lib. Q.*, VIII (1938), 373–390, a study based on too little evidence; Margaret B. Korty,

Benjamin Franklin and Eighteenth-Century American Libraries (Philadelphia, 1965); Michael Kraus, *The Atlantic Civilization: Eighteenth Century Origins* (Ithaca, 1949); Aubrey C. Land, ed., *Bases of the Plantation Society* (Columbia, 1969); Julia C. Spruill, *Woman's Life and Work in the Southern Colonies* (Chapel Hill, 1938); Sarah Stetson, "American Garden Books, Transplanted and Native, before 1807," *WMQ* (3), III (1946), 343–369; C. Seymour Thompson, *Evolution of the American Public Library, 1653–1876* (New York, 1957), and Louis B. Wright, "The Purposeful Reading of Our Colonial Ancestors," *ELH*, IV (1937), 85–111. Marcus A. McCorison, ed., *The 1764 Catalogue of the Redwood Library Company at Newport, Rhode Island* (New Haven, 1965), describes a collection to which southern colonials had some access.

Among the specifically or largely southern subjects covering more than one colony are W.D. Houlette, "Plantation and Parish Libraries in the Old South" (Ph.D. diss., Univ. of Iowa, 1933) and "Parish Libraries and the Work of the Reverend Thomas Bray," *Lib. Q.*, IV (1934), 588–604; and Bernard C. Steiner, "Rev. Thomas Bray and His American Libraries," *AHR*, II (1896), 59–75.

Among the several studies of national or regional printing and provincial gazettes, the first, still useful but far outdated in many details, especially regarding the South Atlantic region, is Isaiah Thomas' *The History of Printing in America, With a Biography of Printers, and an Account of Newspapers . . .* (2 vols., 1st ed. Worcester, Mass., 1810; 2d ed. [used here] Albany, 1874). Lawrence C. Wroth's studies, now a little outdated, are also vaulable: e.g., *The Colonial Printer* (Portland, Maine, 1938) and "Printing in the Colonial Period, 1638–1783," in *The Book in America*, ed. Lehmann-Haupt, and "Book Production and Distribution from the Beginning to the American Revolution," *ibid.*, pp. 7–59; Douglas C. McMurtrie, *A History of Printing in the United States: The Story of the Introduction of the Press and of Its History and Influence during the Pioneer Period in Each State of the Union*, Volume II, Middle and South Atlantic States (New York, 1936), contains some materials Wroth does not. Not at all pertinent is Arthur B. Berthold, *American Colonial Printing as Determined by Contemporary Cultural Forces, 1639–1763* (New York, 1970). Clarence S. Brigham's *History and Bibliography of American Newspapers, 1690–1820* (2 vols., Worcester, Mass., 1947) is invaluable; also interesting is Sidney Kobre, *The Development of the Colonial Newspaper* (Gloucester, Mass, 1960). Rollo G. Silver's *The American Printer, 1787–1825* (Charlottesville, 1967) is focused on a later period but sheds considerable light on printing before 1764. Some of the essays are pertinent in David Kaser, ed., *Books in America's Past: Essays Honoring Rudolph H. Gjelsness* (Charlottesville, 1966). Three recent compilations are especially useful: G. Thomas Tanselle, *Guide to the Study of United States Imprints* (2 vols., Cambridge, Mass., 1971); Ray O. Hummel, Jr., *Southeastern Broadsides before 1877: A Bibliography* (Richmond, 1971), though it omits Maryland; and J.A. Leo

Lemay, *A Calendar of American Poetry in the Colonial Newspapers and Magazines and the Major English Magazines through 1765* (Worcester, Mass., 1970). One should also see Christine Cook, *Literary Influences in Colonial Newspapers, 1704–1750* (New York, 1912).

Maryland: Books, Libraries, and Reading

Thanks to Lawrence Wroth and his successors, a great deal is known about books and printing in Maryland, although many of its most interesting inventory book lists remain in official manuscript repositories. Especially and generally useful are Elizabeth Baer, comp., *Seventeenth Century Maryland, a Bibliography* (Baltimore, 1949) and Lawrence C. Wroth, *A History of Printing in Colonial Maryland, 1686–1776* (Baltimore, 1922), the latter of which contains more than its title suggests. William H. Browne, et al., eds., *The Archives of Maryland* (60 plus vols. to date, Baltimore, 1883–   ), contains some useful oblique references but very few if any inventories of books. The Reverend Thomas Bray's several works on libraries were particularly directed at Maryland; they include his *Proposals for the Encouragement and Promotion of Religion and Learning in the Foreign Plantations* (London, 1695), *Bibliotheca Parochialis* (London, 1697), and *An Essay Towards Promoting All Necessary and Useful Knowledge Both Human and Divine* (London, 1697), besides later works. Bernard C. Steiner, ed., *The Reverend Thomas Bray: His Life and Selected Works Relating to Maryland* (Baltimore, 1901), is a necessary accompaniment to Bray's works and indeed includes some of them. The several studies growing from Joseph T. Wheeler's "Literary Culture in Colonial Maryland, 1700–1776" (Ph.D. diss., Brown Univ., 1939) are indispensable: "Thomas Bray and the Maryland Parochial Libraries," *MdHM*, XXXIV (1939), 111–137, 246–265; "The Laymen's Libraries and the Provincial Library," *MdHM*, XXXV (1940), 60–73; "Books Owned by Marylanders, 1700–1776," *MdHM*, XXXV (1940), 337–383; "Reading Interests of the Professional Classes . . . , The Clergy," *MdHM*, XXXVI (1941), 184–188; *idem* "Lawyers and Doctors," 281–301; "Reading Interests of Maryland Planters and Merchants . . . ," *MdHM*, XXXVII (1942), 26–41, 291–310; "Reading and Other Recreations of Marylanders, 1700–1776," *MdHM*, XXXVIII (1943), 37–55, 167–180; "Literary Culture in Eighteenth Century Maryland, 1700–1776," *MdHM*, XXXVIII (1943), 273–276. Others, including some concerned with cultural background, are *America's First Public Library: The Annapolitan Library of St. John's College* (Annapolis, 1930); Charles A. Barker, *The Background of the Revolution in Maryland* (New Haven, 1940); Charles B. Clark, ed., *The Eastern Shore of Maryland and Virginia* (3 vols., New York, 1950); John W. Garrett, "Seventeenth Century Books Relating to Maryland," *MdHM*, XXXIV (1939), 1–39; [Theophilus Grew], *The Maryland Almanack . . . 1733 . . .* [Annapolis, 1732 etc.]; Phebe R. Jacobsen, *Quaker Records in Maryland* (Annapolis, 1966); Lubov Keefer, *Baltimore's Music: The Haven of American Composers* (Baltimore, 1962); Sarah J. Klein, "The History and Present Status of the Library of St. John's College, Annapolis" (M.A. thesis, Catholic Univ., 1952); Henry F. Thompson, "Maryland at the End of the Seventeenth Century," *MdHM*, II (1907), 163–171; J. Donnell Tilghman, "Wye House," *MdHM*, XLVIII (1953), 89–108; Edwin Wolf, 2nd, "The Library of Edward Lloyd IV of Wye House," *Winterthur Portfolio* (Charlottesville, 1969), 87–121; and Lawrence C. Wroth, "The Maryland Merchant and His Friends in 1750," *MdHM*, VI (1911), 213–240.

Maryland: Printers, Imprints, and Newspapers

The books by Baer, Brigham, and Wroth mentioned above, especially Wroth's *History of Printing in Colonial Maryland*, are basic. Wroth contains sketches and lists of imprints of all the printers of the period. For William Parks as printer, see the bibliography in J.A. Leo Lemay, *Men of Letters in Colonial Maryland* (Knoxville, Tenn., 1972); Lawrence C. Wroth, *William Parks, Printer and Journalist of England and Colonial America* (Richmond, 1926); William H. Castles, Jr., "The *Virginia Gazette*, 1736–1766: Its Editors, Editorial Policy, and Literary Content" (Ph.D. diss., Univ. of Tennessee, 1962); and Cook, *Literary Influences*. For William Nuthead, see Wroth, *History*; and for Jonas Green, Wroth, *History*, and Lemay, *Men of Letters in Colonial Maryland*. For the *Maryland Gazette*, both Parks' and Green's, see A.O. Aldridge, "Benjamin Franklin and the *Maryland Gazette*," *MdHM*, XLIV (1949), 177–189; Martha G. Howard, "The *Maryland Gazette*, an American Imitator of the *Tatler* and *Spectator*," *MdHM*, XXIX (1934), 295–298; Nicholas Joost, " 'Plain-Dealer' and *Free-Thinker*: A Revaluation," *AL*, XXIII (1951), 31–37, and "William Parks, Benjamin Franklin, and a Problem of Colonial Deism," *Mid-America*, n.s. XXIII (1952), 313; *Two Hundred Years of the Maryland Gazette, with Notes and Illustrations of Historical Maryland*, ed. Charles M. Christian and Thomas L. Christian ([Annapolis?], Sept. 29, 1927). The extant issues of the Parks *Maryland Gazette* have been reproduced in photostat by the John Carter Brown Library, those of the later Green *Gazette*, on microfilm by the Yale University Library.

Virginia: Books, Libraries, and Reading

For Virginia there is nothing comparable to the work by Baer and Wroth for Maryland, for William Clayton Torrence's *A Trial Bibliography of Colonial Virginia* (2 pts., Richmond, 1907–1908, 1908–1909) has been long outdated. Earl G. Swem's *Virginia Historical Index* (2 vols., Roanoke, 1934–1936) is of great help on almost any question. There is, however, a far greater body of individual studies and edited documents than exists for any other southern colony. Most of it can be listed in alphabetical order under author: Susie M. Ames, "Law-in-Action; The Court Records of Virginia's Eastern Shore," *WMQ* (3), IV (1947), 177–191, and her *Reading, Writing, and Arithmetic in Virginia*, 350th Anniv. Hist. Booklet no. 15 (Williamsburg, 1957) are but two of this scholar's work bearing to some extent on the present subject; for medical books and reading, Wyndham B. Blanton's *Medicine in Virginia in the Seventeenth Century* (Richmond, 1930) and *Medicine in Virginia in the Eighteenth Century* (Richmond, 1931); for "Books in Colonial

Virginia" see the references to inventories printed in the historical magazines as Swem (above) lists them; for seventeenth-century libraries and books, an excellent general source is Philip A. Bruce's *Institutional History of Virginia in the Seventeenth Century* (2 vols., New York, 1910), based on personal examination of hundreds of extant inventories in manuscript in county records. Richard B. Davis, "Jefferson as Collector of Virginiana," *SB*, XIV (1961), 117–144, traces some of the major books and reading from periods earlier than Jefferson's own; Edward Eggleston, *The Transit of Civilization from England to America in the Seventeenth Century* (New York, 1901), offers pertinent suggestions and some data; Joseph and Nesta Ewan, in *John Banister and His Natural History of Virginia* (Urbana, 1970), trace and identify some of the books still extant from one of America's earliest science book collections; *The Journal and Letters of Philip Vickers Fithian*, ed. H.D. Farish (Williamsburg, 1943), includes a title list of one of the great colonial libraries, that of Councilor Robert Carter; *William Fitzhugh and His Chesapeake World, 1676–1701*, ed. Richard B. Davis (Chapel Hill, 1963), includes titles of dozens of books Fitzhugh ordered and shows reading habits; Appleton P.C. Griffin, ed., *A Catalogue of the Washington Collection in the Boston Athenaeum* (Boston, 1897), includes some titles from earlier Custis libraries and is significant in itself; *The Henley-Horrocks Inventory*, ed. Fraser Neiman, Botetourt Bibliog. Soc. Publ. no. 1 (Williamsburg, 1968), shows a professor's collection; W.D. Houlette, "The Byrd Library," *Tyler's Q.*, XVI (1934), 100–109, is a discussion rather than a listing; John M. Jennings, "Notes on the Original Library of the College of William and Mary in Virginia, 1698–1705," *PBSA*, XLI (1947), 258–267, contains an annotated list of Governor Nicholson's library, and Jennings' *The Library of the College of William and Mary in Virginia, 1693–1793* (Charlottesville, 1968) is equally valuable; Susan M. Kingsbury's *Records of the Virginia Company of London* (4 vols., Washington, D.C., 1906–1935) reveals a great deal about the earliest books at Jamestown; John Gwilym Jones has edited and translated and commented upon *Goronwy Owen's Virginian Adventure: His Life, Poetry, and Literary Opinions, with a Translation of His Virginian Letters*, Botetourt Bibliog. Soc. Publ. no. 2 (Williamsburg, 1969), and also lists some of his books; Lucy T. Latané, *Parson Latané, 1672–1732* (Charlottesville, 1936), lists books on pp. 73–76; Maurer Maurer, "The Library of a Colonial Musician," *WMQ* (3), VII, (1950), 39–52, analyzes the Cuthbert Ogle books, as does John W. Molnar, "A Collection of Music in Colonial Virginia: The Ogle Inventory," *Musical Quarterly*, XLIX (1963), 150–162; touching upon books and reading is C.G. Charles Moss, "Education in Colonial Virginia, Formal and Informal," in *Education in the South*, ed. R.C. Simonini, Jr. (Farmville, Va., 1959), pp. 97–119; John M. Patterson, "Private Libraries in Virginia in the Eighteenth Century" (M.A. thesis, Univ. of Virginia, 1936) analyzes several dozen libraries and gives some statistics; William S. Powell, "Books in the Virginia Colony before 1624," *WMQ* (3), V (1948), 177–184, uses Kingsbury and other sources for his study; George H. Reese, "Books in the Palace: The Libraries of Three Virginia Governors," *Virginia Cavalcade*, XVIII (1968), 20–31, writes of three late-colonial collections, two after 1763; George K. Smart, "Private Libraries in Colonial Virginia," *AL*, X (1938), 24–52, gives one of the best brief studies of book collections; E. Millicent Sowerby's monumental compilation, *Catalogue of the Library of Thomas Jefferson* (5 vols., Washington, D.C., 1952–1959), is a treasure house of comments on dozens of earlier libraries and on the books in them as well as indicative of the variety in the South's greatest pre-1800 library; Mary N. Stanard, *Colonial Virginia: Its People and Customs* (Philadelphia, 1917), lists many libraries and the number of volumes shown in inventories; Nora M. Turman and Mark C. Lewis, eds., "Inventory of the Estate of Argall Yeardley of Northampton County, Virginia, in 1655," *VMHB*, LXX (1962), 410–419, show the titles in the small library of the son of an early governor; Frank Tyrer, "Richard Blundell in Virginia and Maryland," *VMHB*, LXVIII (1960), 429–447, indicates through quoted letters the book-securing habits of one family; C. Malcolm Watkins, *The Cultural History of Marlborough, Virginia: An Archaeological and Historical Investigation of the Port Town of Stafford County and the Plantation of John Mercer . . .* (Washington, D.C., 1968), includes lists of books from Mercer's great library; Edwin Wolf, 2d, "The Dispersal of the Library of William Byrd of Westover," *PAAS*, LXVIII (1958), 19–106, is a revealing account and checklist of extant Byrd volumes; and Louis B. Wright's *The First Gentlemen of Virginia: Intellectual Qualities of the Early Ruling Class* (San Marino, 1940), a charming and most useful study, and his "The 'Gentleman's Library' in Early Virginia: The Literary Interests of the First Carters," *HLQ*, I (1937), 3–61, including two annotated library lists; "Pious Reading in Colonial Virginia," *JSH*, VI (1940), 383–392, are all vital.

Virginia: Printers, Imprints, and Newspapers

Though there is no such book for Virginia as Wroth's *History of Printing in Colonial Maryland*, there are useful studies of varying length. Torrence's *Trial Bibliography of Colonial Virginia* is still useful for a beginning study of imprints, and one looks forward to its successor now in process of compilation. Wroth's *William Parks* is even more useful for Virginia than for Maryland. Another half-century-old list is of some use, Earl G. Swem's *A Bibliography of Virginia: Part I, Containing the Titles of Books in the Virginia State Library Which Relate to Virginia and Virginians, the Titles of Those Books Written by Virginians, and of Those Printed in Virginia*, Bull. Va. St. Lib., VIII (1915), 31–767. Briefer are Douglas C. McMurtrie, *The Beginnings of Printing in Virginia* (Lexington, Va., 1935); Bertha M. Frick, "A History of Printing in Virginia, 1750–1783, with a List of Virginia Imprints for That Period," (M.S. thesis, Columbia Univ., 1933); August Klapper, *The Printer in Eighteenth-Century Williamsburg*, Williamsburg Craft Series (Williamsburg, 1955); Rutherfoord Goodwin, "The Williamsburg Paper Mill of William Parks the Printer," *PBSA*, XXXI (1937), pt. 2, 21–44; and C. Clement Samford and John M. Hemphill, II, *Bookbinding in Colonial Virginia*, Williamsburg Research Series (Williamsburg, 1966). The nearest to an overall study of the provincial newspaper is Castles, "The *Virginia Gazette*,

1736–1766," but shorter pieces are enlightening, as R.M. Myers, "The Old Dominion Looks to London," *VMHB*, LIV (1946), 195–217; George H. and Judith Gibson, "The Influence of the *Tatler* and the *Spectator* on the 'Monitor,'" *Furman Studies* issue of *Furman Univ. Bull.*, n.s. XIV (Nov., 1966), 12–23; Richard A. Overfield, "Science in the *Virginia Gazette*, 1736–1780," *The Emporia State Research Studies*, XVI, no. 3 (March, 1968), 1–53; and Robert D. Arner, "The Short, Happy Life of the Virginia 'Monitor,'" *EAL*, VII (1972), 130–147.

North Carolina: Books, Libraries, and Reading

Several histories and background studies contain material on books and reading, among them R.D.W. Connor, *History of North Carolina* (Vol. I of six, Chicago, 1910); W.H. Foote, *Sketches of North Carolina Historical and Biographical* . . . (New York, 1846); Frank L. Hawks, *History of North Carolina* (2 vols., Fayetteville, N.C., 1857–1858); Hugh T. Lefler, *A Guide to the Study and Reading of North Carolina History* (Chapel Hill, 1955); David D. Oliver, *The Society for the Propagation of the Gospel in North Carolina* (Raleigh, 1910); James S. Purcell, Jr., "Literary Culture in North Carolina before 1820" (Ph.D. diss., Duke Univ., 1950); William L. Saunders, ed., *Colonial Records of North Carolina* (10 vols., Raleigh, 1886–1890); and James Sprunt, *Chronicles of Cape Fear River* (Raleigh, 1914). Helpful are Mary L. Thornton, *A Bibliography of North Carolina, 1589–1956* (Chapel Hill, 1958), and J.B. Grimes, *North Carolina Wills and Inventories* (Raleigh, 1912). On books and libraries see also J.G. deRoulhac Hamilton, "Governor Thomas Burke," *The North Carolina Booklet*, VI (1906), 122, for titles of the governor's books; and Stephen B. Weeks, "Libraries and Literature in North Carolina in the Eighteenth Century," *AHA, Annual Report for 1895* (Washington, D.C., 1896), pp. 169–267.

North Carolina: Printers, Imprints, and Newspapers

There is a fair amount on printing: Douglas C. McMurtrie, *Eighteenth Century North Carolina Imprints, 1749–1800* (Chapel Hill, 1938); "The First Twelve Years of Printing in North Carolina, 1749–1760," *NCHR*, X (1933), 214–340; "Pioneer Printing in North Carolina: A Detailed Account of the Early Printers, 1749–1800," *National Printer Journalist*, L, no. 11 (Nov., 1932), 26–27, 84–85 [rpt., Springfield, Ill., 1932]; George W. Paschal, *A History of Printing in North Carolina: A Detailed Account of the Early Printers* (Raleigh, 1946); William S. Powell, "Eighteenth-Century North Carolina Imprints: A Revision and Supplement to McMurtrie," *NCHR*, XXXV (1958), 50–73, and his *Patrons of the Press: Subscription Book Purchase in North Carolina, 1733–1850* (Raleigh, 1962, orig. in *NCHR*); Wesley H. Wallace, "Cultural and Social Advertising in Early North Carolina Newspapers," *NCHR*, XXXIII (1956), 281–309; Stephen B. Weeks, *The Press of North Carolina in the Eighteenth Century with Biographical Sketches of Printers and an Account of the Manufacture of Paper and Bibliography of the Issues* (Brooklyn, N.Y., 1891), and his "Supplement to My Bibliography of the Eighteenth Century in my *Press of North Carolina in the Eighteenth Century*," *AHA, Annual Report for the year 1895* (Washington, D.C., 1896), 261–267; and John H. Wheeler, "Press of North Carolina from 1749 to 1851," in *Historical Sketches of North Carolina* (Philadelphia, 1851), pp. 112–116.

South Carolina: Books, Libraries, and Reading

Several general and cultural histories, biographies, and papers contain significant material on books and reading: Frederick P. Bowes, *The Culture of Early Charleston* (Chapel Hill, 1942); Carl Bridenbaugh, *Cities in the Wilderness: The First Century of Urban Life in America, 1625–1742* (New York, 1938 and 1955); Gertrude Foster, "Documentary History of Education in South Carolina" (13 vols., Ph.D. diss., Univ. of South Carolina, 1932): *The Papers of Henry Laurens . . .* , ed. Philip M. Hamer, George C. Rogers, Jr., et al., (5 vols. to date, Columbia, 1968–1976); Arthur H. Hirsch, *The Huguenots of South Carolina* (Durham, N.C., 1928); *Letterbook of Eliza Lucas Pinckney, 1739–1762*, ed. Elise Pinckney (Chapel Hill, 1972); Sir Edward Midwinter, "The Society for the Propagation of the Gospel and the Colonial Church in America: the Carolinas," *HMPEC*, IV (1935), 231–239; Mrs. St. Julian Ravenal, *Charleston: The Place and the People* (New York, 1925); George C. Rogers, Jr., *The History of Georgetown County, South Carolina* (Columbia, 1970); D.D. Wallace, *The History of South Carolina* (3 vols., New York, 1934); and Joseph I. Waring, *A History of Medicine in South Carolina, 1670–1825 . . .* (Columbia, 1964). Indispensable is Robert J. Turnbull, *Bibliography of South Carolina, 1563–1950*, esp. Vol. I, 1563–1814 (Charlottesville, 1956). The Department of Archives of South Carolina contains will books and inventories used in the present chapter sometimes in the original and sometimes in typescript copies now in the South Caroliniana Library of the University of South Carolina. Useful are the edition by J.H. Easterby et al. of *The Colonial Records of South Carolina* (Columbia, 1951–   ), Easterby's *Guide to the Study and Reading of South Carolina History: A General Classified Bibliography* (Columbia, 1950), and his *History of the Saint Andrews Society of Charleston, S.C., 1729–1929* (Charleston, 1923); Caroline T. Moore and Agatha A. Simmons, *Abstracts of the Wills of the State of South Carolina*, Vol. I (Columbia, 1960); and John H. Moore, *Research Materials in South Carolina: A Guide* (Columbia, 1967). Specifically concerned with one or more libraries are *A Catalogue of the Books in the Charlestown Library Society* (London, 1750) and *A Catalogue of Books Belonging to the Charlestown Library Society* (Charleston, 1770–1772, with Supplement and a *Catalogue of Books {of} John Mackenzie*); Anne King Gregorie, "The First Decade of the Charleston Library Society," *Proc. S.C. Hist. Assoc.*, 1935, pp. 3–10; Edgar L. Pennington, "The Beginnings of the Library in Charles Town, South Carolina," *PAAS*, XLIV (1934), 159–188, and "Original Rules and Members of the Charlestown Library Society," *SCHM*, XXIII (1922), 163–170; Virginia Rugheimer, "The Charleston Library Society," *Southeastern Librarian*, V (1955), 137–140, 154, and "Charleston Library Society," *SAB*, VIII (1942), 4–5; Mabel L. Webber, "The Georgetown Library Society,"

SCHM, XXV (1924), 94–100. More general are Frances L. Spain, "Libraries of South Carolina: Their Origins and Early History, 1700–1830" (Ph.D. diss., Univ. of Chicago, 1944), and "Early Libraries in Pendleton," *SCHM*, L (1949), 115–116; and Walter B. Edgar's "The Libraries of Colonial South Carolina" (Ph.D. diss., Univ. of South Carolina, 1969), "Notable Libraries of Colonial South Carolina," *SCHM*, LXXII (1971), 105–110, 174–178, and "Some Popular Books in Colonial South Carolina," *SCHM*, LXXII (1971), 227–235, include tables, lists of titles, and chapters on the uses made of books.

South Carolina: Printers, Imprints, and Newspapers

Several of the books and essays just mentioned touch on printing and newspapers. For the principal journal of the period, Hennig Cohen, *The South Carolina Gazette, 1732–1775* (Columbia, 1953), is indispensable, for it includes printers, imprints, contents of newspapers, and other materials. For Robert Wells and his 1758–1764 *South-Carolina Weekly Gazette* there is something in Edgar, Thomas, Wroth, and McMurtrie, though only three issues, two of them fragmentary, of this latter newspaper are extant. Douglas C. McMurtrie has several brief studies, among them "A Bibliography of South Carolina Imprints, 1731–1740," *SCHM*, XXXIV (1933), 117–137, and "The First Decade of Printing in South Carolina," *The Library*, n.s., XIII (1933), 425–452. Then there are Richard P. Morgan, *A Preliminary Bibliography of South Carolina Imprints, 1731–1800* (Clemson, S.C., 1966); Jeanne Denyse Mosimann, "A Checklist of Charleston, South Carolina. Imprints from 1731 to 1799 with a Historical Introduction" (M.S. thesis, Catholic Univ., 1959); and A.S. Salley, "The First Presses of South Carolina [with a list of South Carolina imprints from 1735 to 1771]," *PBSA*, II, (1907/8), 28–69.

Georgia: Books, Libraries, and Reading

Background studies also containing some factual data on books are E.M. Coulter, *Georgia: A Short History* (Chapel Hill, 1960); E.M. Coulter and Albert B. Saye, eds., *A List of Early Settlers of Georgia* (Athens, Ga., 1949); Harold E. Davis, "A Social History of Georgia, 1733–1776" (Ph.D. diss., Emory Univ., 1972); and *DeBrahm's Report of the General Survey of the Southern District of North America*, ed. Louis De Vorsey, Jr. (Columbia, 1971). Concerned directly with books and libraries are Allen D. Candler and Lucien Knight, eds., *The Colonial Records of the State of Georgia* (26 vols., Atlanta, 1904–1916) (referred to below as Candler, *Col. Rec. Georgia*), and original and photographic copies of inventories in the State Archives and in the University of Georgia Library; *Abstracts of Colonial Wills of the State of Georgia, 1733–1777* (publ. by Colonial Dames of America for the Dept. of Archives and History, Atlanta, 1962); Berry Fleming, "199 Years of Augusta's Library: A Chronology," *GaHQ*, XXXIII (1949), 124–181, which includes a catalogue of Augusta's first library; Azalea Clizbee, comp., *Catalogue of the Wymberley Jones De Renne Library of Wormsloe, Isle of Hope, near Savannah, Georgia* (Wormsloe, 1931); Oscar Wegelin, comp., *Books Relating to the History of Georgia in the Library of Wymberley Jones De*

Renne of Wormsloe, Isle of Hope, Chatham County, Georgia (Savannah, 1911); Robert V. Williams, "George Whitefield's Bethesda: The Orphanage, the College, and the Library," *Library History Seminar No. 3, Proceedings 1968* (Florida State Univ., Tallahassee); and *Journals of Henry M. Muhlenberg*, trans. by Theodore G. Tappert and John W. Doberstein (3 vols., Philadelphia, 1942–1958), Vol. II, 596, including some discussion of J.J. Zubly's library. The most recent study is Harold E. Davis, *The Fledgling Province: Social and Cultural Life in Colonial Georgia 1733–1776* (Chapel Hill, 1976).

Georgia: Printers, Imprints, and Newspapers

Betty Jane Daniel, *Georgia Imprints, 1763–1799: A Study of the Form and Subject Matter of Early Printing in Georgia* (M.S. thesis, Emory Univ., 1952, publ. 1955 by Univ. of Rochester Press as ACRL Microcard no. 47); Patricia Ann Libbey, "A Preliminary Checklist of Savannah, Georgia, Imprints, 1763–1837, with a Historical Introduction" (M.S. thesis, Catholic Univ., 1958); Douglas C. McMurtrie, "Located Georgia Imprints of the Eighteenth Century Not in the De Renne Catalogue," *GaHQ*, XVIII (1934), 27–65; and "Pioneer Printing in Georgia," *Ga HQ*, XVI (1932), 77–113. A book-length study by Alexander A. Lawrence, *James Johnston, Georgia's First Printer* (Savannah, 1956), reveals a great deal about the man and his work.

NOTES

1. Bruce, *Inst. Hist. Va.*, I, 440–441. Bruce believes the estimate of twenty thousand most conservative. He based his figures on the hundreds or thousands of inventories he examined in Tidewater Virginia.

2. Investigators agree that religious books, particularly certain titles to be noted below, were the first or prime requisite of almost every reader. See such studies as Wright, *First Gentlemen of Virginia*, passim, and his "The 'Gentleman's Library' in Early Virginia," pp. 3–61, "Pious Reading," pp. 383–392, and "Purposeful Reading," pp. 85–111; Smart, "Private Libraries in Colonial Virginia," *AL*, X (1938), 24–52; Bruce, *Inst. Hist. Va.*, I, 402 ff.; Wheeler's several studies of Maryland noted in the bibliography above, and the few suggestions of inventories in *Archives of Md.*; Edgar, "The Libraries of Col. S.C.," passim; Spain, "Libraries of S.C.," etc. The present writer's examination of manuscript materials of many kinds and locations is suggested in this chapter's bibliography above. This examination in the main bears out conclusions already printed—as far as they go.

3. Wright, "Purposeful Reading," pp. 86–87; and "Pious Reading," pp. 383–392.

4. Robbins, *The Eighteenth-Century Commonwealthman*. See also Colbourn, *The Lamp of Experience*. Of both these books more later. For some pre-Revolutionary uses of the Whig-Tory writers, see Homer D. Kemp, ed., "The Pre-Revolutionary Virginia Polemical Essay: The Pistole Fee and the Two-Penny Acts Controversies" (Ph.D. diss., Univ. of Tennessee, 1972).

5. Edgar, "Libraries of Col. S.C." The present writer would suggest publication of *all* known book inventories of each colony (a not impossible task) and then a study or analysis, including such useful statistical information as Edgar has presented, with their obvious and accessible sources. This procedure would allow the future scholar to make his own assessments along the lines he wished to follow, which might or might not be similar to Edgar's. Even a sampling shows that one of Edgar's appendices, "Notable Libraries of Colonial South Carolina," pp. 105–110, does not contain statistics on all libraries valued at £50 or more, an admittedly questionable criterion in itself. One notes at random at least half a dozen other libraries valued at a little less than £50 but obviously far larger and more valuable than a considerable percentage of those so valued. For the Maryland inventories, see below.

6. Samuel Miller, *A Brief Retrospect of the Eighteenth Century* (2 vols., rpt., New York, 1970), II, 492–506.

7. Keyes, "Col. Lib. and Dev. Sect. Differences," pp. 373–390. The principal favorable comment for this study is that it affords hints of methods of approach which might well be considered in some future more complete analyses based on much more data from inventories and other sources.

8. Printed in Charleston by Robert Wells, the main catalog in 1770 and the appendix in 1772. Along with it goes the catalog of the books of John Mackenzie, deposited with the Library Society for its use until the projected College of Charleston should open its doors, at which time the books were to go to that institution. In 1750 in London a briefer catalog of the Society's books had been printed. See below.

9. Quinn, ed., *The Roanoke Voyages, 1584–1590* (2 vols., London, 1955), II, 615.

10. Barbour, ed., *The Jamestown Voyages 1606–1609* (2 vols., Cambridge, Eng., 1969), II, 393.

11. *Ibid.*, I, 229–230, Wingfield's "Discourse."

12. The best study of these works is Powell, "Books in Va. before 1624," pp. 177–184. Kingsbury, ed., *Records Va. Co.*, passim, is his principal source. There is no complete account of books sent to the colony in this period, partly because the records themselves are fragmentary.

13. This was probably the edition of *The Practise of Pietie* sent, though another published in London in 1619 was a condensed collection of sermons. See Powell, "Books," p. 177.

14. Kingsbury, ed., *Records Va. Co.*, III, 389, 403; and Powell, "Books," pp. 178–180. Powell identifies all these works at least tentatively as to proper titles and dates of publication.

15. Kingsbury, ed., *Records Va. Co.*, III, 576; and Powell, "Books," pp. 180–181. Kingsbury (I, 421) indicates that the Perkins volumes were three in folio and that the map was "of Sr Walter Rawlighes."

16. Powell, "Books," pp. 181–182.

17. Kingsbury, ed., *Records Va. Co.*, IV, 271. Zacharias Ursinus' *Catechisme*, published in 1591, appears in a number of later southern libraries.

18. Kingsbury, ed., *Records Va. Co.*, III, 507; and Alexander Brown, *First Republic in America* (Boston, 1898), p. 460.

19. Richard B. Davis, "Volumes from George Sandys's Library Now in America," *VMHB*, LXV (1957), 450–457. The known extant volumes from Sandys' library may or may not ever have been at Jamestown. Certainly they were used in the 1632 second folio edition commentaries.

20. Kingsbury, ed., *Records Va. Co.*, III, 222.

21. Bucke, in *VMHB*, XXV (1917), 225–238; Yeardley, in McIlwaine, ed., *Minutes Council and Gen. Court of Col. Va.*, p. 166.

22. "A Virginia Minister's Library, 1635," ed R.G. Marsden, *AHR*, XI (1905/6), 328–332.

23. Stanard, *Col. Va.*, p. 296; Bruce, *Inst. Hist. Va.*, I, 433.

24. Stanard, *Col. Va.*, pp. 296 ff.; for the silkworm book, see Samuel Hartlib's MS. notes in the Lambeth Palace Lib. copy of his book, where the four hundred copies sent to Virginia are mentioned. In 1652 the title (altered in 1655) was *A Rare and New Discovery of a Speedy Way, and Easy Manner . . . for the feeding of Silk-worms in the Woods on the Mulberry-Tree-Leaves in Virginia*. In the 1655 edition (pp. 27–28) in a letter of 1654 Edward Digg(e)s describes his use of mulberry leaves in feeding the worms. The letter is more hopeful than indicative of actual silk production, though there was to be later a little silk in Virginia.

25. *VMHB*, II (1894/5), 235–236; Wright, *First Gent. Va.*, p. 237; Stanard, *Col. Va.*, p. 297. A full inventory has not been located though the will is in the Lancaster County Court Records, Wills, 1709–1727, p. 416.

26. Nora M. Turman and Mark C. Lewis, eds., "Inventory of the Estate of Argoll Yeardley of Northampton County, Virginia, in 1655," *VMHB*, LXX (1962), 410–419.

27. Bruce, *Inst. Hist. Va.*, I, 435; York County Records, Va. St. Lib., vol. 1664–1772.

28. Bruce, *Inst. Hist. Va.*, I, 427–428; Blanton, *Med. in Va. in the Seventeenth Century*, pp. 89–90. Both rely on Va. St. Lib., Rappahannock County Records, vol. 1677–1682, p. 75. Bruce also cites the German-language collection of Dr. Nicholas Hack of Accomack County, and the same man's considerable number of Latin and English titles. Hack was a native of Cologne.

29. For Littleton, Bruce, I, 432, and Va. St. Lib., Accomack County Records, vol. 1676–1790, p. 295; for Porter, Stanard, *Col. Va.*, p. 297.

30. For Carter, Wright's "The 'Gentleman's Library' in Early Virginia," pp. 3–61, which includes two Carter inventories with identifications of abbreviated titles.

31. Accomack County, Book of Deeds and Wills, 1692–1715, inventory being recorded February 11, 1696/7 (printed in *WMQ* [2], XXIII [1943], 298–308). My categorical figures are approximate, for many books here and elsewhere obviously might be classified under more than one heading. I have used the Va. St. Lib. copy of the inventory.

32. Jennings, *Library of William and Mary*, and his edition of the catalog, "Notes on the Original Library of the College of William and Mary," pp. 239–

267. The Catalogue, endorsed May 1695, is in the Fulham Palace Archives in the Lambeth Palace Lib.

33. Bruce, *Inst. Hist. Va.*, I, 439; Wright, *First Gent. Va.*, p. 140; *WMQ* (1), VIII (1900), 230–231.

34. Inventory *WMQ* (1), III (1894/5), 133–134; *Tyler's Q.*, X (1929), 163–165. Spicer had been justice of the peace and burgess also. See *William Fitzhugh*, ed. Davis passim, and Wright, *First Gent. Va.*, pp. 140–142.

35. Edmund and Dorothy Berkeley, *The Reverend John Clayton, a Parson with a Scientific Mind* (Charlottesville, 1965), p. 4, quoted in Ch. III above: "for want of bookes they read men the more."

36. See will of Sherwood, *WMQ* (1), XVII (1909), 270–273, and Ambler Papers, Va. Hist. Soc. MS. photocopy. The date is February 7, 1697/8 [or 1699]. At least one scholar has declared his intention of devoting a full-length biographical study to this controversial early Virginian, evidently an embezzler in England, who became a power in the colony.

37. *Archives of Md.*, IV, 35; I, 119. Actually the archivists of the Maryland Hall of Records inform the writer that very few of their numerous inventories for the whole colonial period have been printed. Though the published Maryland *Archives* are the most complete for any southern colony, the series does not contain the many book lists actually in existence. Work is going on. Alan Day of the University of Edinburgh has made notes on all inventory legal material. The "St. Mary's City Commission" is sponsoring a complete study of four counties in the period 1658–1705, which will show what estates over this period contained books, the values of investments in books, and the distribution across the range of total estate values.

38. *Ibid.*, IV, 74, 75, 83, 87–88, 91, 94, 98–99. See note 37.

39. *Ibid.*, III, 96; IV, 320–321; LIV, 102. Calvert (1606–1647) was the brother of the Proprietor Lord Baltimore. For Calvert, see *DAB*.

40. *Ibid.*, LIV, 107.

41. April 3, 1669, in *MdHM*, XXV (1930), 43–53, from holograph letter in Dr. Williams' Library, London, Baxter Letters, Vol. III, f. 261. The present writer has analyzed six interesting inventories of the seventeenth century which survive only in the Hall of Records MSS. They fall between 1660 and 1709/10 (even the last actually made up of seventeenth-century books). The 1669 inventory (Testamentary Proceedings 3, f. 282) of the library of Dr. Thomas Cheek of Talbot County shows in its twenty-odd titles a physician's library with the usual religious works for a layman and Hartlib's *Compleat Husbandry*. John Jones' lawyer's (Inventories and Accounts, 5, f. 113) is even briefer, mostly the parcel-of-books type with some law and history; Philip Calvert's in 1682 (Testamentary Papers, Box 90, f. 12) is a two-part inventory showing Hartlib, Rushworth and many legal works, Quintilian, medical manuals, and a few classics. Captain Thomas Coursey of Kent County in 1701 (Inventories and Accounts, 21, f. 285), a lawyer, had a curious mélange of naval law, sermons, legal writing, and Aesop; his brother Henry Coursey in 1707 (Inventories and Accounts, 27, ff. 94–95) owned a good deal of history and law, Martial, an herbal, some medical books, and the usual layman's re-

ligious works. Both the Coursey libraries had probably originated in the books of their father, Henry, Sr., chief judge of probate of the colony. Nathaniell Taylor's collection, discussed in the text below, is in Inventories and Accounts, 32C, ff. 159–166, a long list.

42. *Archives of Md.*, XX, 212. A month and a half earlier the Council recorded the receipt of several volumes for training militia (*ibid.*, 211–212, etc.).

43. The literature on Dr. Bray and his work, especially his libraries, is voluminous. Besides Bray's own publications on libraries mentioned in the bibliography above, see Steiner, ed., *The Rev. Thomas Bray*; Wheeler, "Thomas Bray and the Maryland Parochial Libraries," pp. 246–265, and "Booksellers and Circulating Libraries in Colonial Maryland," pp. 111–137; and Thompson, "Maryland at the End of the Seventeenth Century," pp. 163–171. For references to studies of Bray in his relation to the S.P.G. and S.P.C.K. see the bibliographies and notes for Chs. V and VI below. A recent sketchy survey containing in its appendices valuable library lists and analyses, is Charles T. Laugher, *Thomas Bray's Grand Design: Libraries of the Church of England in America, 1695–1785* (Chicago, 1973).

44. See note 43. The list for the one parish shown covers pp. 260–265.

45. Curiously this longer-than-average list does not appear in the 1702 (?) table of Maryland libraries drawn up by Bray.

46. See Steiner, ed., *The Rev. Thomas Bray*, pp. 153–156; Wheeler, "The Laymen's Libraries and the Provincial Library," pp. 60–73.

47. The collections as received differed in some details from Bray's inventories, as for example in the laymen's collection sent to St. James' Parish. See Wheeler, "The Laymen's Libraries and the Provincial Library," pp. 67–68.

48. See *ibid.*, pp. 68–73; *America's First Public Library*, p. 17. The authorities of St. John's have graciously allowed the author to have a microfilm copy of the cards from the Annapolitan Library, now housed in the Maryland Hall of Records. The only known copy of the 1847 St. John's catalog shows many or most of the same titles. The Annapolitan was Bray's only genuinely general or provincial library of any great size. The libraries of the other cities to the north and south were parochial. The library at Charleston, for example, was made public probably as early as 1700, three years after the Annapolitan was in public use, but it never rivaled the Maryland one in size. For the seventeenth century only the collections at Harvard and William and Mary rival it, and they were not really public.

49. That is, none of these survives among the four-hundred-plus extant volumes.

50. Hanway's book is used in at least one southern eighteenth-century writer's work. See Richard B. Davis, ed., *The Colonial Virginia Satirist* (Philadelphia, 1967), pp. 27, 39n. The first edition of four volumes seems to have been in 1753.

51. Weeks, "Libraries and Lit. in N.C.," p. 177. One early settler brought a 1599 Geneva Bible.

52. Jean Freeman, "Early Libraries in North Carolina," *North Carolina*

Libraries, n.v. (June 1958), 125–127; Blackwell Robinson, "Libraries Attest to Culture of Colonial North Carolina," [Raleigh] *News and Observer*, Friday, April 17, 1964, p. 17.

53. Brett's list in the Lenox Collection, Ms. Div., NYPL, is "A Catalogue of Books . . . Towards founding a Parochial Library at St. Thomas Parish in Pamlico North Carolina," p. 125, from a letter to the Bishop of London of October 21, 1703. Bath may have had the greatest concentration of population at the time in the province.

54. A.S. Salley, ed., *Narratives of Early Carolina, 1650–1708* (New York, 1911), pp. 184–185. Newe probably referred to John Ray's *Methodus Plantarum Nova* (London, 1682, octavo), a work later to be found in a number of southern collections in the eighteenth century, and much in demand by plant collectors amateur and professional.

55. Spain, "Libraries of S.C.," pp. 33–34. Another book was "Cambridge Concordance" (the half-title for *A Concordance of the Holy Scriptures together with the Books of the Apocrypha* [1698]), published under varying titles from at least 1630 into the eighteenth century. It was used by Anglicans and dissenters alike.

56. S.C. Dept. Archives and History, Will Book I, 1692–1703, pp. 111, 128, 154, 208, 214, 281 (Adams, p. 287); Moore and Simmons, *Abstracts of Wills of S.C.*, I, pp. 14 ff.

57. There are several accounts of the library: e.g., Spain, "Libraries of S.C.," pp. 24–32; Pennington, "The Beginnings of the Library in Charles Town," pp. 159–187. Pennington documents both dates and titles from S.P.G. and South Carolina legislative records. The list of books sent to Charleston is in *Bibliotheca Provinciales Americanae*, II, 58–78 (film in LC). As noted above, Bray's expenditure for the Charleston library was little more than one-third of what he spent on Annapolis but even then far more than he spent on any other colonial library in the whole world (including Africa and India).

58. Spain, "Libraries of S.C.," pp. 30–32; Houlette, "Parish Libraries," pp. 605–607.

59. *Gazette of the Grolier Club*, n.s., no. 16 (June 1971), pp. 3–71.

60. Wheeler, "Reading and Other Recreations of Marylanders," pp. 51–54, 168–170,

61. Edgar, "Libraries of Col. S.C.," p. 21.

62. *America's First Public Library*, p. 11; Jennings, *Lib. of William and Mary*, passim.

63. Wheeler, "Booksellers and Circulating Libraries in Colonial Maryland," pp. 113–114, and *Md. Gaz.*, September 2, 1762.

64. Edgar, "Libraries of Col. S.C.," pp. 59, 81; *South Carolina and American General Gazette*, January 20, July 20, 1767.

65. Cohen, *S.C. Gaz.*, 1732–1775, pp. 138–139, 145, 149. These are advertisements, though the last is a list of miscellaneous volumes Carne had lent (by December 17, 1763) "to persons whose names I have forgot." If he did have a lending library, it was conducted on a very unbusinesslike basis. The *S.C. Gaz.* on April 27, 1765, indicates that at that time George Wood had

books "lent out to read." For libraries in some way connected with schools see the preceding chapter. For example, the Winyaw Indigo Society of Georgetown, S.C. (1740) founded a library as well as a school.

66. Edgar, "Libraries of Col. S.C.," pp. 83–85, and State Archives.

67. This library has been written about many times, as the bibliography for this chapter under South Carolina indicates. See esp. the articles by Rugheimer, Gregorie, Spain, and Edgar, and the 1750 and 1770–1772 catalogues. The London 1750 *Catalogue* (published by W. Strahan) shows approximately 323 titles, several different from those shown in 1770.

68. *A Short Description of the Province of South Carolina* . . . (London, 1770), p. 37. The author then proceeds to give the "Intentions of the Society as printed about two years ago" as a preamble to the rules imposed.

69. "Libraries of Col. S.C.," pp. 90–91. See also the London 1750 *Catalogue*, which Edgar apparently had not seen. Miss Virginia Rugheimer, Director of the Charleston Library Society, was not aware of its existence until I brought it to her attention. Copies are at Duke, Michigan, and the Library of Congress.

70. My count is slightly different from Edgar's (p. 88), probably because of what each of us considered as separate titles. Edgar points out, rightly, I think, that Ramsay's estimate of six thousand volumes when the library was burned during the Revolution is too high. Ramsay may have included Mackenzie's books, which still would not bring the figure even near to that he gives. The 1750 catalogue was of course a much briefer list.

71. Quincy is quoted many times in Carl Bridenbaugh, *Myths and Realities: Societies of the Colonial South* (New York, 1963). See especially pp. 173 and above.

72. The list is given in Saunders, ed., *Col. Rec. N.C.*, II, 465–467, but in more accurate form in Joseph B. Cheshire, Jr., *Sketches of Church History in North Carolina* (Wilmington, N.C., 1892), pp. 157–159, and Purcell, "Literary Culture in N.C.," pp. 465–467; also given in Weeks, "Libraries and Lit. in N.C.," pp. 189–191. Some North Carolina historians believe the library was never accepted officially by anyone and was included in the four hundred volumes Moseley left when he died. As already noted, several have believed this was the remnant of the Bath-Brett provincial-parochial library of which Moseley was a trustee in 1715. Weeks (p. 192) gives some good arguments against this latter view, showing other sources from which it may have been secured. One argument Weeks might have used but did not is that the titles in the Brett and Moseley inventories differ quite considerably.

73. Dean Harold E. Davis of Georgia State University pointed out to me that this list had been published in an appendix to a German doctoral dissertation, Hermann Winde, "Die Frühgeschichte der Lutherischen Kirche in Georgia" (Ph.D. diss., Martin Luther Institute of Halle-Wittenberg, 1960), pp. 216–225. Dr. Davis' own dissertation, "Social History of Georgia," is also well worth examining. In amended form it has been recently published as *The Fledgling Province: Social and Cultural Life in Colonial Georgia, 1733–1776* (Chapel Hill, 1976).

74. See H.E. Davis, "Social History of Georgia," pp. 318–319.

75. Fleming, "199 Years of Augusta's Library," pp. 124–128 [also separate pamphlet]. *DeBrahm's Report*, ed. De Vorsey, pp. 143–144; Candler, *Col. Rec. Georgia*, XXXI, 325; XXXIII, *412–413*.

76. Fleming, "199 Years of Augusta's Library," pp. 127 ff., traces the history of the arrival of books in Georgia, including some titles from 1732. He shows that in 1757 the Reverend Bartholomew Zouberbuhler in Savannah was holding the library (which required a catalog of fifty-six pages), a gift to the province, as a public library.

77. Robert V. Williams, "George Whitefield's Bethesda," pp. 62–66. For a catalog of the library, see Inventory Book F, pp. 509–529, Archives of Georgia, and Davis, "Social History of Georgia," pp. 322–324. Dean Davis informs me that this is another inventory badly needed in print.

78. Williams, "George Whitefield's Bethesda," pp. 65–66.

79. *Ibid.*, pp. 61–63.

80. E.g., R.B. Davis, "Jefferson as Collector of Virginiana," pp. 117–144. See also Davis chapter on slightly later "Reading and Libraries" in *Intellectual Life in Jefferson's Virginia, 1790–1830* (Chapel Hill, 1964), pp. 71–118.

81. The pertinent parts of this investigation, originally a doctoral dissertation, were published in *MdHM* during 1939–1943. Some of the sections, as separate essays, have already been cited in the bibliography for this chapter. See note 37 above. Wheeler publishes some inventories and refers to or summarizes others, though he did not cover all eighteenth-century lists and only incidentally a few from the seventeenth. As the archivists of the Maryland Hall of Records point out, however, most of their library inventories have not yet been printed anywhere. Many aspects of the library-reader relation will have to be re-evaluated when this is done. Wheeler does not indicate how or why he used some libraries and ignored others, such as Nathaniell Taylor's (see note 41 and text above), though he may possibly have considered this particular one too early. It is of course eighteenth-century.

82. "Private Libraries in Colonial Virginia," pp. 24–52.

83. For Quaker items in the inventory of William Mauduit (c. 1750) of Prince Georges County, planter and proprietor of a general store, see *MdHM*, XXXV (1940), 344. Mauduit's books are by no means all Quaker tracts.

84. *Ibid.*, p. 344. Dalton's is *The Country Justice . . .* , and Nelson's *The Office and Authority of a Justice of the Peace*.

85. *Ibid.*, p. 349.

86. Wheeler, "Reading Interests of the . . . Clergy," pp. 184–188. In many instances, as in the case of the life of Marlborough and the histories of the kings, several anonymous works have similar titles. John Campbell's was probably the most popular study of Prince Eugene and the Duke of Marlborough, but there were several others, and Campbell's is usually mentioned without the author.

87. *Ibid.*, pp. 189–192. Bacon died in 1768. Of course most of the library was collected much earlier. For more on this important man see the general index.

88. Bacon had both a bound and an unbound copy of his own compilation of laws.

89. Also in Wheeler, "Reading Interests of the . . . Clergy," p. 195.

90. Letter to the writer of November 14, 1972, with summary of his findings.

91. Wheeler, "Reading Interests of . . . Lawyers," pp. 281, 296. Five of Bordley's letterbooks are in the Md. Hist. Soc. Wheeler quotes other passages from the Bordley letters mentioning Bolingbroke, Rollin, Sale's Koran, etc.

92. See *Gentleman's Progress: The Itinerarium of Dr. Alexander Hamilton, 1744*, ed. Carl Bridenbaugh (Chapel Hill, 1948), passim; J.A. Leo Lemay's "Hamilton's Literary History of the *Maryland Gazette*," *WMQ* (3), XXIII (1966), 273, and his *Men of Letters in Colonial Maryland* (Knoxville, 1972), passim.

93. Wheeler, "Reading Interests of . . . Doctors," pp. 299 ff.

94. Callister himself writes of sitting at the bedside of the (perhaps deistical) dying Morris, and reading at Morris' request Plato's *Phædo*, from which the dying man seemed to take philosophic comfort. See HC to the younger Robert Morris many years later, December 17, 1764, Md. Diocesan Lib. (housed now in Md. Hist. Soc.), and Wheeler, "Reading Interests of Maryland Planters and Merchants, 1700–1776," pp. 28–29.

95. Wheeler, "Reading Interests of . . . Planters and Merchants," pp. 30–33; Oswald Tilghman, *History of Talbot County, Maryland, 1661–1861* (2 vols., Baltimore, 1915, 1967), I, 89, etc. Tilghman infers from Callister's letter that he was a loyal Whig and quite liberal (deistic) in religion. The *Md. Gaz.* advertisement for return of books is in the issue of February 10, 1757. Similar notices from other owners appear in all the southern gazettes: e.g., *Md. Gaz.*, Oct. 21, 1747, the list of Thomas Go[u]gh which was mostly satire (*Shamela, Tale of a Tub, Gulliver, Devil upon Two Sticks*, and an "Ovid Travestie").

96. Printed in Wheeler, "Reading Interests of . . . Planters and Merchants," pp. 39–41, presumably from the Callister Papers in the Md. Dioc. Lib. See note above as to a copy of the Bay Psalm Book.

97. Wheeler, "Reading Interests of . . . Planters and Merchants," pp. 291–295. Generous extracts from the letterbooks appear in *MdHM*, XVIII–XXVII (1923–1932), passim.

98. Wheeler, "Reading Interests of . . . Planters and Merchants," pp. 296–301, with dates of letters and orders.

99. *Ibid.*, pp. 301–308. Letterbooks and other materials are in the Md. Hist. Soc. and elsewhere. Some portions have been published in the *MdHM*.

100. Wheeler, "Reading and Other Recreations of Marylanders," pp. 51–54.

101. *Ibid.*, pp. 168–170. The list appears in Talbot County Inventories 139–141, Riber I B3 folio 351–356. In "The Library of Edward Lloyd IV of Wye House," pp. 87–121, Edwin Wolf, 2nd, points out that this late (1796) eighteenth-century Maryland library is larger than any of those earlier considered by Wheeler, for it numbered what must have been more than 2,500 volumes, and though it contained the standard histories, travels, etc., it had a

greater proportion of fiction than any analyzed by Wheeler. Also, and more significant, the dates of publication of most of the volumes and the knowledge that for several generations the Lloyds had collected books point to the probability that before the end of the colonial period the library was already at least as large as the best of other Maryland collections. Wolf's article contains an annotated bibliographical catalog of the library as it was quite recently. See also McHenry Howard, "Wye House, Talbot County, Maryland," *MdHM*, XVIII (1923), 293–297.

102. Wheeler, "Reading and Other Recreations of Marylanders," pp. 176–180. Both men assembled large libraries again later in England and were noted as scholars and antiquarians.

103. *WMQ* (1), III (1894/5), 251.

104. *William Fitzhugh*, ed. Davis, pp. 49–50, passim. See the discussion below of the library of Fitzhugh's friend Ralph Wormeley II.

105. For Waugh, Stanard, *Col. Va.*, p. 305; for Custis and Shropshire, "Accomack County Wills and Inventories," and *VMHB*, X (1902/3), 400–401; for Hay, *VMHB*, X (1902/3), 395; for Lee, Stanard, *Col. Va.*, p. 299; for Mackie, *VMHB*, VII (1899/1900), 358–363; for Cox, *VMHB*, X (1902/3), 398. Thompson's "Glaneck" is probably a muddled capsuling of Glanvill and Horneck (Glanvill's editor), the latter in 1681 bringing out an edition of the works of the famous writer on witchcraft (see *VMHB*, X [1902/3], 399).

106. Many of these and scores of others are listed in *VMHB*, X (1902/3), 389–405. Others came from Virginia-published sources given in the bibliography for this chapter above. For Buckner, see Stanard, *Col. Va.*, p. 300.

107. Drayton, Reade, and Yates are to be found in *VMHB*, X (1902/3), 389–405. The Robertson inventory is in the Va. Hist. Soc., MSS 5:3/R 5456:1, "Catalogue of my Books."

108. John Gwilym Jones, *Goronwy Owen's Virginia Adventure: His Life, Poetry, and Literary Opinions, with a Translation of His Virginian Letters*, Botetourt Publication no. 2, Botetourt Bibliographical Society, College of William and Mary (Williamsburg, 1969). The Appendix (pp. 32–35) contains the inventory of his books.

109. Smart and Patterson have been cited in both bibliography and text of this chapter. W.D. Houlette, "Plantation and Parish Libraries in the Old South," pp. 68ff., is also listed in the bibliography.

110. See the studies by Smart, Patterson, Houlette, and Edgar in the bibliography of this chapter. Edgar gives the statistical tables with titles under these divisions in his Appendices II, III, V, VI, with little attention paid to the "unknown" category.

111. Since this rough count was made, several other fairly large or large libraries have come to the author's attention. Williamsburg physician-apothecaries not otherwise mentioned include Dr. Kenneth McKenzie, who died before 1759 and had about one hundred volumes, primarily medical; and in the 1780s Dr. Robert Brown of Richmond had 574 volumes along with medical apparatus. See Harold B. Gill, Jr., *The Apothecary in Colonial Virginia* (Williamsburg, 1972), pp. 77–81. Actually Wythe's collection, be-

queathed to Jefferson and at least in part incorporated into the latter's great library, is not here counted among major eighteenth-century gatherings. R.A. Brock (as editor, *The Official Letters of Alexander Spotswood* [2 vols., Richmond, 1882, 1885], pp. x–xi) names the owners of some twenty-five large libraries for some of which we have no detailed list or evidence. Among those named by Brock are Byrd, Mercer, Sir John Randolph, George Mason, John Herbert, Pendleton, Col. Theodorick Bland, John Mayo, William Stith, Benjamin Waller, Robert Bolling, Jr., Robert Bolling (also called Jr.) of Chellowe, Ralph Wormeley, and John Page. Several of these, such as Page, lived long past 1763. I have found evidence of others he does not name. One may be fairly sure that Brock was estimating without full evidence for several of these, as I have done, but he is probably right for every name he mentions.

112. Whether sterling or currency (in South Carolina the former was worth almost seven times the latter), the sum places the value alongside that of the large South Carolina libraries containing more than two hundred volumes. See Edgar, "Libraries of Col. S.C.," pp. 218–226.

113. See Sowerby, *Catalogue of the Library of Thomas Jefferson*, V, 395.

114. For Fitzhugh's inventory, see *Register of Overwharton Parish, Stafford County, Virginia, 1723–1758*, ed. George H.S. King (Fredericksburg, Va., 1961), p. 225.

115. Stanard, *Vol. Va.*, p. 302. A Fitzhugh genealogical chart in the author's possession so identifies this Henry. He married Lucy Carter, daughter of Robert "King" Carter.

116. See Spotswood will in Spotswood Papers, Duke Univ. Lib. Manuscripts, and *The Official Letters of Alexander Spotswood*, ed. Brock, I, xv–xvi; also Jennings, *Lib. of William and Mary*, pp. 48, 88.

117. For Mitchell, see Ch. VII below; Edmund and Dorothy Berkeley, *Dr. John Mitchell, the Man Who Made the Map of North America* (Chapel Hill, 1974), pp. 21, 82–83, 259; and the sketches in *DAB* and *DNB*. The *Va. Gaz.* notice says "A Curious Collection of Books, in most sciences, particularly Physic, Surgery, and Botany; in *Greek, Latin, French and English*." Gordon W. Jones ("The Library of Doctor John Mitchell of Urbanna," *VMHB*, LXXVI [1968], 441–443) picks out twenty-nine of the titles Mitchell must have owned in Virginia by studying his references in the three scientific papers he published while living in the colony. Bacon, Boerhaave, Dillenius, Hippocrates, Linnaeus, Newton, John Ray (*Historiae Plantarum* and *Wisdom of God*), and Locke are among them.

118. Stanard, *Col. Va.*, pp. 305–306; *Va. Gaz.* (Purdie and Dixon), June 8, 1769. E.L. Goodwin, *The Colonial Church in Virginia* (Milwaukee, 1927), p. 267, shows the Reverend William Dunlop as minister of Stratton-Major Parish, King and Queen County, 1768–1779. The announcement that his books ran into "Several thousand" is made in an advertisement that he would take a few boys to tutor as he taught his own children. For the first William Dunlop's library, see below.

119. Sowerby, *Catalogue of the Library of Thomas Jefferson*, V, 201, 254.

120. Professor Henson kindly supplied the author with Xerox copies of

card titles of all the books he had been able to trace. He believes a great many of Bland's books went to the College of William and Mary after the death of George Wythe, despite the fact that Jefferson was supposed to inherit Wythe's library. Suggestions of this possession by the college appear in various letters of the period. The Bland books had all been borrowed by Wythe, Henson believes. Also he thinks there were many more Bland books bought by Jefferson which have not as yet been identified.

121. Griffin, ed., *Catalogue of the Washington Col.,* passim. Two of Stith's sermons (1745/6 and 1753), the 1756 *Treaty* with the Catawba and Cherokee Indians (1756), and the 1744 Lancaster, Pennsylvania, *Treaty* with the Six Nations (1744) are among the valuable Williamsburg imprints Washington possessed. He also had a copy inscribed to him by Jonathan Boucher, the author of the 1792 *A View of the Causes and Consequences of the American Revolution,* the schoolmaster of Washington's stepson, Jacky Custis.

122. Sowerby, *Catalogue of the Library of Thomas Jefferson,* passim; Davis, "Jefferson as Collector of Virginiana," passim, and *Intellectual Life in Jefferson's Virginia, 1790–1830* (Chapel Hill, 1964), pp. 90–94.

123. For a sketch of Waller, see James A. Servies and Carl Dolmetsch, eds., *The Poems of Charles Hansford* (Chapel Hill, 1961), pp. xvii–xix. See also the Waller verse and letter manuscripts in the archives of Colonial Williamsburg, Inc.

124. See J.A. Leo Lemay's "Robert Bolling and the Bailment of Colonel Chiswell," *EAL,* VI (1971), 103, 121, and his *Calendar of American Poetry,* passim and Index.

125. Perhaps the best evidence lies in the literary and other allusions in the two manuscript miscellanies (primarily poetry) which Professor Lemay is now editing. But one miscellany of Bolling's from the Huntington Lib. (Brock MS. 73) contains two pages of books to be ordered (pp. 157–158) and those listed under subject as being in his library (pp. 159–165).

126. See Chs. V and VI below for much more about Davies and his writings. *A Catalogue of Books in the Library of the College of New Jersey January 29, 1760* (Woodbridge, N.J., 1760, reprinted Princeton Univ. Lib., 1949), contains "The Design of the Publication" on pp. iii–iv.

127. Houlette, "Plantation and Parish Libraries in the Old South," pp. 88–89, and *WMQ* (2), X (1910), 74.

128. See *HLQ,* II (1938/9), 1–35, for essay on Lee and the inventory, with the short titles expanded whenever possible. Also see Wright, *First Gent. Va.,* pp. 212–234.

129. For his library and petition of 1715 to Governor Spotswood to practice law, see *VMHB,* XVII (1909), 147–150. He translated Arthur Blackamore's poem on Spotswood's transmontane expedition. The fragment of Pole's version published in the *Southern Literary Messenger* (II, 258) differs markedly from the George Seagood translation printed in the *Md. Gaz.* in 1729. The *SLM* fragment is accompanied by an editorial comment that among his papers is a briefer love poem addressed to Chloe (there is still in the Va. Hist. Soc. a manuscript poem with such a dedication).

130. This is a suggestion the Ewans make in *John Banister and His Natural History of Virginia*, pp. 118–119. The inventory is in *WMQ* (1), II (1893), 250–252.

131. For the two Colston inventories, *WMQ* (1), III (1894/5), 132; for McCarty's, *WMQ* (1), VIII (1899), 19–22. See also Wright, *First Gent. Va.*, pp. 144–146.

132. Also in 1732 John Cargill of Surry County, who left 275 bound books and newspapers and pamphlets, some lent out. See Stanard, *Col. Va.*, p. 305.

133. See John McGill, comp., *The Beverley Family of Virginia* (Columbia, 1956), p. 747. Here are listed some of his major estates in Spotsylvania, Orange, and Essex counties. His library is said to have come in part from his father. "Harnaby's Rhetorick" is almost surely a mistake for "Farnaby's."

134. Latané, *Parson Latané*, pp. 73–76.

135. See Robbins, *The Eighteenth-Century Commonwealthman*, pp. 128–132, for a good summary of what Shaftesbury was doing in the *Characteristicks*. Patterson, "Private Libraries in Va.," p. 77, finds *Télémaque* the most popular novel in the libraries he examined; that is, most frequently present.

136. See for inventory and tombstone epitaph, *WMQ* (1), XV (1906/7), 275–279.

137. *WMQ* (1), III (1894), 132; also Patterson, "Private Libraries in Va.," appendix, p. 2.

138. Molnar, "A Collection of Music in Colonial Virginia: The Ogle Inventory," pp. 150–162; Maurer, "The Library of a Colonial Musician," pp. 39–52; inventory in *WMQ* (1), III (1894/5), 252–253, and York County Records, September 15, 1735. Actually, Ogle's items may barely reach the minimum of one hundred "volumes" considered in this section of the present chapter.

139. For Waller, *WMQ* (1), VIII (1899), 77–79. Smart's and Keyes' studies of southern libraries employ Waller's as a good example of the Virginia library. See also the catalog of his books from Virginia which Joseph Ball ordered to be sent to him in England in 1755.

140. *VMHB*, XVII (1909), 404–412.

141. *Ibid.*, XVIII (1910), 181–186. In the same year the Reverend William Key of Lunenberg left 168 volumes (Stanard, *Col. Va.*, p. 305).

142. Stanard, *Col. Va.*, pp. 305, 306.

143. Inventory in *Tyler's Q.*, IX (1928), 97–104.

144. *VMHB*, XIV (1907), 323; IV (1896/7), 289, and Prince George County Records, vol. 3, p. 287.

145. For the diary, see *The Diary of Colonel Landon Carter of Sabine Hall, 1752–1778*, ed. Jack P. Greene (2 vols., Charlottesville, 1965), passim.

146. For the title pages, see Colonial Williamsburg Microfilm M-188. There is also at Colonial Williamsburg a typed copy of the titles, with indices for authors and titles. The title pages themselves with Carter's inscriptions or holograph signatures and comments are fascinating. A few of the volumes are late and belonged to another member of the family.

147. Accomack County [Deeds], Wills, etc. 1692–1715, XI, Pts. 2 & 3, Reel 7, pp. 331–335, "Inventory of Estate . . . recorded Jany 1708," copy in Va. St.

Lib. For Makemie, see *DAB* and William B. Sprague, ed., *Annals of the American Pulpit* (9 vols., New York, 1859–1869), III, 1–4.

148. See Susie M. Ames, "Law-in-Action: the Court Records of Virginia's Eastern Shore," *WMQ* (3), IV (1947), 182. Also Accomack County [Deeds], Wills, etc., 1692–1715, XI, Pt. 1, 250–258; Pt. 3, 301–304, 334.

149. *WMQ* (1), III (1894/5), 251. For mention of dozens of other medical libraries owned by Virginians in the eighteenth century, see Blanton, *Med. in Va. in the Eighteenth Century*, pp. 93–114. Blanton gives the medical titles in several libraries, including those of William Fleming, Kenneth Mackenzie, David Black (noted above), John Bowser, Alexander Reade, and laymen William Byrd II, John Parke Custis, and Daniel Parke Custis. He also gives the number of medical books in the libraries of Wormeley, Lee, Berkeley, Hub(b)ard, Herbert, Cocke, Dunlop, and John Waller. See also Ch. VII below.

150. See Davis, *Intellectual Life in Jefferson's Virginia*, pp. 96–97.

151. Wright, *First Gent. Va.*, pp. 187–211. Wright says he comes nearest to the picture or image of the fabled cavalier.

152. Inventory, *WMQ* (1), II (1893), 169–174. Bruce, *Inst. Hist. Va.*, I, 426, analyzes the library, and Standard, *Col. Va.*, pp. 500 ff., comments on its contents.

153. For two or three studies of Byrd's library, see the bibliography for this chapter. The manuscript list of abbreviated titles is printed in *The Writings of Colonel William Byrd of Westover in Virginia Esqr.*, ed. J.S. Bassett (New York, 1901), pp. 413–443, in which one full page and two parts of lines of the manuscript are omitted. Bassett printed his list from a copy of a copy. The Library Company of Philadelphia holds this manuscript catalog. Essays of significance on the library are Carl R. Cannon, "William Byrd II, of Westover," *Colophon*, n.s. III (Spring 1938), 291–302; Charles Campbell, "The Westover Library," *Va. Hist. Reg.*, IV (April 1851), 87–90; Houlette, "The Byrd Library"; G.R. Lyle, "William Byrd, Book Collector," *Am. Bk. Collector*, V (1934), 163–165, 208–224; St. George L. Sioussat, "The *Philosophical Transactions* of the Royal Society in the Libraries of William Byrd of Westover, Benjamin Franklin, and the American Philosophical Society," *PAPS*, XL (1949), 101–111; Wolf, "Dispersal of the Library of William Byrd"; and Louis B. Wright, "The Byrds' Progress from Trade to Genteel Elegance," in *First Gent. Va.*, pp. 333–338. There is more on the reading and library in Pierre Marambaud, *William Byrd of Westover, 1674–1744* (Charlottesville, 1971), passim. See also Edwin Wolf, 2d, "Great American Book Collectors to 1800," *Gazette of the Grolier Club*, no. 16 (June 1971), pp. 3–69. Edwin Wolf, 2d, *The Library of James Logan of Philadelphia, 1674–1751* (Philadelphia, 1974), has recently edited the catalog of the Logan library with magnificent annotation. Wolf counts or shows 2,185 titles in 2,651 volumes, smaller than the Byrd collection.

154. Wolf, "Dispersal of the Library of William Byrd," pp. 21–22.

155. *Ibid.*, pp. 43 ff., and the Ewans, *John Banister*, pp. 130–137.

156. *First Gent. Va.*, p. 336.

157. See Richard B. Davis, "William Byrd: Taste and Tolerance," in *Major Writers of Early American Literature*, ed. Everett Emerson (Madison, Wis., 1972), pp. 151–177.

158. For Mercer, see C. Malcolm Watkins, *Cultural History of Marlborough*; and Richard B. Davis, ed., *The Colonial Virginia Satirist* (Philadelphia, 1967). Watkins' book, published by the Smithsonian Institution, includes among its appendices several of the John Mercer manuscript accounts and library lists now in the Bucks County Historical Society in Doylestown, Pennsylvania. There is also a sketch of Mercer in *VMHB*, XIV (1907), 232–235. The Va. Hist. Soc. has copies of a John Mercer Account Book (MSS 5:3/M 5 345:1 and MSS 1c 4485 a from the Bucks Co. Hist. Soc.). Alfred P. Jones, *The Ohio Company: Its Inner History* (Pittsburgh, 1958), and Lois Mulkearn, ed., *George Mercer Papers Relating to the Ohio Company of Virginia* (Pittsburgh, 1954), also include much John Mercer material. Then the "*Virginia Gazette* 1750–1752," already mentioned, shows a great many Mercer purchases.

159. The *Va. Gaz.* advertisement states that twelve hundred volumes are at home and four hundred on loan. Inventory lists (Bucks Co. Hist. Soc. Collections printed in Watkins, *Cultural History of Marlborough, Va.*) between 1768 and 1771 give the buyers' names beside each group of books, most of the purchasers being from Mercer's own family or his neighbors. On August 29, 1771, there appeared in the *Va. Gaz.* a list of books left after three or four years of sale. It still contained 67 folios, 14 quartos, 261 octavos or duodecimos, and many copies of Mercer's own *Abridgement*, as well as broken sets spoiled because volumes had been borrowed. Thus more than 350 volumes remained after extensive purchasing.

160. *Journal and Letters of Philip Vickers Fithian*, ed. Farish, p. 157. The inventory is included in an appendix to this volume, pp. 285–294. Patterson, "Private Libraries in Va.," pp. 56–57 and Appendix, gives a brief general analysis of the collection. The diary is our best account of life on a Northern Neck plantation. For Carter's career as a fairly typical planter, see Louis Morton, *Robert Carter of Nomini Hall, A Virginia Tobacco Planter of the Eighteenth Century* (Williamsburg, 1941).

161. *Journal and Letters of Philip Vickers Fithian*, ed. Farish, p. 35. The letter in which this comment is made is addressed to a Presbyterian clergyman.

162. Weeks, "Libraries and Lit. in N.C.," p. 173.

163. *Ibid.*, pp. 184–186. Weeks personally went through scores of inventories of the 1750–1772 period and gleaned what he could from them. Grimes, *N.C. Wills and Inventories*, was to come later.

164. Jones Family Papers, LC, April 9, 1722.

165. *Ibid.*, p. 206.

166. Grimes, *N.C. Wills and Inventories*, pp. 477, 559.

167. Weeks, "Libraries and Lit. in N.C.," p. 206.

168. S.P.G. Correspondence, "B" 5, "North and South Carolina," June 15, 1762. Also in Saunders, ed., *Col. Rec. N.C.*, VI, 728. The present writer has

examined all the original southern colonial correspondence in the S.P.G. Lib. in London.

169. Grimes, *N.C. Wills and Inventories*, p. 488 etc.; Weeks, "Libraries and Lit. in N.C.," 206–210; Houlette, "Plantation and Parish Libraries in the Old South," II, 69, lists Martin's titles, most of them belles lettres with some history.

170. For his titles, see J.G. de Roulhac Hamilton, "Governor Thomas Burke," pp. 121–122. The volume of verse by Burke recently edited by Richard Walser, *The Poems of Governor Thomas Burke* (Raleigh, 1961) shows that Burke was well acquainted with the political history of his time, the belletristic forms and fashions, and the classics.

171. Letter of George Stevenson to the writer, June 29, 1972, containing references to the *Register* of Christ's Hospital; and in the *SCHM*, XII (1911), 72–212, and A.S. Salley, ed., *Journals of the Commons House of Assembly, 1682–1735* (21 vols., Columbia, 1907–1946), 1702, passim; 1703, p. 90. The Christ's Hospital records show Moseley as born in St. Giles' Cripplegate, London, in 1682, son of merchant tailor John Moseley. Byrd's histories of the Dividing Line give a prejudiced characterization of Moseley when he and Byrd were fellow-commissioners in surveying the boundary. At first Byrd respected him a great deal more than the other Carolinians but eventually found him too "plausible," perhaps because Moseley was as interested as Byrd in securing lands along the boundary. Both died owning thousands of acres of this border land, most of it in North Carolina. For Moseley see also E.G. McPherson, "Edward Moseley; A Study in North Carolina Politics" (M.A. thesis, Univ. of North Carolina, 1925), pp. 6–14.

172. *MdHM*, XXI (1926), 248–249.

173. Grimes, *N.C. Wills and Inventories*, pp. 317–318. This will is dated in 1745.

174. The manuscript inventory is in the North Carolina Dept. of Archives and History, Secretary of State's Office, Inventories and Estates 1748–1754 (S.S. 887, pp. 52–58). There is a good sketch of Allen in Samuel A. Ashe, *Biographical History of North Carolina* (Greensboro, N.C., 1906), V, 1–7.

175. Weeks, "Libraries and Lit. in N.C.," pp. 198–205; Saunders, ed., *Col. Rec. N.C.*, XXIII, 289.

176. Grimes, *N.C. Wills and Inventories*, pp. 560–564.

177. See Desmonde Clarke, *Arthur Dobbs, Esquire, 1689–1765* (Chapel Hill, 1957), pp. 199, 207, etc. Dobbs' personal papers, including manuscript writings and inventories of books, are now in the Public Records Office in Belfast, Northern Ireland. I am indebted to Mr. W.H. Crawford, Deputy Keeper of that office, for a Xerox copy of the inventories which is somewhat more legible than the microfilm reels at the University of North Carolina.

178. A microfilm of this manuscript is in the Sou. Hist. Col. of the Univ. of North Carolina at Chapel Hill.

179. The library was destroyed by fire at Fort George, New York, in 1773. See Jeremy North, *The Library of William Tryon, Royal Governor of North Carolina* (New Bern?, n.d.). I am indebted to Mr. Donald R. Taylor, Curator

of Education at Tryon Palace, for a mimeographed copy of the book list.

180. For the inventory, see Grimes, *N.C. Wills and Inventories*, pp. 490–494. For his corrspondence with Laurence Sterne, *The Letters, Sermons, and Miscellaneous Writings of Laurence Sterne*, ed. George Saintsbury (2 vols., London, 1894), II, 53–55. See also Weeks, "Libraries and Lit. in N.C.," p. 211; Malcolm Ross, *The Cape Fear* (New York, 1965), pp. 67, 99; Saunders, ed., *Col. Rec. N.C.*, VII, 279; XVI, 514.

181. James Milner (1709–1772) of Halifax, N.C., is buried in the town in which he lived. He left his landed estate in England to a brother Arthur and all his Greek and Hebrew books to the Reverend William Willie and the remainder of his books to other heirs. A volume bearing his armorial bookplate with the motto "Societas Scientia Virtus" survives in the Univ. of North Carolina's North Carolina Collection. The Huntington Lib. has at least one other. Apparently Milner's heirs were Loyalists. A few references to him appear in the *Va. Gaz.* and the *Col. Rec. N.C.* For the inventory, see Grimes, *N.C. Wills and Inventories*, pp. 514–522. For more on Milner as man and essayist, see Lemay, "Robert Bolling and the Bailment of Colonel Chiswell," p. 123, note 20.

182. A sketch of Reed appears in Gertrude S. Carroway, *Crown of Life: History of Christ Church, New Bern, N.C., 1715–1940* (New Bern, N.C., 1940), pp. 47–49, 95–97.

183. For a description, see Barbara B. Rehder, "Development of Libraries in the Lower Cape Fear," *Lower Cape Fear Hist. Soc. Bull.*, VII, no. 2 (Feb. 1964), 5 pp. (without numbering). For copies of the library cards of the Lillington-Moseley-Hasell collection the present writer is indebted to John B. Flowers III of the Univ. of North Carolina Lib. Rehder says there are about 150 volumes in the collection, perhaps an earlier count. She traces briefly the history of the library, which began in that of Edward Moseley discussed earlier (one volume only is now at Chapel Hill). An undated clipping from the *North Carolina Library Bulletin*, by Col. Frederick A. Olds, gives the story of the recovery of the library from an old house (copy in Univ. of North Carolina Lib.).

184. Elizabeth Gray Vining, *Flora: A Biography* (Philadelphia, 1966), p. 144; Duane Meyer, *The Highland Scots of North Carolina* Tercentenary Commission Publication (Raleigh, 1963), pp. 60, 68.

185. Edgar, pp. 18–19. The values are in South Carolina currency, about one-sixth or one-seventh that of the pound sterling.

186. See Frank J. Klingberg, ed., *The Carolina Chronicle of Dr. Francis LeJau, 1706–1717* (Berkeley, 1956), passim.

187. E.g., MSS S.P.G. "A," vol. 17, pp. 125–126.

188. South Caroliniana Lib., SC Arch., Rec. Sec. Prov., C (1722–1724), 216–217. Some of the South Carolina reference notes in the following were from typescript copies in the South Caroliniana, or Univ. of South Carolina Lib., others from the S.C. Dept. of Archives and History originals (S.C. Archives). The author is indebted to Professor Walter B. Edgar of the Univ. of South Carolina for assistance in regularizing them. "SC Arch." refers of

course to the South Carolina Archives in the State Dept. of Archives and History, though as noted sometimes to archival copies elsewhere.

189. Except in the most obvious cases, titles are here spelled and worded as in the original inventories. For these, see SC Arch., Misc. Recs. 1727–1729, 26–29.

190. Will made out August 1, 1732, and probated April 7, 1735, SC Arch., WPA Transcript of Charleston County Wills, 3 (1731–1737), 140–141. See Moore and Simmons, *Abstracts of Wills of S.C.*, I, 200.

191. SC Arch. There are hundreds: "Parcels," R(2) (1753–1756), 200, 212, 223, e.g., 271; "Old Books," S (1756–1758), 360; T (1758–1761), 25, 135, 237.

192. Arthur H. Hirsch, *The Huguenots of Colonial South Carolina* (Durham, N.C., 1928), p. 155.

193. SC Arch., Inventories, II (1736–1738), 79–80.

194. E.g., Burtinhead Boutwell of Prince Frederick Parish. See Edgar, "Libraries of Col. S.C.," pp. 155–156, and SC Arch., Inventories (1763–1767), pp. 328–330.

195. G.C. Rogers, Jr., *History of Georgetown County, South Carolina* (Columbia, 1970), describes Serré's as "a fine library," citing SC Arch., Inventories, LL (1744–1746), 223–229.

196. Hirsch, *The Huguenots of South Carolina*, pp. 155 ff. and Edgar, "Libraries of Col. S.C.," p. 219. Edgar lists Tissot or Tessot as a clergyman: SC Arch., Inventories, V (1761–1763), 521–522.

197. Edgar, "Libraries of Col. S.C.," pp. 111–113; SC Arch., Inventories (1740–1743), pp. 187–190. See also Richard Yeadon, *History of the Circular Church* (Charleston, 1853), p. 3; David Ramsay, *History of the Independent or Congregational Church of Charleston, S.C.* (Philadelphia, 1815), p. 14.

198. 1728, 1729, SC Arch., Rec. Sec. Prov., G (1729–1731), 81–85. This inventory is in two parts, with different dates.

199. Bowes, *Culture of Early Charleston*, pp. 57–58.

200. See SC Arch., Inventories, Charleston County (1740–1743), 83–92, for complete list of titles.

201. These are in SC Arch., Inventories, LL (1744–1746), 27–28; SC Arch., Inventories, T (1758–1761), 171–172, and SC Arch., Inventories, Y (1769–1771), 180–182.

202. *Letterbook of Eliza Lucas Pinckney*, ed. Pinckney, passim.

203. *Papers of Henry Laurens*, eds. Hamer, Rogers, et al., I, 369–382, inventory of John Laurens' estate.

204. Rogers, *History of Georgetown County, South Carolina*, p. 101, and SC Arch., Inventories, R (1) (1751–1753), 527–531.

205. SC Arch., Inventories, R (1) (1751–1753), 403–408. See Edgar, "Libraries of Col. S.C." Bowes gives Inventories, Charleston County, LXXIX, 383–385.

206. SC Arch., Inventories, R (2) (1753–1756), 279–284; also see Edgar, "Notable Libraries of S.C.," p. 108, and "Libraries of Col. S.C.," pp. 149–152; Hirsch, *Huguenots*, p. 156. Purry was murdered in 1754.

207. 1756. SC Arch., Inventories, R (2) (1753–1756), 531–532.

208. SC Arch., Inventories, T (1758–1761), 244–246.

209. Edgar W. Knight, *A Documentary History of Education in the South before 1860* (5 vols., Chapel Hill, 1949–1953), I, 354–367.

210. Given in Foster, "Documentary History of Education in S.C.," II, appendix 5.

211. SC Arch., Inventories, K-K (1739–1743), 289–302. See also Edgar, "Notable Libraries of S.C.," p. 108. Edgar says the value was £107.7.6. The greater sum may include other objects, as pictures and portraits.

212. Edgar, "Libraries of Colonial S.C.," p. 134; SC Arch., Inventories, MM (1746–1748), 169–172.

213. Edgar, "Libraries of Colonial S.C.," pp. 136, 137, 180; Edgar, "Notable Libraries of S.C.," p. 106. Also SC Arch., Inventories, R (2) (1755–1756), 369–370.

214. The advertisement of the library is quoted in *SCHM*, VI (1905), 177–178. SC Arch., Inventories R (1) (1751–1753), 72–81, contains the inventory. Edgar, "Libraries of Colonial S.C.," p. 220 gives merely the "library of books" and the 915 pamphlets valued at £800. My own look at the list was in Univ. S.C. Lib. typescript, Inventories, Charleston County (1753–1756).

215. Bowes, *Culture of Early Charleston*, pp. 58–59; SC Arch., Inventories, Charleston County, LXXIX, 86–89, and Univ. S.C. Lib. typescript, Inventories, Charleston County (1751–1753), A-80, Pt. 1. Edgar gives the reference as SC Arch., R (1) (1751–1753), 72–76. For a sketch of Wragg, see Edgar, "Libraries of Colonial S.C.," pp. 102–107 and notes.

216. Edgar, "Notable Libraries of S.C.," pp. 110, 123–125. Edgar says 174 titles, eighty classed as "French Books"; SC Arch., Inventories, R (2) (1753–1756), 101–107.

217. See SC Arch., Inventories, S (1756–1758), 105–110. Later is given the price the books brought at vendue and the names of the purchasers, all prominent in the province. See Edgar, "Notable Libraries of S.C.," p. 108, and S.C. Arch., Film No. J.R. 4377, Inventory (1756–1758).

218. My copy is Univ. S.C. Lib. typescript, Inventories, Charleston County (1758–1761), vol. 8, which lists titles, number of volumes in each, and size of books, with value about £350. But see SC Arch., Inventories, T (1758–1761), 374–379.

219. SC Arch., Inventories, Y (1769–1771), 13–18; Edgar, "Libraries of Col. S.C.," pp. 116–118, and "Notable Libraries of S.C.," p. 107.

220. My copy is from SC Arch., Inventories, W (1763–1767), 278–286, dated August 6, 1765. See also Edgar, "Libraries of Col. S.C.," pp. 106–111, for discussion of this list in relation to the man's active life. My own rough count indicates more titles and volumes than I have given above, where I am relying on Edgar.

221. For Stuart's books see SC Arch., Inventories X (1768–1769), 101–104. For a sketch of Stuart, see John R. Alden, *John Stuart and the Southern Colonial Frontier* (Ann Arbor, 1944), pp. 174–175; and Edgar, "Libraries of Col. S.C.," pp. 119–123. For Chanler's own library see above.

222. Edgar, "Libraries of Col. S.C.," pp. 125–128; SC Arch., Inventories, X (1768–1769), 83–85. The Charleston *General Gazette* of September 11, 1767, advertises fifty-four titles from Stuart's library, only four of which correspond to those in the inventory.

223. SC Arch., Inventories, X (1768–1769), 273–277; Edgar, "Libraries of Col. S.C.," pp. 114–116.

224. SC Arch., Inventories, Y (1769–1771), 74–84. For Seaman, see Mabel Webber, "Death Notices for the *South Carolina American General Gazette* and Its Continuation in the *Royal Gazette*," *SCHM*, XIV (1915), 89. For the books, Edgar, "Libraries of Col. S.C.," pp. 128–138, and "Notable Libraries of S.C.," p. 108. Seaman left the South Carolina Society £500 sterling, and he was a member of the Charleston Library Society.

225. Webber, "Death Notices," *SCHM*, XVII (1916), 48; Edgar, "Libraries of Col. S.C.," pp. 161–164, and "Notable Libraries of S.C.," p. 107. Also SC Arch., Inventories, & (1772–1776), 54–57. "Boyer's *French Dictionary*" is a shortcut title and author. The author, Abel Boyer, compiled the *Royal Dictionary* and *Dictionnaire Anglais-Français*, either of which might be meant by the inventory description.

226. Letter from S. C. Archives Dept. to the present writer as to the lack of detailed inventory. See *DAB* and Edgar, "Notable Libraries of S.C.," p. 107. In a notice in the *S.C. Gaz.*, March 8, 1740, see the remark that "they chiefly consist of Divinity, History, and Law." A briefer notice appeared December 23, 1745, of public vendue at the house of the late Mrs. Trott. SC Arch., Inventories, Charleston County, LL 170; Moore and Simmons, eds., *Abstracts of Wills of S.C. . . .* , I, 285. Of the six which Edgar values at £1,000 or more, only four were really of the colonial period. For newly edited Trott material, see L. Lynn Hogue, ed., "An Edition of Eight Charges Delivered, at So Many Several General Sessions, & Gaol Deliveries: . . . 1703 . . . 1707 by Nicholas Trott, Esq.: Chief Justice of South Carolina" (Ph.D. diss., Univ. of Tennessee, 1972).

227. Edgar, "Libraries of Col. S.C.," p. 221, gives some as SC Arch., Inventories, T (1758–1761), 445–453, but indicates only the values as shown.

228. SC Arch., Inventories, V (1761–1763), 97–105. A John Rattray appears in the *S.C. Gaz.*, Feb. 26, 1750. See also Hamer and Rogers, eds., *Papers of Henry Laurens*, III, 117n, for John Rattray, who had plantations at Pon-Pon and on Indian land. The inventory gives only the total value.

229. Mackenzie's inventory in SC Arch., Inventory Book Z, pp. 64–74, is unitemized as far as books are concerned. I am indebted to Mrs. Terry S. Helsley, Assistant Reference Archivist, S.C. Dept. of History and Archives, for this reference. For Mackenzie as polemical Whig essayist, see Edgar, "Libraries of Colonial S.C.," pp. 198–200, etc.

230. Edgar, "Libraries of Col. S.C.," pp. 140–149, 223–224.

231. For such booklists see Hennig Cohen, *The South Carolina Gazette, 1732–1775* (Columbia, 1953), pp. 121–156.

232. See text above and Harold E. Davis, "A Social History of Georgia," pp. 328, etc., and *The Fledgling Province*, pp. 176–186. Davis refers especially

to the five excellent libraries DeBrahm knew of within a few miles of Savannah, or in the town. See epigraphs for this chapter.

233. Univ. of Georgia Special Collections, Telamon Cuyler Collection. I am indebted to Mrs. William Tate of the Special Collections Department for securing Xerox copies of this and other literary inventories for me. Some I examined for myself in this collection several years ago. For Rigby, see *Abstracts of Colonial Wills of Georgia*, p. 118. Also Coulter and Saye, eds., *List of the Early Settlers of Georgia*, pp. 36, 43.

234. See Inventory Book F, pp. 282–288, in Georgia Dept. of Archives and History (which supplied the author with a photostatic copy in 1972), and H.E. Davis, *The Fledgling Province*, pp. 182–183.

235. See Inventory Book F, pp. 392–397, and Davis, "A Social History of Georgia," p. 328.

236. For Zubly, see *DAB* and Sprague, *Annals of the American Pulpit*, III, 219–222. Zubly may have moved to Georgia before 1760.

237. *Journals of Henry M. Muhlenberg*, trans. Tappert and Doberstein, II, 596.

238. Davis, "A Social History of Georgia," p. 317.

239. See *ibid.*, pp. 324–325, for Davis' tables of statistics and his warning that the 57 percent of all inventories of this period showing books does not mean that such a large proportion of the population owned reading matter, for probably many of the less literate or illiterate filed no wills or inventories at all.

240. Univ. of Georgia, Telamon Cuyler Col., December 15, 1758.

241. *Ibid.*, n.d.

242. McMurtrie, "Pioneer Printing in Georgia," pp. 77–112.

243. "The Libraries of Col. S.C." and "Some Popular Books in Col. S.C.," pp. 174–178.

244. *The Old and New Testament Connected in the History of the Jews and Neighboring Nations* (1716–1718). Edgar, "Some Popular Books in Col. S.C.," confining himself to the larger or more valuable libraries of the eighteenth century, finds in order of popularity William Burkitt's edition of the New Testament, then *The Whole Duty of Man*, Hervey's *Meditations*, and Tillotson's sermons. An inclusion of smaller and earlier libraries (his earliest is from the 1720s) might vary the order of popularity considerably. For South Carolina the order of the first three titles might hold, at least for most of the eighteenth cenutry to 1776, despite the nonconformist element in the colony.

245. For Blair's, Davies', and Whitefield's *Sermons* see Ch. VI below.

246. See other chapters for these men, and of course above in this chapter for some of the titles in Carter's library.

247. *Good Newes from Virginia*, 1613 (London, 1613).

248. Edited with introduction by Richard B. Davis, in *WMQ* (3), XVII (1960), 371–394.

249. See Ch. VI below. Bacon's sermon of October 1753 in favor of a charity school contains even more direct biblical marginal references.

250. Manuscript in Houghton Lib., Harvard Univ. For discussion of sermons, see Ch. VI.

251. Copy in Maryland Diocesan Lib., Md. Hist. Soc.

252. Steiner, *The Reverend Thomas Bray*, pp. 67–70.

253. Nelson Rightmyer, *Maryland's Established Church* (Baltimore, 1956), p. 166.

254. For discussion of this work, see Chapter VI below. It was edited by Thomas J. Pears, Jr., and published by the Presbyterian Hist. Soc. in Philadelphia in 1941.

255. Wright, *First Gent. Va.*, p. 221, gives titles of other textbooks or manuals.

256. "Some Popular Books in Col. S.C.," p. 176.

257. Wright, *First Gent. Va.*, p. 203.

258. "Donald Robertson's School, King and Queen County, Va., 1758–1769," *VMHB*, XXXIII (1925), 194–198, 288–292; XXXIV (1926), 141–148, 232–236; XXXV (1927), 55–56, etc. Most of the entries are simply for subject and in some instances refer to tuition paid for in a particular subject.

259. See Richard B. Davis, "The Gentlest Art in Seventeenth Century Virginia," *TSL*, II (1957), passim.

260. (Columbia, 1964), pp. 85, 205, 373–374, dates varying.

261. See Waring, *Hist. of Med. in S.C.*, p. 85, for a list of some of Mottet's books. Presumably it is his library advertised in the *S.C. Gaz.* of Oct. 2, 1762 (Waring gives Oct. 16, probably a later printing of the same list).

262. Blanton, *Med. in Va. in the Seventeenth Century*, pp. 105–107, 309–318; the Evans, *John Banister*, pp. 74, 75, 141, 154, passim; the Berkeleys, *The Reverend John Clayton, a Parson with a Scientific Mind*, pp. 40–50, 62–67, etc.

263. Blanton, Ch. VI, "Reading and Writing," in *Med. in Va. in the Eighteenth Century*, pp. 93 ff. See also note 111 above for libraries of Brown and McKenzie and the obvious use of the predominantly medical volumes in actual practice. Gill, *The Apothecary in Colonial Virginia*, pp. 77–81.

264. Robbins, *The Eighteenth-Century Commonwealthman*, and Edgar, "Libraries of Col. S.C.," passim. Edgar laments Colbourn's failure to utilize or analyze most southern libraries. Since Colbourn never gets to South Carolina, he fails to mention classic examples of the use of history in the essays of Henry Laurens and John Mackenzie. For the latter, see the discussion in Edgar, "Libraries of Colonial S.C." pp. 198–200, the *S.C. Gaz.* and William H. Drayton, ed., *The Letters of Freeman, etc.* (London, 1771), pp. 38, 111.

265. George B. Watts, "Marmontel's Vogue in America," pp. 267–269; Mary-Margaret Barr, *Voltaire in America*; many studies of Locke, including Colbourn's *Lamp of Experience* and Merle Curti's "The Great Mr. Locke, America's Philosopher," *HL Bull*, XI (1937), 107–152; Leon Howard, "Early American Copies of Milton," pp. 169–179, and George Sensabaugh, *Milton in Early America*; Fredric M. Litto, "Addison's *Cato* in the Colonies," pp. 431–

449; Edward A. Richards, *Hudibras in the Burlesque Tradition*; Paul M. Spurlin, *Montesquieu in America* and *Rousseau in America*.

266. John Dunn, in "Politics of Locke in England and America," in *John Locke*, ed. Yolton, pp. 45–80, claims that Locke *On Government* was relatively unread in America before 1750, feeling that here was a cultural lag.

267. *WMQ* (1), II (1893), 172.

268. See Lemay, "Hamilton's Literary History of the *Maryland Gazette*," p. 280, note 25. For Dulany, see Aubrey C. Land, *The Dulanys of Maryland* (rpt., Balitmore, 1968), pp. 82–83, and the *Right* (Annapolis, William Parks). An investigation of editions of Locke's *Works* now in the BM shows that the "Two Treatises" was in the 1714 edition published by John Churchill and Samuel Manship and in their 1722 edition, as well as in the 1727, 1740, and later editions from various publishers. Among those who had the *Works* by the 1730s were Robert Beverley of Virginia and Samuel Johnston of North Carolina. The *Works* is probably also the "Locke" or "John Locke" in many inventories.

269. For uses by the major Virginia political writers such as Landon Carter and Bland, see Homer D. Kemp, "The Pre-Revolutionary Virginia Polemical Essay," passim. For Locke and Blair, see Parke Rouse, Jr., *James Blair of Virginia* (Chapel Hill, 1971), passim, and Michael G. Kammen, ed., "Virginia at the Close of the Seventeenth Century: An Appraisal by James Blair and John Locke," *VMHB*, LXXIV (1966), 141–169.

270. For a chart of the "Diffusion of Printing" through the thirteen colonies, see Wroth, *The Colonial Printer*, p. 15.

271. Bruce, *Inst. Hist. Va.*, I, 402–403, points out that in 1680 the Virginia Assembly had authorized Nuthead to print the Acts passed in that year. See also Hening, *Statutes*, II, 517–518.

272. For Buckner, see *William Fitzhugh*, ed. Davis, pp. 103–106n; and Wroth, *The Colonial Printer*, pp. 38–39, and *History of Printing in Col. Md.*, p. 210. Wroth points out that the Virginia governors by 1690 were told they could license a press, but certainly Nuthead's experience discouraged printers and possible sponsors for another forty years.

273. The edition here referred to is that of the American Antiquarian Society, published in Albany, N.Y., in two volumes in 1874. Thomas' report on Maryland printing is in I, 320–329.

274. Wroth, *The Colonial Printer*, p. 40, points out that this form was discovered as recently as 1934, twelve years after publication of his *History of Printing in Col. Md.*

275. Wroth, *History of Printing in Col. Md.*, pp. 165–167.

276. For Parks, see Wroth, *William Parks, The Colonial Printer*, and *History of Printing in Col. Md.*, pp. 59–74; Thomas, *History of Printing*, II, 320–321; Castles, "The *Virginia Gazette*."

277. See Wroth, *William Parks*, pp. 10–12, for the summary of evidence and argument.

278. For Green, see Wroth, *History of Printing in Col. Md.*, pp. 75–94, and Lemay, *Men of Letters in Colonial Maryland*, pp. 193–212.

279. Wroth, *History of Printing in Col. Md.*, pp. 95–110. He seems to have had it finished by 1758. Completely printed by 1766, the title page bears the date 1765.

280. *Ibid.*, pp. 85–87. Rind was soon appointed public printer in Virginia.

281. Wroth, *William Parks*, pp. 16–18, 43–44. Markland's poem has been reprinted a number of times, e.g., in facsimile with an introduction by Earl G. Swem (Roanoke, 1926) and in more easily accessible form in Richard B. Davis, C. Hugh Holman, and Louis D. Rubin, eds., *Southern Writing* (New York, 1970), pp. 242–246. Gooch's *A Charge* is reproduced in facsimile in Wroth, *William Parks*, pp. [31–34]. One should remember that a poem by J. Dumbleton celebrated the first southern colonial paper mill, established in Williamsburg by Parks about 1743/4.

282. Reprinted in 1920 in Heartman's Historical Series, ed., Earl G. Swem, and in 1930 by the Facsimile Text Society, New York, ed. Ralph L. Rusk. Neither editor knew then of Dawson's authorship.

283. Thomas, *History of Printing in America*, I, 334–335; Castles, "The *Virginia Gazette*," pp. 47–62; Wroth, *The Colonial Printer*, 43, 67; Frick, "History of Printing in Va.," pp. 59–77, etc.

284. The original ledger or daybook is now at the Univ. of Virginia, with copies in several university and institutional libraries such as Colonial Williamsburg, Inc. Castles tells more of Hunter than do the printed sources. Hunter's distinguished work in the postal service is surveyed, pp. 56–60.

285. Castles, "The *Virginia Gazette*," pp. 60 ff.; Frick, "History of Printing in Va.," pp. 59–77. Knight, *Doc. Hist. Ed. in the South*, I, 500 ff., dates a printed copy of the *Statutes* as 1728. The revised *Charter . . . and Statutes* is indeed Hunter's imprint of 1758. The Latin-English *Statutes* dated 1728 are probably a London printing. Parks' 1736 edition was in Latin and English.

286. For the essays, see Kemp, "The Pre-Revolutionary Virginia Polemical Essay," passim. For the sermons, see Ch. VI below.

287. See Kemp, passim, and for briefer discussion Ch. VI below. The story of Royle's troubles because of his refusal to print a 1763 pamphlet by Camm is told by Kemp and also by Castles in "The *Virginia Gazette*," p. 66.

288. For an account of the technical side of printing in the provinces, see Klapper, *The Printer in Eighteenth-Century Williamsburg*.

289. For binding connected with the Virginia printing establishments, see Samford and Hemphill, *Bookbinding in Colonial Virginia*, which contains interesting photographs of binding done by Parks in both Annapolis and Williamsburg, and by William Hunter, John Stretch, and Thomas Brend in Williamsburg.

290. For the several essays and pamphlets of North Carolina printing see the bibliography for this chapter, especially McMurtrie, *Eighteenth Century N.C. Imprints*, and Powell, "Eighteenth-Century North Carolina Imprints: A Revision and Supplement to McMurtrie," pp. 50–73.

291. McMurtrie, *Eighteenth Century N.C. Imprints*, pp. 12 ff.

292. In 1938 McMurtrie had never located a copy of the work, but Powell has located and reprinted in facsimile the unique Duke University copy

(Raleigh, State Dept. of Archives and History, 1961), with an enlightening introduction. Powell also located many actual copies of McMurtrie's mere titles and added more on his own.

293. McMurtrie, *Eighteenth Century N.C. Imprints*, pp. 40 ff. Davis' most significant publications, at least outside official records, are Moore's, Hermon Husband's, and others' political tracts, and Davis' own *The Office and Authority of a Justice of the Peace* (1774) and his humorous work *The First Book of the American Chronicles of the Times* (also 1774). His *North Carolina Gazette* and his 1764 *North Carolina Magazine* were not really successful. But more on the former below.

294. McMurtrie, "Bibliography of S.C. Imprints," pp. 117–137, and "First Decade of Printing in S.C.," pp. 425–452; Cohen, *S.C. Gaz.*, passim, and other items in the bibliography of this chapter.

295. McMurtrie, "First Decade of Printing in S.C.," pp. 425–428. The Webb imprint survives in a P.R.O. copy.

296. (Richmond, Virginia St. Lib., 1971), p. 201. The earliest South Carolina broadside Hummel lists is of 1744, but McMurtrie cites two copies of one of those of 1732 as being in the P.R.O. The second, also in the P.R.O., McMurtrie believes to be Whitmarsh's on the basis of type similarity.

297. McMurtrie, "Bibliography of S.C. Imprints," pp. 120–124. Richard P. Morgan, *Prelim. Bibliog. of S.C. Imprints*, notices two 1732 Whitmarsh items not in McMurtrie.

298. William Friedman, "The First Librarian in America," *Lib. Journ.*, LVI (1931), 902–903, Timothy had already edited a German-language newspaper in Pennsylvania. Cohen, *S.C. Gaz.* (pp. 223–248), gives a full account of the Timothys as printers.

299. McMurtrie, "Bibliography of S.C. Imprints," p. 132. A recent facsimile edition, edited by Frank Baker and George W. Williams, was published in 1964 jointly by the Dalcho Historical Society of Charleston and the Wesley Historical Society of London.

300. *A True and Historical Narrative of the Colony of Georgia in America* (1741, reprinted several times, including the edition by Clarence L. Ver Steeg [Athens, Ga., 1960]). For the motivations of the authors see chapters IX and X below.

301. See Cohen, *S.C. Gaz.*, pp. 170–171.

302. Despite insistence of the *S.C. Gaz.* that "The Poem of Indico" would be published (advertised as late as November 3, 1759), there is no evidence that it ever was.

303. For Morgan's checklist, see the bibliography for this chapter above.

304. Edgar, "Libraries of Col. S.C.," p. 6.

305. McMurtrie, "Pioneer Printing in Georgia," pp. 77–113; Wroth, *The Colonial Printer*, pp. 48–51; and other items in the bibliography for this chapter, including Lawrence, *James Johnston, Georgia's First Printer*.

306. Johnston was given or allowed certain perquisites in his office, such as having a monopoly on selling Acts of Assembly to others than provincial officers. On the same date as the first issue of the *Gazette* Governor James

Wright assented to an appropriation act which included an allowance to the printer of £50, the first part of his salary. The place of Johnston's apprenticeship is unknown.

307. George C. McMurtrie, *The First Printing in Georgia* (Metuchen, N.J., Charles F. Heartman, 1927).

308. All extant issues of Parks' *Maryland Gazette*, 1728–1734, save a few recently discovered, have been issued in photostat by the John Carter Brown Lib. There is a file in the library of the Univ. of Tennessee, among other institutions.

309. The issue is no longer extant, but this "prospectus" is reprinted in the *Virginia Hist. Reg.*, VI (1853), 20–22.

310. Lemay, for example, in *Men of Letters in Colonial Maryland* and in his "Hamilton's Literary History of the *Maryland Gazette*," pp. 273–285, already has connected scores of pieces with their authors. In editing a Virginia poet of the period, he is now identifying a number of verses in British and American magazines and newspapers. Though much by Davies and Mercer and Byrd in Virginia and Cook and Cradock and Bacon and Hamilton in Maryland has been identified, undoubtedly much by each of these and by other men has not. The first great step for all colonies is Lemay's own *Calendar of American Poetry*.

311. Davis, ed., *The Col. Va. Satirist*, passim.

312. Lemay, "Robert Bolling and the Bailment of Colonel Chiswell," pp. 99–142.

313. See Joost, " 'Plain-Dealer' and *Free-Thinker*: A Revaluation," pp. 31–37; Aldridge, "Benjamin Franklin and the *Maryland Gazette*," pp. 177–189; Lemay, *Men of Letters in Colonial Maryland*, pp. 115–118; the *Md. Gaz.*; and the *Penna. Gaz.*, nos. 13, 74, 76, 79, 81, 82, 83, and 85.

314. Cooke, *Literary Influences*, p. 159, however, with Aldridge, also considers the series deistic.

315. Thanks to the microfilming of all known copies some years ago by the Yale Univ. Lib., a number of repositories in this country have Green's *Gazette* on film. As noted above, a few more copies have been discovered since this filming was done. There are two number ones, that dated in January and a second published on April 26. From the latter date publication was uninterrupted until the Stamp Act crisis of 1765.

316. See films of the *Md. Gaz.*, and Lemay, *Men of Letters in Colonial Maryland*, pp. 199–202.

317. This rollicking hedonistic verse has been republished at least two or three times in the past decade.

318. The last is in the issue of March 10, 1763, with the statement that it had been published in Virginia in September 1761 and than many persons had requested that it appear in the *Md. Gaz.* Carter tells of his experiments with the plant. Two long articles on insects signed "C" Lemay believes were written by Henry Callister.

319. For more on Green as man and writer, see Lemay, *Men of Letters in*

Colonial Maryland, pp. 193–212, and Wroth, *Hist. of Printing in Col. Md.,* pp. 75–94.

320. Castles, "The *Virginia Gazette,*" pp. 26–28, notes that Parks was aware of previous suspicion of printing in Virginia and was resolved to be more than extraordinarily careful not to offend officialdom.

321. It is worth noting that the *Va. Gaz.* and the *S.C. Gaz.* were frequently quoted in the newspapers of the middle colonies and New England and even in the British *Gentleman's Magazine.*

322. The first few issues are missing. Our earliest extant "Monitor" is no. 6, in the issue of September 10, though one writer gives as an example "No. 3." For the "Monitor" essays, see Castles, "The *Virginia Gazette,*" pp. 193–202; the Gibsons, "The Influence of the *Tatler* and the *Spectator* on the 'Monitor,'" pp. 12–23; and Lemay, *Men of Letters in Colonial Maryland,* p. 115. Parks omitted "The Monitor" when more important "news" filled the paper. See also Arner, "The Short Happy Life of the Virginia 'Monitor,'" pp. 130–147, and Ch. IX below.

323. Professor Lemay has located nos. 1, [2?], 3, 9, 10, 16, 17, 18, and 19 in other provincial newspapers from New Hampshire and Massachusetts on south. Several survive in three or four newspapers. The present writer's Xerox copies of all of them are dated 1756–1757. Number 10 also appears in the *Md. Gaz.* and the *N.Y. Gaz.*

324. See Clinton Rossiter, "Richard Bland: The Whig in America," *WMQ* (3), X (1953), 45.

325. Castles, "The *Virginia Gazette,*" pp. 176 ff., discusses the various kinds of religious and moral essays and identifies some of the probable contributors.

326. Castles identifies "Dymocke" tentatively as John Camm. Others have shown that he was rather the Reverend John Robertson.

327. Overfield, "Science in the *Virginia Gazette,*" pp. 1–52.

328. Kobre, *Dev. of the Col. Newspaper,* pp. 83–84.

329. It is an incomplete voice in more senses than one, for there are tremendous gaps of years in the extant issues of the *Virginia Gazette.* One repeats, it was normally the voice of the legislative ruling class, though the Centinel and Davies-Dymocke controversies show that the editor was allowed or allowed himself considerable freedom of intellectual movement in certain directions.

330. The Duke University Library has the six in photostat, as do other North Carolina libraries. The originals are in the State Department of Archives and History in Raleigh.

331. See Wroth, *The Colonial Printer,* p. 48; McMurtrie, *Hist. of Printing in the U. S.,* II, 337 ff. Thomas (*History of Printing in America,* II, 166) says that Davis' *N.C. Gaz.* printed issue no. 1 in December 1755. The issue he describes is not one of those included in the collection of six noted above. Thomas says the paper was published for about six years and then discontinued.

332. See the microfilm of all known issues of South Carolina newspapers from 1732 to a period long after 1763 produced by the Charleston Library Society; also Thomas, *History of Printing in America,* I, 340–351; Wroth,

The Colonial Printer, pp. 43–48; and above all Cohen, *S.C. Gaz.* For something on Wells' newspaper towards the end of the colonial period (in 1758), see Thomas, *History of Printing in America*, pp. 343–344; and Edgar, "Libraries of Col. S.C.," p. 6 and passim.

333. It is worth noting that the *S.C. Gaz.* of August 8, 1748, has three and one-half columns of quotations from Trenchard and Gordon's *Cato's Letters* on "The Right and Capacities of the People to judge of Government."

334. Wells opened his bookshop in 1754. See Bowes, *Culture of Early Charleston*, pp. 66–67; Thomas, *History of Printing in America*, I, 343–344; Edgar, "Libraries of Col. S.C.," p. 6 ff.; Cohen, *S.C. Gaz.*, p. 5n and passim (see Index). Edgar found Wells' journal a most useful supplement to Timothy's.

335. Quoted from Bowes, *Culture of Early Charleston*, p. 97, from the *S.C. & American General Gazette* of June 20, 1766. Only three issues of Wells' *S.C. Weekly Gazette* are known to exist: February 7, 1759 (no. 12); October 31, 1759; and December 10, 1760 (see Clarence S. Brigham, *History and Bibliography of American Newspapers, 1690–1820* [2 vols., Worcester, Mass., 1947], II, 1041–1042). For the involvement of this paper and the *S.C. Gaz.* in the pre-Revolutionary essay controversies, see *Papers of Henry Laurens*, eds. Hamer, Rogers, et al., III, passim.

336. McMurtrie, "Pioneer Printing in Georgia," pp. 84–85; and Lawrence, *James Johnston, Georgia's First Printer*, passim. A thorough study of the *Georgia Gazette* is needed.

337. *Travels through the United States of America* (1799), quoted in Davis, *Intellectual Life in Jefferson's Virginia, 1790–1830* (Chapel Hill, 1964), p. [71].

338. This is an impressionistic, not a statistical conclusion, for there is no way of making the latter sort at present.

CHAPTER FIVE: RELIGION: ESTABLISHED,
EVANGELICAL, AND INDIVIDUAL

BIBLIOGRAPHY

The notes on the text of this chapter include many references to individual periodical essays and to books used only once or twice. The bibliography of colonial religion is so vast that this can only be a selective bibliography, pointing out books and a few essays which have proved most useful.

General studies of varied value are Alan Heimert, *Religion and the American Mind from the Great Awakening to the Revolution* (Cambridge, Mass., 1966), which is considered specifically in text and notes; Winthrop S. Hudson, *American Protestanism* (Chicago, 1961); W.W. Sweet, *Religion in Colonial America* (New York, 1942); W. Noel Sainsbury et al., eds., *Calendar of State Papers, Colonial Series, America and the West Indies* (10 vols., London, 1860–1908); H. Shelton Smith, Robert T. Handy, and Lefferts A. Loetscher, eds., *American Christianity: An Historical Interpretation with Representative*

Documents, I, 1607–1820 (New York, 1960); and W.S. Perry, ed., *Historical Collections Relating to the American Colonial Church*, I, *Virginia* (privately printed, 1870), IV, *Maryland and Delaware* (1878), largely but not entirely Anglican in materials.

Useful in general for Virginia are Daniel J. Boorstin, *The Americans: The Colonial Experience* (New York, 1958) pp. 97–143; W.W. Hening, ed. *Statutes at Large of Virginia* (13 vols., Richmond, 1809–1823); Alexander Brown, ed., *Genesis of the United States* (2 vols., Boston, 1890), and *The First Republic in America* (Boston, 1898); Peter Force, ed., *Tracts and Other Papers* (4 vols., New York, 1947); H.R. McIlwaine, ed., journals, minutes, and other records (see notes for individual items); Richard L. Morton, *Colonial Virginia* (2 vols., Chapel Hill, 1960); and Louis B. Wright, *The First Gentlemen of Virginia* (San Marino, Calif., 1940). For Maryland especially valuable are Charles A. Barker, *The Background of the Revolution in Maryland* (New Haven, 1940); and William H. Browne et al., eds., *The Archives of Maryland* (Baltimore, 1883–   ). For North Carolina Mattie E.E. Parker, ed., *North Carolina: Charters and Constitutions* (Raleigh, 1963); W.L. Saunders, ed., *The Colonial Records of North Carolina* (6 vols., Raleigh, 1886–1888); and Stephen B. Weeks, *The Religious Development of the Province of North Carolina* (Baltimore, 1892); Hugh T. Lefler and Albert R. Newsome, *North Carolina: The History of a Southern State* (Chapel Hill, 1954). For South Carolina useful are the series of records of Assemblies and other legislative and judicial agencies edited by A.S. Salley and by J.H. Easterby, et al.; R.B. Carroll, *Historical Collections of South Carolina* (2 vols., New York, 1836); Anne King Gregorie, ed., *Records of the Court of Chancery of South Carolina, 1671–1729* (Washington, D.C., 1950); the histories of Alexander Hewatt, Edward McCrady, and especially D.D. Wallace, *The History of South Carolina*, I (New York, 1934). For Georgia, Allen D. Candler, and Lucien Knight, eds., *Colonial Records of the State of Georgia* (26 vols., Atlanta, 1904–1916); and Reba C. Strickland, *Religion and the State in Georgia in the Eighteenth Century* (New York, 1939).

The Anglicans. For the earliest years, Susan M. Kingsbury, ed., *Records of the Virginia Company of London* (4 vols., Washington, D.C. 1906–1935), contains a great deal. For relationship to the state, see Elizabeth H. Davidson, *The Establishment of the English Church in the Continental American Colonies* (Durham, N.C., 1936). For missionary effort, see text and notes and David Humphrey, *An Historical Account of the Incorporated Society for the Propagation of the Gospel in Foreign Parts* (London, 1730; rpt., New York, 1873); Charles F. Pascoe, *Two Hundred Years of the S.P.G.: An Historical Account of the Society for the Propagation of the Gospel in Foreign Parts* (2 vols., London, 1901); and H.P. Thompson, *Into All Lands: The History of the Society for the Propagation of the Gospel in Foreign Parts* (London, 1951). There is also considerable discussion and material on earlier efforts in text and notes for the section of this chapter on the seventeenth century. For Virginia there are several books of value: G.M. Brydon, *Virginia's Mother*

Church and the Political Conditions under Which It Grew, I (Richmond, 1947), II (Philadelphia, 1952); F.L. Hawks, *Contributions to the Ecclesiastical History of the United States of America*, I, *A Narrative of Events Connected with the Rise of the Protestant Episcopal Church in Virginia* (New York, 1836); Philip A. Bruce, *Institutional History of Virginia in the Seventeenth Century* (2 vols., New York, 1910); E.L. Goodwin, *The Colonial Church in Virginia* (Milwaukee, 1927); William Meade, *Old Churches, Ministers, and Families of Virginia* (2 vols., Philadelphia, 1857); Perry, *Historical Collections*, I, *Virginia*; and the histories of the colony mentioned in the notes, by William Stith, Hugh Jones, and Robert Beverley. For Maryland, Nelson W. Rightmyer, *Maryland's Established Church* (Baltimore, 1956); G.L. Petrie, *Church and State in Early Maryland* (Baltimore, 1892); and Perry, *Historical Collections*, IV, *Maryland*. For South Carolina, Frederick Dalcho, *An Historical Account of the Protestant Episcopal Church in South-Carolina* (Charleston, 1820). For North Carolina and Georgia, see items in the notes for this chapter.

The question of an Anglican episcopate is discussed in many essays and historical documents listed in the notes. Carl Bridenbaugh, *Mitre and Sceptre: Transatlantic Faiths, Ideas, Personalities and Politics, 1689–1775* (New York, 1962), almost completely ignores the southern colonies in his study; much more useful is Arthur L. Cross, *The Anglican Episcopate and the American Colonies* (Cambridge, Mass., 1924; orig. ed., 1902). For items on Christianizing and educating the Negro, see note 161 ff. For witchcraft, see the notes on the section so entitled. For Puritanism and puritanism and their relation to Anglicanism, see below. Babette Levy's *Early Puritanism in the Southern and Island Colonies* (Worcester, Mass., 1960) is the one book dealing with this subject for the whole region, but there are monographs and other studies of smaller compass listed in the notes.

The Presbyterians. The principal general studies are Charles A. Biggs, *American Presbyterianism: Its Origin and Early History* (New York, 1885); Ernest T. Thompson, *Presbyterians in the South, I: 1607–1861* (Richmond, 1963); Leonard J. Trinterud, *The Forming of an American Tradition: A Re-examination of Colonial Presbyterianism* (Philadelphia, 1948). For Virginia, W.H. Foote, *Sketches of Virginia Historical and Biographical*, 1st ser. (orig. ed., Philadelphia, 1850; rev. ed., Richmond, 1966) is entirely concerned with the early Presbyterian church in Virginia. W.H. Foote's *Sketches of the North Carolina Historical and Biographical*, ed. Harold J. Dudley (orig. ed., New York, 1846; rev. ed., New Bern, N.C., 1966) is useful but largely concerned with years after 1763. George Howe, *History of the Presbyterian Church in South Carolina* (2 vols., Columbia, 1870) contains a good deal about Independents, Puritans, and Huguenots as well as Presbyterians.

For the Great Awakening in the South, there are many materials. Several of the sermons and tracts on both sides of what was in part a controversy will be examined in the next chapter. Many of the books already mentioned are also useful on this subject: Briggs, *American Presbyterianism*; Thompson,

Presbyterians in the South, I; Trinterud, *Forming an American Tradition;* Cross, *The Anglican Episcopate;* Foote, *Sketches of Virginia,* 1st. ser., and *Sketches of North Carolina;* Dalcho, *Historical Account of the Protestant Episcopal Church in S.C.;* Howe, *History of the Presbyterian Church in S.C.;* Meade, *Old Churches;* Brydon, *Virginia's Mother Church,* II; Hening, ed., *Statutes.* As a comprehensive examination, though it considers only one colony, the best book is Wesley M. Gewehr, *The Great Awakening in Virginia, 1704–1790* (Durham, N.C., 1930). Smith, Hardy, and Loetscher, eds., *American Christianity,* I, provide pertinent documents and helpful introductions. H.R. McIlwaine, *The Struggle of Protestant Dissenters for Religious Toleration in Virginia* (Baltimore, 1894) is an older study still worth consideration. Two essays should be mentioned: Leonard W. Labaree, "The Conservative Attitude toward the Great Awakening," *WMQ* (3), I (1944), 331–352; and Gerald J. Goodwin, "The Anglican Reaction to the Great Awakening," *HMPEC,* XXXV (1966), 343–371. A controversial book of vital concern here is Heimert, *Religion and the American Mind,* which equates New England Calvinism with true liberalism and both with the revivalists. Alan Heimert and Perry Miller, eds., *The Great Awakening: Documents Illustrating the Crisis and Its Consequences* (Indianapolis, 1967) includes more representative southern figures of the Great Awakening than Heimert's earlier book and some of their writing, but like *Religion and the American Mind* it is a badly balanced book, for in both the New England mind is equated with the American mind, some of the editors' own documentary evidence to the contrary. Much the same is true for several other anthologies of materials of the Great Awakening, as those edited by Richard L. Bushman (New York, 1970); J.M. Bumsted (Waltham, Mass., 1970); and Darrett B. Rutman (New York, 1970). More or less peripheral studies are L.H. Butterfeld, "Elder John Leland, Jeffersonian Itinerant," *PAAS,* n.s. LXII (1952), 155–242; Richard Niebuhr and Daniel D. Williams, eds., *The Ministry in Historical Perspective* (New York, 1956); Alexander Hamilton's *Itinerarium,* ed. Carl Bridenbaugh (Chapel Hill, 1948), details of a journey to the north by a Marylander in the revival years; and Weeks, *Religious Development of North Carolina.*

For the greatest of the Presbyterians, Samuel Davies, the materials are voluminous yet unsatisfactory. Badly needed is a definitive study of his work in the ministry, including the battle for religious toleration in Virginia, the full story of his labors for education at Princeton, and above all a comprehensive critique of the literary and theological quality of his sermons, tracts, and poems. Perhaps what are the two best studies to date remain unpublished: George H. Bost, "Samuel Davies: Colonial Revivalist and Champion of Religious Toleration" (Ph.D. diss., Univ. of Chicago, 1942), which includes an excellent though not quite complete bibliography of Davies' writings; and Robert S. Alley, "The Reverend Samuel Davies: A Study in Religion and Politics, 1747–1759" (Ph.D. diss., Princeton Univ., 1962). Brief and barely touching upon some phases of Davies' activities is G.W. Pilcher, *Samuel Davies: Apostle of Dissent in Colonial Virginia* (Knoxville, Tenn., 1971). Useful appraisals are in Foote, *Sketches of Virginia*, pp. 119–307; Gewehr, *Great Awakening in Virginia*, pp. 68–105; Heimert, *Religion and the American Mind*, pp. 75, 173–174, 222–237; J.E. Pomfret, "Samuel Davies" in *DAB*; William B. Sprague, ed., *Annals of the American Pulpit* (9 vols., New York 1857–1869), III, 140–146; and most general histories of Presbyterianism and religion in the colonial period. A recent good edition, G.W. Pilcher, ed., *The Reverend Samuel Davies Abroad: The Diary of a Journey to England and Scotland, 1753–1755* (Urbana, 1967), replaces the abbreviated and at times inaccurate text in Foote's *Sketches of Virginia*. Valuable periodical essays are George H. Bost, "Samuel Davies, Preacher of the Great Awakening," *JPHS*, XXVI (1948), 65–86; "Samuel Davies as President of Princeton," *JPHS*, XXVI (1948), 165–181; and "Samuel Davies, the South's Great Awakener," *JPHS*, XXXIII (1955), 135–155; G.W. Pilcher, "Samuel Davies and Religious Toleration in Virginia," *The Historian*, XXVIII (1965), 48–71. For discussions and bibliography of Davies' sermons, tracts, and poems see Chapters VI and IX.

The Quakers. Though much has been written of the Quakers, a thorough study needs to be made, through an examination of letters and minutes of Monthly and Yearly Meetings, of their place in southern colonial religious history and education. A few books give some space to southern Friends and their activities: Rufus M. Jones, *The Quakers in the American Colonies* (new ed., New York, 1962); Thomas E. Drake, *The Quakers and Slavery* (New Haven, 1950); Samuel H. Janney, *History of the Religious Society of Friends* (4 vols., Philadelphia, 1860–1867); Frederick B. Tolles, *Quakers and the Atlantic Culture* (New York, 1960); and the journals of John Burnyeat, George Fox, Thomas Story, and William Edmundson commented upon in the text and notes for this chapter. Babette Levy, *Early Puritanism in the Southern Colonies*, includes the Quakers as one of her "Puritan" sects and gives them considerable attention.

The Baptists. The great proportion of the literature of Baptist history is concerned with a period later than the one under study. Something of the colonial period is discussed in O.K. and Marjorie Armstrong, *The Indomitable Baptists: A Narrative of Their Role in Shaping American History* (Garden City, N.Y., 1967). For Virginia, see Garnett Ryland, *The Baptists of Virginia, 1699–1926* (Richmond, 1955); and Robert B. Semple, *A History of the Rise and Progress of the Baptists in Virginia* (Richmond, 1810; rev. ed. of G.W. Beale, 1894). For North Carolina, George W. Paschal, *History of the North Carolina Baptists, I, 1663–1805* (Raleigh, 1930). For South Carolina, Leah Townsend, *South Carolina Baptists, 1670–1805* (Florence, S.C., 1935). For the other colonies, see text and notes for this chapter.

The German Groups. The Moravians are discussed at some length in text and notes for this chapter and Chapter VIII. Smaller sects are also discussed in text and notes of this chapter. The Lutherans have written about themselves more extensively than some of their brethren: for example, William J. Finck, *Lutheran Landmarks and Pioneers in America* (Philadelphia, 1913); C.W. Cassell, W.J. Finck, and E.O. Henkel, *History of the Lutheran Church in Virginia and East Tennessee* (Strasburg, Va., 1930); W.K. Boyd and Charles A. Krummel, "German Tracts Concerning the Lutheran Church in North Carolina during the Eighteenth Century," *NCHR*, VII (1930), 79–147, 225–282; and William E. Eisenberg, *The Lutheran Church in Virginia, 1717–1962* (Roanoke, 1967), G.D. Bernheim, *History of the German Settlements and of the Lutheran Church in North and South Carolina* (Philadelphia, 1872). For the Georgia German and Swiss sects, see note 216 below.

The Huguenots, small in number, have maintained a pride in their heritage and have written much on themselves, though most of it is social rather than religious history. Earl G. Swem, comp., *Virginia Historical Index* (2 vols., Roanoke, 1934–1936) includes a great deal of data citation on the Virginia Huguenots, and the present chapter discusses them in connection with Anglicans and Presbyterians. In South Carolina they have had their own periodical and a good study of their early history, Arthur H. Hirsch, *The Huguenots of South Carolina* (Durham, N.C., 1928). The deists of the colonial South have received little attention, but representative primary material has been presented in text and notes here. The special group, the Labadists of Bohemia Manor, have received attention in Bartlett B. James, *The Labadist Colony in Maryland* (Baltimore, 1899); and Mark Holloway, *Heavens on Earth* (London, 1951), a study of utopian experiments. There is also information on them in *MdHM* and in various histories of the colony, as well as in *Archives of Maryland*. Though the Jews were in most of the colonies from the beginning, their numbers were so small that little or nothing has been written about their group history in the colonial South. Pertinent books are Leon Hühner, *Jews in America in Colonial and Revolutionary Times* (New York, 1959); Jacob R. Marens, *The Colonial American Jew, 1492–1776* (3 vols., Detroit, 1970); and Barnett Elzas, *The Jews of South Carolina from the Earliest Times to the Present Day* (Philadelphia, 1905). Except in Maryland, the Roman Catholics were as rare or as isolated as the Jews in the colonial South. They appear frequently in the *Archives of Maryland*, in various histories, and in J. Hall Pleasants, ed., *Narratives of Early Maryland, 1683–1684* (New York, 1910). See text and notes for other books and essays.

NOTES

1. Quinn, ed., *The Roanoke Voyages*, II, 531n.
2. See Kingsbury, ed., *Records Va. Co.* These volumes were printed in large part from the manuscripts in the LC and were formerly in the possession of William Byrd II and Thomas Jefferson and others. Most are official copies made when the Crown was seizing all the data of the Company just before or

after its dissolution in 1624. Other pertinent materials from various sources are also included.

3. "Letters Patent to Sir Thomas Gates ... ," dated April 10, 1606. The full text is printed in William Stith, The History of the *First Discovery and Settlement of Virginia* (Williamsburg, 1747), Appendix no. 1, pp. A–1–8.

4. Stith, *History of the First Discovery*, p. A-22.

5. For Virginia Company manuscript copies of the Oaths of Allegiance and Supremacy of the year 1607 see Kingsbury, ed., *Records, Va. Co.*, III, 4–5.

6. *Ibid.*, Va. Co., III, 14. Abbreviations have been expanded.

7. Brydon, *Virginia's Mother Church*, I, 11–13, and Goodwin, *Col. Ch. in Va.*, pp. 280, 281.

8. John Smith, "Advertisements for the Unexperienced Planters of New-England, or any where" [orig. ed., London, 1631], in Smith, *Works* II, 957–958. For other references to Hunt, see this edition, passim, referred to hereafter as Smith, *Works*.

9. *Ibid.*, I, lxxxviii and lxxvii.

10. It has also been suggested that William Strachey or the Reverend Richard Bucke wrote it.

11. In 1967 the prayer was still repeated in the rebuilt stockade at Jamestown.

12. From William Strachey, *For the Colony in Virginia Britannia Lawes Divine Morall and Martiall* (London, 1612; pp. 66–68), reprinted in Force, *Tracts*, III, no. 2; and *Lawes Divine, Morall and Martiall, etc. Compiled by William Strachey*, ed. David H. Flaherty (Charlottesville, 1969), pp. 98–101.

13. Apparently Bucke had at least one associate, Nicholas Glover. See Goodwin, *Col. Church in Virginia*, pp. 256, 272, 299. Brydon (*Virginia's Mother Church*, I, 16) thinks the second clergyman was William Mease.

14. *A Voyage to Virginia in 1609: Two Narratives, Strachey's True Reportory and Jourdain's Discovery of the Bermudas*, ed. Louis B. Wright (Charlottesville, 1964), pp. 79–80.

15. For Whitaker, see William H. Littleton, "Alexander Whitaker (1585–1617) 'The Apostle of Virginia,'" *HMPEC*, XXIX (1960), 325–348; H.C. Porter, "Alexander Whitaker: Cambridge Apostle to Virginia," *WMQ* (3), XIV (1957), 317–343; Brydon, *Virginia's Mother Church*, I, 24 ff.; Goodwin, *Col. Ch. in Va.*, p. 316; Meade, *Old Churches*, I, 76–78; Levy, *Early Puritanism in the Southern Colonies*, pp. 99–100.

16. Littleton, "Alexander Whitaker," p. 344. The three letters are to William Crashaw, 1611 (printed in Brown, ed., *Genesis of the United States*, I, 497–500); to Sir Thomas Smith, 1612 (in *Good Newes from Virginia* [London, 1613; modern ed. SF&R], pp. D2$^{r&v}$); to William Gouge, 1614, in part in Ralph Hamor, *A True Discourse of the Present Estate of Virginia* (London, 1615, two variant issues), pp. 59–61. The sermon-letter printed in *Good Newes from Virginia* was written in 1612.

17. The second passage is from the first issue of Hamor's *A True Discourse of the Present Estate of Virginia*, the first from a second issue in the same place in the text (see Porter, "Alexander Whitaker," p. 339). The original

letter probably contained both passages and was cut for reasons of space by the printer or publisher of Hamor's volume. The second passage may have given offense to High-Churchmen in England and therefore was neatly deleted and replaced.

It is perhaps worth recalling here that church and lay historians point out that Hakluyt and Purchas and perhaps others thought service in the colonies would be a fine way of getting rid of troublesome puritans at home and of using them profitably. We presume that this had nothing to do with Whitaker's "call" to America, though it was probably a factor in the appointment of several later ministers.

18. *Virginia's Mother Church*, I, 22.

19. *Ibid.*, I, 28; Kingsbury, ed., *Records Va. Co.*, IV, 521. The "two without" were Wickham and Maycock, both well-educated men. The archbishop did have the right to license a minister of Genevan or Presbyterian ordination to hold a parish and administer the sacraments. This right remained *as law* in England until after the Restoration. It continued *in practice* in Virginia until the last Presbyterian incumbent of a parish died in 1710. See Goodwin, *Col. Ch. in Va.*, pp. 281, 331.

20. *The Present State of Virginia* [1724], ed. Richard L. Morton (Chapel Hill, 1956), p. 98. Levy (*Early Puritanism in the Southern Colonies*, pp. 101–102) offers some evidence that Hawte Wyatt and his contemporary George Keith (not the later Quaker) were nonconformist.

21. For more on these Indian-white relations, see Chapter II.

22. H.R. McIlwaine et al., eds., Journals H.B. *Va. . . . , 1619–1658/9* (Richmond, 1915), introd. Actual journals of these earliest meetings do not survive. What legislation was enacted we learn through surviving reports and appeals sent to the Company or the King.

23. Brydon, *Virginia's Mother Church*, I, 83–85.

24. Hening, ed., *Statutes*, I, 123 etc. The fines may have taken the place of the earlier and harsher laws for nonattendance, but probably they applied only to first offenders.

25. For example, James City, Charles City, and Elizabeth City, which have kept the word *City* in their county names to this day.

26. Hening, ed., *Statutes*, I, 149, and Brydon, *Virginia's Mother Church*, I, 88.

27. Brydon, *Virginia's Mother Church*, I, 93.

28. Brydon (*ibid.*, I, 43–46, etc.) explains the history of the nomination of rectors in England and under the Virginia Company. Originally the Company had the right of appointment and presumably of "induction," but the Council in Virginia challenged this right successfully even in Sir Francis Wyatt's administration and had their own way. As the parishes proliferated and the congregations and vestries were made up of men who owned their own land, the vestries chose the clergy and failed to present them to the governor for induction, as apparently they were required by law to do within a reasonable period of time. If they did not, the governor was to present and induct. By 1697 probably no governor had pushed this matter, though the Archbishop

of Canterbury said he had the right. As William Byrd II drily remarked to the Archbishop, Virginia was not England. See Perry, ed., *Historical Collections*, I, 47, "The Conference at Lambeth." Blair's role is never entirely clear, or one might say he never urged an induction except his own at Bruton Parish, and there the case was never settled. In the eighteenth century a governor occasionally did try to induct against a vestry's wishes, as Spotswood did. Maryland's vestries were chosen somewhat differently, and since in principle they had little to do with choice of a clergyman, they were considered primarily as holders and managers of church property. In North and South Carolina the vestries upon occasion chose ministers and opposed induction; at certain periods they were self-perpetuating. But their duties and privileges varied from time to time more than in Virginia. See Davidson, *Estab. of the Eng. Church in the Colonies*, pp. 29, 52–53, 54–55, 61, 65, 88. For Spotswood's refusal to induct Blair in Williamsburg and the eminent British legal opinion on both sides, see Brydon, *Virginia's Mother Church*, I, 344–353.

29. A fourth, Sir William Gooch, reveals in his letters to his brother, the Bishop of Norwich, that he never trusted Blair in ecclesiastical or other matters.

30. Perry, ed., *Historical Collections*, I, pp. 252–253, 261–368, and Brydon, *Virginia's Mother Church*, I, 376–377. Robert Beverley (*The History and Present State of Virginia*, ed. Louis B. Wright [orig. ed. 1705; Chapel Hill, 1947], p. 264) states that he never heard the clergy complain of anything save the precariousness of their livings.

31. Meade, *Old Churches*, I, 151, quoted with agreement in Boorstin, *The Americans*, p. 129. See also Bruce, *Inst. Hist. Va.*, passim, and Jack D. Owen, "The Virginia Vestry: A Study in the Decline of the Ruling Class," (Ph.D. diss., Princeton Univ., 1947). As suggested, vestry books reveal a great deal about lay-clerical relations and about the personnel of the vestries, *e.g.*, C.G. Chamberlayne, ed., *The Vestry Book of Christ Parish*, 1663–1767 [Middlesex County] (Richmond, Va., 1927). The Christ Church vestry in the later seventeenth century included Sir Peyton Skipwith, Sir Henry Chicheley, Major-General Robert Smith, Captain Christopher Wormeley, and Robert Beverley. Among its clergy were the able Deuel Pead (see notice of his sermon in the next chapter), Robert Yates, and Bartholomew Yates. The minutes of these vestry meetings indicate discussion of care of orphans and the poor, tithes, salary of clergy, choice of clergy, the sacraments, and sermons, and include a copy of Pead's parting deed of gift to the parish. Besides the several printed vestry books, others remain in manuscript in such places as the Va. Theol. Sem. in Alexandria, the Va. Hist. Soc., the Va. St. Lib., the Univ. of Va., the Md. Hist. Soc., the S.C. Hist. Soc., the Univ. South Caroliniana Soc., other state libraries, and the LC. Some of the original books are still held by parishes, though usually copies have been procured by library repositories.

32. Brydon, *Virginia's Mother Church*, I, passim; Jones, *The Present State of Virginia*, ed. Morton, pp. 125–126. Jones mentions that some parishes were long vacant because of the badness of the tobacco, which gave room for dissenters, especially Quakers (p. 125).

33. Though there were a few notorious cases, Virginia never seems to have had the trouble with clerical behavior experienced in the Carolinas and Maryland, where the men were usually inducted. This is not to say that vestries in the other southern colonies did not frequently stand upon their "rights."

34. McIlwaine, ed., *Minutes Council and Gen. Court Col. Va.*, p. 481.

35. Rightmyer, *Maryland's Established Church*, pp. 6, 177, 194; Goodwin, *Col. Ch. in Va.*, p. 261; Levy, *Early Puritanism in the Southern Colonies*, pp. 140–141. James received a regular annual salary; Cotton was paid for each visit. Though there is no proof that Cotton was as strongly Calvinist or even Puritan as his immediate predecessors and successors in Hungar's Parish in Accomack County, Virginia, his widow married in succession two noted nonconformists, Nathaniel Eaton, deposed head of Harvard, and Francis Doughty, of whom more later.

36. Rightmyer, *Maryland's Established Church*, p. 4, quotes. See also George Petrie, *Church and State in Early Maryland* (Baltimore, 1892), pp. 6–8.

37. See *Archives of Md.*, IV, 35; E.D. Neill, *Terrae Mariae* (Philadelphia, 1867), p. 67. The servants were reading the sermons of the famous Puritan preacher, "Silver-tongued" Smith.

38. *Archives of Md.*, I, 119, Assembly Proceedings 1641. A little later the proportion of Catholic and Protestant members of the Governor's Council leans toward the Catholics. It will be noted below that three of Ger(r)ard's sons-in-law were leaders of the 1689 Protestant Rebellion.

39. Rightmyer, *Maryland's Established Church*, p. 7, and Petrie, *Church and State in Early Md.*, passim.

40. A good deal has been written on capital-letter Puritanism in the early years, and printed and unprinted county records include much more. John B. Boddie, *Seventeenth Century Isle of Wight County, Virginia* (Chicago, 1938) has much on Isle of Wight and Nansemond County Puritans. Useful are David R. Randall, *A Puritan Colony in Maryland* (Baltimore, 1886); Brydon, *Virginia's Mother Church*, I; George B. Scriven, "Religious Affiliation in Seventeenth Century Maryland," *HMPEC*, XXV (1956), 220–229; and above all Levy, *Early Puritanism in the Southern Colonies*, though she makes no distinction between puritans and Puritans, always using the capital *P*.

41. Levy, *Early Puritanism in the Southern Colonies*, p. 108.

42. *Ibid.*, p. 123.

43. *Ibid.*, p. 126. There is a curious newspaper or periodical (now in the Va. Hist. Soc.) item by strong Anglican Peter Heylyn (*Mercurius Aulicus . . . The 35 Weeks ending Aug. 31, 1644*, p. 1136, etc.) which accuses Sir Francis Wyatt of having "covenanted" with the Puritans in Virginia against the royal governor. Wyatt had immediately preceded Berkeley in 1639–1641 in a second term as governor and had always been at least mildly puritan. It is alleged that Wyatt led a rebellion which was at first successful but finally was put down. In other words, Wyatt was accused of being leader in a movement which almost aligned Virginia with the British Commonwealth in 1641–1642. This story was written two days before Wyatt was buried at

Boxley in Kent in 1644. How much truth is in the charge is unknown, but certainly many of Wyatt's kin took the Puritan side during the wars (see Richard B. Davis, *George Sandys, Poet-Adventurer* [London and New York, 1955], passim), his widow was a friend of Richard Baxter, and his manuscript writings reveal a kind of piety which may have been at least puritan (see Earl of Romney, Wyatt MSS, Deposit, BM). Actually Peter Heylyn wrote for the journal as a royalist propagandist (see "Peter Heylyn," *DNB*).

44. Levy, *Early Puritanism in the Southern Colonies*, pp. 126–130. See various printed records of General Court and Council and House of Burgesses, and Ronald Bayne, "Thomas Harrison, D.D." in *DNB*, who states that Harrison was Berkeley's chaplain and gives much more on his brilliant subsequent career (until 1662). John Cotton in "The Way of Congregational Churches Cleared" [1646] (in Larzer Ziff, ed., *John Cotton on the Churches of New England* [Cambridge, Mass., 1968], p. 272) does claim that the "missionaries" sent from New England "mightily stirred" Harrison to their way of thinking, which of course suggests he was before then an orthodox Anglican. Harrison did not die until 1682.

45. *Virginia and Maryland, Or, The Lord Baltamore's printed Case, uncased and answered* (London, 1655; reprinted in Force, *Tracts*, II, no. 9), pp. 28–29.

46. Levy, *Early Puritanism in the Southern Colonies*, p. 133. This estimate is based on various surviving papers. Not all the settlers were from *southeastern* Virginia, See also Randall; *Puritan Colony in Md.*

47. For these men, especially Doughty, see Levy, *Early Puritanism in the Southern Colonies*, pp. 139–149. Of course Nathaniel Eaton was a sort of renegade Puritan.

48. Some other short titles (the full titles being more revealing of content but well nigh interminable) of contemporary contributions to this and related conflicts are *The Lord Baltemore's Case* (London, 1653); the answer to it, *Virginia and Maryland, Or . . .* (London, 1655); [Roger Heamans], *An Additional brief Narrative Of a late Bloody Design Against the Protestants in Ann Arundel County, and Severn* (London, 1655); John Hammond, *Hammond versus Heamans, Or, an Answer* (London, [c. 1656]); Lionel Gatford, *Publick Good Without Private Interest* (London, 1657), strongly Anglican, and more concerning Virginia than Maryland; Francis Howgill, *The Deceiver of the Nations Discovered* (London, 1660), by a successively Anglican-Independent-Anabaptist-Quaker clergyman, and showing intolerance of the Quakers in Maryland. These are noted here rather than in the next chapter because they seem to be concerned usually more with church polity than doctrine or conversion. It perhaps cannot be emphasized too much that distinction between noncomformists and Low-Churchmen, between puritans and Puritans, was rarely absolute in the South any more than it was in old England in the seventeenth century. Almost surely many Low-Church Anglicans were a part of this rebellion as they certainly were leaders in the later 1689 Protestant Rebellion in Maryland.

49. Bruce E. Steiner, "The Catholic Brents of Colonial Virginia: An Instance of Practical Toleration," *VMHB*, LXX (1962), 387–409; and *William Fitzhugh*, ed. Davis, passim.

50. For Quakerism in all the southern colonies, see Levy, *Early Puritanism in the Southern Colonies*, chapters on Virginia and Maryland; Jones, *Quakers in the American Colonies*; Brydon, *Virginia's Mother Church*, I; Sweet, *Religion in Colonial America*, esp. pp. 153–166. Levy's book is somewhat confusing because she uses the terms *Puritan* and *Puritanism* to cover so many varieties of Protestant dissent.

51. For records of the treatment of Quakers, see McIlwaine, ed., *Minutes Council and Gen. Court Col. Va.*, pp. 353–354, 413–414, 415–416; Kenneth L. Carroll, "Quakerism on the Eastern Shore of Virginia," *VMHB*, LXXIV (1966), 170–189.

52. Levy, *Early Puritanism in the Southern Colonies*, pp. 155–156; Boddie, *Seventeenth Century Isle of Wight*, Ch. VIII, "The Quakers," pp. 111–123. See also the records of Monthly and Yearly Meetings from the mid-seventeenth century until past the Revolution in the Va. St. Lib. The Meetings were held at Chuckatuck, Nansemond, Henrico, Isle of Wight, Blackwater (Surry County), and many other places, including some later ones north of the James. See also John Burnyeat, *The Truth Exalted in the Writings of That Eminent and Faithful Servant of Christ John Burnyeat* (London, 1691); George Rofe, *A True Believer's Testimony of the Work of True Faith* ... (London, 1661) [done in Maryland and Virginia]; George Fox, *The Journal of* (Cambridge, 1911); William Edmundson, *A Journal of the Life, Sufferings, and Labour of Love in the Work of the Ministry* (London, 1715); Thomas Story, *A Journal of the Life of Thomas Story: Containing an Account of his Remarkable Convincement ... and also of his Travels and Labours in the service of the Gospel* ... (Newcastle-upon-Tyne, 1747, and later eds.); Kenneth L. Carroll, "Maryland Quakers in the Seventeenth Century," *MdHM*, XLII (1952), 297–313; Delmar L. Thornbury, "The Society of Friends in Maryland," *MdHM*, XXIX (1934), 101–115.

53. The colonial records of both colonies have many references to Presbyterians before 1700. General histories are Thompson, *Presbyterians in the South*, I; Briggs, *American Presbyterianism*; Trinterud, *Forming an American Tradition*; Sweet, *Religion in Colonial America*; and J.H. Gardner, Jr., "Beginnings of the Presbyterian Church in the Southern Colonies," *JPHS*, XXXIV, (1956), 36–52. For Virginia, see Foote, *Sketches of Virginia*, 1st ser.; Brydon, *Virginia's Mother Church*, I; A.B. Altanfather, "Early Presbyterianism in Virginia," *JPHS*, XIII (1929), 267–281. For North Carolina, see Foote, *Sketches of North Carolina*, ed. Dudley; and bibliography in Thompson, *Presbyterians in the South*, I, pp. 597–608.

54. Leon Hühner, "The Jew in Virginia from the Earliest Times to the Close of the Eighteenth Century," in *Jews in America in Colonial and Revolutionary Times*, pp. 189–194.

55. Levy, *Early Puritanism in the South*, pp. 224–226; Holloway, *Heavens*

on Earth, pp. 32 ff.; and James, *Labadist Colony in Maryland*. Their first appearance in Maryland was about 1679.

56. Michael G. Kammen, "The Causes of the Maryland Revolution of 1689," *MdHM, LV* (1960), 293–333. For its Virginia repercussions, see *William Fitzhugh*, ed. Davis, passim, and Fairfax Harrison, "Parson Waugh's Tumult," in his *Landmarks of Old Prince William* (rev. ed., Berryville, Va., 1964), pp. 127–142.

57. Kammen, "Causes," pp. 321–322: Rightmyer, *Maryland's Established Church*, pp. 10–13, 173–176; *Archives of Md., V*, 111–116; 330, 332; LI, 243; VIII, 159; VII, 135–38, etc.; Newton D. Mereness, "John Coode" in *DAB*; and various histories including Charles A. Barker, *Background of the Revolution in Maryland* (New Haven, 1940). Rightmyer's sketch (pp. 173–176) discusses *in extenso* Coode's alleged Angican ordination and proves that he was indeed in Holy Orders. Mereness presents a largely unfavorable picture. Kammen seems judiciously balanced. A recent Columbia dissertation on Coode is said by Kammen to present its subject in a most favorable light.

58. Parker, ed., *North Carolina: Charters and Constitutions*, pp. 74–89, esp. p. 77, and Locke's "Fundamental Constitutions," *1668*, pp. 128–140.

59. Locke, "Fundamental Constitutions," p. 202. This, it turned out, did not mean formal establishment as in Virginia. For the Anglican did not become the *legal* church of North Carolina until 1701. See Weeks, *Religious Development of North Carolina*, pp. 1–12, and Spencer Ervin, "The Anglican Church in North Carolina," *HMPEC, XXV* (1956), 102–161.

60. Weeks, *Religious Development of North Carolina*, p. 20, shows that Roger Green, "Clarke," was granted permission by the Virginia House of Burgesses in 1653 to settle in what is today Bertie County, N.C. Weeks argues that *Clarke* was a term never used in referring to a dissenting clergyman, only Anglican. He finds no evidence that Green exercised any ministerial function.

61. *Ibid.*, 32–33.

62. For the religious history of South Carolina see, among others, Wallace, *Hist. of S.C.*, I, passim; Dalcho, *Hist. Acc. Prot. Epis. Ch. in S.C.*; Howe, *Hist. Presby. Ch. in S.C.*, 2 vols.; Edward McCrady, *The History of South Carolina under the Proprietary Government, 1670–1719* (New York, 1897), and *The History of South Carolina under the Royal Government* (New York, 1899); Hirsch, *The Huguenots of South Carolina*; Elzas, *The Jews of S.C.*; *Carolina Chronicle: The Papers of Commissary Gideon Johnston, 1707–1716*, ed. Frank J. Klingberg (Berkeley, 1946), and *The Carolina Chronicle of Dr. Francis LeJau, 1706–1777* (Berkeley, 1956), ed. Frank J. Klingberg; Alexander Hewatt, *An Historical Account of the Rise and Progress of South Carolina and Georgia* (2 vols., London, 1779); Carroll, ed., *Hist. Collections of S.C.*; Townsend, *S.C. Baptists*; Bernheim, *Hist. of German Settlements and Lutheran Church in N. and S.C.*. See also various denominational historical journals, the *SCHGM*, and the various colonial records of South Carolina edited by A.S. Salley, J.H. Easterby, et al., cited in these notes.

63. Dalcho, *Hist. Acct. Prot. Epis. Ch. in S.C.*, p. 26; Howe, *Hist. Presby. Ch. in S.C.*, p. 70.

64. Howe, *Hist. Presby. Ch. in S.C.*, pp. 70–126. Townsend, *S.C. Baptists*, thinks this date early.

65. Wallace, *History of S.C.*, I, 149.

66. Howe, *Hist. Presby. Ch. in S.C.*, pp. 126–127. Elzas, *The Jews of S.C.*, asserts that there were Jews in Charleston by 1695.

67. Scriven, "Religious Affiliation in Seventeenth Century Maryland," p. 229.

68. P. 69. Much of what here follows, especilay concerning Virginia in the earlier years, may be found in greater detail in Richard B. Davis, "The Devil in Virginia in the Seventeenth Century," *VMHB*, LXV (1957), 131–149.

69. "Observations," in Lyon G. Tyler, ed., *Narratives of Early Virginia, 1606–1625* (New York, 1907), p. 6. See Davis, "The Devil in Va.," pp. 132–133.

70. Letter of Aug. 9, 1611, in Brown, ed., *Genesis*, I, 498–499, and letter of July 28, 1612, in *Good Newes from Virginia*, p. 24. A century later John Lawson, in a less credulous fashion, goes to great lengths to describe the "Conjurations" of North Carolina Indians (*A New Voyage to Carolina*, ed. Hugh T. Lefler [Chapel Hill, 1967]), passim.

71. George L. Kittredge, *Witchcraft in Old and New England* (Cambridge, Mass., 1929), p. 363.

72. Its earlier and shorter form was *Philosophical Considerations Concerning Witchcraft* (1666). For Perkins, see *The Works of* (1618 ed.), III, 607–652.

73. See Davis, "The Devil in Va.," pp. 138–141.

74. McIlwaine, ed., *Minutes Council and Gen. Court Col. Va.*, p. 476.

75. *Archives of Md.*, III, 306–307. See also Francis H. Parke, *Witchcraft in Maryland* (n.p., 1937, an enlargement of an essay in *MdHM*), pp. 1–4. British records indicate that many alleged British witches were accused of bringing storms upon ships in the North Sea or other coastal waters. See Davis, "The Devil in Va.," p. 142.

76. McIlwaine, ed., *Minutes Council and Gen. Court Col. Va.*, p. 504. Only the summarizing notes of Conway Robinson remain as evidence.

77. E.D. Neill, *The Founders of Maryland* (Albany, 1876), pp. 137–140. This is a record of a Westmoreland County, Va., court, just across the Potomac from Maryland. Washington seems to have been a passenger on the ship and Prescott its owner. For the documents, see Parke, *Witchcraft in Md.*, pp. 6–8.

78. McIlwaine, ed., *Minutes Council and Gen. Court Col. Va.*, p. 504. No other information exists.

79. In MS. "Acts of Grand Assemblie holden of James Cittie," Jefferson Collection, LC; also in Hening, ed., *Statutes*, II, 166–167; and G.L. Chumbley, *Colonial Justice in Virginia* (Richmond, 1938), pp. 129–130.

80. Hopkins was himself hanged as a witch in 1647.

81. Louis D. Scisco, "The First Church in Charles County," *MdHM*, XXIII (1928), 155–162, and *Archives of Md.*, LX, xxix–xxx.

82. *Archives of Md.*, XLIX, 486, 508.

83. *WMQ* (1), III (1895), 163–166; I (1893), 70; *Lower Norfolk County Antiquary*, I (1895–1896), 20–21, 56–57; Bruce, *Inst. Hist. Va.*, I, 284; Essex County Orders, etc., 1692–1695, pp. 240, 246–247 (in VSL).

84. The best collection of records of this case are in George L. Burr, ed., *Narratives of the Witchcraft Cases, 1648–1706* (New York, 1914), pp. 435–442. See also *WMQ* (1), III (1895), 99–100, 190–192, 242–245; and Davis, "The Devil in Va.," pp. 146–147.

85. Wright, *The First Gentlemen of Virginia*, p. 181, and *William Fitzhugh*, ed. Davis, p. 177 (letter of April 22, 1686).

86. Parke, *Witchcraft in Md.*, pp. 9–10; *Archives of Md.*, Proceedings of the Assembly, 1666–1676, II, 425–426.

87. Parke, *Witchcraft in Md.*, pp. 35–37.

88. *Ibid.*, pp. 33–35. Parke locates the various accused as to counties.

89. Tom Peete Cross, "Witchcraft in North Carolina," *SP*, XVI (1919), 217–287, gives an entertaining account of Anglo-American witchcraft in general. He records a great many survivals of folk beliefs regarding witches and conjuring in the nineteenth and early twentieth centuries in North Carolina, but almost nothing from the legal records of the colonial period.

90. For Ann _____ vs. Sarah _____, *NCHGR*, II (1901), 207. The writer intentionally omitted the names, he tells us. For Susannah Evans, *NCHGR*, III (1903), 57–58, 68–69; for Martha Richardson, *NCHGR*, III (1903), 56–57. For the jury, Jesse F. Pugh, "The Genial Mariner, Captain Cornelius Jones," in *Three Hundred Years along the Pasquotank, A Biographical History of Camden County* (Old Trap, N.C., 1957), 15–18. See also *Col. Rec. N.C.*, 2nd ser., IV, ed. Wm. S. Price, Jr. (Raleigh, 1974), 66, 70, 96.

91. P. 167; also Lefler, ed., 1967, p. 169, mentions "murder" and "witch" in the same breath, but the implication of execution is doubtful.

92. Wallace, *History of S.C.*, I, 177.

93. See *The Carolina Chronicle of Dr. Francis LeJau*, ed. Klingberg; Arthur H. Hirsch, "Reverend Francis LeJau, First Rector of St. James Church, Goose Creek, S.C.," *Huguenot Society of South Carolina Transactions*, XXXIV (1929), 25–29; Edgar L. Pennington, "The Reverend Francis LeJau's Work among the Indians and Negro Slaves," *JSH*, I (1935), 442–458.

94. *The Carolina Chronicle of LeJau*, ed. Klingberg, pp. 25, 30.

95. See T.D. Jervey, "Nicholas Trott," in *DAB*; A.S. Salley, "Judge Nicholas Trott," *The State* (Columbia), March 18, 1923; J.N. Heyward, *Nicholas Trott, Attorney General, Chief Justice of the Court of Common Pleas . . .* (n.p., n.d., in University South Caroliniana Lib.); Wallace, *History of S.C.*, I, 176–177.

96. *History of S.C.*, I, 177.

97. "Eight Charges," Charleston Library Society, page numbers obliterated. These appear, with an excellent introduction and notes, in L. Lynn Hogue, ed., "An Edition of 'Eight Charges Delivered, at So Many Several General Sessions, & Gaol Deliveries: Held at Charles Town . . .'" (Ph.D. diss., Univ. of Tennessee, 1972). Hogue has recently published on Trott.

98. Kittredge, *Witchcraft in Old and New England*, pp. 367–372.

99. Bridenbaugh's *Mitre and Sceptre* and Cross's *The Anglican Episcopate* are the two principal books. Bridenbaugh's 1962 study is an avowed attempt to reexamine all aspects of the question. It almost ignores the southern colonies, for it really is concerned with the socio-politico-religious effects on the northeastern and middle colonies, particularly as a strong factor leading to the desire for independence. For a review pointing out some of its many inadequacies see *AQ*, XV (1963), 592–593, by Percy G. Adams. Far better balanced is Cross's 1902 (rev. 1924) book. Most useful are the files of the S.P.G. in London (copies of most but not all are in the LC) and various documents (including unpublished letters) in Virginia and Maryland repositories. Phases of the question are discussed in Hugh Jones, *The Present State of Virginia* (1724), and Hartwell, Blair, and Chilton, *The Present State of Virginia and the College* (1727). See also Brydon, *Virginia's Mother Church*, I and II, passim; Rightmyer, *Maryland's Established Church*, pp. 172, etc.; Perry, ed., *Historical Collections*, I and IV, passim; Morton, *Colonial Virginia*, II, 820–821; Spencer Ervin, "The Established Church in Colonial Maryland," *HMPEC*, XXIV (1955), 262–263; R.L. Hilldrup, "The Need of a Bishop in Virginia in 1706 as Seen by a Layman: A Letter of Graham Frank to Thomas Sherlock, Bishop of London," *HMPEC*, XXVI (1957), 165–172.

100. Cross, *The Anglican Episcopate*, pp. 8 ff. Laud in 1638 made arrangements to send a bishop to New England to combat and control the nonconformists, but the outbreak of troubles at home thwarted his design.

101. *Ibid.*, p. 23, and Sainsbury, ed., *Cal. St. Papers, Col., 1661–1668*, pp. 400–401.

102. Bodleian Tanner MSS 114, f. 79; and *Archives of Md.*, V, 130–132.

103. For several possible reasons for this division of functions, see Cross, *The Anglican Episcopate*, pp. 4–5.

104. Brydon (*Virginia's Mother Church*, I, 57, 232) says also the "greatest," with Commissary Bray of Maryland. I am not even sure he was among the ablest, considering at least two South Carolina commissaries. Certainly he was the craftiest, the least scrupulous. For a recent balanced account of Blair, see Park Rouse, Jr., *James Blair of Virginia* (Chapel Hill, 1971).

105. See Rightmyer, *Maryland's Established Church*, pp. 37 ff., 165, etc., and Bernard C. Steiner, *The Reverend Thomas Bray: His Life and Selected Works Relating to Maryland* (Baltimore, 1901).

106. *Archives of Md.*, XXII, 255, November, 1698; Rightmyer, *Maryland's Established Church*, p. 38.

107. See note 99 above and general bibliography for this chapter.

108. London, 1662, reprinted in Force, *Tracts*, III, no. 15, 19 pp., dedicated to the Bishop of London. See also Brydon, *Virginia's Mother Church*, I, 100–101.

109. P. 18.

110. Copies of the charter are in All Souls College, Oxford, and the Bodleian (Tanner MSS), in Latin. The charter is translated into English in *VMHB*, XXXVI (1928), 45–53. Cross (*The Anglican Episcopate*, p. 90) mistakenly says the man was ready to be sent from England.

111. *WMQ* (2), II (1922), 157–161; Royal Society MSS M. 1. 36a, dates February 1, 1665, and June 12, 1668, from Ware River, Mock-Jack Bay.

112. The original announcement and requests for information and Moray's petition survive in BM MSS Harleian 3790, ff. 1–4.

113. Perry, ed., *Historical Collections*, I, 31. See also (Ch. VI below) [Morgan Godwyn's] *Some Proposals Toward the Propagation of the Gospel in Our American Plantations* (London, 1708, written twenty years earlier), the publication of a twenty-year-old tract by an editor interested in seeing that bishoprics are set up in America.

114. S.P.G. "A" Books, Vol. VII, p. 105.

115. Cross, *The Anglican Episcopate*, pp. 91–92. Hunter earlier hoped to be lieutenant-governor of Virginia. When he became governor of New York he wrote Swift that the land (at Burlington, N.J.?) had been bought for a bishop's seat in his new province. Here the matter seems to have ended. Brydon (*Virginia's Mother Church*, II, 59), curiously, says that not one word was uttered in Virginia in favor of a bishopric between 1701 and 1776. He simply had not noticed the evidence. See in text immediately below, though Jones' plea may actually have been written in England, a mere technicality in this situation.

116. Ed. Morton, 127. See also Morton's own comments, pp. 25, 26, 256 in this edition. Morton indicates (p. 26) that seventeen years later Jones had changed his mind on this subject.

117. R.L. Hilldrup, "Need of a Bishop in Va. in 1756," *HMPEC*, XXVI (1957), 165–172. The MS is in P.R.O., H.C.A. 30/258, Bundles of Intercepted Letters. Brydon clearly did not see this letter and had overlooked the Hugh Jones plea.

118. Rightmyer, *Maryland's Established Church*, pp. 39–41. Bray MSS, Sion College, London. The date actually may be after Bray's visit to Maryland.

119. A little later, in 1703, a committee of the society formulated a statement, "The Case of Suffragan Bishops briefly proposed," and referred it to the attorney-general without result (Cross, *The Anglican Episcopate*, pp. 100–101). Rightmyer (*Maryland's Established Church*, pp. 38–39) thinks a coalition of Low-Church Whig politicians and dissenters prevented Bray's consecration. The society took other steps toward having a bishop settle in America.

120. Whether the bishopric was requested for a particular colony, a group of colonies, or the whole of British America has not usually been differentiated in this chapter for two reasons: 1) it is generally not at all clear from the request as to what the prospective bishop's jurisdiction should be, and 2) the problem of concern here is primarily that of bishopric or no bishopric in America, for part or for whole makes not too much difference. If it had ever come down to the actual appointment of a bishop in one colony and not in or for another, there would have been special problems it is useless to consider here.

121. Rightmyer, *Maryland's Established Church*, pp. 79–81, 172; Cross, *The Anglican Episcopate*, p. 105; Perry, ed., *Historical Collections*, IV, 128, 231–232, 244–246. Bordley stated to the S.P.G. in 1725 that though the

colonies wanted a bishop, they did not want Henderson, who was "turbulent and haughty" (Perry, ed., *Historical Collections*, IV, 253). A letter of Wilkinson to the Bishop of London on September 9, 1724 observes that he understands that two bishoprics are planned for America, one in the "Western Islands" and the other in Virginia. He suggests that Maryland is more central than Virginia (Perry, ed., *Historical Collections*, IV, 245).

122. Rightmyer, *Maryland's Established Church*, p. 84.

123. *Ibid.*, p. 84.

124. The Bishop's letter of May 11, Doddridge's of May 14. Perry, ed., *Historical Collections*, I, 373, 375.

125. For the last colonial attempt at a bishopric for Virginia see Brydon's "James Horrocks and the American Episcopate" in his *Virginia's Mother Church*, II, 341–364. Brydon draws the distinctions between what the appointment of a bishop for any southern colony as opposed to a northern colony would have made for clergy and people. This is another evidence that Bridenbaugh's posed situation in *Mitre and Sceptre* simply has little or no relevance for the southern colonies.

126. For the history of the S.P.G., see Humphry, *Hist. Account of the S.P.G.*; Pascoe, *Two Hundred Years of the S.P.G.*; Thompson, *Into All Lands*; Cross, *The Anglican Episcopate*; Brydon, *Virginia's Mother Church*, esp. I, 216–221; Rightmyer, *Maryland's Established Church*; Bridenbaugh, *Mitre and Sceptre*; both works edited by Klingberg as *Carolina Chronicle . . .*; Perry, ed., *Historical Collections*, IV.

The manuscript records of the correspondence and reports of missionaries in the S.P.G. Lib. in London are of enormous value. Copies of most but not all are in the LC. The Fulham Palace Papers are now housed in the Lambeth Palace Lib. The correspondence of both the archbishop and the bishop is frequently with the S.P.G. For Bray, see Steiner, *Thomas Bray*, and the Bray manuscripts in the Sion College Lib.

127. Edgar L. Pennington, "Dr. Thomas Bray's Associates and Their Work among the Negroes," *PAAS*, n.s. XLVIII (1938), 311–403.

128. Apparently in the first decade of the century some S.P.G. missionaries were in Maryland, and that province, through its direct connection with Dr. Bray, received a good deal of help from the organization.

129. The S.P.G. apparently handled the S.P.C.K.'s distribution of books and did a good deal of distribution on and of its own. For Dr. Bray's plan and establishment of libraries, see Ch. IV. Much of the correspondence to the S.P.G. and the Bishop of London includes pleas for copies of the Book of Common Prayer, the Bible, the Psalter, *The Whole Duty of Man*, and Tillotson's *Sermons*, as well as other works aimed at controverting desim, Presbyterianism, etc.

130. Though theoretically there was considerable difference between the two, it is difficult to distinguish them in the colonies. In Maryland, for example, the clergy usually gathered at visitations and did just what the Virginians did in conventions. See Perry, ed., *Historical Collections*, I and IV.

131. *Ibid.*, ed., I and IV, passim.

132. The whole matter is not as simple as this, but this seems the basis of the conflict. Blair was jealous of the prerogatives of all governors, as noted. He wanted to rule the colony, and when he found he could not under Andros, Nicholson, and Spotswood, he managed to get rid of them. Gooch, though he never trusted Blair, made it a point to get along with the commissary in the latter's old age. One gathers that at times Blair was in favor of a bishopric, perhaps when he thought he had a good chance of securing the position. As to induction, even so pious a churchman as Nicholson had been loath to carry it out against the wishes of a vestry. He knew he would stir a hornet's nest if he did so.

133. The librarian of Lambeth Palace writes that he finds no replies from North Carolina in 1724.

134. Rightmyer, *Maryland's Established Church*, pp. 61–63; *Archives of Md.*, XXIX, 361–363; Perry, ed., *Historical Collections*, IV, 74 ff., 196–233. For another set of somewhat differing questions see Rightmyer, pp. 65–68 and Perry, IV, 88 ff., 96 ff., 131 ff., 190 ff.

135. Maryland and Virginia were prosperous enough, as noted above, to attract S.P.G. missionaries who became parish priests. Therefore this plea of inadequate salaries cannot be accepted at face value for most parishes.

136. Brydon, *Virginia's Mother Church*, I, 517–534, from P.R.O., C.O. 5/1314, Pt. 2, 63. Northey's opinion appears in Perry, ed., *Historical Collections*, I, 127–128.

137. The questions propounded seem to have been the first action for the colonies on the part of Edmund Gibson when he became Bishop of London in 1723. See Fulham Palace Papers, IX, ff. 160–167, 169–170, etc., Lambeth Palace Lib.; Perry, ed., *Historical Collections*, I, 261–334, and IV, 180–232. Mr. E.G.W. Bill, librarian at Lambeth, has rechecked the South Carolina replies for me (May 3, 1968). For analysis of the Virginia reports, see Brydon, *Virginia's Mother Church*, I, 374–391.

138. See Ch. III, on Education. At least the Maryland clergy put more emphasis on the secondary schools.

139. *Virginia's Mother Church*, II, 55. Before the end of Gooch's administration in the late 1740s all parishes seem to have had clergy.

140. Governor Drysdale's 1726 accurate list of parishes shows fifty-three. Between 1724 and 1726 a few had been dissolved or divided. Brydon (*Virginia's Mother Church*, I, 375) calculates that fifty-one was probably the number in 1724.

141. Apparently some parishes willing to induct in 1704 had done so since that time.

142. Ed. Morton. Morton's notes and introduction are most useful. Also he differentiates among the three Hugh Joneses, who have been confused in Chesapeake Bay ecclesiastical history.

143. In 1719. See above.

144. A sort of textbook. Two other books he mentions having written, on Christianity and on mathematics, are not known to have been published.

145. P. 127.

146. E.g., Henry Cabot Lodge, *A Short History of the English Colonies in America* (rev. ed., New York, 1881), pp. 54, etc.

147. "A True Account of a Conference at Lambeth, Dec. 27, 1697," in Perry, ed., *Historical Collections*, I, 36–65. The Archbishop of Canterbury, the Bishop of London, Commissary Blair, John Povey, William Byrd II, Richard Marshall, and Benjamin Harrison, Jr., were attempting to straighten out ecclesiastical affairs in Virginia. Sir Edmund Andros had been accused by Blair of many illegal procedures regarding the church during his governorship.

148. *Old Churches*, I, 167.

149. For Urmstone, see Rightmyer, *Maryland's Established Church*, p. 216; and Stephen B. Weeks, *Church and State in North Carolina, 1711–1776,* (Baltimore, 1893) p. 16.

150. See Rouse, *James Blair of Virginia*; Samuel R. Mohler, "Commissary James Blair, Churchman, Educator, and Politician of Colonial Virginia" (Ph.D. diss., Univ. of Illinois, 1944); Meade, *Old Churches*, I, 154–156, 157–165 (a sympathetic view); Edgar L. Pennington, *Commissary Blair*, Soldier and Servant Ser. (Hartford, Conn., 1936); Perry, ed., *Historical Collections*, I, passim; Brydon, *Virginia's Mother Church*, I, 273–326 (the ablest account); Earl G. Swem, "James Blair," in *DAB*; Morton, *Colonial Virginia*, passim. Blair was born in Scotland *c.* 1656 and died in Virginia in 1743. For his work in founding the College of William and Mary, see Ch. III. Rouse's study above is a good first step in assessing Blair, but it is not sufficiently detailed to be comprehensive.

151. *Virginia's Mother Church*, I, 273.

152. *Ibid.*, I, 275.

153. Dalcho, *Hist. Acct. Prot. Epis. Ch. in S.C.*, pp. 77 ff. For more detail see Klingberg, ed., *Carolina Chronicle: Papers of Gideon Johnston.*

154. *Carolina Chronicle: Papers of Gideon Johnston*, p. 16.

155. Dalcho, *Hist. Acct. Prot. Epis. Ch. in S.C.*, pp. 98, 168–171, 176, etc.; Cross, *The Anglican Episcopate*, p. 80; Edgar L. Pennington, "The Reverend Alexander Garden," *HMPEC*, III (1934), 48–55; Quentin Begley, "The Problems of a Commissary: The Reverend Alexander Garden of South Carolina," *HMPEC*, XX (1951), 136–155.

156. For Indians, see Chapter II; for Negroes, below in the present chapter.

157. Saunders, ed., *Col. Rec. N.C.*, II, 125–128.

158. Richard B. Davis, ed., "A Virginia Colonial Frontier Parish's 'Poor' Petition for a Priest," *HMPEC*, XXXV (1966), 87–98.

159. Printed from S.P.G. MSS, III, February 1, 1716/17, No. 28, p. 229, in *Carolina Chronicle: Papers of Gideon Johnston*, ed. Klingberg, pp. 163–164.

160. *The Poems of Charles Hansford*, eds. James A. Servies and Carl R. Dolmetsch (Chapel Hill, 1961), pp. ix–xix. In one poem, "My Country's Worth," Hansford celebrates "The gentry of Virginia," of whom he claims he is not one because of his "low place and station/Tied down to labor, education wanting." (p. 57).

161. The best brief study of the subject is Mary G. Goodwin, "Christianizing and Educating the Negro in Colonial Virginia," *HMPEC*, I (1932), 143–

152. Also see J.B. Lawrence, "Christianizing the Negro in the Colony of Georgia," *GaHQ*, XIV (1930), 41–57; Perry, ed., *Historical Collections*, I and IV, passim; Wallace, *History of S.C.*, I, passim; Brydon, *Virginia's Mother Church*, I and II, passim; Klingberg, ed., both his works called *Carolina Chronicle . . .*; Foote, *Sketches of Virginia*, 1st ser., passim; Jones, *The Present State of Virginia*, ed. Morton, pp. 99, 105, 116, 229, 230; Thompson, *Presbyterians in the South, I*, passim; Lefler and Newsome, *The History of a Southern State: North Carolina*, pp. 117–118, 124; Sirmans, *Colonial South Carolina*, pp. 14, 99, 142; Frank J. Klingberg, *An Appraisal of the Negro in Colonial South Carolina: A Study in Americanization* (Washington, D.C., 1941), passim; Edgar W. Knight, ed., *A Documentary History of Education in the South before 1860*, I (Chapel Hill, 1949), 62, 90–97, 114–115, 205. Most suggestive is Winthrop D. Jordan, *White over Black: American Attitudes toward the Negro, 1550–1812* (Chapel Hill, 1968), passim, esp. e.g., pp. 210–211.

For Quaker work in instruction and conversion there is a little in the journals of Burnyeat, Edmundson, and Woolman; in Jones, *The Quakers in the American Colonies*, under Slavery; in Henry J. Cadbury, "Negro Membership in the Society of Friends," *JNH*, XXI (1936), 151–213; in Levy, *Early Puritanism in the Southern Colonies*, passim; and a very little in Zora Klain, *Quaker Contributions to Education in North Carolina* (Philadelphia, 1925).

162. Goodwin, "Christianizing and Educating the Negro," pp. 143–145.

163. Parker, ed., *North Carolina: Charters and Constitutions*, pp. 150, 164, 229, 239.

164. *William Fitzhugh*, ed. Davis.

165. Brydon, *Virginia's Mother Church*, I, 187. Godwyn's *A Supplement to the Negro's & Indians Advocate* (London, 1681) was directed particularly to owners of slaves in the West Indies, but he included the southern colonies too. Godwyn challenges many evidently voiced objections. *Some Proposals* is on the same subject. In 1685 he published a sermon he had preached at Westminster Abbey on "Trade preferr'd before Religion and Christ," another blast at the plantations.

166. The letter is reprinted in full in Brydon, *Virginia's Mother Church*, I, 511–516 (original 1680 ed., pp. 167–172). Deputy governor Moryson of Virginia called the letter "a virulent libel."

167. Perry, ed., *Historical Collections*, I, 277–361.

168. *Ibid.*, IV, 292–307. Ten thousand copies of the 1727 Pastoral Letter of the Bishop of London had been distributed by the S.P.G. See Dalcho, *Hist. Acct. Prot. Epis. Ch. in S.C.*, pp. 103–114.

169. This school lasted for fourteen years under the devoted care of Robert Carter Nicholas, treasurer of the colony. Goodwin, "Christianizing and Educating the Negro," pp. 148–149.

170. William P. Harrison, *The Gospel Among the Slaves. A Short Account of the Missionary Operations among the African Slaves of the Southern States* (Nashville, 1893), p. 52. For more on these schools, see Ch. III above and Klingberg, *The Negro in Colonial S.C.*, pp. 101–122, etc.

171. Strickland, *Religion and State in Georgia*, pp. 130–131; Lawrence, "Religious Education of the Negro in the Colony of Georgia," pp. 49–57.

172. *Carolina Chronicle of LeJau*, ed. Klingberg, pp. 8, 149.

173. *Carolina Chronicle: Papers of Gideon Johnston*, ed. Klingberg, p. 123, and Klingberg, *The Negro in Colonial S.C.*, pp. 6–7.

174. See Ch. VI for these sermons.

175. *The Secret Diary of William Byrd of Westover, 1709–1712*, ed. Louis B. Wright and Marion Tinling (Richmond, 1941), p. 202, entry for July 9, 1710.

176. *Journal and Letters of Philip Vickers Fithian, 1773–1774*, ed. H.D. Farish (Williamsburg, 1943), pp. 119, 147, 199.

177. *The Journal of John Harrower, an Indentured Servant in the Colony of Virginia, 1773–1776*, ed. E.M. Riley (Williamsburg, 1963; New York, 1963), pp. xviii, 48, 124.

178. *The Diary of Landon Carter of Sabine Hall, 1752–1778*, ed. Jack P. Greene (2 vols., Charlottesville, 1965), II, 941. See also I, 174, 292, 295, 378; II, 925. Carter always sent to church all those inclined to go; the rest he held at work at home to keep them out of mischief.

179. March 1755. Foote, *Sketches of Virginia*, 1st ser., pp. 285–286, 289.

180. *Ibid.*, pp. 172, 220, 284–293, 358–359, 365, etc.

181. Foote, *Sketches of North Carolina*, references to Caldwell, pp. 61, 81, etc.; to Davies, pp. 158, 213, 215, 219, 221 ff. Though Foote in his Virginia volume devotes a good deal of space to Negro conversion, he says almost nothing about it in this North Carolina companion work, certainly for the colonial period.

182. Howe, *Hist. Presby. Ch. in S.C.*, I, 240–241, 244–246. See also Ch. VI below, tracts.

183. Howe, *Hist. Presby. Ch. in S.C.*, I, 248.

184. Thompson, *Presbyterians in the South*, I, 39. This held true generally for Virginia, for after Davies' time the Presbyterians of the Northern Neck and Tidewater gradually dwindled.

185. Jones, *The Quakers in the American Colonies*, pp. 162–163; 321; 327; Levy, *Early Puritanism in the Southern Colonies*, passim; Drake, *The Quakers and Slavery*, passim; Cadbury, "Negro Membership in the Society of Friends," pp. 151–213.

186. *Journal* (London, 1775), pp. 64, 72, etc.

187. "Negro Membership in the Society of Friends," pp. 167, etc. Also in a personal letter from Henry J. Cadbury to the author, May 10, 1969[8].

188. For earlier-eighteenth-century Presbyterianism in the South see Thompson, *Presbyterians in the South*, I; Trinterud, *Forming an American Tradition*; Brydon, *Virginia's Mother Church*, I and II; Foote, *Sketches of Virginia*, 1st ser., and *Sketches of North Carolina*; Howe, *Hist. Presby. Ch. in S.C.*; and Sweet, *Religion in Colonial America*.

189. Howe, *Hist. Presby. Ch. in S.C.*, I, 163; Thompson, *Presbyterians in the South*, I, 32.

190. Also prominent in the Great Awakening controversies a decade later.

For Smith, see Clifford K. Shipton, *Sibley's Harvard Graduates, VII, 1722–1725* (Boston, 1945), 569–585. See Smith's letter of October 12, 1730, quoted in Howe, *Hist. Presby. Ch. in S.C.*, I, 191, and Thompson, *Presbyterians in the South, I*, 35. Howe notes that the records of most of the purely Presbyterian churches have not survived.

191. A good example is H.C. Bradshaw, *History of Prince Edward County, Virginia . . .* (Richmond, 1955), which employs many original documents and rare printed materials.

192. Sweet, *Religion in Colonial America*, pp. 274–275, 281; Brydon, *Virginia's Mother Church*, II, 143, offers evidence that it began as a great movement within the Anglican church (Whitefield and the Wesleys being among its leaders), and of course in a sense this is true. For a concise bibliography of the Great Awakening in the South, see the general bibliography for this chapter above.

193. John Gillies, *Memoirs of the Rev. George Whitefield* (rev. and corrected, Middletown, Conn., 1838); Albert D. Belden, *George Whitefield—the Awakener: A Modern Study of the Evangelical Revival* ([London], 1930); Sprague, ed., *Annals of the American Pulpit*, V, 94–108. For tracts and sermons, see Ch. VI below.

194. Cf. Heimert (*Religion and the American Mind*, p. 36), who states (as though Whitefield had never met Garden before) of a later visit: "Whitefield stormed into Charleston, where he called on Garden and upbraided him for failing to preach against the 'sinful diversions' of the deep-South metropolis." Something remotely resembling this did happen, but only after Garden had given the "arrogant and ignorant" (see below) Whitefield every chance to behave with Anglican decency.

195. Goodwin, "The Anglican Reaction to the Great Awakening," pp. 343–371.

196. *Ibid.*, p. 360.

197. Brydon, *Virginia's Mother Church*, II, 148. Brydon admits this assumption may be based on inconclusive evidence.

198. John Gillies, ed., *Memoirs of the Reverend George Whitefield*. Revised and corrected (Middletown, Conn., 1838), p. 44.

199. Garden's letters are discussed in Ch. VI.

200. *Memoirs*, p. 100; Howe, *Hist. Presby. Ch. in S.C.*, pp. 231, 234–236, etc.; Dalcho, *Hist. Acct. Prot. Epis. Ch. in S.C.*, pp. 128–132. Whitefield protested the court had no jurisdiction, as he was of Georgia. Whitefield, in addition to the violations of church decorum and doctrine mentioned above, had not used the Book of Common Prayer in services. See Garden's point of view in Alexander Garden, *The Doctrine of Justification . . .* (Charleston, 1742), p. 69.

201. In fact, the *Md. Gaz.*, the *Va. Gaz.*, and the *S.C. Gaz.* contain much of the most interesting "literary" material growing out of Whitefield's part in the great revival in America.

202. Howe, *Hist. Presby. Ch. in S.C.*, p. 219, and discussed in Ch. VI below.

203. For the story of Hanover County Presbyterianism and Davies, see

Foote, *Sketches of Virginia*, 1st ser., pp. 119–309; Thompson, *Presbyterians in the South*, I, pp. 52–61; Sweet, *Religion in Colonial America*, pp. 293–301.

204. For the materials on Davies, see the general bibliography for this chapter above; for his sermons, discussion and bibliography, see Ch. VI.

205. See the general bibliography for this chapter above. Some of Davies' and Doddridge's letters are included in Perry, ed., *Historical Collections*, I, passim.

206. See Ch. VI for discussion of these sermons.

207. Yet note the strong Calvinism of his "Charity and Truth United," six letters in 1755 in reply to the sermon "The Nature and Extent of Christ's Redemption" by President Stith of William and Mary. See Ch. VI below.

208. For clear definitions and concise discussions of the meanings of the theological terms *Calvinism, Arminianism, Arianism, Pelagianism, Socinianism,* and *Deism,* see the Introduction to Heimert and Miller, eds., *The Great Awakening*, pp. xiii–xx.

209. As two of their historians put it, the Baptists were the peculiar benefactors of the spiritual movement led by the Presbyterian Tennents. See the Armstrongs, *The Indomitable Baptists*, p. 77.

210 See Gewehr, *Great Awakening in Virginia*, pp. 106 ff.; and Semple, *History of the Baptists in Va.*, passim. Gewehr divides the Awakening in Virginia into Presbyterian, Baptist, and Methodist phases, only the first of which falls in the period before 1764.

211. Smith, Handy, and Loetscher, eds., *American Christianity: I, 1607–1820*, pp. 360–366; Paschal, *Hist. N.C. Baptists, I, 1663–1805*, 204–223.

212. Sweet, *Religion in Colonial America*, pp. 210 ff.

213. Orange County Will Book 1, page 84. For Spotswood's group, men who came to be miners, see William J. Hinke, "The First German Reformed Colony in Virginia: 1714–1750," *JPHS*, II (1903), 1–17, 98–110, 140–150; for an account of their Sunday services, see Brydon, *Virginia's Mother Church*, II, 84. For other Lutheran groups, see William P. Huddle, *History of the Hebron Lutheran Church in Madison County, 1717–1907* (New Market, Va., 1908); Cassell, Finck, and Henkel, *Hist. Lutheran Church in Va. and East Tenn.*; Finck, *Lutheran Landmarks*; Brydon, *Virginia's Mother Church*, II, 78–116, where the various German religious groups in Virginia are distinguished and their history briefly traced.

214. Actually the names Salem and Wachovia were originally those of separate Moravian settlements. See Adelaide L. Fries, "The Moravian Contribution to Colonial North Carolina," *NCHR*, VII (1930), 1–14; Adelaide Fries, *The Road to Salem* (Chapel Hill, 1944), and as ed., *Records of the Moravians in North Carolina*, I (Raleigh, 1922), passim; Edward M. Holder, "Social Life of the Moravians in North Carolina," *NCHR*, XI (1934), 167–184. A number of Moravian missionary diaries have been published in *VMHB*, XI and XII. See also Brydon, *Virginia's Mother Church*, II, 78–116.

215. Lefler and Newsome, *The History of a Southern State*, pp. 78–81, 130–131; Boyd and Krummel, "German Tracts," pp. 79–147, 225–282.

216. See Friedrich, Baron Von Reck and J.M. Bolzius, *An Extract of the*

Journals of Mr. Commissary Von Reck . . . (London, 1734, in Force, *Tracts,* IV, no. 5); the *Urlsperger Tracts, 1735–1740,* Vol. I (printed in Germany c. 1740?; in Univ. of Georgia Lib.); John J. Zubly, *Eine Predigt* and *Eine Leicht-Predig* (Germantown, 1747, 1749). It should be remembered that Zubly was a Swiss and probably a Presbyterian minister who originally came to South Carolina. Recently a number of the German letters and journals of these men have been translated and republished in this country: e.g., *Henry Newman's Salzburger Letterbooks,* trans. and ed. George F. Jones (Athens, Ga., 1966); "John Martin Bolzius Answers a Questionnaire on Carolina and Georgia," trans. and ed. Klaus G. Leowald, Beverly Starika, and Paul S. Taylor, *WMQ* (3), XIV (1957), 218–261; XV (1958), 228–252; G.F. Jones, "John Martin Bolzius Reports on Georgia," *GaHQ,* XLVII (1963), 216–219. See also J.M. Hofer, "The Georgia Salzburgers," *GaHQ,* XVIII (1934), 99–117.

For the Moravians, see Adelaide L. Fries, *The Moravians in Georgia, 1735–1740* (Raleigh, N.C., 1905); William Harden, "The Moravians of Georgia and Pennsylvania as Educators," *GaHQ,* II (1916) 47–56.

217. See Ch. VI below. The names in South Carolina of Hugh Swinton Legaré and Basil Lanneau Gildersleeve, among many others, testify to these men's Huguenot ancestry.

218. Rod W. Horton and Herbert W. Edwards, *Backgrounds of American Literary Thought* (New York, 1952), p. 56, and Herbert M. Morais, *Deism in Eighteenth Century America* (New York, 1934), passim.

219. A.O. Aldridge, *Benjamin Franklin and Nature's God* (Durham, N.C., 1967).

220. For example, Charles Chauncy in Massachusetts, Samuel Quincy in Charleston, James Maury and others in Virginia and Maryland. See Smith, Handy, and Loetscher, eds., *American Christianity,* I, 374–418.

221. Perry, ed., *Historical Collections,* I, 331.

222. *VMHB,* XXXII (1924), 332–333.

223. Text from George M. Brydon, "The Antiecclesiastical Laws of Virginia," *VMHB,* LXIV (1956), 262–263; also in *VMHB,* XXXVI (1928), 376–377.

224. Brydon, "Antiecclesiastical Laws," p. 263.

225. McIlwaine et al., eds., *Journals H.B. Va., 1727–1734, 1736–1740,* pp. 338–339.

CHAPTER SIX: THE SERMON AND THE RELIGIOUS TRACT

BIBLIOGRAPHY

The authors, titles, and dates of most colonial sermons and tracts printed in America may be found in Charles Evans et al., *American Bibliography: A Chronological Dictionary . . . . From . . . 1693 . . . to 1820* (14 vols., Chicago and Worcester, Mass., 1903–1959) and its various supplements, referred to as

Evans. Texts of the Evans items are available on microcard in most major libraries in the monumental collection sponsored by the American Antiquarian Society and edited by Clifford K. Shipton. Most of the items printed in Great Britain are listed in the *Catalogue* of the British Museum.

Whenever possible the original or a photoduplicate copy has been used, and in most instances of rare items the location of the original copy employed is indicated in the note accompanying the title. Especially useful for printed works were the libraries of the Maryland Historical Society, the Virginia Historical Society, the University of North Carolina, the University of South Carolina, the University of Virginia, the Library of Congress, the John Carter Brown Library, the American Antiquarian Society, the State of Virginia, the Library Company of Philadelphia, the General Theological Seminary of New York, Duke University, the Huntington Library, the S.P.G. Library, the British Museum, and Lambeth Palace Library.

A pleasant surprise was the discovery that a considerable number of manuscript sermons of the colonial South are still in existence. The largest collection of these is that of the Maryland Diocesan Library of the Protestant Episcopal Church, now on deposit in the Maryland Historical Society. To these have recently been added approximately one hundred manuscript sermons of the Reverend Thomas Cradock, of which more below. The University of Virginia, Harvard University, the Huntington Library, the Library of Congress, Duke University, and the Maryland Historical Society (in its own files), are among the repositories holding others. A few manuscript tracts exist in the same institutions. By no means all the manuscript or printed sermons in existence have been discussed or even mentioned in the present chapter, though an attempt has been made to refer to some work of every author of sermons or tracts of any significance. Undoubtedly a number have been missed, for though the author has inquired from as many church historical societies as he could locate, as well as from institutions other than those mentioned above and from individuals, he has probably missed several repositories. There is no complete or nearly complete bibliography of American colonial religious literature—that is, of religious writing, and certainly none of southern colonial sermons and tracts. For the present chapter several score sermons and other discourses apparently unknown to religious historians have been unearthed and presented, and in numerous instances where title was known but no copy, a copy has been located.

The general studies of some value were in general the same as those listed for Chapter V. Especially useful in this chapter were W. Fraser Mitchell, *English Pulpit Oratory from Andrewes to Tillotson: A Study of Its Literary Aspects* (New York, 1962); Perry Miller, *The New England Mind: The Seventeenth Century* (New York, 1939) and *The New England Mind: From Colony to Province* (Cambridge, Mass., 1953); Louis B. Wright, *Religion and Empire: The Alliance between Piety and Commerce in English Expansion,*

1585–1625 (Chapel Hill, 1943) and *The First Gentlemen of Virginia* (San Marino, 1940); Rufus M. Jones, *The Quakers in the American Colonies* (new ed., New York, 1962); H. Shelton Smith et al., eds., *American Christianity, I, 1607–1820* (New York, 1960); William S. Perry, ed., *Historical Collections Relating to the American Colonial Church, I, Virginia* (privately printed, 1870); *IV, Maryland and Delaware* (1878), largely but not entirely Anglican; Alan Heimert, *Religion and the American Mind from the Great Awakening to the Revolution* (Cambridge, Mass., 1966); Alan Heimert and Perry Miller, eds., *The Great Awakening* (Indianapolis, 1967); Peter Force, ed., *Tracts and Other Papers* (4 vols., New York, 1947); Ernest T. Thompson, *Presbyterians in the South, I, 1607–1861* (Richmond, 1963), and William B. Sprague, ed., *Anuals of the American Pulpit* (9 vols., New York, 1859–1869).

FOR MARYLAND, essential are Nelson Rightmyer, *Maryland's Established Church* (Baltimore, 1956), and Lawrence C. Wroth, *A History of Printing in Colonial Maryland, 1686–1776* (Baltimore, 1922), both of which contain a great deal on clergymen and their writings. FOR VIRGINIA, most important are William Meade, *Old Churches, Ministers, and Families of Virginia* (2 vols., Philadelphia, 1857); G.M. Brydon, *Virginia's Mother Church, I* (Richmond, 1947), *II* (Philadelphia, 1952); E.L. Goodwin, *The Colonial Church in Virginia* (Milwaukee, 1927); William H. Foote, *Sketches of Virginia, Historical and Biographical*, 1st ser. (rpt., Richmond, 1966); Wesley M. Gewehr, *The Great Awakening in Virginia, 1740–1790* (Durham, N.C., 1930); Alexander Brown, ed., *Genesis of the United States* (2 vols., Boston, 1890), and *The First Republic in America* (Boston, 1898), these last for primary materials. FOR NORTH CAROLINA William L. Saunders, ed., *The Colonial Records of North Carolina* (6 vols., Raleigh, 1886–1888), and other items listed in Chapter V. FOR SOUTH CAROLINA, Frederick Dalcho, *An Historical Account of the Protestant Episcopal Church in South-Carolina* (Charleston, 1820), and George Howe, *History of the Presbyterian Church in South Carolina* (2 vols., Columbia 1870). Both contain material on denominations and writing other than those mentioned in their titles. FOR GEORGIA, see materials listed in the general bibliography and notes for Chapter V.

On major writers or preachers and the situations which inspired their writing there is considerable comment in the preceding chapter and its notes. Major and even some minor figures are commented upon in both Chapters V and VI. The terms "Old Side" and "Old Light" and their opposites, "New Side" and "New Light," are used interchangeably, for so they were used by older southern religious historians. Though in the North there was a distinction in meaning between the terms, this did not hold true in or for the southern colonies.

If the specific location of a copy of a colonial tract or sermon is not given in the notes, the item referred to was read from the AAS microcards mentioned above. When possible, for printed materials southern locations are given, for these copies and their availability are not sufficiently known among scholars.

NOTES

1. *Puritan* and *puritan*, *Puritanism* and *puritanism*, are used to denote somewhat differing religious concepts in this chapter and that preceding. For a definition of these forms as here used, see the asterisked footnote in Ch. V, p. 632.

2. Wright, *Religion and Empire*, pp. 45–56; Howard M. Jones, "The Colonial Impulse: An Analysis of the Promotion Literature of Colonization," *PAPS*, XC (1946), 146–161.

3. For abstracts of this and many of the sermons immediately following referred to, see Brown, ed., *Genesis*, passim, and Wright, *Religion and Empire*, pp. 90–101. Though the author has read the complete texts in the BM or elsewhere, he has attempted to refer to an edition or abstract more easily available in America.

4. Edited by Wesley F. Craven, *A Good Speed to Virginia* has been reprinted with R. Rich's *Newes from Virginia* by SF&R (New York, 1937).

5. Brown, ed., *Genesis*, I, 255–256.

6. Text from *ibid.*, I, 372.

7. Robert L. Hickey, "Donne and Virginia," *PQ*, XXVI (1947), 181–192, and Wright, *Religion and Empire*, pp. 110–111. It may be worth observing that in 1625 Samuel Purchas in *Hakluytus Posthumous, or Purchas His Pilgrimes* (20 vols., Glasgow, 1906), XIX, 218–287, used the form of a puritan sermon in his "Virginia's Verger," a description of the benefits England will derive from Virginia and Bermuda.

8. See Ch. V above, for a discussion of this matter and of Whitaker's other writings and religious conduct.

9. Mitchell, *English Pulpit Oratory*, pp. 136 ff. Perry Miller and Alan Heimert, whose studies of New England preaching have been referred to in the preceding chapter and will be again in this, agree with or accept these divisions or labels, though by explicit statement or implication they often reduce them to two. This is especially true of Miller (*The New England Mind*, p. 333), who describes the plain Puritan and the ornate "symphonic" Anglican (or metaphysical).

10. *The New England Mind*, p. 332.

11. Alan Heimert, *Religion and the American Mind*, passim. See also Heimert and Miller, eds., *The Great Awakening*.

12. As noted above, Perkins died soon after Whitaker's arrival at Trinity College.

13. Louis B. Wright, *The First Gentlemen of Virginia*, passim. See below.

14. Mitchell, *English Pulpit Oratory*, passim; Miller, *The New England Mind*, passim.

15. *The New England Mind*, pp. 332–333.

16. Clarence H. Faust and Thomas H. Johnson, eds., *Jonathan Edwards: Representative Selections, with Introduction, Bibliography, and Notes* (rev. ed., New York, 1962), p. cx.

17. William S. Powell, "Books in the Virginia Colony before 1624," *WMQ* (3), V (1948), 177–184; Wright, *First Gent. Va.*, passim.

18. Bayley was Bishop of Bangor. For the book in libraries, see Wright, *First Gent. Va.*, p. 240, and ten other citations. Wright points out that almost any Virginian who owned books at all had this in his library, perhaps more because it showed the way to attaining the good life than for its specific puritanism.

19. *The New England Mind*, pp. 4 and passim. The edition presented was in English, translated in 1610.

20. E.g., in the libraries of Argall Yeardley (1655), Arthur Spicer (1700), Charles Colston (1724), Robert ("King") Carter (1732), and William Claiborne (1654).

21. Nine editions appeared between 1603 and 1618, "His sermons were not so plain but that the piously learned did admire them, nor so learned but that the plain did understand them," says J.B. Mullinger, "William Perkins," *DNB*.

22. G.G. Marsden, ed., "A Virginia Minister's Library, 1635," *AHR*, XI (1905/6), 328–332.

23. *Archives of Md.*, V, 172–173; LIV, 102.

24. Wright, "Pious Reading in Colonial Virginia," *JSH*, VI (1940), 388, and "The 'Gentleman's Library' in Early Virginia: The Literary Interests of the First Carters," *HLQ*, I (1937), 41, 55; also Cohen, *S.C. Gaz.*, pp. 133, 148.

25. Lucy T. Latané, *Parson Latané, 1672–1732* (Charlottesville, 1936).

26. Among other studies of Tillotson as preacher see Mitchell, *English Pulpit Oratory*, passim; Louis G. Locke, *Tillotson: A Study in Seventeenth Century Literature* (Copenhagen, 1954), passim; and Alexander Gordon, "John Tillotson," *DNB*. Wilkins is best known for *The Principles of Natural Religion*. He was an early exponent of the plain style as practiced and encouraged by the Royal Society. His own plain style also owed something to Perkins.

27. See e.g., Miller, *The New England Mind*, passim.

28. Locke, *Tillotson*, p. 67.

29. For Pead's sermon, see "A Sermon Preached at James City in Virginia the 23d of April 1686 . . . , by Deuel Pead . . . ," ed. Richard B. Davis, *WMQ* (3), XVII (1960), 372–394. For Pead, see Davis; also Meade, *Old Churches*, I, 358–359; Goodwin, *The Colonial Church in Virginia*, pp. 297–298; *The Parish Register of Christ Church, Middlesex County, Virginia, from 1653 to 1812* (Baltimore, 1964), pp. 31, 34, 39; and Rightmyer, *Maryland's Established Church*, pp. 19, 207 (though there is an error in dating here which Mr. Rightmyer and the present writer have checked).

30. *Archives of Md.*, VII, 543, 562, 565, 568, 570.

31. Meade, *Old Churches*, I, 358. and *Parish Register of Christ Church*, passim.

32. Compare titles of these last two with those of evangelists like Davies and Whitefield a generation later.

33. Blathwayt Papers, XIV, no. 3, Archives of Colonial Williamsburg.

Knowing of this letter, the present writer searched for the sermon for some years. It finally turned up, listed in the Virginia 350th Anniversary Survey Reports of 1956.

34. It was printed, as noted above, with introduction and original dedication and text, in 1960.

35. It is interesting to compare Pead's nautical imagery with that of the earlier seventeenth-century Puritan Thomas Shepard and later eighteenth-century Presbyterian Samuel Davies. Like Pead, they used it extensively. Most of Shepard's is of biblical derivation, as is some of Pead's. For Shepard, see Bonnie L. Strother, "The Imagery in the Sermons of Thomas Shepard" (Ph.D. diss., Univ. of Tennessee, 1968), pp. 112 ff. Davies uses the grander aspects of ocean-nature, especially the storm, to produce the sublime. Davies' images are a mixture from his own experience and from the Bible. As a pre-Romantic his emphases and uses are different from those of Shepard or Pead.

36. Bodleian Lib., Additional Manuscripts, A 31, Oxford. Summ. Cat. no. 30143.

37. See Fairfax Harrison, "Parson Waugh's Tumult," in *Landmarks of Old Prince William* (rev. ed., Berryville, Va., 1964), pp. 127–142.

38. Published London, 1685.

39. McIlwaine et al., eds., *Journals H.B., Va.,* 1659–1693, pp. 338, 385, 395, 416.

40. P.R.O. C.O. 5/718 ff. 71–76. Joseph spoke against drunkenness, adultery, swearing, and Sabbath-breaking, and on loyalty to kings as "the Lord's anointed."

41. Peregrine Coney, M.A. Cambridge, 1688, B.D. Oxford, was in Virginia with Nicholson in 1704. In Maryland he was not only the governor's chaplain but rector of the Annapolis parish. For the sermons, see *Archives of Md.,* XIX, 40, 313, 316, 362, and Wroth, *History of Printing in Col. Md.,* pp. 10, 14, 162. Coney preached another fast-day sermon in May 1695, and the Rev. John Huett (chaplain of the Assembly in 1692) preached with him in 1694, but there is no record of either of these sermons being printed. For more on Coney and Huett, see Rightmyer, *Maryland's Established Church,* pp 17, 173, 192, and Goodwin, *Co. Ch. in Va.,* p. 261.

42. For Nicholett, see *Archives of Md.,* II, 159 ff.; Rightmyer, *Maryland's Established Church,* pp. 17, 205; Thompson, *Presbyterians in the South, I,* p. 19. It is possible that Nicholett may have been in Anglican orders. For Thomas Story, see *A Journal of the Life of Thomas Story: Containing an Account of his Remarkable Convincement . . .* (Newcastle upon Tyne, 1747; and later editions). For his work in Great Britain later, see Thomas Story's *Discourses in the Assemblies of Quakers* (taken in shorthand) (London, 1738), and *DNB.*

43. Wroth (*History of Printing in Col. Md.,* p. 163) thought in 1922 that this was the oldest extant Maryland imprint, but now the Library of Congress has a copy of *A Complete Body of the Laws of Maryland,* which may be as old or older, and there may be more recent acquisitions in Maryland libraries which antedate it. For more on the sermon, see Wroth, pp. 20–22, 162–163;

and for text, Bernard C. Steiner, ed., *The Reverend Thomas Bray: His Life and Selected Works Relating to Maryland* (Baltimore, 1901), pp. 99–122.

44. Steiner, ed., *Rev. Thomas Bray*, pp. 120–121.

45. Perry, ed., *Historical Collections*, I, 124–127.

46. See *Carolina Chronicle: The Papers of Commissary Gideon Johnston, 1707–1716*, ed. Frank J. Klingberg (Berkeley, 1946), passim; Dalcho, *Hist. Acc. Prot. Epis. Ch. in S.C.*, pp. 54–56; John R. Moore, "Defoe's 'Queries upon the Foregoing Act': A Defense of Civil Liberty in South Carolina," in *Essays in History and Literature* (Chicago, 1965), pp. 139–140, 150–151.

47. Rightmyer, *Maryland's Established Church*, pp. 171, 220; Wroth, *History of Printing in Col. Md.*, p. 165.

48. Frank L. Hawks, *History of North Carolina* (2 vols., Fayetteville, N.C. 1857–1858), II, 298–299.

49. Rightmyer, *Maryland's Established Church*, pp. 168, 189–190; *Archives of Md.*, XXVII, 536. Again the sermons are lost.

50. Reprinted in *Collections of the Protestant Episcopal Historical Society* (New York, 1851), pp. 37–54, and by E.L. Pennington, ed., "The Journal of the Reverend George Keith, 1702–1704," HMPEC, XX (1951), 346–487.

51. *The Quakers in the American Colonies*, pp. 457–458, passim; Alexander Gordon, "George Keith," *DNB*; Rufus M. Jones, "George Keith," *DAB*; Edgar L. Pennington, "The Journal of the Reverend George Keith, 1702–1704," HMPEC, XX (1951), 346–487. A different reprinting of Keith's *Journal of Travels from New-Hampshire to Caratuck, Coll. Protestant Episcopal Hist. Soc.* (New York, 1851) gives (p. 52) the titles of ten treatises he "wrote and Published in Print, in North America . . . in the years 1702, and 1703, to 1704," and in the same journal he gives the circumstances of the delivery of the sermon in Annapolis and its being printed at the insistence of and paid for by one of his auditors. In the *Journal* (p. 52) he lists three sermons and seven tracts printed in America, this Maryland sermon the only southern item in presentation or printing. See note 240 below.

52. Boston, B. Green for Benj. Eliot. For Makemie see Thompson, *Presbyterians in the South*, I, 20–23; Sprague, *Annals of the American Pulpit*, III, 1–4; Ernest T. Thompson, "Francis Makemie," *DAB*. Makemie published in the same year as the sermon *A Narrative of a New and Unusual American Imprisonment of Two Presbyterian Ministers and Prosecution of Mr. Francis Makemie* (reprinted in Force, *Tracts*, IV, no. 4). See selection in Smith, Handy, and Loetscher, eds., *American Christianity*, I, 256–261.

53. The text of the whole sermon is reprinted in *Collections of the New York Historical Society*, III (this reference p. 423).

54. "Clergy Ordained and Licensed for the American Colonies from 1699 to 1710," *Notes and Queries*, 5th ser., IX (March 22, 1884), 221–222, and VMHB, VII (1899), 312; W.A.R. Goodwin, *The Record of Bruton Parish Church* (Richmond, 1941), p. 132; *The Secret Diary of William Byrd of Westover, 1709–1712*, ed. Louis B. Wright and Marion Tinling (Richmond, 1941, p. 439). Goodwin (*Col. Ch. in Va.*, p. 297) identifies him as Zechariah Paxton, and Wright and Tinling follow. He preached at Bruton in 1710

on one of a succession of Sundays with five other men, including Commissary Blair, who were being considered as minister of the parish. Blair was elected soon after, on December 28. Byrd probably heard Paxton the next year when he was simply a visiting minister.

55. Though the pages are in good condition, they are dark with age and do not photograph well. The Harvard-Houghton librarian probably picked up the volume in Great Britain.

56. It may be of some interest that St. John's, Hampton, an eighteenth-century church possesses today the earliest Communion silver of use in this country. It was used at Smith's Hundred in 1618. See George M. Brydon, *Religious Life in Virginia in the Seventeenth Century*, Jamestown 350th Anniv. Hist. Booklet no. 10 (Williamsburg, 1957), for illustration following p. 24.

57. In *Memoirs of a Huguenot Family: Translated and Compiled from the Original Autobiography of the Rev. James Fontaine, and Other Family Manuscripts ... with an Appendix* (New York, 1853), pp. 311–324. For Peter Fontaine, see Goodwin, *Col. Ch. in Va.*, pp. 269–270; *William Byrd of Virginia: The London Diary (1717–1721) and Other Writings*, ed. Louis B. Wright and Marion Tinling (New York, 1958), passim; *Another Secret Diary of William Byrd of Westover, 1739–1741 ...*, ed. Maude H. Woodfin and Marion Tinling (Richmond, 1942), passim; *The Prose Works of William Byrd of Westover ...*, ed. Louis B. Wright (Cambridge, Mass., 1966), passim; *William Byrd's Histories of the Dividing Line betwixt Virginia, and North Carolina*, ed. W.K. Boyd and Percy G. Adams (New York, 1967), passim.

58. See William Byrd, *The Secret Diary, Another Secret Diary*, and *The London Diary*, passim; also the *Histories of the Dividing Line*, ed. W.K. Boyd and P.G. Adams (New York, 1967), p. 17, passim (this contains the "Secret History").

59. Perry, ed., *Historical Collections*, I, 154–182.

60. *Ibid.*, I, 172–173.

61. *Ibid.*, I, 219, 221–222. Apparently the commissary always opened the convention with a sermon preached by himself.

62. For Blair, see Ch. V, text, and note 150; also Parke Rouse, *James Blair of Virginia* (Chapel Hill, 1971); Daniel E. Motley, *Life of Commissary James Blair, Founder of William and Mary College* (Baltimore, 1901); Moses C. Tyler, *History of American Literature, 1607–1765* (2 vols. in one, New York, 1895), II, 261–263; and Donna Walter Netherland, "Imagery in the Sermons of James Blair" (M.A. thesis, Univ. of Tennessee, 1967). For the founding of the College of William and Mary, see Ch. III.

63. The 1722 edition in the British Museum, 227, f. 7, bound in red leather with the royal arms on each volume, is apparently George III's copy. Robert Carter of Corotoman had Blair's sermons in his library (Wright, "The 'Gentleman's Library' in Early Virginia," *HLQ*, I [1937], 49), but listings of "Blair's Sermons" in later eighteenth-century inventories and catalogues must usually refer to the works of the Scot Hugh Blair (rhetorician and preacher) and his discourses. Probably Meade (in *Old Churches*, I, 22, 25, 54) is referring to Hugh Blair.

64. One of the Dawsons wrote on February 28, 1748, to Dr. Thomas Wilson, Dean's Yard, Westminster, that Blair's sermons were not yet in his hands. On March 22, 1749/50, Wilson wrote that he had received the sermons but had been too ill and busy to read them. This correspondence, including at least one other letter on the subject, is in the Dawson Papers, LC. Attempts to locate the sermon manuscripts at the Abbey or Westminster School have been unsuccessful.

65. In the edition of 1740, p. xx. All later references are to the 1740 four-volume edition. Copy in the library of the Univ. of Virginia.

66. I, xxxi, xxxii.

67. J.M. Rigg, "Daniel Waterland," *DNB*.

68. I, vi–viii. Waterland cites examples of Blair's emphasis in good works "as necessary Conditions to Salvation" and of our growth in grace. He gives as examples "Of the Value of Good Works," "What Makes a Good Work," "Of False Prophets," and "Of Enthusiasm."

69. I, 233.

70. *Old Churches*, I, 155.

71. II, 110.

72. Not probable, for Blair would have known that in print he would be detected and accused of plagiarism. Maury's sermon is in manuscript.

73. III, 151.

74. Sprague, ed., *Annals of the American Pulpit*, V, 9. For Meade and Tyler, see notes and bibliography above.

75. Netherland, "Imagery in the Sermons of James Blair," pp. 17, 55, etc.

76. *Ibid.*, pp. 79–80; and Heimert, *Religion and the American Mind*, p. 215.

77. For these items, see respectively Bruce, *Inst. Hist. Va.*, I, 20–21; Va. Hist. Soc., Old File, Lightfoot-Minor Papers; Thomas A. Glenn, *Some Colonial Mansions and Those who Lived in Them* (2 vols., Philadelphia, 1898–1900), I, 242–243; Dawson Papers, LC (Delivered at Williamsburg, Christmas Day 1732; December 19, 1736; December 24, 1738; and August 17, 1740; on "Rejoicing in the Lord"); Dawson Papers, LC, 12½ pages, beginning "Yes verily, and by God's help so I will . . ." (a confirmation sermon).

78. Perry, ed., *Historical Collections*, I, 45, 418.

79. These sermons are among the manuscripts in the Brock Collection, Box 120, HEH. For Selden, see Goodwin, *Col. Ch. in Va.*, p. 305. Goodwin does not locate Selden in Henrico Parish until 1752. I am indebted to the Reverend George J. Cleaveland, D.D., Registrar of the Diocese of Virginia, for aid in identifying the probable author of both discourses.

80. For the most detailed study of Stith, see Toshiko Tsuruta, "William Stith, Historian of Colonial Virginia" (Ph.D. diss., Univ. of Washington, 1957).

81. Williamsburg: Printed and Sold by William Parks, M. DCC. XLV–VI. "Published at the Request of the House of Burgesses" appears on the title page, as it does on his other two sermons.

82. Williamsburg: Printed and Sold by William Hunter, 175[2?]. Stith was still rector of Henrico Parish, according to the title page.

83. Williamsburg: Printed and Sold by William Hunter. MDCCLIII, 32 pages.

84. Lyttleton, later first Baron Lyttleton, was known as "the good Lord Lyttleton." He is perhaps best known as the author of *Letters from a Persian* (1735) and his *Dialogues of the Dead* (1760), and he wrote and edited dozens of other books, including poems. Lyttleton was at Christ Church, Oxford, while Stith was at the university, a fact which Stith mentions.

85. Stith gives the title of Davies' pamphlet in a footnote: *The Impartial Trial, impartially Tried, and convicted of Partiality* (quotation from page 47). It was published at Williamsburg in 1748. Davies in turn was to answer Stith's sermon after the latter's death. See below, *Charity and Truth United.*

86. Pp. 31–32.

87. Brydon, *Virginia's Mother Church*, II, 309–310; also Meade, *Old Churches*, II, 44.

88. "A Dissertation on Education in the Form of a Letter from James Maury to Robert Jackson, July 17, 1762," ed. Helen D. Bullock, *Papers of the Albemarle County Historical Society*, II (1941–1942), 36–60; for his letters, Ann Maury, ed., *Memoirs of a Huguenot Family* (New York, 1853), pp. 379–442. James Maury was the son of Mary Ann Fontaine.

89. Quoted in "A Dissertation," ed. Bullock, pp. 36–38.

90. Perry, ed., *Historical Collections*, I, 364.

91. Apparently he had an upper church and a lower church, for he most frequently employs the initials U.C. and L.C. with his dates.

92. The two sermons on prayer were preached five times between 1743 and 1766.

93. Preached ten times between 1745 and 1762.

94. Preached at least six times between 1746 and 1755.

95. Marked as "Taken from the deserted residence of Bishop Green. July 11th . . . Jackson, Miss." The handwriting *may* be the same as that of the others.

96. This sermon, a late one, was preached six times between 1761 and 1764.

97. Preached 1764–1767.

98. For Maury as essayist of ideas, see Ch. IX below. For the Parson's Cause and Maury's part in it, see this chapter below (mention only) and Brydon, *Virginia's Mother Church*, II, passim. For Jefferson's opinion of Maury, see *The Papers of Thomas Jefferson*, ed. Julian P. Boyd, et al. (Princeton, 1950–), Vols. VI, VII, passim.

99. Brydon, *Virginia's Mother Church*, II, 341–364, "James Horrocks and the American Episcopate."

100. *Upon the Peace. A Sermon Preach'd at the Church of Petsworth, In the County of Gloucester, On August the 25th, The Day Appointed by Authority for the Observance of that Solemnity* . . . Williamsburg: Printed by Joseph Royle, MD CCLXIII, p. 7.

101. Rightmyer, *Maryland's Established Church*, pp. 155–156; Callister Papers, Md. Diocesan Lib.; Lawson Papers, LC.

102. Rightmyer, *Maryland's Established Church*, p. 158; Elihu S. Riley, 'The Ancient City': *A History of Annapolis in Maryland* (Annapolis, 1887), p. 132; Oswald Tilghman, *History of Talbot County Maryland, 1661–1861* (2 vols., Baltimore, 1915), I, 272–300; Perry, ed., *Historical Collections*, IV, passim; Ethan Allen, "Rev. Thomas Bacon," *Am. Q. Ch. Review*, XVII (1865), 430–451.

103. Rightmyer, *Maryland's Established Church*, p. 166; Sprague, *Annals of the American Pulpit*, V, 85–88. He appears to be mentioned in verses in the *Md. Gaz.* See also *MdHM*, LIX (1964), 388–390.

104. Rightmyer, *Maryland's Established Church*, p. 169. Some of his poems are in the Md. Hist. Soc. Lib. See also Rosamond R. Beirne, "The Reverend Thomas Chase, Pugnacious Parson," *MdHM*, LIX (1964), 1–14.

105. Rightmyer, *Maryland's Established Church*, pp. 177–178; *Md. Gaz.*, June 2, 1747, and July 23, 1752; Sprague, *Annals of the American Pulpit*, V, 111–117.

106. Rightmyer, *Maryland's Established Church*, p. 185; Frederick L. Weis, *The Colonial Clergy of Maryland, Delaware, and Georgia* (Lancaster, Mass., 1950).

107. Rightmyer, *Maryland's Established Church*, p. 213; Lawrence C. Wroth, *James Sterling, Priest, Poet and Prophet of Empire* (Worcester, Mass., 1931), and "James Sterling," *DAB*; J.A. Leo Lemay, *Men of Letters in Colonial Maryland* (Knoxville, 1972). Also, for MSS, see BM MSS Egerton 1764; Lambeth Palace-Fulham MSS American, III, 244–245.

108. With the possible exceptions of the printed collections of Blair and Davies.

109. Rightmyer, *Maryland's Established Church*, p. 193. The manuscript copy of the sermon in the Md. Hist. Soc. was made in 1843 from what was probably a decaying original. Bordley died in London undergoing an operation for the stone.

110. Md. Hist. Soc., Vertical File. About 37 pp., some fragmentary.

111. Md. Diocesan Lib., 18 pp. During the Revolution Addison was a Loyalist who went to England for a time but did not give up his parish, probably because his relatives made up most of it.

112. BM 4486. a. 24.

113. See also the comments on these sermons and one idea of their significance in Winthrop D. Jordan, *White Over Black: American Attitudes toward the Negro* (Chapel Hill, 1968), pp. 182, 191–192.

114. Copies, BM 225. g. 19 and Gen. Theol. Sem., New York, formerly in the Md. Diocesan Lib.

115. Wroth, *History of Printing in Col. Md.*, p. 202, recorded the title from the *Md. Gaz.* with the note "No copy recorded." Heimert (*Religion and the American Mind*, p. 166) remarks that "not surprisingly many of the Liberal clergy [and he refers primarily to the New England-middle colonies] were among the earliest patrons of English Masonry in the colonies. For the Liberal mind was clearly disposed to the classic and medieval distinction between esoteric and exoteric knowledge."

116. Copy in Md. Diocesan Lib. In it are advertised the *Two Sermons* and the *Four Sermons*. LC, 28 pages, including appendices.

117. In this parish and later in All Saints, Frederick County, he established charity schools. See Ch. III.

118. BM 4486. aa. 77, pp. 16.

119. Wroth, *History of Printing in Col. Md.*, p. 204. But a copy does survive in the Md. Diocesan Lib., 47 pages.

120. Preached ten times between 1751 and 1771, on occasion the whole, the first part, and the second part.

121. BM 4476. a. 37. The manuscript in the Md. Diocesan Lib. of the first sermon has the annotation by the Reverend Ethan Allen that it was a copy of the original lent to him by Dr. Thomas Walker. For Cradock's sermons, see David C. Skaggs and F. Garner Ranney, "Thomas Cradock's Sermons," *MdHM*, LXVII (1972), 179–180, and David C. Skaggs, "Thomas Cradock and the Chesapeake Golden Age," *WMQ* (3), XXX (1973), 93–116. The mirthful sermon was preached on St. George's Day, a sort of Fourth of July for the Englishmen of the colony.

122. These lines are from the nineteenth-century manuscript copy, pp. 3–4. Much more of like tenor follows. This sermon occupies only six printed and four close-packed small-hand manuscript pages. To those who would not join in the celebration, the preacher says, "Procul, procul absunt profani, away, away, with them." The manuscript and printed text agree word for word, but the manuscript is modernised in capitalization and punctuation. See Skaggs, "Thomas Cradock," p. 102. This sermon has recently been reprinted in Richard B. Davis, C. Hugh Holman, and Louis Rubin, eds., *Southern Writing, 1585–1920* (New York, 1970), pp. 136–140.

123. Manuscript in the Md. Diocesan Lib. The date is probably between 1743 and 1763. Skaggs, "Thomas Cradock," p. 102, feels that this sermon is at least in part a reply to Benjamin Franklin's *Proposals Relating to the Education of Youth in Pensilvania*.

124. Md. Diocesan Lib., 24 pages. His preface is clearly to the reader, not the hearer. David C. Skaggs has recently printed this sermon with introduction and annotation as, "Thomas Cradock's Sermon on the Governance of Maryland's Church," *WMQ* (3), XVII (1970), 630–653.

125. P. 6.

126. For example, Susquehannah Parish and its late unworthy incumbent are alluded to.

127. Though undated, they are almost surely between 1743 and 1763, 6 and 21 pages respectively. Both are in the Md. Diocesan Lib. MSS.

128. Those in manuscript are in the Md. Diocesan Lib., 16+ and 16 pages respectively. That preached from Hebrews 13:14 may just possibly not be his, though attributed to him by the Reverend Ethan Allen, collector of the manuscripts.

129. Printed by Jonas Green. Copy in the Gen. Theol. Sem., New York, 30 pages.

130. Copy in the John Carter Brown Lib., 22 pages, plus an essay by Dr.

Alexander Hamilton on Liberty continuously paginated with the sermon through p. 27.

131. The Annapolis edition was printed by Jonas Green, copy in the Univ. of Virginia Lib., 47 pages. The London edition was by Whiston and White, copy in the BM, 30 pages. The passage quoted below is from the London edition, differing slightly in spelling and italics from the Annapolis edition.

132. It should be remembered that George Whitefield while in Maryland noted that Sterling had felt the call of the Great Revival. Whitefield intimates that Sterling was ready to act in the cause, but that the Anglican clergyman was not suited to be a revivalist preacher. See Ch. V.

133. Described from the *Md. Gaz.* by Wroth, *History of Printing in Col. Md.*, p. 191. Wroth quotes the divisions of the sermon given in the advertisement. Jones is said to have carried on a running feud with the Jesuits in his parish and to have used this sermon is one weapon, or bit of ammunition, in the war.

134. See Rightmyer, *Maryland's Established Church*, p. 208. The sermon is in manuscript in the Md. Diocesan Lib. Interlinear comments are difficult to decipher. The author preached it six times between 1763 and 1776.

135. Printed by James Davis. Only known copy, Library Company of Philadelphia (formerly in Pa. Hist. Soc.). The title page may be mutilated, but the "To" would seem to be a printer's error for an "A." Smith was an M.A. of Trinity College, Dublin, ordained by the Bishop of London in 1747.

136. For more on Smith, see Saunders, ed., *Col. Rec. N.C.*, V, 665, 696, 961–962; VI, 58–60, 222, 312–313, 710; *Classified List of the Records for the Society for the Propagation of the Gospel* (London, 1898), p. 850.

137. J.S. Purcell, Jr., "Literary Culture in North Carolina before 1820" (Ph.D. diss., Duke Univ., 1950), p. 192; Douglas McMurtrie, *Eighteenth Century North Carolina Imprints, 1749–1800* (Chapel Hill, 1938), knew of no extant copy of either. Four hundred copies of the former, preached before the General Assembly, were printed. See also Saunders, ed., *Col. Rec. N.C.*, VI, 684, 688, 823, 955.

138. Printed in part in Heimert and Miller, eds., *The Great Awakening*, pp. 47–61.

139. Edgar L. Pennington, "The Reverend Samuel Quincy, S.P.G. Missionary," *GaHQ*, XI (1927), 157–165; Jay B. Hubbell, *The South in American Literature, 1607–1900* (Durham, N.C., 1954), pp. 75–76. In *CMHS*, 2d ser. II (1824, reprinted 1846), 188–189, in a letter to Edmund Quincy in Massachusetts, Samuel signs himself "your affectionate kinsman."

140. Copy in Univ. South Caroliniana Lib. Printed and sold by John Draper.

141. Heimert and Miller, eds., *The Great Awakening*, pp. 481–482. Part of the sermon appears on pp. 482–489.

142. See Patrick Henry's description of these methods as employed in Hanover County by Robinson, Roan, and Blair (he might have added the Tennents). Gewehr, *Great Awakening in Virginia*, p. 60.

143. *Baltimore Literary and Religious Magazine*, VI (1840), 52–53, etc. quoted in Thompson, *Presbyterians in the South*, I, p. 74. See Thompson

also (pp. 73–74) for Craig's disapproval of New Side or New Light methods, and for his long sermons extending from the midday dinner hour to sunset.

144. See John G. Herndon, "John Thomson," *JPHS*, XX (1942), 116–158, XXI (1943), 34–59; H.C. Bradshaw, *History of Prince Edward County, Virginia* . . . (Richmond, 1955), p. 16; Thompson, *Presbyterians in the South*, I, passim; Foote, *Sketches of Virginia*, 1st ser., passim; Gewehr, *Great Awakening in Virginia*, passim; Heimert, *Religion and the American Mind* (where at least one sermon is quoted), passim.

145. See Preface. The text is I Corinthians III:12, 13.

146. Foote, *Sketches of Virginia*, 1st ser., pp. 137–138; Gewehr, *Great Awakening in Virginia*, pp. 54–56.

147. For Finley, see Sprague, ed., *Annals of the American Pulpit*, III, 96–101; H.E. Starr, "Samuel Finley," *DAB*; Heimert, *Religion and the American Mind*, passim; Heimert and Miller, eds., *The Great Awakening*, pp. 152–167 (selection); and Foote, *Sketches of Virginia*, 1st ser., pp. 142–143.

148. MS. in Duke Univ. Lib., pp. 38. According to Mrs. Virginia R. Gray of Duke, Ker lived in Rowan County and had been ordained at Princeton. He later removed to Somerset County, Maryland.

149. For Chanler, see Howe, *Hist. of the Presby. Ch. in S.C.*, I, 219, 240. In Virginia the Regular and Separate Baptists fought for a time somewhat along lines of Old Side vs. New Side Presbyterians, though the alignments, since one group of Baptists was Arminian, were never quite the same as those of the Presbyterians.

150. Printed by D. Fowle, for Kneeland and Green, 43 pages. For Chanler's doctrinal tract, see below.

151. A mimeographed copy of the diary is in the Duke Univ. Lib. The sermon outlines are in the Univ. South Caroliniana Lib.

152. Charles-Town, printed by Peter Timothy, 1745.

153. For record of this occasion, see Egmont Manuscripts, Univ. of Georgia, V. 14203, pt. 1 (vol. 4), p. 26.

154. *The Works of John Wesley* (rpt. of 1872 ed., Grand Rapids, Mich., n.d.).

155. Heimert, *Religion and the American Mind*, p. 53, from Patrick Tailfer, et al., *A True and Historical Narrative of the Colony of Georgia*, ed. Clarence L. Ver Steeg (Athens, Georgia, 1960), p. 11. See Ch. IX below.

156. London, printed by James Hutton, 1738, 23 pages.

157. Printed by James Hutton, 19 pages.

158. Printed by W. Bowyer for James Hutton, etc., viii plus 25 pages.

159. Boston, N.E. Re-printed and Sold by Kneeland and Green and Harrison, 15 pages. Copy in HEH.

160. By Fleet for Harrison. London original printing.

161. See, e.g., Cohen, *S.C. Gaz.*, passim; and Lester J. Cappon and Stella F. Duff, *Virginia Gazette Index* (2 vols., Williamsburg, 1950).

162. Josiah Smith is one of the relatively neglected figures of colonial American religious history. The most complete sketch appears in Clifford K. Shipton, *Sibley's Harvard Graduates*, VIII (Boston, 1945), 569–585. This

essay has some facts but is hopelessly parochial in trying to make a transplanted New Englander out of Smith. See also Howe, *Hist. of the Presby. Ch. in S.C.*, I, 185, 205–206, 232, 260, 454, 461; and Heimert and Miller, eds., *The Great Awakening*, pp. 62–69 (including selection from his sermon on Whitefield). Smith was of the Harvard class of 1725.

163. In *The Greatest Sufferers not always the Greatest Sinners* (Boston, 1730), Preface, and pp. 16 ff. Actually he was *defending* New England because it had recently suffered a catastrophic earthquake, which was *not* caused by its sins, Smith argues.

164. Shipton, *Sibley's Harvard Graduates*, VIII, 575–576; and Howe, *Hist. of the Presby. Ch. in S.C.*, pp. 190–191 (which quotes at length a letter from Smith to Colman of October 12, 1730).

165. Shipton, *Sibley's Harvard Graduates*, VIII, 576.

166. Smith's New England biographer entirely fails to recognize the fact that Smith was *not* the first to open his church doors in Charleston to Whitefield. Garden did, as Commissary Blair also did in Virginia.

167. The bibliography of his writings included at the end of the biographical sketch in Shipton's *Sibley's Harvard Graduates*, pp. 583–585, is certainly not complete as far as newspaper publication is concerned, and probably not for pamphlets and collected works.

168. Copy in Kendall Collection, Univ. South Caroliniana Lib.

169. Copy in LC, ii plus 44 pages.

170. Copies in Duke Univ. Lib. and LC, ii plus 21 pages.

171. Copy in Duke Univ. Lib., 14 pages.

172. Copy in Duke Univ. Lib., 31 (2) pages.

173. Printed by Lewis Timothy. Copy in Univ. South Caroliniana Lib., 16 pages.

174. First ed. in LC, 16 pages; 2d ed. in HEH, 25 pages.

175. Copy in American Antiquarian Society, vi plus 20 (1) pages. Also a Charleston edition of 1765, copy at Yale, vi plus 22 pages.

176. See Shipton, *Sibley's Harvard Graduates*, VIII, 584. There were also other northern American editions.

177. Glasgow. Smith's sermon, pp. 11–28.

178. Heimert and Miller, eds., *The Great Awakening*, p. 63.

179. *Ibid.*, pp. 67–68; *Fifteen Sermons*, p. 20. There is a long excerpt from the sermon in Howe, *History of the Presbyterian Church in S.C.*, I, 233–234.

180. See Sermon XV, Copy in Univ. South Caroliniana Lib., "The Effects of Divine Fury"; and Howe, *History of the Presbyterian Church in S.C.*, I, 229.

181. Copy in Mass. Hist. Soc., 14 pages (2).

182. For Davies, see the general bibliography in Ch. V. Perhaps the best bibliography of his sermons is that included in George H. Bost, "Samuel Davies, Colonial Revivalist and Champion of Religious Toleration" (Ph.D. diss., Univ. of Chicago, 1942), but it is not complete for publication of individual sermons. The eighteenth-century three- and five-volume editions are useful for the introductory material, but the several editions printed after 1811 contain nineteen more sermons of great importance. For this study,

the editions of London, 1792, and New York, 1841, have been used. All references unless otherwise specified are to the 1841 edition.

183. The 1841 edition (3 vols., New York) with an essay on the life and times of Davies by Albert Barnes, "containing all the author's sermons ever published," does not quite live up to this claim.

184. See the general bibliography for this chapter for Heimert, Foote, and Sprague. Albert Barnes' sketch in the 1841 edition includes "The characteristics of President Davies as a preacher," I, xxxvi–x/v, much of it quotations from Davies. Tyler, *History of American Literature*, II, 241–244, quotes somewhat from the sermons.

185. For the present, see George W. Pilcher, *Samuel Davies, Apostle of Dissent in Colonial Virginia* (Knoxville, 1971). Craig A. Gilborn, "The Literary Work of the Reverend Samuel Davies" (M.A. thesis, Univ. of Delaware, 1961), is a brief survey of Davies' writing. See also George H. Bost, "Samuel Davies, Preacher of the Great Awakening," *JPHS*, XXVI (1948), 65–86, primarily an historical sketch, and his "Samuel Davies, The South's Great Awakener," *JPHS*, XXXIII (1955), 135–156. The recent *Samuel Davies* by Pilcher, contains no significant analyses of Davies' sermons or of Davies as sermon writer.

186. See *Collected Poems of Samuel Davies*, ed. Richard B. Davis (Gainesville, Fla., 1968), Introduction. Unfortunately only a fraction of these hymns survive.

187. Foote, *Sketches of Virginia*, 1st ser., pp. 301–303.

188. Cf. Heimert, *Religion and the American Mind*, Chapter II, "The Work of Redemption," pp. 59–94.

189. "The Crisis," *Sermons*, III, 77.

190. *Sermons*, I, 316.

191. *Ibid.*, I, 338–356, 357–383.

192. *Ibid.*, I, 339. Liberals like Byles in New England spoke against the "uncouth jargon" and "affected phrases" of this sermon, meaning its sublimity, which drew audiences emotionally. Heimert, *Religion and the American Mind*, p. 218.

193. *Sermons.*, I, 387.

194. *Ibid.*, III, 222, "On the Defeat of General Braddock."

195. *Ibid.*, III, 372.

196. *Ibid.*, Sermons XXXI, "Dedication to God argued from Redeeming Mercy"; XXXII, "The Christian Feast"; XXXVII, "The Divine Perfections Illustrated"; LIII, "A Sight of Christ the Desire and Delight of Saints in all Ages"; and LV, "The Gospel-Invitation." For the hymns, see *Collected Poems of Samuel Davies*, ed. Davis.

197. Respectively XLVI, LVI, LVII.

198. Sermon XXIX.

199. E.g., sermons II, III, IV, V, XIX, XXI, XLIII, LXXXI.

200. *Sermons*, II, 287, number XLIII, "The Vessels of Mercy and the Vessels of Wrath Delineated."

201. XXII, XXIII, XXVII, and LXXIV.

202. These are respectively LXXVII, LXXVIII, XXXIV, LIX, LX, LXVI, LXVII, LXX, LXXI, LXXIX, and LXXXII.

203. Copy in Brock Collection, HEH.

204. See extract of Davies' letter of Oct. 2, 1750, in Perry, ed., *Historical Collections*, I, 369, and Davies' sermon LXXX, "Christians Solemnly Reminded of Their Obligations."

205. LXXXII, "The Apostolic Farewell Considered and Applied," *Sermons*, III, 490–493.

206. Heimert, *Religion and the American Mind*, p. 345. See *Sermons*, I, 194.

207. LXI, LXII, LXIII, and LXIX, in *Sermons*, III, 41–99, 215–232.

208. *Sermons*, III, 215–216.

209. *Ibid.*, III, 222.

210. *Ibid.*, III, 47.

211. *Ibid.*, III, 62.

212. *Ibid.*, III, 77.

213. *Ibid.*, III, 88.

214. *Ibid.*, III, 91.

215. *Ibid.*, III, 94–95.

216. *Ibid.*, III, 99.

217. See C.C. Hall, ed., *Narratives of Early Maryland, 1633–1684* (New York, 1910), passim; Elizabeth Baer, comp., *Seventeenth Century Maryland, Bibliography* (Baltimore, 1949); Father White in *Calvert Papers No. 3*, Md. Hist. Soc. (Baltimore, 1899) and Father White's *Relatio Itineris*, Md. Hist. Soc. (Baltimore, 1874). For titles see Baer.

218. Given in Hall, ed, *Narratives of Early Maryland*, pp. 118–144.

219. N.p., pp. 3–16. See Lathrop C. Harper, *A Maryland Tract of 1646*, reprinted from *Bibliographical Essays: A Tribute to Wilberforce Eames* (Freeport, N.Y., 1967), 8 pp. The evidence points to Father Richard Blount, Provincial of the English Society of Jesus, as the author.

220. For a concise discussion of the situation, see Hall, ed., *Narratives of Early Maryland*, pp. 183–186.

221. P. 12. Photostat copy in John Carter Brown Lib., from original in BM.

222. Copy, BM 8175. a. 35. The titles of all these pamphlets have been reduced to about one-fourth their full length. The pamphleteers must all have been in London at the time they published.

223. Reprinted in Force, *Tracts*, III, no. 15. "R.G." has also been said to stand for Robert Gray but all the evidence points to Roger Green.

224. Gordon Goodwin, "Morgan Godwyn," *DNB*; Goodwin, *Col. Ch. in Va.*, p. 272; Brydon, *Virginia's Mother Church*, I, 175, 186–188, 198, 202, 205; Bruce, *Inst. Hist. Va.*, I, 206, etc. E.D. Neill, *Virginia Carolorum* (Albany, 1886), pp. 342–343.

225. Published in London in that year. It is said to have been preached in various other London churches also.

226. Curiously Bruce (*Inst. Hist. Va.*, I, 206) passes this off as a Puritan

diatribe and says that "the intemperate Godwyn" dedicated it to Cromwell! Copy of Godwyn's book in BM, 867. d. 22.

227. *Virginia's Mother Church*, I, 187.

228. P. 167.

229. Copy, BM 864. f. 30.

230. Copy, BM 1369. f. 37.

231. Perry, ed., *Historical Collections*, IV, 4–7.

232. This broadside exists in the P.R.O.

233. The title page gives the original imprint as William Nuthead's at "St. Maries" in Maryland for "The Protestant Association."

234. An "Epistle to the Reader" of July 26, 1692, is dated "At Rehobeth in Pocamok Maryland." Pp. 5–19 are "A True Copy of George Keith's Paper, Delivered to Mr. George Layfield, at Pocamok in Mary-Land."

235. Perry, ed., *Historical Collections*, IV, 32 ff. Much more of this sort appears in the *Archives of Md.*, passim.

236. These two are reprinted in Steiner, *The Rev. Thomas Bray*, pp. 174–182, from the printed folio sheets in the Sion College Lib. (the letter at least apparently dated 1700 or before), probably not published in Maryland.

237. *Ibid.*, pp. 209–229, from London 1700 edition.

238. *Ibid.*, p. 228.

239. See Moore, "Defoe's 'Queries upon the Foregoing Act,'" pp. 133–154.

240. See *Collections of the Protestant Episcopal Historical Society for the Year 1851* (New York, 1851), pp. 1–54, for one reprinting of the *Journal*; a well-edited edition is Pennington, "The Journal of the Reverend George Keith," pp. 346–487. Original printed by Joseph Dawning for B. Aylmer. See note 51 above.

241. Wroth, *History of Printing in Col. Md.*, pp. 177–178; Perry, ed., *Historical Collections*, IV, 130 etc.; Rightmyer, *Maryland's Established Church*, pp. 64 ff. Copy of pamphlet in John Carter Brown Lib. Henderson and the elder Daniel Dulany appear to have been the principals in the economic-religious dispute carried on primarily through Philadelphia newspapers, magazines, and pamphlets. See Dulany's "Sermon," *The Traditions of the Clergy Destructive of Religion* (March 1731/2), dedicated to Henderson. Henderson as "The Extinguisher" replied in the *American Weekly Mercury* (April 12 and 20). For this controversy also are useful *Archives of Md.*, XXXVIII, 148, 453–460; William W. Manross, comp., *The Fulham Papers in the Lambeth Palace Library* (Oxford, 1965), Part One, Vol. III; and other issues of *American Weekly Mercury* or *Pa. Gaz.*, 1731–1732, under various pseudonyms.

242. Advertisement in *S.C. Gaz.*, Oct. 2, 1749. See Cohen, *S.C. Gaz.*, p. 170.

243. Jones, *The Quakers in the American Colonies*, pp. 300–301.

244. The edition here used is that of London, 1752, in the Univ. of Tennessee Lib. Her work is dated from Charleston, 30th of Tenth Month, 1747. There was also a Bristol 1751 edition.

245. She says she had been brought up in the Church of England.

246. Also no place given. Copy in Univ. of Tennessee Lib.

247. A copy of the Philadelphia, 1759, edition is in the Virginia State Library and references here are to that edition. See Alexander Gordon, "Samuel Bownas," *DNB*, for his other writings, and Jones, *The Quakers in the American Colonies*, passim.

248. Pp. 133–134. The governor may have been Francis Nicholson, and "the Snake" is not hard to identify. Such a work would not have been out of keeping with Nicholson's zealous Anglicanism. The *BM Cat.* ascribes an anti-Quaker pamphlet, *The Snake in the Grass* (London, 1696, 1697, 1698), to Charles Leslie, famous theological controversialist (see *DNB*). It was answered by Joseph Wyeth, Quaker writer, in *Anguis Flagellatus: or a Switch for the Snake* (London, 1699). Certainly *The Snake* well represented Nicholson's views.

249. N.p., n.d. Copies in the Univ. South Caroliniana and Univ. of North Carolina libraries.

250. William E. Eisenberg, *The Lutheran Church in Virginia, 1717–1962* (Roanoke, 1967), pp. 11–13, and *VMHB*, XIV (1906), 147ff.

251. Title above text: "An Answer to the Several Pleas against Infant Baptism." Photocopy in the Univ. of North Carolina Lib., pp. 39. Stephen B. Weeks, "Libraries and Literature in the Eighteenth Century," *AHA, Annual Report for the Year 1895*, p. 262, identifies the author. Though he had not seen the tract, Weeks states that four copies were sent to the S.P.G. and four hundred distributed in the province. In *Church and State in North Carolina* (Baltimore, 1893), p. 37, Weeks mentions Stewart again.

252. Incidentally, Whitefield valued him highly, even pro-revival commentators aver. For Bryan, see Howe, *Hist. of the Presby. Ch. in S.C.*, I, 244–246, etc.; and D.D. Wallace, *South Carolina: A Short History* (Columbia, 1961), p. 184.

253. The tract has 171 pages.

254. See, e.g., "Johan Martin Bolzius Answers a Questionnaire on Carolina and Georgia," eds. Klaus G. Loewald, et al. *WMQ* (3), XIV (1957), 218–261; XV (1958), 228–252; "John Martin Bolzius Reports on Georgia," trans. and ed. G.F. Jones, *GaHQ*, 47 (1963), 216–219 (original printed in German in 1740).

255. For Zubly's later pamphleteering and preaching career, see E.M. Coulter, *Georgia: A Short History* (Chapel Hill, 1960), pp. 124–130. Zubly was an ardent patriot who was elected to the Continental Congress but refused to go all the way to independence. See also Marjorie Daniel, "John Joachim Zubly," *DAB*.

256. Copy in Univ. South Caroliniana Lib. The same year had appeared in London Clarke's *An Essay on the Number Seven. Wherein the Duration of the Church of Rome and the Mahometan Imposture; the Time also of the Conversion of the Jews; and the Year of the World for the Beginning of the Millenium; and the First Resurrection of the Martyrs, are attempted to be*

Shown. The *Prophetic Numbers* is an "ingenious" fitting together of scriptural passages to make the author's point.

257. *Hist Acc. Prot. Epis. Ch. in S.C.*, pp. 180–183.

258. Copy in Univ. South Caroliniana Lib., pp. vii, 445. The full title runs the whole page.

259. Howe, *Hist. of the Presby. Ch. in S.C.*, I, 219. It is also probably the southern colonies' first theological treatise.

260. All three of Husband's pamphlets have been reprinted in K. Boyd, ed., *Some Eighteenth Century Tracts Concerning North Carolina* (Raleigh, 1927), pp. 193–396. *Some Remarks* is also excerpted in Heimert and Miller, eds., *The Great Awakening*, pp. 636–654. Also see *WMQ* (3), XXXIV.

261. Copy in Univ. South Caroliniana Lib., pp. 54.

262. See Heimert and Miller, eds., *The Great Awakening*, pp. 505–515, for a selection from Croswell's *What is Christ to me, if he is not mine? Or a Seasonable Defense of the Old Protestant Doctrine of Justifying Faith . . .* (Boston, 1745).

263. Copy in Univ. South Caroliniana Lib., pp. 70, (1).

264. Bishop of London to Doddridge, May 11, 1751, in Perry, ed., *Historical Collections*, I, 371. Davies' letter is in Perry, pp. 368–371. Davies himself wrote directly to the Bishop of London. See Foote, *Sketches of Virginia*, 1st ser., pp. 120–122, 167, 173, 180–206, 284–295.

265. Perry, ed., *Historical Collections*, I, 383, 384–386, 395, 396. Davies at times corresponded directly with the bishop. See also letters Davies was to deliver to the Bishop of London in Dawson Papers, LC.

266. Williamsburg: William Parks, 1747.

267. Bost, "Samuel Davies: The South's Great Awakener," p. 139. Bost refers to an unsigned article in *The Biblical Repository and Princeton Review*, IX (1837), 363–364.

268. Copy in the Va. Hist. Soc. A good selection from this essay is in Heimert and Miller, eds., *The Great Awakening*, pp. 376–392.

269. For location of editions and copies, see Union Catalogue, LC.

270. Edited by Thomas C. Pears, Jr. (Philadelphia, 1941), an offprint from *JPHS*, XX (1941), 191–323.

271. P. 217.

272. P. 219.

273. P. 296.

274. Pp. 309–310.

275. *Virginia's Mother Church*, II, 295. Brydon certainly exaggerates the existence of a clique of Oxonians.

276. See Richard L. Morton, *Colonial Virginia* (2 vols., Chapel Hill, 1960), II, Chapters XXVII, "The Parsons' Cause—The Clergy and the Commissary"; XXVIII, "The Parson's Cause—The College and the Visitors"; XXIX, "The Two-Penny Act, the Clergy, and the Committee of Correspondence"; XXX. "The Parsons' Cause, the Committee of Correspondence, and the Con-

stitution," 751–819. Morton adds the episcopacy and other matters to the causes of friction.

For a well-edited and perceptive treatment of all the essays in the Pistole Fee and Parsons' Cause–Two-Penny disputes, see Homer D. Kemp, "The Pre-Revolutionary Virginia Polemical Essay: The Pistole Fee and the Two-Penny Acts Controversies," (Ph.D. diss., Univ. of Tennessee, 1972). Accurate texts of all the essays here mentioned and a few other minor ones are given in Kemp's edition. Camm, Carter, and Bland as controversial writers are treated at some length. Kemp disagrees with Bernard Bailyn (see note 289 below) on several interpretations and estimates of these men's abilities and on their characteristics as writers.

277. Brydon, *Virginia's Mother Church*, II, 301; Morton, *Colonial Virginia*, II, 795.

278. Edited by Jack P. Greene (2 vols., Charlottesville, 1965). See Chapter IX below for discussion of this work.

279. Copy in Va. St. Lib. Not listed in Evans but in Bristol's *Supplement*. See also Jack P. Greene, "Landon Carter and the Pistole Fee Dispute," *WMQ* (3), XIV (1957), 66–69.

280. The bishop's letter to the Board of Trade is given in Perry, ed., *Historical Collections*, I, 461–463. For an analysis of the charges and pointing out of their inaccuracy, see Brydon, *Virginia's Mother Church*, II, 304–308.

281. Clinton Rossiter, "Richard Bland: The Whig in America," *WMQ* (3), X (1953), 33–79. The ascription from Jefferson is to be found in an appended note of a letter dated July 25, 1775, in the Charles Campbell Papers, Duke Univ.

282. Signed from "Jordan's / March 20, 1760."

283. Morton, *Colonial Virginia*, II, 804–806; H.R. McIlwaine et al., eds., *Journals H.B. Va.*, 1758–1761, p. 188, etc.

284. Printed by Jonas Green. The first part of the appendix contains a correspondence wherein Camm tries to persuade Joseph Royle of Wiliamsburg, public printer of Virginia, to publish his pamphlet. Royle declines because of its "Satyrical Touches upon the Late Assembly." Imperfect copy in LC.

285. These pieces were reprinted in Bland's *The Colonel Dismounted* as Appendices I and II. The issue of the *Va. Gaz.* including Bland's letter is not extant.

286. Page 30.

287. Called Part the First, 29 pages.

288. The pamphlet was long taken to be without satiric intent and was ascribed to Camm, but Eckenrode and Torrence give reasons, now obvious, why it is Bland's (see Wroth, *History of Printing in Col. Md.*, p. 219, and Kemp, "Pre-Rev. Va. Polemical Essay"). It is reprinted in Bernard Bailyn, ed., *Pamphlets of the American Revolution. Volume I. 1750–1765* (Cambridge, Mass., 1965), pp. 292–354. There was a final shot by Camm in 1765, *Critical Remarks on a Letter Ascribed to Common Sense . . . with a Dissertation upon Drowsiness* (Williamsburg), but it seems to have aroused little interest be-

cause it was concerned with matters rapidly being outdated.

289. Bailyn, ed., *Pamphlets of the American Revolution*, I, "The Colonel Dismounted," pp. 319–320.

290. Cf. *Ibid.*, p. 297.

Chapter Seven: Science and Technology, Including Agriculture

Bibliography

Over the past quarter of a century I have examined manuscripts for this chapter and copied many of them or had them photographed, from repositories in England, Scotland, Northern Ireland, the Republic of Ireland, and the United States. Since this project was begun, many of the primary sources have appeared in print, a fact which makes even this tentative and necessarily inconclusive chapter easier in reference than some other sections of this book. The subject, as the subjects of some of the other chapters, could have been developed into several volumes.

Three recent printed general guides, one of them a history in itself, have been most useful: Whitfield J. Bell, Jr., *Early American Science: Needs and Opportunities for Study* (Williamsburg, 1955); Brooke Hindle, *Technology in Early America: Needs and Opportunities for Study* (Williamsburg and Chapel Hill, 1966); and Raymond P. Stearns, *Science in the British Colonies of America* (Urbana, 1970). The emphasis in the first two of these, however, seems to be on the northeastern and middle colonies to the neglect of the southern, almost surely because of inadequate available information. Generally useful also have been Brooke Hindle, *The Pursuit of Science in Revolutionary America, 1735–1789* (Chapel Hill, 1956) and Theodore Hornberger, *Scientific Thought in the American Colleges, 1638–1800* (Austin, 1945). General histories or studies of American agriculture, technology, and medicine are totally inadequate in their treatment of the southeastern colonies, if they treat them at all, though a number will be mentioned below.

Several books ostensibly on British science, including gardening, actually contain some of the most useful and significant material on American plants, cultivation, and workers in the field: James Britten, *The Sloane Herbarium*, ed. J.E. Dandy (London, 1958), deals with a great many botanists in the colonies; Evelyn Cecil, *A History of Gardening in England* (London, 1916); H.N. Clokie, *An Account of the Department of Gardening in the University of Oxford* (Oxford, 1964); R.H. Fox, *Dr. John Fothergill and His Friends: Chapters in Eighteenth Century Life* (London, 1910); G.E. Fussell, *Old English Farming Books from Fitzherbert to Tull, 1523 to 1730* (London, [1947]) and *More Old English Farming Books from Tull to the Board of Agriculture, 1731–1793* (London, [1950]); George Edwards, *Gleanings of Natural History, Exhibiting Figures of Quadrupeds, Birds, Insects, Plants &c. . . . in Fifty Copper Plate Prints* (3 vols., London, 1758); R.W.T. Gunther, *Early English*

Botanists and Their Gardens . . . Goodyer, Tradescant, and Others (Oxford, 1922); Miles Hadfield, *Gardening in Britain* (London, 1960), and *Pioneers in Gardening* (London, 1955), Derek Hudson and Kenneth W. Luckhurst, *The Royal Society of Arts, 1754–1954* (London, 1954); Arthur A. Lisney, *A Bibliography of British Lepidoptera, 1608–1799* (London, 1960); George Pasti, Jr., "Consul Sherard: Amateur Botanist and Patron of Learning, 1659–1728" (Ph.D. diss., Univ. of Illinois, 1950); Lester S. King, *The Medical World of the Eighteenth Century* (Chicago, 1958); James E. Smith, ed., *A Selection of the Correspondence of Linnaeus and Other Naturalists* (2 vols., London, 1821); Agnes Arber, "A Seventeenth Century Naturalist: John Ray," *Isis*, XXXIV (1943), 319–324; Norman Brett-James, *The Life of Peter Collinson, F.R.S., F.S.A.* (London, [1926?]); W. Noel Sainsbury et al., eds., *Calendar of State Papers, Colonial Series, America, and the West Indies* (42 vols., London, 1860–1953); Raymond P. Stearns, "James Petiver, Promoter of Natural Science c. 1669–1718," *PAAS*, LXII (1952), 243–379; and Charles E. Raven, *John Ray, Naturalist, His Life and Works* (Cambridge, Eng., 1942).

Bibliographies of some use (besides those in Hindle and Bell noted above) are Robert B. Austin, *Early American Medical Imprints, 1668–1820* (Washington, D.C., 1961); [William C. Sturtevant, comp.], *American Indian Medicine: Bibliography* (Washington, D.C., 1957); Jack P. Greene, *The American Colonies in the Eighteenth Century, 1689–1763* (New York, Goldentree Bibliographies, 1969); Alden T. Vaughan, *The American Colonies in the Seventeenth Century* (New York, Goldentree Bibliographies, 1971); and index, Lester J. Cappon and Stella Duff, *Virginia Gazette Index* (2 vols., Williamsburg, 1950).

General works on American natural history include June R. Butler, "America: A Hunting Ground for Eighteenth Century Naturalists with Special Reference to Trees . . . ," *PBSA*, XXXII (1938), 1–16; John Ellis, *Directions for Bringing Over Seeds and Plants . . .* (London, 1770); Frederick Brasch, "The Newtonian Epoch in the American Colonies (1680–1783)," *PAAS*, n.s. XLIX (1939), 314–442; "The Royal Society of London and Its Influence upon Scientific Thought in the American Colonies," *Sci. Monthly*, XXXIII (1931), 336–355, 444–469; and *The Royal Society of London and Its Influence upon Scientific Thought in America* (Washington, D.C., 1931); Peter Force, ed., *Tracts and Other Papers Relating Principally to . . . . the Colonies in North America . . .* (4 vols., Washington, D.C., 1836–1840; 1947; also reprinted Gloucester, Mass., 1963); S.G. Brown Goode, "The Beginnings of Natural History in America," in *Bio. Soc. Washington Proc.*, III (1884–1886), 35–105 [also U.S. Nat. Mus. Report, 1897, pt. 2, 357–406]; Jerry Stannard, "Early American Botany and Its Sources," in *Bibliography and Natural History Essays*, ed. T.R. Buckman (Lawrence, Kans., 1966); Mattie M. Russell, "The Naturalist Explorers' Interpretation of the Southeastern United States from 1700 to 1900" (Ph.D. diss., Cornell Univ., 1947); Winthrop Tilley, "The Literature of Natural and Physical Science in American Colleges from the Beginning to 1765" (Ph.D. diss., Brown Univ., 1933); William M. and Mabel S.C. Smallwood, *Natural History and the American Mind* (New York,

1941); Roderick Nash, *Wilderness and the American Mind* (New Haven, 1967).

In agriculture and horticulture see Lewis C. Gray, *History of Agriculture in the Southern States to 1860* (Washington, D.C., 1933); Avery O. Craven, *Soil Exhaustion as a Factor in the Agricultural History of Virginia and Maryland, 1606–1860* (Urbana, 1926); [Anon.] *American Husbandry Containing an Account of the Soil, Climate, Production . . . {of the} Colonies in North America and the West Indies by an American*, ed. Harry J. Carman (2 vols., London, 1775; rpt. New York, 1939); Aubrey C. Land, ed., *Bases of the Plantation Society* (Columbia, 1969); Everett E. Edwards, "American Agriculture: The First Three Hundred Years," *Yearbook of Agriculture, 1940* (Washington, D.C., 1941), pp. 171–191; U.P. Hedrick, *A History of Horticulture in America to 1860* (New York, 1950), an especially useful volume; Sarah Stetson, "American Garden Books Transplanted and Native, before 1807," *WMQ* (3), (1946), 343–369; Alice B. Lockwood, comp. and ed., *Gardens of Colony and State . . . before 1840* (2 vols., New York, 1934), perhaps more useful for the next chapter; Philip Miller, *The Gardener's Dictionary* (abridged ed. of 1754; rpt. New York, 1969), most useful; Carolyn Miller, "Recapturing the Charm of a Colonial Garden," *Americana*, I (1973), 18–21; Joseph C. Robert, *The Story of Tobacco in America* (New York, 1949); Robert T. Young, *Biology in America* (Boston, 1923).

Medicine: Though one scholar devoted most of his career to the history of American medicine, except for the Virginia and South Carolina colonies little has been written concerning the southeast. The material for those two areas will appear in the bibliography of each colony. But see Otho T. Beall, Jr., "Aristotle's Master Piece in America: A Landmark in the Folklore of Medicine," *WMQ* (3), XX (1963), 207–222; Whitfield J. Bell, "Medical Practice in Colonial America," *Bull. Hist. Med.*, XXI (Sept.–Oct. 1957), 442–453; John B. Blake, "Diseases and Medical Practice in Colonial America," in *History of Medicine in America: A Symposium*, ed., Felix Marti-Ibañez (New York, 1958), pp. 34–54; James H. Cassedy, "Meteorology and Medicine in Colonial America: Beginnings of the Experimental Approach," *Journ. Hist. Med.*, XXIV (1969), 193–204; Albert Deutsch, *The Mentally Ill in America: A History of Their Care and Treatment in Colonial Times* (New York, 1949); John Duffy, *Epidemics in Colonial America* (Baton Rouge, 1953), and "Yellow Fever in Colonial Charleston," *SCHM*, LII (1951), 189–197; Maurice B. Gordon, *Aesculapius Comes to the Colonies* (Ventnor, N.J., 1949), comprehensive but to be used with caution; Samuel Lewis, "List of American Graduates in Medicine in the University of Edinburgh from 1705 to 1866, with their Theses," *NEHGR*, XLII (April 1888), 157–160; Howard A. Kelly, *Some American Medical Botanists Commemorated in our Botanical Nomenclature* (Troy, N.Y., 1914); Edward B. Krumbhaar, "The State of Pathology in the British Colonies of North America," *Yale Journ. Biology and Med.*, XIX (1947), 801–815; J.A. Leo Lemay, "Franklin's 'Dr. Spence': The Reverend Archibald Spencer (1698?–1760), M.D.," *MdHM*, LIX (1964), 199–216, also important in the history of electricity; Francis R. Packard, *History of Medicine in the United States* (2 vols., New York, 1931, 1963); Richard H. Shryock, *Medical Licensing in America, 1650–1965* (Baltimore, 1967), *Medicine and Society in America, 1660–1860* (New York, 1960), and *Medicine in America: Historical Essays* (Baltimore, 1966); James Thacher, *American Medical Biography* (Boston, 1828); and others under separate colonies.

Zoology and Paleontology: Many books and essays discuss various aspects of colonial southern zoology and paleontology, though in most instances the discussion is a minor portion of a survey of natural history in general. The major work on colonial ornithology is Elsa G. Allen, "The History of American Ornithology before Audubon," *Trans. APS*, XLI, pt. 3, 1951, pp. 385–591, and "New Light on Mark Catesby," *The Auk*, LIV (1937), 348–363; George Frick and Raymond P. Stearns, *Mark Catesby: The Colonial Audubon* (Urbana, 1961); T.P. Harrison, *John White and Edward Topsell: The First Watercolors of North American Birds* (Austin, 1964); O.A. Stevens, "The First Descriptions of North American Birds," *Wilson Bull.*, XLVIII (1936), 203–215; and some representative studies of only one colony or of a single-colony figure. George G. Simpson should be noted on "The Beginning of Vertebrate Paleontology," *Trans. APS*, LXXXVI (1942), 130–188, and "The Discovery of Fossil Vertebrates in North America," *Journ. Paleontology*, XVII (1943), 26–38. See also Harry B. Weiss, *The Pioneer Century of American Entomology* (New Brunswick, N.J., mimeographed, 1936).

Geology: For geology, see George P. Merrill, *The First Hundred Years of American Geology* (New Haven, 1924), and G.W. White, "Early American Geology," *Sci. Monthly*, LXXVI (1953), 134–141.

Technology and Industry: Technology and industry again are treated most extensively in the separate studies of crafts and manufactures, but there are some fairly useful comprehensive works: J.L. Bishop, *A History of American Manufactures from 1608 to 1860* (3d ed., 3 vols., New York, 1966); Silvio A. Bedini, *Early American Scientific Instruments and Their Makers* (Washington, D.C., Smithsonian Instn., 1964); Howard I. Chapelle, *The History of American Sailing Ships* (New York, 1935); Victor S. Clark, *History of Manufactures in the United States, Vol. I, 1607–1860* (rpt. New York, 1949); John W. Oliver, *History of American Technology* (1607–1955) (New York, 1956); Alfred C. Prime, *The Arts and Crafts in Philadelphia, Maryland, and South Carolina* ([Philadelphia?], 1929); John W. Reps, *Tidewater Towns: City Planning in Colonial Virginia and Maryland* (Williamsburg and Charlottesville, 1972); T.A. Richard, *A History of American Mining* (New York, 1932); A[braham] Wolf, *A History of Science, Technology, and Philosophy in the 16th and 17th Centuries*, new ed. Douglas McKee (London, 1950); and L.B. Cohen, *Some Early Tools of American Science* (Cambridge, Mass., 1950).

For the crafts alone much has been written about individual projects or types but most of it concerns work outside the South. Carl Bridenbaugh, *The*

Colonial Craftsman (Chicago, 1961), though brief is still indispensable. Individual colonies are represented in William De Matteo, *The Silversmith in Eighteenth-Century Williamsburg*, Craft Series (Williamsburg, 1956); George B. Cutten, *The Silversmiths of North Carolina* (Raleigh, 1948), and *The Silversmiths of Georgia* (Savannah, 1958); much more comprehensive is E. Milby Burton, *South Carolina Silversmiths, 1690–1860* (Rutland, Vt., 1968); and C. Clement Samford and John M. Hemphill, II, *Bookbinding in Colonial Virginia*, Williamsburg Research Series (Charlottesville and Williamsburg, 1966). Printing is discussed in earlier chapters.

General Backgrounds and Special Approaches: A number of general works touch upon intellectual life in the colonies: Merle Curti, *The Growth of American Thought* (New York, 1943 and later eds.); Margaret Denny, "The Royal Society and American Scholars," *Sci. Monthly*, LXV (1947), 415–427; *De Brahm's Report of the General Survey in the Southern District of North America*, ed. Louis De Vorsey, Jr. (Columbia, 1971); Michael Kraus, *Intercolonial Aspects of American Culture on the Eve of the Revolution* (New York, 1928), and *The Atlantic Civilization: Eighteenth Century Origins* (Ithaca, 1949); Theodore Hornberger, "Acosta's *Historia Natural y Moral de las Indias*: A Guide to the Sources and Growth of the American Scientific Tradition," *Texas Studies in English*, XIX (1939), 139–162; Leo Marx, *The Machine in the Garden: Technology and the Pastoral Ideal in America* (New York, 1964), especially useful on a few southern writers and always provocative; William D. Stahlman, "Astrology in Colonial America: An Extended Query," *WMQ* (3), XIII (1956), 551–563; Raymond P. Stearns, "Colonial Fellows of the Royal Society of London, 1661–1788," *WMQ* (3), III (1946), 208–268; Harry Woolf, *The Transit of Venus: A Study of Eighteenth-Century Science* (Princeton, 1959); Harvey Wish, *Society and Thought in Early America: A Social and Intellectual History of the American People through 1865* (New York, 1950); Louis B. Wright, *Cultural Life in the American Colonies, 1607–1763* (New York, 1957), especially Chapter X.

Cartography: Halfway between craft and true art, cartography has received more attention than many other aspects of southern colonial civilization or production. Foremost among scholars of the subject is William P. Cumming, represented here by his "Geographical Misconceptions of the Southeast in the Cartography of the Seventeenth and Eighteenth Centuries," *JSH*, IV (1938), 476–492, and *The Southeast in Early Maps* (Chapel Hill, 1962). *De Brahm's Report*, ed. De Vorsey, just mentioned; [Anne Freudenberg et al.], *Notes to Accompany A Facsimile of John Speed's "A Map of Virginia and Maryland, 1676"* (Charlottesville, [1962]); and Fairfax Harrison, *Landmarks of Old Prince William* (rpt. Berryville, Va., 1964), all contain reproductions of early maps and discussions of them. See also Henry Harrisse, *The Discovery of North America: A Critical, Documentary, and Historic Investigation with An Essay on the Early Cartography of the New World, Including Description of Two Hundred and Fifty Maps or Atlases Existing or Lost, Constructed before the Year 1536* ... (Amsterdam, 1961); Erwin Raisz, "Outline of American Cartography," *Isis*, XXVI (1937), 371–389; Henry Stevens and Roland Tree, "Comparative Cartography: Exemplified in an Analytical and Bibliographical Description of Nearly One Hundred Maps and Charts of the American Continent Published in Great Britain during the Years 1600 to 1850," in *Essays Honoring Lawrence C. Wroth*, introduction by W.S. Lewis (Portland, Me., 1951), pp. 305–363; James C. Wheat and Christian F. Brun, *Maps and Charts Published in America before 1800: A Bibliography* (New Haven, 1969); Justin Winsor, ed., *Narrative and Critical History of America* (8 vols., Boston, 1884, etc.), Vols. III and V; and P. Lee Phillips, *A List of Maps of America in the Library of Congress Preceded by a List of Works Relating to Cartography* (Washington, D.C., 1901).

Virginia-Maryland cartography has received individual attention: J.L. Kuethe, "A Gazetteer of Maryland," *MdHM*, XXX (1935), 310–325, compiled in part from Herrman's map; Edward B. Mathews, "The Maps and Mapmakers of Maryland," in *Maryland Geological Survey*, Vol. II (Baltimore, 1898); Reps, *Tidewater Towns*, noted above, containing interesting plats and plans in facsimile; P. Lee Phillips, "Some Early Maps of Virginia and Their Makers, Including Plates Relating to the First Settlement of Virginia," *VMHB*, XV (1908), 71–81, and "Virginia Cartography," *Smithsonian Miscellaneous Collections*, no. 1039 (1896), pp. 1–85; Walter W. Ristow, *Captain John Smith's Map of Virginia* [to accompany engraving facsimile] (Washington, D.C., 1957); L.D. Scisco, "Notes on Augustine Herrman's Map," *MdHM*, XXXIII (1938), 343–351; Earl G. Swem, "Maps Relating to Virginia in the Virginia State Library and Other Departments of the Commonwealth with the 17th and 18th Century Atlas-Maps in the Library of Congress," in *Virginia State Library Bull.*, vol. 7, nos. 2 and 3, April–July 1914 (Richmond, 1914), pp. 37–229, still the most useful descriptive bibliography of Virginia maps; Coolie Verner, "The First Maps of Virginia, 1590–1673," *VMHB*, LVIII (1950), 3–15, and "The Several States of the Farrer Map of Virginia," *SB*, III (1950), 281–284. Useful also is Edmund and Dorothy Berkeley, *Dr. John Mitchell, the Man who Made the Map of North America* (Chapel Hill, 1974).

Maryland: Miscellaneous

Elizabeth Baer, comp., *Seventeenth Century Maryland: A Bibliography* (Baltimore, 1949) is eminently useful for the first half of the period, but there is nothing comparable for the colony for the eighteenth century. William H. Browne et al., eds., *The Archives of Maryland* (60–plus vols. to date, Baltimore, 1883–   ) contains much on the subject scattered through many volumes; Charles A. Barker, *The Background of the Revolution in Maryland* (New Haven, 1940), has pertinent material. Several descriptions of the colony contain scientific and technological materials, as Anon., "Eighteenth Century Maryland as Portrayed in 'Itinerant Observations' of Edward Kimber," *MdHM*, LII (1956), 315–336; *Gentleman's Progress: The Itinerarium of Dr. Alexander Hamilton, 1744*, ed. Carl Bridenbaugh (Chapel Hill, 1948); C.C. Hall, ed., *Narratives of Early Maryland, 1633–1684* (New York, 1910); John Hammond, *Leah and Rachel; or, the Two Fruitful Sisters Virginia and Maryland* (London, 1656); "Maryland in 1699: A Letter from the Reverend Hugh Jones," ed. Michael G. Kammen, *JSH*, XXIX (1963), 362–372; Anon., "Maryland in 1720," *MdHM*, XXIX (1934), 252–255; Elihu S. Riley, "*The Ancient City.*" *A History of Annapolis, in Maryland, 1649–1887* (Annapolis, 1887); Bernard C. Steiner, *Descriptions of Maryland*, Johns Hopkins Stud. Hist. & Polit. Sci., Series XXII, nos. 11–12 (Baltimore, 1904). Work on agriculture and gardening includes Edith R. Bevan, "Gardens and Gardening in Early Maryland," *MdHM*, XLV (1950), 243–270; C.P. Gould, *Land System of Maryland, 1720–1765*, Johns Hopkins Stud. Hist. & Polit. Sci., Series XXXI, no. 1 (Baltimore, 1913). Maryland medicine is studied or presented in Eugene F. Cordell, *The Medical Annals of Maryland* (Baltimore, 1903); Thomas S. Cullen, *Early Medicine in Maryland* (Baltimore, [1927? 15 pp.]); John R. Quinan, *The Medical Annals of Baltimore from 1608 to 1880* . . . (Baltimore, 1884); George B. Scriven, "Maryland Medicine in the Seventeenth Century," *MdHM*, LVII (1962), 29–46, and his "Doctors, Drugs, and Apothecaries of Seventeenth Century Maryland," *Bull. Hist. Med.*, XXXVII (1963), 516–522; also Bernard C. Steiner, "A Contribution to the History of Medicine in the Province of Maryland, 1631–1671," *Johns Hopkins Hosp. Bull.*, XIII (1902), 192–198. There is considerable Maryland material in the *Philosophical Transactions* of the Royal Society in both the seventeenth and the eighteenth century, e.g., "Part of a Letter from the Reverend Mr. Hugh Jones . . . Concerning Several Observables in Maryland," XXI, no. 259 (1700), 436–441; and "Remarks by James Petiver, on Some Animals, Plants, & c. Sent to Him from Maryland by the Reverend Mr. Hugh Jones," XX, no. 246 (1699), 393–406. Earl C. May, in *From Principio to Wheeling, 1715–1945: A Pageant of Iron and Steel* (New York, 1945) gives a romanticized picture of Maryland's first iron. For other materials on this subject see the footnotes below. An agricultural aid was Abraham Milton, *The Farmer's Companion, directing how To Survey Land after a new and particular Method* . . . (Annapolis, 1761), and the province's business is considered in Margaret S. Morris, *The Colonial Trade of Maryland, 1689–1715*, Johns Hopkins Stud. Hist. & Polit. Sci., Series XXXII (Baltimore, 1914), and Vertrees J. Wyckoff, *Tobacco Regulation in Colonial Maryland* (Baltimore, 1936).

Virginia: Natural History

Men and their work in this area are discussed by Mea Allen, *The Tradescants: Their Plants, Gardens, and Museums, 1570–1662* (London, 1964); Clarence W. Alvord and Lee Bidgood, eds., *The First Explorations of the Trans-Allegheny Region by the Virginians, 1650–1674* (Cleveland, 1912); John Banister, "Some Observations Concerning Insects Made in Virginia A.D. 1680 with remarks by Mr. James Petiver," *Philos. Trans.*, XXII, no. 270 (March–April 1701), 807–814, and "The Extracts of Four Letters . . . to Dr. Lister . . . ," *Philos. Trans.* XVII, no. 198 (March 1693), 667–672; Edmund and Dorothy Berkeley, "Another 'Account of Virginia' by the Reverend John Clayton,"

VMHB, LXXXVI (1968), 415–436; *John Clayton, Pioneer of American Botany* (Chapel Hill, 1963); *The Reverend John Clayton, A Parson with a Scientific Mind* (Charlottesville, 1965); Benjamin S. Barton, "Memorandum of the Life and Writings of Mr. John Clayton, the Celebrated Botanist of Virginia," *Philad. Med. and Physical Journal*, Pt. 1, II (1805), 139–145; Robert Beverley, *The History and Present State of Virginia*, ed. Louis B. Wright (Chapel Hill, 1947); Joseph Ewan, "First Fern Records from Virginia: John Banister's Account of 1679–1692," *American Fern Journal*, LIII (Oct.-Dec. 1963), 138–144; Joseph and Nesta Ewan, *John Banister and His Natural History of Virginia* (Urbana, 1970); Lyman Carrier, "Dr. John Mitchell, Naturalist, Cartographer, and Historian," *AHA, Annual Report for 1918*, I (Washington, D.C., 1918), 201–209; [once attributed to John Mitchell], *American Husbandry*, ed. Harry J. Carman (2 vols., London, 1775; rpt. New York, 1939); "John Mitchell to Peter Collinson," *Philos. Trans.*, XLIII, no. 424 (1744), 102–158; "John Mitchell to Cadwallader Colden," ed. Theodore Hornberger, *HLQ*, X (1946–1947), 411–417; Theodore Hornberger, "The Scientific Ideas of Dr. John Mitchell," *HLQ*, I (1946–1947), 277–296; John F. Dorman and James F. Lewis, "Dr. John Mitchell, F.R.S., Native Virginian," *VMHB*, LXXVI (1968), 437–440; Gordon W. Jones, "Doctor John Mitchell's Yellow Fever Epidemics," *VMHB*, LXX (1962), 43–48, and "The Library of Doctor John Mitchell of Urbanna," *VMHB*, LXXVI (1968), 441–443; "John Mitchell to Benjamin Franklin," *Colden Papers*, III, 151–154, in *Coll. N.-Y. Hist. Soc. 1919*; Herbert Thatcher, "Dr. Mitchell, M.D., F.R.S., of Virginia," *VMHB*, XXXIX (1931), 126–135, 206–220, XL (1932), 48–62, 97–110, 268–279, 335–346; XLI (1933), 59–70, 144–156; the Berkeleys, *Dr. John Mitchell*, and more on Mitchell in *DAB*; Hindle, *Pursuit of Science*; Stearns, *Science in the British Colonies of America*; the Berkeleys, *John Clayton*; and Blanton, *Medicine in Virginia in the Eighteenth Century* (Richmond, 1931); [Robert Fellows], "The Expedition of Batts and Fallam. John Clayton's Transcript . . ." in Alvord and Bidgood, *First Explorations*, pp. 183–205; [William Byrd?], *Natural History of Virginia*, trans. and ed. R.C. Beatty and William J. Mulloy (Richmond, 1940); Gary Dunbar, "Assessment of Virginia's Natural Qualities by Explorers and Other Settlers," in *Virginia in History and Tradition* (Farmville, Va., 1957), pp. 65–84; Eileen W. Erlanson, "The Flora of the Peninsula of Virginia," *Papers Michigan Acad. of Science, Arts, and Letters*, vol. 4, pp. 115–182; Richard M. Jellison, "Scientific Enquiry in Eighteenth Century Virginia," *Historian*, XXV (1963), 292–311, which covers much more than natural history; Hugh Jones, *The Present State of Virginia*, ed. Richard L. Morton (Chapel Hill, 1956); J.J. Murray, "A Brief History of Virginia Ornithology," *Raven*, IV (March 1933), 2–11; Richard A. Overfield, "Science in the *Virginia Gazette*," *Emporia State Research Studies*, XVI, no. 3 (March 1968), 5–53, which also includes medicine and other sciences; Earl G. Swem, "Brothers of the Spade: Correspondence of Peter Collinson and John Custis, *PAAS*, LVIII, pt. 1 (1949), 17–190; William Strachey, *The Historie of Travell into Virginia Britania*, eds. Louis B. Wright and Virginia Freund (London, 1953); John Tradescant, *Musæum Tradescantium; or, A Collection of Rarities Preserved at South-Lambeth neer London* (London, 1656); Maude H. Woodfin, "William Byrd and the Royal Society," *VMHB*, XL (1932), 23–24, 111–123; Sarah P. Stetson, "John Mercer's Notes on Plants," *VMHB*, LXI (1953), 34–44; Edward A. Wyatt, IV, "Dr. James Greenway, Eighteenth Century Botanist of Dinwiddie County, with an Account of Two Generations of His Descendants," *Tyler's Q.*, XVII (1935–1936), 211–220; Conway Zirkle, "John Clayton and our Colonial Botany," *VMHB*, LXVII (1959), 284–294.

Virginia: Physical and General Science, Horticulture and Agricultural Staples

Galen W. Ewing, "Early Teaching of Science at the College of William and Mary in Virginia," *Journ. Chemical Educ.*, XV (1938), 3–15 (rpt. *Wm. & Mary Bull.*, XXXII, no. 4 [April], 1938); Hugh Jones, "Reasons and Uses of the Georgian Calendar . . ." (B.M. Add. MSS 2183); George W. White, "Geological Observations of Captain John Smith in 1607–1614," *Illinois Acad. of Sci. Trans.*, XLVI (1953), 124–132.

John Bonoeil, *Observations to be Followed, for the Making of fit rooms . . . {for} Silkworms . . . Mulberry Trees . . .* (London, 1620); N.F. Cabell, "Early History of Agriculture in Virginia," *De Bow's Review*, XXIV (1858), 280–284, 411–421, 542–549; S.W. Fletcher, "A History of Fruit Growing in Virginia," *Virginia Fruit (Thirty-Seventh Annual Meeting of the Virginia Horticultural Society, December 6, 7, 8, 1932)*, XXI (1933), 109–119; Edward Digges, "Extract of a Letter [on Silk]," *Philos. Trans.*, I (1665), 694–698; Mary Frances Goodwin, "Three Eighteenth-Century Gardens: Bartram, Collinson, Custis," *VQR*, X (1934), 218–233; [Samuel Hartlib], *Glory Be To God on High . . . A Rare and New Discovery of a Speedy Way . . . for the Feeding of Silk-Worms in the Woods, on the Mulberry-Tree-Leaves in Virginia* (London, 1652), and *The Reformed Virginia Silk-Worm . . .* (London, 1655); Charles E. Hatch, Jr., "Mulberry Trees and Silkworms: Sericulture in Early Virginia," *VMHB*, LXV (1957), 3–61; Melvin Herndon, *Tobacco in Colonial Virginia: "The Sovereign Remedy,"* Jamestown 350th Anniv. Hist. Booklet no. 20 (Williamsburg, 1957); [John Randolph], *A Treatise on Gardening By a Citizen of Virginia* (Williamsburg, 1924, rpt. of the 3d ed. of 1826); E. Smith, *The Compleat Housewife . . . Receipts* (Williamsburg, 1742).

Virginia: Medicine

There is more on Virginia medicine than on that of any other colony. The principal works are those of Wyndham B. Blanton, *Medicine in Virginia in the Seventeenth Century* (Richmond, 1930); "Epidemics, Real and Imaginary . . . , and Other Factors Influencing Seventeenth Century Virginia's Population," *Bull. Hist. Med.*, XXXI (1957), 452–462; and *Medicine in Virginia in the Eighteenth Century* (Richmond, 1931). See also *The Apothecary in Eighteenth-Century Williamsburg* (Williamsburg, Craft Series, 1970); Harold B. Gill, *The Apothecary in Colonial Virginia* (Williamsburg Research Series, Williamsburg and Charlottesville, 1972); Charles E. Gilliam, "Mount Malado," *Tyler's Q.*, XX (1939), 138–142; Edward Ingle, "Regulating Physicians in

Colonial Virginia," *Annals. Med.*, IV (1922), 248–250; Thomas P. Hughes, *Medicine in Virginia, 1607–1699*, Jamestown 350th Anniv. Hist. Booklet no. 21 (Williamsburg, 1957); Bernard G. Hoffman, "John Clayton's Account of the Medicinal Practices of the Virginia Indians," *Ethnohistory*, XI (1964), 1–40; Richard M. Jellison, "Dr. John Tennent and the Universal Specific," *Bull. Hist. Med.*, XXXVII (1963), 336–346; Gordon W. Jones, "The First Epidemic in English America," *VMHB*, LXXI (1963), 3–10, and his essays on Dr. John Mitchell; William B. Maxwell, "The True State of the Smallpox in Williamsburg, February 22, 1748," *VMHB*, LXIII (1955), 269–274; Genevieve Miller, "European Influences on Colonial Medicine," *Ciba*, VIII (1947), 54–521, and her "Smallpox Inoculation in England and America: A Reappraisal," *WMQ* (3), XIII (1956), 476–492; and John Tennent, *An Essay on the Pleurisy* (Williamsburg, 1736), and his other works mentioned in text and notes.

Virginia: Manufacturing, Industry, Crafts

R.A. Brock, ed., *The Official Letters of Alexander Spotswood . . . 1710–1722* (2 vols., Richmond, 1885); Lester J. Cappon, ed., *Iron Works at Tuball: Terms and Conditions for their Lease as stated by Alexander Spotswood . . .* (Charlottesville, Tracy W. McGregor Library, Univ. of Virginia, 1945); Leonidas Dodson, *Alexander Spotswood, Governor of Colonial Virginia, 1710–1722* (Philadelphia, 1932); Charles E. Hatch, Jr., and T.G. Gregory, "The First American Blast Furnace . . . ," *VMHB*, LXX (1962), 259–296; Kathleen Bruce, *Virginia Iron Manufacture in the Slave Era* (New York, 1931); Charles E. Hatch, Jr., "Glassmaking in Virginia, 1607–1625," *WMQ* (2), XXI (1941), 119–138, 227–238; Jacob M. Price, "The Beginnings of Tobacco Manufacture in Virginia," *VMHB*, LXIV (1956), 3–29; and Cerinda W. Evans, *Some Notes on Shipbuilding and Shipping in Colonial Virginia*, Jamestown 350th Anniv. Hist. Booklet no. 22 (Williamsburg, 1957).

North Carolina: Miscellaneous

Percy G. Adams, "John Lawson's Alter Ego—Dr. John Brickell," *NCHR*, XXXIV (1957), 313–326; John Archdale, *A New Description of that Fertile and Pleasant Province of Carolina* (London, 1707); John Brickell, *Natural History of North Carolina*, new introduction, Carol Urness (New York, 1969); Desmond Clarke, *Arthur Dobbs, Esq., 1689–1765 . . .* (Chapel Hill, 1957); Beth G. Crabtree, *North Carolina Governors, 1585–1958* (Raleigh, 1958); [John Crafford], *A New and Most Exact Account of the Fertiles{sic} and Famous Colony of Carolina* (Dublin, 1683, [also for South Carolina]); W. Neil Franklin, "Agriculture in Colonial North Carolina," *NCHR*, III (1926), 538–574; Paul Hulton et al., eds., *The American Drawings of John White, 1577–1590* (2 vols., London and Chapel Hill, 1964); John Lawson's *A New Voyage to Carolina* (London, 1709), ed. Hugh Lefler (Chapel Hill, 1967); Lawrence Lee, *The Lower Cape Fear in Colonial Days* (Chapel Hill, 1965); Hugh Meredith, *An Account of the Cape Fear Country, 1731 . . . ,* ed. Earl G. Swem (Perth Amboy, N.J., 1922); David B. Quinn, ed., *The*

Roanoke Voyages, 1584–1590 (2 vols., London, 1955); A.S. Salley, ed., *Narratives of Early Carolina, 1650–1708* (New York, 1911); William L. Saunders, ed., *The Colonial Records of North Carolina* (26 vols., Raleigh, 1886–1907); James Sprunt, *Chronicles of the Cape Fear River, 1660–1916* (2d ed., Raleigh, 1916); George W. White, "Thomas Hariot's Observations on American Geology in 1588," *Illinois Acad. Sci. Trans.*, XLV (1952), 116–121. See also Stearns, *Science*, and Gordon, *Aesculapius*.

South Carolina: Natural History

Many of the persons and their labors here listed overlap into medicine and agriculture and other areas: Edmund and Dorothy Berkeley, *Dr. Alexander Garden of Charles Town* (Chapel Hill, 1969); Frederick P. Bowes, *The Culture of Early Charleston* (Chapel Hill, 1942); Laura M. Bragg, "Bibliography of the Sylva of South Carolina," *Bull. Charleston Museum*, VI, no. 8 (December 1910), 61–68, etc.; Mark Catesby, *The Natural History of Carolina, Florida, and the Bahama Islands* (2 vols., London, 1731–1747); for Crafford, see North Carolina bibliography just above; Margaret Denny, "Naming the Gardenia," *Sci. Monthly*, LXVII (1948), 17–22, and her "Linnaeus and His Disciple in Carolina, Alexander Garden," *Isis*, XXXVIII (1948), 161–174; "Early Letters from South Carolina upon Natural History," *SCHM*, XXI (1920), 3–9, 50–51; Pierre G. Jenkins, "Alexander Garden, M.D., F.R.S. (1728–1791), Colonial Physician and Naturalist," *Annals Med. Hist.*, X (1928), 149–158; Chapman J. Milling, ed., *Colonial South Carolina: Two Contemporary Descriptions by Governor James Glen and Doctor George Milligen-Johnston* (Columbia, 1951); Thomas Nairne?, *A Letter from South Carolina: Giving an Account of the Soil, Air, Product, Trade* . . . (2d ed., London, 1718); [John Peachie], *Some Observations on the Herb Cassing; imported from Carolina* . . . (London, 1695); for Salley, ed., *Narratives of Early Carolina*, see North Carolina bibliography just above; Mary B. Prior, ed., "Letters of Martha Logan to John Bartram, 1760–1763," *SCHM*, LIX (1958), 38–46; *Letterbook of Eliza Lucas Pinckney, 1739–1762, ed. Elise Pinckney* (Chapel Hill, 1972); Raymond P. Stearns, "The Charles Town Scientific Community," in *Science*, pp. 593–619; Joseph I. Waring, ed., "Correspondence between Alexander Garden, M.D., and the Royal Society of Arts," *SCHM*, LXIV (1963), 16–22, 86–94. See also physicians just below.

South Carolina: Medicine and related Science

R.C. Aldredge, "Weather Observers and Observations at Charleston, South Carolina, 1670–1871," *Charleston Year Book 1942*, pp. 189–257; St. Julien R. Childs, *Malaria and Colonization in the Carolina Low Country, 1526–1696* (Baltimore, 1940), and "Notes on the History of Public Health in South Carolina, 1670–1800," *Proc. S.C. Hist. Assoc., 1932* (1933), 13–22; Lionel Chalmers, *An Account of the Weather and Diseases of South Carolina* (2 vols., London, 1776); John Duffy, "Eighteenth-Century Carolina Health Conditions," *JSH*, XVIII (1952), 289–302, and his "Yellow Fever in Colonial Charleston"; James Killpatrick, *A Full and Clear Reply to Doctor Thomas Dale. . . . Im-*

proprieties of Blistering . . . Small-Pox . . . (Charles-Town, 1739); John
Lining, *A Description of the American Yellow Fever Which Prevailed at
Charleston in South-Carolina in . . . 1748* (Philadelphia, 1799, orig. by Timothy, Charleston, 1753); Everett Mendelsohn, "John Lining and his Contribution to Early American Science," *Isis*, LI (1960), 278–292; John Moultrie,
Dissertatio Medica Inauguralis, de Febre Maligna biliosa Americae (Edinburgh, 1749); Marguerite Steadman, "John Lining, Southern Scientist," *GaR*,
X (1956), 334–345; Joseph I. Waring, *A History of Medicine in South Carolina, 1670–1825* (Columbia, 1964), the single most valuable work on medicine
and other sciences in the province, and his essays, "James Killpatrick and
Smallpox Inoculation before 1914 in Charlestown," *Annals Med. Hist.*, n.s. X
(1938), 301–308, "The Influence of Benjamin Rush in the Practice of Bleed-
ing in South Carolina," *Bull. Hist. Med.*, XXXV (1961), 230–237, "Medicine
in Charleston 1750–1775," *Annals Med. Hist.*, n.s. VII (1935), 19–26, "An
Incident in Early South Carolina Medicine," *Annals Med. Hist.*, n.s. I (1929),
608–610, and other essays incorporated into his *History*.

South Carolina: General, Agricultural, Industrial, etc.

Robert J. Turnbull, *Bibliography of South Carolina, 1563–1950*, Vol. I, 1563–
1814 (Charlottesville, [1956]); Mabel L. Webber, "South Carolina Almanacs
to 1800," *SCHM*, XV (1914), 73–81; Henning Cohen, *The South Carolina
Gazette* (Columbia, 1953), and "A Colonial Topographical Poem," *Names*,
I (1953), 252–258; David Doar, *Rice and Rice Planting in the South Carolina
Low Country* (Charleston, 1936); *The Papers of Henry Laurens*, ed. Philip
M. Hamer, George C. Rogers, Jr., et al. (5 vols. to date, Columbia, 1968–
1976); C. Robert Haywood, "Mercantilism and South Carolina Agriculture,
1700–1763," *SCHM*, LX (1959), 15–27; *The Carolina Backcountry on the
Eve of the Revolution: The Journal and Other Writings of Charles Woodmason, Anglican Itinerant*, ed. Richard J. Hooker (Chapel Hill, 1953); *The
Writings of Christopher Gadsden*, ed. Christopher Walsh (Columbia, 1966);
and the publications of the South Carolina Historical Commission and the
files of the *South-Carolina Gazette* and other early newspapers.

Georgia: Miscellaneous

[T. Bowman], *A Compendium of the Whole Art of Breeding, Nursing, and the
Right Ordering of the Silk-Worm . . .* (London, 1733); Joseph Ewan, "Silk
Culture in the Colonies, with Particular Reference to the Ebenezer Colony
and the First Local Flora of Georgia," *Agricultural History*, XLIII (1969),
129–141; Allen D. Candler and Lucien Knight, eds., *The Colonial Records of
the State of Georgia* (26 vols., Atlanta, 1904–1909); *De Brahm's Report*
mentioned under *General Backgrounds . . .* above; E.M. Coulter, *Georgia: A
Short History* (rev. ed., Chapel Hill, 1960); Bertha S. Hart, "The First Garden
of Georgia," *GaHQ*, XIX (1935), 325–332; Alexander Hewatt, *An Historical
Account of the Rise and Progress of the Colonies of South Carolina and
Georgia* (2 vols., London, 1779); James W. Holland, "The Trustees Garden

in Georgia," *Agricultural Hist.*, XII (1938), 271–291; R.P. Hommel, "The History of Andrew Duché, Huguenot Potter of Georgia and Virginia," Va. Hist. Soc., Old File T-4 V typescript carbon; Francis Harper, ed., "Diary of a Journey through the Carolinas, Georgia, and Florida [by John Bartram]," *Trans. APS*, n.s. XXXIII, pt. 1 (1942), 1–120; Edith D. Johnston, "Dr. William Houstoun, Botanist," *GaHQ*, XXV (1941), 325–339, and *The Houstouns of Georgia* (Athens, Ga., 1958); Joseph Krafka, Jr., "Medicine in Colonial Georgia," *GaHQ*, XX (1936), 326–394; "Johann Martin Bolzius Answers a Questionnaire on Carolina and Georgia," eds. Klaus G. Loewald, Beverly Starika, and Paul S. Taylor, *WMQ* (3), XIV (1957), 218–261; Horace Montgomery, ed., *Georgians in Profile: Historical Essays in Honor of E.M. Coulter* (Athens, Ga., 1958), especially on Governor Henry Ellis; Hester W. Newton, "The Agricultural Activities of the Salzburgers in Colonial Georgia," *GaHQ*, XVIII (1934), 248–263; David M. Potter, Jr., "The Rise of the Plantation System in Georgia," *GaHQ*, XVI (1932), 114–135; Trevor R. Reese, *Colonial Georgia: A Study in British Imperial Policy in the Eighteenth Century* (Athens, Ga., 1963); Patrick Tailfer et al., *A True and Historical Narrative of the Colony of Georgia*, ed. Clarence L. Ver Steeg (rpt. Athens, Ga., [1960]); J. Calvin Weaver, "Early Medical History of Georgia: Georgia as a Colony," *Journ. Med. Assoc. Ga.*, XXIX (1940), 89–112; Robert C. Wilson, *Drugs and Pharmacy in the Life of Georgia, 1733–1959* (Athens, Ga., [1959]), including some biographical sketches.

Notes

1. For something of these early investigations of natural history and the exchange of plants begun by 1493 between the Old and New Worlds, see Stearns, "Old Science in the New World," in *Science in the British Colonies of America* (hereafter referred to as *Science*), pp. 19n–43, which devotes space to Oviedo, Acosta, and Monardes; Hedrick, *Hist. of Horticulture*; Goode, *Beginnings of Nat. Hist.*, U.S. Nat. Mus. Report, 1897, pt. 2 (Washington, D.C., 1901) (referred to hereafter in this edition); Howard M. Jones, *O Strange New World: American Culture: The Formative Years* (New York, 1964).

2. For a succinct account of English and European early herbalists and/or botanists, see Stearns, *Science*, pp. 44–83, which surveys the situation up to the time of the founding of the Royal Society. For other commentators on Anglo-European Renaissance natural history, see the bibliography for this chapter and the notes below.

3. From the preliminary page of *Musæum Tradescantium* (facsimile, Oxford, 1925). See also Mea Allen, "The Touchstone of Virginia," in *The Tradescants*, Ch. XIX, pp. 157–162, and "Payanketank and Poruptank," Ch. XX, pp. 163–173. Aso see the Ewans, *John Banister*, passim; and Stearns, *Science*, p. 49n. The 1925 facsimile of the *Musæum* omits pp. 74–78 of the original, the contents of which are printed with the earlier portion as one of the appendices

of Allen's study. And see Gunther, *Early English Botanists and Their Gardens*, pp. 165, 197, 233, 334–354, 370.

4. Allen, *The Tradescants*, pp. 119, 266; Richard B. Davis, *George Sandys, Poet-Adventurer* (London and New York, 1955), p. 193n. In 1625 Sandys returned to London, undoubtedly taking a collection of American marvels with him. His letter or letters to John Tradescant have disappeared: only the specific proof that they were written remains. Sandys' philosophical commentaries in his translation of Ovid's *Metamorphoses* (Oxford, 1632) indicate the traveler-poet's interest in Indian lore and customs and in the New World environment.

5. Stearns, *Science*, pp. 69–71, considers Hariot's report disappointing because it displays no knowledge of the latest scientific developments. He seems to forget for the moment how useful it was to early observers in the seventeenth century. Curiously, Stearns implies that John Smith was a better scientist (p. 71). True, Smith may have been a better observer in that he had the opportunity and did record things Hariot did not, but in later centuries he was more widely read primarily for reasons other than scientific history.

6. See below; Stearns, *Science*, pp. 71–72; and White, "Geological Observations of John Smith," pp. 124–132 (which include cartography).

7. Strachey's indebtedness is considered in S.G. Culliford, *William Strachey, 1572–1621* (Charlottesville, 1965), passim; Strachey, *Historie of Travell*, passim; Philip L. Barbour, ed., *The Jamestown Voyages under the First Charter, 1606–1609* (2 vols., Cambridge, Eng., 1969), II, 324–325; Stearns, *Science*, pp. 74–77. Two of Strachey's other writings, the "True Reportory" (in *A Voyage to Virginia in 1609*, ed. Louis B. Wright [Charlottesville, 1964]) and *For the Colony in Virginia Britannia Lawes Divine, Morall and Martiall*, ed. David H. Flaherty (Charlottesville, 1969) also contain some scientific observations though incidentally.

8. Hatch, "Mulberry Trees and Silkworms," pp. 3–61; Fletcher, "Fruit Growing in Va.," p. 11. For more on the silkworm see below; Hartlib's two books mentioned in the bibliography for this chapter; E[dward] W[illiams], *Virginia More Especially the South Part thereof Richly and truly Valued* (London, 1650); both Hartlib and Williams in Force, *Tracts*, III, xi and xiii. See also Ewan, "Silk Culture in the Colonies," pp. 129–141.

9. Hatch, "Mulberry Trees and Silkworms," pp. 51–53, who points out that Digges was by no means the only cultivator of silk in Virginia in the 1650s, though he was the most successful. See also "An Extract of a Letter, containing some Observations, made in the ordering of Silk-Worms, . . . from the ingenious Mr. *Edward Diggs*," *Philos. Trans.*, I, no. 2 (April 1665), 26–27. Digges died in 1674/5 at the age of 54. He was the son of Sir Dudley Digges, Bart., Master of the Rolls under Charles I; and Edward was himself governor of Virginia. See also Bruce, *Econ. Hist. Va.*, I, 365–370; II, 416.

10. Hammond, *Leah and Rachel*, in Force, *Tracts*, III, xiv, 19 ff.; Williams, *Virginia*, pp. 51–53. In 1648 Richard Bennett made twenty butts of fine cider from his own apples, and about the same time Captain [?] Mathews, "an old

Planter of above thirty years standing," was producing fine hemp, flax, grain and cattle. See [Sir William Berkeley], *A Perfect Description of Virginia* (London, 1649), in Force, *Tracts*, II, viii, 13–15.

11. Gunther, *Early English Botanists and Their Gardens*, pp. 346–358. On pp. 370–371 Gunther gives a "List of Seeds Imported from Virginia, 1636 . . . rec'd from Mr. Morrice," March 18, 1646.

12. For the *Hortus Siccus*, Bodleian Ashmole MSS 1405 (Va. 350th Anniv. Survey Report, no. x.94); for Digges' present of silk, BM Egerton 2543, f. 22 (*ibid.*, no. 172); for the opossum, BM Harleian 6494, f. 193 (*ibid.*, no. 307); for Hoare, Bodleian Ashmole MSS 242 (my photostat of drawing); and for Maverick, E.D. Neill, *Virginia Carolorum* (Albany, 1886), p. 131. The drawing signed by Hoare states, "This Apperition I see in Verginia at Blonte Point in James River one wensday the 14[th?] of ffebey: 1648/9 . . . is Conserd to bee on 37dr:30":Lattitud." The King had Thomas Povey inform Digges (March 2, 1660) that he would be pleased to have plants and simples for his garden from Virginia (BM Add. MSS 11411, f. 24; Va. 350th Anniv. Survey Report, no. 376).

13. "William Byrd Title Book," *VMHB*, XLVIII (1940), 36n.

14. There is a great deal of printed material on the objectives and foundation of the Royal Society, the principal being Thomas Birch's *The History of the Royal Society of London* . . . (4 vols., London, 1756–1757), and C.R. Weld, *A History of the Royal Society* (2 vols., London, 1848). A succinct statement is in Stearns, *Science*, pp. 84–114. For further bibliography see Stearns' notes, pp. 85 ff. Both Stearns and the present writer are indebted to the unpublished manuscript Journal-Books and Letter-Books in the Royal Society library, as well as to the BM Sloane MSS, the printed *Philos. Trans.*, and other manuscripts in scattered places, as the Linnean Society.

15. Lists and discussions of North American colonial Fellows of the Royal Society are given in Margaret Denny, "The Royal Society and American Scholars," pp. 415–427; William L. Sachse, *The Colonial American in Britain* (Madison, Wis., 1956), pp. 154–178; Stearns, *Science*, pp. 162ff., and list of members, pp. 708–711. Stearns is in the older historical tradition of assigning disproportionate importance to anything from New England and being supercilious or condescending toward anything done south of the Susquehanna. He writes Maryland scientific history off quickly as being of no importance and gives relatively little space to such significant figures as Banister, Lawson, Beverley, the two John Claytons, Lining, Chalmers, and others to be mentioned below, any one of whom deserved membership before half of those on his list. He assigns the controversial Virginian Dr. John Tennent to Pennsylvania. The three contributions from Virginia to appear in Volume I of the *Philos. Trans.* were by Digges, Silas Taylor, and Moray.

16. Stearns, *Science*, pp. 117–161. Quite a different point of view appears in F.G. Kilgour, "The Rise of Scientific Activity in Colonial New England," *Yale Journal of Biology and Medicine*, XXII (1949), 123–128. Much has been made of Cotton Mather as a pioneer figure in American medicine by Beall and Shryock, Hornberger, and Stearns (*Science*, pp. 403–406). The gen-

eralization that Mather was the first native American with a philosophical approach to medicine and the first to advance beyond being merely a field agent for European scientists may certainly be challenged or discounted because the "native-born" may be balanced by dozens of southerners who showed some of these qualities and spent all their active years in America.

17. The itemized list is printed in Stearns, *Science*, pp. 694–698, from a copy in the Royal Society Archives, Classified Papers, 1660–1770, XIX, no. 48.

18. See note 9 above and Letter-Book, I, 241–242, and Guard-Book, M-I, no. 36a, as well as *Philos. Trans.*, I, no. 12 (May 7, 1665), 201–202, and *WMQ* (2), II (1922), 157–161, for Moray.

19. Reproduced from the Royal Society's collection in *WMQ* (2), II (1922), 157–161. Sir Robert Moray (1600–1673) was a founder of the Royal Society. The quotation is from page 160 of *WMQ*.

20. In XI, no. 126 (June 20, 1676), 623–626; reprinted at Oxford in 1904. The original is in the Royal Society Classified Papers, 1660–1740, VII (1), no. 18. See Stearns, *Science*, pp. 180–183.

21. Catlett is sketched briefly in Harrison, *Landmarks of Old Prince William*, p. 34, and in Douglas L. Rights and William P. Cumming, eds., *The Discoveries of John Lederer* (Charlottesville, 1958), pp. 87n–90. The original letter is in the archives of the Colonial Williamsburg Foundation. Catlett apparently acted with Lederer as co-leader of the expedition and its surveyor and natural-history man. One phrase of his letter is in a cipher which Mrs. Helen Bullock solved.

22. Several of Ludwell's letters are in IV, V, and XX (1896, 1897, 1912) of the *VMHB*, with originals in the Huntington Lib., the London P.R.O., and the Bodleian. See also Sainsbury, ed., *Cal. St. Papers, Col., 1661–1668*, p. 475, and Howard M. Jones, *The Literature of Virginia in the Seventeenth Century* (rev. ed., Charlottesville, 1968), pp. 77–79.

23. Clayton is discussed in a number of places, and his writings appear in the *Philos. Trans.* of the Royal Society or the BM MSS. Stearns, *Science*, pp. 183–195, gives a good succinct account of his activities in Virginia, and Edmund and Dorothy Berkeley have in *The Reverend John Clayton* given the most extensive account of his life and printed his writings in the same volume, from print or manuscript, with a good bibliography. Clayton's son, Robert, a distinguished writer and bishop in Ireland, preserved many of his father's papers, some by making fresh copies.

24. The Berkeleys, *The Reverend John Clayton*, pp. xxi, 11. John Evelyn describes demonstrations with his vessel before the Royal Society in 1682 by Dr. Dennis Papin (*ibid.*, pp. xxi–xxiin).

25. The account is reprinted from BM MS. Sloane 4432, f. 9 in the Berkeleys, *The Reverend John Clayton*, pp. 68–77; a somewhat different version appears in Alvord and Bidgood, eds., *The First Explorations*, pp. 183–195. The Royal Society's Journal-Book (no. 8, p. 223) abbreviates many words which were given in full by Clayton. The journal was read before the Society Aug. 1, 1688.

26. The version printed by the Berkeleys, *The Reverend John Clayton*, pp. 21–39, is that of Bishop Robert Clayton's copy of his father's MS.

27. Printed by the Berkeleys, *The Reverend John Clayton*, pp. 105–121, from the Royal Society Classified Papers C2.23/1–11. In slightly differing version it appeared in *Philos. Trans.*, XVIII (1694), 121–135.

28. Read but not published until the Berkeleys included it in *The Reverend John Clayton* (pp. 122–127) from the original in the Royal Society Archives C2.23/11–14.

29. Published in the Berkeleys, *ibid.*, pp. 128–131. The original of the former is in the Royal Society Archives C2.24, the latter in the BM MSS 243 f. 150 [Article 28], according to the Berkeleys for the last, "A Copy of a Register Book of the Royal Society."

30. Stearns, *Science*, pp. 195–211, and the Ewans, *John Banister*. The latter include an extensive biographical sketch, a study of the use and disposition of Banister's works, a list of books from his library, and a thoroughly annotated edition of his published and unpublished writings, including "Of the Natives" discussed in Ch. II above. Both Stearns and the Ewans recognize the wide range of Banister's interests. The Ewans give a good picture of the natural-history circle of Oxford and London from which Banister probably received his interest and training.

31. Britten, *Sloane Herbarium*, ed. Dandy, p. 50, described more fully in the Ewans, *John Banister*, pp. 29–31.

32. The Ewans, *John Banister*, pp. 98–108, 118–126; for location of his manuscripts, pp. 402–403.

33. *Ibid.*, pp. 68–69.

34. BM Sloane MS. 3321, ff. 3v–4v, reproduced in Ewans, *John Banister*, pp. 74–75. This is a fragment only, and a copy in Doody's hand.

35. BM Sloane MS. 3321, f. 7, published in the Ewans, *John Banister*, pp. 80–84.

36. BM Sloane MS. 3321, f. 8, printed in the Ewans, *John Banister*, pp. 99–101.

37. Stearns, *Science*, pp. 210–211; also the Ewans, *John Banister*, passim, on whom Stearns relied heavily. The Ewans (pp. 154–160) show some typical uses of Banister's material by later botanists.

38. The Ewans, *John Banister*, pp. 117–265; Insect-Arachnid, pp. 272 ff.

39. Goode, "Beginnings of Nat. Hist. in America," p. 385. See the Ewans, *John Banister*, pp. 279–280, for a list of manuscripts and drawings of Insects and Arachnida.

40. The Ewans, *John Banister*, pp. 308–309.

41. BM Sloane MS. 3343, f. 58, etc. including ff. 97–274; also in Va. 350th Anniv. Survey Report no. 73, Sloane MS 3328 ff. 88–89.

42. W.S. Perry, ed., *Historical Collections*, I (Hartford, Conn., 1870), 29–32, and Fulham Palace Papers 14, item no. 59, for letter to the Bishop of Lichfield. For that to the archbishop, see MS. in Fulham Papers, V. VI, Virginia 1626–1723, in Lambeth Palace Lib.

43. Considering his brief life span in Maryland, there is considerable ma-

terial on the first Hugh Jones. Stearns has produced some of his letters in "Petiver," pp. 294–303, passim, and in *Science*, pp. 263–268. Recently edited by Kammen is "Maryland in 1699," a letter from Jones. Also in the *Philos. Trans.* are communications from Jones, as in XX, no. 246 (1699), 393–406. More complete MS. copies of Jones' communications are in BM Sloane MSS, the Ashmolean at Oxford, the Royal Society's various Guard-Books and Letter-Books, and the Fulham Palace Papers at Lambeth. Stearns, *Science*, pp. 268–269, gives two reproductions of dried plants from Maryland, one of Jones' which has never been fully identified.

44. For Vernon, see Stearns, "Petiver," pp. 303–307, and *Science*, pp. 268–271, and printed and MS. material in BM and Royal Society, Blathwayt Papers, XV, no. 3 (Colonial Williamsburg Foundation). For Krieg and Isaac, see Stearns, "Petiver," pp. 307–310, and *Science*, pp. 271–274; and the same MS. collections noted for Vernon. The anonymous 1705–1706 "Narrative" is printed in *AHR*, XII (1907), 327–340 from BM Sloane MS. noted in the text above. Stephen Bordley's letter to Petiver is in BM Sloane MS. 3321, f. 194. For a sketch of Bordley, see Nelson Rightmyer, *Maryland's Established Church* (Baltimore, 1956), pp. 162–163. Bordley's letter mentions his accidentally seeing directions Petiver had sent to a Mr. _____. Stearns says that the letter miscarried and that when it reached Petiver the latter tried to reach Bordley, who had by then lost his enthusiasm. Actually Bordley was dead. Clearly Stearns never fully identified Bordley.

45. Stearns, *Science*, p. 293, discusses North Carolina's participation in the Royal Society's activities, or the lack of it, in half a sentence. Wilson's pamphlet is reprinted in Salley, ed. *Narratives of Early Carolina, 1650–1708* (New York, 1911; rpt. 1953), pp. 161–176.

46. In Salley, ed., *Narratives of Early Carolina*, pp. 127–134, and *Coll. S.C. Hist. Soc.* (1897), pp. 456–462.

47. Joseph Dalton to Anthony Lord Ashley, from "Charles Town upon Ashley river," in Sainsbury, ed., *Cal. St. Papers Col., 1669–1674*, pp. 319–321, from Shaftesbury Papers, Section IX, Bundle 48, no. 87.

48. Letter in Univ. of Edinburgh Lib., La. II. 718/1, in four large pages. Mathews offers to reveal to the medical botanist all he himself has already learned.

49. Newe's letters of May 17 and 29 and Aug. 23, 1682, are printed from Bodleian MS. Rawlinson D. 810 in the *SCHM*, VIII (1907), 120 ff. and in Salley, ed., *Narratives of Early Carolina*, pp. 179–187. Newe mentions that a new herbal appeared just as he left England, probably John Ray's *Methodus plantarum nova* (London, 1682).

50. Copy of Peachie's letter, NYPL, Sabin 86676. See Stearns, *Science*, p. 293, for Cox. Several papers of this period from Carolina are preserved in the Journal-Book, Classified Papers, and Register-Book of the Royal Society.

51. For brief sketches of these and most other South Carolina collectors, see Britten, *Sloane Herbarium*, ed. Dandy, passim. Stearns, who mentions the 1698 botanizing in Hampstead in London may be confusing Bohun father and son, but the evidence points to the younger man being frequently in Britain on

business. Petiver in *Musei Petiveriani* in 1703 acknowledged plants from Bohun. See also J.K. Small, "Botanical Fields, Historic and Prehistoric," *Journ. N.Y. Bot. Garden*, XXIX (1928), 149–179, 185–209, and Stearns, *Science*, p. 295. Though I have personally examined the Sloane MS. letters, the references to them are most easily accessible usually in Britten, *Sloane Herbarium*, and Stearns, *Science* and his "Petiver." Professor Joseph Ewan has seen in a copy of "Petiver's Works" presented by Sloane to John Bartram a description of a Carolina "Caseworm" brought to Petiver by Bohun, with a description of its habitat. Bohun, who went back to England in 1701, returned to Carolina in 1709 but did no more collecting.

52. For Francklyn, see Britten, *Sloane Herbarium*, p. 131, and Stearns, *Science*, p. 295. For Halsteed, etc., see Britten, passim, and BM Sloane MS. 4063, f. 18; for Rutherford, Britten, pp. 196–197. Their letters to Petiver are also among the Sloane MSS.

53. Clifford K. Shipton and J.L. Sibley, *Biographical Sketches of the Graduates of Harvard University*, IV (Cambridge, Mass., 1933), 101–106; *SCHM*, XXI (1920), 4; Britten, *Sloane Herbarium*, p. 159 and plate 53. The letters are in BM Sloane MSS 4063, ff. 132, 155; 4064, ff. 4, 69, 148, 150, 155, 192, 233, 258. Stearns, *Science*, opp. pp. 300–301, has photographs of two of Lord's dried specimens now in the Sloane Herbarium gathered in 1704 and 1707.

54. For Henchman, see Stearns, *Science*, pp. 297, 303–305, and Britten, *Sloane Herbarium*, p. 159 under "Joseph Lord." Shipton and Sibley, *Biog. Sketches Graduates of Harvard*, IV, 297–298. Henchman's letter is in BM Sloane MS. 334, ff. 196–199, recorded in Royal Society Journal-Book, XI, 106.

55. Stearns, "Petiver," pp. 345–346, 363–364, and *Science*, pp. 298–299. Her letters are among the Sloane MSS. Her "Account of Animals and Shells from Carolina," edited by Petiver, appeared in *Philos. Trans.*, XXIV, no. 299 (May 1705), 1952–1960. The one other known South Carolina correspondent of Petiver in this early period is Thomas Pinckney, who on May 20, 1704, wrote that he was forwarding a small box from his friend Mr. Lord (BM Sloane MS. 4064, f. 11). For a letter of Mrs. Williams and several from Joseph Lord see "Early Letters from South Carolina upon Natural History." pp. 3–9, 50–51.

56. *A New Voyage to Carolina by John Lawson*, ed. Hugh T. Lefler (Chapel Hill, 1967), pp. xvi, xl–xlii; Stearns, "Petiver," p. 335, and *Science*, pp. 305–306.

57. My own copy of the letter from BM Sloane MS. 4063 f. 79 agrees with that printed in Lefler, ed., *A New Voyage*, pp. 267–268, rather than the version in Stearns, *Science*, p. 306, or "Petiver," p. 336.

58. Britten, *Sloane Herbarium*, p. 154.

59. Lefler, ed., *A New Voyage*, p. xviii, who like Stearns is uncertain of the date of Lawson's appointment, which may have been while he was in London in 1709.

60. *A New Voyage*, ed. Lefler, pp. 96–171, for text. For comment regarding Lawson's observation, see U.P. Hedrick, *Hist. of Horticulture*, pp. 122–124.

61. For a succinct critical summary of *A New Voyage*, see Stearns, *Science*, pp. 313–315.

62. For the Lawson-Petiver letters see *A New Voyage*, ed. Lefler, pp. 267–273 (BM Sloane MSS 4064, ff. 214, 249, 267, 271; Britten, *Sloane Herbarium*, pp. 44, 154 (and MS. refs.).

63. Stearns, *Science*, pp. 280 ff. The Journal-Books and *Philos. Trans.* from 1697 are full of contributions by Byrd and other Virginians or sent by visitors in that province. See also Pierre Marambaud, *William Byrd of Westover, 1674–1744* (Charlottesville, 1971), pp. 80–83. For Byrd letters to Sloane and others, see the list in Marambaud, pp. 282–287, and in the manuscripts of the BM Sloane Collection and the Royal Society. Petiver seems never to have got a reply to his several letters to Byrd, who preferred to answer through Sloane.

64. The most elaborate study is Frick and Stearns, *Mark Catesby*, but see also Stearns, *Science*, pp. 286–288, 315–316, the manuscripts of the Royal Society and the BM Sloane Collection, and the Berkeleys, *John Clayton, Pioneer*, pp. 201n, passim. It is pointed out that Cocke arrived in 1710, two years before his wife and her brother Mark.

65. Frick and Stearns, *Catesby*, pp. 8–10. The reasoning here seems to this reader unconvincing. There appear to be numerous other ways in which early acquaintanceship, if it did exist, might have occurred. Stearns, *Science*, p. 286n, avers that Frick has discovered more persuasive evidence of Catesby's early association with Ray since the biography appeared. See also Britten, *Sloane Herbarium*, pp. 110–113. For list of seeds sent to Dale, see BM Sloane MS. 3339.

66. For a bibliography of various editions of the *Natural History* and of Catesby's other published writings, see Frick and Stearns, *Mark Catesby*, pp. 109–111. I am indebted to the biography and to Stearns' *Science* for much of what is said of Catesby, though I have also used the manuscript correspondence and other items in the British Museum and the Royal Society, several Virginia sources in that state's historical society, and the Bodleian. The interested reader should look also at Butler, "America: A Hunting Ground for Eighteenth-Century Naturalists," pp. 3–5, and Allen's "History of American Ornithology," passim, and "New Light on Mark Catesby," pp. 348–363. Recently the Beehive Press of Savannah, Georgia, has published a handsome full-size facsimile, with some colored plates but unfortunately not a complete text, edited by George F. Frick and Joseph Ewan.

67. Royal Society, Classified Papers IV (2). 4 and MSS L. 6. 44. See Stearns, *Science*, p. 276, which finds Lewis' communications in the Journal-Books, Guard-Books, and Letter-Books of the Society. They or some of them were published in *Philos. Trans.*, XXXVII, no. 418 (March-May 1731), 55–69, 69–70; and XXXVIII, no. 429 (July-Oct. 1733), 119–121.

68. Stearns, *Science*, pp. 275, 277–278; Royal Society Letter-Books and Journal-Books; and Britten, *Sloane Herbarium*, p. 202. Sloane's Lloyd was probably Edward Lloyd III, member of the Council and of a most distinguished family. He was probably the son of the Philemon Lloyd elected F.R.S. 1722.

See Oswald D. Tilghman, *Hist. Talbot County Md., 1661–1861* (2 vols., Baltimore, 1915; rpt. 1967), I, 132–146.

69. Jones Family Papers, III (LC).

70. For Symmer's (Seymour, Symor) letters and list, see BM Sloane MSS 4054, ff. 304, 306 (for 1732); 4061; f. 158 (c. 1737); 4019, ff. 69–70 (for c. 1737); and Blanton, *Med. in Va. in the Eighteenth Century*, pp. 372–376, etc. See Blanton's chapter on "Botany and Medicine" and the discussion in the text below of southern colonial medicine. Stearns fails to note Symmer in either *Science* or "Petiver"; he also ignores Booth of Stafford County.

71. Letter dated April 2, 1735, in Bristow Papers, 22953, Va. St. Lib.

72. Most of the surviving letters are from Collinson to Custis: in Earl G. Swem's "Brothers of the Spade: Correspondence of Peter Collinson of London, and John Custis, of Williamsburg, Virginia, 1734–1746," *PAAS*, LVIII, pt. 1, 17–190. There are other letters than the exchange of the two persons named in the title.

73. For Isham Randolph, see Jonathan Daniels, *The Randolphs of Virginia, "America's Foremost Family"* (Garden City, N.Y., 1972), pp. 40 52–53, passim, and H.J. Eckenrode, *The Randophs: The Story of a Virginia Family* (New York, 1946), passim, esp. p. 146. Isham's presence is noted in all three of the extant William Byrd diaries, from 1709 through 1741, both in Virginia and in London, and frequently in the Byrd correspondence printed and in manuscript. See also "Brothers of the Spade," ed. Swem, p. 166, and "Letters of Isham Randolph," *WMQ* (2), VI (1926) 314, and *VMHB*, XIV (1907), 226, etc.

74. See Eckenrode and Daniels in note 73 just above, and John Custis' letter of 1734 from the Custis Letter-Book in LC, printed in "Brothers of the Spade," ed. Swem, pp. 38–40.

75. One recalls that Thomas Jefferson's library included many books from that of his great uncle Sir John (see E. Millicent Sowerby, comp., *Catalogue of the Library of Thomas Jefferson* [5 vols., Washington, D.C., 1952–1959], passim, esp. the index in Volume V).

76. Hindle, *The Pursuit of Science*, pp. 28, 30. For recent study of the *Flora Virginica*, see the Berkeleys, *John Clayton, Pioneer*, pp. 64–70, 128–145, and Stearns, *Science*, pp. 554–558.

77. The Berkeleys in *John Clayton, Pioneer* (pp. 138–150) offer persuasive and perhaps conclusive evidence, with their conclusions based on surviving fragments of Clayton's planned revision, that it was greatly superior to that which did appear. Stearns, *Science*, p. 558, agrees that Clayton's own manuscript second edition was superior to that published.

78. Journal-Book, XIV, 383 (December 11, 1729). See Stearns, *Science*, p. 556. For Clayton's marriage, children, plantation, library, and living conditions see the Berkeleys, *John Clayton, Pioneer*, pp. 22–40.

79. Quoted in the Berkeleys, *John Clayton, Pioneer*, pp. 56–57, from Catesby's *Natural History*, II, Appendix, 116. No correspondence between Catesby and Clayton appears to have survived, though there is abundant evidence that they did exchange letters as well as natural materials.

80. Both the 1739 and the 1743 sections were republished in facsimile by the Arnold Arboretum (Cambridge, Mass., 1946), and the 1762 edition by the Arboretum in the same year.

81. Neither name appears on the fragmentary rolls of the first American Philosophical Society, but contemporary letters indicate their membership. See Berkeleys, *John Clayton, Pioneer*, pp. 95–97.

82. Linnaeus' Corresp., Vol. XVII Supplement, in Linnaean Society, London.

83. See the Berkeleys, *John Clayton, Pioneer*, pp. 171–172. As recently as 1906, Earl G. Swem avers ("Brothers of the Spade," p. 176) Clayton letter-books and other papers existed in the hands of descendants in Chesterfield County, Virginia. Swem sought for them without success in 1929. The papers included two volumes of manuscript neatly copied and prepared for the press and a *Hortus Siccus*, folio, also prepared for the press with marginal notes and directions for an engraver (the Berkeleys, *John Clayton, Pioneer*, p. 171).

84. Berkeleys, p. 169; Benjamin S. Barton, "Memorandum of the Life and Writings of Mr. John Clayton, the Celebrated Botanist of Virginia," *Philad. Med. and Physical Journal*, Part 1, II (1805), 139–145. Barton's memoir should be read carefully by anyone interested in the history of American science.

85. Barton's statement is quoted by the Berkeleys, *John Clayton, Pioneer*, p. 198; see also the Gronovius-Linnaeus Correspondence, LC, XV, 442, also quoted in the Berkeleys, p. 177.

86. The Berkeleys, *John Clayton, Pioneer*, pp. 174–175.

87. *Notes on the State of Virginia*, ed. William Peden (Chapel Hill, 1954), p. 42; *Thomas Jefferson's Garden Book, 1766–1824*, ed. Edwin M. Betts (Philadelphia, 1944), passim (the quotation on p. 647).

88. Actually a great many monographs and essays have been devoted to Mitchell, for which see bibliography for this chapter above. The most extensive and comprehensive was Thatcher's, a curiously assorted gathering of a good deal of data. In 1974, however, Edmund and Dorothy Berkeley published the first full-length study, *Dr. John Mitchell, the Man who Made the Map of North America*. They considered all phases of his activity. See also Lawrence Martin's sketch in *DAB*. Of those essays mentioned in the bibliography Hornberger's "The Scientific Ideas of John Mitchell" is especially useful, as is Lyman Carrier's "Dr. John Mitchell, Naturalist, Cartographer, and Historian."

89. For proof of place and time of birth see Dorman and Lewis, "Doctor John Mitchell, F.R.S., Native Virginian," pp. 437–438. Others earlier have suggested somewhat timidly that Mitchell was born in the Old Dominion. Stearns, *Science*, p. 539, goes along with those who have guessed Mitchell's birthdate as about 1690, twenty-one years too early. Dorman and Lewis show that he did not leave Virginia until after January 8, 1745/6. He was in England by June 2, 1746, as Collinson notes (Herbert Thatcher, "Dr. John Mitchell, M.D., F.R.S. of Virginia," *VMHB*, XXXIX [1931], 127).

90. Original in Edinburgh Univ. Lib. Printed in Herbert Thatcher, "Dr. Mitchell," *VMHB*, XL (1932), 50–57.

91. See *Va. Gaz.*, November 14, 1745, and *Tyler's Q.*, VIII (1926/7), 286,

for the advertisement of Mitchell's property for sale at Urbanna: a large herb and plant garden; furnishings of an apothecary's shop and a small chemical laboratory; and a choice collection of books in several languages. In his 1738 letter he remarks, however, on his want of a [comprehensive?] botanical library. See also Jones, "The Library of Doctor John Mitchell," pp. 441–443.

92. The essay in *Philos. Trans.*, XLV, no. 489 (London, 1750), 541–563 (received November 17 and 24, 1748). For the best estimate of his significance as a botanist see Hornberger, "Scientific Ideas," pp. 278–283, and Stearns, *Science*, pp. 539–544.

93. Stearns, *Science*, pp. 544–545. The July 8 paper was printed in its entirety in Thatcher, "Dr. Mitchell," *VMHB*, XL (1932), 338–346. See also Hornberger, "Scientific Ideas," pp. 285–286, and the Berkeleys, *Dr. John Mitchell*, passim, but see the Berkeleys on authorship of these books.

94. For Dobbs and the Venus's flytrap, see Joseph Ewan, "'The Most Wonderful Plant in the World' [Darwin]," in *Sonderdruck aus Festschrift für Claus Nissen* (Guido Pressler, Wiesbaden, 1973), pp. 173, 183.

95. The best succinct account of the Charleston naturalists is Stearns, *Science*, pp. 593–619. For Dr. Garden and his circle, see the Berkeleys, *Dr. Alexander Garden*; for the medical men and their botanical interests, Waring, *Hist. of Med. in S.C.*, passim. For Lucas and others individually see items in this chapter's bibliography and in the notes below. For Gregg, see Smith, ed., *Correspondence of Linnaeus*, I, 189.

96. Letter of April 7, 1742, in Amer. Philos. Soc., Waring, *Hist of Med. in S.C.*, pp. 183–184, and pp. 204–206. Dale's will speaks of Gronovius as his friend, a statement which probably means there had been a long correspondence and perhaps earlier personal intimacy.

97. *Papers of Henry Laurens*, ed. Hamer, Rogers, et al. (Columbia, 1972), III, 958–959; Dering, BM Sloane MSS 4049, f. 151 and 4050, f. 199; Standish, BM Sloane MS. 4049, f. 250; Jenner, BM Sloane MS. 4056, f. 272; Yonge, Duke MSS, C.C. Pinckney to Yonge, February 4, 1746/7. See also the Berkeleys, *Dr. Alexander Garden*, in the text below.

98. Royal Society of Arts, Guard-Book II, 62, for Woodmason to RSA of May 23, 1763; for Garden to RSA of February 17, 1759, RSA Guard-Book IV, 38. Other letters are in RSA Guard-Book III, 252, 96; V, 28, etc.

99. Garden is represented in thirteen manuscript collections in Great Britain and America and has been the subject of a number of studies of various phases of his work. See Stearns, *Science*, pp. 599–619, and the Berkeleys, *Dr. Alexander Garden*, the latter including a good bibliography of Garden's own work and of that on him. For other material, see bibliography for this chapter above and various notes below. Waring, *Hist. of Med. in S.C.*, p. 221, gives 1725 as the date of Garden's birth.

100. For more on American observations on this plant see the Berkeleys, *Alexander Garden*, pp. 29–31. *Essays and Observations* was the journal of the Philosophical Society of Edinburgh. Philip Miller, who cultivated pinkroot, may have got the seeds from Garden.

101. See Stearns, *Science*, pp. 604–605, and the Berkeleys, *Dr. Alexander*

Garden, pp. 36–37 ff., passim. See also the Royal Society of Arts manuscript "American Correspondence . . . 1755–1840" and the Berkeleys, *Dr. Alexander Garden*, p. 56n.

102. Frick and Stearns, *Mark Catesby*, pp. 75–77; Stearns, *Science*, pp. 605–606; the Berkeleys, *Dr. Alexander Garden*, pp. 56–57, 75, 132–133, 164.

103. The Berkeleys, *Dr. Alexander Garden*, pp. 193–197.

104. *Ibid.*, pp. 330–333; Stearns, *Science*, pp. 618–619.

105. *De Brahm's Report*, ed. De Vorsey, passim. De Brahm describes South Carolina flora in some detail, with the implication that it is the same as that of Georgia. The *Report* was written in the early 1760s. For Houstoun and Millar, see Stearns, *Science*, pp. 326–333. See also Ewan, "Silk Culture in the Colonies, with Particular Reference to the Ebenezer Colony and the First Local Flora of Georgia," pp. 137–138. For a synopsis of Bolzius' report, see this Ewan article, pp. 140–141.

106. Allen, "Hist. of Amer. Ornithology," pp. 386–591, devotes many pages to the European backgrounds of the study of birds in America. Hariot's work is touched upon in Ch. I above. In addition to the Stephen Lorant and Hulton et al. editions of Hariot-White illustrations noted above, see Thomas P. Harrison, *John White and Edward Topsell: The First Water Colors of North American Birds* (Austin, Tex., n.d. [1964]).

107. Text in the Berkeleys, *The Reverend John Clayton*, pp. 93–104. See Allen, "Hist. of Amer. Ornithology," pp. 459–461; and the Ewans, *John Banister*, p. 60.

108. For Banister, the Ewans, *John Banister*, passim; for Lawson's list, *A New Voyage*, ed. Lefler, pp. 140–155.

109. For Catesby as ornithologist, see Allen, "Hist. of Amer. Ornithology," pp. 463–478; and Frick and Stearns, *Mark Catesby*, pp. 54–64, 112–113, etc. Most of the single essays listed by Frick and Stearns have been read for this study, but actually Allen, and Frick and Stearns, supersede them. Allen, pp. 465–467, lists one hundred different birds (she is using Catesby's names as published in the American Ornithological Union's Check-List of North American Birds, 4th ed. Lancaster, Pa., 1931). She notes that nine other birds are illustrated in the Appendix to Volume II of Catesby's *Natural History*. The number 113 is from Frick and Stearns, p. 56.

110. *Philos. Trans.*, XLIV, pt. 2 (1747), 435–444, and *Gentleman's Magaine*, XVIII (1748), 447–448. See Frick and Stearns, pp. 43–44, 63–64.

111. "Mark Catesby and the Nomenclature of North American Birds," *The Auk*, XLVI (1929), 447–454.

112. See reproduction in Allen, "Hist. of Amer. Ornithology," p. 493. This is from Pennant's *Arctic Zoology* (1784–1785).

113. See the Berkeleys, *John Clayton, Pioneer*, pp. 56–57, for the text of the description of the whippoorwill, and see the Berkeleys, *Dr. Alexander Garden*, for the further references to Garden's natural-history contributions, pp. 305–312.

114. Among the serials, *Philos. Trans.* of the Royal Society (and its manuscript records) and the *Gentleman's Magazine*, contained a number of brief

observations on mockingbirds, hummingbirds, and other varieties—descriptions which supplement the more complete book-length studies already mentioned.

115. P. 385. Petiver had acknowledged Banister's help in *Musae Petiveriani* . . . and other works. See Stearns, *Science*, pp. 264 ff. For two of Petiver's observations from Banister, or Banister's own sent to Petiver, see *Philos Trans.*, XVII (1693), 671–672, and XXII (1701), 807–814; also the Ewans, *John Banister*, pp. 272–307, for the Insect and Arachnid Catalogue and other insect work.

116. *A New Voyage*, ed. Lefler, pp. 131–140. Joseph Lord had frequently sent Petiver boxes of insects (e.g., see letter from Lord to Petiver, January 16, 1701/2, in BM Sloane MS., 4063, ff. 132).

117. Frick and Stearns, *Mark Catesby*, p. 82. For the South Carolina references, see the Berkeleys, *Dr. Alexander Garden*, pp. 81–84, 95–96, 128–130.

118. Quinn, ed., *The Roanoke Voyages* I, 330–331, 355–357, 398–462.

119. A convenient source for all three (Percy, Perkins, and Smith) in a recently meticulously edited assemblage is Barbour, ed., *The Jamestown Voyages under the First Charter, 1606–1609:* for Percy, I, 130; Perkins, I, 161; and Smith, II, 348–350.

120. Kingsbury, ed., *Records Va. Co.*, III, 307–309. See Ch. I above for exaggerated descriptions of the natural marvels of the southern colonies.

121. This essay is reprinted with notes in the Berkeleys, *The Reverend John Clayton*, pp. 105–121. The manuscript from which they printed is in the Royal Society Archives, Classified Papers c.2.23/1–11. It was published in *Philos. Trans.*, XVIII (1694), 121–135, and has also been printed in Force, ed., *Tracts*, III, xii, pp. 35–45.

122. See the Ewans, *John Banister*, passim, for his work in the other areas. For his molluscs, see pp. 308–325; for his fossils, see the section below.

123. Frick and Stearns, *Mark Catesby*, pp. 76–85, including identifications of the subjects of the thirty-three fish plates, and Stearns, *Science*, passim. For correspondence concerning animals, see other letters in BM Sloane MSS and the Royal Society's various manuscript records.

124. BM Sloane MSS 4054, ff. 304–306; 4061, f. 158; 4019, ff. 69–70, dated 1736–1737.

125. Thus Hornberger, "The Scientific Ideas of Dr. John Mitchell," does classify this essay; see also Stearns, *Science*, pp. 545–547. Mitchell's essay is in *Philos. Trans.* XLIII, no. 424 (1744), 102–150.

126. Swem, ed., "Brothers of the Spade," pp. 61, 75–76. Byrd and others believed the snake had the power to charm. See Stearns, *Science*, p. 581.

127. Ed. Louis B. Wright (Chapel Hill, 1947), pp. 146–156.

128. White, "Thomas Hariot's Observations on American Geology in 1588," pp. 116–141; Quinn, ed., *Roanoke Voyages*, I, 314–387, passim; Stearns, *Science*, p. 69.

129. Barbour, ed., *The Jamestown Voyages*, II, 338, passim, from *A Map of Virginia*. Smith's *Description of New England* contains less geological information. In *The Generall Historie* he gives in greater detail a report on mines

discovered in the Chesapeake Bay exploration and more on the falls of the Potomac. See White, "Geological Observations of John Smith," pp. 124–132.

130. Strachey, *Historie of Travell*, ed. Louis B. Wright and Virginia Freund (London, 1953), p. 40; also quoted in Stearns, *Science*, p. 75. For Strachey's indebtedness to Smith and others, see the Wright and Freund edition, pp. xxxi, xxxii, and Barbour, ed., *Jamestown Voyages*, II, 324–325.

131. For Glover, *An Account of Virginia* (reprinted from *Philos. Trans.*, June 20, 1676, by B.H. Blackwell, Oxford, 1904), p. 11. *The Discoveries of John Lederer . . .* , ed. Rights and Cumming (Charlottesville, 1958), p. 10.

132. The Berkeleys, *The Reverend John Clayton*, pp. 57–59. Clayton sent to Richard Waller, secretary of the Royal Society, a fossil "just as it was taken out of the earth without refining." This was apparently fossil alum. See *ibid.*, pp. 128–129.

133. *Ibid.*, pp. 60, 64, 79, 89, 90, etc. See also White, "Early American Geology," pp. 132–138. Clayton's observations on both vertebrate and invertebrate fossils were quoted approvingly in England as late as 1778.

134. In 1636 Samuel Maverick reported the skeleton of a whale found eighteen feet below the surface of the James River sixty miles above its mouth. In his 1632 edition of the *Metamorphoses* George Sandys mentions finding sea shells on mountain tops as Ovid had done. Later Catesby in his *Natural History* mentions fossil shells and vertebrae found in Virginia and Carolina. For identification of Banister's friends see the Ewans, *John Banister*, pp. 330–338.

135. Jellison, "Scientific Enquiry in Eighteenth Century Virginia," pp. 292–311. For Byrd letters see Swem, ed., *Va. Hist. Index*. A good general essay is Pierre Marambaud, "William Byrd I: A Young Virginia Planter in the 1670's," *VMHB*, LXXXI (1973), 131–150. In Marambaud's *William Byrd of Westover, 1674–1744*, there is something on the father's interests. See also Woodfin, "William Byrd and the Royal Society," pp. 23–24, 111–123.

136. *History*, ed. Wright, pp. 123–128; White, "Early American Geology," p. 138; Stearns, *Science*, p. 209. The Ewans, *John Banister*, p. 311, point out that Beverley's geology owes something to Banister.

137. Jones' 1696 letter appears in Stearns, "Petiver," pp. 297–300, the extracts from his 1698/9 letter in *Philos. Trans.*, XXI, no. 259 (Dec. 1699), 436–442. For original letters see Royal Society MSS; for Petiver's comment on Jones, *Musae Petiveriani . . .* (1699), nos. 418–419, etc.

138. *Philos. Trans.*, XIX, no. 232 (Sept. 1697), 674–676. Sloane believed he had seen the living creature in Jamaica (see Royal Society Journal-Book, X, 45).

139. BM Sloane MSS 4041, f. 202, and 4068, f. 54; also in Royal Society Letter-Book, XIV, 239–240 and Journal-Book, XI, 179 (presented to the Royal Society December 7, 1709). See letters to and from Sloane printed in *WMQ* (2), I (1921), 186–200.

140. For Lord, in other matters as well as this, see text above and note 53; for Lawson, *A New Voyage*, ed. Lefler, p. 271. The Resolves are in Stearns, *Science*, pp. 310–312, from BM Sloane MSS.

141. The quotations are from the *Natural History*, II, xii. Frick and Stearns,

Mark Catesby, p. 74n, point out that a Thomas Jenner's discovery near the falls of the James River may have been almost contemporaneous with Catesby. See also Frick and Stearns, *Catesby*, pp. 72–73, for a summary of the geological observations and speculations.

142. Royal Society MSS L.6.44, entered Jan. 4, 1732. All contractions except ampersand have been expanded. Stearns locates it in Journal-Book XV, 213–214. See also below.

143. See *Va. Gaz.*, and Jellison, "Scientific Enquiry in Eighteenth Century Virginia," pp. 301–302.

144. *Papers of Henry Laurens*, ed. Hamer, Rogers, et al., II, passim.

145. The sermon appears in Davies' *Sermons on Important Subjects* (3 vols., New York, 1828), III, 132–144.

146. Lemay, "Franklin's 'Dr. Spence,'" pp. 199–216. N.H. Heck, *Earthquake History of the United States* (rev. ed. Washington, D.C., 1958), p. 21, in his chart of earthquakes of the eastern U.S. shows the 1755 earthquake as felt slightly in Maryland, and another of 1758 noticed in Annapolis. He describes the latter as lasting thirty seconds, preceded by subterranean noises. He also notes a 1699 tremor felt in what is today West Tennessee.

147. Barbour, ed., *The Jamestown Voyages*, I, 129; II, 334–335.

148. Bodleian Ashmolean MSS 242, f. 126; 423, f. 220. The 1667 bears on the back a name like [Edward?].

149. To Arlington, in Alvord and Bidgood, eds., *The First Explorations*, pp. 177–178, from P.R.O., Col. Papers, XXV, no. 4; to Berkeley, printed in *VMHB*, XIX (1911), 250–254. For Digges' directions, see Stearns, *Science*, p. 698.

150. Printed in the Berkeleys, *The Reverend John Clayton*, pp. 40–80. It was printed originally in *Philos. Trans.*, XVII (1963), 781–789. Original MSS of Clayton's letters on Virginia do not seem to have survived.

151. Listed in Baer, comp., *Seventeenth Century Maryland*. James A. Baer's *A Checklist of Virginia Almanacks, 1732–1850* (Charlottesville, 1962) lists only those printed in the colony.

152. *The Present State of Virginia*, ed. Morton, pp. 34–36.

153. Jones, in Guard-Books and Letter-Books of the Royal Society, 1699/1700. Lewis' letter from Annapolis survives in Royal Society Classified Papers, IV (2). 4 Stearns, *Science*, p. 276 says the letter was presented March 4, 1730/1. Stearns points out that Isaac Greenwood of Harvard College sent a more sophisticated account based upon telescopic views and read at the same time. For Lewis' see *Philos. Trans.*, XXXVII, no. 418 (March-May, 1731), 69–70. The earliest recorded report of Lewis from Maryland to the Royal Society is of October 25, 1725, concerning an explosion in the air at Patapsco (see J.A. Leo Lemay, *Men of Letters in Colonial Maryland* [Knoxville, Tenn., 1972], p. 127).

154. Royal Society Manuscripts, Journal-Book, XXII, 90. For more on Brooke and his medical contributions see Stearns, *Science*, p. 278, and text of the present chapter below.

155. *A New Voyage*, ed. Lefler, passim. See index under *climate* and *weather*.

156. Frick and Stearns, *Mark Catesby*, p. 72. The authors acknowledge their indebtedness to George W. White's unpublished study of Catesby as a geologist.

157. BM Sloane MS. 4057, f. 20, and *WMQ* (2), I (1921), 186–200.

158. The MS. is in the Royal Society Journal-Book, XXI (1751–1754), 47. For excerpts see the Berkeleys, *John Clayton, Pioneer*, pp. 115–116, 210.

159. See Stearns, *Science*, pp. 333–335, and W.W. Abbott on Ellis in *Georgians in Profile: Historical Essays in Honor of Ellis Merton Coulter*, ed. Horace Montgomery (Athens, Ga., 1958), pp. 17–19.

160. Garden's description is quoted apparently in full in the Berkeleys, *Dr. Alexander Garden*, pp. 309–312. For comments on Garden's friendship with Ellis and Pennant and his investigations of meteorological conditions, see the Berkeleys, passim. For the comet, see Stearns, *Science*, p. 609, and Royal Society Journal-Book, XXIII (1759), 572–573.

161. For Lining and his work, Waring, *Hist. of Med. in S.C.*, pp. 254–260, and a list of his published writings, p. 366. See also Stearns, *Science*, pp. 595–598, and the Berkeleys, *Dr. Alexander Garden*, passim. For his medical theories and electrical experiments, see below. His unpublished letters are in the Linnean Society, London, and the Royal Society Journal-Books. See also Aldredge, "Weather Observers and Observations," pp. 204–218, which contains his 1753 letter to the Royal Society; and Everett Mendelsohn, "John Lining and His Contribution to Science," pp. 278–292.

162. Waring, *Hist. Med. S. C.*, pp. 188–198, 364; Stearns, *Science*, pp. 597–599; Aldredge, "Weather Observers and Observations at Charleston, pp. 219–223.

163. James H. Cassedy, "Meteorology and Medicine in Colonial America, pp. 193–204.

164. *The Diary of Colonel Landon Carter of Sabine Hall, 1752–1778*, ed. Jack P. Green (2 vols., Charlottesville, 1965), passim. There are scores of index entries under both astronomy and weather. William Small purchased scientific apparatus for the College of William and Mary which might have been useful in meteorology.

165. Stearns, *Science*, p. 540; Hornberger, "Scientific Ideas of John Mitchell," pp. 291–295.

166. Hindle, *Pursuit of Science*, p. 31. "An Account of an extraordinary Storm of Hail in Virginia . . . communicated by William Fauquier, Esq; F.R.S." (read November 9, 1758). Fauquier's other contributions are listed in Hindle. The younger Fauquier's letter is in the Archives of the Colonial Williamsburg Foundation.

167. Page sent weather observations to the APS (see MS. Communications, Natural Philosophy, I, 4). In the *Va. Gaz.* (Purdie and Dixon) of several dates in 1769 he wrote of the Transit and of the College's lack of interest. For Page, see Hindle, passim, and Stearns, *Science*, p. 664; William S. Dunstan, III, "Rosewell, an Unfulfilled Dream," *Va. Cavalcade*, XX, no. 2 (1970), 16–17; and Davis, *Intellectual Life in Jefferson's Virginia*, pp. 178, 195. For *Va. Gaz.* notices of the 1769 Transit of Venus, see Overfield, "Science in the *Va. Gaz.*,"

pp. 35–39, with more listings of other reports on astronomy. In one essay another Virginian disagrees with Page's method and result, but apparently he had not personally observed the transit.

168. Much more could be said of Jefferson as meteorologist. See *Notes on the State of Virginia*, ed. Peden; *The Papers of Thomas Jefferson*, ed. Julian P. Boyd et al. (Princeton, 1950–   ), passim; *Thomas Jefferson's Garden Book*, ed. Betts, passim; *Thomas Jefferson's Farm Book*, ed. Edwin M. Betts (Princeton, 1953), passim; Edwin T. Martin, *Thomas Jefferson, Scientist* (New York, 1952), pp. 131–147. Peden's edition of the *Notes* and Martin contain some of Jefferson's weather charts.

169. See Hornberger, *Scientific Thought in the American Colleges, 1638–1800*, passim.

170. For the apothecary, see histories of medicine by Blanton and Waring listed in the bibliography of this chapter and Gill, *The Apothecary in Col. Va.*, passim.

171. Hornberger, "The Scientific Ideas of John Mitchell," pp. 295–296; Overfield, "Science in the *Va. Gaz.*," pp. 46–47; Cappon and Duff, *Va. Gaz. Index*, passim.

172. Hindle and many others have had Spencer's Christian name wrong. The best account of his life and lectures is Lemay, "Franklin's 'Dr. Spence,'" pp. 199–216. Lemay feels that Spencer only aroused Franklin's interest but did not personally help him begin his work in electricity.

173. J.A. Leo Lemay, *Ebenezer Kinnersley, Franklin's Friend* (Philadelphia, 1964), passim. Stearns, *Science*, p. 509, states that Kinnersley lectured in South Carolina. Lemay does not agree.

174. A summary of the contents of these *Va. Gaz.* essays is in Overfield, "Science in the *Va. Gaz.*," pp. 42–52.

175. Waring, *Hist. of Med. in S.C.*, p. 259; Lemay, *Kinnersley*, pp. 55, 78; Bowes, *Culture of Early Charleston*, pp. 83–84. For Dömjén, see Lemay, *Kinnersley*, pp. 61, 62, 73; Cohen, *S.C. Gaz.*, p. 87; Bowes, *Culture of Early Charleston*, pp. 84–85.

176. For Garden, the Berkeleys, *Dr. Alexander Garden*, pp. 257–259; for Evans, Stearns, *Science*, p. 514, and Lemay, *Kinnersley*, p. 72n.

177. See Franklin's essay sent to Dr. Mitchell, dated in MS. April 29, 1749, printed later in *Experiments and Observations on Electricity . . .* (London, 1774, as Letter V) and reprinted in *Benjamin Franklin's Experiments*, ed. Bernard Cohen (Cambridge, Mass., 1941), pp. 201–211. See Royal Society Journal-Book XXIV (December 20, 1759), 454–455. The letters between Franklin and Mitchell of the 1745 period are printed in *The Papers of Benjamin Franklin*, III and IV (New Haven, 1961), passim. They fail to show that Franklin's paper was laughed at or that Dr. Mitchell so stated.

178. BM Additional MSS 38823, ff. 1–8.

179. Quinn, ed., *The Roanoke Voyages*, I, 52–58.

180. *Ibid.*, I, opp. p. 461 [figure 7], and II, 847–848.

181. *Ibid.*, I, opp. 460 [figure 6], and II, 846; for engraving, see Cumming, *The Southeast in Early Maps*, plate 14 and p. 96.

182. Most easily accessible, though somewhat distorted, are the watercolor reproductions in Stephen Lorant, ed., *The New World* (New York, 1946). True to color and edited with careful notes is Paul Hulton et al., eds., *The American Drawings of John White, 1577–1590*. See also Ch. I above. Cumming, *The Southeast*, p. 15, discusses the influence of some of the early geographers on White. Quinn, ed., *Roanoke Voyages*, II, 846–872, discusses the details and history of these first maps. Cumming, pp. 113–134, describes John Smith's map of "Ould Virginia" in the 1624 *Generall Historie*. It was engraved by Robert Vaughan, who may have combined Hariot, White, and Smith in the outlines and detail. This map is reproduced in the Bradley-Arber edition of the *Travels and Works of Captain John Smith*, I, 342.

183. The colored drawing of 1608 entitled "A Chart of K. James's River, in Virginia," is in BM, Cotton Augustus, I, Vol. II.46. The 1607 letter accompanying the original drawing has been reproduced a number of times, most recently in Barbour, ed., *The Jamestown Voyages*, I, 104–107.

184. Reproduced (folded in) in Barbour, *The Jamestown Voyages*, I, opp. p. 239; also see Brown, ed., *Genesis*, I, 456.

185. Coolie Verner, "The First Maps of Virginia, 1590–1673," *VMHB*, LVIII (1950), 8–12; reproduced in many places, among them Barbour, ed., *The Jamestown Voyages*, II, opp. 374. See also Swem, "Maps Relating to Virginia," p. 44. One of the most detailed accounts of Smith's 1612 map is in Mathews, "Maps of Md.," pp. 347–360. See also Ristow, *Captain John Smith's Map of Virginia*, a detailed essay written to explain the accompanying map in facsimile.

186. Reproductions sometimes in reduced size appear in Hall, ed., *Narratives of Early Maryland*, frontispiece; in Mathews, "Maps of Early Md.," pp. 361–363. See also Verner, "The First Maps of Virginia," p. 12. Verner mentions several of the derivative maps before 1650.

187. Verner, "The First Maps of Virginia," pp. 13–14; Mathews, "Maps of Early Md.," pp. 363–365 (including facsimiles); Swem, "Maps Relating to Virginia," p. 48; Cumming, *The Southeast*, pp. 141–142. Cumming lists it as drawn by John Ferrar (Virginia's parent) and gives some arguments for this identification. Cumming also points ou that it was first engraved for the third edition of Williams' *Virginia . . . Richly . . . Valued* (original 1650; this ed. 1651). Some copies of Edward Bland's *Discovery of New Brittain* (see Ch. I above) have this map. See also Verner, "The Several States of the Ferrar Map," pp. 281–284 (here Verner mentions an original MS. draft of the engraving).

188. For Comberford maps, see Cumming, *The Southeast*, pp. 144–145 and plate 32 (fascimile); for Shapley-Hilton and Horne, pp. 147–148; for unpublished 1670–1671 charts and maps, pp. 148–149.

189. For Alsop's map, see Mathews, "Maps of Md.," pp. 365–368; for Lederer, Cumming, *The Southeast*, p. 150, and Cumming, ed., *The Discoveries of John Lederer*; for Herrman, Verner, "The First Maps of Virginia," pp. 14–15; Cumming, *The Southeast*, pp. 152–153; Mathews, "Maps of Md.," pp.

368–386; Swem, "Maps Relating to Virginia," p. 52; and Scisco, "Notes on Augustine Herrman's Map," pp. 343–351. One more map of 1688/89, by Cadwallader Jones of the Northern Neck, is of some significance as an improvement on the Lederer map. See Harrison, *Landmarks of Old Prince William*, pp. 607–612, and his essay in *VMHB*, XXX (1927), 323–340.

190. For the Carolina maps, Cumming, *The Southeast*, pp. 154–155; for the Virginia and Maryland map, see *Notes to Accompany a Facsimile of John Speed's A Map of Virginia and Maryland 1676* (Charlottesville, 1962), pp. 2–4 and the facsimile map. John Ogilby's appeared in his *America* (London, 1671). See also Cumming, "Geographical Misconceptions of the Southeast," pp. 484, 489. For the miscellaneous maps of the latter part of the century, see Cumming, *The Southeast*, pp. 152–153, 162–163, 179–180. The original Mathews map is BM Add. MSS 5415.24. A colored photocopy is in the LC.

191. Stearns, *Science*, pp. 146–148, 181, 189–190, 307; *A New Voyage*, ed. Lefler, passim.

192. These are fairly typical of small-area plans or plats or maps listed by Cumming, *The Southeast*, (pp. 173, 176). There are several others. See draft of Williamsburg by Theodorick Bland, surveyor, 11 x 12 inches from the P.R.O. in London reproduced in Lyon G. Tyler, *Williamsburg, the Old Colonial Capital* (Richmond, 1907), p. 20.

193. Cumming, *The Southeast*, pp. 179, 180–181. Crisp, though evidently a resident of London, received six hundred acres of land as recompense (plus ten guineas). Moll's greatest European-made map of the southeast appeared in 1715 (Cumming, *The Southeast*, pp. 181–183); see also Harrison, *Landmarks of Old Prince William*, pp. 613–617.

194. Cumming, *The Southeast*, pp. 183–184, 185.

195. For the Virginia maps mentioned, some printed in the eighteenth and others in the nineteenth century and some remaining in manuscript, see Swem, "Maps Relating to Virginia," pp. 58–60, and Mathews, "Maps of Md." p. 306. See P.R.O. Carolina-Virginia 1728, etc., boundary maps. For the Hoxton map, see Mathews, "Maps of Md.," pp. 386–388, and for the Mayo 1737 map, sometimes called the Byrd map, *ibid.*, pp. 388–391.

196. Cumming, *The Southeast*, pp. 192–197.

197. *Ibid.*, pp. 198–200, 200–202.

198. Swem, "Maps Relating to Virginia," pp. 60–61, describes three or four states of this map, one a copy on parchment in the Va. St. Lib., the distinctions not quite clear from the details given.

199. Cumming, *The Southeast*, pp. 216–217. The first map is in the London P.R.O., the second at the Univ. of Virginia.

200. See Coolie Verner, "Checklist of Eighteenth-Century Editions of the Fry and Jefferson Map," in *The Fry and Jefferson Map of Virginia and Maryland* (Charlottesville, 1966), pp. 13–19, which includes discussions and fold-in facsimiles of the 1754 and 1794 printings. See also Cumming, *The Southeast*, pp. 219–221, in some respects more accurate than Verner; and Mathews, "Maps of Md.," pp. 391–394.

201. Walter Klinefelter, "Lewis Evans and His Maps," *Trans. APS*, n.s. LXI, pt. 7 (1971), 43–50; Swem, "Maps Relating to Virginia," p. 63; Mathews, "Maps of Md.," pp. 395–398.

202. Cumming, *The Southeast*, pp. 223–224; Hornberger, "The Scientific Ideas of Dr. John Mitchell," pp. 289–291; the Berkeleys, *Dr. John Mitchell*, passim.

203. Cumming, *The Southeast*, pp. 54–55, 227–228; *De Brahm's Report*, which contains thirty-nine reproductions of his plans, charts, and maps.

204. See Cumming, *The Southeast*, p. 236, and *The Memoirs of Lieut. Henry Timberlake*, ed. Samuel C. Williams (Marietta, Ga., 1948), for a facsimile fold of the map after page 17.

205. See Swem, "Maps Relating to Virginia," pp. 67–68, for description and the texts of Henry's three major petitions. For contemporary comment, see *Va. Gaz.* (Rind), September 27, 1770.

206. For William Clark's self-acquired cartographic skill and his maps, see Paul Russell Cutright, *Lewis and Clark: Pioneering Naturalists* (Urbana, 1969), pp. 37–39, 455–456. For Hutchins, see Hindle, *Pursuit of Science*, pp. 179, 243, 318–319.

207. Quinn, ed., *The Roanoke Voyages*, I, 135, 213, 334; II, 612. Blanton, *Med. Va. in the Seventeenth Cent.*, p. 3, tells of death of Dr. Henry Kenton in the Chesapeake Bay region in 1603.

208. Barbour, ed., *The Jamestown Voyages*, I, 232; II, 375, 377, etc. Wotton is listed once as "gentleman" and once as "Master" and is also referred to as "our Chirurgeon generall"; Wilkinson is not listed as "gentleman" at all. Dr. Russell is always listed as "gentleman."

209. Shryock, *Medicine and Society in America*, pp. 2–4; Gill, *Apothecary in Col. Va.*, pp. 7–15. As Shryock points out, physicians in Philadelphia as well as southern towns felt compelled to operate apothecary shops.

210. Blanton, *Med. Va. in the Seventeenth Cent.*, pp. 7–11.

211. See John Donald Wade on Bohun in *DAB*; Smith *Works*, passim; Kingsbury, ed., *Rec. Va. Co.*, I and II, passim; Blanton, *Med. Va. in the Seventeenth Cent.*, pp. 11–16; Brown, ed., *Genesis*, II, 830–831. See also Gill, *Apothecary in Col. Va.*, pp. 16–17.

212. Blanton, *Med. Va. in the Seventeenth Cent.*, pp. 16–24; A.C. Gordon, Jr., in *DAB*; Charles E. Gilliam, "Mount Malado," pp. 138–142.

213. Blanton, *Med. Va. in the Seventeenth Cent.*, pp. 24–30; Smith, *Works*, II, 564–586. Blanton names many others of these early surgeons and physicians and apothecaries with references to records of their labors.

214. Blanton, *Med. Va. in the Seventeenth Cent.*, passim, esp. pp. 260–297.

215. Scriven, "Md. Med. Seventeenth Cent.," pp. 29–46, and his "Doctors, Drugs, and Apothecaries," pp. 516–522; Quinan, *Med. Annals of Baltimore*; Gordon, *Aesculapius*, pp. 229–245; Cullen, *Early Med. in Maryland*, passim. The terms "barber" and "surgeon" were used in early Maryland, but no evidence indicates that they referred to the person of both occupations.

216. Waring, *Hist. of Med. in S.C.*, pp. 7, 10–13, etc.; Childs, *Malaria and*

Colonization in Carolina Low Country, pp. 133–264, who concludes that malaria did not materially affect development of the colony.

217. Waring, *Hist. of Med. in S.C.*, pp. 9–17.

218. Quinan, *Med. Annals of Baltimore*, pp. 11–52, etc.; Gordon, *Aesculapius*, pp. 232–237; Lemay, *Men of Letters in Colonial Maryland*, esp. pp. 240–244, etc.

219. Lemay, *Men of Letters in Colonial Maryland*, pp. 240–244, traces the history of this medical dispute, quotes from Hamilton's *Defence*, and locates the other essays in the controversy. For Hamilton, see also Gordon, *Aesculapius*, pp. 233–236, and Carl Bridenbaugh, ed., *Gentleman's Progress: The Itinerarium of Dr. Alexander Hamilton, 1744* (Chapel Hill, 1949), pp. xiii, xix–xx. Bridenbaugh says Kearsley half apologized at the end of the dispute.

220. Gordon, *Aesculapius*, pp. 234–236, for Stevens and Wiesenthal; for Spencer, Lemay's "Franklin's 'Dr Spence,'" pp. 199–216.

221. Summarized in Blanton, *Med. Va. in the Eighteenth Cent.*, p. 45.

222. Ingle, "Regulating Physicians Col. Va.," pp. 248–250; Blanton, *Med. Va. in the Eighteenth Cent.*, pp. 25–29. For attempts made in this law to separate quackery from medicine, see partial text in Gill. *The Apothecary in Col. Va.*, pp. 24–26; Hening, ed., *Statutes*, IV, 509–510; Blanton, *Med. Va. in the Eighteenth Cent.*, pp. 396–402.

223. Gill, *The Apothecary in Col. Va.*, pp. 53–56. Gill seems to confuse Drs. George Gilmer Sr. and Jr. See also his "Pharmaceutical Equipment," pp. 67–81. Gill, pp. 92–94, gives a list of Williamsburg apothecaries, half of them working after 1763.

224. *Ibid.*, pp. 95–115. His portrait is in the Winterthur Museum, reproduced in *ibid.*, before p. 64.

225. Overfield, "Science *Va. Gaz.*," pp. 9–31; Blanton, *Med. Va. in the Eighteenth Cent.*, pp. 60–66.

226. Tennent in Blanton, *Med. Va. in the Eighteenth Cent.*, pp. 119–129; Mitchell, Blanton, p. 116, and Hornberger, "The Scientific Ideas of Dr. John Mitchell," pp. 282–296; Mitchell to Franklin, Colden Papers 1743–1747 in *N-Y Hist. Soc. Coll. 1919* (New York, 1920), pp. 151–154, and edited by Theodore Hornberger, *HLQ*, X (1946–1947), 411–417. See below and Gordon W. Jones, "Doctor John Mitchell's Yellow Fever Epidemics," pp. 43–48.

227. Blanton, *Med. Va. in the Eighteenth Cent.*, pp. 220–236.

228. All these men are discussed in Waring, *Hist. of Med. in S.C.*, passim. See also Cohen, *S.C. Gaz.*, pp. 46–48; Waring, "Kilpatrick and Smallpox Inoculation in Charlestown," pp. 301–308, which includes a list of Kilpatrick's writings; Waring, "Medicine in Charleston, 1750–1775," pp. 19–26; Robert Seibels, "Thomas Dale, M.D., of Charleston, S.C.," *Annals Med. Hist.*, n.s. III (1931), 50–57. Professor J.A. Leo Lemay has gathered new materials on Kilpatrick-Kilpatrick. Stearns, *Science*, pp. 594 ff., summarizes all these men's careers but makes some errors regarding their education. There are anonymous or pseudonymous essays on smallpox and inoculation in the *S.C. Gaz.* of several dates in 1731/2 and 1738. On August 4, 1759, appeared one on whooping cough, discussing the relation of weather to the disease.

229. Robert B. Austin, *Early American Medical Imprints* (Washington, D.C., 1961), p. 48; Stearns, *Science*, p. 598; Waring, *Hist. of Med. in S.C.*, pp. 188–197, and list of writings on Chalmers, p. 364; Aldredge, "Weather Observers and Observations at Charleston," pp. 219–222.

230. Stearns, *Science*, pp. 599–619; the Berkeleys, *Dr. Alexander Garden*, passim; *Corresp. of Linnaeus*, ed. Smith, I, 282–283; Jenkins, "Alexander Garden, M.D., F.R.S. (1728–1791), Colonial Physician and Naturalist," pp. 149–158; Waring, *Hist. of Med. in S.C.*, pp. 221–236.

231. Reports on Georgia colonial medicine are entirely inadequate. Suggestive are Wilson, *Drugs and Pharmacy in Georgia*, passim; Gordon, *Aesculapius*, pp. 484–511; Weaver, "Early Med. Hist. of Ga.," pp. 89–112; Krafka, "Med. Col. Ga.," pp. 232–236; *Detailed Reports of the Salzburger Emigrants Who Settled in America . . . Edited by Samuel Urlsperger*, ed. and trans. George F. Jones and Hermann J. Lacher, (II and III, 1734–1736, Athens, Ga., 1969 and 1972); and *Henry Newman's Salzburger Letterbooks*, ed. Jones, (Athens, Ga., 1966), passim. Wilson includes brief biographical sketches.

232. The most comprehensive study is Duffy, *Epidemics in Col. Am.* See also Cassedy, "Meteorology and Medicine in Col. Am." pp. 193–204; Shryock, *Med. and Society in America*; and Blake, "Diseases and Med. Practice in Col. Am.," pp. 34–54. Several essays and chapters concerned with situations in individual colonies are noted below.

233. Blanton, "Epidemics Real and Imaginary . . . Influencing Seventeenth Cent. Va.'s Population," pp. 454–462, and his *Med. Va. in the Seventeenth Cent.*, pp. 32–77. See also Duffy, *Epidemics in Col. Am.*, pp. 69 ff.; Blake, "Diseases and Med. Practice in Col. Am.," pp. 35–40.

234. Jones, "Doctor John Mitchell's Yellow Fever Epidemics," pp. 43–48. Jones sees no real yellow fever epidemic in Virginia until after the Revolution. The Berkeleys, *Dr. John Mitchell*, pp. 79–81, see Weil's disease as more in keeping with Mitchell's pathological findings.

235. Much of this section comes from Blanton, *Med. Va. in the Eighteenth Cent.*, pp. 50–70. See also Duffy, *Epidemics in Col. Am.*, pp. 74–75. For an annual account of Virginia diseases, including some suggestions of epidemics, see Dr. Sequeyra's journal of 1745–1781 in Gill, *The Apothecary in Col. Va.*, pp. 95–115. For Tennent, see Jellison, "Dr John Tennent and the Universal Specific," pp. 336–346.

263. Scriven, "Md. Med. Seventeenth Cent.," pp. 38–46; Gordon, *Aesculapius*, pp. 233–236.

237. *A New Voyage*, ed. Lefler, passim. Lawson observes that the red men do not appear to be addicted to agues or fevers.

238. Saunders, ed., *Col. Rec. N.C.*, V, 940–941. There were of course minor epidemics, as the one in North Carolina in 1712 Governor Spotswood of Virginia mentions in a letter to the Board of Trade (*The Official Letters of Alexander Spotswood*, ed. R.A. Brock [Vol. I, Richmond, 1882], p. 169).

239. See Waring, "A Sketch of Medicine in South Carolina, 1670–1700," *Journ. S.C. Med. Assoc.*, XXXVII (1941), reprinted without pagination 1941, and his *Hist. of Med. in S.C.*, pp. 11–17.

240. Thomas Cooper and David M. McCord, eds., *The Statutes at Large of South Carolina* (10 vols., Columbia, 1836–1841), II, 152; see also Edward McCrady, *Hist. S.C. under the Proprietary Government, 1670–1719* (New York, 1897), pp. 308–309.

241. Act reprinted in Waring, *Hist. of Med. in S.C.*, Appendix, pp. 333–334.

242. Quoted in Waring, *Hist. of Med. in S.C.*, p. 39.

243. Waring, *Hist. of Med. in S.C.*, pp. 48–91. See also Duffy, *Epidemics in Col. Am.*, passim, esp. p. 93.

244. Krafka, "Med. Col. Ga.," pp. 342–344; Duffy, *Epidemics in Col. Am.*, pp. 90–93; Wilson, *Drugs and Pharmacy in Georgia*, pp. 40–65.

245. Duffy, *Epidemics in Col. Am.*, pp. 156–160; 179–182, 192–193, 224, 241–242.

246. May 31, 1737, Virginia to London, BM Sloane MS. 4055, f. 112, printed in *WMQ* (2), I (1921), 196.

247. See such books as Henry Nash Smith, *Virgin Land: The American West as Symbol and Myth* (Cambridge, Mass., 1950); Marx, *The Machine in the Garden*; Charles L. Sanford, *The Quest for Paradise: Europe and the American Moral Imagination* (Urbana, 1961).

248. Quinn, ed., *The Roanoke Voyages*, I, 105–106, 315, 337–346, 421–423; and Lorant, *New World*, pp. 264–265 [full-page engraving].

249. Barbour ed., *The Jamestown Voyages*, passim; Cabell, "Early Hist. Agriculture in Va.," pp. 281–284; and Edwards, "American Agriculture: The First Three Hundred Years," p. 174.

250. *Historie of Travell*, ed. Wright and Freund, passim.

251. Kingsbury, ed., *Rec. Va. Co.*, I, 483, 510; III, 581–582; IV, 125 ff.; Fletcher, "Hist. of Fruit Growing in Va.," pp. 109–119; Edward Digges, "Extract of a Letter," *Philos. Trans.*, I, (no. 2, April, 1665), 26–27; Hatch, "Mulberry Trees and Silkworms," pp. 3–61.

252. The Ewans, eds., *John Banister*, pp. 340–372.

253. The Berkeleys, *The Reverend John Clayton*, pp. 59–67, 80–83, etc.; Cabell, "Early Hist. Agriculture in Va.," pp. 546–547, etc.

254. Ed. H.D. Farish, pp. lvi–lxi, 8–9.

255. Beverley, *History*, ed. Wright, pp. 314–319.

256. Ed. Richard L. Morton, passim.

257. *Letters from America by William Eddis*, ed. Aubrey C. Land (Cambridge, Mass., 1969), pp. 61–65.

258. See *American Husbandry*, ed. Carman, pp. 292–303; also Land, ed., *Bases of the Plantation Society*, passim, and the Berkeleys, *Dr. John Mitchell*, passim.

259. For the history of tobacco, see works listed in the bibliography for this chapter by Robert, *The Story of Tobacco in America*, etc., passim; and Jerome E. Brooks, *Tobacco: Its History Illustrated in Books . . . in the Library of George Arents, Jr.* (5 vols., New York, 1937–1952), I, 86, 87; II, 3, and his *The Mighty Leaf: Tobacco through the Centuries* (Boston, 1952), passim;

Cabell, "Early Hist. Agriculture in Va.," pp. 542–547; and Herndon, *Tobacco in Colonial Virginia: "The Sovereign Remedy."*

260. See figures quoted in Land, ed., *Bases of the Plantation Society*, pp. 20–21; also for figures see Brooks, *The Mighty Leaf*, pp. 53–55.

261. *A True Discourse of the Present Estate of Virginia* (London, 1615), p. 24; Rolfe's *A True Relation of the State of Virginia left by Sir Thomas Dale Knight . . . 1616* (New Haven, 1961), facsimile of manuscript and letter-press text, p. 37.

262. For Maryland, see Wyckoff, *Tobacco Regulation in Col. Md.*, passim; Brooks, *The Mighty Leaf*, pp. 99–102, ff. Oroonoko is often spelled Orinoco or Oronoco or Oronoko. For North Carolina, see Franklin, "Agriculture in Col. N.C.," pp. 553–554.

263. Sirmans, *Col. S.C.*, pp. 55–57 and passim; Franklin, "Agric. in Col. N.C.," pp. 556–557; Edwards, "American Agriculture," pp. 185–186; *Detailed Reports . . . Salzburger Emigrants . . . by . . . Urlsperger*, trans. and ed. Jones and Lacher, pp. 94, 210; *De Brahm's Report*, ed. De Vorsey, pp. 162–163.

264. *Papers of Henry Laurens*, ed. Hamer, Rogers, et al., passim; *Letterbook of Eliza Lucas Pinckney*, ed. Pinckney, passim; Sirmans, *Col. S.C.*, pp. 130, 155, 227, 269.

265. Sirmans, *Col. S.C.*, passim; *Papers of Henry Laurens*, I, II, III, passim; *Letterbook of Eliza Lucas Pinckney*, ed. Pinckney, passim; *De Brahm's Report*, ed. De Vorsey, p. 72; *The Writings of Christopher Gadsden, 1746–1805*, ed. Richard Walsh (Columbia, 1966), pp. 83, 220; Chapman J. Milling, ed., *Colonial South Carolina: Two Contemporary Descriptions by . . . Glen . . . and . . . Milligen-Johnston* (Columbia, S.C., 1951), passim; Land, *Bases of Plantation Society*, pp. 89–95; Edwards, "American Agriculture," p. 186.

266. Fletcher, "Fruit Growing in Va.," pp. 110–115; Hedrick, *Hist. of Horticulture*, pp. 97–107. Governor Berkeley is said to have had 1,500 apple trees at Green Spring by 1642.

267. See Ch. IV above on various colonial inventories; also the reprint of the 1754 edition of Miller, and Stetson, "American Garden Books," pp. 343–369.

268. Hedrick, *Hist. of Horticulture*, pp. 133 ff. Dr. Alexander Garden was interested in several sorts of useful plants. See Waring, ed., "Corresp. between . . . Garden . . . and the Royal Society of Arts," pp. 16–22, 86–94.

269. Holland, "The Trustees Garden in Georgia," pp. 271–298; Hart, "The First Garden of Georgia," pp. 325–332; Hedrick, *Hist. of Horticulture in America*, p. 136. See chapter on agriculture in R.B. Davis, *Intellectual Life in Jefferson's Virginia, 1790–1830* (Chapel Hill, 1964, or Knoxville, 1972).

270. Miller, *Gardener's Dictionary*, passim; Sowerby, comp., *Catalogue of the Library of Thomas Jefferson*, I, 323–373; *Jefferson's Garden Book*, ed. Betts, passim, and *Jefferson's Farm Book*, ed. Betts, passim; Appleton P.C. Griffin, comp., *A Catalogue of the Washington Collection in the Boston Athenaeum* (Boston, 1897), passim; and Stetson, "American Garden Books," pp. 343–353.

271. See *American Husbandry*, ed. Carman, passim, and Hornberger, "The Scientific Ideas of Dr. John Mitchell," p. 295.

272. Stetson, "American Garden Books," pp. 356–358, and [John Randolph], *A Treatise on Gardening By a Citizen of Virginia*, passim.

273. Davis, *Intellectual Life in Jefferson's Virginia*, pp. 153–160; Sowerby, comp., *Catalogue of the Library of Thomas Jefferson*, I, 332–336; Craven, *Soil Exhaustion as a Factor in the Agricultural History of Va. and Md.*, pp. 12–76.

274. Barbour, ed., *The Jamestown Voyages*, II, 382–384, 397–399, 418–420, 451–453.

275. Kingsbury, ed., *Rec. Va. Co.*, III, 105, 128, 317, 474–475, 496, 531, 536, 640–650; IV, 15, 68, 92, 108, 143, 227, 230, 279, 281, etc.

276. *De Brahm's Report*, ed. De Vorsey, p. 161; Bishop, *Hist. Amer. Manufactures*, pp. 320, 356–360, who cites silk production to indicate that it was a thriving industry in Georgia, North Carolina, and South Carolina in the 1760s; J. Paul Hudson, *A Pictorial Booklet on Early Jamestown Commodities and Industries*, Jamestown 350th Anniv. Hist. Booklet no. 23 (Williamsburg, 1957), pp. 46–47; Hatch's work noted above; Edward Digges, "Extract of a Letter"; Gray, *Hist. Agric. in Southern States*, pp. 3–61, pp. 22, 184; Hindle, *Technol. in Early Amer.*, p. 79; Oliver, *Hist. Amer. Technol.*, pp. 21 ff; Ewan, "Silk Culture in the Colonies," pp. 137–138.

277. See histories of Virginia from Smith through Jones, the advertisements in the various provincial gazettes for brewers and of beer; the laws of the provinces and the instructions sent by the Board of Trade to governors. Also Hudson, *Pictorial Booklet on Early Jamestown Commodities*, p. 60, which describes a 1625–1660 structure for brewing and distilling. Bruce, *Econ. Hist. Va. Seven. Cent.*, II, 211–214, points out the brewhouses in operation in the colony before 1625 and the use of locally grown grain and native plants in the public brewhouses.

278. *Papers of Henry Laurens*, ed. Hamer, Rogers, et al., III, 126, letter of September 20, 1762; Lawson, *A New Voyage*, ed. Lefler, p. 267; Bishop, *Hist. Amer. Manufactures*, pp. 244–265.

279. Milling, ed., *Col. S.C.*, p. 57; Carl Bridenbaugh, *Myths and Realities: Societies of the Colonial South* (rpt., New York, 1963), p. 142; "Johann Martin Bolzius Answers a Questionnaire on Carolina and Georgia," ed. Loewald, Starika, and Taylor, *WMQ* (3), XV (1958), 247.

280. C. Malcolm Watkins, *The Cultural History of Marlborough, Virginia* . . . (Washington, D.C., 1968), pp. 55–56, 58, 178.

281. *The Diary of Landon Carter*, ed. Greene, II, 1118, etc.

282. Bruce, *Econ. Hist. Va. Seven. Cent.*, II, passim; Bishop, *Hist. Amer. Manufactures*, pp. 266–273; Hudson, *Pictorial Booklet on Early Jamestown Commodities*, p. 42, who says one reason for failure of viniculture was spoilage of wine on long voyages to England. He states that by 1675 viniculture had waned in Virginia. But see Beverley below, and instructions to governors from the time of the Virginia Company to that of the last royal governor of Georgia. For early attempts see Brown, ed., *Genesis*, I, 335.

283. Beverley, *History*, ed. Wright, pp. 133–136; Bruce, *Econ. Hist. Va. Seven. Cent.*, I, 471; *The Journal of John Fontaine*, ed. Edmund P. Alexander (Williamsburg, 1972), pp. 85–86, passim.

284. *Papers of Henry Laurens*, ed. Hamer et al., III, 98. From 1746 Laurens was importing cider. For Hugh Jones' comments, see his *Present State of Virginia*, ed. Morton, pp. 78, 138, 199; *William Fitzhugh and His Chesapeake World*, ed. Davis, pp. 175, etc.; Watkins, *Cultural Hist. Marlborough*, p. 62; Bruce, *Econ. Hist. Va. Seven. Cent.*, II, 214.

285. *The Diary of Landon Carter*, ed. Greene, II, passim; *Detailed Reports . . . Salzburger Emigrants . . . by . . . Urlsperger*, trans. and ed. Jones and Lacher, II, 47, 111; III, 44, 70, 103, 307.

286. Bridenbaugh, *The Colonial Craftsman*, p. 13; Marcus W. Jernegan, *Laboring and Dependent Classes in Colonial America*, (rpt., New York, 1965), pp. 11–13. Bolzius in Georgia in 1734, speaking of the skilled craftsmen among the Salzburgers, remarks, "One of us can make do as a cooper," probably because these settlers had not yet got into export crops. See "Bolzius Answers a Questionnaire," ed. Loewald, Starika, and Taylor, p. 246.

287. Hartwell, Blair, and Chilton, *The Present State of Va., and the College*, ed. Farish, pp. 9–10.

288. Ivor Noël Hume, *Here Lies Virginia: An Archaeologist's View of Colonial Life and History* (New York, 1963), pp. 208–209; Hudson, *Pictorial Booklet on Early Jamestown Commodities*, p. 52. A long pewter spoon handle bearing Copeland's name, date, and town was unearthed at Jamestown.

289. The Jamestown glassworks receive cursory attention in almost every history of American general or glass manufacture. National Park historians seem to believe the discovery of the second site might answer some questions but admit that it may now be in the river—under water. For the glassworks, see J.C. Harrington, *Glassmaking at Jamestown: America's First Industry* (Richmond, 1952); Hume, *Here Lies Virginia*, pp. 196–204; Hudson, *Pictorial Booklet on Early Jamestown Commodities*, pp. 23–25; Kingsbury, ed., *Rec. Va. Co.*, II and III, passim; Davis, *George Sandys, Poet-Adventurer*, passim, esp. Sandys' letters; Bruce, *Econ. Hist. Va. Seven. Cent.*, II, 159, 340, 440–443; Hatch, "Glassmaking in Va.," pp. 119–138, 227–238; George S. and Helen McKearn, *American Glass* (New York, 1941), pp. 75–76, point out that there were between 1609 and 1739 only five or six attempts to produce glass in what is now the United States. They count the two Jamestown attempts but know nothing of Berkeley's probable glass factory.

290. Hume, *Here Lies Virginia*, pp. 144, 204–206.

291. Brown, ed., *Genesis*, I, 398; Barbour, ed., *The Jamestown Voyages*, I, 156. The two editors translate the sentences regarding iron manufacture somewhat differently. Actually Lane and Hariot from Roanoke Island also sought for iron ore and found some. See "A brief and true report," ed. Quinn, *The Roanoke Voyages*, I, 331.

292. Hatch and Gregory, "The First American Blast Furnace," pp. 259–296; Hume, *Here Lies Virginia*, pp. 24, 48, 49, 137, 154, 206, 207; Bruce, *Econ.*

Hist. Va. Seven. Cent., II, 451–453, summarizes the activity in the iron industry in the rest of the seventeenth century.

293. See the semipopular account by May, *Principio to Wheeling*, and the better-documented Henry Whitely, "The Principio Company," *PMHB*," XI (1887/8), 63–68, 190–198, 288–295. Whitely points out that the original group of Principio investors were Britishers and that the first Maryland Principio furnace came at about the same time as Spotswood's.

294. *Iron Works at Tuball*, pp. 3–22; Harrison, *Landmarks of Old Prince William*, pp. 207–221, 426–427, 434–435; Dodson, *Alexander Spotswood*, passim; *Official Letters of . . . Spotswood*, ed. Brock, passim; *Journal of John Fontaine*, ed. Alexander, pp. 87–88, 101–103. For North Carolina iron, see L. J. Cappon, "Iron-making—A Forgotten Industry of North Carolina," *NCHR*, IX (1932), 332ff.

295. See note 293, esp. Whitely and May; Bridenbaugh, *The Colonial Craftsman*, p. 17; Louis Morton, *Robert Carter of Nomini Hall* (Williamsburg, 1941), pp. 166–172; Dulany letters in *MdHM*, XVI (1921), 43–50; Clark, *Hist. Manufactures in U. S.*, I, passim; Watkins, *Cultural Hist. Marlborough*, pp. 23–25, 47, 162, 193 (Mercer's relations with Nathaniel Chapman, manager of the Accokeek works, and purchases of pots, etc.); Hugh Jones, *Present State of Virginia*, ed. Morton, passim (covering Spotswood's works).

296. For the best text of "A Progress to the Mines" see *The Prose Works of William Byrd of Westover*, ed. Louis B. Wright (Cambridge, Mass., 1966), pp. 339–378. For his early experiences with iron, see *The Secret Diary of William Byrd of Westover, 1709–1712*, ed. Louis B. Wright and Marion Tinling (Richmond, 1941), passim. Bruce, *Va. Iron Manufacture in the Slave Era*, pp. 12–16, summarizes Byrd's journey and comments on economic and technical aspects of the industry at the time. Bruce also points out the Prince William County furnaces at Neabsco Creek and at Occoquan 1738 and 1760 and later to 1781 (pp. 18–22).

297. Bridenbaugh, *The Colonial Craftsman*, pp. 24–26, 185. Bibliography for Zane is given at p. 185. For other evidences of Virginia iron manufacture see Cappon and Duff, comps. *Va. Gaz. Index*. There was some iron work in the lower colonies: see Alston Deas, *The Early Ironwork of Charleston* (Columbia, 1941). Early North Carolina iron works are noted in Cappon, "Iron-making," pp. 331–348.

298. Bridenbaugh, *The Colonial Craftsman*, pp. 18–20, 184. See *Va. Gaz.* and *Md. Gaz.* for 1769, 1770, 1772, 1777; *WMQ* (1) XI (1908), 245.

299. *Jeffersonian America: Notes on the United States . . . 1805–6–7 and 11–12*, ed. Richard B. Davis (San Marino, Calif., 1954), pp. 151–152.

300. Bruce, *Econ. Hist. Va. Seven. Cent.*, II, 426–439; Evans, *Notes on Shipbuilding and Shipping in Col. Va.*, passim. Evans includes advertisements of early ships offered for sale.

301. Chapelle, *Hist. Amer. Sailing Ships*, pp. 6–31, 222–231, 273; Lemay, *Men of Letters in Colonial Maryland*, p. 133; Bishop, *Hist. Amer. Manufactures*, pp. 78–85.

302. Hume, *Here Lies Virginia*, pp. 208–225.

303. Bridenbaugh, *The Colonial Craftsman*, pp. 28–29, believes they were making glazed pottery by 1756, but a recent study by the Moravians themselves points to a mid-1760s date. By 1771 they were making Queen's Ware at Salem. For Maryland, see Prime, *Arts and Crafts in Philadelphia, Maryland and South Carolina*, pp. 112–125.

304. Hommel, "The History of Andrew Duché, Huguenot Potter of Georgia and Virginia," (see bibliography for this chapter above).

305. De Matteo, *The Silversmith in Eighteenth-Century Williamsburg*, passim.

306. Bridenbaugh, *The Colonial Craftsman*, pp. 122–123, 143; Hume, *Here Lies Virginia*, pp. 225–228. Hume notes that no gold has been found at Jamestown, and less silver than at Williamsburg. See also Cohen, *S.C. Gaz.*, pp. 54–57; Watkins, *Cultural Hist. Marlborough*, pp. 39, 44 (who mentions a Fredericksburg silversmith named Robert Jackson); Louis B. Wright et al., *The Arts in America: The Colonial Period* (New York, 1966), pp. 319–344; Burton, *South Carolina Silversmiths*, passim, and the works by De Matteo and Cutten on other colonies.

307. Cutten, *The Silversmiths of North Carolina*, passim, and *The Silversmiths of Georgia*, passim; also Burton, *South Carolina Silversmiths*, passim.

308. Bridenbaugh, *The Colonial Craftsman*, pp. 142–143, 206; Cohen, *S.C. Gaz.*, pp. 54–57. The latter lists advertisements of dozens of other highly skilled artisans of Charleston, including the engraver of Moseley's map of North Carolina. Above all, see E. Milby Burton, *Charleston Furniture, 1700–1823* (Columbia, 1955). Burton gives good reasons why most of the furniture made in Charleston in the eighteenth century did not survive.

309. Bedini, *Early Scientific Instruments and Their Makers*, pp. 54–55; Bridenbaugh, *The Colonial Craftsman*, p. 142.

310. Lawrence C. Wroth, *A History of Printing in Colonial Maryland, 1686–1776* (Baltimore, 1922), pp. 72–73, etc.; Samford and Hemphill, *Bookbinding in Colonial Virginia*, passim; Bridenbaugh, *The Colonial Craftsman*, p. 121; "The Paper Mill," *VMHB*, VII (1899–1900), 442–444; *Va. Gaz.*, July 26, 1744; and August Klapper, *The Printer in Eighteenth-Century Williamsburg*, Williamsburg Craft Series (Williamsburg, 1955), passim.